STUDIES IN MODERN DRA
VOL. 3

THE PINTER ETHIC

GARLAND REFERENCE LIBRARY
OF THE HUMANITIES
VOL. 2237

Studies in Modern Drama

KIMBALL KING
Series Editor

THE PINTER ETHIC

The Erotic Aesthetic

Penelope Prentice

GARLAND PUBLISHING, Inc.
A member of the Taylor
& Francis Group
New York & London / 2000

Published in 2000 by
Garland Publishing Inc.
A member of the Taylor & Francis Group
29 West 35th Street
New York, NY 10001

10 9 8 7 6 5 4 3 2 1

Library of Congress Cataloging-in-Publication Data

Prentice, Penelope.
The Pinter ethic: the erotic aesthetic / Penelope Prentice.
p. cm. — (Studies in modern drama ; v. 3) (Garland reference library of the humanities ; vol. 2237)
ISBN 0–8153–3909-7 (hbk: alk. paper)
ISBN 0-8153-3886-4 (pbk: alk. paper)
1. Pinter, Harold, 1930– —Criticism and interpretation. 2. Pinter, Harold, 1930– —Ethics. 3. Ethics in literature. I. Title. II. Series. III. Series: Garland reference library of the humanities ; vol. 2237.

Printed on acid-free, 250-year-life paper
Manufactured in the United States of America

Dedication

This book is dedicated to my family who have devoted the most to me and to my work:

To my parents Olga and Edwin Prentice.

To my husband James Grunebaum and to our son, Jason Grunebaum.

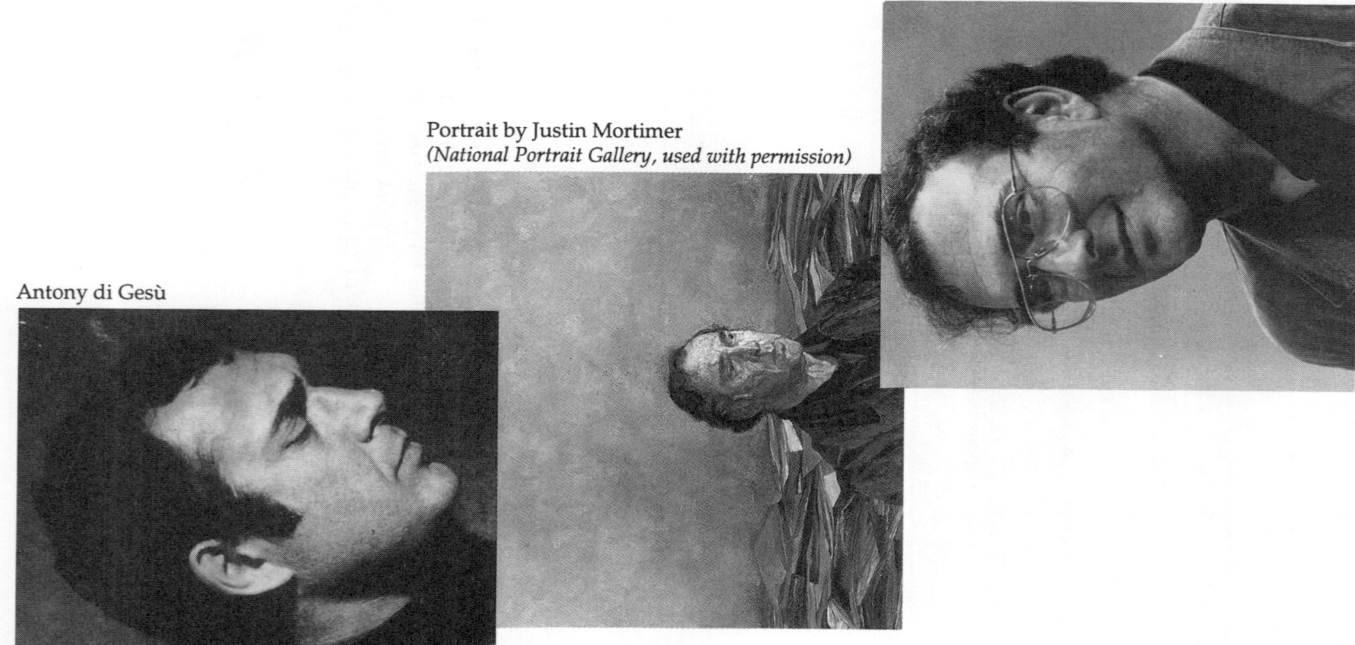

Antony di Gesù

Portrait by Justin Mortimer
(National Portrait Gallery, used with permission)

Ivan Kyncl

Contents

General Editor's Note

The Pinter Ethic: The Erotic Aesthetic explores the ways in which Harold Pinter's plays revise the vision, the masternarrative by which his characters and we, as audience, live. A comprehensive analysis of his work, including his most recent play *Moonlight* and recently published early novel, *The Dwarfs*, this book is indispensable in showing how Pinter's vision illuminates the methods by which drama engages an audience and by which he redefines love and justice. The present volume not only tracks Pinter's dramatic insights into causes of human violence, suffering, and destruction but also traces the development of the ethic through the core vision that dramatizes those life-engendering attitudes, values and actions required for survival. This insightful reading of Pinter's plays and screenplays engages the reader as the author demystifies what has previously puzzled Pinter scholars and critics: the uses of mystery and the multiple ambiguities. An analysis of the mystery and surface conflicts convey the core vision and show how that vision reawakens consciousness of love's knowledge—the knowledge (of self and the work) and actions required not only to survive but to thrive: transforming the vision into an erotic ethic.

This book ultimately links private love to public and global justice. In the 1980s, responding to global brutalities—human torture and warfare—and campaigning on behalf of human freedom, Pinter asked whether any writer could change the way we see the world or act in it. In 1993 he answered that question with the delightful and disturbing *Moonlight*. By removing the hero/heroine (and destructor) from the stage/page to the audience, this play assumes and evokes greater agency, empowering the audience by dramatizing the daily life-and-death choices that we all bear. The final *Moonlight* chapter, thus, earns Penelope Prentice's closing line summarizing the play as an "act of love." The book returns us to Pinter's work with deepened appreciation of love and justice, and, equally, returns us to life with renewed appreciation of the choices and responsibility we all possess in creating just life. As general editor I have watched

The Pinter Ethic: The Erotic Aesthetic grow from a text intended primarily for scholars, critics, audiences, theater professionals, and writers into a book intended for the general reader and observer of contemporary life.

Penelope Prentice, an award-winning poet and playwright, is also an established Pinter scholar, author of *Harold Pinter: Life, Work and Criticism,* (York Press) with Pinter criticism appearing in *Drama and Discussion,* in *Twentieth Century Literature* and *The Pinter Review.* She has had productions of over a dozen of her twenty plays in New York City, Buffalo, and elsewhere, including *Collector of Beautiful Men, Thriller,* and the off-off Broadway *Transformational Country Dances.* Recipient of a MacDowell fellowship and an Edward Albee Foundation Fellowship for playwriting, she helped head the original planning of the first International Women Playwrights' Conference and serves on the board of the International Women Playwrights' Center. A Professor of English at D'Youville College in Buffalo, New York and currently President of the New York College English Association, she gives readings and writing workshops around this country and Canada and is completing two new plays, *City of No Illusions* and *Ex.*

Her contribution to Garland's *Studies in Modern Drama* series attests to the variety and complexity of Pinter's work and is helpful as a volume that reassesses crucial aspects of his achievement.

Kimball King

Preface

The German art critic Anton Ehrenzweig said that the function of art is to delight and to disturb. How else than by delighting does a play hold an audience or continue to live? How other than by disturbing does it move an audience to confront unexamined received values or to act on them? I was stunned when I first saw *The Birthday Party* in the 1960s at the Jane Addams' Hull House Chicago premiere. I knew I had seen a play that changed the course of twentieth-century drama, and I wanted to find out why. The new physics with its fractal geometry would have to intervene to provide the metaphor that would adequately describe the remarkable structure which conveys the vision in Harold Pinter's plays. But that evening in the theatre changed my life.

When, for his 60th birthday in 1990, I received from Harold Pinter a copy of his novel *The Dwarfs,* written in his early 20s but published for the first time that year, I realized that he knew from the beginning what he was attempting aesthetically and ethically. *The Printer Ethic* aims to describe that aesthetic and ethic at the core of his work: the values and the vision in his plays.

W. H. Auden once said that among those he likes he can find no comparison, but among those he loves they all make him laugh. Not the least of my attraction to Pinter's work is that it makes me laugh—often. I had been raised in a comic tradition, hearing George Bernard Shaw at my mother's knee, and from my father, philosophy, particularly Bertrand Russell, and history—I remember best the Borgias. I read Freud beginning at ten, primarily for his emphasis on sex, and clearly the erotic undertones in Pinter's plays remain a portion of my attraction to his work.

That first night watching *The Birthday Party* I was both more delighted and deeply disturbed than I had ever remembered being in the theatre. I had seen something more real and simply funnier than anything else I had seen on stage. But I also knew my laughter was provoked by something original: fearful, more immediate, and of our time.

I blithely assumed that it was just a matter of time before the next great dramatist showed up. I had not yet dared enter that arena as a playwright and did not yet know that great playwrights don't grow on trees. When I caught on to that fact I nearly stopped going to the theatre for almost a decade because nothing else I saw measured up to Pinter's work in depth, honesty, resonance, and sheer pleasure. Immediately after Pinter had completed *À la Recherche du Temps Perdu: The Proust Screenplay,* I read Proust with a similar result—no other fiction writer offers a reader another lifetime in this one.

This task must have been inspired by my early reading of Shaw's *Quintessence of Ibsenism* and by Beckett's slender *Proust* which reads like a familiar second journey through Proust's tome, condensing that pleasure to seventy-two pages yet capturing Proust's essence. My aim is to trace a similar brief journey, to summon the heart of Pinter's work, a reading or re-reading of his plays, preserving its emotional depth charge in order to appreciate where we are moved—to what new place.

An attentive viewing or a careful reading of a Pinter play requires little or no commentary. His plays, like all drama, move the head through the heart a long distance in a remarkably short space of time, but the impact can be missed by those who respond only intellectually. My first experience teaching Pinter's work in downtown Chicago to college students from around the world, some of whom had read little and had seen less theatre, was the same as Edward Albee's when he took a young street boy to see Beckett's *Endgame.* Quite simply, the boy got it. My students understood much that many critics often failed to appreciate for the same simple reason—they responded to the play not merely intellectually but wholly: with their hearts and their heads.

Although critics who demand an explanation of his plays frequently accuse Pinter of silence or evasiveness about his work, some of the most illuminating observations remain Pinter's own. In defense of Pinter's seeming reticence, the late Alan Schneider who directed *The Dumb Waiter, The Collection,* and *One for the Road* remarked, "If you write deeply enough, of course there will be resonances, but these have to be discovered from the outside. The more profoundly a guy writes, the less he's aware of the larger implications." ("Pinterview," 69) Yet over twenty years ago after first collecting Pinter's interviews and essays, I immediately saw how among the dozens of books and thousands of articles about his work, some of the best insights into Pinter's work remain his own. Because Pinter wishes to avoid inaccuracy and redundancy, he gives few interviews, but together with his essays they provide some of the best insights into nearly every aspect of his writing.

Pinter's early interviews disclosed to me his boyhood appreciation of T. S. Eliot and Dostoevsky, my own first real literary loves at 14 and 15; and revealed Pinter's stand as a conscientious objector, which also struck a chord. My father, a conscientious objector in World War II at a time it was not permissible for an atheist, said he did not wish to carry a gun to kill another young man with a wife and children. But because in college he had been obligated to join the Reserve Officer Training Corps, he was offered a lieutenant's rank and the opportunity to serve in Eisenhower's First Army Headquarters where, he later said, he would have been, "drinking champagne through the war." He chose instead to go to jail. He consented, however, to serve by accepting the duties of a medic and at the end of the war in the liberation force was sent to Buchenwald to tend to the living. When he came home he never spoke of his war experiences. His silence remains more powerful than anything he could have said.

I believe now that part of my continued attraction and commitment to Pinter's work is his dramatization of the unspeakable. His plays culminating in *Party Time, The New World Order,* and *Moonlight* offer some of drama's best understanding of the causes of human violence and destruction as well as an appreciation of what is necessary for a sustained peace or for any "new world order" to be achieved.

Early on I realized that no serious dramatic writer who comes after Pinter can ignore his influence. To do so would be to confine oneself to nineteenth-century forms and attitudes which have become codified, stale, dead. Donald Pleasence compares playing Davies, the tramp in *The Caretaker,* to "being in the first performance of Chekhov's *The Three Sisters* or *The Cherry Orchard.*" (Sweeney, 8) Unlike any other English-speaking dramatist of this century, Harold Pinter has created an accurately realistic, rich and distinguished body of work, with a breadth that is comically tragic, large, uniquely his own, and in a special sense, complete. It is all there, the whole of life.

I wish first to thank Kimball King at the University of North Carolina for proposing this project and for his valued commentary, my parents Olga and Edwin Prentice for their careful readings of the many drafts, and Colin G. A. Brezicki of Ridley College, Canada, for his bold suggestions. I wish also to thank George Bishop at D'Youville College and to express appreciation to D'Youville College for substantially funding three research grants enabling me to meet with Harold Pinter in London, Los Angeles, and New York, and for a 1991–92 sabbatical to complete this book. I am deeply indebted to Harold Pinter for his encouragement of my writing. In 1979, during the previews of *Betrayal,* he asked to look at my first play slated for a reading and production in New York. Although he was extremely busy and anxious about his own opening, he took the time to read my work and to make very specific suggestions. I was astounded and can only hope to be guided by his extraordinary generosity.

I wish to extend special and deep thanks to John Mulryan, editor of *Cithara,* Francis Gillen, editor of *The Pinter Review,* William McBrien, editor of *Twentieth Century Literature,* and Saad Elkhadem at York Press for their careful reading and insights and for permission to reprint portions of published material. I wish to cite my advisor, the late Stanley Clayes, editor of *Drama and Discussion,* the Prentice-Hall anthology of drama, for first soliciting my commentary on Pinter for the volume, and to thank Prentice-Hall for permission to reprint "The Ironic Con Game." I also wish to acknowledge Carl Dennis, Leslie Fiedler, Anthony Hunt, and Marcia and David Lamb for their reading of the *Moonlight* chapter, and to express my appreciation to Lynnette McClive and the late Sr. Virginia Carley for their support and reading of early drafts of this book, and Robert L. Nielson for his research. I would like to thank Evelyn Wolf for her meticulous reading and Jamie Milliron for her reading and commentary. I offer special thanks to Michael Basinski and Robert Bertholf at the Poetry/Rare Books Collection at the State University of New York at Buffalo, to Leon D. Shkolnik and Charlene Mirabella at the D'Youville Library, and express my appreciation to the many other librarians who assisted in this work at Loyola University of Chicago, Northwestern University, The University of Chicago, Newberry Library, SUNY Buffalo. The Library of Congress, the Victoria and Albert Museum, and especially the librarians in charge of maintaining the clipping files at the New York Library of the

Performing Arts at Lincoln Center. I also wish to thank Mary Jean Irion at the Chautauqua Institute for supplementing a playwright-in-residence invitation with an opportunity to deliver "The Pinter Ethic," a paper seminal to this book.

Finally I offer my deepest gratitude to my husband James Grunebaum who made an extraordinary sacrifice early in his career as a philosophy professor so that I could remain in Chicago to finish my dissertation on Harold Pinter's plays. At a time when academic positions were already scarce or nonexistent, he turned down permanent positions to accept a one-year appointment at Northwestern so that I could remain in Chicago to complete my work immediately after my advisor, on leave in Italy for a year, returned. Without that year, almost wholly devoted to research and writing, I would not have been able to finish this book. I remain grateful to my husband and to our son Jason for their participation in all my work all these many years.

The Pinter Ethic: Overview

With Heisenberg's uncertainty early in the twentieth century and the dropping of the bomb at the end of World War II came an end to nineteenth-century form and the belief in happily-ever-after predictable symmetries. Other forms and ideas challenge the earlier century's already deteriorating belief in man's power to be master of his fate, captain of his soul. One defining stance of postmodernism is individual impotence in the face of global wars, pollution, disease which could destroy all.

The resultant paralysis that can occur when any animal feels threatened with loss of control over self and surroundings has led some writers to reflect the human as a doomed creature on a doomed planet. Already breaking with traditional form well before Pinter's work, Samuel Beckett's *Endgame* seems set in the aftermath of nuclear holocaust—the only hopeful sign, the life form sighted outside paralleling the minimally hopeful leafing of the tree in *Waiting for Godot*. More recently, both American playwright Sam Shepard and British playwright David Hare return to fairly traditional forms to convey an apocalyptic vision: Shepard with a mythical resonance from *Curse of the Starving Class* onward reflects the death of the American dream, while David Hare's plays, culminating in *The Secret Rapture*, diminish or destroy all dreams.[1] In works such as these love and justice, which might empower human life, are generally absent or lost, and nothing in the work points to how balance might be realized or restored.

In contrast, Harold Pinter's plays combine a focus on love and justice that presents an ethic expressed in new forms which challenge those currently received reflections of human powerlessness. Through that focus and form, his plays convey a vision both darker and more delightful which suggests that, on the contrary, a human being's attitudes and actions at the private level may have profound implications for action on the public and even global levels of life.

Harold Pinter's work from the beginning has concerned itself with love in the Western tradition as an erotically charged attraction between two people which reaches or fails to achieve fulfillment. That tradition of romantic love has become so internalized for contemporary audiences that it is only necessary to place a woman and man on the same page or stage and the reader/audience automatically wants them to get together. The love evoked in Pinter's work, sometimes expressed as the bond of friendship or familial love, is frequently love remembered between a man and woman, the greatest good, but often already past. Yet throughout, love functions powerfully in the present as the wellspring that drives all else. It is the desire for love and respect that ignites and fuels the struggle for power *over* others, a conflict waged to gain a position which seemingly might win another's esteem.

That struggle for power unleashes an equally powerful concern with justice. Pinter's most recent work dramatizes that love without justice is not love, nor is justice, without love, justice. The position is not revolutionary. Aristotle in his *Ethics* already reflects that connection which runs through Western values. (V–VI) Justice in Pinter's work operates both in that general, overarching sense of the just as the fair, and in its more specific forms of retributive, and recently, distributive justice. The connection between love and justice becomes most explicit in later plays such as *Mountain Language* where love displays a selfless, unconditional generosity rare in the early work. That love transforms into a power which sustains human bonds through extreme adversity and the worst injustice—torture. Love's connection with justice in Pinter's work dramatizes an enlarged definition of love.

The Pinter Ethic places primary emphasis on the major full-length plays. Divided into three parts, the book traces the development and variations in the expression of the ethic through the Pinter canon, touching on his screenplays, novels, poetry, essays, Pinter's own salient commentary and some neglected interviews which further an appreciation for the aesthetics and ethics of his work.

The brief biography summarizes major events which shaped the values the plays dramatize and examines Pinter's adolescent work and novel *The Dwarfs* as remarkably early expressions of the aesthetics and ethics formative to his plays. The introduction situates the discussion within the context of Pinter's achievement and examines *The Dumb Waiter's* portrayal of Pinter's dominant/ subservient conflict as seminal to any larger appreciation of his values. Part One opens with a discussion of *The Birthday Party* which offers a paradigmatic portrayal of the values and actions which define the ethic in Pinter's plays. Part One also tracks the variations in the dramatization of the ethic in the other early plays. Parts Two and Three trace that development in the middle and recent plays.

The development of Pinter's ethic played out through the power struggle in the dominant/subservient conflict falls into roughly three phases, each separated by the locus of the threat of violence: the outside source(s) of destruction. That axis shifts, evolving first from focus on the private, then the communal and finally the global levels.[2] Pinter's dramatization of the dominant/subservient conflict primarily as a private battle between individuals within the confines of hermetically sealed rooms in his early work opens out in the middle work to the communal level and in the later work to a focus on global power sources. His most recent plays go further still, fusing a triple focus on power, love and justice at all three levels: the private, public, and global.

As in any highly organic artistic development, there can be no absolute demarcation between the phases of Pinter's plays. The latest plays continue to exhibit elements primarily associated with the earliest, and the earliest seminally contain his later global concerns. Where the early plays *The Dumb Waiter* and *The Birthday Party* already poise the conflict toward a larger organization or power in the world, his latest work, focused on global powerplays, remains a battle fought between individuals. In addition to the focus shift from private to global concerns, what also shifts is both the intensity of the conflict and its implications for the audience, obliquely addressed as a responsible witness.

Awareness of the locus of threat as it evolves in Pinter's plays enhances appreciation for his considerable achievement in the development of the ethic: the innovation and integrity in that progression toward a focus on global justice.

In Pinter's earliest work, from *The Room, The Birthday Party, The Dumb Waiter, The Caretaker,* through *The Homecoming,* even when the initial threat of violence may appear to come, as in *The Birthday Party* and *The Dumb Waiter,* from a larger organization distant and unseen, the overriding primary focus in the early plays remains on the private level of conflict; individuals, often living at the margins of society, jockey for position over one another myopically until the all-consuming struggle escalates into a deadly battle for power and survival. What it means to be a good person is tested in that battle, but any question of justice abides almost exclusively in the private hands of private individuals.

The early phase, focusing primarily, sometimes exclusively, on the private level, ends with *The Homecoming*, a pivotal play, and Pinter's first major work where a woman gains dominance and something positive—her freedom.

Pinter's middle plays occupy a liminal position where attention to the private level subtly moves toward but not fully into the public sphere in the three full-length plays of that period: characters in *Old Times*, *No Man's Land*, and *Betrayal* all assume positions of responsibility in the larger community where what happens privately may have public repercussions. But the reverse seldom obtains. However successful the characters are publicly, who they are and what they do in that larger world—producer, poet, publisher—can provide no protection for the character's private self in the struggle for love or power. Moreover, being publicly acclaimed as good within one's profession, as a successful poet or publisher, may neither link to being good privately nor serve as an index of the quality of one's public work. The successful, off-stage writer Spinks in *Betrayal* is deemed over the hill by his publisher, and his private life, despite Emma's romantic interest in him, may be in shambles. Pinter explores the many levels at which a character may or may not be a good person evidenced dramatically in action.

The full-length plays among the middle work, frequently referred to as memory plays, also retain the drive and impetus of the earlier dominant/subservient struggle but introduce as equally important the force of memory, the past's ability to encroach upon the present with an attendant role in the future. What is remembered often threatens to engulf and overtake what is currently happening, and indeed, as in *Landscape* and *Silence*, it does. *Old Times*, *No Man's Land* and *Betrayal* all focus on loves past and present, where when memory threatens to invalidate past well-being it may destroy present happiness. By questioning what characters believe they remember, the conflict dismantles the illusions which sustain characters' lives no less nakedly than in the early plays. All three full-length plays of the period also explore the more elusive aspects of the powerplays among private levels of the comfortable, publicly visible middle class, where any hidden threat from a larger organization or society is almost entirely internalized, even seemingly absent, and where the conflict for power turns on who remembers what correctly—a conflict which is, however, no less deadly.

Although the conflict may not actually threaten characters' lives or even public position in the outer world, almost all, once stripped of illusion, lose some portion of the self that makes life worth living. Moreover, when the conflict, now couched in the subtlety of middle-class courtesy, re-emerges in the full-length liminal plays, it does so with a fierce vengence as unrelenting as in the early plays.

Finally, Pinter's latest work shifts focus away from the individual and communal level of struggle to target agents of national and international forces empowered to institute murder, torture or nuclear war.

For the past decade Pinter's work for the stage has taken a generally more somber tone, finding expression for his political and global concerns in eight one-acts plus two sketches. *Family Voices*, *Victoria Station*, and *A Kind of Alaska* return primary focus to the private level but do so with added dimension and implication in the larger world. *Precisely,* a sketch in which two men argue the kill power of a nuclear war, confronts that global issue head on. *One for the Road*, dramatizing the brutal torture of a man and his wife culminating in the murder of their child, represents Pinter's first major explicit break with his earlier contempt for agit prop, political drama, yet Pinter also reminds us of that play's connection to very early work such as *The Dumb Waiter* in dramatizing the abuse of authority. *One for the Road* remains his most horrifyingly violent portrayal of that abuse in a hierarchical system until *Mountain Language,* which, inspired by the suffering of the Kurds, details the brutal torturing to death of several victims for speaking their native, mountain language.

With the recent torture plays, the one-act *Party Time* and the sketch *The New World Order,* Pinter's plays recursively cycle, or more correctly spiral to another plane, which allows the audience to maintain a triple focus on the private, public and global causes, implications and consequences of violence resulting from dominant/ subservient power struggles.

In Pinter's *Party Time,* where power brokers party while they squelch an insurrection outside, and in *The New World Order,* where two torturers hint at the brutalities they are about to inflict upon a blindfolded, seated man, Pinter links love and justice in surprisingly fresh ways. These later plays infuse a reminder of love into this bleakest of all human landscapes—the torture of one human being by another. Through the portrayal of love, the plays become a call for a redefinition of love as it is generally communicated through the received values of Western romance and friendship. The ethic in Pinter's plays distills most simply to a dramatization of love and justice; through the delineation of power and the abuse of authority the plays end in awakening an enlarged view of love as they provoke a demand for action to bring about justice.

Moonlight, Pinter's most recent full-length play, depicts Andy, a dying man, who served the state as a civil servant, Bel, his wife, their daughter Bridget, and their two estranged sons, Jake and Fred, who serve the state by preserving the status quo through covert violence. The grown children, who never address their parents, further cement the connection between private love and public justice. Bridget appears alone on stage to open and close the play, addressing the audience with her memories and images from her unconscious, to frame both the play and the questions with which the play leaves the audience. Through Bridget, a voice from the nether of the dead, the play articulates a fresh vision, conveyed through her directly to the audience, and that vision addresses and speaks more directly to the audience at conscious and subconscious levels, offering us the clearest insights into Pinter's ethic and aesthetic through the dramatization of love. Though the sons no longer speak to their father, their separation from family also speaks to the audience by raising questions that dramatize how choices made by an ordinary citizen at home fuel decisions and actions of global powers.

The title and subtitle, *The Pinter Ethic: The Erotic Aesthetic,* would seem to make large claims for Pinter's work. *Moonlight* offers and requires a fresh vision, a fresh way of seeing both Pinter's plays and life. The title, *The Pinter Ethic,* might seem to suggest that there is something unique about the ethic which Pinter presents when in fact, as argued throughout this book, the ethic in Harold

Pinter's work rests on traditional Western virtues as they promote, rather than destroy life. The characters in his work, often struggling to preserve identity and, by extension, to survive, engage in a conflict that becomes a life-and-death battle. What Pinter's plays dramatize as destructive and inimical to survival, however, is the vision which informs almost all characters' action.

The core vision, expressed through the surface dominant/subservient conflict, is revealed as unconsciously driven by an impulse to survive, which, paradoxically, destroys. Paradox is, however, only *apparent* contradiction. The vision which Pinter's characters live by—to do good, and to destroy what is not good—would seem noble enough. Even his torturers (especially his torturers) torture the innocent not out of sadistic malice but from what they perceive as divinely inspired cleansing. Characters act in ignorance of the destructive nature of the received vision they live by which informs all destructive action at all levels of human relationship—from friendship, marriage, family, and community to the institutions of torture and destruction and the states invested with the right of protecting its citizenry.

Pinter's characters act from a vision which situates what is not good only in others. His plays dramatize how failing to acknowledge what is not good in the self (but instead viewing and promoting the self as superior to others, often in the name of love and justice) can only destroy relationship and the self. Moreover, the characters reveal that through misguided vision their perceived love is not only limited but destructive. Though they perceive themselves benignant creatures impelled by love, they are driven by a very limited love, in a text where love is dramatized as the generative force of connection to others and community. That limited love, balanced almost equally by a lack of love, becomes a destructive force resulting in estrangement from the self, others, and, thus, is destructive of relationship and community. What Pinter's work calls for is a revision of that destructive vision: a re-seeing the vision which the characters and we in the audience live by.

To see the destructive vision clearly is both to revise the vision and to see what vision is necessary to promote survival rather than destruction. The clearest and fullest expression of the destructive vision comes in *Moonlight*. Andy, who says he is "good" and has lead a life which "harmed no-one," dramatizes how a life lived blind to the destructive us-versus-them vision that informs his action, severs his relationship with almost everyone he has loved. More horrifying, that destroying vision becomes the primary legacy he leaves his children and larger community. The ethic in Pinter's work, thus, goes beyond what Virgina Woolf in *Mrs. Dalloway* called the "atheist's religion" of doing good for the sake of good. In Pinter's ethic, doing good is dramatized as urgently required for survival.

To survive requires a revised vision which informs action that enlarges our concept of love and, as Pinter's later work dramatizes, links love to justice.

The centrality of love in Pinter's ethic throughout his work suggested the subtitle, *The Erotic Aesthetic*. Love as Eros, a life-promoting force, appears in Pinter's plays in all its guises—from the passionately ecstatic to familial love and friendship—all connected at root in the desire for survival. Through the appreciation of love and of Pinter's portrayal of love, which is enlarged to link with justice, this study of Pinter's ethic is, finally, no less about the aesthetic, the beauty in Pinter's plays. As the subtitle is intended to imply, the ethic and the aesthetic are wedded through the erotic. That recognition carries the further concomitant appreciation of love's connection to death and destruction.

Understanding that connection can begin here in the acknowledgement that the subtitle of this book was inspired by Wendy Doniger O'Flaherty's considerable scholarly achievement in *Siva: The Erotic Ascetic*.[3] Her book, a compilation and analyses of myriad, seemingly endless, variants of the Hindu Siva myth, cites the many contradictory (even fabricated and spurious stories!) which, as she points out, all can contribute to a deeper understanding of Siva's mysteries. Similarly, *The Pinter Ethic* examines the many conflicting and contradictory statements of Pinter's character which evoke larger truths.

Nearly all self-referential statements that the characters make, such as Andy's claim that he "harmed no-one," almost always summon recognition of the opposite truth. That recognition serves as a cautionary reminder to any viewer, reader, or critic to examine any seemingly definitive conclusions about Pinter's work, which may contain opposite truths.

O'Flaherty's subtitle, *The Erotic Ascetic,* also evokes appreciation of the wholeness contained in what at first appears seeming contradictory opposites in her study of Siva: the erotic and ascetic. That understanding leads to the larger appreciation of how

Siva, Lord of the Universe and creator of life, can also be the destroyer. Reconciliation of those seeming opposites, at the center of all religion, also informs the core vision of Pinter's *Moonlight*. Where religion posits responsibility for creation and death with divinity, Pinter's plays reveal other mysteries: hidden human responsibility for destruction and death as well as for the reverse: for survival. The source of that destruction is the received vision which informs all action. That vision is destructive but unconscious. So long as it remains hidden from consciousness, it cannot promote survival or creation. By revealing the received vision and making it manifest in consciousness, as Bridget does in *Moonlight,* and delivering it directly to the audience, Pinter's work summons a fresh vision, one which requires another view of love, productive of generation rather than destruction. In doing so, as this work later argues, *Moonlight* becomes an act of love.

Naming a thing an act of love, even in poetry, becomes a statement that has to be earned and can only be hard won. To make such a statement in a scholarly work of criticism might seem extravagant. But Pinter's work, viewed and read with the pleasure it can engender and the disturbing vision that can provoke change in the audience, becomes an act. Revising our vision revises our action, and thus *Moonlight* assumes the agency of a lover, enlarging the lives of the other(s), whose agency is similarly empowered. How *Moonlight* delivers its fresh vision can be understood by attending to the images we see and hear.

Moonlight frontally addresses our own desires and loves through all the characters' many professions of love and love's ecstasy and through the play's genius, Bridget. She opens and closes the play speaking from Psyche's interior realm of memories, dream and unconscious vision. Bridget, as genius, an engendering catalyst, is guardian of a place (her home), of intuition, and of the unconscious and the play's vision. She guards the play's vision by *not waking* her parents (by analogy, to any other vision). She also consciously preserves the received vision by remembering. She is a voice from the past; though she would be a grown woman during the time of much of the play's action, when she appears to us alone on stage, she is 16. She is also a voice of the past who addresses us in the present with the horror she believes she escaped: recalling her parents' love and her nightmare vision of a journey through a warscape of "skeletons in ditches" and "burning." Though consciously she says she does not wish to wake her parents, trapped in the past, ironically it is her vision (delivered as we shall more fully see later as a question and through mystery) that wakes us, as audience, to a fresh vision to inspire our action.

She stands before us at the end not like a magic genii of ancient fairy tale, who performs tasks impossible for us or who can grant three wishes, but as one who summons our wishes into consciousness—our desires for love, friendship, fellowship and for survival within community and among all our neighboring communities, which, these days, is the world.

Bridget, unconsciously, performs the greatest revision of all in Pinter's work. In giving us her vision, she brings the destructive vision into our consciousness by provoking us at the end with unanswered questions only we can answer. In doing so, Bridget transfers heroic agency from the stage to the audience.

The fresh vision summons us to acknowledge choices where we assumed we have none. Assuming that we have "nowhere to go," like Stanley in *The Birthday Party,* is to exile ourselves from agency in the mistaken belief that we have no choices. Bridget's vision will at first seem mysterious. Confronting that mystery, and all the many mysteries in the play, leads to the larger mystery that delivers the core vision. Thus the vision is conveyed as a question.

Both the question and answer return us to the riddle of the sphinx with a slight shift in emphasis.[4] The answer is not "man," but "we, as man and woman." In our own time, the riddle for a free society is posed not for some extraordinary hero to answer in order to deliver our community from pestilence and destruction; it is posed for each of us to acknowledge and assume our own responsibility and agency in all actions which destroy. That knowledge leads to the vision necessary for survival. The knowledge required begins in self-knowledge. The lifting of ignorance requires all knowledge, from knowledge of self to knowledge of the larger world. Ignorance of the received vision is the form that malice assumes in Pinter's work. Failing to know ourselves in time and falling into Stanley's misguided belief that "there's nowhere to go," we may be forced to assume Oedipus's own ironically self-proclaimed sentence. Putting out our eyes, when, too late we see the terrible truth, we exile ourselves. The image is comic. The whole world cannot go into exile; there is nowhere else at the moment to go to off the planet Earth.

Bridget's message is merely a description of what she sees as safe—a retreat from the world where she has no agency or even expressed desire. Thus she offers no didactic message in the form of a finger pointing out what is wrong at the surface in our actions, then wagging that finger at us to beckon us to mend our ways and change. Instead, awakening consciousness of the received, destructive vision reveals its own reverse constructive side and at a much deeper level. Knowing ourselves, knowing the world and seeing the vision that informs all our action, transforms into love's knowledge: the vision that can reverse destructive action.

By reversing the vision which informs our action and inspiring the desire and courage to act differently, *Moonlight* revises the way we see and receive drama, beginning with the pleasure we take away from drama, defined in Aristotle's notion of drama's tragedy.

The tragic pleasure is that of pity and fear. . . . (1453)

Moonlight adds another dimension to tragedy's fear and pity: hope. While it is argued later that Oedipus, in blinding himself acknowledges his responsibility and thus dignifies human responsibility, as our surrogate, *Moonlight* offers and requires not reflected agency, assumed by a hero, but our own actual agency. Pinter's work throughout dramatizes what is finally the greatest human tragedy—one human being destroying another, blindly believing such destruction is undertaken in love or by what some of the characters in *Moonlight* believe is rooted in human "nature," which in this play assumes the force of fate. Recognizing human destruction as rooted in an unconscious, destructive vision allows us a vision of choices we did not know we had.

Seeing choices we were not conscious we had restores trust in our own agency. How? The fearful and destructive vision, once seen clearly, contains its opposite, revealing how almost all actions, from the most private within the family to the largest choices made in governing public policy, are choices between life and death.

The received vision is not didactically delivered to us as a chastening admonition nor an apocalyptic warning that can stun an already overwhelmed human creature into paralysis. But the fresh vision, which the play trusts us to see and claim, comes as a gift that empowers by admitting hope; seeing and confronting clearly the truth, however disturbing, liberates. Seeing the core vision that engenders destructive actions can promote actions which promote survival.

The Pinter Ethic: The Erotic Aesthetic can be read in many ways and begun almost anywhere, but the Introduction with its appreciation of Pinter's achievements seem to be indispensable in any reading as does the final chapter on *Moonlight* and the Conclusion. The chapters on *The Dumb Waiter, The Birthday Party, The Homecoming, One for the Road* and *Party Time* are key to appreciating the central conflict and the vision of power, love and justice. The aim in this book is to engender the provocative disturbing delight of seeing or reading Pinter's work. More importantly, it is intended to return the reader to his work with greater appreciation and understanding. The *Moonlight* chapter acknowledges Pinter's work within the long tradition beginning with *Oedipus,* through *Everyman* and *Hamlet,* and shows how this work has effected a global shift in the way we view, read, and write plays.

If as Toni Cade Bambara said (as will be later noted to a different end), we are all writing the same play, then access to Pinter's ethic and aesthetic contained in *Moonlight's* vision, revises the way we view and appreciate much current drama and film and will surely continue to inspire other writers. The book is intended not only for the audience, critic, actor, director and for other writers but for anyone reading contemporary literature and, in that fuller sense, reading contemporary life and death played out on the private, public and world stage. Finally, it serves that far greater function: recognition that Pinter's work returns us all to life different, more deeply appreciative of our own possibilities.

NOTES

1. In Shepard's plays, from *Curse of the Starving Class* onward, food which might nourish the body is trashed on stage, and the home, as a family dwelling which might sustain and develop both body and spirit, may literally explode. Hare's work, culminating in *The Secret Rapture,* unleashes a predatory Margaret Thatcher clone, Marion French, whose administration and the mega-business her government represents bulldoze over those who may be well-intentioned environmentalists or small business people but are

powerless to act. Such is Marion's gentle sister Isobel, whose death is related to and indirectly results from her sister's myopic greed. Marion's turning to her husband with erotic desire in the wake of her sister's funeral cuts whatever disturbance and recognition Marion feels confronting Isobel's "ghost" with irony.

2. While it might be interesting to compare the development of Pinter's work with Foucault's three stages of authority and punishment described in *Discipline and Punish,* it is the differences which are most informative. Where Foucault identifies the third and present stage of the development of authority and punishment as amorphous and ubiquitous and concludes by looking into a cynical black hole without hope for change, Pinter continues to examine specific acts and specific causes for abuses of authority (and punishment), situating responsibility within both the individual as well as a global worldview which promotes misguided destruction.
3. I am indebted to Jason Grunebaum for recommending the book to me.
4. The riddle of the Sphinx is, "What walks on four legs in the morning, two legs at noon and three legs at night?" The answer is "man."

Harold Pinter: Biography

1930–1940: "Every Time We Evacuated I Took My Cricket Bat with Me."

As a young man Harold Pinter appears to have performed a Cinderella transformation without a fairy godmother or Pygmalion to sculpt or script him. Born in Hackney 10 October 1930, Harold Pinter grew up at 19 Thistlewaite Road on a street of identical, orange-brick row houses in the bustling, working-class East London of small shops near a foul-smelling soap factory, but by the age of thirty was acknowledged by some as England's foremost playwright, made a Commander of the Order of the British Empire, and by his forties and fifties acclaimed as one of the world's leading dramatists. In a real sense, however, the values and vision of the man who would alter the course of the aesthetics and ethics of drama in the twentieth century were already in evidence in nascent form even in his grammar school juvenilia, and astonishingly well developed in his one novel *The Dwarfs,* begun when he was twenty.

Born to Hyman "Jack" and Frances (née Moskowitz) Pinter, a Jewish family who emigrated to Britain via Eastern Europe, possibly Hungary or Poland in the early twentieth century, Harold Pinter honors his childhood in the East End as spent in a "living community" with "a living language." (Sherwood, n.p.) His late father worked twelve hours a day as a ladies' tailor, lost his business, then went to work for someone else, and served as an air raid warden during the war. His late mother, whom he describes as a good cook and "the very opposite of a Jewish Matriarch," kept a lovely backyard garden, one happy site of his earliest boyhood imaginings. (Gussow, "Conversation [Pause] with Harold Pinter," 43) There in the back garden at the age of six or seven, Harold began to make up stories with imaginary characters and "to have long dramatic interludes" and "a very real relationship with them." (Sherwood, n.p.)

While there is nothing remarkable about imaginary friends in the childhood of any writer, Harold's experience with violence was early, immediate, and indelible. Before his first decade was out, at the age of nine during World War II, he was evacuated to a castle in Cornwall without his parents. He recalls the "marvelous grounds" on the sea looking out on the English Channel with twenty-four other boys. He says "it wasn't quite so idyllic as it sounds, because I was quite a morose little boy," and it was also terrifying. ("Two People in a Room," 35) From the ages of nine to fourteen, when he was evacuated to Cornwall and elsewhere, his parents visited him whenever they could, at great expense at a time they had no money.

In 1944 a the age of fourteen he returned home to see his first flying bomb in the street: "It looked like a tiny airplane. It was an innocent-looking thing. It just chugged along. And then I saw it come down." (35) At other times he opened the back door to find the garden in flames.

1940–1950: "I Was Aware of the Suffering and the Horror of War, and by No Means Was I Going to Subscribe to Keeping It Going."

As a child, Harold found the whole experience of being evacuated and returning home to London during the bombing "very disturbing" and "frightening." (35) Yet he did not eschew or shun violence but confronted it. From about the age of fourteen, whenever he was in London he began frequenting the cinema and especially enjoyed American gangster movies. His early war experience, coupled with his early confrontation and exploration of violence in literature and film, provided the nexus of aesthetic and ethical concerns that later developed in his plays.

If Harold acquired unforgettable contacts with violence in his early years, he also developed a life-long passion for cricket, a sport he would share with Samuel Beckett and, later, Tom Stoppard. "Every time we evacuated, I took my cricket bat with me." (36) That love of sport has continued in Ping Pong, squash, and, more recently, tennis. At thirteen he had his first love affair.

In his early youth Harold also formed a closely bonded friendship, a "remarkably enjoyable association with five other boys." (Kathleen Tynan, 9) He describes it as "a great relief, I remember, that they knew what I was on about." But the friendship also included, "[r]uthless mutual confrontations," and, as he says of his autobiographical play *The Dwarfs*, derived from his novel by the same name, betrayal. (9) Yet of that group, two who emigrated to Canada remained his closest friends: Henry Woolf, who went on to teach at the University of Saskatchewan, and Morris Wernick, who taught in Sault Sainte Marie and later in Burlington, Ontario.

During those years the neighborhood Hackney Downs Grammar School which Harold attended on scholarship became the locus of his intellectual and artistic pursuits. Never merely a sensitive or shrinking artist, even in school Harold balanced academic and literary production with competitive physical activity and excelled in all areas. He played football and cricket and competed in track, setting school sprinting records. He also wrote lyric poetry and began acting. He played Macbeth and Romeo under English master Joseph Brearley, "a brilliant man ... obsessed with the theatre," who recognized his talents and became Harold's acknowledged most valued source of early encouragement. ("Two People in a Room," 35) Harold also exhibited a formidable intellect and wide range of reading. His school essays already display an impassioned interest in the larger world.

Taken together Harold's poems, essays and speeches not only prefigure the scope of his mature work, ranging from the romantic and realistic to the violent, but embrace the two poles of what would become his central concerns: love and destruction. His lyric poems "Dawn" and "O Beloved Maiden" express a young man's desire and concern with love, while his essay "Blood Sports," his speeches "A United Europe Would Be the Only Means of Preventing War" and "War Is Inevitable" address violence and destruction in the world. In at least one early piece describing a cockfight, love and destruction merge, as they would to a quite different end, in his most recent work:

> They are clawed to insanity. Their tongues are limp in blood. . . . One sinks wearily to the floor and dies. And sharper than the claws of the cock are the nails of a lady digging into the arm of a man. (Kroll, 74)

In addition to love and violent destruction, Harold's early writing also delineated a third area of interest, equally significant: aesthetics. Specifically he focused on literature and film. His school essay "James Joyce" praises Joyce's work from *A Portrait of the Artist as a Young Man* through *Finnegans Wake,* and his speeches "Realism and Post-Realism in the French Cinema" and "In View of Its Progress in the Last Decade, the Film Is More Promising in Its Future as an Art Than the Theatre" evince a range of knowledge poised toward the future of that art and his contribution to it. The only academic subjects he says he was interested in pursuing further were English language and literature, and the only universities he seriously considered were Oxford and Cambridge. But to attend university at that time it was necessary to know Latin, and he did not. He left school at sixteen.

He describes himself as "fed up and restless" and says, "I was mostly in love at the time and tied up with that." (Bensky, 354) A first turning point toward his career came when he saw Donald Wolfit in *King Lear.* So deeply impressed was he by his performance, he went back to see the actor-manager of a traveling theatre company perform Lear five more times. That profound impression determined the course of his next decade and the rest of his life.

Harold won a grant to RADA, the Royal Academy of Dramatic Arts, but did not study seriously. In that "terrible atmosphere of affectation and unreality, ankle bands and golden hair," he skipped class to watch cricket trials; after three months he faked a nervous breakdown and dropped out for months without informing either his parents or those funding him. ("*Caretaker's* Caretaker," 76) He later attended the Central School of Dramatic Arts and again dropped out. But his considerable reading had already taken hold.

When Pinter was asked if the drama schools were of any use he replied, "None whatsoever. It was just living," but he quickly added, "I was reading, for years, a great deal of modern literature, mostly novels." Early in his career he lists Dostoevsky, Joyce, Hemingway, and Henry Miller "at a very early age, and Kafka." (Bensky, 354) Elsewhere he cites the early influence of Dylan Thomas, Dos Passos, George Barker, Yeats, Eliot and Proust. He also mentions William Burroughs, Raymond Chandler and the poets Gerard Manley Hopkins, Philip Larkin, Pope, and Donne. *One Hundred Poems by One Hundred Poets,* Pinter's collection of poetry which he selected and edited, indicates some preferences among traditional poets. He enjoys reading poetry aloud. Later, during the Broadway production of *The Homecoming,* Pinter brought with him fourteen books, indicating omnivorous reading preferences: Joyce's *Letters;* Alain Robbe-Grillet's *La Maison de Rendez-vous;* Jane Bowles' *Plain Pleasures;* Edna O'Brien's *Casualties of Peace;* Edward Albee's *A Delicate Balance; The Story of O;* Robert Shaw's *The Man in the Glass Booth; The New Poetry,* edited by A. Alvarez; *The Poems of John Donne; Love Poems* by Thomas Hardy; *The Less Deceived* and *The Whitsun Weddings* by Philip Larkin and *The Selected Letters of Dylan Thomas.* ("Two People in a Room," 34) While he denied an early influence of Ionesco or Brecht, claiming he did not know Ionesco's plays or Beckett's, he already knew and deeply admired Beckett's prose. He has expressed admiration for playwrights Edward Albee, Edward Bond, Joe Orton, John Mortimer, N.F. Simpson, Peter Weiss, Heathcote Williams, Arthur Miller, Tennessee Williams, David Storey, Simon Gray, David Mercer, and Ionesco. His deepest admiration was for the late Samuel Beckett with whom he formed a long and close friendship, calling Beckett, in the festschrift *Beckett at Sixty,* "the finest writer now writing." (86) Pinter's more recent reading reflects the ethical concerns that have become the core of his activity and later plays. His list of book recommendations contributed to *The Observer* included: *Night* by Eli Wiesel, *In Dark Time* edited by Nicholas Humphrey and Robert Jay Lifton, *Nunca Mas,* the Argentinean Nation Commission report, *Semites and Anti Semites* by Bernard Lewis and *The Drowned and the Saved* by Primo Levi. He has consistently endorsed *Requiem for a Woman's Soul* by Omar Rivabella. (Knowles 1989, 26) His other loves in art and music include a passion for the art of Francis Bacon and an appreciation of the music of Boulez and Webern, of American Jazz, Miles Davis, Thelonious Monk and of a number of contemporary composers and performers, including the Beatles and Peter Gabriel. He puts Bach at the head of the list. But no biography can trace the artistic influences nor catalogue the prodigious reading of a man who says, "I read all the time." (Bensky, 354) Perhaps most telling are that the only sketches hanging in his study are one of Joyce and one of Beckett. He says that if he had one of Yeats it would hang there, too.

As a reader and writer, he was accorded automatic esteem and the privacy to write in the homes of friends he visited. "Jewish families had a great respect for education," he says and he recalls writing from about the age of twelve. He remembers once visiting his friend Henry Woolf who was out when he arrived, so the family gave him tea and cakes while he waited, and when he asked for paper, saying, "Something's just come across my mind," he says, "They supplied me with paper and I wrote away. We sat in absolute silence for about forty-five minutes with them smiling and nodding because a good Jewish boy was writing something." (Kroll, 78)

As a Jew, often carrying books and therefore taken for a communist, Harold's confrontation with violence continued after the war during the fascists' return to power. He witnessed elderly Jews attacked on the street. On his way to attend a Jewish club, he encountered gangs carrying broken milk bottles waiting under a railway arch or gathering in the Ridley Road Market near Dalston Junction. "*We* didn't have any milk bottles," he says. (Bensky, 363) He frequently talked his way past the gangs. Sometimes he fought.

After the war when he was called up to do National Service, he refused. He found "the idea of rearming was preposterous" and said, "I was aware of the suffering and of the horror of war, and by no means was I going to subscribe to keeping it going." ("Two People in a Room," 25) His parents who were "wonderfully encouraging" when he became an actor were, however, "worried" when he became a conscientious objector. (Kroll, 76) He had two tribunals, two trials, and was released both times with fines which his father, who respected his position, paid. At his second tribunal, while others brought ministers to speak on their behalf, because Pinter had no religious beliefs by that time, he took his close friend Morris Wernick, and he recalls the "immortal speech" he made to secure his freedom. That intense bond of youthful friendship informs work from the early novel *The Dwarfs* and the plays *The Basement* through *Monologue, Old Times* and *Betrayal.* The bond sometimes ends in disillusionment or, as in *Reunion*, in healing. Hans, a young Jewish boy during World War II, now an old man seeking knowledge of his boyhood friend Konradin, a German aristocrat, fears he had become a Nazi. In the end Hans discovers that Konradin had not betrayed their childhood friendship or ideals but was executed as a result of his participation in an attempted death plot against Hitler.

1950–1960: "At That Time Acting Was the Only Way I Could Conceive of Earning Any Money."

For the next decade under the stage name David Baron, Harold Pinter toured England and Ireland, acting in over ninety plays. In response to an advertisement after he left the Central School of Speech and Drama, Pinter joined Anew McMaster's Shakespeare touring company in Ireland, playing Horatio, Bassanio, Edgar, Edmund, Macduff, Iago, Cassio, Creon in *Oedipus*, Sir Robert Chiltern in *An Ideal Husband*, Lord Windermere in *Lady Windermere's Fan* and John Worthing in *The Importance of Being Earnest*. In *Mac*, Pinter's tribute to Anew McMaster written after McMaster's death in 1962, Pinter details with characteristic raw honesty the exuberant man with the love Pinter bore his early mentor at a "time acting was the only way I could conceive of earning any money." He says, "I never imagined that writing would gradually take over." (Dean, 312)

Harold Pinter took the name Pinta and da Pinta, possibly his original family name, for his earliest published poetry. *Kullus*, a dialogue, appeared in 1949 in *Poems*, and his first published poems "New Year in the Midlands," "Chandeliers and Shadows," "Rural Idyll" and "European Revels," appeared in *Poetry London*, and "The Second Visit," in *The Window* in 1950. That year he began his novel, *The Dwarfs*.

While he was touring with Anew McMaster, Pinter chanced upon Beckett's writing, beginning what would ten years later become a close friendship:

> I was one of the very first people, believe it or not, in England who came across Beckett. I was in Ireland at the time with Mac and I picked up a copy of *Irish Writing*, a little magazine—the editor was there before me, I must admit. And there was a piece of Beckett's, a fragment from *Watt*, and I'd never heard of him. It really rang in my head. (Bakewell, 631)

Pinter's amazement was immediate:

> I looked at this and went cross-eyed and really saw double and I was amazed … How do we put it? The top ten and all that. He's the boy all right. He can write everyone else under the table.

> But what can I say, Beckett was an absolute knockout for me. It wasn't a matter of saying I see. This is something quite new. This is something I must attend to. It was the most ... terrible chord struck in me at the time. I was about nineteen I think. It was terrible, terrible business to read that fragment but I went on to read Beckett a great deal. (Kitchen and Mayersberg, n.p.)

When he returned to London no one had heard of Beckett, and no library possessed a copy of his work. When he finally found a copy of *Murphy* in the Battersea Public Reserve Library in 1949, last signed out in 1939, he took it. "I still have that particular copy. No one missed it." (631)

Later in Paris during the run of *The Caretaker* Roger Blin introduced Pinter to Beckett. Pinter says he had written to Beckett in 1959 "and got an extremely nice letter back. So then I was in a position of meeting him. The longshot of it is I came into his hotel and he was very vigorous and chatty and extremely affable and extremely friendly and we spent the whole *night* together. And that was really ... very good. And since then, we've really seen quite a lot of one another." (Gussow, "A Conversation ... ," 218) During plans to collaborate on a film with Beckett and Ionesco, Pinter said: "He's a wonderful writer, but a very generous man too. Splendid chap. I'm privileged to be working with him on a film." (Kitchen and Mayersberg, n.p.) Beginning with *The Homecoming*, Pinter began to send his work to Beckett, who occasionally made suggestions. Like Beckett, one of the rare playwrights who made few or no changes after writing or during rehearsal, Pinter says he cut only one speech in *Silence*—at Beckett's suggestion but not until he himself heard it in rehearsal.

In 1953, after touring Ireland for almost two years, Pinter joined Donald Wolfit's company where he first met the actress Vivien Merchant, born Ada Brand Thomson.[1] She took Vivien as her stage name out of her admiration for actress Vivien Leigh and took Merchant after her brother, a Merchant Marine. Pinter later joined other repertory companies touring in provincial theatres in England throughout the fifties. Originally hired as a juvenile, Pinter confesses he was "quite good at being sinister in a smiling way." (Kroll, 78) When asked what influence his acting had on his plays Pinter replied, "I think I certainly developed some feeling for construction, which believe it or not, is important for me, and for speakable dialogue," adding, "I had a pretty good notion in my earlier plays of what would shut an audience up; not so much what would make them laugh; that I had no idea about." ("Writing for Myself," 173)

Commenting on Pinter's comedy, the late Joseph Losey, who directed several of Pinter's screenplays, pointed out that Pinter's humor is often overlooked. One of Pinter's closest friends, the late Robert Shaw, called Pinter himself "a mixture of Groucho Marx and T.S. Eliot." (Kroll, 81) Pinter, at that time, named Jack Benny as the comedian he most admired: "I saw Benny thirty years ago at the Palladium. And I've never forgotten it—his timing, his pauses, his silences." (81) But when asked if he aims for laugh lines when he writes, Pinter says he does not. Asked if he ever laughs while working on a play, he confesses sometimes, when he is writing.

Clearly he appreciates his own humor and wishes others to do so. His decision to produce *The Hothouse*, which had remained unproduced for thirty years, was based on the play's laughter-producing comedy. He found when he reread the play "as a stranger" that he "laughed quite a lot," and he says, "in consequence I thought of bringing it out." (Gussow, "Harold Pinter: I Started with Two People in a Room," IV, 7) He had a similar reaction to seeing *A Night Out*, a play he had earlier deemed not very successful, but more recently when he saw it again, he laughed a lot.

Asked to comment upon the observation that he had invented the comedy of menace or the comedy of dread, he denied the whole question of invention: "Anything one writes can't be new," yet while he assents, "You've just got your individual way of saying it, what has been said and must have been said for centuries;" he adds, "There is comedy in life and there is menace in life, and I think the two things certainly go together—to a certain extent." Importantly, he cautions, "But there comes a point where things cease to be funny." (Tynan, n.p.)

Pinter acknowledges that his comedy, informed by terror, links the comic and tragic through the horror and absurdity beneath:

> I think what I try to do in my plays is get to this recognisable reality of the absurdity of what we do and how we behave and how we speak. The point is people laugh at absurdity, because it is recognisable and secondly it verges on the unknown. We don't quite know where this absurdity is fixed. Of course it isn't fixed anywhere. The fact that it's verging on the unknown leads

> us to the next step which seems to occur in my plays; there's a kind of horror about it and I think that this horror and absurdity go together. (Wildman, n.p.)

He believes his work is "funnier than is generally acknowledged," by critics and wishes audiences might "have been encouraged to enjoy themselves." (Nightingale, n.p.)

Meanwhile as a young actor in the early 1950s, Pinter continued writing hundreds of poems, short prose pieces including "The Examination," getting about a dozen pieces published in literary magazines. Between morning rehearsals and evening performances, he says he was able "to get down with considerable enjoyment in the afternoon to writing." (Tynan, n.p.)

Pinter gained much else besides "an ear for speakable dialogue" and "a sense of construction" from his time as an actor. In his praise for his mentor Anew McMaster, he reveals some of the many values that accrued to him as an actor: from respect for Mac's business acumen and admiration for his art of acting, to some of the deepest values his own writing embraces. Pinter praises Mac's practicality, describing him as a man who regarded himself as "a working man," as Pinter would later describe himself. Like Pinter who continues to teach his audiences and to stretch the form at nearly every turn, Mac "respected his occupation and never stopped learning about it, from himself and from others." He adds:

> He was not any kind of dreamer. He was remote from the Celtic Twilight. He kept a close eye on the box-office receipts. (*Mac*, 17; cf., Pete's argument in the novel *The Dwarfs* with Mark's saying, "I've got nothing but contempt for the till." [79])

Pinter was deeply impressed with the precision, the accuracy, the artistry of both McMaster and Wolfit. He recalls McMaster's Othello as "the finest Othello I have seen." Though "his age was always a mystery," he thinks he was in his sixties:

> But on stage in *Othello* he stood well over six foot, naked to the waist, his gestures complete, final, nothing jagged, his movement of the utmost fluidity and yet of the utmost precision: stood there, dead in the center of the role, and the great sweeping symphonic

> playing would begin, the rare tension and release within him, the arrest, the swoop, the savagery, the majesty and repose. His voice was unique: in my experience of an unequaled range. (*Mac*, 84)

Of Wolfit's Oedipus at Colonus Pinter speaks of the same kind of "precision" that "impressed" him in a gesture Wolfit made with a cloak: "He waited for *the* moment, which was always the same moment, nevertheless the tension waiting for it each night was always pronounced. What got me was the accuracy of these people in what they were doing, their instinct for the moment when things were to happen." (Bakewell, 82) That regard for accuracy, precision, and "the moment when things would happen" translated directly into his own writing.

But Pinter idealizes, sentimentalizes, and romanticizes no one, neither his mentors, his characters, nor himself. He has referred to himself as a "Bastard. A bastard human being." (Nightingale, n.p.) He acknowledges that Mac "was capable, of course, of many indifferent and offhand performances." (*Mac*, 12) Pinter's unfiltered honesty toward both positive and negative qualities in the living people he admired informs his greatest characters, in fact, nearly all his characters. That ability to encompass and to hold in tension those opposing qualities functions in his work like a Hegelian dialectic but without a synthesis. Mac, as Pinter recalls him, embodies extremes of ugliness and beauty. Pinter allows us to see Mac at the outset without his teeth and at his roaring worst yet enhances appreciation for the respect, admiration, and the love he had for the man, for his vitality, which all by itself is portrayed as a virtue, and for his overwhelming generosity—Mac's "true liberality of spirit." That vitality (which informs Pinter's Max and Mac in *The Homecoming*) and that generosity, traditionally regarded as the crowning virtue, together form the capstone of the ethic in Pinter's work:

> He was a realist. But he possessed a true liberality of spirit. He was humble. He was a devout anti-puritan. He was a very great pisstaker. He was a great actor and we who worked with him were the luckiest people in the world and loved him. (*Mac*, 19)

In 1956 Pinter again met Vivien Merchant, this time playing opposite as Rochester to her Jane Eyre. That year they were married. A year later he wrote his first play, *The Room*.

Pinter had earlier mentioned the play to his friend, actor Henry Woolf, then a student in the drama department of Bristol University. When Woolf solicited the play for production, Pinter said he hadn't written it yet and couldn't possibly write it in time. He wrote it in four days.

Pinter's first dramatic image came at a party in London when he was taken to a room where he saw one loquacious, literate man serving food to another man, burly and silent. Those two people became Rose and Burt in *The Room.*

Until that production, aside from his work published in literary magazines, only a few friends had ever seen what he had written, and Pinter had never seen anything of his performed. He describes the experience of sitting in the audience the first time as "remarkable," adding, "I wanted to piss very badly throughout the whole thing, and at the end I dashed out behind the bicycle shed." (Bensky, 351–2) Afterwards he says, "I was profoundly disoriented and got totally drunk." (352) His excitement, he confesses, was coupled with violence: "They found me in the lavatory attacking this actor who was twice my size. It was just the shock of the birth of one's work in a public arena." (Kroll, 78) He says, "[B]ut what I'm really talking about is the dizziness of the event to a young man. I never quite recovered from that. I realized I was a marked man." (Schiff, 303) He adds, [however], "Watching first nights, though I've seen quite a few by now, is never any better. It's a nerve-wracking experience. It's not a question of whether the play goes well or badly. It's not the audience reaction, it's *my* reaction." (Bensky, 352) The play was later produced in London at the Hampstead Theatre Club, directed by Pinter starring Vivien Merchant as Rose. But Pinter was "very encouraged by the response of that university audience," yet he admits that "no matter what the response had been I would have written *The Birthday Party,* I know that." (Bensky, 352)

In January 1958 *The Room* was entered in a festival of university drama where the late *Times* critic Harold Hobson, one of the judges, was so impressed he reviewed the play. When Michael Codron heard about it, he asked at once if Pinter had a full-length work. Pinter had just finished *The Birthday Party.* Although Pinter confesses he nearly gave up on it "because the characters were so horrible," he finished it and went on that same year to write *The Dumb Waiter,* which premiered at Frankfurt-am-Main, Germany, in

1959. (Tynan, n.p.) Like *The Room*, his plays *The Birthday Party, The Caretaker, The Homecoming*, and several early sketches also began in biographical remembrance. *The Caretaker* was informed by several tramps Pinter had met, one in particular who he says, "did most of the talking when I saw him." (Bensky, 353) *The Homecoming* began with a friend who had gone abroad to teach, then married and had three children without telling his father. "Then one day I knew he was going to come home and have to tell his father." (Bakewell, 631) But as in all his work the initial image transforms to communicate a point far beyond the simple story line and, like an umbilical cord, falls away: "When it *does* happen, the image itself—I mean the real thing—becomes dead very quickly." (631)

In 1957 Pinter wrote *The Birthday Party,* triggered on tour by filthy digs he shared with a young man who claimed to have been a concert pianist. When Pinter asked the man why he stayed, he replied, "There's nowhere to go." (Bakewell, 631) That man informed the character Stanley; their slovenly landlady became Meg. After a successful tour of Oxford and Cambridge, *The Birthday Party* produced by Michael Codron opened at the Lyric Theatre, Hammersmith, London, to be "massacred" by the critics, with one exception: Harold Hobson.

Typical of the early reviews was the bewilderment critics felt at the mystery, anything that could not be easily categorized and explained: "Sitting through *The Birthday Party* at the Lyric, Hammersmith, is like trying to solve a crossword puzzle where every vertical clue is designed to put you off the horizontal. It will be best enjoyed by those who believe that obscurity is its own reward ... Not nearly as witty as Simpson's *The Resounding Tinkle* nor nearly as chilling as Ionesco's *The Lesson. ...* " (Shulman, 9)

Hobson, however, recognized the mystery as the play's strength: "The fact that no one can say precisely what it is about, or give the address from which the intruding Goldberg and McCann come, or say precisely why it is that Stanley is so frightened by them is, of course, one of its greatest merits. It is exactly in this vagueness that its spine-chilling quality lies. If we knew what Miles had done, *The Turn of the Screw* would fade away. As it is Mr Pinter has learned the lesson of the Master. Henry James would recognize him as an equal." (Hobson, 11)

Yet Pinter consistently insists he has "never willfully hidden any piece of information out of whim or mischief":

> I learn about the characters from what they say. You can't force characters to say something that would be untrue to them. Then it flops. You're inventing it. It's so obviously phony. If I'm going to hide information or force a man to say something which he wouldn't say, the whole thing would drop to pieces at my feet. (Crist, 80)

The mystery in Pinter's work conveys a deeper philosophy. To establish truth, Pinter, like the twentieth-century scientist, shuns causal relationships (simplistic explanations which distort and falsify) in favor of high correlations which create mystery and ambiguity that express his more complex view of time and reality:

> The most we know for sure is that the things which have happened have happened in a certain order: any connections we think we see, or choose to make, are pure guesswork. Life is so much more mysterious than plays make it out to be. And it is this mystery which fascinates me: what happens between words and what happens when no words are spoken. (John Russell Taylor, "Accident," 184)

American playwright David Freeman praises the realistic use of mystery and asserts it is difficult to achieve:

> Whenever the apparent action becomes mysterious but still retains a realistic surface, we are drawn to it. To make a character both real and mysterious is difficult, and it makes magic on the stage. (A letter, by permission of the author)

When Hobson wrote his now-famous review of *The Birthday Party,* aware of the bad notices and not even sure the play would still be running when his review appeared, he believed Pinter's name and the play would be seen elsewhere:

> Deliberately, I am willing to risk whatever reputation I have as a judge of plays by saying that *The Birthday Party* is not a Fourth, not even a Second, but a First, and that Mr Pinter, on the evidence of this work, possesses the most original, disturbing and arresting talent in theatrical London. . . . (11; ellipses mine)

Hobson's analysis bears rereading as one of the most perceptive not only of the surface tension but of the deeper values and vision communicated in the subtext:

> There is only one quality that is essential to a play. It is the quality that can be found both in *Hamlet* and in *Simple Spyman.* A play must entertain; it must hold the attention; it must give pleasure. Unless it does that it is useless for stage purposes. No amount of intellect, of high moral intent, or of beautiful writing is of the slightest avail if a play is not in itself theatrically interesting. Theatrically speaking *The Birthday Party* is absorbing. It is witty. Its characters . . . fascinating. The play, which consists, with all kinds of verbal arabesques and echoing explorations of memory and fancy, of the springing of a trap, is first rate. The whole play has the same atmosphere of delicious, impalpable and hair-raising terror which makes *Turn of the Screw* one of the best stories in the world. (11)

Hobson recognized that at depth the characters faced the void:

> Mr Pinter has got hold of a primary fact of existence. We live on the verge of disaster. One sunny day whilst Peter May is making a century at Lords against Middlesex ... and the old men are dozing in the Long Room, a hydrogen bomb may explode. This is one sort of threat. But Mr Pinter's is of a subtler sort. It breathes in the air. It cannot be seen, but it enters the room every time the door is opened. There is something in your past—it does not matter what—which will catch up with you. Though you go to the uttermost parts of the earth, and hide yourself in the most obscure lodgings in the least popular town, one day there is a possibility that two men will appear. They will be looking for you and you cannot get away. And someone will be looking for *them,* too. There is terror everywhere. (11; ellipses mine)

Hobson understood that the plight of both pursued and pursuer was identical and further appreciated not only the principal source of the play's delight, its comic wit, but the comedy's connection to the horror it makes endurable:

> Meanwhile it is best to make jokes (Mr Pinter's jokes are very good) and to play blind man's buff, and to bang on a toy drum, anything to forget the slow approach of doom. (11)

The play closed after a week. That year Pinter's son Daniel was born.

The work of that third decade of Pinter's life spanning his early to his late twenties had provided the proving ground that defined the values of the rest of his work. His novel *The Dwarfs* written in his early twenties already laid out his artistic demands aesthetically and ethically. The novel centers on the close friendship of three young men, Pete, Mark and Len, and Pete's girlfriend Virginia, whom he slowly rejects in his attempt to educate her, till Mark appropriates her, betraying Pete. Through Pete, the novel defines the self through action at three levels: in Pete's relation to himself, to friends, and, finally, to the larger world.

It is impossible to argue that the novel, as a work of fiction, articulates Pinter's aesthetic intentions. Nor does the novel offer an ethical treatise. Yet many of the subtle issues of ethics and aesthetics, later internalized and dramatized in his plays, are given expression only here in his writing. The topic, of friendship betrayed, launches the discussion that marks the beginning point defining the aesthetics and ethics, two major issues that would fuse in Pinter's later work in a single linked topic: love and justice.

When Mark betrays Pete's friendship confessing he slept with Virginia, Pete slams Mark's "morality": his "bedmanners" and "integrity." Yet Pete acknowledges that Mark's morality has no bearing on his own:

> But it's your integrity that's in question and you haven't proved that you're worth it. (181)

Pete however, considers himself as "worth it" and views his own survival as a virtue; were he killed he asks if it "might be not only an overwhelming disaster for me, but an irreplaceable lack in the sum total of human knowledge, and an irreparably lost opportunity for creating good?" (181) Pete might be voicing the aspiration of any emerging writer. While Pete possesses the insight to appreciate Mark's betrayal as resulting from "frustration and hate," he notes his own duty to survive "at all costs," and ends in linking his lost love with justice: "It was a question of overriding justice." (181)

Pete's high self-regard requires of a friend an equal. But when Pete asks Mark if he chose him as a friend, "Because you considered me your equal?" he himself answers, "Not by a long chalk." (176) Pete places high demands on friendship insisting, "The function of a friend," must be "that of an ambassador to yourself from yourself," adding, "Then he's a man of your soul." (177)

If equality is the basis for friendship, Pete cites his own admiration as a quality he brings, yet he adds to the gratitude he feels for their friendship a caveat:

> But if you get inside and eat my stomach I will always bite back—
> in spades. (179)

Pete moves from the topic of friendship, where ethics are played out privately, to the subjects of aesthetics and public ethics. Speaking from the aesthetic center of the novel's controversy, Pete also places rigorous demands on every element in art from the smallest to the largest:

> Every particle of a work of art should crack a nut, or help form a pressure that'll crack the final nut. (77)

Where an actual nut cracker "gives off heat and friction which is incidental," art must burn clean without excess heat or friction. But at every point Pete ties his demand for economy, image and structure to the larger idea:

> Each idea must possess stringency and economy and the image, if you like, that expresses it must stand in exact correspondence and relation to the idea. Only then can you speak of utterance and only then can you speak of achievement. (77)

Already conscious of the function of form, Pete as spokesperson for the nascent aesthetic in Pinter's work, nicely defines what is later described here by the fractal geometry, the remarkable structure of Pinter's plays where each momentary friction point reflects the conflict manifested in the work as a whole (see 4ff). The resultant resonance of that structure gives richness to the subtext and points to the larger end Pinter's economy serves. That larger end, as Pete demands, situates economy and efficiency within the context of the relationship of the play's action to a changing world.

Throughout, Pete opposes mere abstraction and argues for grounding ideas in life. One great source of the power in Pinter's plays comes from his ability to allow audience identification with the smallest to the largest emotions, intentions and actions of each character within very specific situations—not abstract theory. Pete accuses Mark of not "paying enough attention to what goes on around you." When Mark asks if he means "headlines," Pete says, "There's more to it than that." (78) He accuses Mark of "operating on life and not in it," (79) reversing Teddy's admonition to his family in *The Homecoming,* to "operate on things and not in things." (61) Although Teddy accuses them of getting lost in life, he has removed himself from life to the abstract world of theory.

If, as Chekhov says, in comedy characters overcome their weaknesses, Pinter's plays redefine both comedy and tragedy. His characters neither overcome nor even acknowledge their weaknesses, yet Pinter's expression remains comic. Beneath the deadly seriousness he recognizes his essentially comic take on life informs what he writes:

> If I write about myself or you, we're going to be funny. Everything is funny. The greatest earnestness is funny. Even tragedy is funny. The point about tragedy is that it is no longer funny. It's funny, and then it becomes no longer funny. (Wildman, n.p.)

Pinter never uses humor to distance himself or his audience from pain or suffering or from confronting the deeper and essentially tragic vision of life. Instead the comedy leads an audience directly to that inescapable point where it is necessary to confront the worst.

Not only is Pinter's comedy throughout informed by the terror it makes bearable, but as in Shakespeare's great tragedies, his plays release tragedy's special power of "transfiguring all that dread." Pinter describes that relationship between tragedy and transfiguration in *Mac* as he recalls McMaster's performances of Othello and Lear:

> [H]e understood and expressed totally the final tender clarity that is under the storm, the blindness, the anguish. For me his acting at these times embodied the idea of Yeats' line: "They know that Hamlet and Lear are gay, Gaity transfiguring all that dread." (*Mac,* 15)

Pinter concludes, "Mac entered into this tragic gaiety naturally and inevitably." (15)

Through Pete as a voice for aesthetic values, Pinter like George Bernard Shaw measured himself against Shakespeare, but unlike Shaw remained wholly grounded in life, took Shakespeare as a touchstone for some basic values, but saw that the worldview had shifted. That paradigm shift requires not merely a revision of ideas and intention but of action.

Pinter, however, also appreciated the powerful forces opposing his characters' actions from within and without. If in comedy characters overcome weaknesses, Pete, discussing Shakespeare's morality, understands that in tragedy, (as in many of Pinter's plays) characters are overcome by their strengths:

> Leave Hamlet out of it. He's another story. But the others, Othello, Macbeth and Lear, are men whose great virtues are converted by their very superfluity into faults. (132)

In *Tragedy and the Theory of Drama*, Elder Olsen similarly defines the classic tragic hero as "hoist by his own petard," destroyed not by his weaknesses but by his own strengths.

Yet in Pinter's plays, the characters' refusal to recognize their own "territorial limitations" resulting from their lack of self-knowledge also destroys them. The test of virtue, as Pete knows, can come only in action which is then evaluated "by common justice":

> And when they have to act … , they're found to be lacking. When they're called to account by common justice they're wrong. (132; ellipses mine)

Paradoxically, Pete recognizes:

> At the same time, of course, they're right. They're right according to our admiration and sympathy. But that's to look at them in no way morally. (132)

In *The Dwarfs* Pete explicitly introduces two concepts central to the ethic throughout Pinter's work: responsibility and action.

> We're sympathizing with what they are when unhampered by the responsibility of action. (132)

While the emphasis on responsibility recurs throughout Pinter's interviews and essays, it remains almost unspoken in any of Pinter's plays and appears only by negation, by its absence, its failure, in the dramatic action. But Pete also understands why in Shakespeare's plays characters' virtue tested in action fails:

> The necessity of action smothers their virtue. They cease to be morally thinking creatures. Lear, Macbeth and Othello are all forced, in one way or another, to account for what they do and they all fail to do it. (132)

Pete, like Pinter, refuses to view "good and evil as abstractions" apart from specific human circumstances of life, or to see art as a refuge, sanctuary, or an activity which sets the artist, hero, or audience apart from the world, even the mundane, practical matters basic to existence. Pete finds Mark's saying, "I've got nothing but contempt for the till," hardly admirable. Insisting that Mark's notion of morality must be grounded both in his present surroundings and in the larger community, Pete castigates Mark for his solipsism: "You can't live safely tucked up in a test tube." (77) He then deduces that same point from his observations of Shakespeare's greatest tragic characters' morality nested within the larger social system:

> All they can see is the natural process of cause and effect working in a system of which they have ceased to be a part. They fall away from this system by lack of a social virtue. By not thinking for others. (133)

The lack of "social virtue" and the failure of "thinking for others" contrasts with Pinter's own compassion, his ability so completely to enter the hearts and heads of all his characters. Pinter's own most powerful destructors, like Shakespeare's, are limited in their ability to do so:

> In each case, the initial thinking for others was superficial and unrealized, delusive. Their unique qualities gave them, if you like, the power of dispensation over others. So they thought. (133)

But Pete cautions:

> [A]s all things are qualified by relevant circumstances, so they considered they were not responsible to a code of morality which did not take them into account. (133)

While Pete insists that those in power must see themselves as a part of the rest of life rather than apart from it, he also recognizes Shakespeare's tragic characters' paradoxical inability to disassociate from the "machine"—unexamined, received morality—as a source of their own destruction:

> Where these geezers slip up is that they try to overcome the machine of which they remain, whether they like it or not, a part. The machine, if you like, is morality, the standards of the majority. It seems to me that Shakespeare justifies both the man and the machine. (133)

Pinter's work justifies neither the man nor the machine, yet in presenting with compassion both those who support and oppose the machine, his plays dramatize insights into a central cause for almost all human destruction.

Pinter remains neither an apologist for the machine—the morality of the majority and its representatives wherever the machine requires addressing—nor for the man who fails to see, to know his own limitations and, failing to address those limitations when he can, is destroyed.

If Shakespeare does justify both the man and the machine, Mark wonders, "How can it be said that he's a moral poet?" Mark himself answers by defending Shakespeare as nondidactic, not explicitly a moralist: "I mean, look what he does. Look at the way he behaves. He never uses a communication cord or a lifebelt, and what's more, he never suggests he's got one handy for your use or his." (133) Pinter's work offers neither a "lifebelt" nor a message. Mark further praises Shakespeare as a dramatist too complex to make moral judgments, which he terms a form of bankruptcy:

> How can moral judgments be applied when you consider how many directions he travels at once? Hasn't he got enough troubles . . . ? [H]e turns down blind alleys, he stews in his own juice, and he nearly always ends up by losing all hands. But the

> fabric, mate, never breaks. The tightrope is never at less than an even stretch. He keeps in business, that's what, and if he started making moral judgments he'd go bankrupt like the others. (133)

But it is Pete who drives the ethical point further—that Shakespeare did not foist a prescriptive ethic, an ideal like a template upon his characters:

> [H]e didn't measure the man up against the idea and give you hot tips on the outcome. (133–4)

Pinter returns the discussion to friendship as Pete drives the question of responsibility further and at the same time opens discussion of friendship to aesthetics and ethics by articulating the way real friendship is destroyed when an ideal ("so ... they can fit your requirements") is imposed:

> Where they fail to do so, contempt, by your own logic, is the only outcome. It's their epitaph. They become an academic exercise in failure. Not because they themselves have necessarily failed, but simply that in attempting to retain what is their own, they have failed you. (176)

Yet Pete does not jettison all criteria for morality, but praises Shakespeare for avoiding abstractions:

> —He laid bare, that's all. I'd defy any man who said he saw good and evil as abstractions. He didn't. (134)

Pete concedes that like Shakespeare "we must retain some standards by which to measure the whole business":

> If we had no terms of reference, the experience would be lost. (134)

That morality which undergoes its severest test only in action, Pete acknowledges, is likely to obliterate "our own moral sense."

> And if you take that obliteration as bad, you can call Shakespeare an immoral poet. (134)

Pete reverses his original position on Shakespeare as a moral poet and introduces to "responsibility" and "action" the third important term in the ethic—"choice":

> *[A]s a man of choice he's finally obliged to accept responsibility for his actions. You could say then, that in so far as he points that out, he is a moral poet.* (134; italics mine)

It is at least in that same sense—through a character's responsibility for choice and action—that Pinter is a moral poet. Like Shakespeare's characters, his are attacked on all sides as well as by forces unknown and unknowable.

When Pete next reverses position on Shakespeare as a moral poet it might be tempting for an American to take Pete's seeming contradiction and quote Whitman's: "Do I contradict myself?/Very well I contradict myself./(I am large. I contain multitudes.)" (76) But Pinter's seeming contradictions, like the seeming polar opposites of his characters, are of a different order, and again reflect, like a Hegelian dialectic, an ability to embrace and contain opposites. Yet, unlike Hegel, Pinter provides no stated synthesis, no comfortable resting position that clarifies a correct position between those two poles.

Opposing dichotomies remain unreconciled, not as implacable oppositions but as acknowledged extremes in all human intention and action that are not sanitized by an idealized, sentimental vision or fiction. Moreover, as Pete concludes, one's weaknesses do not diminish the validity of one's strengths: "Your faults don't make your virtues any less true." (136) Refusing abstraction as distortion and simplification, Pinter allows within each character both paired opposites—the strengths and weaknesses—to stand *within a specific context* allowing audiences, as an equal partner, to draw their own conclusions.

In a key observation Pete opposes mere theory untested in action as sterile:

> Well, I don't see how good and evil can be defined by contemplation of the results of particular actions. Good is a productive state of mind, if you like, as well as a social virtue. But a productive state of mind in some circumstances may become quite sterile in others. Good and evil, they're both qualified by circumstances. (132)

Like Kant, who points out that we have only three choices in life, a choice of attitude, intention and action, Pete assesses that mere attitude ("contemplation of the results of particular actions," to define good or evil) or intention ("a productive state of mind") is insufficient to define morality without action ("a social virtue") which requires social intercourse with the world. Pete concludes that good and evil can be "neither arbitrary nor static." (132)

No moral relativist, Pinter draws the distinction between the standards working within a dynamic "living moment" and that desire to fix statically or to supply an abstract moral precept (which can neither apply in difficult cases nor remain standing unqualified by circumstances). The final emphasis in Pinter's work remains on action—the living moment. Pete says: "The point is, I want living to uphold me." (136) He concludes, "Experience is the testing ground." (178)

Like Oedipus, Lear and Othello, Pinter's characters, though they may fail in their responsibility, are revealed as responsible beings through their action and, in conveying that responsibility to the audience, dignify the human position in the world.

1960–1970: "When You Can't Write, You Feel You've Been Banished from Yourself."

Pinter's emphasis on action carried over to his own life. His own choices and action during the early years of his writing career required a test no less courageous than any his characters faced at that time. But where his characters often retreat to seek static comfort and shelter in attempts to save themselves, Pinter took risks to preserve his art.

In the wake of the disastrous reception of *The Birthday Party,* the BBC's Donald McWhinnie called Pinter into his office to say he had just read *The Birthday Party* and was deeply disturbed by the play. He then offered Pinter a commission. Although Pinter wrote *A Slight Ache,* which aired in July with Vivien Merchant as Flora, and also *A Night Out,* which aired in March with Vivien Merchant as Sally and with Pinter himself as Seeley, Pinter rejected McWhinnie's offer of the full-time employment that regular writing for television offered. In 1960, at a time when Pinter was living in a basement flat in Notting Hill Gate, writing with a baby on his knee and, when unemployed as an actor, working as a caretaker, doorman, snow shoveler, street salesman and dance-hall bouncer, he turned down an opportunity almost any other writer would jump at and risked what few would. Pinter and his wife, who had just been offered acting positions at the Alexandria Theatre in Birmingham, moved instead to Chiswick in order to remain in London for their work. Although Pinter was most grateful for McWhinnie's interest in his work, when McWhinnie offered him a secure income from television contracts, Pinter refused the offer to maintain his freedom as a writer.

The decision immediately proved correct. In 1959 his first screenplay from the Robin Maugham novel *The Servant* had opened in London, launching Pinter's film-writing career. He read his short prose fiction "The Examination" on BBC *Third Programme*, *The Collection*, with Vivien Merchant as Stella, opened at the Aldwych Theatre, London, and he received the Italia prize for best television play. The following year, 1960, beginning his next decade in theatre as a playwright, *The Dumb Waiter* and *The Room*, with Vivien Merchant as Rose, were produced as a double bill at Hampstead Theatre Club, which remains a staging ground for his work, and later transferred to the Royal Court Theatre. That same year *The Birthday Party* and *A Night Out* were produced on television; *The Caretaker* premiered at the Arts Theatre Club, then transferred to the West End, Duchess Theatre, and opened at Dusseldorf Schauspielhaus. That year *The Dwarfs* as a radio play was broadcast on the BBC. *Night School*, originally written for radio, was successfully broadcast on television in 1960 with Vivien Merchant as Sally but withheld by Pinter from publication in collections until 1967 when it appeared in revised form. *The Birthday Party* opened in 1960 at Actors' Workshop, San Francisco. In London, Pinter won *The Evening Standard* Award for *The Caretaker*, which opened the following year at the Theatre de Lutece, Paris, and in New York at the Lyceum Theatre, where it went on to win the Page 1 Award of the Newspaper Guild of New York.

The Caretaker's critical acclaim reversed Pinter's fortunes as a playwright. During the next five years he would continue to win prizes, write and produce short plays, and write for the screen. In 1965 the film *The Caretaker*, directed by William Friedkin, starring Alan Bates, Robert Shaw and Donald Pleasence won the Silver Bear at the Berlin Film Festival, a Certificate of Merit at the Edinburgh

Festival, and the next year opened in New York under the title *The Guest*. That year he read the short story "Tea Party" on the BBC *Third Programme* and also won the British Screenwriters' Guild award for *The Servant*, written originally for director Michael Anderson. Adapted from the novel by Robin Maugham, *The Servant* was directed by Joseph Losey and featured Dirk Bogarde as Barrett the servant, Sarah Miles as Vera, and playwright Alun Owen as the curate. He wrote his screenplays as he did his plays—claiming he did not know how the script would end till he finished it. From the beginning of his film career, Pinter insisted on *carte blanche*, and he used his screenplays to explore concerns expressed in his plays, often in heightened form.

But it would not be for five years after *The Caretaker*, until 1965, that his next full-length play, *The Homecoming*, was written and produced. That intervening gap between full-length plays would set a writing pattern that continues to haunt him to the present. Not a daily writer, Pinter writes intuitively, only when an image, inspiration or voice strikes. The interim periods have remained a kind of purgatory for him. Adapting novels for film and television has remained one way to continue writing throughout his career.

During that five-year period Pinter did, however, continue to write plays that have become standard one-act fare. In 1963 *The Lover*, with Vivien Merchant as Sarah, was broadcast by Associated Redifusion and won the Prix Italia for Television Drama at Naples, then opened with *The Dwarfs*, adapted from his unpublished novel, at the Arts Theatre Club, London. Nine sketches, *Last to Go, Applicant, Request Stop, That's Your Trouble, That's All, Interview, Trouble in the Works, The Black and White*, and *Dialogue for Three*, several with Vivien Merchant, were broadcast in 1964 on BBC *Third Programme*. Although Vivien Merchant performed most of the major female roles in his plays from *The Room* through *The Homecoming* and *Old Times*, when Pinter was asked whether he wrote those parts specifically for her, he said never, that she was cast just because she was a very good actress.

"Good writing excites me and makes life worth living," Pinter says, (Bensky, 364) adding, "I regard myself as nothing more than a working man." ("Speech: Hamburg," 3) He works organically, from an initial image, never plotting out in advance, but he requires that the initial image be fertile and hopes it is alive. Like the vitality he admires in living people and that his greatest characters possess,

Pinter insists, "Theatre should be a living moment. Something is happening then, and it's self explanatory. What it means is what it says, what the characters say." (Tynan, n.p.)

He claims he writes by listening to his characters for clues, however he notes, "[T]hey don't arrange and select. I do the donkey work. But they carry the can." ("Harold Pinter Replies," 9) He cautions: "I'd like to make quite clear at the same time that I don't regard my own characters as uncontrolled, or anarchic. They're not. The function of selection and arrangement is mine," and he adds:

> I pay meticulous attention to the shape of things, from the shape of a sentence to the overall structure of the play. This shaping, to put it mildly, is of the first importance. But I think a double thing happens. You arrange *and* you listen, following the clues you leave for yourself, through the characters. ("Writing for the Theatre," 82)

In describing his writing process, he says, "I don't analyse a play as I go along," adding, "I only formulate conclusions after I've written the play." (Kathleen Tynan, 8) He says he has been "very fortunate" in working with directors such as Peter Hall at the Royal Shakespeare Company and at the National. Together, he says they "have found that the image must be pursued with the greatest vigilance, calmly, and once found, must be sharpened, guarded, accurately focused and maintained," emphasizing, "the key word is economy, economy of movement and gesture, of emotion and its expression, both internal and external in specific and exact relation to each other, so that there is no wastage and no mess." ("Speech: Hamburg," 4)

However, he says flat out, "I distrust theory." (3) He has always spoken out against the reductive application of labels. In distant echo of T. S. Eliot's Prufrock who inveighs against "the eyes that fix you in formulated phrase" to leave you "pinned and wriggling on the wall," (5) Pinter says, "We don't carry labels on our chests, and even though they are continually fixed to us by others, they convince nobody." ("Writing for the Theatre," 80) While he is understandably disturbed by negative criticism, he also confesses he finds little of use from professional critics, though amateur critics sometimes strike a chord.

Pinter has little sympathy for baffled critics who have continued to misunderstand or to misinterpret his work by reductively labeling it in purely symbolic terms:

> When a character cannot be comfortably defined, or understood in terms of the familiar, the tendency is to perch him on a symbolic shelf, out of harm's way. Once there, he can be talked about but need not be lived with. In this way, it is easy to put up a pretty efficient smoke screen, on the part of the critics or the audiences against recognition, against an active and willing participation. ("Writing for the Theatre," 80)

Mystery and ambiguity are heightened by one of Pinter's important contributions to characterization: his refusal to supply artificial biographical information.

> A character on stage who can present no convincing argument or information as to his past experience, his present behavior or his aspiration, nor give a comprehensive analysis of this problem is as legitimate and as worthy of attention as one who, alarmingly, can do all these things. (80–81)

Like any master who trusts his audience, Pinter objects to "the specter of the author looming above his characters, telling the audience at every stage just what they are to think of them." ("Mr. Harold Pinter—Avant-Garde Playwright and Intimate Revue," 4) Director Peter Hall tells about meeting Ethel Merman at a party after the *Old Times* premiere:

> She talked to me about *Old Times* as if she'd seen a Neil Simon play. She had no problem with the play—she understood it from beginning to end. Meanwhile a famous intellectual was wandering around the party saying, "What does it mean?" (Kroll, 77)

Pinter's plays require a response from the whole being, not just the head. A purely intellectual response misses half the show.

Pinter's unselfconscious and unplotted writing method requires the highest degree of self trust. He claims he usually starts at the beginning of a play and generally writes three drafts striving for clarity and economy of both word and gesture, for proportion, shape, consistency of mood, and, paramount, structure and form. He generally writes rather rapidly, and as his worksheets reveal, his revisions almost always compact, clarify, sharpen, and heighten.

Despite his refusal to draw conclusions while writing, he reverses position during rehearsal and becomes very exacting:

> When we get down to working practically with actors I'm extremely curious and, in fact, fascinated by how I myself have arrived at certain conclusions. I never ask myself why while I'm writing. But when we get down to rehearsing, I am able to give reasons. In rehearsing, we do go into detail. (Crist, 83)

What is significant about his writing process, which does not map out form in advance nor greatly rearrange afterward, is the resultant tight structure, razor-sharp ambiguity, and complexity of character.

Just as he is careful never to make characters say what they would not say, he avoids explicitness and explanation: "The explanation is necessarily false." ("Pinter on Pinter," 11) He identifies one source of his plays' power as the characters' life-and-death situations: "I'm dealing with these characters at the extreme edge of their living—where they are pretty much alone." (Tynan, n.p.) Speaking of the three kinds of pain he has suffered through his characters, he notes the pain occurs both when he falsifies them and when he strikes at the truth:

> I have witnessed *their* pain when I am in the act of distorting them, of falsifying them, and I have witnessed their contempt. I have suffered pain when I have been unable to get to the quick of them, when they willfully elude me, when they withdraw into the shadows. And there's a third and rarer pain. That is when the right word, or the right act jolts them or stills them into their proper life. When that happens the pain is worth having. ("Speech: Hamburg," 4)

He concludes: "Characters always grow out of all proportion to your critical conception of them, and if they don't the play is a bad one." ("Harold Pinter Replies," 10)

Characters in drama grow only through what they do and say, and Pinter is perhaps most famed for his characteristic dialogue, that quotidian speech which remains nevertheless poetic: both compressed and lyrical. As the discourse in *The Dwarfs* reveals, the characters Pinter admires express themselves with fresh phrases, as opposed to characters whose clichéd language and hackneyed actions reflect an unexamined morality. BBC critic Hallam Tennyson early recognized Pinter's dialogue as one great source of his power:

> Now Pinter seems to me to achieve this universal effect through very original means. The dialogue, which appears on the surface so inarticulate and restricted, opens up unexpected depth. Through a careful placing of words, through repetitions and rhythm which is punctuated by frequent silences, he creates a tremendous tension and mystery and at times even poetry. (Tennyson, n.p.)

Tennyson concludes:

> Without a single pretentious word or strained gesture, he brings his poetry and tragedy right into the heart of a London suburb. (n.p.)

Critics puzzled by Pinter's characters' dialogue have stayed only at the surface, labeling it "failure to communicate," and miss the deeper intent. Pinter resists "that tired, grimy phrase" as well as "non-communication," and "inability to communicate" ("Writing for the Theatre," 82), but instead insists "there is a deliberate evasion of communication" because "[c]ommunication itself between people is so frightening" that characters will do what they can to avoid it but he emphasizes that his characters do communicate "on a deeper level":

> There is something happening underneath the dialogue invariably in all the works I've written. (Tynan, n.p.)

That deeper level, Pinter asserts, is not metaphor or symbol but the subtext where "below the word spoken, is the thing known and unspoken," where "under what is said, another thing is being said." ("Writing for the Theatre," 82) He says, "The speech we hear is an indication of that which we don't hear ... a necessary avoidance ... which keeps the other in its place." (82) He concludes, "One way of looking at speech is to say that it is a constant stratagem to cover nakedness." (82)

Mystery and ambiguity, aside from their technical functions, serve a special thematic function in Pinter's work to force attention to the subtext:

> Between my lack of biographical data about them and the ambiguity of what they say lies a territory which is not only worthy of exploration but which it is compulsory to explore. ("Writing for the Theatre," 82)

For Pinter, pauses, halting speech and silence are as much communication as language: "When true silence falls we are still left with echo but are nearer nakedness." (82) He notes, "There are two silences. One when no word is spoken. The other when perhaps a torrent of language is being employed." (82) Pinter also points out that the pauses and halting speech convey deep emotions: "The more acute the experience the less articulate its expression." (82) He says he is "interested in emotion which is contained, and felt very, very deeply." (Gussow, "A Conversation ... ," 128)

While Pinter concedes that occasionally actors apparently benefit from a dot and pause rehearsal, he sees pauses not as merely stops or formal stresses but as an organic part of the action: "The pause is a pause because of what has just happened in the minds and guts of the characters. They spring out of the text. They're not formal conveniences or stresses but part of the body of the action." (129) At the other extreme he speaks of the "dangerous territory," of going over the top with lyricism: "You can fall on your ass very easily in attempting to express in, if you like, 'lyrical' terms what is actually happening to people." (130) He says that he thinks in pictures when he writes, claiming that while he writes he views the work from the perspective of the footlights, but when he is finished he walks through all the parts.

When asked if he is ever tempted to go back and revise a play, he says not once the play exists: "I have to respect that life. I could do it damage by fooling about with it." (Gussow, "Harold Pinter: I Started with Two People in a Pub," 7) While Pinter admits he may never have given "full service" to any of his plays, he also argues that no play, not even *Hamlet*, is perfect. He regards himself as a traditional playwright. Although he admits the decision to bring down the curtain comes as "pure instinct" when "the rhythm seems right" and when "the action calls for a finish," Pinter, like any poet, gives special attention to closure: "I'm very fond of curtain lines, of doing them properly." (Bensky, 359) Finally his writing achieves what he describes of Losey's direction of *Accident*: "No matter how much you see and guess at there is always something more." (Taylor, 184)

Pinter is one of those fortunate writers who does not have a trunk full of unpublished paper. Nearly everything he has written has been performed and published. But by 1968, only a decade into his public writing career, he was already complaining of writer's "constipation," and describing the torment of those fallow periods he says:

> When you can't write you feel you've been banished from yourself. ("Speech: Hamburg," 4)

Just as his characters and the people he admires embrace opposite qualities without reconciling them, Pinter, too, describes himself as someone who both loves and is nauseated by words, as someone both delighted by and sick of them, and even by his own plays. He says, "Given this nausea, it's very easy to be overcome by it and step back into paralysis." But, customarily, Pinter attempts to confront whatever seems difficult: "But if it is possible to confront this nausea, to follow it to its hilt, to move through it and out of it, then it is possible to say that something has occurred, that something has even been achieved." ("Writing for the Theatre," 81) When Pinter locates his characters and discovers the proper words he says, "You know they're going to make your life hell," but adds, "And while it may be hell, it's certainly for me the best kind of hell to be in." ("Speech: Hamburg," 3) Even while Pinter regards writing for the theatre as "the most difficult thing," (Kitchen and Mayersberg, n.p.) writing remains for him "a kind of celebration." ("Speech: Hamburg," 3)

Pinter remains his severest critic, yet he recalls confronting one of the worst receptions from a living audience with a laugh. During opening night of *The Caretaker* in Germany, when, as is customary, the author takes a bow with the cast, he remembers he was "booed violently ... by the finest collection of booers in the world":

> I thought they were using megaphones, but it was pure mouth. The cast was as dogged as the audience, however, and we took thirty-four curtain calls, all to boos. (80)

He confesses he was "strangely warmed by all this," and admits, "now, whenever I sense a tremor of the old apprehension or expectation, I remember Dusseldorf, and am cured." ("Writing for the Theatre," 80)

1965 was a golden year for Pinter. *The Homecoming* opened with Vivien Merchant as Ruth at the Aldwych Theatre, London, and was later produced in Paris and Boston. *The Collection* and *The Lover* were performed in double bill in Paris. *The Collection,* featuring Vivien Merchant as Stella in its first televised performance, was later co-directed by Harold Pinter and Peter Hall, and *The Lover* featured Vivien Merchant as Sarah in both the first television and stage productions. Pinter won the British Film Academy Award for the best screenplay for the adaptation of Penelope Mortimer's novel *The Pumpkin Eater,* which starred Anne Bancroft as Jo, Peter Finch as Jake, Cedrick Hardwicke as Mr. James and Maggie Smith as the children's nanny, Philpot. *The Birthday Party* was revived that year at the Aldwych Theatre, London. Pinter also played Garcia in Sartre's *No Exit* on BBC Television and heard *Tea Party,* with Vivien Merchant as Wendy, broadcast by BBC I in the series *The Largest Theatre in the World.* That year he was awarded the distinguished Commander of the Order of the British Empire (C.B.E.).

Very early in his career he defined himself as an intensely private man, and he has remained reclusive from the press and interviews. Even his closest friend, fellow actor and writer the late Robert Shaw, respected him as a man no one just drops in upon. The Harold Pinter who had left behind forever the East End of London, the unemployed actor's jobs and his home in the Notting Hill Gate basement, made a rare transformation more rapidly and completely than most when he moved to the five-story Nash house in Regent's Park where he and his first wife threw parties that included Sir John Gielgud and the Beatles' Paul McCartney.

Pinter never had any illusions about poverty or the privileged class, the relation of class to justice, or the importance of appearing privileged as communicated through speech and diction. In his New York reading where he read backward through his work from *Betrayal* and *The Homecoming* to *The Caretaker* and *The Birthday Party,* his voice stripped back to the lower-class accent of the streets and, reading Goldberg, the Yiddish accents of his youth. In the television production *Pinter People* he relates two incidents revealing his attitude toward class and its relationship to justice. Once he recalls, he was nearly arrested for singing in noisy Covent Garden at four in the morning by a policeman who "just didn't like the look of us. We didn't have ties on, I think, or something. British coppers are the same as New York restaurants, really." (*Pinter People*, n.p.) When he was quite young, he also remembers being drunk in the road in Fleet Street, being picked up roughly by a policeman who said, "What the hell do you think you're doing?" Pinter replied, "Constable, please, excuse me. I'm on my way home," and he says:

> [I] spoke in the best voice I could find ..., and immediately he brushed me down and called me Sir and found me the next bus you know. If I'd have said, "Uh, now, wait a minute I'm uh, you know, just 'appen to be wondering about," or something he'd have had me. This class thing, you know. But you can't expect this in any way to be a just world, surely, in any kind of sense. I don't. I don't yearn for ... Oh, justice, I mean what is interpreted as justice, quite often is intolerable, of course, because of all the suffering it creates indeed. I have no kind of expectation of the world growing better in any way. The world remains as it is. (*Pinter People*, n.p.)

Pinter, who at that time called himself "a man of the theatre," understood the value of educated-sounding, privileged speech, and he would make an even more complete break from his origins than Teddy, the professor in *The Homecoming*, could have dreamed. Yet unlike Teddy who escapes and disparages his lower-class family, Pinter remained sympathetic with the less privileged and those who remained in the community of his birth.

In 1967 as the decade drew to a close *The Homecoming* opened at The Music Box in New York and swept awards: claiming both an Antoinette Perry (Tony) Award and The New York Drama Critics' Circle Award for best play, the Whitebread Anglo-American Award for the best play on Broadway and American Library Association "Notable Books of 1967 Award." The first London and New York productions and the film version were directed by Peter Hall with Paul Rogers as Max and Vivien Merchant as Ruth.

The year before, in 1966, *The Quiller Memorandum*, adapted by Pinter from *The Berlin Memorandum* by Adam Hall, was released featuring George Segal as Quiller, Alec Guinness as Pol, Senta Berger as Inge, and Max von Sydow as Oktober. In 1967 Pinter was also awarded a Cannes Jury Prize for his screenplay for *Accident* adapted from the novel by Nicholas Mosley, directed by Joseph Losey, with Dirk Bogarde as Stephen, Michael York as William, Jacqueline Sassard as Anna, Vivien Merchant as Stephen's wife Rosalind, Nicholas Mosley as Hedges and Harold Pinter as Bell. *Tea Party,* commissioned by the European Broadcasting Union, transmitted under the title, *The Largest Theatre in the World,* featured Vivien Merchant as Wendy and later paired with *The Basement* (originally *The Compartment* for Grove Press Project 1), first presented by BBC-TV in 1967, featuring Harold Pinter as Stott. That year Pinter also directed Robert Shaw's *The Man in the Glass Booth* in London.

If Pinter does not reveal more about himself it is because he tells us all we need to know. He insists he is not so different from other men and lists as his main interests: language—his work in theatre and films, reading—watching and playing cricket, and drinking. He adds, sex: "I'm surely not uncommon, by no means a rare example of the human race when I say that I like sex … " (Gussow, "A Conversation … ," 127) Yet he remains, despite free use of sexual epithets employed as weapons by his torturers, circumspect in his attitude toward the language of sex:

> I do object to one thing to do with sex: this scheme afoot on the part of many "liberal-minded" persons to open up obscene language to general commerce. It should be the dark secret language of the underworld. There are very few words—you shouldn't kill them by overuse. I have used such words once or twice in my plays, but I couldn't get them past the Lord Chamberlain. They're great, wonderful words, but must be used very sparingly. (Bensky, 365)

He also once cautioned that an overemphasis on sex can become cloying:

> Sexual relations as now discussed in 1976 so continually are a pain in the ass. Sex has become like a supermarket. I say let's get on with it personally. Some friends pointed out to me a man who was supposed to be a great lover—stamina, that old thing. I advised these people to think of this chap and a woman screwing forever and ever and ever. I think that's a terrifying image, and that's where so many people's minds seem to be nowadays. That poor young man doesn't know what fate has in store for him. As the old Bible says, there's a time for this and a time for that. (Kroll, 81)

That image of perpetual sex would recur in his filmscript *The Comfort of Strangers,* but Pinter's call for proportion, *sophrosyne*—that ancient Greek virtue, the term for moderation—applies to his ethic throughout.

Pinter, who till now had claimed he was not political, would soon become so. In 1968 when he refused to make cuts in *Landscape* in keeping with the Lord Chamberlain's demand against offending language, the stage version at Royal Shakespeare Company was abandoned, but an unaltered version was performed on BBC's *Third Programme. The Tea Party* and *The Basement* opened at the East Side Playhouse, New York, and *The Birthday Party* film opened.

The decade closed with *Night,* featuring Vivien Merchant as Woman, first performed in an evening of one-acts called *Mixed Doubles* at the Comedy Theatre, London. *Landscape,* along with the brief one-act *Silence,* which he says took him longer than any other play to write, opened at the Aldwych Theatre, London. *The Caretaker* opened at the Theatre Moderne, Paris, and *Pinter People,* the Grove Press cartoon film of *Trouble in the Works, The Black and White, Applicant* and *Last to Go,* aired on television. *The Homecoming* as a film opened in 1969.

1970–1980: "I Think We're All Very Close to Tramps"

Pinter's early characters from *The Room* and *The Birthday Party,* through *The Caretaker* and *The Homecoming* (except for Teddy and Ruth who have escaped) are primarily those marginalized by society without power to influence the larger world or even alter their most immediate surroundings: to secure shelter. Yet Pinter portrays them with respect, even profound compassion. He says:

> I think we're all very close to tramps, we all come down to the same thing in the end. (Tynan, n.p.)

While in the next decade Pinter's characters ascend, upwardly mobile, into spheres allowing them to assume positions of responsibility in the community, their private needs and desire for respect and love remain a constant across all his social scales.

During the 1970s Pinter's attention focused on the past's role in the present: "What interests me a great deal is the mistiness of the past," which, when dramatized in the present tense of drama, is not the past but the present. ("Writing for the Theatre," 81) Pinter's fascination with "mistiness" of the past and "the impossibility of verifying it" developed early: "A moment is sucked away and distorted, often even at the time of its birth":

> Apart from any other consideration, we are faced with the immense difficulty, if not the impossibility, of verifying the past. I don't mean merely years ago, but yesterday, this morning. What took place, what was the nature of what took place, what happened? If one can speak of the difficulty of knowing what in fact took place yesterday, one can I think treat the present the same way. What's happening now? We won't know until tomorrow or in six months time, and we won't know then, we'll have forgotten, or our imagination will have attributed quite false characteristics to today. (81)

For Pinter it is impossible for two people to view the same experience in the same way:

> We will all interpret a common experience quite differently, though we prefer to subscribe to the view that there's a shared common ground, a known ground. I think there's a shared common ground all right, but that it's more like a quicksand. (81)

The seventies would produce three full-length Pinter plays: *Old Times*, *No Man's Land* and *Betrayal,* a considerable achievement. That decade, which opened with the Shakespeare Prize of the University of Hamburg, was a transitional period in his work and a turbulent time in his life. In 1975 Vivien Merchant, his wife of almost twenty years, sued for divorce naming the brilliant, beautiful and prolific author Lady Antonia Fraser as correspondent, creating a scandal that rocked London society. She dropped the suit when he chose to live with Lady Antonia, then she refused to grant the divorce Pinter now requested. *Betrayal*, the play written at the end of that decade, moves from the end of a love affair to the passionate beginning, stretching the form of drama as *The French Lieutenant's Woman* would in film at the beginning of the next decade.

During that decade of the seventies Pinter continued to act, to direct, to write short plays and screenplays, and to garner prizes. He appeared in 1975 in *Rogue Male* BBC-TV, in Beckett's *Rough for Radio*, and in 1977 in *Two Plays* by Vaclav Havel. He also turned more and more to directing. In 1970 he directed Simon Gray's *Butley* and Joyce's *Exiles* in London; in 1974, John Hopkins' *Next of Kin* in London, and the film *Butley*; in 1975, Simon Gray's *Otherwise Engaged* in London, and again, in 1977, in New York. That year he directed *Blithe Spirit* at the National's Lyttleton, William Archibald's *The Innocents* in New York, Simon Gray's *Rear Column* in 1978 at the Globe, London, and also Gray's *Close of Play* in 1979 at the National, in London.

In addition to his three full-length plays, Pinter also wrote the short play *Monologue*, broadcast on BBC-TV in 1973. In 1971 *Old Times* opened in London, directed by Peter Hall with Vivien Merchant as Anna, and in New York with Pinter's friend Robert Shaw as Deeley playing opposite his wife Mary Ure as Kate with Dorothy Tutin as Anna. The play was performed at the Theatre Montparnasse, Paris, and the Billy Rose, New York, and the following year, at Thalia Theatre, Hamburg. *No Man's Land* opened at the National Theatre at the Old Vic in 1975 and transferred to the West End, Whyndham Theatre. The play, directed by Peter Hall, starred Ralph Richardson as Hirst and John Gielgud as Spooner. *Betrayal* opened at the National Theatre, Lyttleton, and in New York, at the Trafalgar in 1979.

Pinter also wrote both the screenplay for F. Scott Fitzgerald's *The Last Tycoon*, which opened in New York in 1975, and his unfilmed but published 1977 *À la Recherche du Temps Perdu: The Proust Screenplay*, distilled from the seven volume novel. In the preface he describes writing it as "the best working year of my life." He went on in 1978–9 to adapt Aidan Higgins's novel *Langrishe, Go Down* for broadcast by BBC-TV. The television film starred Jeremy Irons as Otto, Judy Dench as Imogen Langrishe, and Harold Pinter as Barry Shannon.

During that decade Harold Pinter was also heaped with honors and awards. In 1970 he was made an Honorary Fellow of the Modern Language Association and received an honorary degree from Reading University. In 1972 an honorary degree was conferred upon Pinter by the University of Birmingham. He was also awarded an Hon. D. Litt. from both Glasgow and East Anglia, and in 1979 from Stirling.

He continued to receive awards and honors in film and in the theatre. He received the 1969 Palme d'Or (Best Picture) for *The Go-Between* at the Cannes Film Festival. In 1971 Pinter won the British Film Academy Award for that screenplay. He adapted *The Go-Between* from the novel by L.P. Hartley, directed by Joseph Losey with Julie Christie as Marian, Alan Bates as Ted, Margaret Leighton as Mrs. Maudsley, and Michael Redgrave as Colston. In 1973 he was appointed an Associate Director to Peter Hall at the National Theatre. That year he received the Vienna Prize and the Austrian State Prize. In 1975 he received the National Board of Review Best English-Language Film Award for *The Last Tycoon* adapted from the novel by F. Scott Fitzgerald, directed by Elia Kazan, and featuring Robert De Niro as Monroe Stahr, Tony Curtis as Rodriguez, Robert Mitchum as Pat Brady, Jeanne Moreau as Didi, Jack Nicholson as Brimmer, Donald Pleasence as Boxley, and Angelica Houston as Edna. The year the decade closed he won the Society of West End Theatres Award for *Betrayal.*

1980–1990: "If You Shake Hands with Murderers You Have No Moral Commitment."

The decade of the eighties opened with a look back. *The Hothouse,* written over twenty years before, was produced for the first time at the Hampstead Theatre, moved to the Ambassador, was broadcast on BBC-TV, and opened in America at Provincetown in 1982 and in New York at the Playhouse Theatre. That decade began with fresh happiness in his private life: in 1980 Vivien Merchant received a *decree nisi,* freeing him to marry Lady Antonia Fraser. But the happiness was not without deep grief. Within several years her former husband Sir Hugh Fraser would die from lung cancer and Vivien Merchant, from chronic alcoholism.

Pinter's writing for stage was confined to one acts and sketches. And though he continued to direct and champion the work of other playwrights, by the end of the decade he would vow to devote even less time to the time-consuming task of directing. He continued to win honors and prizes, and his writing for screen and other media surged as did his political involvement.

His new work for the stage included the 1981 *Family Voices,* aired on BBC Radio 3, a radio play with three voices, featuring Peggy Ashcroft. *Other Places,* a triple bill that included *Victoria Station* and *A Kind of Alaska,* inspired by Oliver Sack's compassionately written book *Awakenings,* opened at the National Theatre. *One for the Road,* directed by Pinter, opened at the Hampstead Theatre Club, London, featuring Jenny Quayle as Gila, Alan Bates as Nicolas and the following year was included in *Other Places* at the Manhattan Theatre Club, New York, where it was directed by Alan Schneider just before his untimely death in 1984. It was later performed in a reading in New York by Pinter himself. Pinter's short sketch *Precisely* was broadcast by the BBC in *The Big One* and published in a collection under that same title. His prose tribute to two men he most admired in cricket and in theatre, McMaster the actor and Wellard the batsman, entitled *Players: Mac and Arthur Wellard,* was broadcast by the BBC in 1985. In 1986 he co-edited the *P.E.N. Anthology of New Poems* and *100 Poems by 100 Poets.*

Harold Pinter continued to be both revered and derided by critics. *Betrayal* won the 1980 New York Drama Critics' Circle Award for best foreign play. He received the 1982 Pirandello Prize, Italy. In 1981 he shared with Tennessee Williams the Commonwealth Award, Washington, D.C., for distinguished service in dramatic arts. The following year he was awarded an honorary doctorate from Brown University, Providence, Rhode Island; the Ennio Flaiano; Award for Screenwriting and the Donatello Prize, Italy, for *The French Lieutenant's Woman,* which he adapted from the novel by John Fowles, directed by Karel Reisz with Meryl Streep doubling as Sarah Woodruff/Anna, Jeremy Irons as Charles Smithson/Mike and Penelope Wilton as Sonia. He received the British Theatre Association Award in 1983 and in 1985 and the Bobst Award in 1984. That year he was awarded an Hon. D. Litt. with Lady Antonia Fraser from Hull University, where he delivered his "Address to Hull University Congregation." He was also made a Fellow of the Royal Society of Literature and an honorary member of the American Academy and Institute of Arts and Letters, an honorary member of the American Academy of Arts and Sciences in 1985, and an Honorary Fellow at Queen Mary College in 1987.

During the eighties he wrote more screenplays than in any previous decade. In 1981 *The French Lieutenant's Woman,* opened, and in 1983 the film version of *Betrayal.* In 1984 he adapted Joseph Conrad's novel *Victory* for the screen (unproduced). In 1985 he wrote the screenplay *Turtle Diary* adapted from the novel by Russell Hoban, the author of the children's books *The Story of Hester Mouse: Who Became a Writer.* The film was directed by John Irvin with Glenda Jackson as Neaera, a children's book writer; Ben Kingsley as William, a bookstore clerk; Michael Gambon as George Fairbain, the Zookeeper; Eleanor Bror as Miss Neap, a tenant in William's building; and Harold Pinter as Man in Bookshop. In 1987 he adapted Margaret Atwood's novel *Handmaid's Tale* for film starring Natasha Richardson, Richard Duvall, Fay Dunaway and Elizabeth McGovern; in 1988, Fred Uhlman's *Reunion,* with Jason Robards as Hans; and Elizabeth Bowen's *The Heat of the Day* for television broadcast 1990 starring Patricia Hodges as Stella, Michael York as her lover Robert, and Michael Gambon as Harrison. All three films address causes of violence and authoritarian repression: *Handmaid's Tale* in the future, *Reunion* in Nazi Germany, and *Heat of the Day* in World War II England. In 1989 he also wrote the screenplays for Kafka's *The Trial* and Ian McEwan's *The Comfort of Strangers* directed by Paul Schrader, starring Christopher Walken, Rupert Everett, Natasha Richardson and Helen Mirren addressing causes of homicidal violence at the most private level.

Pinter continued to act in some of his own work and to direct the work of playwrights he admired. He played Deeley in October and November 1985 in the *Old Times* American tour, and Goldberg in *The Birthday Party,* recorded 24 February 1986 for the BBC TV. He directed Simon Gray's *Quartermaine's Terms* at Queen Theatre in 1981, and Robert East's *Incident at Tulse Hill* at the Hampstead Theatre Club in 1984. That same year he also directed Giraudoux's *The Trojan War Will Not Take Place* at the National and Simon Gray's *The Common Pursuit* at the Lyric. He directed Lauren Bacall in Tennessee Williams's *Sweet Bird of Youth* in Brighton, June 1985, and in 1986, Faye Dunaway in Donald Freed's *Circe and Bravo* in London.

The year 1985 represented a public turning point for Pinter when he visited Turkey with American playwright Arthur Miller at the request of PEN to intervene on behalf of academics being held as political prisoners. He wrote *One for the Road* in direct response to their torture. At a party one night Pinter was appalled when two young Turkish women dismissed his concern with torture as resulting from his active imagination, suggesting that the torture was deserved because the prisoners "were probably communists." (Appleyard, 13) He went home and wrote the play. Eleven years earlier the overthrow of the democratically elected Marxist Allende regime in Chile and theWestern hypocrisy had outraged him. He became an active member in both the CND, the Campaign for Nuclear Disarmament and in Amnesty International, the British based human rights watch organization, crusading on behalf of prisoners of conscience. His 1988 the remorseless *Mountain Language,* which he directed at the National and dedicated to his wife Antonia, continues to dramatize the inescapable horrors of torture. Recent work like the sketch *Precisely,* with its indictment of nuclear armament, is outright political in its statement. He was shocked to learn in 1984 that a new location for his cricket club, the idyllic cricket pitch in the Chilterns outside High Wycomb in rural England, is directly over the three-story underground bunker, the American headquarters of nuclear operations in Europe, replacing Stuttgart as the nuclear strike command.

Pinter's concern over the abrogation of human freedom translates into his recent work as a plea to act: "I think it is more and more evident everyday that we are becoming very, very close to any other damn police state." (Appleyard, 13) At times he sounds despairing: "I think all the plays I've written are attempts to understand people behaving in certain contexts," adding, "You see now I do feel that there will be no writing, no entertainment, no drama whatsoever in a very short time unless we recognize the realities of the world in which we live. I think we'll be very lucky to get to the end of this century." (13)

1990—2000: "Can Any Playwright Enlarge Our Point of View, Our Understanding of the World We Live in and Mankind?"

On 10 October 1990 Harold Pinter turned sixty. The decade of the nineties like the eighties began with a look back. The unpublished novel *The Dwarfs,* written thirty years earlier, finally appeared in print; his prose and poetry were reissued in a new volume. *The Homecoming, The Caretaker* and *Betrayal* were revived that season. As a poetry editor at Greville Press, which published in 1989 work of Edna O'Brien and Nicaraguan poet Gioconda Belli, Pinter was instrumental in 1990 in bringing out the uncollected poems of W. S. Graham, and chapbooks of poetry by David Wright and by Turkish poet Nazim Hikmet.

In his May 1990 television speech "Oh, Superman," Pinter delivered a scathing attack against the U.S. involvement in Central and South America and the British complicity that has allowed, even perpetuated, atrocities against human rights and basic human needs. He also helped promote publication of José Coronel Urtecho's poem *Panels of Hell* dedicated to Frente Sandinista. Yet in lighter contrast, in the summer of that same year, Pinter directed Jane Stanton Hitchcock's satirical comedy *Vanilla*.

Together Pinter and Lady Antonia Fraser were recipients of honorary degrees from Sussex University, she for her contributions to the writing of history, he for his contributions to the university. He adapted Kazuo Ishiguro's novel *Remains of the Day* for director Mike Nichols for the screen.[2] In 1992 Pinter directed *Party Time* for Channel 4, broadcast 17 November, and his script of *The Trial* was filmed, directed by David Jones. In November Pinter opened as Hirst in *No Man's Land,* directed by David Leveaux, at the Almeida Theatre, London to great reviews. In 1993 he directed David Mamet's *Oleanna* which opened 30 June to a great stir. But 1992 brought him sorrow, the death of his mother, survived by his father who turned ninety.

The public celebration of his birthday that began in 1990 has continued into the decade beginning with the "Harold Pinter at 60—A Birthday Party," where the BBC for the first time ever devoted a whole evening to a living British playwright. To mark Harold Pinter's birthday and achievement, an International Pinter Festival was held in the spring 1991 at Ohio State University, and *The Pinter Review* slated a commemorative issue in honor of his sixtieth year. Late on the last night of the conference, an acting company from Goldsmiths' College, University of London, gave a staged reading of the new Pinter script, *Party Time,* with Nesta Jones as Charlotte. With *Party Time,* Pinter's plays had entered the world of the powerbrokers, not merely the torturers, the lackeys of those at the helm of the machine—but the men and women directing the course of events in the larger world. In the fall of that year he wrote the sketch *The New World Order.* In 1992 the University of London, Queen Mary's College, opened the Harold Pinter Theatre dedicated by Queen Elizabeth II.

In his plays of the 90s, Pinter's concern with love and violence now explicitly linked love to the larger question of justice and brought into focus a lens through which all of his work could be viewed with a fresh perspective. Pinter's focus on those in power, the self-delusion in the name of idealism which promotes the destruction of others, reveals the destructive power of seeming good intentions when unaccompanied by love and justice.

One for the Road, begun in "passion and rage," and written with compassion for the suffering of those involved, focuses on the family destroyed by torture because, as Pinter says, "The family suffers in final terms—not only does that person suffer—and my god does he suffer—so does the rest of the family." (Nightingale, n.p.) In *Mountain Language* a mother's visit to her imprisoned, tortured son dramatizes the endurance and the courage of both, hers no less than his, for the physical attack she silently suffers during her interminable wait for the few minutes with her son. When families visit in prison, Pinter says, "those three or four minutes are a lifetime to people who haven't seen each other." (n.p.)

Pinter's concern for the plight of prisoners of conscience has thrust him beyond the theatre, championing the poetry of the long-imprisoned Nazim Hikmet, corresponding with Vaclav Havel in the early eighties when he was still in prison, and more recently touring Nicaragua as a guest of the Sandinistas, opening his Campden Hill home to Nicaraguan president Daniel Ortega, writers Salman Rushdie, Ian McEwan, John Mortimer, Germaine Greer, David Hare, Margaret Drabble and Michael Holroyd, many of whom had met in the late eighties to form what they called the 20th June Society, named for the date they first convened. (Schiff, 220)

After Pinter visited Turkish prisoners he returned to describe what had happened to the families and people imprisoned, "the ruin of people's lives as so pervasive," but he also accepted the responsibility as his own and ours. He says, "Most of us sleepwalk through the day," adding:

> People have no idea what's going on at any particular moment. (Nightingale, n.p.)

But equally he castigates himself for "sleepwalking" for ten years. It was the military coup in Chile, he says, that woke him up. While he describes himself as a "critical, independent minded" person, he also admits that even after standing as a conscientious objector, he swallowed the World War II "propaganda—the war would be the last war." (n.p.) In 1945 at the age of fifteen he was already able to "join in an understanding of a new world," he says but now confesses he was "totally mislead. The cold war began before the hot war was over." (n.p.)

While he occasionally lapses into muttering that "everything is too late," he continues to write and to support his selected causes. But when he talks about responsibility, as always he sees it as both the individual's as well as the society's:

> The power's been taken and willingly given. (n.p.)

He says we have given the politicians so much power, "we're going to have a hell of a time getting it back." (n.p.) How is it possible to reclaim power? Through knowledge and action, he replies.

Pinter's own political campaigning on behalf of human freedoms through PEN, the Campaign for Nuclear Disarmament and Amnesty International extended, during the decades of the late eighties and nineties, to include The International Committee for the Defense of Salman Rushdie, the British Defense and Aid Fund for Southern Africa petitioning for the freedom of Nelson Mandela. He also campaigned for the freedom of many other political prisoners including Vladimir Bukovsky, Abbas Cheblak and Mordechai Vanunu; he assisted The Miners Families Appeal; he has spoken and written widely in support of the democratically elected Sandinista government in Nicaragua, and was invited to address the House of Commons to launch the "500 Years of Resistance Campaign" in counter-protest of the Christopher Columbus anniversary celebrations in the U.S.A.. He has also condemned the brutalities of the *intifada*, spoken out against Clause 28, the Official Secrets Act to outlaw "promotion" of homosexuality, protested the government's proposal to abolish the Greater London Council for the arts and has been a subscriber to the Index on Censorship. Yet when asked if he now writes from a political perspective—something Pinter not only earlier shunned in his own plays but would have walked out on in someone else's—he replied, "The problem with writing from a particular point of view is that the play is written before it is written, which is to say it's dead. Not alive." (Nightingale, n.p.)

He also says, "I would be very irritated with myself if I said I was a political playwright." (n.p.) He distinguishes between his and didactic work, reminding that his work has been from the beginning anti-authoritarian. Citing his conscientious objector status and early disapproval of the military, he concludes, "I didn't see why I should be told what to do. By anyone." (n.p.)

When asked what he hopes his work will accomplish he says he hopes people will want "to investigate to find out what is happening," and will be moved to action:

> I feel as a citizen of the world everyone has a responsibility to find out what is going on, to speak of it, to act on it. (n.p.)

When pressed to specify what action, he says he hopes people "will at least contribute to Amnesty International." (n.p.) He concludes by placing emphasis on the importance of maintaining dignity and common sense.

He also takes to task those who do not want to know about violence, those who say, "I'm too sensitive." He points to "the fact [that] the people subjected to torture are equally sensitive. The person too sensitive to read about it is neither dead nor suffering." (n.p.) He holds men and women equally culpable. When asked if he believes women are less violent than men he cited the monster of Belsen, the woman torturer. (n.p.)

Pinter makes no claims for his own moral superiority, nor does he embrace or envision utopian change. "It's the pain that one throws around, that one gives to other people, that's intolerable," he says. "It's quite impossible to cease to inflict pain. One's very presence inflicts pain. I think there's no end to the respect one must give to other people." (Kroll, 81) But he acknowledges, "That's very demanding.":

> I'm not talking about universal love—that's a load of shit. A friend of mine is fond of using the word love in that way. He's very active politically and I said he clearly felt a kinship with his fellows and acted on it. And he surprised me by saying "Well, so do you." I had to take a moment's rest on that and decided that perhaps I did. (81)

Laughing, he then added, "I'm much more selective than my friend. But I couldn't deny that I felt a certain kind of kinship with some of my fellows." (81)

While Pinter remains deeply concerned about the destruction and death of others, he remains remarkably cool and without illusions about his own death:

> I'm not afraid of dying. I think the heart stops and that's it, absolutely. I shall regret it. I mean I shall regret the leaving life. But who wouldn't? Just the same as everyone in that respect. I've no special things about dying. (*Pinter People*, n.p.)

Pinter's influence continues to live on in the work of many other playwrights. His impact is inestimable. By the 1970s it was already clear that it was not possible to be a Western playwright in the twentieth century without an intimate knowledge of Pinter's work. At that time Joe Orton, David Mercer, and younger playwrights, from David Mamet and Tom Stoppard to Simon Gray, acknowledged their debt to Pinter. Pinter's work runs the full gamut of emotions, from joy, anger, despair, pity and terror, to the erotic, but is also a late twentieth-century phenomena—he continues to write amazingly compressed, sparse, but powerfully rich drama for a busy world and through the late sixties, seventies and eighties such varied playwrights as Noel Coward, Neil Simon, Alan Ayckbourn, David Hare and Tennessee Williams paid tribute to Pinter. Many less well-known playwrights he has promoted have expressed gratitude to Pinter for his inspiration and encouragement and many other emerging and established playwrights in the 1990s have publicly thanked him, including Howard Brenton, Caryl Churchill, Christopher Hampton, Winsome Pinnock, Nick Darke and Charlotte Keatley. (McFerran, 19) Tennessee Williams simply called him "the best living playwright."

In an early interview Pinter was asked whether he thought the theatre was finished. He replied, "It's not finished while I'm alive." (Kathleen Tynan, 8)

For Pinter it is never enough simply to write a new work. He has to take the form somewhere new, extend our sympathy, enlarge our vision. Pinter's concern is that he can no longer be comic in the old way. When he talks about the world wide success of *The Birthday Party* after its initial failure he says:

> And I think one of the reasons is that Goldberg is actually quite endearing. You know he's a bastard, but you still enjoy the joke of him. Well, I can't conceive writing another Goldberg. I think the problem might be for me that I know much more now about what is happening in places like Turkey and Guatemala. So the joke is in fact over. I can't write that way anymore because the joke is no longer funny. (Schiff, 303)

Yet in 1989 before a New York audience of thousands after his solo reading of *One for the Road*, Pinter publicly admitted that he wished he could write another full-length play. But in a 1990 BBC interview, he dismissed those who proclaimed that his playwriting was over as "absolute nonsense." (Wolf, 71) Harold Pinter added, "I've got plenty left in me, I think." Since then he wrote *Party Time* and *The New World Order*. What comedy exists in those plays is almost always horrifying.

Then, after twelve years since his last major work for stage *Betrayal,* Harold Pinter wrote *Moonlight*. Between Christmas and the new year, straddling 1992 and 1993 produced a ninety-four page typescript, playing an hour and a half. The play was immediately scheduled to premiere at London's Almeida Theatre in the early autumn 1993. *Moonlight* is both darker and more comically delightful than any other recent work of Pinter's. His concern with private love and global justice coalesces to offer a new vision, dramatizing how choices at the private level connect to public decisions, how each human choice may become an ethical choice between what is either life enhancing or destructive.

He confronts in his writing what was and remains most disturbing to him, as it must be to other reasonable, reflective people—the violence and destruction one person or a people inflict upon another. He takes that most disturbing area of human interaction as his subject and dramatizes insights into its root causes in the human psyche and action, exploring what may be possible to awaken and change in ourselves and in others. He also appreciates how changing what is darkest and most destructive may also require changing what is most pleasurable and productive—the way we love. His recent work extends that portrayal of love into its public domain—justice.

Nadine Gordimer in her 1992 Nobel Lecture quotes Camus, expressing what she calls "the credo for all writers," which aptly describes Pinter's work:

> One either serves the whole of man or one does not serve him at all. And if man needs bread and justice, and if what has to be done must be done to serve this need, he also needs pure beauty, which is the bread of his heart. (21–22)

Pinter's work not only attempts to "serve the whole of man"—both "bread and justice," and "the bread of the heart"—but dramatizes what is best among human strengths and virtue by also allowing his audience to see what is worst. And he does so in ways that continue to fascinate and, even in his darkest plays, delight.

Out of the ashes of destruction of the Second World War and its aftermath, Pinter confronted and continues to explore issues of power, love, and justice. Placing stringent demands on his writing, he concludes with a question:

> Can any playwright enlarge our point of view, our understanding of the world we live in and mankind? (Nightingale, n.p.)

Earlier, on 25 December 1991, *the Independent* published the nineteen-year-old Pinter's conscientious objector speech. Written in the late 1940s, that speech already articulated the full force of his independent thinking that would inform the actions of the political conscience he has become half a century later:

> It is useless speaking of policies or sentiments or defense against aggression, for all these words will mean nothing in a final and eternal extinction. . . . To join an organization whose main purpose is mass-murder, whose conception of true human values is absolutely nil, speeding on the utter degradation of a prematurely fatigued man, and whose result and indeed ambition is to destroy the world's very, very precious life, is completely beyond my human understanding and moral conception. (15 Knowles, *The Pinter Review* 1992, 85; ellipses in original).

The year 1992 saw two productions of *No Man's Land,* one at the Almeida, starring Harold Pinter as Hirst, and the other on radio, with Michael Hordern as Hirst, Dirk Bogarde as Spooner, Keith Allen as Forster and Bernard Hill as Briggs. That year also produced a televised version of *Party Time,* a rebroadcast of the televised *The Lover* starring Vivien Merchant, and a production of

The Birthday Party in Glasgow. *Ten Early Poems* was rediscovered and published by Greville Press Pamphlets. Pinter was represented as the character Hector Duff, the celebrated playwright, in Simon Gray's *Unnatural Pursuits,* for the BBC2 broadcast in December. An important interview, "The 22 from Hackney to Chelsea," with Barry Davis, Yiddish editor of the *Jewish Quarterly* (Winter 1991/1992, 9–17), appeared in which Pinter described the Holocaust as "the most appalling thing that has ever happened." In that interview, in which he identified with the suffering of Jewish artists such as Paul Celan, Nelly Sachs, Primo Levi and Elie Wiesel, Pinter also criticized Israeli policy on the Occupied Territories and used a phrase he and his group of Hackney friends had first used in the 1940s: "That's what they're doing, they're dropping the Atom Bomb to keep the world clean for democracy." That phrase would appear as "you're keeping the world clean for democracy" in *New World Order.* Also in 1992, Pinter's portrait was unveiled at the National Portrait Gallery.

Earlier in February 1991, at a London ad hoc International War Crimes Tribunal to arraign President Bush for war crimes in the Persian Gulf, Pinter read his stunning poem "American Football," subtitled "A Reflection upon the Gulf War":

> Hallelujah!
> It works.
> We blew the shit out of them.
> We blew the shit right back up their own ass
> And out their fucking ears.
>
> It works.
> We blew the shit out of them.
> They suffocated in their own shit!
>
> They are eating it.
>
> Praise the Lord for all good things.
>
> We blew their balls into shards of dust,
> Into shards of fucking dust.
> We did it.
>
> Now I want you to come over here and kiss me on the mouth.

It was an odyssey of years before he was finally able to get it published in *The Bomb,* which featured a cover story interview with Edward Albee. In March Pinter's article "The Shameful Truth" accompanied photographs by Susan Meiselas, and later introduced her film on U.S. policy in South America, which Pinter called "the US policy of vicarious military and economic aggression, subversion and destabilization in the name of 'Freedom and democracy." (Pinter, "Shameful Truth," World *BBC Magazine of Mankind*, March N. 58.; Knowles, 1992,94) With broader international references Pinter delivered this material in May to the Oxford Union Debate with, "This House Regrets America's Role as Policeman to the World." (Knowles, 1992, quoting from typescript sent by Pinter) On *The Late Show,* Pinter introduced the Guatemalan Rigoberta Menchu, a thirty-three-year-old self-educated Mayan peasant, as a candidate for the Nobel Peace Prize, which she was awarded in October. Her book *I Rigoberta Menchu* catalogs the torture, hanging, burning and destruction of her family "and a whole people, mostly as a direct result of United States foreign policy since, yet again, the overthrow of a democratically elected president, Jacobo Arenz, in 1954." (Knowles, 1992, 4–95) In April Pinter was honored at the Chilean embassy in London, with the insignia of Grand Officer, the Chilean Order of Merit, for "his support for the Chilean people in their fight to recover democracy."

In 1993, on what must be viewed as a momentous occasion, Pinter donated his archive, sixty boxes of personal manuscripts, to the British Library, giving scholars for the first time access to original drafts of *The Birthday Party, The Caretaker, Betrayal* and other plays, his novel *The Dwarfs* and his screenplay of *Victory*. Although he knew American universities would have exceeded the estimated value of one million pounds, Pinter "always admired what the British Library did and stood for." He was accompanied at the induction by his wife, Lady Antonia Fraser, with library officials Dr Brian Lang and Sir Anthony Kenny. Later in 1993 *No Man's Land* successfully transferred to the Comedy Theatre from the Almeida with Pinter as Hirst, "a kind of inverted doppleganger of Spooner." (Knowles, 1993–1994, 15) Pinter directed David Suchet and Lia Williams in David Mamet's *Oleanna,* insisting on using Mamet's original ending. (conversation with Pinter)

A second momentous occasion that year was the production of *Moonlight,* Pinter's first new play in fifteen years. Directed by

David Leveaux, with Claire Skinner as Bridget, Anna Massey as Bell, Michael Sheen as Fred, Douglas Hodge as Jake, Jill Johnson as Maria and Edward de Souza as Ralph; Pinter brought Ian Holm back to the stage after decades-long absence to play Andy. Holm would later perform an extraordinary Lear on stage and for a BBC/production. Once again Pinter proved the most insightful critic of his own work on the topic of Bridget, the daughter in the play. When director David Leveaux asked Pinter "if the somnambulist young woman who opens *Moonlight* was dead," Pinter replied, "That would seem to be the case." (Knowles, 1993–1994, 122, quoting from the *Observer,* 12 Sept. 1993, n.p.) He told Leveaux, "I want to put my cards on the table about one thing. There are many things I don't know about the play, but I have a strong feeling Bridget is dead." (Knowles, 1993–1994, 124) But "would seem" and "strong feeling," to describe Pinter's conviction, crack open a sliver of doubt.[3]

In 1993, the *Observer* published Pinter's scathing "The US and Salvador," naming the United States as "the missing protagonist" responsible for the seventy-five thousand dead: "The United States subsidized the Salvadorean government to the tune of $6 billion throughout the 1980s," he said, detailing activities of U.S. "advisers" in the "field" that "ranged from a strategic concept which applied to the whole of Central America down to more specific and precise recommendations. These included the most efficient methods of skinning alive, castration and disembowelment [. . .], employed in order to defend Christianity and democracy against the devil." (*Various Voices,* 187–188; ellipses throughout in brackets mine) He protests President Cristiani's amnesty that allowed not only "the army officers and government ministers" to walk free, "but also two soldiers [imprisoned] for the murder of the Jesuits and five imprisoned for the rape and murder of four American churchwomen in 1980," and he then names the "quite substantial body of [. . .] American 'Military advisers' " that also walk free: "CIA, Elliot Abrams, former head of the US Latin American Desk, Jeane Kirkpatrick, former US ambassador to the United Nations, former Secretary of State Al Haig, and ex-Presidents Reagan and Bush." He admits that the information was "notoriously hard to come by" until the UN Commission report was published, and asks what would bring about a U.S. congressional investigation. He answers himself, "nothing." "There is one good reason for this. The US has long assumed a position as the world's moral centre, the world's 'Dad.' This is so deeply embedded in official American thinking that to tear this assumption apart would be to perform an operation without anaesthetic. The US Congress and media would, I believe, find this insupportable." (188) When he asks, "Why did these people in El Salvador die? They died because [. . .] they dared to question the status quo, the endless plateau of poverty, disease, degradation and oppression which is their birthright." (188–189) "On behalf of the dead," he says, "we must regard the breathtaking discrepancy between US government language and US government action with the absolute contempt it merits," and concludes, "The US has done really well since the end of the Second World War. It has exercised a sustained, systematic, remorseless and quite clinical manipulation of power worldwide, while masquerading as 'a force for universal good.' It's a brilliant, even witty, certainly highly successful con-job." (189)

In 1994, eighteen years after the first major 1975 London revival of *The Birthday Party,* Sam Mendes directed the second revival at the National Theatre with Dora Bryan as Meg, Trevor Peacock as Petey, Anton Lesser as Stanley, Emma Amos as Lulu, Bob Peck as Goldberg and Nicholas Woodson as McCann. Alan Ayckbourn, who had played Stanley in the Scarborough theatre after the original Lyric, Hammersmith production, recalls in his memoirs, "We read the play and thought he was barking mad. It made absolutely no sense whatever. . . . But what helped us was that the author was directing it . . . passionate in his belief that his play would work." (Knowles, 1993–1994, 123). That early 1959 production, which ran for three months in Stephen Joseph's Theatre-in-the-Round tour to Birmingham and Leicester, Ayckbourn notes, brought audiences, "not packed," but "the production was received . . . with extraordinary rapt fascination, really electric. People did enjoy it, in part for the seeming allegory: people started, there and then, coming up to him afterwards and saying, 'I see this as a sort of metaphor for the British economy,' and he would go 'Mmhmmmmm, mmhmmmm,' and look very interested. But would never, ever mention anything other than the characters to us." (Knowles, 1993–1994, 124)

Also in 1994 Pinter, with Anthony Astbury and Geoffrey Godbert, the other editors at Greville Press, published a striking volume, *99 Poems in Translation*. He contributed to the first issue of *Red Pepper,* which would in 1996 publish his "Carribean Cold War," denouncing the United States on several fronts, among them attempts to bring down a Cuba that had attempted a distributive justice to right the "grotesque economic polarization." Despite the U.S. embargo, Cuba has educated its children to high literacy rates and survived because, Pinter believes, the people are possessed of "a formidable centre of pride, faith and solidarity." (*Various Voices,* 192) Pinter appeared at the Hackney Empire with actress Julie Christie, poet Benjamin Zephaniah and others in a program in aid of "the Campaign to Free Vanunu," the Israeli imprisoned for revealing Israel's secret plutonium plant. Pinter's name appeared protesting the government's savage cutbacks on arts funding, and, with Edward Albee, Arthur Miller, Toni Morrison, Kurt Vonnegut and others, he signed the Anglo-American protest against the murder of thirteen journalists in Turkey that pleaded for the democratic right of free speech. Pinter again brought attention to the politically sanctioned atrocities and murder of Archbishop Romero while saying mass, and the slaughter of six Jesuit priests in "Archbishop Romero's Ghost Can be Avenged," in the 28 March issue of the *Observer* (24).

The second half of the 1990s saw the most extensive festivals of Pinter's work globally, his plays staged in Dublin and Barcelona, a major retrospective of Pinter films in London and the Pinter 2000 Conference in London. In May 1994 the Dublin festival staged *The Dumb Waiter, Betrayal, One for the Road, Old Times, Moonlight* and *Landscape*. Pinter gave a reading of *Mountain Language* at Cardiff's Festival of Literature in October. In April of that year, on the TV arts program *Omnibus* devoted to John Gielgud, Pinter acknowledged that he had modeled Gielgud's Spooner in *No Man's Land* on W. H. Auden, whom he had met just before the 1974 production. (Knowles, 1995–1996, 155) Robert Altman, director of the 1987 film of *The Room* for television in Montreal, describes using a house with the number 73 instead of 7, as specified in the script, and says that Pinter's "angry reactions really amazed me, and it actually hurt my feelings to discover that he had put me in the category of someone who tampers with his work." (155–156) Two of Pinter's scripts did not go forward: his screenplay for the Holocaust narrative *The Diaries of Etty Hillesum* was not filmed, and his screenplay for Nabokov's *Lolita* was rejected by director Adrian Lyne, who had commissioned it, over disagreement on the nature of Lolita's dialog; the screenplay went to David Mamet.

Following playwright Alun Owen's death in 1994, his tribute to Pinter, first published in the 25 April 1968 *Evening Standard* resurfaced: "Harold is the most honest man I know and the most scrupulous observer of the truth." (7) In November Pinter joined eighty-six playwrights, including Edward Bond, Peter Shaffer and Arnold Wesker, protesting the decreasing number of new plays produced each year. Other letters Pinter wrote included his 30 September 1994 plea in *the Independent* for clemency for Mordechai Vanunu, the Israeli who disclosed details of Israel's production of nuclear weapons, after having served eight years of an eighteen-year sentence in conditions described by Amnesty International as "cruel, inhuman and degrading." (18) In June, in response to the assasination of several Kurdistan journalists, the arrest of a staff of one hundred, and the torture of many, Pinter, along with Noam Chomsky, Arthur Miller in a letter to *The Independent* pointing out that since Turkey was a signator to the Copenhagen Declaration, requested that Britain send observers to the trial of the Turkish journalists to address the freedom of expression agreed to in the Copenhagen Declaration. In response to the *Times Literary Supplement* review of Noam Chomsky's *World Orders, Old and New,* Pinter points out that no mention was made of U.S. policy in Nicaragua, and he counters the reviewer Ken Jowitt's citation of a political theorist who "emphasizes the structural, not evil, basis of American actions in Central America and Iraq" with his rejoinder: "I . . . emphasize the dead, those murdered in the conduct of a foreign policy not in the least hysterical or haphazard, but one carefully considered and precisely intended—lucid, systematic and clinical. But I suppose to speak of the dead is to commit a naive error of taste and to demonstrate a lack of historical—and structural—perspective." (17 February, 5). He expresses his warning in the 1995 "Poem"

> Don't look.
> The world's about to break.
> Don't look.
> The world's about to chuck out all its light
> And stuff us in the chokepit of its dark,

That black and fat and suffocated place
Where we will kill or die or dance or weep
Or scream or whine or squeak like mice
To renegotiate our starting price. (*Various Voices,* 159)

"Renegotiate" and "starting price" seem key, as we "dance" at the edge of destruction but may have an opportunity to "renegotiate," to start over.

In March Harold Pinter was honored to receive the David Cohen British Literature Prize for his lifetime achievement in literature, and *the Times* quoted portions of his acceptance speech, including, "And thank you, Hackney Library." (18 March 1995, 18) Earlier, in January, in the *Daily Telegraph,* revising upward his praise of Pinter as "our greatest living playwright," John Casey in "The Master's Hand," calls Pinter "One of the best English playwrights," noting how few other distinguished dramatists England has had since the Renaissance, and he concludes, "We should rejoice that this authentic genius of our stage is living amongst us." (Knowles, 1994–1995, 156, quoting John Casey, "The Master's Hand") In an interview with David Sexton of the *Daily Telegraph,* Pinter mentioned that he had recently received for his political commitment the Frederick II Medal, which made him a citizen of Rome. Pinter also said of the Holocaust, "The thing is never far from my mind," adding, "We did appreciate that it was only by the skin of our teeth that it wasn't happening to us. Whether you liked it or not, you were part of the whole thing." (Knowles, 1994–1995, 159, quoting David Sexton who interviewed Pinter for the *Daily Telegraph,* n.p.) Further addressing violence in film and theatre, Pinter reviled Quentin Tarantino's use of violence as entertainment as "truly demeaning." "It undermines the spirit and intelligence too, because it falsely represents the real thing. The real thing is appalling and this stuff on film and television is just fun. Therefore I deplore it, I find it actually disgusting." (Knowles, 1994–1995, 159) Yet Tarantino in *Pulp Fiction* would seem to know his Pinter. In contrast, Pinter praised Sarah Kane's play *Blasted*, which was cast by critics as filth and pornography for the moment when an ex-soldier traumatized by war eats the eyes of a victim: "Sara Kane was facing something actual and true and ugly and painful—therefore received the headlines saying this play should be banned." (Knowles, 1995–1996, 159) In his acceptance speech for the British Literature Prize, Pinter revised the origin of his family. Until that time his family had been reported to be Portuguese, Da Pinta, or Spanish, having survived the Inquisition, information without confirmation that came from one aunt, and he contrasted this with his understanding from others in the family that all four of his grandparents were Eastern European and "came from Odessa, or at least Hungary or perhaps even Poland." Significantly, in that speech he also quoted long passages recited to him by Joseph Brearley on their walks, among them, passages from Webster's *The White Devil* and *The Duchess of Malfi,* notably, the speech the Duchess's husband addresses to his tortured and now dead wife that begins, "What would it pleasure me to have my throat cut / With diamonds[. . .]? / I know Death hath ten thousand several doors" and concludes with the husband's wish for his own death: "So I were out of your whisperings." His reference to the Duchess's "whisperings," her lines spoken as an echo from beyond the grave telling the truth of the atrocities of her death, seems to evoke Rebecca's echo words in *Ashes to Ashes,* spoken perhaps as a medium for the Holocaust dead and disappeared everywhere, when she says, "I don't know of any baby."

The year 1995 also saw the publication by Nick Hern of Mel Gussow's important *Conversations with Pinter,* spanning twenty years of highly selected, collected and rare interviews by one of Pinter's most perceptive theatre critics. Pinter disposes of us/them dichotomies when he says, "Being encouraged to look 'over there,' we quite obviously draw a blank about what is happening in our lives. You have the rhetoric of the free, the Christian, the democratic, but underneath the rhetoric what you have is excrement, vomit, urine, blood, mutilation, horror, depravation, poverty." (73)

One reported anecdote in *the Times* revealed an incident in Pinter's life that prefigured the Waiter in *Celebration*—Pinter was fired from the National Liberal Club as a waiter when he overheard several guests talking about T. S. Eliot and he joined them, "at some length. So I was caught talking to the clients, as it were. They didn't complain, but the head waiter did." (Knowles, 1994–1996, 161) In June and July the *Guardian* published two of Pinter's poems. One, "Cricket at Night," offers an allegory on blindness of political leaders in the destruction caused in their covert activities: "They are dying to pass a new law / Where blindness is deemed to be sight." (*Various Voices,* 160). In "The Other Guy," the second poem, "it's the other guy who's dying" a holy death in a war "he is banking on. . . . To glue him to a country / Where girls and boys contend / That the dead come back from dying." The poem ends with the awful finality of "dying out of love," a love that kills, "A love that holds him breathless / And burns him in his grave." (*Various Voices,* 161) "Girls," a short story that opens with a reported story about a girl who goes to her professor and says that girls like to be spanked, appeared in the October *Granta* and *the Sunday Times*. (*Various Voices,* 97–98)

Two major 1995 productions were mounted, one of *Old Times* starring Julie Christie as Kate (Pinter was responsible for bringing her back to the stage after a long absence), directed by Lindy Davies at the Wyndhams Theatre, London, and the other, *The Hothouse,* starring Harold Pinter as Roote, the menacing director of a mental institution, directed by David Jones at the Theatre Royal, Bath. *The Proust Screenplay* was produced on BBC Radio 3 in December, and there was a production of *The Homecoming* at the Haymarket Theatre, Leicester. Pinter directed Reginald Rose's *Twelve Angry Men* at Bath, which later transferred to the Comedy Theatre, London, and Ronald Harwood's *Taking Sides* at the Criterion Theatre, London, dramatizing Wilhelm Furtwängler's decision to remain in Nazi Germany on grounds of the separation of arts and politics.

Pinter, along with Margaret Drabble and Ben Okri, through the Writers in Prison Committee of International PEN, demonstrated outside the Nigerian High Commission on the tragic execution by Nigerian authorities of playwright Ken Saro-Wiwa, a long-standing champion of the rights of southern Nigerian tribal people against state-sponsored exploitation and the pollution by oil companies such as Shell. His last words, "Lord take my soul, but the struggle continues," inspired Pinter's, "murder is the most brutal form of censorship." (Knowles, 1994–1995, 167) Pinter also protested in opposition to capital punishment, the execution on the basis of disputed evidence of ex–Black Panther Mumia Abu-Jamal, held on death row in a U.S. prison for thirteen years. Pinter, with Billie Whitelaw, read from *Voice of Conscience: Poems from Oppression* at St. James Church, Piccadilly in September. In May he received an honorary doctorate in Sofia, Bulgaria, and in his acceptance speech, "A War of Words," he talked about how his characters use language "to disguise what they think and feel." He reflected, "In the world in which we live, words are often employed to distort or deceive or to manipulate as they are to convey actual and direct meaning." ("A War of Words," *Red Pepper* 24–25). On the BBC TV's Laurence Olivier Awards in February, Pinter received a special prize for his lifetime achievement to theatre, and he announced the completion of his new play *Ashes to Ashes.*

The year 1996 saw a major retrospective of Pinter's films at the National Film Theatre, the Michael Billington authorized biography, *The Life and Work of Harold Pinter,* another new play, *Ashes to Ashes,* and the revival of *The Homecoming* at the Lyttleton Theatre. Pinter's production of *Twelve Angry Men* moved to London's Comedy Theatre, and he acted in Hugh Whitmore's *Breaking the Code,* starring Derek Jacobi as Alan Turing, the man who broke the Enigma code that turned World War II around. Pinter also appeared in the film of Jez Butterworth's *Mojo.*

In May the first production of *Ashes to Ashes* was presented as part of the Otoño Pinter Festival of his work in translation in Barcelona, where Pinter gave an important interview, "Writing, Politics and *Ashes to Ashes.*" (*Various Voices,* 58–70) At another festival, Palermo's *Noveccento,* Pinter directed the Italian premier of *Ashes to Ashes,* which toured Italy with Adriana Asti from Visconti's *Old Times* starring as Rebecca.

In June, armed and uniformed men were seen entering a North London Kurdish community center, which raised an alarm that brought sharpshooters and a police helicopter to the roofs. The police brought out four hooded prisoners with guns pointed at their heads—members of a Kurdish theatre group, Ueni Yuasam, or New Life, rehearsing for Pinter's *Mountain Language,* his play about people hooded and tortured for speaking their forbidden mountain language. Pinter's comment: "The line between fiction and reality sometimes becomes very blurred." (Knowles, 1997–1998, 166, quoting from The *Guardian,* 21 June 1999, 2)

In 1997 Pinter joined in a letter of protest against the closing of the Atrush refugee camp in south Kurdistan, and appeared with Doris Lessing and others in reading from their own and other banned works. Pinter's "Picking a Fight with Uncle Sam" attacks U.S. foreign policy. Pinter called for repeal of the Police Bill, supporting Vanessa Redgrave's Charter for Basic Rights. He also joined other playwrights in censuring Director General of the BBC John Birt's intention to merge radio and televison program-making, including a bimedia drama department in order to meet the commercial demands of digital broadcasting.

His early review sketch *The Black and the White* appeared with a new one, *God's Own District,* about an American woman proselytising in London to convert the populace. Two poems alluding to international atrocities appeared: "Order" and "The Old Days." "Fascist order 'requires the blood of disorder,' while the good old days were those when 'all the democracies' were complicit in the murderous suppression of anything deemed lefty." (Knowles, 1997–1998, 167) Pinter's 1953 poem "Latest Reports from the Stock Exchange" resurfaced, beginning with an "All quiet on Wall Street" and ending with "6:30 Moscow 9 for 71 including the hat trick." (*Various Voices,* 78)

The Michael Billington biography, *The Life and Work of Harold Pinter,* appeared with clarifications and revelations about Pinter's life, including his close relationship with David Mercer, with whom he formed Shield Productions and whose early death Pinter felt very deeply, as well as the fact that *Betrayal* was informed not by his affair with Antonia Fraser as some supposed but by a much earlier affair with Joan Bakewell, whose early interview with Pinter provided some of Pinter's most illuminating insights into his work. The biography corrects the early information on Pinter's mother's maiden name, it was not Mann but Moskowitz. (Billington, 150a)

In the biography, what Pinter describes of *Party Time* applies to his most recent play *Celebration,* "I see a society where people are obsessed with their own health, with their own well being, and that leads them to a moral indifference to what is happening in the society outside, and to the fact that their comfort depends upon other people's depravation." (Billington, 134) Pinter's response to injustice is revealed as immediate and early in his life. Pinter revealed to playwright Donald Freed a most telling story. As a boy of fourteen, when Harold went to the tailor's shop where his father worked to deliver his lunch, the foreman commanded his father, "Pinter get back to work." Harold, appalled, made a rude gesture at the man. His father slapped his face and said, "I have to work here." (Billington, 344–345) That slap may have resounded around the world in Pinter's work and, coupled with Pinter's own fighting spirit, may have informed his admiration for those who fight "against savage and pitiful odds." It may also be why, at some level, he holds partially responsible for their downfall all those (save his torture victims) who, like Stanley in *The Birthday Party,* do not succeed in their fight (because they do not know themselves and are not articulate) or who, like the Waiter in *Celebration,* refuse to assert themselves and instead accept subservience.

Ashes to Ashes, written after Pinter's reading of Gitta Serenely's *Albert Speer: His Battle with Truth,* received its first London production at the Ambassadors Theatre, directed by Harold Pinter with Lindsay Duncan as Rebecca and Stephen Rea as Devlin. Rebecca and her monster lover opened new territory in the relationship between victim and victimizer in Pinter's work. *The Homecoming* opened at the Lyttelton Theatre, with Roger Michell directing David Bradley as Max, Michael Sheen as Lenny, Sam Kelly as Sam, Eddie Marsan as Joe, Keith Allen as Teddy and Lindsay Anderson as Ruth.

Another Pinter Festival was mounted in Dublin in 1997, following the success of the 1994 Dublin Festival. It included a BBC radio production of *Old Times* and *Victoria Station,* and Pinter directed Simon Gray's *Life Support.* The Gate Theatre presented *No Man's Land, Ashes to Ashes, A Kind of Alaska* and *The Collection,* with Pinter playing Harry. He read at a symposium there from many of his full-length plays. Pinter, as a man of the theatre who went to school in Shakespeare, for the first time offered his 1950's "A Note on Shakespeare," an avalanching somersault of tumbling praise from a very young Pinter who appreciated from the start the wedded opposites contained in truth—the fecund "open wound," that produces Shakespeare's work, but whose source we "cannot determine and calculate" if we are to "approach Shakespeare's work in its entirety." (*Various Voices,* 5) But, Pinter says, as we approach that open wound:

> One discovers a long corridor of postures: fluid and hardened at the quick; gross and godlike; putrescent and copulative [. . .] fanatical; paralytic; voluptuous; impassive; musclebound; lissom; virginal; unwashed; bewildered; humpbacked; icy and statuesque. All are contained in the wound [. . .] whose pain he does not attempt to eradicate. He amputates, deadens, aggravates at will, within the limits of a particular piece, but he will not pronounce judgement or cure. (*Various Voices,* 5)

Pinter delivers his highest lyrical praise for Shakespeare with a naked freshness and precision that might equally describe his own work: "He can only rely on a 'few well chosen words' to bring him through any doubtful patch." He calls Shakespeare "a malefactor; a lunatic; a deserter, a conscientious objector; a guttersnipe; a social menace and an Anti-Christ" but says, "He belongs, of course, ultimately, to a secret society, a conspiracy, of which there is only one member: himself." The "Note," prefiguring the important Shakespeare passages in Pinter's novel *The Dwarfs,* ends with "The fabric never breaks." (*Various Voice,* 6, 7)

In 1997 Harold Pinter wrote the screenplay for *The Dreaming Child,* adapted from the Karen Blixen/Isak Dinesen story in *Winter's Tales*. An attempt to produce *The Lover* in a bilingual production was halted at the Toronto Drama Festival. But a London production of *The Lover,* under Michael Billington's direction, appeared at the Battersea Arts Centre.

In March 1998 BBC Radio 4 broadcast *Old Times* under Ned Chaillet's direction, with Julia Ormond as Kate, Cheryl Campbell as Anna and Michael Pennington as Deeley, and also produced *Victoria Station* with Paul Rogers as the Controller and Martin Jarvis as the Driver, under John Tydeman's direction. On Pinter's birthday, 10 October 1998, in the *Times Literary Supplement,* Pinter's poem "Death," following the death of Pinter's own father, was published, an imaginative questionnaire beginning "When was the dead body found?" (*Various Voices,* 165)

Pinter's name appeared in a letter protesting Germany's decision to halt the Musa Anter Peace Train at the Belgian border, preventing its reaching Turkey and the Kurds. (Knowles, 1997–1998, citing the *Independent,* 29 Sept. 1998, 13) In another letter Pinter protested the uncorroborated reports of Kurdish threats of poison bombs to the United Kingdom. (Knowles 1997–1998, citing the *Observer,* 10 Oct. 1991 n.p.) In court, Pinter served as a character witness for one of a group arrested for protesting against Britain's arms sales to Turkey. Pinter appeared as an Iranian tramp in a staged reading of Ghazi Rabihavi's new play *Look, Europe!* about Iranian dissident writer Faraj Sarkoohi facing a death sentence in Iran, which as vice-president of PEN Pinter had earlier addressed in appealing for freedom of expression in Iran. Pinter, with Vanessa Redgrave and others, protested legal sanctions of various parliamentary acts that increase governmental control but decrease justice by criminalising civil liberties. Pinter pleaded for compassion to be shown to Abdul Onibiyo, who fell under the Asylum Act when he overstayed his leave from his country and was deported to Nigeria, (letter, the *Independent,* 10 July 1998, 21) and he supported the campaign to decriminalise cannabis. (letter, the *Independent on Sunday,* 5 Oct. 1998, 1) Pinter joined the Cuba Solidarity march in London after Che Guevara's reburial, and he supported "In Praise of Freedom" at Chelsea Town Hall. (Knowles, 1996–1997, citing the *The Independent on Sunday,* 19 Oct. 1998, and *The Independent,* and 9 Feb. 1998) He briefly reviewed Sharon Beder's *Global Spin* (on the exploitive alliance of governments and multinationals) and *An Embarrassment of Tyrannies: 25 Years of Index on Censorship* ("Global Spin") His own criticism of New Labour appeared in *Red Pepper,* reported by the *Independent.* ("Attack on Labour", 19) Pinter's speech before the Emergency Committee on Iraq meeting in the House of Commons aimed an attack focusing on the death of children in the Gulf War and subsequently children "dying by [U.S.] sanctions in a war sanitised by political propaganda from government with a certain kind of complicity in the media" and he denounced the United States as "a bovine monster run out of control," referring to the "humiliation" of the British government's "lapdog support of Clinton." (Knowles, 1997–1998, citing the *Independent,* 13 February 1998) Several days later, in an open letter to Prime Minister Blair, Pinter invited Blair to review the U.S. record on human rights since 1945, which Pinter compared with that of Saddam Hussein's. (Grove, 1998, 20)

Finally, from 1997 to 2000, Pinter's work on all fronts, including theatre and film, was productive and his writing was greatly honored. After the 1997 screenplay for *The Dreaming Child* and his 1998 collection *Various Voices,* Pinter appeared in 1999 in Patricia Rozema's film adaptation of *Mansfield Park* as the patriarch Sir Thomas Bertram, an aristocratic slaveholder, compassionate, benevolent, powerful, even wise, but a man whose slaves have been sexually abused and tortured. Yet, when confronted by Fanny Price with his eldest son's drawings of that torture during his son's near fatal breakdown and illness, presumably provoked by some guilt, he unflinchingly asks his son's forgiveness, sells his slaves, and with an added irony, goes into tobacco at the end. Pinter's role displays a quintessentially interesting Pinter mix of wisdom and ignorance, cunning, perversion, insecurity and kindness—all driven by a desire to retain power and augment wealth yet driven also by what seems ethically right. In August 1999 Pinter completed the remarkable new play *Celebration,* which he directed at the Almeida Theatre in a double bill with his first play, *The Room,* which can from 16 March to 29 April 2000. *Celebration's* cast included Keith Allen as Lambert, Andy de La Tour as Matt, Lindsay Duncan as Prue, Susan Wooldridge as Julie, Steven Pacey as Russell, Lia Williams as Suki, Thomas Wheatley as Richard, Indira Varma as Sonia, Danny Dyer as Waiter, Nina Raine as Waitress 1 and Katherine Tozer as Waitress 2. *The Room* featured Lindsay Duncan as Rose, Steven Pacey as Bert, Pinter's boyhood friend Henry Woolf as Mr Kidd, Lia Williams as Mrs Sands, Keith Allen as Mr Sands and George Harris as Riley, with set design by Eileen Diss. He appeared in the film of Beckett's Catastrophe with John Gielgud, shot on Gielgud's ninety-sixth birthday and directed by David Mamet. Pinter adapted Shakespeare's *King Lear* for the director Tim Keth. His unproduced screenplay "Remembrance of Things Past" playing at the Royal National Theatre in the 2000–2001 season, was adapted by him and DiTrevis. In 2000, he also performed in the film of John Le Carre's *The Tailor of Panama.* In October 2000, Michael Gambon starred in the West End revival of *The Caretaker,* directed by Patrick Macbar. For his work in theatre, on 24 May 1997 Pinter received the *Sunday Times* Award for Literary Excellence, which acknowledged that his work is "an essential part of the education of any schoolchild studying English literature and will remain so." (Knowles, 1997–1998, citing the *Sunday Times,* 27 April 1998) Printer received a BAFTA Fellowship from the British Academy of Film and Television Arts, and in 1998 he was made a Companion of Literature by RSL, the Royal Society of Literature.

NOTES

1. Vivi*a*n occurs as a variant spelling in the dedication to *The Birthday Party,* Grove Press edition.
2. When the project's $26 million dollar budget was too high for Columbia, the script was revised by Ruth Prawer Jhabvala for a James Ivory-Ismail Merchant production with Anthony Hopkins and Emma Thompson costing $11.5 million. (Nightingale, 11)
3. In 1995 Pinter wrote a very short fictional sketch, "Short Story," which begins, "There was another daughter who died. I'm thinking of finding out a Little more about that." (*Various Voices,* 96)

Introduction to the Second Edition: "Fought Against Savage and Pitiless Odds"

This past decade, England's greatest living dramatist, Harold Pinter, has continued his trajectory to Cinderella himself out of the ashes of World War II to light a way for others in the twenty-first century. He transformed childhood war trauma—terror, loneliness, and rage—into courage and compassion to become a fearless conscience of the world. No other Western dramatist better understands causes of human violence or dramatizes conflict with such far-reaching, illuminating insight to confront and resolve it. He deploys his global fame to question received ideas of power and responsibility everywhere.

His new plays *Ashes to Ashes* and *Celebration,* written since the first edition of this book was published, constitute the main focus of additions to this new edition. Together with his screenplay for *The Dreaming Child,* adapted from the Karen Blixen/Isak Dinesen story, and his remarkably well researched essays, letters and speeches, many collected in the 1998 *Various Voices: Prose, Poetry, Politics 1948–1998,* Pinter's recent published writing, interviews and plays entertain and assault with a crash course in global politics that reveals how Pinter has redressed in writing almost every major, current, global injustice. Publicly. Eloquently. Remorselessly. His ability to catapult himself into the palaces of princes and presidents affords in his plays horrifying glimpses into the halls of power that compel audiences and readers to summon courage to confront the most important issue of our time: peace. At every level, from the most intimate and domestic to the geopolitical within and between nation-states, his fiercely passionate writing confronts conflict in every beat to raise questions of responsibility that he fearlessly answers daily with his life, as we must with ours.

To see and read everything that Pinter has written and done this past decade is to be changed—utterly. Each question raised in his plays, when answered, leads only to larger questions, which, after each play's end, require us to answer with action. Where *Ashes to Ashes* dramatizes past atrocity and its role in the present, *Celebration* dramatizes present power structures with their ongoing, destructive implications for current and future atrocity. In *Ashes to Ashes* Rebecca recounts to Devlin, the man she lives with, witnessing and receiving brutal treatment committed by a man during atrocities suggestive of the Nazi Holocaust. Although she claims that man adored her, and she calls the unnamed man her most intimate friend, in the end she becomes one of the women whose baby is torn from her arms. Why does this woman, safely ensconced in a middle-class suburb, who admits "nothing bad" has ever happened to her, confess a "remembrance" she is too young to have experienced and then claim there was no baby? In *Celebration,* Julie and Lambert celebrate their wedding anniversary with Prue and Matt while tearing into one another in a restaurant. Seated at another table are Russell and Suki, a woman Lambert notices and casually remarks he once "fucked." Russell and Suki join them at Lambert's request. Who are these people? What provokes their unremitting, malicious animosity and destruction? *Celebration,* a delightfully witty jewel among Pinter's plays, reveals how the puzzles, questions and mystery through his work point to larger mysteries of life: love and destruction.

Pinter's recent political writing speaks with the urgency of one who has experienced and continues to bear witness to suffering throughout the world and feels time is running out. Where the fall of Adam and Eve in Milton's *Paradise Lost* becomes the fall of mankind and loss of paradise that also admits redemption and the possibility of a greater paradise within, the fall of the characters in Pinter's new plays signal an earthly fall into destruction that takes us all with them and where the only savior on the horizon may be the self. Or, as argued earlier, his work provokes, demands that we become our own best hero—if we are to survive and thrive. These new plays compel us to seek and seize power for productive ends at every level, often where we fear we have none. He dramatizes how giving in to fear or indifference is to relinquish power to destructors. We ignore Pinter at our peril. But to recognize him as a conscience of the world is not to neglect his delightfully disturbing comedy that makes the terror bearable, his wit that continues to ignite laughter, the flashpoint of insight, a brave genius in whose presence we discover courage to locate our own genius.

As Pinter is becoming recognized as one of England's greatest dramatists ever,[1] it might be easy to say that Pinter has in the past decade gone from being a National Treasure to a World Treasure, one of the great living dramatists anywhere. But as playwright Jack Gelber is eager to remind us, *The Homecoming* catapulted Pinter into world fame very early on. (conversation with Gelber) And while his human rights work is a continuation of his 1986 political awakening—when, with Arthur Miller, he visited Turkish political prisoners on behalf of PEN—he has conducted that work at ever-accelerating speed and on almost all fronts. Certainly Pinter's receipt of the *Sunday Times* Award for Literary Excellence in 1997 acknowledges him to the world as one of England's master playwrights of all time.

What new insights and direction does Pinter this past decade offer to light a way into the future?

These new plays frontally assault global issues, dramatizing in *Ashes to Ashes* past holocaust and present, in *Celebration,* those who profit from ongoing violence and atrocity. There are many first appearances here in Pinter's plays, among them the admissions from dominant characters of vulnerability, Rebecca's and Devlin's in *Ashes to Ashes,* along with her admission that she has no authority to tell her terrible story. In these new plays, women, half the world's population, consciously or unconsciously dramatize two poles of the question of the complicity of women and their responsibility in perpetuating destruction. Where Rebecca accepts responsibility for atrocity she never participated in, the women in *Celebration* neither wish for nor claim agency or responsibility in countering destruction from which their husbands, and they, profit. Yet now at the forefront is a voiced sexual liberation, approaching the sort enjoyed by the American actress Anna in *The French Lieutenant's Woman*—all the women in these new plays, and in *The Dreaming Child,* proudly acknowledge (or invent), even flaunt, past lovers. But in *Celebration,* Suki, for this, is still called "whore," so that, while the women approach a sexual parity with the men, (are no longer nor have ever been in Pinter's work keepers of the morality, where chastity is the sole virtue accorded women,) they do not approach political or economic equality, and they share with the men little power. While love is a thing of the past in both plays, where loveless lust and sex are deployed verbally as weapons throughout, the subtle emphasis on children, unseen, absent or lost, serves as a reminder that both plays are about the future.

To appreciate the unprecedented achievements of Pinter's past decade—his plays, screenplays, essays and speeches—is to understand how he has heightened and tightened almost every issue he confronted in his first three decades in theatre, in film and as a man of the world. He has remained true to, but expanded, his vision: the awful paradox that the very strength necessary to survive, the ability to assert the self, when driven by a desire to overpower others inevitably destroys the relationship, often but more subtly and insidiously, destroys the self, and in these plays, violence begets retaliatory violence down through generations into the future. Where his early plays dramatized the inevitably horrifying consequences of hierarchy, more recently he delivers that point in person: in his writing and his presence as a writer in the world, as vice-president of PEN, in his participation and service in so many other organizations and private fronts. That now famous sympathy he early expressed for all of his characters he now extends to those suffering injustice everywhere: from Central and South America, especially Salvador, Nicaragua and Chile, to the Persian Gulf, Eastern Europe, Africa and Israel, to Cuba, "after over thirty-five years of the most ruthless economic violence, thirty-five years of unremitting and virulent hostility from the US," and to U.S. Blacks, to the U.S. underclass, "fifty million in poverty" and "the one and a half million" prisoners, those "3,000 on death row [. . .], abused and condemned in the thirty-eight states that practice the death penalty" and to single mothers everywhere condemned to poverty. (*Various Voices,* 191, 193)

Pinter even expresses a certain sympathy, as understanding, for those, like Nicolas the torturer in *One for the Road,* who *perpetuate* violence and injustice by seeing them as people who often know not what they do, "but [are like Nicolas] as a deluded man, possessed, religiously. . . . He's enacting a religious and political obsession, and I feel very sorry for him. He's an absolute disaster, but the society he's speaking for is in itself a disaster." (62) And if Nicolas and those like him fight to retain what position, power and seeming security they possess, they do so out of fears and insecurities no different from those of Pinter's first characters,

Rose in *The Room* and Stanley in *The Birthday Party.* In his newest work the comic wit creates a strange, new sympathy for the attractiveness and attraction of those powerfully responsible for perpetuating atrocity.

The struggle for dominance has expanded or, more correctly, dissolved in his two most recent plays to the assertion of power for power's sake. The men in *Celebration,* despite their claims as "peacekeepers," are without ideals or an ethic to do good, without community or social consciousness or conscience, aside from how what they do fills their own coffers, protects their own country's corporations; and they bully to retain power only to bloat the ego and to divert attack from the self. Of course what's at stake remains survival, although any obvious physical danger to these characters in both plays seems laughably slight. But where in the past a character's desire for power was represented by a position wedded to some overarching belief (even the tramp Davies in *The Caretaker* fights to protect his rules of decorum as he attempts to attain shelter to survive), in these new plays even the fanatical beliefs of the Party Timers and torturers who want to keep "the world clean for democracy," are reduced to mouthed, crypto beliefs, defined by negation and doublespeak. Peace is war, as the American cartoonist Sorel said "Keeping the world safe for hypocrisy." Devlin's lashing out in *Ashes to Ashes* at Rebecca's lack of belief in God does not forward his positive faith, but expresses only his fear of living in a godless world. Lambert and Matt in *Celebration* justify their moneymaking and lives in terms of their work as "peacekeepers," although, more accurately, warmongering keeps them in business at unimaginable profit—where gain and greed for greed's sake remain the prime motives. The real threat is to the future: the children.

Unlike Shakespeare's ambitious heroes and villains, Pinter's characters continue to fight most fiercely not *to gain* what they do not have, but *to maintain* what they already possess. From Rose in *The Room* to the destructors in *Party Time* and *Celebration,* they hang tightly onto their status quo—but to do so is to careen toward destruction, and now on a scale unmeasurable.

The weapons characters deploy against one another in these plays, preeminently language, continue to evolve, turning more deliberately pernicious, unconsciously habitual and unrelenting, but not lethal—words shot like the full-metal-jacket combat bullets designed to pass through, wound and thus distract their fellow combatants rather than to explode interiorly like hydrashocks to kill. Instead, corrosive complaint is doled out in equal measure with "honeyed phrases" and "pisstaking," that quintessentially British witty derision, dished out to "dis" everyone and to keep lessers in place. Attack that is aimed at, and comes from, all quarters for the first time is mounted and acknowledged as a full-frontal assault to keep at bay any threat to the self. Yet here, all attack is intended to wound deeply without destroying the adversary—most often the personnearest the self: a life partner, sibling, in-law or spouse.

These are plays of wounded people wounding those nearest to them without doing them to death. To do so would terminate their most intimate relationships, revealed as a parasitic symbiosis. Thus, one seeks to possess what one already has, even if one does not want it, as language brilliantly becomes a triple-edged sword, cutting down multiple targets at once. Prue's simple, erotic gesture, to kiss Richard, the restaurant's host, "on the mouth," cuts Richard, cuts her husband, Matt, and his brother, Lambert, when her action incites her sister Julie to kiss Richard, too, thus, effectively cutting all the men. The deep, often hidden agenda in many of Pinter's past plays, the erotic as love, is reduced here to loveless lust. In this psychological warfare, past loves, mentioned as memory, serve to incite jealousies in the present while revealing love among all these characters as a mere remembrance of things past. And, as Pinter dramatizes, where there is no love there can be no justice.

With the playing field expanded from a room and party rooms to off-stage battlefields of the world, and the arsenal of the on-stage characters expanded to include real weapons of mass destruction, these players in *Celebration* are now the boys who broker the guns, drugs and money that run the world. In a restaurant, the "best in the world," these men allude only in code to their clandestine activities with guns and drugs. As "peacekeepers" they "don't carry guns" (as strategist/brokers they don't have to), but are on the receiving end of "some of the best tea in China." Pinter, who like any master trusts and accords his audiences the dignity to "get it," has never himself assumed a morally superior position, having reminded us that he is just another "bastard human being," complicit, as are we, in the destruction, but he assumes responsibility as a citizen of the world, speaking out with courage while delivering the word in his plays, without any of the explicit detail and directive of his essays, in what may seem to some like code. "It's . . . our duty as citizens . . . to exercise acts of critical scrutiny upon that use of language . . . fascinatingly pernicious . . . which keeps thought at bay." (*Various Voices,* 70)

Stanley in *The Birthday Party* is quashed, Pinter reminds us, because "he was not articulate." More recently Pinter also said in response to a question, "You asked what can the man in the streets do. I think what we can do, since we're all men and women of the street, is simply to keep it right there (*touches his forehead*) and try to articulate it." (*Various Voices,* 70)

What hope these new plays hold out, as always, is ours, our responsibility, redeemed by acknowledging both the "bastard" and hero inextricably intertwined in the self. Here in the new work we are beyond complexity as ambiguity. Where in the past the father in *The Homecoming* might express love for his wife at one moment, loathing, the next, here they exist simultaneously. The Waiter in *Celebration* describes his grandfather, a friend to all the early-twentieth-century artistic and political notables, as "a Christlike figure." He proudly boasts of him as "a man of the world" yet subtly reveals him as tinged with a touch of the fascist. And by association, the Waiter obliquely admits his own complicity in destruction—as the boasting grandson of a man who played poker with Churchill and Mussolini, just as opposing generals might meet for a toast before a battle, but here denoting that they (and he, and we) were/are all in bed together.

One source of primal power in Pinter's plays is conflict that confronts the villain in us all. Pinter unleashes his own primal terror with compassion to inflict an awakened consciousness on his audience, many of whom he understands may know firsthand nothing of the reality of life under siege—those living in the suburban safety zones created by post-World War II returning veterans, an option closed to Viet Nam veterans several decades later. The same Pinter who loved gangster movies as a teenager, who reminds us of the thrill of the torturer Nicolas in *One for the Road* ("Imagine having all that power"), continues to enjoy playing the villain on stage, and perhaps enjoys appearing the heavy in life.

He admits, "So while I'm 'enigmatic, taciturn, terse, prickly explosive and forbidding,' I've also enjoyed my writing life, and indeed my life to the hilt." (*Various Voices,* 49) He sported a little Hitlerian moustache for his role as the famed poet Hirth in the recent London revival of his play *No Man's Land* and relished his acclaimed performance as a slaveholder in the film *Mansfield Park*. When I went with my young son, Jason, to meet Harold in Los Angeles, where we went to see him play Deeley in *Old Times,* as we approached Harold, dressed in a customary warm weather costume—white jacket, black shirt, black pants and dark glasses (the alternative to his familiar all black)—Jason remarked, "He looks like a hit man." That forbidding appearance, which I would not have noticed as such, is perhaps cultivated to assure necessary privacy and may parallel what polite readers read as an abrasive tone in his forthrightly written political confrontations with the Western powers—the forceful tone he must use in his off-stage political writing to be heard.

Pinter's recent work takes us beyond ambiguity, or even yin/yang wholeness, appearing less like light and dark halves than it seemingly resembles a Jackson Pollock full-color splatter painting. As such, these plays that seem more rawly honest in that dramatization of what may at first seem merely puzzling, communicate a wholeness that is nicely expressed in the implied answer to C. K. Williams's question posed in his poem "Risk" from his recent volume *Repair:* "Difficult to know whether humans are inordinately anxious/about crisis, calamity, disaster, or unknowingly crave them." (29) The answer requires acknowledging *both*. Pinter's recent plays similarly confront the "unknowingly" of desire: that we don't know, that we rarely wish to face the fact that we might simultaneously both—crave *and* fear disaster—as genius solutions almost always prove: not either/or but *both/and* choices.

These plays of the past decade offer a new complexity of paired opposites contained in a single person not simply at different times but simultaneously, where revulsion and desire exist entwined together not as warring opposites, or even shoulder to shoulder along a continuum, but in many shades and colors, seemingly imbedded in the DNA of each cell. In *Heartbreak House,* Shaw says, "People don't have their virtues and vices in sets: they have them anyhow: all mixed," which is what Pinter gives us so much more richly. Yet Pinter's portrayal of these opposites doesn't signal ambiguity or endorse the destructive. Fintan O'Toole, analyzing Pinter's political commitment in the 7 October 1999 issue of the *New York Review of Books,* quotes Beckett as angrily complaining to his biographer, James Knowlson, of charges of ambiguity in *Catastrophe* (Beckett's response to Vaclav Hável's persecution): "There's no ambiguity there at all. He's saying 'you bastards, you haven't finished me yet.'" ("Our Own Jacobean," 28–29) The same could describe Pinter's fierce political stance.

As Pinter's biographer Michael Billington points out, "What is commendable about Pinter is that his political anger gets more, not less, intense with the years. In his mid-sixties, by which time most people have long retreated into private life, he seems to feel the pain of the world more acutely than ever." He adds in a note on his impassioned integrity, "Pinter does not rent his conscience out for hire. He tries to focus his protest on areas where he feels Britain and the West have a direct responsibility." (Billington, 372, 373)

Pinter asserts, "We are in a terrible dip at the moment, a kind of abyss, because the assumption is that politics are all over. That's what the propaganda says. But I don't believe the propaganda. I believe that politics, our political consciousness and our political intelligence are not all over, because if they are, we are really doomed. I myself can't live like this. I've been told so often that I live in a free country. I'm damn well going to be free. By which I mean I'm going to retain my independence of mind and spirit, and I think that's what is obligatory of us all." (*Various Voices,* 60)

In stark contrast to his political writing and these new plays, where the anger and violence on the private level is a measure of the violence done to others on the public, Pinter's own private life is not marked with niggling conflict. His wife, Antonia Fraser, notes, "There's never any rage or anger of the 'Where's my shirt?' variety. Harold for all his combativeness is completely unexplosive." The unchecked and excessive drive for dominance, which his plays dramatize as propelled by insecurity to expose how dangerous is a little insecurity, also seems absent in Pinter. Jennifer Mortimer, who grew up with Harold, remarks on his position among his closest friends, the gang of five boys at Hackney Downs Grammar School, "Harold wasn't fighting for supremacy. He was just floating to the top because of his genuine interest and love and talents. His parents must have been so wonderful to him because he has never, ever really doubted himself." (Billington, 387, 59)

Yet publicly Pinter has fought and must continue to fight against all odds. When the Waiter in *Celebration* at the end says his grandfather knew the artists in their wounds, "where they fought against savage and pitiless odds," he might have been talking about

Pinter, like any artist who reaches the widest possible audience: with an emphasis on *fought*. What else can we wish but that Pinter keep up the good fight on all fronts.

Along with his signature conflict, his powerplays expressed in inimitable witty Pinter dialogue, mystery best defines Pinter's work. As leader of the pack, Pinter has had to walk off a gangplank in each new play, demanding of himself to keep walking—figuratively walk on water, that is, with nothing underfoot, with no path, heading where no one has lead before except himself, and of course, audience and critics can't always be expected to keep up on the first round. While his work continues to puzzle and mystify, in these plays the many puzzles and unresolved questions edge us closer to larger mysteries of life.

The mystery of characters' inexplicable, puzzling remarks are still frequently dismissed by scholars and critics as revealing epistemological impossibility (How can we know the truth? Wholly. What can we know?) And the tired old label, theatre of the absurd, continues to perpetuate itself, slapped on what's not immediately and easily understood. Mystery in Pinter's work actually frequently signals concealed conflict beneath the surface and in these new plays ultimately exposes what for the first time a character, the Waiter in *Celebration* calls, "the mystery of life." Mystery signals the big questions in that abundant tangle of questions these plays raise about confronting human violence productively, and also—and equally importantly—about leaving almost nothing unquestioned. These plays question all human relations, values, desires, power and all intimate bonds: between siblings, lovers, husbands and wives. Thus, the plays ultimately question love and justice among the loveless. Is justice possible among those who do not love? As the private becomes one with the political in Pinter's work, in the relationships between these people conflict lurches toward destruction along a parallel course among nation-states. In *Celebration,* the only reciprocal love reported is Lambert's, long past but set in a present landscape where all bonds of intimacy are now broken, lost, unobtainable. And yet there is a longing for communion with another, the intimate contact and connection experienced only briefly in the past in moments of youthful romance in its young-in-one-another's-arms glory. Now, in these plays, love remembered presents itself as an outgrown hormonal rush for Suki, a painful, wrenching, a longing for Rebecca and for

Lambert, signals in stark relief only love's absence in the present, denied in the future. Why? Questions abound, not as puzzles for a puzzle's sake, but integral to the core mystery. Why does Rebecca unprovoked in *Ashes to Ashes* call Devlin a "fuckpig," call the siren "beautiful," tell her lover, "put your hand around my throat"? What do these men in *Celebration* do? Why the mutual animosity? In these plays we confront that space where love and destruction meet.

Appreciating the awful mystery of life requires not merely difficult, hard choices, but the even more impossible both/and alternatives: confronting the paradox of our own joy in destruction. Why, after all, do we come to theatre, or seek entertainments in film, sports or TV, if not for the promise of conflict, of seeing some vicarious disaster, and, receiving that felt/thought shock of recognition, perhaps feeling how confronting conflict can transform, can free us from fear? Momentarily. Pinter's plays come closer than any other contemporary dramatist's to offering, I believe, Aristotle's notion of catharsis, without in the least letting us off the hook with a comfortable feeling of resolution of conflict. Because the conflict isn't out there. It is ours.

Mystery, contained in the present, speaks to our future, but remains more deeply imbedded in the past among these characters, who are more vulnerable, honest, yet finally also more delightful and malicious. Each question answered only raises a larger one. As we begin to realize why Rebecca tells the story, as a conscience of the past, she raises further questions about the joys of victimization, and at some level acknowledges her responsibility in atrocity.

Rebecca, in *Ashes to Ashes* a young-middle-aged woman, living now, more than half a century after the Nazi Holocaust, "remembers" bearing witness, then being forced to participate in unspeakable acts. Her "action," the story she tells, distantly resonates with the young, intelligent, informed, attractive wife in Arthur Miller's *Broken Glass,* an American Jew during World War II who mysteriously takes to her bed paralyzed. Unable to walk, she assumes a crippling guilt that displaces the responsibility she, like most of us, is unable to commandeer to counter overwhelming forces of destruction on another continent across an ocean, but which her sympathetic doctor and husband nevertheless choose to deny or ignore. What can she do to halt the advance of Hitler and his death camps after *Kristallnacht,* The Night of Broken Glass, when windows of Jewish storefronts and homes were smashed? Are we equally paralyzed before such brutality? Where does courage to confront such brutality come from? That seems a central question in *Ashes to Ashes*.

Though set in the present, recalled by a woman too young to have participated in the Nazi Holocaust, Pinter's play journeys through an imagined, startlingly and rarely acknowledged juncture, the shared space in the relationship between victim/survivor and victimizer: the erotic joys of power. Where earlier *One for the Road* dramatized the joys of the torturer, his pleasure in his power "to keep the world clean for Democracy," this play provocatively reveals the erotic element in the powerlessness as well. Rebecca's insistence that the man who commanded her to "Kiss my fist" also adored her resonates with Sylvia Plath's "Daddy"—"Every woman adores a Fascist/the boot in the face the brute brute force of a brute like you"—and while such an attitude may scarcely seem to apply to any of us at a conscious level, yet it unconsciously carries an erotic power to move us all; unacknowledged, it retains its power to destroy. *Paradise Lost* reminds us that sin and evil in the form of the beautiful Lucifer/Satan, *must* be attractive in order to tempt. Collectively, the characters in both plays exhibit almost all the traditional seven deadly sins: pride, wrath, gluttony, lust, sloth, greed and envy, but come up short on the traditional virtues: wisdom, prudence, temperance, friendship, love and justice. Even temporal faith, defined as trust is impossible. Without a center of a self they can trust, characters are propelled to fight more fiercely for things they already possess. But we can sympathize with what they show us of ourselves. Again, to acknowledge warring opposites in the self, among our generally held received beliefs, is a portion of that self knowledge, together with a knowledge of the real world, required to confront the deadly questions of conflict we all face as we claim we seek peace.

But is Rebecca, aside from making her story real for Devlin and for us, paralyzed into inaction? If so, why? In the end, when she acknowledges responsibility for handing over the baby, she claims a moral responsibility, but what of justice? Just as Swiss banks in acknowledging responsibility for keeping holdings of Holocaust survivors fulfill moral responsibility, without subsequent action they commit no justice. Have the women in *Celebration* gone further, ceased even to desire agency or justice? If so, what do they want? Those are the very questions we must confront before we can claim courage.

These plays are about that rarely acknowledged interface between opposites in the self where the erotic meets the destructive, desire butts up against revulsion, normalcy with nightmare, reality with the invented and the imagined, that, unless acknowledged, carries the detonating charge for destructive, explosive force. Recently, while working on a documentary film on recovery from rape/incest, considered the most intractable trauma because recovery is generally deemed impossible, I asked Harold, as an active member of Amnesty International, his experience on recovery from trauma. He answered with a question, something to the effect: What if they enjoy it? At first I was incensed, but he cited Louis Malle's film *Murmurs of the Heart* about mother-son incest, forcing me to reconsider and to recall research I'd encountered decades earlier that concurred in some instances on the topic of incest. But of course not rape/incest. Pinter's new plays are about looking at almost all relationships and values from another perspective, about seeing our daddys' and our grandfathers' acts anew to better acquaint us with ourselves—to discover present responsibility. But if we "forget," rather than "remember" as Rebecca attempts, these plays ask us how we can claim responsibility and power in the future.

Pinter's most recent play, *Celebration,* telegraphs only scant information about what these characters do to contribute to global destruction. Less obvious is that we, who are probably invested in global commodities, are complicit with them. Yet, the way the privileged characters in *Celebration* treat one another in their family parallels the way they treat community, country and the world: them family and community have no meaning. Pinter says, "The essence of England was, as I said, punishment, and making money. Mrs Thatcher, I remind you said immortally: 'There's no such thing as society,'" which according to Pinter means, "We have no obligation or responsibility to anyone but ourselves." Certainly that describes the celebrants in *Party Time,* and even more so in *Celebration*. What such a view inevitably leads to, he says, is "the poor have become the enemy of the rich," then adds, they have always been. Those who rebel against injustice are punished in the name of preserving democracy. He asks, What is "democracy that helps people murder their own citizens?" (*Various Voices,* 67, 68, 65)

Thus, these new plays about the present are really about the future, revealed in Pinter's women and children.

Pinter's women in these two plays, hardly docile, give almost as good as they get, but none commandeers any power for change, nor do they seek any agency to do so. Rebecca in *Ashes to Ashes* musters guilt and great feeling, insisting she's deeply upset by the events she describes, babies torn from their mothers, while the pampered women in *Celebration* do charity work, not out of love but in obligation to their class, casting alms to the poor kept in poverty by their husbands' economic strategies. The women in *Celebration* otherwise fiddle while the world burns, taking only sniper-fire potshots at their husbands, responsible also for brushfire wars and conflagrations, but the women never target the conflagration. Yet, the women are central to all else, certainly to the future through their children, with whom connection seems to be severed. Where they fondly recall their children in their cuddly childhood, they seem to take no part in their grown children's lives or affection. Instead, these women, like Sarah in *The French Lieutenant's Woman,* flaunt admissions of youthful lust (and still win the label "whore") but to a vastly different end. Where Sarah invents a premarital affair to elevate her outsider status that gains her her freedom to invent her self while also enchanting the young Smithson to win his respect and love, these women flaunt sexual encounters and make sexual overtures to rouse their partners' jealousy, using sex as yet another weapon in the arsenal of mutual attack. Like their men, arrested in a lusty adolescent sexuality, they also seem to have become revirginated into a preadolescent no man's land. Yet, they can only react by lashing out, and only score a hit with subordinates.

Certainly Pinter, like Shakespeare, creates strong women, and Michael Billington, along with many others (such as Victor L. Cahn in *Gender and Power in the Plays of Harold Pinter*), sees Pinter's women as "agents of change." (Freed, *The Pinter Review* 1997–1998, 128) "Pinter's women possess a greater imaginative understanding of suffering," Billington notes in an interview with the playwright Donald Freed, "and I think that motif reaches its fulfillment in *Ashes to Ashes*." He insists on Pinter's women's strength: "A constant factor" is his "belief women do have, as a sex, a physical and psychological resilience and a much greater imagination than men." (Freed, 130 cf. Ben and Gus, where women "don't hold together" as well as men). "Pinter's men are nearly always plagued by some form of duty, insecurity, uncertainty about their identity, whereas the woman in Pinter's plays time and time again have a greater degree of control and authority," a comment that might apply to Rebecca. "The woman can reconcile her social and sexual self very easily, her roles as wife and mistress. But the man cracks under the strain of living the double life." (Freed, 130) That hardly applies to *Celebration,* where the women seem condemned to be ex-mothers, marginal wives, and "Nobody's sweetheart," while Lambert fondly remembers a past love, and invites Suki, a one-time sex partner, to his anniversary table after announcing to his assembled company he "fucked" her when she was eighteen.

Billington further describes Pinter's women as rebels, and, citing Dusty in *Party Time,* "as agents of opposition to this ruthless world of male oppression that is going on. She is active in her protest and will not be silenced in any way. And it just seems he is suggesting women have a capacity for anger and rage and a refusal to enlist in male barbarism that is very significant and important and therefore seems to be quite logical that he goes on in *Ashes to Ashes* to show Rebecca as the conscience of history." (Freed, 131)

Freed concurs: "What happens to men without women is precisely called either war, at the macrocosm, or family in the microcosm. Max and his boys. [in *The Homecoming*]." (Freed, 131)

Cahn, who in *Gender and Power in the Plays of Harold Pinter* argues that the battles are for power and language is used for protection, hasn't met the women in *Celebration,* who use language offensively as an assault weapon. Battles are conducted at two levels, conscious and unconscious, and women may be "propelled by biological forces of which they may not be aware." (Cahn, 6) Cahn sets out to make us aware of them. He confronts to Arlene Sykes', "Does Pinter say anything more about women than they are mothers, wives, and whores? Not, I think, a great deal" but notes, "women are saved by their mystery . . . vitality." (Cahn, 6; Sykes, 106) He concedes that women are in conflicts with men are "exacerbated by sexual desire, repulsion and jealousy" and that the conflicts "take place largely apart from political or economic territory." (Cahn, 7) Yet, he finds no narrowness to this view of women as excluded from political and economic power; nor does anyone ask if women exclude themselves.

"Mystery," Cahn says, "troubles men more than women," and he claims that women unfortunately "are forced to seek from men the emotional sustenance that men are often unable to provide." But, because of their natures, "distinct values and desires," he suggests Pinter's women don't desire agency in their struggle for power. (Cahn, 7, 8) As Kimball King points out in his review of Cahn's book, "Cahn makes a persuasive case for the importance of gender conflict in Pinter's works, but we must not forget that the home 'battleground' on which it is waged is booby-trapped with lies and posturing." King cites *Betrayal:* "It is risky to believe Emma when she tells Jerry she is carrying Robert's (and not Jerry's) child; for she has preceded her announcement by asking him if he had ever considered getting a divorce. Jerry's strong negative response could easily have influenced Emma to 'decide' the paternity issue without his help." (King, *The Pinter Review* 1995–1996, 199)

Pinter's women, with their "greater awareness, both of their own natures and of the nature of men," have, Cahn insists, an understanding that "gives women a strength, a capacity of survival, that the male characters lack," and such a woman seeks dominance "as her only means of achieving the psychological wholeness and integration she desires and demands for herself as a person." (Cahn, 133) Wholeness might seem a starting point, or a means to an end, but hardly an end in itself. Wholeness doesn't necessarily imply agency or action. But he believes Pinter dramatizes a refinement of sensibility and portrays women with sympathy.

Even Pinter contributes to the consensus that women are more resilient than men, with greater emotional and imaginative depth, in emotional battles and that "women are nicer," acknowledging that women seldom commit the atrocities men do except when acting as men, in the concentration camps. He quotes Kingsley Amis, "Women are so much nicer than men/No wonder we like them." Although his wife finds that patronizing, he says, "Nevertheless in my plays women have always come out in one way or another as the people I feel something towards which I don't feel towards men." When asked, "That's a very male point of view, isn't it?" he replies, "Why not?" (*Various Voices,* 61)

No one seems to notice his women are largely ineffectual: ineffective in gaining what they want for themselves, any agency over what seems important to their lives or the future of their own families, children or community. Nor is anyone asking, Why not? What do Pinter's women want? Perhaps William Blake answered, a century before Freud, when he asked the same question and answered, "The Lineaments of gratified desire." In the same poem,

Blake also asks what men want and gives the same answer. Pinter's work, too, returns us to love as gratified desire and a productive relationship between equals, although Rebecca insists, protesting too much, "The last thing I want is to be anybody's sweetheart." Hers is one of those self-referential statements, like almost all in Pinter's work, that signals the truth resides in the opposite.

More recently, many of Pinter's women (and men) not only do not indicate what they want, but don't seem to want anything at all—other than maintaining what they already possess. Consider John Stuart Mill's observation in *On the Subjection of Women* that one reason women did not excel in the arts and elsewhere is that, while all the men he knew who achieved acclaim had wished to be famous as children, women were not even permitted to wish for it. These women don't even wish to wish for agency, and certainly don't know how to claim that power. To praise Dusty in *Party Time* for fearlessly confronting perpetrators of atrocity and torture is not to praise her superior imagination or greater emotional depth but to ignore that what propels her is her close-hand experience with it—her brother Jimmy is the one being tortured and is about to die at the hands of her host and his other guests. She has *no power* to save him. To what extent is it her responsibility to claim power? Can she claim power? If so, how?

Is Pinter subtly confronting these issues concerning half the population of the world, as some contemporary women writers are doing more explicitly, to awaken women as well as others who are oppressed to their own responsibility? Barbara Kingsolver in *The Poisonwood Bible* and Lauren Belfer in *City of Light* set their novels in the past to illuminate ongoing oppression in the present, less to register complaint against men than to expose the CIA responsibility for the death of the popularly elected Lumumba, or to explore the power of the wealthy oligarchy who really run the show beneath the veneer of elected officials in turn of the century Buffalo and in the country. Patricia Rozema, the writer and director of the film *Mansfield Park,* joins a host of recent screenwriters presenting strong, successful, independent women who fight for and win both love and some measure of justice for themselves and for others. Pinter accepted the role of the aristocratic slaveholder patriarch exposed in the film for his atrocity by his young ward and niece, Fanny Price, who boldly shows him the face of his atrocity in his own son's graphic drawings that witness his sexual exploitation and torture. Pinter similarly exposes to us the powerbrokers in *Celebration* as those in charge who really run the world. Interestingly, in his plays through *Betrayal,* which moved back in time to youth, Pinter's men and women seemed largely contemporary with him, roughly his own age, and continue to grow older as he did, but after *Betrayal,* his characters, including those women partnered with others sexually, remain under fifty, and except for the asexual Margaret Thatcher clone in *Party Time,* none of his women can effect change for the future. Contrast his women to those of Leslie Marmon Silko in *Almanac of the Dead,* set in the present, which casts two beautiful, sexually active, postmenopausal, native American women who not only possess an awakened consciousness but take revolutionary action against oppression.

In her book *A Kind of Alaska: Women in the Plays of O'Neill, Pinter, and Shepard,* Ann C. Hall cogently argues that Pinter's plays "illustrate the limits of the stereotypical roles in the phallic economy." (55) The suggestion is that Pinter is conscious of his choices that awaken an audience to the limits society places on women, and Hall seems to see in his dramatization of women a "hint at hope for the oppressed position of women he has so exquisitely depicted." (90) In her favorable review of Hall's argument, Judith Roof rightly concludes, "Hall seems somewhat undecided, finally, about what Pinter's plays reveal about gender, highlighting instead their sense of paradox and unsettling irony." (132–133).

Yet, comedy laced through some of *Ashes to Ashes* and almost all of *Celebration* reveals a leveling of the playing field between men and women. The women's acerbic wit that often provokes and matches the men's in a comic Laurel and Hardy thrust-and-parry stichomythia reveals possibilities for the women's greater participation than they claim. Pinter wrenches language in ways he claims he learned from radio, "knowing that language is to be turned on its head and kicked up the arse," and frees the language of both men and women. (Knowles, *The Pinter Review,* 1997–1998, 180) Pinter's comedy deploys simple slot-slipping comic technique to achieve that end: slipping unexpected words into a slot occupied in received discourse by another. In *Ashes to Ashes* Devlin praises Rebecca's "green *fingers*" (for the idiomatic, green "*thumb*"). Prue claims her sister Julie can make a better sauce with "one hand stuffed between her legs" (for "one hand tied behind her back"). Both shifts comically transmit erotic overtones. Prue complains that her mother-in-law wouldn't give her "the drippings off her nose," and the Waiter, that his grandfather was James Joyce's godmother.

While Pinter claims, "I think I write quite affectionate humour" (as opposed to cruel humor), created by affection for his characters, he also says, "When we recognize the ugliness of people, we see the ugliness of ourselves." He sees laughter as "very much a question of recognition of our own worst characteristics. So," he admits, "I've actually contradicted myself. I've said laughter is created by true affection; it's also created by quite the opposite, by a recognition of where we are ugly." (*Various Voice,* (62) The puerile, often scatological, vaudeville music hall comedy works to displace received meaning and wrench consciousness to awareness of fresh levels of action required in the plays' larger intentions by pointing to the deeper levels at which Pinter's comedy works.

The screaming mothers at the train platforms whose babies are torn from their arms in *Ashes to Ashes* is a horrifying reminder of the Slaughter of the Innocents, which was played for comedy in early English mystery plays where, when the soldier comes to spear a child on his sword, a mother says you shall not take my *bairn,* then shoves the child's naked bottom in the soldier's face. Although we might not laugh today at that gesture, or find it believably effectual, yet early mystery plays, like later morality plays as popular entertainment, reveal, in this interesting juncture between comedy and the violent conflict of atrocity, the alliance between comedy, conflict and courage.[2]

Laughter remains a flash point of insight necessary for fresh action. At a recent, nearby college production of *The Room,* I was surrounded by students at the intermission who said that they had heard me and my husband laughing during the performance, knew I got it, and could I please answer some questions about the play. It seems appropriate that Pinter should couple his first play, *The Room,* with his most recent, *Celebration,* in its first London production, since they both portray people clinging to what is most familiar to maintain their status quo: Rose to her room, and the celebrants, less obviously, to their place at the table at this restaurant, the best in the world.[3] Comedy and conflict in Pinter's work conspire to create a generosity and optimism necessary for productive change.

The wellspring of the primal power in Pinter's work, the terrifying, yet wittily delightful, life-and-death conflicts, originates at the conjunction of comedy and conflict. These polar opposites create a breadth and depth captured in Western theatre's ancient icons of drama, the laughing and crying masks, emblems of fear and desire. Comedy and conflict representing contradictory, yet essential human emotions—terror and joy—drive almost all human thought and action. Pinter, unlike a Neil Simon, never uses humor to distance himself from pain, but to convey truths and make the terror bearable. At the point of insight where we see our darkest side there is a generosity as a form of trust in being able to laugh at our own ugliness and an optimism that we can change in that trust.

Pinter's work continues to puzzle, and we appreciate how, in the unanswered and seemingly unanswerable questions his work has provoked from the beginning, we are tossed into the great mysteries. But much that at first appears puzzling may not be, even in these new plays, after a closer look at the work.

A young colleague of mine, about to teach *The Dumb Waiter* and puzzled, asked, *What's it all about?* I handed him the chapter here, simply a close textual reading. When he returned, he exclaimed, *It's all so obvious!* as if he hadn't needed any analysis at all. That is precisely the point. My hope is that a reader who finishes reading a chapter on a play should think, *Oh, that's obvious,* always was—and that so much lurking just below the surface awaits to summon us more deeply into Pinter's work. This book is intended not only for scholars, students, critics and audiences, it is equally aimed at directors, actors, and other theatre professionals who continue to find it useful. Intended to be read wholly or in part, the introductions provide the main starting point, and may be guide enough so that much of what at first appears puzzling becomes obvious.

The Pinter Ethic is not intended to explain the inexplicable mysteries Pinter is so famous for, the Big Questions nobody has answers for, but for what concerns us most intimately and globally: life and death, good and evil, sex and violence, above all, love—and by extension— justice. The book, like his plays and other writings, is intended to point us in the direction of ourselves, with some trust we can and will productively confront some of the questions he raises.

Along with this new introduction, the second edition of *The Pinter Ethic: The Erotic Aesthetic* contains a chapter on Pinter's most recent work: his plays *Ashes to Ashes* and *Celebration,* his screenplay *The Dreaming Child,* adapted from the Karen Blixen/Isak Dinesen story in *Winter's Tales,* as well as *Various Voices: Prose, Poetry, Politics 1948–1998.* Several recent books on Harold Pinter, which again verify that Pinter offers the best insight into his own work, include Mel Gussow's important collection of Pinter interviews, *Conversations with Pinter,* and the eloquent, respectful, authorized

Michael Billington biography, *The Life and Work of Harold Pinter*, which confronts and clears up some mysteries about Pinter's life, presenting stripped of lies, evasions and disguises, then perpetuated in the scholarship. *The Pinter Review,* now publishing drafts of Pinter's plays, requires special commendation, as do the editors Francis Gillen and Steven H. Gale and regular contributors Susan Hollis Merritt for the bibliography and Ronald Knowles for the annual "Pinter in London" update, who have all dedicated their lifetimes to forwarding an understanding and appreciation of Pinter's work and seeing to his nomination for the Nobel Prize which I believe he should receive for his insights into violent conflict.

The fractal geometry that conveys the parallels and resonances between the private and public in Pinter's dominant/subservient conflict in each beat, each scene, each act and each play as a whole, now become powerplays that more directly engage and resonate with the audience through mystery. As the new plays seem to many in his audiences to remain as puzzling, or even more puzzling, than earlier work, they may seem to act as a Rorschach where we must supply answers to the questions with our own actions. That does not mean that the plays can mean anything, that the questions and clues don't require meticulous attention, but throughout Pinter's plays, as he says of Shakespeare's plays, "the fabric never breaks," and in that tension is the spell and the magic his work does in speaking directly to the soul. We may "get it" without knowing it, without knowing anything more than we are disturbed, delighted, moved.

The best guide to Harold Pinter's work remains his own, and in his plays about winning and power, we are the rich recipients of a knowledge and wisdom about ourselves and the world because of his writing—in a world where the center not only does not hold but there is no center. Perhaps never was. He can say in one play "the best man wins," and in the second, "fuck the best man. " In the awful mystery of life, where the "best man" enters much of his recent work to play on friendship and on betrayal to remind us of what is best. Love and its public aspect, justice, remain the heartbeat of his work.

Without love, chaos is come again. And with chaos can come a cry for order sometimes manifested as totalitarianism. The real risk is less annihilation, than what may be worse—loss of freedom—already ongoing. "Murder is the most brutal form of censorship" he says, people imprisoned and put to death because they're writers. (*Various Voices,* 70) Martin Luther King said, "When the world looks back on the twentieth century, they will weep not for the atrocities that took place, but for the silence of the good people."[4] Pinter's courage, his truth telling, his showing us ourselves as we might not wish to see ourselves, onstage and in our world, also gives us what best hope we have of becoming our best selves.

I wish to thank James Morgan, the editor in chief, and Kimball King, the series editor, for their support and suggestions, Angela Cheyne, Harold Pinter's assistant, as always, for her gracious assistance; Charles A. S. Ernst and Lynn Mistretta for the generosity of their meticulous editing; Mia Zamora, the editorial assistant, Judy Ashkenaz, Deborah Klenotic, Marian Corkett, and Jeanne Shu for their fine editing and production assistance; Leon Shkolnick, director of the library at D'Youville College, Ava Edah, reference director, Cheryl Lajds, and Linda Hall for their generous assistance in researching and locating information; my mother, Olga Prentice, for her careful reading; Leslie and Sally Fiedler for their direction and encouragement; John Mulryan and Ann Goldsmith for insights on Milton and allegory; Donald Savage for his suggestions on medieval drama; Harold Pinter for keeping me abreast of his work; and, with my deepest gratitude, my husband, James Grunebaum.

Pinter is only seventy on 10 October 2000. Those of us who have been fortunate enough to know him, to work with him, to receive his generous support, to know the delight of his work intimately, and who continue to be inspired and moved by his genius, will wish him to be like Shaw and Sophocles, writing through his nineties.

NOTES

1. Acknowledged during presentation of his award for the David Cohen British Literature Prize, March 1995, and the *Sunday Times* Award for Literary Excellence, May 1997.
2. I am indebted to Donald Savage for the connection between the Slaughter of the Innocents and comedy.
3. Ironically, the restaurant in the play is informed by Pinter's favorite, The Ivy (in conversation with the author.)
4. William F. Schultz, quoted in the Amnesty International letter, "Breaking the Cycle of Violence: Meeting the Human Rights Challenge of the 21st Century" (November 24, 1999)

PART ONE

The Early Work: Power as a Private Affair

Introduction: Pinter's Achievement—Form and Innovation

What Yeats, Pound, and Eliot did for poetry in the early twentieth century, Harold Pinter later did for drama. He transformed it in ways that have yet to be fully articulated. He leveled easy distinctions between villain and victim, redefining each by rerouting our focus to include understanding, even compassion for both, and in doing so established a basis for an ethic where both bear responsibility. He sounded the realistic speech of ordinary people in spare dialogue rendered poetic and stamped it indelibly his own. His dialogue and its menace, more than any other aspect of his work, have attracted the label "Pinteresque," suggestive of "Kafkaesque," and his work is distinguished by being more deeply disturbing and unnerving than almost any other contemporary playwright's. Yet his plays are simultaneously counterbalanced with that special delight of a high comic wit and a consistently resonant subtext. What is happening on several levels beneath the surface of the text is often more important than what is occurring on the surface. But Pinter remains a master of holding audience attention on level one.

Pinter's innovations do not stop there. He eliminated the "Who-asked-you's," that contrivance of drama whereby two characters enter at the start of a play to supply answers to questions the audience has not asked about an off-stage character or an anticipated or past event. In dispensing with unnecessary exposition, Pinter's work creates both a seductive mystery and an elliptically concise structure, tighter yet more complex than that of almost any other dramatist. Like any master he trusts his audiences to understand his text and subtext without road signs.

Equally important Pinter has challenged, extended, even changed the structure of contemporary drama on three levels—at the surface, and below: both laterally and vertically. On the surface his plays such as *Old Times*, where Anna is both present and not present at the opening, *Betrayal*, begun at the end of a love story, and his filmscript for *The French Lieutenant's Woman*, intersticing a nineteenth-century cinema love story with the contemporary love affair between the two actors playing the lovers in the film within the film, are just a few works which have inventively stretched the surface structure in ways that contribute new forms to contemporary drama and film not merely for form's sake, but to raise profound questions about the nature of time, memory, and perhaps most important, the nature of love.

On two deeper levels, laterally and vertically, Pinter's plays, expressed through a fractal geometry, have also contributed a highly organic dramatic depth structure.

Pinter's dominant/subservient conflict which embeds his signature on every breath and beat provides the actuating impulse and basis for all ethical choice in his plays. That conflict, conveyed through the fractal geometry, operates laterally from the smallest element to the play as a whole and vertically from the private to the global levels. The resulting organic structure directly challenges any view of human powerlessness.

Fractal geometry offers a simple, elegant metaphor to describe the tightly organic form which consistently structures Pinter's work from the earliest to the most recent. Organically, fractal geometry might be compared to the way DNA, encoded in every cell, manifests itself on the structures we can see of a living organism. The term "fractal," coined in 1975 by mathematician Benoit Mandelbrot during his investigations of irregularity and chaos, was devised to describe his conclusion that the degree of irregularity remains constant over different scales; in chaos theory the degree of irregularity a snail might trace following the coastline of England would be the same a geographer might record in mapping it. More simply, fractal geometry exhibits an analogy to crystalline form, where the shape of the invisible crystal at the molecular level bears a shape identical to the macroscopic crystal form we actually see. Fractal geometry's theory that the degree of irregularity remains constant across scale, elsewhere defined as "self-same over scale," (Gleick, 98) provides an analog that nicely describes Pinter's unique lateral and vertical structuring of conflict that provides the essential force in his work.

Laterally, in Pinter's plays the central conflict for power, inscribed on all elements from the smallest to the largest, is the "self-same" conflict which drives his work across scale to propel each beat, each scene, each act, through the arc of the play as a whole. The lateral structure reveals how a character's smallest choice and its consequences may have resounding but identical consequences within the larger arc of the whole play's action.

Vertically, the same dominant/subservient conflict in Pinter's work serves as the constant which crosses the three levels in which we all live: the private level of self, family, friends and lovers which provides the foundation for all else; the public level of community where we work and play; and finally the global level of world affairs, which in return impinges on all our lives. The vertical structure dramatizes how human choice and action on the private level may have public, even global, repercussions.

Through his multidimensional fractal geometry, Pinter's plays create a four-dimensional world with a depth and resonance seldom if ever achieved elsewhere with such economy. Chaos theory's concept of fractals provides a construct that illuminates how the organic structure in Pinter's work weds the ethic to the aesthetic keeping the ethic in the conflict alive before the audience at all times.

Chaos theory unlocked yet other surprises suggestive for appreciation of Pinter's work. The logarithms in the fractal geometry used to map the irregularities in chaos theory to measure the onset of turbulence or irregularity in chaos were applied across wildly divergent disciplines: from that point when, for example, cigarette smoke smoothly ascending from a cigarette in an ashtray or water steadily dripping from a faucet becomes irregular, to irregularities in weather patterns, the stock market, the human heart beat, schizophrenic behavior and the occurrence of rime icing on an airplane wing. What once appeared to be chaotic now appears to have a previously unsuspected underlying order, and one great contribution of chaos theory was the discovery of order in chaos: both within a single entity under observation and among disparate entities and systems. Taken together both conclusions (that the degree of irregularity remains the same across scale and the discovery of chaos theory's application to disparate systems) open access to a fresh perspective in appreciating the ethical implications of the vertical structure of Pinter's work and its suggestive application to life.

From Pinter's earliest to his most recent work, the choices characters make that promote destruction privately—from Gus in *The Room*, to Stanley in *The Birthday Party*, and more obviously to Jimmy in *Party Time,* the nameless blindfolded victim in *The New World Order* and the father and sons in *Moonlight*—resonate at all levels with repercussions which allow us to see ethical connections between the private and global spheres.[1] The choices Pinter's characters exhibit are recognizably our own, and chaos theory's ability to apply fractal geometry to widely divergent systems and disciplines provocatively connects Pinter's insights into the source and consequences of conflict to ethical implications in life.

What Pinter does with form is remarkable in dramatizing how the final destruction of an individual character is fractally contained in the ongoing dynamic of each momentary and minute conflict in a struggle to achieve respect, love and power. Yet Pinter repeatedly dramatizes how attempts to dominate another inevitably destroy relationships on the private level, organizations on the public level, and governments at the global level. In his most recent work the fractal geometry finally links power and justice with love.

Both the destroyed and destroyer, in all but several most recent plays, bear responsibility for the destruction and the downfall of relationships, revealing at all levels what cannot work and why. Yet through the implications of the fractal geometry Pinter's work also suggests what might work. His plays simultaneously value the old virtues of love and friendship and promote courage and justice, while they call for and celebrate change in both the definitions of love and justice and in the actions necessary to implement them.

Finally, however, no simple analog can adequately describe how Pinter's organic integrity extends to include life itself. The range of his organic unity encompasses the pulses in life, a heart that is time, in harmony with the subsurface, subcommunication beat of our existence—our anxieties and fears, not only the fear but the passion and delight. For almost anyone watching plays generally, even the most realistic plays, it is nearly impossible not to be aware at some moment that what is being observed is theatre. To watch Pinter's work seems to be to watch life itself. Because even the surface action of his work taps into the same sources of action as life, there appears to be no intruding artifice.[2]

Pinter has done much more than this brief sketch indicates. Any analysis of a single attribute of Pinter's work is limiting, distorting and may falsify; it may ignore a salient aspect of his work, such as the resonant subtext which also distinguishes Pinter as a dramatist, or it may overlook the often hilarious comedy, or, capturing the wit, neglect the terror beneath, which almost always informs the best comedy. But, because Pinter's work is so organic in both structure and theme, a deep understanding of almost any essential aspect of his work may take an audience or reader everywhere —to an appreciation of all other significant elements.

A balanced appreciation of Pinter's achievement and the ethic that bonds his work at center requires comprehension of his values, voice and vision. *The Pinter Ethic* describes the values fused through voice and action that form the aesthetic which conveys Harold Pinter's vision.

Pinter's most extraordinary contribution is his vision. A vision encompasses the totality of a writer's work, conveying a view of human nature that reflects the cause of human action and subsequent interaction with the world; specifically defined, a vision addresses the question: What actuates human beings? More directly, What motivates characters to act? Are characters driven by selfish ambitions or inspired by ameliorist desires for the welfare of others and the self? Or by both? In drama and in fiction characters may be impelled to act from duty or desire, from exhaustion or despair, from necessity, a preordained fate or even gratuitously from whimsy, without any design but a wayward response to chance. What vision of human action does Pinter reflect?

Pinter's characters are consistently driven by a desire for love and respect, which ultimately transforms into a struggle for survival. They attempt to maintain a position in the world to gain respect and love through power over others.

The love that drives action in Pinter's work aligns with the classic definitions of love and friendship defined by Aristotle as a relationship between equals in beauty, strength and wisdom but is most often defined by its absence—as unachievable in dominant/subservient relations. His work also strains against mere courtly, nineteenth-century, twentieth-century and Hollywood notions of romantic love as not going far enough.[3]

Pinter's plays recognize love as a force in destruction whenever the attempt to gain love and respect, used to maintain a relationship, is manifested in the struggle for dominance. That struggle projects itself as the self-same cause for violence and destruction of relationships at all levels. Yet his plays also celebrate love as a driving force toward justice.

What sets Pinter's work apart from that of almost any other twentieth-century dramatist is that at the center his ethic is wedded to his aesthetic. Aesthetically the struggle for dominance functions as both primary theme and dramatic technique.

Thematically, that struggle provides the axial center which drives all else in the play: themes of sight and blindness, mystery, time, space and reality as well as his special use of comedy. Technically the struggle rivets audience attention throughout. Techniques range from verbal skirmishes to brutal violence and death.

Deeply embedded in the very techniques and themes which create the beauty and power that enthrall are the values and the action raising the questions which ultimately define the ethic: What does it mean to be a good person?

If the first virtue of the virtuous person is to survive (else how can one help others?), then the struggle to assert oneself is absolutely necessary to promote any other virtue. But Pinter's vision, which reflects a hierarchical, dominator society developed over centuries in Britain, as in Japan, explores the inherent destructive force in that struggle. Hierarchy, maintained so long as most subscribe to it, insured that many people living on a tiny and now crowded island could continue to get along. While some thinkers believe hierarchy is inevitable in all primates, others contend, as Pinter's work dramatizes, that time has run out on that system and that by its very binary structure it is programmed to self destruct.

Thus the terrible paradox at the core of Pinter's work dramatizes how the very impulse to survive, when unchecked and driven by a quest for dominance that equates identity with position, may be the very impulse which may destroy all.

What values and action define the ethic in Pinter's work?

The ethic in Pinter's plays defines itself, as it must in drama, by action. It is expressed through the values and action held up for audience admiration as best promoting life and welfare of both the characters and audience. Pinter's recent work, dramatizing increasing concern for action informed by courage, love and justice (which recognizes and respects the welfare of the individual), focuses on those qualities necessary for human survival. But rather than offering exemplars of those life-promoting qualities, which serious post-Renaissance drama and literature rarely does, Pinter's work often defines those qualities by negation, by showing what action is not ethical and why it does not work.

Key to understanding Pinter's ethic in his over thirty plays and sketches and most of his sixteen screenplays is the theme of dominant/subservient relationships—one character's struggle to assert dominance over another. Characters battle for position on the implicit assumption that maintaining or gaining an advantage is required to gain the love and respect of others and to preserve one's own sense of self-worth, superiority and, ultimately, identity. Who will gain dominance, Ben or Gus in *The Dumb Waiter*, the intruders or Stanley in *The Birthday Party,* Anna and Deeley or Kate in *Old Times,* the powerbrokers or Jimmy tortured in *Party Time*, the torturers or their blindfolded, mute victim in *The New World Order?*

Almost all the major techniques that fuel the central conflict, from the benign to the lethal, appear paradigmatically in *The Dumb Waiter*. To appreciate the operation of the dominant/subservient conflict in this play is to understand its critical role in the dramatization of the ethic in all Pinter's other plays.

Notes

1. Although characters who are destroyed may appear without choice and may seem to convey a vision of human powerlessness, closer, careful reading of action and structure reveals that the opposite is generally, however subtly, communicated. Even in Pinter's most recent torture plays, *One for the Road*, *Mountain Language*, *Party Time*, and *The New World Order*, where torture victims are powerless to secure their own freedom, Pinter continues to explore questions of responsibility and love, linking the power of human love to sustain life through the worst injustices, thus, as we shall see, transferring responsibility to the audience.
2. I am indebted to Colin Brezicki for the suggestion of why this is so; moreover it is frequently pointed out that the reverse effect is also true, that when Pinter enters a room or when an audience exits his work, his dialogue becomes ours, that people are suddenly conscious of how we speak like Pinter's characters.

3. Here beauty, the lowest and least important element, is followed at a higher level by strength, both physical and moral, and finally crowned by wisdom, which encompasses both knowledge and experience. Ideally friendship and love can only be achieved by people who manifest all three.

The Dumb Waiter: Paradigmatic Dramatization of Conflict—Toward a Definition of The Pinter Ethic

Ben and Gus, two hit men, await kill orders, but instead of orders, matches appear under the door. Discussion about their purpose leads to argument till Ben, the senior partner, strikes Gus. The dumb waiter next arrives with orders, not the expected orders but orders for food that the men nevertheless attempt to fill. The dumb waiter repeatedly ascends empty until the men send up what food they have brought. A voice at the other end rejects the food—Ben again strikes Gus. The men receive yet another in a series of food orders they are unable to fill. While Gus is out of the room, Ben finally receives the awaited order to proceed as usual, presumably as the two had just rehearsed it, then calls Gus. When Gus enters, stripped of waistcoat and gun, Ben levels his gun at him. One of the killers becomes an intended victim.

Why?

What puzzled critics called willful mystification or glibly labeled theatre of the absurd is in reality a manifestation of the carefully constructed ambiguity which redefines villain and victim in Pinter's portrayal of the dominant/subservient conflict. The audience is led to a sympathy for one hired killer, Gus, and indeed, quite subtly to a sympathy for both, as the play demystifies the power of the seeming villain as bluff coupled with inertia of motion. Once set in action, both characters remain in action, dramatizing also the partial responsibility of the seeming victim to know what is happening in order to overcome inertia and to act to prevent his own destruction.

"There's no question of hero and villain," says Pinter, who sees both the individual and society as equally culpable:

> I'm afraid society is a pattern which does kill and crab and confine, and that at the same time the individuals who make the society do the same to themselves by conforming to their own habits continually day after day and year after year. (Sherwood, n.p.)

What also rescues Pinter's dominant characters from charges of villainy is the fact that he likes all of his characters, and never patronizes or diminishes any. To do so only diminishes a writer. He says, "[E]very single character, even a bastard like Goldberg in *The Birthday Party* I care for." (Bensky, 361) Even the torturer Nicholas in *One for the Road* expresses a human fondness for nature and family. Exceptions occur both in the recent *Mountain Language, Party Time* and *The New World Order* as well as in the early play Pinter discarded for twenty years, *The Hothouse,* his most blatant and perhaps most didactic early portrayal of the dominant/subservient conflict.

Pinter sees communication as central to the conflict—not the inability to communicate as commonly noted but "a deliberate evasion of communication." ("Pinterview," 69) He says communication "is so frightening" that it results in "continual cross talk" to evade it. When the matches mysteriously appear under the door, Ben, the senior partner, interprets the event literally, arguing that the matches arrived to light the kettle. But there is no gas. As Pinter notes, the characters deliberately argue whether the correct usage is "Light the kettle" or "Light the gas" in order to avoid the real issue: "that they are *both* in fact frightened of their condition, of their situation, of their state." (Tynan, n.p.; italics mine) Ben terminates the "Light the kettle/Light the gas" argument by striking Gus.

It is important to note violence in Pinter's work ensues when a character attempts to *maintain* rather than to gain dominance. As in nearly all Pinter's work, much of the violence which at first appears mysterious (why does Ben strike Gus?) is linked to the struggle to maintain dominance. Ben *strikes* Gus only when Gus's questions threaten his authority. The final culmination of violence in the play (Ben may shoot Gus) is fractally consistent with the earlier violence—each time Ben's position as senior partner is seriously threatened he strikes out at his subordinate, Gus. Thus Ben's aiming his gun at Gus subtly registers the degree of threat he feels aimed at himself. When interviewed about violence in his work, Pinter traced it to the dominant/subservient conflict. "The world *is* a pretty violent place." He adds:

> I think what you're talking about began in *The Dumb Waiter*, which from my point of view is a relatively simple piece of work. The violence is really only an expression of the question of dominance and subservience ... I wouldn't call this violence so much as a battle for positions, it's a very common, everyday thing." (Bensky, 362–3; ellipses mine)

It is not surprising that the innocuous disagreement over usage in the "Light the kettle/Light the gas" dispute escalates into the threatened destruction of a subservient character. Technically at every turn the struggle for dominance generates dramatic tension equal to or greater than the threat from the unseen superior, repeatedly raising the question: Will Ben maintain authority over Gus? He will try, in this ironic con game, even if he has to kill him. The cause of the violence and the consequences of subsequent destruction remains the same from Goldberg and McCann's collision with Stanley in *The Birthday Party* to Des and Lionel's torture of the unnamed victim in *The New World Order*.

Within a dominant/subservient relationship, characters are by definition symbiotically dependent upon each other, and equally, the tension between the two inextricably links to the threat from above. Gus submits to Ben's authority, which largely derives from having someone to dominate. Mutual dependence, a precarious basis for a relationship, can thrive only so long as the dominant character, Ben, can maintain his superior position without threat from outside forces and without question by the subservient character, Gus. Since outside forces are seldom absent and since Gus is unwilling and unable to remain wholly subordinate, changes which must occur are bound to destroy the relationship and may obviously destroy Gus.

Dramatic tension, further enhanced by violence as the natural by-product of the struggle for dominance, escalates because both characters fight with the reflexive action of trained athletes whenever their values meet a challenge. What makes for conflict is that their values are radically different. Ben subscribes to the authority manifested in the organization sending them; Gus questions it.

Pinter's dominant and subservient characters, embracing different values and intentions, see the world differently, draw different insights and conclusions, facing off on opposite sides of a struggle which automatically engenders conflict. The mainspring of the tension in Pinter's plays, provided by the opposing attributes of the dominant and subservient characters, dramatizes their seemingly opposite concerns.

The dominant character asserts control, does not question authority, cannot allow his own authority to be questioned, will not feel pity for others or permit others to feel sympathy for him, but he is blind to the limitations of blindly obeying orders, to the intrinsic worthlessness of his position and to the meaninglessness of their shared situation. The subservient character's questions, which threaten the dominant character's position are without a principle, a plan, or the ability to subvert it and only invite attack upon himself.

The dominant character, Ben, must always retain confidence and command, while the subservient character, Gus, may admit doubt and offer sympathy for weakness that the dominant character must refuse. Ben expresses contempt for doubt and weakness which he must attempt to eradicate. When Gus admits he has difficulty talking to their superior, Wilson, Ben charges, "Scrub round it, will you." (101; unless otherwise noted, all references are to first American editions)

Equipped at the outset with his ranking position as senior partner, Ben, even in the first moments of the opening scene, evinces his superior rank, positioned as he is on the bed above Gus, who is on the floor. Ben's first response to Gus when Gus exits to the lavatory is disapproval—"he glares after him." (89) Ironically Ben can remain dominant only so long as he continues to be wholly subservient to the organization, and he is.

Ben's selecting and reading aloud newspaper accounts about killing and death dramatize his willing compliance with authority, any authority; when Gus questions one newspaper account, Ben returns, "It's down here in black and white." (86) Nor can Ben evince sympathy for anyone who happens into a position to get himself killed. "It's enough to make you want to puke," he says of an old man run over by a lorry. Ben never questions an order of a superior, and the questions he aims at Gus, almost exclusively rhetorical, aim at confirming his own authority: "What are you doing, criticising me?" and "Who's the senior partner here, me or you?" (98)

As senior partner, Ben must supply answers or reasons for all events, however uncanny. When the matches mysteriously appear and Gus conjectures, "Well they'll come in handy," Ben, momentarily unthreatened and relaxed, merely raises Gus's conjecture to fact by fleeting agreement: "Well they'll come in handy." (97) Ben's perfect echo of Gus bespeaks his interchangeability with his subordinate. Conjecture again functions as fact as their real fears are deflected into minor concerns—fear over the unscheduled appearance of the matches dissolves into a quarrel about whether the matches were sent "to light the gas" as Gus argues, or "to light the kettle," as Ben maintains. Battle over truth in so relative a matter as usage subordinates their real fear to the importance of maintaining position. Although *Gus* is first to say "light the kettle," Ben appropriates it, defending it as his own in order to defend his position. First Ben resorts to authority: "It's common knowledge," then "It's common usage!" and failing to convince Gus resorts to verbal abuse and bullying as he "vehemently" proceeds: "Nobody says light the gas!" (98) To score the point he asks what the gas lights, grabs Gus by the throat and shouts: "THE KETTLE, YOU FOOL!" Ever a meticulous writer, Pinter tosses in a comic reversal. Ben, relieved and relaxed by having "won," lapses into, "Put on the bloody kettle," usage he just denounced. Being "right" requires only a more forceful assertion of might.

But more is at stake: the truth. In contrast to Ben's vicarious pleasures, reading *about* sports events and other people's news, Gus prefers life firsthand, "a bit of a view," a window. As a result Gus sees many things Ben is blind to until Gus points them out: Gus observes this place is "worse than the last one"; (101) he notices the number of burners on the stove, the orders for food, and the speaking tube next to the dumb waiter. His observations lead to subsequent insights: the fact that the stove has only three burners leads him to conclude that they are not in the basement of a restaurant. Unfortunately the truth behind his conclusions, if applied to their situation, makes their attempt to fill food orders absurd. Yet what other choices do they have?

Ben has no better answers than Gus. More important Ben can entertain no alternatives which do not support his position. When the dumb waiter clatters down for the first time, both men draw their guns; neither knows who sent the orders for steak and sago pudding. When the dumb waiter ascends empty, although it is Gus who shouts, "Give us a chance," (104) *both* men equally desire to comply with the food order; both remain equally mystified. Ben, as senior partner, however, must supply an answer for the mysterious appearance of the dumb waiter. He conjectures, "It probably used to be a café here, that's all." But when Gus raises the crucial question, "WELL WHO'S GOT IT NOW?" Ben can only hedge, "Well that all depends—." (104) Pinter has nicely prepared for the divergent responses of the two men. While Gus continues to question the events, Ben acts on his own conjecture adopting the implicit but untested assumption that the organization is operating the dumb waiter. Uncertainty and an openness to questioning is not a stance Ben can comfortably embrace, and his greatest strength—his reflexive ability to act—constrains development of his character.

Mystery intervenes throughout to undermine Ben's authority revealing his position has no intrinsic value. Technically mystery enhances suspense. Who are Ben and Gus? We learn they are hired killers. Each answer poses new questions. Who sent them? Wilson. Who sent him? The organization. Who runs the organization and for what purpose? The ultimate Who, What and Why remain mysterious, unknown, and possibly unknowable. Thematically, mystery connotes a contemporary world without a Prime Mover where hierarchy and therefore one's position are artificial, man-made, without ultimate value.

What follows in the play is fairly easy to understand. Both the audience and the characters are at first perplexed by the discovery of the dumb waiter as they earlier were by the matches. Ben, not only accustomed to giving orders but also to taking them, responds to these orders for food as he would to any other order from above: reflexively. He leaps to comply. But as the demands from the dumb waiter become increasingly difficult to meet (though they were always impossible) Ben becomes more aggressive in asserting his power over Gus.

Ben's aggression and violence against Gus proceed in direct proportion to his being thwarted both from below in maintaining his position by Gus and by his perception of being threatened from above. Ben can relieve pressure only momentarily by each new resolve to act. Although "they are both relieved at the decision," when Ben resolves, "We'd better send something up," tension only mounts with the impossibility of filling the order. (118) Yet both eagerly try to comply even though they do not know who is issuing the orders. Why? Obviously, if the orders are not being issued by the organization, then the men wish to avoid attracting unnecessary attention to their clandestine activities. If they are issued by the organization, this may be a test the men do not wish to fail. Gus asks, "We're reliable, aren't we?" and says, "We've been through our tests, haven't we?" (118)

When the next order, for Macaroni Pastitsio and Ormitha Macarounada, descends, Ben deflects his renewed frustration by reprimanding Gus for bringing only one Eccles cake and only enough crisps for himself, which to Ben denotes an imbalance in the relationship, an erosion of his power, explaining why he strikes Gus with, "You're playing a dirty game my lad!" (106)

To fill this order for Greek food the men send up all the food Gus brought: "One Lyons Red Label! One Smith's Crisps! One Eccles cake!" and a bottle of milk and a candy bar. (108) Because again threat seems suspended by action, Ben only mildly rebukes Gus for shouting up the hatch—as bad form: "It isn't done." (108) But a moment later new orders for Chinese food appear, and when Gus blurts out the truth, "The larder's bare!" Ben seizes the speaking tube and "with great deference" reveals his absolute respect for the authority of the unknown superior:

> Good evening. I'm sorry to—bother you, but we just thought we'd better let you know that we haven't got anything left. (112)

Although he receives complaints that the cake was stale, the chocolate melted, and the milk sour, he is elated by information which he believes confirms his position and therefore his safety:

> You know what he said? Light the kettle! Not put on the kettle! Not light the gas! But light the kettle! (112)

Ben's victory is both comic and irrelevant. Gus points out, "There is no gas." (113) For the first and only time Ben is both despondent and genuinely questioning: "Now what do we do?" (113) But when Gus sympathizes by providing a tirade against those upstairs who he suspects have plenty of food, Ben refuses sympathy and pulls himself out of despair by his characteristic resolve: to act. He orders Gus to rehearse their plans with him.

The situation is not of course under control. Gus points out that in the rehearsal Ben left out the part where Gus withdraws his gun, then asks, "Why did he send us matches if he knew there is no gas?" (117) Ben responds "nervously" both with a bit of bullying, "What's one thing to do with another?" and, to regain his empty authority, by again hitting Gus, this time "viciously on the shoulder." (117)

Ben's aggression, however, fails to check Gus's questions: "What's he playing these games for?" (118) The unspoken threat implied by Gus's question signals that the game is being played for survival. If they fail to comply with the orders, they may be killed. One of Pinter's great innovations is his double ironic subversion of the stereotypical con game and audience response: portraying both men beneath their opposing actions as equally terrified for their lives evokes audience sympathy not only for both men occupying traditional villain/victim positions within the relationship but at another level for two killers.

When the dumb waiter arrives with another order, (this time for scampi), Gus impulsively again shouts up the truth: "WE'VE GOT NOTHING LEFT! NOTHING! DO YOU UNDERSTAND?" But Ben immediately flings him away and "slaps him hard, back-handed across the chest," with "Stop it! You maniac!" (118) Since Ben cannot permit the truth that they cannot fulfill the order (which signals the weakness of his position), Ben's only alternative, to ignore the box which ominously ascends empty, sends him back to the bed to bury his head in his newspaper, escaping ostrich-like the impending terror. Again he takes "action": "reading" aloud, this time not the stories, but only his response to news now devoid of all meaning: "Listen to this! (*Pause*) What about that, eh? (*Pause*) Kaw!" This last nonsense expletive, "Kaw!" returns the audience recursively to the opening, Ben's first word: the sound a parrot makes.

But Gus's willing participation in Ben's meaningless "reading" registers his equal complicity:

> GUS: Is that a fact?
> BEN: Can you imagine it.
> GUS: It's unbelievable. (119)

The interlude provides a comic spacer, which both diffuses tension and allows it to mount naturally toward inevitable doom.

No evidence suggests that Ben knows in advance who the victim will be. He receives the awaited order while Gus is out of the room, and his response, "Sure *we're* ready," (emphasis mine) signals the audience that both he and Gus are going to do the job. Yet when Gus returns, Ben levels his gun at him, and the two men merely stare at each other without surprise or recognition until the curtain falls.

The ending is both inevitable and astonishing. It is no surprise that Gus, not Ben, stands on the receiving end of the gun. Although the ultimate reasons for the final action remain mysterious, the more immediate reasons are carefully prepared for. Ben, eager to comply with orders from above, finally receives an order he can fill! Gus's stunning entrance as Ben's target and the effectively abrupt closure, which suspends any character shock or recognition, force attention to the precariousness of the relationship in the unresolved dilemma.

Ben must choose whether or not to shoot Gus, but either way he himself may lose. Although Ben's violence culminates in his holding a gun on Gus, if he pulls the trigger, he destroys his own position, which depends upon having someone to dominate. Despite their numerous apparent differences, the obvious irony in this con game is there can be no real winner and possibly nothing to win. If Gus is destroyed, the best Ben can hope is to maintain what he has—his life and some continued position subservient to the organization. The organization may not, however, be sending the orders. If they are, if Ben fails to follow the order to shoot, the implicit threat is that he may almost certainly be killed. Given the capriciousness of the events, there are no guarantees that even by complying with the orders Ben can insure himself against being next on the receiving end. Pinter thus evokes audience sympathy for both.

This world without women would seem to be without friendship or love, but the latter is made conspicuous by the two brief allusions to women. In the "Light the kettle" argument when

Ben challenges Gus's "Light the gas," with "Who says?" Gus, too, argues from authority: "I bet my mother used to say it." (98) When Ben challenges with, "When did you last see your mother?" he asserts the great scam perpetrated by the oppressor worldwide: "I'm only looking after your interests, Gus." (98) The reference to the mother as protector of values and authority arcs forward in Pinter's plays all the way to *The New World Order* where Lionel claims he used to discuss "the theological aspirations of the female" with his mother whom he cites as authority for moral lessons he cannot, however, remember. (4) The other allusion to women in *The Dumb Waiter* comes with Gus's, "I was just thinking about that girl, that's all," (102) a woman they no doubt eradicated for their organization: "She wasn't much to look at, I know, but still. It was a mess though, wasn't it?" Gus's observation, "They don't seem to hold together like men, women," and "Didn't she spread, eh," conveys both subliminal erotic connotations and his own distance from women. Gus telegraphs his fear of women when he specifically couples the topic of killing with the subject of women when he wonders about the girl: "Who clears up after we've gone?" (103) The violence expressed toward women in *The New World Order* makes Gus and Ben's attitude by contrast appear loving.[1] Yet there can be no love, just as there can be no friendship, in a relationship where one must assert position over another. Nor can there be any justice in a system where one must blindly obey the orders of authority and repress any questions aimed at the system or one's own position. But Ben cannot see that either. Instead Ben interprets Gus's curiosity as a challenge he must meet by squelching it. The self-knowledge required as a starting point for the discussion of justice within the ethic in Pinter's work cannot even raise itself as an issue in *The Dumb Waiter*, where a character such as Ben, so wholly unconscious of his own motivation, remains utterly blind to first questions.

Sight and blindness as a theme operates literally and figuratively in defining the opposing positions. The dominant characters from Ben in *The Dumb Waiter* and Goldberg in *The Birthday Party* to Nicholas the torturer in *One for the Road*, interested in facts which support orders dictated by authority, are blind to the larger picture around them and to the essential absurdity both of their situations and of the authority which motivates their actions. If the world does not tally with their prescribed views, they proceed to *act* as if it does. Ben, the dominant senior partner in *The Dumb Waiter,* acts as if the organization for which he and Gus work is in logical control of the situation despite all evidence to the contrary. Goldberg in *The Birthday Party* acts much the same. Nicolas in *One for the Road* never questions authority and is prepared to kill anyone who does.

Mystery and ambiguity further define the central ethic by forcing reexamination of the received values which inform action. The traditional values held up for scrutiny are those commonly associated with chivalry and martial societies in the West—courage, honor, justice, loyalty, friendship and magnanimity. Pinter, like any master, raises rather than answers questions. The questions he poses call for a rerouting of those values to place them in service of a larger humanity, not merely of one or another individual or faction in arbitrary conflictual opposition with others.

Ambiguity, in communication and action, also serves a larger end in Pinter's work to signal a shift away from received us-vs-them values and thinking to dramatize the strengths to be admired and weaknesses to be confronted in both the dominant and the subservient characters in order to promote survival, and beyond that, the welfare and happiness of both the self and others.

Just as *The Dumb Waiter* offers a paradigmatic illustration of the dominant/subservient conflict fractally conveyed in every beat, *The Birthday Party* provides a paradigm for appreciating the ethic in Pinter's work thus offering a better starting point for discussion than Pinter's first play, *The Room.*

Harold Pinter's frontal assault on traditional villain/victim dichotomies, fully played out in the struggle for dominance in *The Birthday Party,* utilizes the traditional villain/victim tension to subvert the stereotype in order to force reexamination and redefinition of those terms.

Pinter's work from the outset to the present awakens an audience to the importance of understanding the source of the desire for dominance in the private level of self if it is to be confronted and acted upon in the service of love or justice on any other level.[2]

NOTES

1. It may be instructive to note how Lionel and Des in *The New World Order* convey a more amiable equality toward one another, and even some mutual empathy, without, however, conveying indications of friendship.
2. From his earliest work, the novel *The Dwarfs*, the plays *The Room, The Dumb Waiter*, *The Birthday Party*, and *The Caretaker*, all characters quest for love and the security of shelter in a world where any justice, often administered by intruders, seems gratuitous, even designed to rob those hopeful of maintaining some human alliance and safe refuge or both.

The Birthday Party: Choice, Action and Responsibility—The Pinter Ethic Defined

Harold Pinter's first full-length play, *The Birthday Party*, challenged serious dramatic literature's traditional portrayal of villain and victim with complexities that demand redefinition of those terms. The unwavering ambiguity which dramatizes the responsibility of *both* the dominant and the subservient characters for the disturbing events of the play disallows any simple equation of the dominant and subservient characters with villain and victim and invalidates easy application of those terms to his work generally. The dominant character, rarely wholly culpable, nor the subservient, wholly pure, embrace different values, engendering opposing resultant action. Those values and the conflicting action held up for approbation and censure define the ethic which informs the entire Pinter canon. Pinter's antipathy for simplistic labels—reductive dualities or thinking which he believes encourage an audience to compartmentalize, distance, and dismiss rather than confront whatever disturbs—extends to his assault on the villain/victim stereotypes. Exposing the individual responsibility of both those characters uncovers the moral responsibility of all other characters as well.

In *The Birthday Party*, Stanley, a seedy, former piano player, lives quietly in a rundown seaside boarding house until two new well-dressed boarders, Goldberg and McCann, enter, displacing him as center of his landlady Meg's household. When Goldberg hears that it is Stanley's birthday, he proposes a party. When Stanley resists, claiming it is not his birthday, the men conduct an inquisition into his past with a viciousness that continues through the party, finally dissolving in a series of violent acts which culminate in McCann's breaking Stanley's glasses and Stanley's choking Meg, then attacking Lulu. The next morning when Stanley comes downstairs dressed like his suit-and-tie adversaries who cart him off in their black van, Stanley has been reduced to a broken, possibly blind, gibbering shell of his former self. Happy birthday.

Did Goldberg and McCann come deliberately to get Stanley, or is Stanley the instrument of his own destruction? Pinter has affirmed and denied both views, and the tightly controlled ambiguity keeps both possibilities alive to the end.

While the most obvious evidence suggests that Goldberg and McCann deliberately come to destroy him, Stanley's fearful response to Meg's news of their coming, his choice to bait his adversaries, to sit down, finally to stay when he might have left, render him almost equally culpable as the men who appear to be stock villains out to destroy him.

Even before they arrive, Stanley's alarm in itself raises the suspicion that the men are deliberately seeking him. Suspicion is heightened when Stanley overhears the men exchange vaguely sinister remarks: "Is this it?" "This is it." (27) The unspecified "job" the men say they plan to perform reinforces that suspicion of their evil intent. So does Goldberg's grim allusion to death: "McCann, what are you so nervous about? Everywhere you go these days it's like a funeral." (28)

While Harold Pinter has supported this view, "For my money, Goldberg and McCann have come down to get Stanley," (Crist, 79) and in a letter to director Peter Wood writes, "They had come with a purpose, a job in hand—to take Stanley away," (3) elsewhere he suggests the opposite: "I would say they worked for a large organization with an office completely above board." (Hewes, 56) Never in the play itself is it resolved whether what happens to Stanley results from a premeditated plot by Goldberg and McCann or from choices Stanley himself makes in his relations with them.

The most convincing evidence we as audience see supports the argument that Goldberg and McCann did not arrive on a premeditated mission but that Stanley initiates and invites his own destruction. As William Friedkin, director of the film version, proposes:

> I believe it entirely possible that Goldberg and McCann had nothing to do with him, that Stanley is entirely the instrument of his own destruction. He starts the inquisition … (Crist, 79)

While Stanley's alarmed denial of Meg's news, "They won't come," (21) heightens suspicion that he believes someone is after him, obvious, better-established reasons also account for his defensiveness.

Prior to Goldberg and McCann's arrival, Stanley's position in Meg's house is like an only child's, so central that any addition will result in a change for the worse. The locus of Meg's attention, almost to the exclusion of her husband Petey, Stanley is taken seriously as he would not be elsewhere. Here he is somebody, elsewhere, nobody. As Pinter notes, "he rules the roost and doesn't do any work, and carries on like an emperor." (Sherwood, n.p.) To leave would be to lose whatever identity comes from the recognition of others.

What prevents Stanley from walking out on the party he does not wish to attend? Inertia. The same inertia earlier prevents his asking his young neighbor Lulu out and later from successfully confronting or fleeing Goldberg and McCann. We watch Stanley's inertia result from his inability to imagine choices. Inertia, which sparked the writing of *The Birthday Party*, is what Pinter as a young actor encountered in the self-delimiting stance of a man with whom he once shared a room in Eastbourne:

> At the end of the week I said to this fellow, who turned out to have been a concert pianist on the pier: "Why do you stay here?" and he said: "There's nowhere else to go." I left with that ringing in my ears. Then about a year later or so I started to write *The Birthday Party*. (Bakewell, 630–31)

But is there, as Stanley says to Lulu, "nowhere to go"?[1] Are there no good choices? Without choice there can be no question of ethical responsibility.

Stanley has and makes a number of choices he is not conscious he makes, most strikingly the many on-stage choices, however small, that result in his larger destruction.

Stanley instigates but loses sparring matches with both Lulu and Meg before the men arrive. "How would you like to go away with me?" he asks Lulu, but when she answers, "Where?" he says, "Nowhere, still we could go." (26) Stanley retreats from every skirmish he initiates, allowing each woman the last word: "You deserve the strap," says Meg to conclude one match. (19) "You're a bit of a washout, aren't you," says Lulu ending another. (26)

But Stanley is not a mere passive victim. While much critical response promotes the view that Stanley, like Joseph K. of Kafka's *The Trial*, is an unwitting victim of a mysterious organization, which Goldberg and McCann, like the Inspectors, represent,[2] we see Stanley make a series of on-stage choices which determine the direction of the action as he tries to discover the identity of the intruders and their reason for coming.

Fearful that they have come for him, Stanley simultaneously attempts to deny and to affirm any past connection with the men. To deny connection would seem to establish Stanley's innocence for some unspecified past deed and disengage their pursuit. But to affirm the connection might give a name and cause to their presence. Yet, however much he wishes to deny it, like Oedipus, he remains committed to uncovering the truth. When Stanley asks whether they have been in Maidenhead or Basingstoke, gone to "Fuller's Tea Shop," and "Boots Library" (although such circumstantial evidence can prove no connection), McCann denies knowing the towns or even such ubiquitously familiar British shops, then claims they never met. The men seem equally determined to deny or conceal any past connection. But the unresolved ambiguity so frustrates Stanley, who would prefer conclusive disproof of any ties, that he ends in provoking McCann:

> (*hissing*). I've explained to you, damn you, that all those years I lived in Basingstoke I never stepped out the door. (42)

Later however, out of Stanley's earshot, Goldberg mentions a visit to Bastingstoke, (27) and recounts to Lulu his jaunts to Fuller's for tea and to Boots for a library book. (50) Yet twice when Stanley confronts McCann directly, "Why are you down here?" McCann answers, "A short holiday." (41) McCann, of course, may or may not be telling the truth.

From the moment they enter the men refer to a "job," a "mission," and an "assignment" to perform, but nowhere does either man specify the job or explicitly link it with what happens to Stanley. Just as Goldberg's evasive double talk veils the nature of the job, Goldberg also implies to McCann that their visit to the resort town may be a vacation stopover unrelated to any job: "I bring you to the seaside. Take a holiday." (27) Even in the final scene before taking Stanley away, McCann says only, "Let's get the thing done and go," (76) never "Let's get the *job* done."

While some aggression during the party may seem premeditated, Goldberg's initial spontaneous suggestion to throw Stanley a birthday party is uncalculated:

> GOLDBERG: Weren't you going to have one?
> MEG: (*her eyes wide*). No.
> GOLDBERG: Well, of course, you must have one. (*He stands.*) We'll have a party, eh? What do you say? (32)

Ambiguity may direct audience sympathy to both the dominant and subservient character but weights it toward the subservient, Stanley, less as victim or underdog who arouses pity for his weakness than as the character often with the clearer sight in honest pursuit of truth, whose opposing struggle provokes admiration for his perseverance and whatever strengths he possesses. The subservient character also more closely resembles the traditional hero as one who courageously embarks on a quest for the benefit of others. Almost all Pinter's characters' quest for truth, however, is quickly deflected to self-preservation, which they rarely achieve.

Because the dominant character's position seldom proceeds from greater strength or wisdom, but primarily from a stronger will to act, Pinter's work reveals the dominant character as the reverse side of the same coin equally struggling with the subservient character for survival.

The dominant and subservient characters, caught in separate worlds, are unable to meet on common ground or to cross-pollinate to any fruitful end.[3] The dominant character has or asserts power but remains blind both to its flimsy source and to his own unexamined values, whereas the subservient character may see correctly, or at least pose the right questions, and cherish virtues of love, honesty and justice but be powerless to promote them or even to defend himself against attack. Those virtues contained in the opposing characters supply the chief values of the ethic in Pinter's work.

Their different strengths are what allows Pinter to sympathize with both and precludes Goldberg, however subtly, from being a stock villain. To say that Pinter sympathizes with both is to say he admires their different strengths and has compassion for their weaknesses. But Pinter does not mistake power for virtue or allow pity for weakness to blind us to a subservient character's need for greater strength. When Stanley succumbs to his interrogators in *The Birthday Party*, we cannot view his defeat as dramatizing the cliché of artist against society. Stanley is not an artist however much he may possess an artist's sensitivity or more honest vision. He has stopped playing the piano and in many ways stopped living.

Equally, we sympathize when Goldberg momentarily steps to the precipice to confront the hollowness of his authority gained by sacrificing private values for public position:

> Learn by heart. Never write down a thing. And don't go too near the water. And you'll find what I say is true.
>
> Because I believe that the world ... (*Vacant.*)...
>
> Because I believe that the world ... (Desper*ate.*)...
>
> BECAUSE I BELIEVE THAT THE WORLD ... (Lost.) ... (78)

But audience sympathy flags when Goldberg retreats, refusing to acknowledge the hollow basis of his authority, refusing in essence to know himself, and reverts instead to commanding others in order to affirm his position and the certainty it seems to supply.[4]

The consequences of the lack of self-knowledge would seem less dire for the dominant character, Goldberg, than for Stanley because in Pinter's work asserting dominance over another remains the primary means characters not only establish identity but survive in a world where to allow oneself to assume a subservient position, for even a moment, can result in annihilation—physical, psychological, or both.[5] And that seems to be precisely the point: such destruction that can happen at any time requires attention to the moment, knowledge of the self and one's circumstance, followed by action and continued vigilance. Moreover, as Pinter's plays subtly reveal, the consequences finally may be equally dire for the dominant character, such as Ben in *The Dumb Waiter*.

Yet the consequences for the dominant character may seem less life threatening because almost invariably it is the dominant character, the character with the least well-developed interior life, who is better equipped to spring reflexively into action, who also maintains power. But as Goldberg's retreat from the void discloses, the dominant character cannot permit himself to develop because he will not permit himself to examine the source of motivation or to feel empathy for others. To do so in Pinter's plays, is to display weakness. Yet maintaining dominance over another in the face of evidence contrary to one's worthiness to do so also hardens ones sympathies, annihilates compassion, and uncovers for the audience the dominant character's position and power as a façade.

Goldberg wins a dominant position over the subservient character Stanley, but in doing so, like Ben in *The Dumb Waiter*, exposes the nature of his victory and private kingdom as essentially worthless: Goldberg becomes boss over nothing.[6]

Pinter is not a philosopher. Nowhere as a dramatist can he or his characters break into a philosophical disquisition declaiming his ethical convictions, nor is there in Pinter's essays any treatise outlining or defining a theoretical ethical position. His essays address specific issues or political events. But lest anyone demand a clear, systematically defined ethic in order to appreciate Pinter's work, it may be helpful to recall that Western philosophers even after three thousand years, have not yet arrived at a universal moral principle. The golden rule may be as close as we come, but cannot discriminate in hard cases. Pinter dramatizes what can only be loosely called a definition, and any idea, as he insists in his novel *The Dwarfs*, requires being tested within a specific situation and in action. His characters illuminate the ethical values in their attitudes, intentions, and, above all, in their actions, which either serve to enhance or to destroy life. The life-enhancing values and actions serve to define the ethic.

Interestingly, however, in Pinter's plays the values which promote survival and human development remain split between dominant and subservient characters so that the outcome of action is almost always destruction. Nevertheless, the plays endorse the separate strengths of both: the subservient character's clear-sighted attention and questioning, honest and courageous quest for truth, love, and justice, and the dominant character's ability to seize power and to act.

By presenting the dominant or subservient positions as an either/or fallacy, a false set of choices, Pinter subtly reveals that Stanley never considers there may be a third choice that combines the strengths of both, while eschewing the limitations of either to avoid the fallacy altogether.[7]

Pinter's characters thus dramatize the necessity for self-knowledge as a basis for all ethical action and further show why that understanding also requires compassion for the other if it is to benefit either the self or anyone else. Without that consciousness that comes from knowledge of self and others, a character may make a choice, then run right past it without realizing its significance or, worse, without registering that any choice has been made at all or, worst of all, that that choice has set subsequent, irreversible action in motion.

Such is Stanley's simple but crucial choice to sit. Ironically, it is in *resisting* Goldberg and McCann's attempts to force him to stay that he seals his fate and thereby chooses to remain at the party.

When Stanley tries to escape before the party McCann threateningly requests but, it is important to note, does not *force* him to stay. Stage directions explicitly indicate Stanley freely backs away from the door when he is given the option to leave, a similar option he earlier refused with Lulu:

> STANLEY *walks around the table towards the door.*
> MCCANN *meets him.*
> STANLEY: Excuse me.
> MCCANN: Where are you going?
> STANLEY: I want to go out.
> MCCANN: Why don't you stay here?
> STANLEY *moves away, to the right of the table.* (39)

Stanley's unfortunate choice to sit, a pivotal mistake assumes the form of *hamartia*, the classical mistake, the error in judgment which in Aristotle's *Poetics* is sometimes translated as "flaw." (Aristotle, 1452)[8] Trapped by his own decision to assume a subordinate position, Stanley steps over an invisible line that ushers in a brutal verbal inquisition.

The significance of Stanley's choice to sit is carefully prepared for earlier when Goldberg and McCann enter and McCann refuses to sit until Goldberg sits. (27) Both McCann and Stanley tacitly recognize that to sit is tantamount to losing position. At first Stanley successfully resists Goldberg's invitation to sit and even deflects his threats.

But then, carelessly, in a casually unguarded moment Stanley arbitrarily chooses to tempt his adversaries. Strolling to a chair at the table, he voluntarily sits. (47) When he cautions, "You'd better watch out," he is already impotent. Why does he tempt fate?

Stanley's impulsive action to assert his freedom, which ironically costs him his liberty, results from a classic combination of pride and lack of self-knowledge. His pride impels him to challenge adversaries who outnumber him, but he does not know himself well enough to see he cannot withstand even verbal abuse because whenever Stanley confronts conflict he does not act but *re*acts. He is thus doomed to fail to outwit a man with a cockroach's tenacity to attack and survive.

Pinter himself links Stanley's lack of self-knowledge to his responsibility. He compares Stanley's illusion to Rose's, whose intruder in *The Room* enters "to upset the balance of everything, in other words, points to the illusion on which she was building her life":

> I think the same thing applies in *The Birthday Party*. Again this man is hidden away in a seaside boarding house ... Then two people suddenly arrive out of nowhere, and I don't consider this an unnatural happening. (Sherwood n.p.; excised material quoted above)

In a letter to Peter Wood, Pinter identifies Stanley's weakness first as one of communication—"But he is not *articulate*;" (3; emphasis in original)—yet ultimately he links Stanley's responsibility to communicate with self-knowledge and truth:

> Stanley *cannot* perceive his only valid justification—which is he is what he is—therefore he certainly can never be articulate about it. He knows only to attempt to justify himself by dream, by pretence and by bluff, through fright. If he had cottoned on to the fact that he need only admit to himself what he actually is and is not—then Goldberg and McCann would not have paid their visit, or if they had, the same course of events would have been by no means assured. (3–4; emphasis in original)

When Stanley sits, his self-selected fall resolves simultaneously both his inner and outer conflicts; his sitting down, a final act of inertia, is the same action which provokes the exterior assault. Both the provocation and inertia originate in allowing others, rather than the self, to affirm identity. His overly defensive reaction all by itself finally invites attack when he says: "Listen. You knew what I was talking about before, didn't you ... ? It's a mistake! Do you understand?" (42)

Stanley, like Gus, questions in order to discover the truth, but his intention extends further. Like a classic hero, Stanley transposes fear for himself to his described concern to benefit others:

> But I have a responsibility towards the people in this house. They've been down here too long. They've lost their sense of smell. I haven't. And nobody's going to take advantage of them while I'm here. (45)

Stanley's expressed concern for others may be a challenge or bluff, but it precipitates the inquisition which Goldberg begins for personal reasons: "If you want to know the truth, Webber, you're beginning to get on my breasts." (46) Violence quickly erupts developing its own momentum which ends in impersonal generalized questions: "What about the Albigensenist heresy?" "What about the blessed Oliver Plunkett?" (51) Pinter describes a similar impetus in a barroom brawl he had with a man who claimed that Hitler did not kill enough Jews:

> "You're talking a load of rubbish," I said.
> "I suppose you're a filthy Yid yourself," he said.
> "Say that again," I said and he did.
>
> I hit him and there was this frozen thing there, then a slice of blood came down his cheek. He hit me, then I laid into him forgetting who he was and what the whole thing was about entirely. (Pugh, 8)

Where Pinter acknowledges that a personal affront may have provided the continuing force in his brawl and asks, "But would I have hit him so hard if he had been talking about Negroes?" (Pugh, 8) Goldberg and Stanley never achieve the self-reflective distance to understand the private level at which they respond to attack. What happens after this turning point was already fractally contained in each beat leading up to it as well as following it in the opposing, defensive offense of both characters.

Interestingly, although Goldberg and McCann may deliver verbal abuse, it is Stanley who delivers the first blow. In extreme, frustrated self-defense, Stanley kicks Goldberg in the stomach, sending him to the floor. But Goldberg's response, delayed by Meg's entrance at that moment, prevents immediate retaliation and suspends his violence until the birthday party when McCann deliberately breaks Stanley's glasses, the cruelest act openly committed because it seems apparently unprovoked. Yet both McCann's seemingly gratuitous striking out and Stanley's assault stem from the same source: self-defense.

Since an outward position almost entirely defines the self, it is no wonder that characters will resort to violence both verbal and physical to maintain that position. Failure to do so results in destruction of the "self." The characters engaged in the conflict lack both distance and clear boundaries so that an offending remark made by one is reflexively seized upon, internalized, then reacted against by the other. But Stanley's questions with which he attempts to maintain his safe, central position in the household, only challenge Goldberg's authority and values and bring about the reverse by further augmenting the struggle against the men who may not have been sent to destroy him.

We see Goldberg and McCann enter the struggle for the same reasons that Stanley initiates it—to preserve identity. But in the end Stanley comes downstairs stripped of his identity, his seedy appearance revised to conform outwardly with the business-like appearance and values of his adversaries Goldberg and McCann.

Thematically, the struggle for dominance dramatizes the frailty of an identity based solely on outward roles and relative position. A character only *apparently* better preserves identity, if, like Goldberg, he is able to achieve dominance, or if, like Petey or McCann, he consents to subservience. If, on the other hand, like Stanley, he is unable to achieve dominance and is unwilling to be subservient, he may be destroyed.

A developed identity requires a balance between an inner and an outward sense of who one is, maintained by a self that mediates between the two. Pinter's description of himself nicely supplies a contrast to his characters:

> When I was a failure I wasn't a failure to me. When I'm a success, I'm not a success to me. (Pugh, 8)

Identity in *The Birthday Party* and in much of Pinter's work, grounded in outward position, remains relative to other people who grant or withhold approval. Resembling the Lacanian description of earliest identity development before the recognition of the self in the mirror as separate from the self mirrored by others, identity in Pinter's plays parallels identity as Len describes, then questions it in the play *The Dwarfs*:

> You are the sum of so many reflections. How many reflections? Whose reflection? Is that what you consist of? (*Three Plays*, 105)

Lacking a strong inner self, Stanley, no differently from Goldberg, seeks approval from those he does not admire: Meg and Lulu. Losing an argument with Meg, Stanley attempts to reclaim authority by reminding her of his former position as pianist:

> Tell me, Mrs. Boles, when you address yourself to me, do you ever ask yourself who exactly you are talking to? Eh? (21)

Meg dimly acknowledges Stanley's equation of identity with his former position when she gives him a toy drum because, as she says, "you don't have a piano." (36) And though Stanley feigns unconcern when Lulu criticizes his dirty appearance, he also courts her approval, however belatedly—as soon as she exits, he washes his face.

Similarly, Goldberg solicits McCann's admiration, flaunting his identity in several pathetically hollow-sounding exchanges:

> GOLDBERG: I would never deny I had a position.
> MCCANN: And what a position!
> GOLDBERG: It's a thing I would not deny. (29)

Goldberg's arrogant self-proclaiming only questions the value of his outer position. But unlike Stanley who resists authority, Goldberg capitulates to society's prescribed constricting rules to maintain what little power he has:

> What do you think, I'm a self-made man? No! I sat where I was told to sit. (77)

The unexamined rules which guide Goldberg's action, like the platitudes with which he expresses them, comprise Goldberg's voice, his choice of language, establishing voice as yet another aspect of the ethic: lazy language translates not only into an index of a character's intelligence and imagination but also of moral fiber. Goldberg's dialogue, like the dialogue of so many of Pinter's dominant characters, consists chiefly of stringing together clichés. Banality, however comical, is equated in the Pinter canon as yet another manifestation of corruption. In school Goldberg claims he was "[t]op in all subjects," yet when he asks, "And for why?" (77) he doesn't know. Instead, resuming his mask he reverts to secondhand phrases, revealing himself as without his own values, voice or vision to guide his action.

Goldberg's empty triumph over Stanley exposes the deeper reality that neither dominance nor subservience provides a sound base for an identity. Goldberg's blind adherence to authority, like Stanley's rebellion against it, mirrors the same unconscious response to received values; both reflexively attack whatever does not conform to that self. The struggle for dominance that defines identity inevitably and irrevocably intensifies into a life-and-death battle over what each character regards as his own deepest values, ultimately indistinguishable from the self.

Those values, explicitly stated or implied, even vaguely defined, form the ethical basis the characters espouse and are willing to defend with their lives. "We're right and you're wrong, Webber, all along the way," (51) says Goldberg when Stanley, broken and unable to see properly, comes down stairs in the end with his snapped and shattered glasses. Being right is expressed literally as sight, a vision which also serves as a metaphor for those values.[9] "It goes without saying you can't see straight," says Goldberg. (51)

Ironically, however, Stanley, the character with the defective vision, who possibly becomes blind in the end, may have the clearest or most far-seeing vision of all, and the suspicion that Stanley's initial intuitive fear of the men may be justified builds unrelentingly to the play's final impression.

If Stanley were in no way superior to any of the others and if he did not struggle against powerful forces he fears, any sympathy for him would be mere pity. Stanley does struggle against those forces in order to see correctly and is superior to the others in his desire and quest for truth against outnumbering forces.

Moreover, Stanley's fear of the men, frequently interpreted as causally connected to their pursuit, presupposes that if the men are after him *he* must be guilty of a crime. But that argument obscures the larger point that Goldberg and McCann may pursue him not for some specific deed but, more frighteningly, out of their blind nature to destroy whatever does not conform to their values—a point which Stanley sees but the others miss.

Stanley's observations, from the smallest details of the house to the larger threat from the men, seem consistently correct. In contrast to the others who commend Meg and her house, Stanley sees that the house is "filthy" (15) and Meg, a "Bad wife"—in the first act she fails to have tea for Petey, (6) in the last, she forgets his breakfast altogether. (70) While Goldberg flatters Meg, and Petey praises her cornflakes as "very nice," Stanley refuses the cornflakes as "horrible" and says, "The milk's off." (15) When he condemns Meg's housekeeping she dusts the table while he eats! Stanley's view is similar to that in a letter Pinter wrote detailing in the Eastbourne boarding house that supplied the setting and the Meg original for *The Birthday Party:*

> I have filthy insane digs, a great bulging scrag of a woman with breasts rolling at her belly, an obscene household, cats, dogs, filth, tea strainers, mess, oh bullocks, talk, chat rubbish shit scratch dung poison, infantility, deficient order in the upper fretwork, fucking roll on. (Bensky, 352)

Most important it is Stanley's view of the house that the audience actually sees. Stanley gains audience sympathy not merely because he is an underdog, but because his honest appraisal and moral vision may deserve to triumph. Stanley's correct evaluation of his surroundings lends credence to his fears and, in turn, makes his struggle a plausible, desirable extension of his values.

Only Stanley sees the threat from Goldberg. While his suspicions provoke Goldberg, Goldberg finally opposes Stanley because Stanley infuriates him the way that a child might whose values attack a position a father sacrificed his life to attain. Stanley's disrespectful attitude and slovenly attire insult Goldberg's chief value—outward appearance. In the end Goldberg and McCann believe that their views and values triumph:

GOLDBERG: It goes without saying, between you and me, Stan, it's about time you had a new pair of glasses. (82)

Stanley sees no better, thanks to the men, and in the end may not see at all. Are Goldberg and McCann blind? Does Stanley initially see more clearly? Ambiguity operates here to suggest both the partial correctness of each vision and set of values. The values the play promotes, distributed between both the dominant and subservient characters, reveal Stanley may possess the correct views but is without power, while Goldberg and McCann achieve power over Stanley but without underlying ethical values.

Goldberg's values, however empty, do endorse asserting oneself and seizing power, which Goldberg does, either out of the momentum of the moment or quite possibly gratuitously. It is that latter possibility, that what happens to Stanley happens for no good reason at all, which makes the events all the more frightening.

Stanley's more honest vision of his immediate world does not extend beyond or even as far as seeing his own appearance as no better than Meg's filthy house. Moreover, whatever the superiority of his values, they do not enable him to act to impose his views on others, to alter his surroundings, or even to remove himself from danger.

In the end Stanley achieves a moral victory but a physical defeat. His fearful view of the men may triumph as correct, but by relinquishing his power over himself, he has been destroyed.

While initially Stanley alone is suspicious of the men, in the end only Meg remains totally blind to Goldberg and McCann's threat.

The belated suspicions of Lulu, then Petcy, about the men lend final credence to Stanley's fears and vision, which seem intuitively sound. When Lulu, who was happily settled in Goldberg's lap at the party, the next morning accuses Goldberg of a sinister sexual assault, he deflects her attack with glib-sounding retorts which perhaps accurately transfer equal responsibility to her:

LULU: (*with growing anger.*) You used me for a night. A passing fancy.
GOLDBERG: Who used who?
LULU: You made use of me by cunning when my defenses were down.
GOLDBERG. Who took them down? (80)

Lulu, as powerless as Stanley to prove Goldberg's evil intent, is left muttering only half-formed suspicions: "I've seen everything that's happened. I know what's going on. I've got a pretty shrewd idea." (81)

Even mild-mannered Petey finally voices distrust as he ineffectually cries out to prevent the men from removing Stanley: "Leave him alone!" Goldberg's "insidiously" turning on Petey with, "Why don't you come with us, Mr. Boles?" has its calculated effect, but his invitation directed against the otherwise innocuous Petey, may do more than any other act to support Stanley's original suspicions. (85) Petey "brokenly" backs down with the empty caution: "Stan, don't let them tell you what to do!"[10] (86)

By the time Petey, who was absent from the party, sees the threat it is too late; Stanley's defenses are gone. Like Stanley, who chose to sit, and Lulu, who sat in Goldberg's lap, Petey may have unconsciously chosen powerlessness by choosing to sit out his life. Is it by chance that Petey's job is setting out chairs so others can sit? The many negative references to sitting serve as a larger metaphor underscoring the need for action. But what action? At the least, an honest assessment of the self, the point emphasized as the play closes dramatizing the opposite: only Meg remains totally blind to the possibly sinister intent of the men, remaining equally blind to who she is.

When Meg returns after the men have taken Stanley away, Petey, trying to shield Meg from the loss and horror, tells one of the few unambiguous lies in the play—that Stanley is still upstairs. But Petey's kindly-intended cover-up and Meg's suspended realization until after the final curtain make what happens to Stanley more horrifying than if he had actually been murdered. When Petey tells Meg, "He's . . . still asleep," he adds, "Let him . . . sleep." (87) Indeed Stanley never wholly awakens to who he is.

But more salient than Petey's lie and more horrifying is Meg's blithe lack of self-knowledge maintained by choice. The final ironic comedy emphasizes not only the folly but the evil of ignorance. The play achieves closure on the dangers of the lack of self-knowledge dramatized in Meg's grimly humorous assertion that at the birthday party she was the "belle of the ball": "Oh it's true. I was. (*Pause*) I know I was." (87)

Her sublimely chipper ignorance, her self-delusion in the face of Stanley's horror, throws us back into the play and to Stanley's mistake in assessing himself. Pinter, in his letter to Peter Wood, stresses that survival requires self-knowledge and vigilance:

> Stanley is the king of his castle and loses his kingdom because he assessed it and himself inaccurately. We all have to be very careful. The boot is itching to squash and very efficient. (4)

That threat of ever-impending destruction, the larger point and the primary focus of Pinter's most recent work, consistently fuses with the lack of self-knowledge on the part of the destructors, which remains the central source of destruction throughout. In the end Goldberg and McCann probably do not know why they destroy Stanley. Goldberg and McCann are as driven by inertia as Stanley. Where he is stymied by inertia of rest, they are impelled by inertia of motion, but both remain equally unaware. Pinter's more recent torturers may supply reasons for their destruction, but explanation never tallies with the larger truths in Pinter's work.

What Pinter's characters know of themselves and of others is not always accurate. What they can and cannot know, and what is true and what is not are not always clear. But the events are never deliberately calculated to create mere confusion or chaos. Instead, a brilliantly developed ambiguity sustained through all levels of the play proliferates into multiple ambiguities which prevent any simple dichotomous conclusions and reflects Pinter's view that living requires vigilance however elusive our knowledge of reality may be:

> A moment is sucked away and distorted, often even at the time of its birth. ("Writing for the Theatre," 81)

Ambiguity raises questions of right and wrong, while simultaneously dramatizing the difficulty of verification. But ambiguity is not synonymous with ambivalence, and neither Pinter's views, nor the play's ambiguity, support moral relativism, a you-are-right-if-you-think-you-are interpretation. No one who sees or reads the play would view what the men do to Stanley as virtuous, nor is Stanley's inability to act commendable. Stanley's desire to know the truth about the men, however, is praiseworthy, if, ambiguously, his fear is not mere paranoia. Ambiguity does not remove questions of right or wrong or moral responsibility but dramatizes the difficulty of knowing the truth, then acting on it.

Ambiguity actually keeps alive the possibility of choice and responsibility. Goldberg and McCann may have just cause and may have deliberately come to get him. But if, like Ben in *The Dumb Waiter*, they are simply obeying orders they do not understand, they may not be wholly or solely responsible for their actions. On the other hand what happens to Stanley in the end may be the final act in a series of actions Stanley himself provokes.

Though the suspicion that Goldberg and McCann intentionally come for Stanley remains strong, it is supported only by circumstantial evidence, while the more subtle indication that Stanley invites his destruction is supported by the dramatized events the audience actually witnesses. Yet even if Stanley overcame his inertia and chose to leave, if the men were deliberately sent to get him, what would prevent them from pursuing him?

Ambiguity generates fear and terror as Stanley's amorphous suspicions and Goldberg and McCann's equivocally ominous actions become all the more terrifying because they cannot be confronted, pinned down, examined, then dismissed. Such menace assumes the proportions of necessity or fate.

Thematically the innate reflexive assertion of dominance to preserve identity, ineffective and ultimately destructive, promotes violence to protect perceived differences and uncovers that violence as an archaic response to differences in a crowded, complex world.

But by evoking the powerful external and internal forces that confront and threaten survival[11] and by allowing characters choice in their actions, Pinter restores dignity to humankind by dramatizing the possibility of individual responsibility. Again emphasizing both the society's and the individual's responsibility for what happens, Pinter contends:

> [T]he hierarchy, the Establishment, the arbiters, the socioreligious monsters arrive to effect alteration and censure upon a member of the club who has discarded responsibility (that word again) towards himself and others ... He does possess, however, for my money a certain fibre—he fights for his life. It doesn't last long, this fight. His core being a quagmire of delusion, his mind a tenuous fusebox, he collapses under the weight of their accusation—an accusation compounded of the shitstained

> strictures of centuries of "tradition." Though non conformist he is neither hero nor exemplar of revolt. Nothing salutary for the audience to identify itself with. And *yet*, at the same time, I believe that a greater degree of identification will take place than might seem likely ... Couldn't we all find ourselves in Stanley's position at any given moment? ("Letter to Peter Wood," 5; interpolation in original, ellipsis, mine)

By deconstructing the equation of the dominant and subservient characters as villain and victim and, further, by dismantling the simple dichotomies they imply, an audience is forced to acknowledge kinship with Stanley.

We do well to walk away from *The Birthday Party* with the feeling of dread, deeply disturbed by what happens to Stanley, realizing that what happens to him could happen to us, aware of the responsibility all bear for the consequences of actions.

Individual responsibility obscured by easy labels of villain and victim promotes a dangerous view of us as "good guys" versus *them* as "villains" and, therefore, "other." Francis Gillen reminds us that Stanley could easily become Meg's torturer. (42) Goldberg's lack of an interior life is not so different from Stanley's, though of a different order and magnitude, and both equally advance the struggle for dominance that can only result in destruction.

The Birthday Party, like *The Dumb Waiter*, reawakens us to the consciousness that in a human relationship there is no winner and no loser; together both win or both lose.

Once the easy labels are removed, it is obvious, on both sides, how dangerous is a little insecurity. But both the dominant and subservient characters also possess strengths, and were we able to combine Stanley's vision and desire for truth with Goldberg's ability to act, we might have a whole person and possibly an exemplar of ethical values and action.

The ethic in Pinter's work, expressed through the dramatization of the dominant/subservient conflict, promotes life-enhancing values of love and justice. *The Birthday Party* dramatizes a need for an ethical set of values to preserve human life but also calls for action to promote those values. The play demands nothing less than a revised world view which retains the traditional virtues of love, friendship, truth, courage and justice but requires self-knowledge as a base and then demands acting forcefully on those values.

Notes

1. Is there "nowhere to go," as Stanley says? Francis Gillen forcefully argues that point, concluding "the real terror of the play is not just that Stanley is destroyed as he is led away at the end of the play, but that he is also destroyed if he remains, that if "it's no good here and no good out there in the world of Monty, then truly Stanley has nowhere to go." (39) What we see instead is that Stanley has and makes many choices, but his overwhelming inertia makes him unwilling to actually go anywhere other than where he is.
2. The majority of critics view Goldberg and McCann as agents from some unspecified organization who deliberately come to remove Stanley for some unspecified or implied crime, sin or amorphous guilt. (Kerr, *Harold Pinter,* 22–23; Esslin, *The Peopled Wound,* 76–77; Hollis, 33–34; Gordon, *Stragetems to Uncover Nakedness,* 21; Almansi and Henderson, 39; Cardullo, 9; Klein, 187, who also sees the intrusion as a game) Others assign Stanley a specific guilt, illness, or inability to reconcile with the rules of society. (Hinchliffe, 54–55; David Thompson, 57; Kauffman, 168; Kirby, 158–9; Steven Gale, 51–59; Merritt in *Pinter in Play* cites Pinter's acknowledgement that the "knock" on Stanley's door "came from my knowledge of the Gestapo," 179, but Merritt's survey of Pinter criticism, without presenting her own critical view, parrots Gabbard's Freudian dream analysis to suggest his guilt, 124, Gordon's "Oedipal 'dilemma' at heart of *The Birthday Party*" and "the crux" of all his work, 110, yet Merritt concludes by linking her own perceived "castration" to her fascination with Pinter's work, 257, citing the break up of her marriage and "'falling in love'" with Pinter," as part of her ongoing commitment, 258, thus allowing her to conclude by emphasizing her Freudian spin on the topic of Stanley's guilt.) Several notable exceptions equate the victim and villain. (Sykes, 10, views the villain and victim as equally vulnerable, but nevertheless sees Goldberg and McCann as arriving for a clear reason which they know; Burkman, 39, views villain and victim equally as victim and believes that Stanley's aggression against Lulu and Meg allies him with the victor/villain; Merritt quotes Irving Wardle, the critic initially credited with the phrase "comedy of menace," with interpreting Pinter's treatment of "destiny" as "an apt motif for an age of conditioned behaviour in which orthodox man is a willing collaborator in his own destruction," 225; but again, if Stanley is merely conditioned,

he is robbed of ethical responsibility.) Interestingly, Pinter chose to work on the screenplay for Kafka's *The Trial* because he finds compelling the struggle of the individual.

3. What Pinter dramatizes seems to echo Yeats's observation in "The Second Coming" describing those caught between unbridgeable dichotomies:

> The best lack all conviction, while the worst
> Are filled with a passionate intensity. (Yeats, 185)

4. Goldberg echoes the closure of T.S. Eliot's "The Hollow Men," but avoids the recognition that his outward position may be intrinsically worthless:

> For Thine is
> Life is
> For thine is the
> This is the way the world ends
> This is the way the world ends
> This is the way the world ends
> *Not with a bang but a whimper.* (Eliot, 57)

5. Gus in *The Dumb Waiter* may die at the end of Ben's gun. Stanley is emotionally and psychologically flayed by Goldberg's ruthless interrogation in *The Birthday Party.* Davies in *The Caretaker* may lose his last chance to find shelter in the world. Certainly Victor and Gila, though they are free to reenter the world at the end of *One for the Road,* are physically and psychologically damaged by the torture and the information that their very young son has been tortured to death.
6. Davies, the tramp in *The Caretaker* whose survival on the street has required one-upmanship, may win the running argument but in the end is simply out, expelled from the last room that might have sheltered him. *The Homecoming* is a pivotal work. Here, Ruth, the intended scapegoat caught between an ineffectual husband and his attacking father and brothers, who would keep her as servant and prostitute, wins over all the others who would dominate her and is the first of Pinter's characters to gain a tangible scrap of victory—her freedom; see also "The Ironic Con Game in *The Dumb Waiter*" and "*The Homecoming* Revisited."
7. I am indebted to Michael Dolzani for this suggestion.
8. Cf.: *The Room* and *The Dumb Waiter* for a similar treatment of "sitting"; in the former the would-be tenant refuses to sit, and when he does, only admits that he has perched; in the latter, Gus's subordinate position to Ben is immediately telegraphed to the

audience in the opening scene by the fact that he is sitting and Ben is standing. Other instances, abound: in "Kullus," *The Homecoming, No Man's Land,* and, perhaps most horrifyingly, the two seated lovers at the end of Pinter's screenplay for *The Comfort of Strangers.* Cf., Shakespeare's Caesar and Antony in *Antony and Cleopatra.*

9. Far more horrifying than the on-stage verbal threats or even McCann's breaking Stanley's glasses is the off-stage violence Goldberg and McCann inflict upon Stanley which we can only imagine when McCann says of Stanley who is upstairs trying to repair his damaged glasses: "He tried to fit the eyeholes into his eyes." (74) Stanley's blindness, like that of Oedipus, renders him naked of all illusion and defenseless. But where Oedipus puts out his own eyes, taking responsibility for acts we have not seen, we actually see that Stanley is not passively robbed of his sight; he relinquishes it through choices he makes, from choosing to sit and tempt his adversaries to engaging in the unequal struggle for dominance.
10. Pinter quoted that line at a reading to stress that he himself has lived his own life by that injunction (3 October 1989, 92nd Street Y Reading and Interview).
11. Pinter has said he does not consider the knock at the door and the taking a person away uncommon, adding that it has been going on for hundreds of years, but more recently while discussing background to *The Dwarfs* he detailed a first-hand experience which informed the act in *The Birthday Party*:

> I suddenly recalled a thing which happened to me, not Mark in the book, but me in real life. I had a group of friends, of which these people in the book are included. And I actually . . . , how can I put this . . . ? I took one of my friend's girlfriends for a walk down to the river Lea one summer evening which I shouldn't have done, you know. This was found out, naturally, and I was invited one day by two men—I know this sounds like *The Birthday Party*, but I happened to know these people, they were my very close friends—and they said, "We're going for a walk, Harold." We got on a bus, silence, dead silence, got to Victoria Park, which is a big park on the way to Bethnal Green in East London. They walked me in silence right into the middle of the park, turned, and left me there. I saw them walk away, and I felt absolutely desolated. I can't think of a more powerful chastisement, really. They had no need to say anything and they didn't. That was my humiliation, and I realized I had betrayed the whole group of people, not only one friend, but the idea of friendship, and this was not going to be tolerated by them. I don't think I've recovered since. (Knowles 1990, 81)

Pinter explores the full range of forces which threaten survival of the individual and humanity from the most private, reflex, inertia, and momentum, to the most public, the suggestion of orders from some unseen power represented by Monty, and over him, the organization with its own ideology and henchmen. By not identifying any cause as *the* real source of threat, Pinter gives full play and interplay to all the complex machinery of destruction that may occur in the name of preservation.

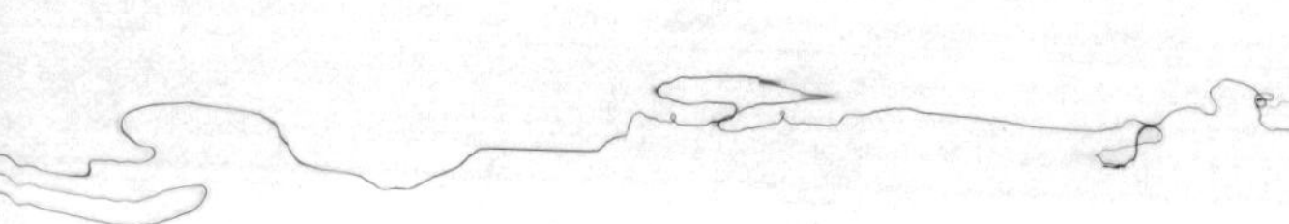

The Room and *The Revue Sketches*: The Ethic in the Early Work—Dominance and Destruction

The Room

Individual responsibility for a character's own destruction was already dramatized on the private level in Pinter's first play *The Room,* a one-act where Rose fights throughout to cling to the illusory safety of her room. The ethic in Pinter's work plays through seemingly endless variations on the dominant/subservient power struggle from this first play where Rose believes she has no choice to Pinter's recent torture plays where a seated blindfolded character in fact may be without choice even to speak out in his own defense. Yet Pinter's latest play *Moonlight* restores the centrality of choice and responsibility as all Pinter's plays preserve choice and freedom at the forefront of the values portrayed.

The Room opens with Rose serving Bert his food, assuring herself as much as him of the superiority of their squalid room as a safe haven. Before Bert exits to make a run in his van, Mr. Kidd, the landlord, arrives on the pretext of fixing the pipes but in fact hoping to deliver a message from a man in the basement who wishes to see Rose. After Mr. Kidd and Bert leave, Mr. and Mrs. Sands arrive, insisting Rose's room is for rent. When they exit, Mr. Kidd returns to press Rose to see the blind Riley, a black man and stranger from the basement, who eventually enters and claims he knows Rose. Bert returns, at first nonplused by Riley, but swiftly, gratuitously, then violently turns upon him, and without clear provocation, apparently kills him, while Rose reports that she has gone blind.

The puzzling cause of Bert's violence bewildered early critics who sought extratextual explanations for his action. But even the briefest summary of the story line which imparts some of the play's disturbing power clarifies a primary source for Bert's violence. By destroying Riley, Bert defends the original configuration of the room, restoring himself and Rose to their nested position: two people, apparently safely alone in a room. Ironically, in ridding himself of the threat Bert exposes their real lack of safety.

When asked what the play is about Pinter said he believed he was saying, "that before you've managed to adjust yourself to living alone in your room, with someone else possibly, then you're not really terribly fit and equipped to go out and fight the battles which are fought mostly in the outside world." (Tynan, n.p.) Pinter's acknowledgement of the cross-scale link between the private and public world reinforces the fractal nature of the blind, offensive defense that propels the conflict throughout, revealing with terrible irony in the end that what Rose most desperately defends is what she really wishes to reject. Pinter notes that Rose repeatedly attempts to defend "the illusion on which she was building her life," but again her lack of essential self-knowledge points directly to the surface lie used to defend a deeper lie:

> This old woman is living in a room which she is convinced is the best in the house, and she refuses to know anything about the basement downstairs. She says it's damp and nasty, and the world outside is cold and icy, and that in her warm and comfortable room her security is complete.
>
> But of course it isn't. (Sherwood, n.p.)

The theme of the intruder as the agent of stripping away illusions of safety and introducing a room's inhabitants to dark, destructive forces they fear, arcs from this play, *The Birthday Party, The Dumb Waiter* and *A Slight Ache* through Pinter's recent screen adaptation of the nightmare world of Kafka's *The Trial*. Pinter says he doesn't consider such intrusion unnatural or surrealistic because it has been happening for the last two to three hundred years. (Sherwood, n.p.)

Rose's choices may seem even more limited than Stanley's, and yet, like Stanley it is through a series of choices which have begun even before the play opens that she serves as midwife to the final violence and possibly to her own destruction.

Rose is more vaguely suspicious of every change than is Stanley, whose suspicions remain focused on the two men. Her generalized, almost paranoid, alarm begins even before the Sandses enter and threaten to rent their room. Rose assures Bert, "If they ever ask you Bert, I'm quite happy where I am." (93) While Bert and Rose first apparently considered but rejected the basement room, Rose becomes more than idly curious about it and more than mildly suspicious about the man who may be living there:

> Those walls would have finished you off. I don't know who lives down there now. Whoever it is, they're taking a big chance. (103)

Outside, even the weather threatens Rose who prefers to stay in: "It's very cold out, I can tell you. It's murder." (91) When Mrs. Sands confirms Rose's fear, "It's murder out," Rose casually invites Mrs. Sands in "to have a warm." (101) Like Goldberg's reference to "a funeral," their reference to "murder" telegraphs a foreboding, subliminal threat faintly laden with a promise of death. Rose's impulsive invitation, as unconscious and seemingly as innocent as Stanley's sitting, is as unthinking as her permitting Riley up after firmly refusing—and as dangerous.

When Rose fails to prompt Mr. Kidd to tell her whether anyone actually lives in the basement, it is with suppressed agitation she finally asks Mrs. Sands (who has just seen the basement), "I was just wondering whether anyone was living down there now." (106)

Rose's worst fear—losing the room—quickly connects to her suspicion that there is a threatening stranger in the basement. In her nightmarishly comic cross talk with Mr. Kidd, she tries to discover why the Sandses think her room is for rent at the same time that he urgently presses her to see Riley:

> ROSE: (Rising). Mr Kidd! I was just going to find you. I've got to speak to you.
>
> MR. KIDD: Look here, Mrs. Hudd, I've got to speak to you. I came up specially.
>
> ROSE: There were two people in here just now. They said this room was going vacant. What were they talking about?
>
> MR. KIDD: As soon as I heard the van go I got ready to come and see you. I'm knocked out. (109)

Although Rose adamantly refuses to admit Riley, arguing that he is a stranger and that she is a respectable woman home alone, she seems *almost* forced to give in when Mr. Kidd threatens that

Riley may come up when Bert is home—a threat all the more weighty because Mr. Kidd, at the stranger's insistence, avoided mentioning Riley in Bert's presence, then waited a week until Rose was alone to deliver Riley's message.

Does Rose know Riley? The past connection between Rose and Riley and his possible threat, like that between Stanley and the guests, can only be guessed. When Riley enters, he claims he has come with a message for Rose: her father wants her home. He then says he wants her home. Although she clearly cannot literally be his daughter, Rose's decision to allow Riley to come up seems unprompted except by the threat from Riley which, like Stanley's fear of Goldberg and McCann, may have a simple, more obvious explanation. Rose may fear Bert's jealousy and wrath.

Nothing Rose is able to discover verifies her fearful suspicion or past connection with Riley. Yet when he says that his name is Riley she counters, "That's not your name," and insists his request to see her was a horrible mistake. (112)

When nothing he does or says seems sinister, she responds more warmly toward him despite her protests. Ultimately, the momentary human warmth Riley offers exposes Rose's fear of losing the room as a lie, concealing the lie by which she lives her life, namely, that she values the room. When Riley asks her to come home she admits the truth: that the room is really a trap:

> The day's a hump. I never go anywhere. (116)

When she puts her hands on Riley's face and neck, she seems to be exploring an avenue of escape from her room, but her hands already employ the gestures of the blind.

When Bert returns and finds Rose's hands on Riley, Bert squashes any possibility for Rose's escape. Bert's outburst of violence may be motivated by jealousy, the result of that intuitive grasp about what is happening that can occur between people who have lived together. But Bert's delayed reaction also suggests some other motivation, the clue to which may be found in the image Pinter says triggered the writing of the play. At a party in London he says he was taken up to a room where he was introduced to two people, both men:

> One carrying on a lively and rather literate conversation, and at the table next to him sat an enormous lorry driver. He had his cap on and never spoke a word. And all the while, as he talked, the little man was feeding the big man—cutting his bread, buttering it, and so on. Well, this image would never leave me. ("*Caretaker's* Caretaker" 76)

Where the two men, transformed into Rose and Bert, are central to both the triggering image and the play's opening is the silence of the man being fed. Like the silence of Mrs. Y in Strindberg's *The Stronger*, Bert's silence conveys power without a single word being uttered. Rose's prattle contrasts as a nervous attempt to fill a vacuum and maintain relationship to the person on whom she is dependent for food and shelter; but Bert seems equally dependent since she spends all her time feeding, clothing and caring for him, actions which convey her concern to him and from which Rose derives her own sense of worth:

> This is a good room. You've got a chance in a place like this. I look after you, don't I, Bert? Like when they offered us the basement here I said no straight off. I knew that'd be no good. The ceiling right on top of you. No, you've got a window here, you can move yourself, you can come home at night, if you have to go out, you can do your job, you can come home, you're all right. And I'm here. You stand a chance. (95)

Is she trying to convince herself or Bert of his good fortune that he has her and the room? The relationship is subtly off balance; she does all the talking, is ten years older than Bert, who likes weak tea while she prefers hers strong, implying that while he appears more independent, Rose may be the stronger. But until he leaves she seems happy enough to remain within the protective walls of the room rather than venture out, and three times she promises Bert she will have cocoa for him when he returns.

Instead, Bert returns to find Rose standing with her hands on Riley. Although Bert registers no affect, he projects a violent sexual energy onto his narrative of driving his van: "She was good. She went with me. She don't mix it with me. I use my hand. Like that. I get hold of her. I go where I go. She took me there. She brought me back." (119) Bert implies that, in contrast to Rose, his van is faithful to him. His response to Riley parallels his reaction to a car in his way: "I bumped him. I got my road. I had all my way." (116)

While nothing demonstrates that any of Bert's sexual interest is focused on Rose, in the absence of Bert's visible affection and of Bert himself, Rose may be responding to the proffered affection of Riley. Although Bert never accuses Rose, who never attempts to explain Riley's presence, he also may realize Rose may no longer be wholly dependent upon him for her care nor as willing to supply his sense of importance. Before he leaves she praises his driving skill, his bravery in going out into the world. (98) But he returns home to discover he can perhaps be replaced by a blind black man whom Bert considers his inferior: "Lice," he calls out as he strikes Riley. (116) Bert may also suspect a past connection between his wife and Riley, who is on the verge of a confession when he is silenced by Bert: "Mr. Hudd, your wife—" (116) Bert strikes him to the floor.

More enigmatic than Bert's violence is Rose's blindness which throws final focus on the dramatization of fear and its intuited causes in half-seen, half-mysterious, half-confirmed forms. Her sudden blindness ironically links her to the blind Riley at the very moment that severs connection between them and dashes any further possibility for her escape. Rose's blindness, like Stanley's and Oedipus's, sends the audience back into the play to see how she was blind to herself and her choices all along.

From the beginning Rose sees herself without choices: if she does not admit Riley into her room, Riley may, as Mr. Kidd threatens, come of his own accord when Bert is home. Rose's attempts to avoid the worst scenario, as did Oedipus, ironically bring on precisely the worst, again giving the final action the inexorable force of fate.

Rose gets what she says she wants: the room. Ironically, that room which she defends as a kingdom is quite subtly revealed as a prison, in part, of her own making.

Pinter's ability to "care for" all his characters sustains a tension which does not preclude caring for some, such as Stanley and Rose, more than such others as Goldberg, McCann, and Bert. Riley might seem to have done nothing to bring down his own destruction, but he is not aligned with the purely innocent torture victims of Pinter's later work. Riley chooses to force himself into Rose's room and senses the risks and dangers because he keeps his distance, perhaps at Mr. Kidd's insistence, till Bert is gone. Bert's violence, though at first appearing gratuitous, is really not puzzling.

Within a patriarchal value system it is enough for Bert to discover his wife or woman alone with her hands on a strange man to elicit and to justify his violent "claim" upon her which requires little or no explanation. The fact that the audience perceives no threat from Riley and that Riley even evokes audience sympathy for his persistence, his desire and his proffered affection call those act-first-ask-later values Bert embodies into question.

Without assigning blame, Pinter evokes in the audience a clear sympathy for Rose as a woman fighting, as it were, for her life: the hermetically sealed room allows her to act with seeming plausibility as if there are no alternatives to that room but also registers the complicity between Rose and Bert as he acts to fulfill her explicit desire: to insure the safety and safekeeping of their lodgings. Rose and Bert, in contrast to Stanley, may claim a physical victory—they can remain in their room—but at the expense of a moral defeat; Riley may be dead, Rose, blind and trapped in their illusory safety.

Where Bert's early silence makes him appear Rose's antagonist and his brutal act at the end would seem to align him with Pinter's other taciturn dominant thugs such as Ben, McCann, the bodyguards in *No Man's Land*, and the torturers in *The New World Order*, a moment's reflection reveals Bert as little more powerful than the nervously protective, garrulous Rose. Fearing and refusing to confront the worst, Pinter's characters discover that the worst inescapably confronts them. For both Rose and Bert, the relationship and illusion of safety have been damaged and unalterably reversed.

Rife with the apparent mystery that made the play seem almost incomprehensible to some early critics, closer analysis dispels much of that mystery which in most of Pinter's early work incidentally served to deflect any charge of didacticism. Pinter denied himself the broad strokes of tipping scales clearly toward any seeming victim against outright villains in favor of dramatizing more complex truths.

As the curtain falls in *The Room*, destruction hangs poised over Bert and Rose even in their extreme attempt to prove their security. Mystery is also a function of Pinter's highly elliptical dialogue, which like Hemingway's, illuminates only the visible tip of the iceberg while evocatively disclosing the hidden subtext below the relationship.

For a first play written in only three or four days when Pinter was twenty-seven, *The Room* remains fine theatre and already raises ethical questions of responsibility. It contains an honest portrayal of the characters' fears coupled with comic touches of Pinter's best dialogue: a single comic line can evoke worlds of deeper subtext. Mr. Sands, for example, refuses his wife's invitation to sit when they first enter, but when he does inadvertently sit and his wife points it out, he denies it: "Don't be silly. I perched." (106) Sitting down in this work, as in Pinter's work generally, is equated with allowing oneself to assume a subservient position. Mr. Sands's comic denial reveals refusal to admit any loss of power to his wife and discloses that inner tension that marks the entire play—a desire to remain comfortable, safe, and in one place, pitted against the equally powerful desire to remain free, to go out into the world, even to seek and confront danger as Bert does and Riley.

On a larger scale that inner tension reflects the tension between permanence and mutability. But Pinter exposes such permanence, when it is equated with security, as false, a result primarily of a limited view of choices.

Already in this early work were marks of Pinter's important contributions to drama; he handles with surety the dramatization of the ambiguous appearance of good and evil, and violence is disclosed as a bully's jealous, even fearful, attempt to maintain territory. His characters live and are never mere contrivances of a puppeteer, so that the resultant realism of Pinter's dialogue, the resonance, and the depth of the subtext all give his work its durability and distinguish him as a dramatist from mere playwrights. Simple attention to what happens in *The Room* demystifies most of what seems initially puzzling. That care repays itself in disclosing the deeper reverberations of subtext where all bear responsibility for the final action.

What *The Room* ironically dramatizes is that the rigid or obsessive desire to maintain the *sine qua non* of existence—shelter—may be the very attitude which produces the action to destroy it when that attitude is attended by a belief that there is no other choice, no way out. Thus Riley's arrival reveals a deeper truth than the one Rose expresses. Though she tries to maintain her shelter this is not what she wants; she truly seeks something no less important—love or affection. Love will, only much later in Pinter's work, inform justice on a larger scale. But here characters dramatize the dishonesty of stated desire and the irony that they cling to what they do not want, implying perhaps they might do well to hold with a loose rein what is truly desired. But first they must know what that is. If human relationship, love, some reciprocity of communication is wanted, it remains unarticulated even while it is dramatized. Here justice remains in the shadow as the self-administered iron fist delivered by Bert, whose power is equaled only by his fear.

The Revue Sketches

Early on Pinter shunned political rhetoric and conclusions: "I wouldn't know where to start on political issues. I'm as confused as anybody else, and maybe even more." (Pugh, 8). Even the question of knowing what occurred during a world event was for him unclear but was transformed into an epistemological question of how we can know at all. "Take the massacres in Africa. How can you determine what took place unless you're on the spot?" (8)

But Pinter was already quick to make the connections between private, communal, and global implications of violence in his early work: "Maybe it's more difficult if you're on the spot. I'm never *surprised* to hear about massacres. You have only to get on a bus and a massacre is taking place ... or [be] in a room." (8)

Such a "massacre" is precisely what is dramatized in the revue sketch *Request Stop* where a woman at a bus stop suffers a slight or imaginary insult, antagonizes others in line until she is isolated, then excised from the group. What happens, as Pinter says, is both funny and sad:

> I want as far as possible to leave comment to the audience, to let them decide whether the characters in situations are funny or sad. Take the woman in *Request Stop.* We've all met them, the people who talk to themselves in crowds, enlarging upon a slight or imagined grievance, making fragmentary attempts to communicate and slipping back into muttered protest. Is the reaction of other people to them as they edge uneasily away, funny or tragic? Obviously it can be both, but I think my job as

> dramatist is simply to present the situation shaped in dramatic terms, and let the audience decide for themselves. ("Mr. Harold Pinter—Avant-Garde Playwright and Intimate Revue," 9)

Even in these thumbnail-sized sketches Pinter's richly layered ambiguity again allows for resonant complexity. In the Woman's familiar-sounding harangue against the Small Man in *Request Stop*, Pinter evokes the uncomfortably comic qualities of the fearful and the powerless attempting to assert self-importance:

> I beg your pardon, what did you say?
> [*Pause.*]
> All I asked was if I could get a bus from here to Shepherds Bush.
> [*Pause.*]
> Nobody asked you to start making insinuations. (93)

When the man does not respond, the Woman's attack quickens to menace, her fear masquerading as anger finds subtextual expression in her defensiveness in the guise of attack:

> I'm not going to stand here and be insulted on a public highway. Anyone can tell you're a foreigner. I was born just around the corner. (98)

In the last line Pinter simultaneously captures the sense of place, class, and British chauvinism which impels his characters to fight so tenaciously at whatever cost to maintain whatever place they assume they have.

The Woman's menace is quickly deflected when another woman to whom she appeals as witness to her injury exits to a taxi without a word. The entire crowd's refusal to respond to the Woman turns the situation that might otherwise be amusingly threatening into one that becomes quietly but comically pathetic. But though the sketch might have legitimately ended when the whole group boards a passing bus and abandons her, Pinter continues it for one more line that rescues the growing pathos with a final comic twist, throwing mystery back over the Woman's previous behavior. When another man approaches, the Woman asks "shyly, hesitantly, and with a smile," if she can get a bus *not* to Shepherds Bush, but to Marble Arch. (99)

Could a woman born "just around the corner" not know the bus to Marble Arch? Does she, like the two tramp women in *The Black and White* live on the street and stand at the bus stop in wait of passersby? With really remarkable economy, Pinter manages to evoke all the shifting responses and, with a swift final stroke, concludes by ambiguously implying several imaginative possibilities to account for the Woman's behavior—all in well under four minutes.

The revue sketches, written in 1959 in the wake of *The Birthday Party's* bad reviews, took Pinter's work out of one room but allowed him some play with concerns of his longer works. When asked how he first got started writing revue sketches, Pinter replied:

> Well, I was asked. Disley Jones, of the Lyric, Hammersmith, had worked with me before on *The Birthday Party*, and when he became involved with planning a new revue for the theatre he asked me if I would care to contribute. I'd never done anything like that before, but I thought about it, and then wrote *The Black and White,* which along with *The Last To Go*, is my favorite sketch. ("Mr. Harold Pinter ... ," 9)

These sketches, as Pinter insists, are primarily about people, the way they talk to one another, what they say, imply or fail to say. Though Pinter's sketches have the strength of presenting real characters, as in any very short work characters are drawn more to familiar types than as individuals, yet, as he notes, they do not attempt to convey any moral stance. But the values emerge:

> As far as I am concerned there is no real difference between my sketches and my plays. In both I am interested primarily in people; I want to present living people to the audience, worthy of their interest basically because they *are*, because they exist, not because of any moral the author may draw from them. (9)

Even though the sketches are not written as a vehicle for a moral, they manage to embrace those values which inform the main concerns of the ethic throughout his work—mystery, sight and blindness, friendship and love, time, space, and identity along with the overriding concern with dominant/subservient relations as an expression of survival.

Even a faint assertion of dominance in the text may be emphasized or exaggerated in production. In *The Pinter People* television production of *Trouble in the Works* which Pinter helped direct while playing Fibbs, the overpowering manager, Fibbs, looms large behind a desk, listening to his insignificantly small employee, Wills, complain that the workers are unhappy and have turned against his products. When Wills with growing confidence explains, "Well, I hate to say it, but they've gone vicious about the high speed taper shank spiral flute reamers," (92) Fibbs, originally drawn to many times the size of Wills, at the end collapses, a much-deflated figure behind his desk, while the now much-inflated figure of Wills looms before Fibbs to inform his boss that what the men want to make is "Love," ("Brandy balls" in the text, (93)) The two men chiasmically exchange positions of power.

This brief sketch might have worked theatrically as a mere comic vehicle for displaying machine tool names charged with sexual connotations: "the brass pet cock," "the gunmetal side outlet relief with handwheel," "the nippled adaptor," "[t]he jaw for Jacob's chuck for use on portable drill," and "bronze draw off cock." The triggering image came from Pinter's own experience:

> So, I did do one day's work in an office once. Half a day. Job with machine part tools. In fact *Trouble in the Works* came right out of that half day's work which made the work in the office well worthwhile. I had to copy down all the names of these machine part tools, extraordinary, half dog points, hemi-spherical rod end and all that lot. (*Pinter People*, n.p.)

But the sketch goes much further than the original image, remaining one of the rare instances in Pinter's work where the clear underdog through a patient persistence wins his point, a kind of justice in the end, and his winning reveals deeper truths: the lie behind the inflated façade of Fibbs's power and the greater importance of love.

Wills confronts a worthy and formidable opponent to win at the closure a contest of wills and the change from "brandy balls" to "Love" pits the mechanical, profit-bearing public values against the humane and private values of love.

After *Trouble in the Works* and beginning with *The Black and White*, *Last to Go*, *Request Stop*, *Special Offer*, *Night*, *That's Your Trouble*, *That's All*, *Applicant*, *Interview* and *Dialogue for*

Three, the dominant/subservient struggle and the tension between values is often less blatant, more subtly executed, sometimes only hinted at or nearly absent.

In *The Black and White* two tramp women in an all-night cafe merely discuss the numbers of the all-night busses and their dread of being taken away. Like Stanley and Rose they cling to the familiar for ballast, identity, as well as seeming security. With little overt contest, the Second Woman cotemporaneously asserts her superior position and voices her fear of strangers:

> I see you talking to strangers as I come in. You want to stop talking to strangers, old piece of boot like you, you mind who you talk to. (95)

Again asserting superiority she claims that when the police took her away they "took a fancy to me"; yet what remains is her own vague fear of being taken away and her distrust of the police, those officials entrusted with keeping the public safety. Nevertheless she maintains her superior edge when the First Woman asks, "Do you think they'd take a fancy to me?" The Second Woman replies, "I wouldn't back on it." (96)

Even in these brief speeches, layered with multiple meanings, Pinter implies there is no safe haven, that the goods of life are by no means necessarily guaranteed by the law to those who do not already possess sufficient goods. The connection between the ethical good and material goods, between welfare and safety, commodities and possession arcs through to *Party Time*. The First Woman admits what only Pinter's subservient characters might, a desire to hold what she has: "I wouldn't mind staying." But she is reminded by the Second, "They won't let you." (97) The tension welling up even in this brief sketch proceeds from the menace of the unknown, containing a barely concealed life-and-death threat of losing it all. Yet beneath their fears lurks some admirable courage in those who nevertheless are able to survive at the margins.

In *Last to Go,* a newspaper seller and customer simply discuss which of the papers will be last to go, but their failure to communicate sounds a deeper note—the difficulty of knowing the truth communicated in verbal discourse. According to Pinter:

> The whole point of *The Last One to Go* [sic] as far as it has a point, in the obvious sense is that the newspaperman and the stallkeeper talk to each other but they never communicate at all, a situation which is both funny and tragic, like any misunderstanding. ("Mr. Harold Pinter ... " 9)

Last to Go evokes a double response without menace as the men simply exchange shoptalk about nothing that seems very important but is essential to each: the jobs that occupy most of these men's lives. The Barman recalls his busy spell, the Man, his last newspaper sold:

BARMAN: Yes, trade was very brisk here about ten.
MAN: Yes, I noticed.
[*Pause*]
I sold my last one about then. Yes. About nine forty-five.
BARMAN: Sold your last then did you?
MAN: Yes, my last 'Evening News' it was. Went about twenty to ten.
BARMAN: Yes.
[*Pause.*]
Sometimes it's the 'Star' is the last to go.
BARMAN: Ah.
MAN: Or the . . . whatsisname.
BARMAN: 'Standard.'
MAN: Yes. (100)

When talk shifts to George, it hardly matters to either man that each has a different "George . . . whatsisname" in mind; they both agree "he must have left the area." (102) Again the resonant subtext evokes epistemological questions about how we know, the nature of knowledge, and what truth can be achieved by verbal communication.

The tension in other sketches comes from the contest of one of the character's scoring a point by being right and achieving a kind of private justice or by overpowering another. In *That's Your Trouble* two men in a park argue whether a man carrying a sandwich board has a headache or back or a leg ache; in *That's All* two old women dispute whether Mrs. A comes for tea on Thursdays rather than Wednesdays; in *Interview* Mr. Jakes, a pornographic bookstore owner, fantasizes about imprisoning his customers because, he concludes, they are all communists; in *Dialogue for Three* the first man recalls a woman he once met as the second man comments upon the weather, and the woman asks if he remembers the first time they met, to which the first man, derailing the banter entirely, replies that the second man reminds him of someone else.

In *Applicant*, excerpted from *The Hothouse*, Miss Piffs viciously interrogates the applicant Lamb during the familiar situation of a job interview, but Pinter pushes the conflict to some imaginative extremes, combining the horrors of an inquisition and physical torment. The most didactic of Pinter's early sketches, it portrays the abuse of authority by a person representing some large organization who uses her position to inflate her identity.

The "essence of efficiency," Miss Piffs, a descendant of Miss Cutts from *The Hothouse*, maintains the upper hand from the first moment. Even without the stage directions indicating that Lamb is "striding nervously about" and without knowing that his name is Lamb, tension proceeds from Lamb's first line—a single word signals Lamb as the subservient character. To Miss Piffs's "Ah, good morning," Lamb responds, "Oh, good morning, miss." But the deferential "miss" places him beneath her as one who in that single word has said too much and said it badly. Unable to match Miss Piffs's forcefulness, he reveals himself as a character headed in a direction opposite hers. (103)

Not only does this sketch examine one public arena open to abuse of authority, the workplace, but it also contains the most blatant of all sexual attacks by one of Pinter's women characters.

One of the few questions Miss Piffs permits Lamb to answer, "Are you Virgo Intacta?" is immediately followed by the more direct, "Do women frighten you?" as she pushes the button for a second jolt of electrical current which propels Lamb to the floor. In *Pinter People* the cartoon character Miss Piffs drifts to a horizontal and superior position above the prostrate Lamb, suggesting a thinly veiled frustrated sexual desire beneath her attack, while negatively equating a female superior position with Miss Piffs's castrating attitude. The sketch points to public justice, or injustice, and questions of sexual ethics.

In *Special Offer* Pinter continues to explore and question received attitudes about women: sex, gender, and role. Inverting received attitudes toward prostitution, the comedy proceeds from a secretary wondering whether an offer she was made while on vacation of men for sale could be true. By reversing the stock situation of women for sale, this sketch is not only comic but makes a more serious satirical commentary on sexual ethics and prostitution. The BBC secretary describes how she was approached by an old crone with men for sale:

> It's an international congress, she said, got up for the entertainment and relief of lady members of the civil service. You can hear some of the boys we've got speak through a microphone, especially for your pleasure, singing little folk tunes we're sure you've never heard before. Tea is on the house and everyday we have the very best pastries. For the cabaret at teatime the boys do a rare dance imported all the way from Buenos Aires, dressed in nothing but a pair of cricket pads. Every single one of them is tried and tested, very best quality, and at very reasonable rates. (73–74)

The secretary's deadpan response addresses sex as a good of life:

> That's very kind of you, I said, but as a matter of fact I've just been on leave, I start work tomorrow and am perfectly refreshed. (74)

The sketch ends stating what is already implied: "Do you think it's a joke . . . or serious?" Yet the discourse emphasizing sex, desire, and love begun in these sketches will develop later into larger issues of love and justice.

Pinter brought to the sketches the same elements that made for greatness in his plays, threading through these brief works those larger concerns: questioning in almost every fractal beat what it means to act responsibly. Peeling back layers of familiar behavior, Pinter brought his incisive comic wit to play upon morality in the familiar institutions of human life to reveal both what we really believe and how we behave when we act on unexamined assumptions. Insisting he was "interested primarily in people," he recognized that the demands made upon actors here were the same as for the multidimensional characters of his plays: "One of the difficulties of my sort of sketch is that it calls for acting performances, not personality displays, like the traditional revue." ("Mr. Harold Pinter . . . ," 4) It is the depth of character which allows audiences to respond seriously to the ethical core of the conflict.

A Slight Ache as Fulcrum: Leveling Dominant and Subservient Roles—The Triumph of Vitality and Truth

In the next group of plays published together, *A Slight Ache, The Collection*, and *The Dwarfs*, along with the later play *The Caretaker*, mystery weighs almost equally with the theme of the intruder to produce the tension in the quest for dominance. In *A Slight Ache*, originally a radio play, Flora's husband, a middle-aged, would-be squire, Edward, invites in and interrogates a completely silent old Matchseller who has been standing at the gate "in all weathers." As Edward wants to know what the man is doing, he attributes certain actions to him: "You're crying," "You're laughing," "You're moving." Although on radio we hear only silence, Pinter felt, "We're pretty certain however that the old man is not doing any of those things." (Sherwood, n.p.) While it seemed to him "inconceivable" that the play could transfer to stage, it did with a single alteration: the Matchseller does make one positive action, but none of the other actions reported by Edward. (Wildman, n.p.) In the end Edward and the Matchseller chiasmically exchange positions as Edward, concerned that the Matchseller may be going blind, reveals it is he himself who may be doing so. When Edward collapses to the floor in the end, Flora steps out into the back garden with the Matchseller.

Written during the year the revue sketches were first presented, *A Slight Ache* contains a freshly imaginative, dense handling of all the themes and techniques already observed in Pinter's earlier plays but this time without any easy distinctions between dominant and subservient character. What is true and what is projection is even less easily discernible. While both the dominant and subservient characters are treated more sympathetically than in previous plays, the focus zooms in on Edward, giving us a more intimate look at him than almost any other of Pinter's dominant characters, allowing us to appreciate both his struggle and the flaw in the anatomy of dominance. Edward, who initially overpowers both the apparently subservient Flora and the Matchseller, reveals a blindness begun as a slight ache in his eyes that ends in his own defeat.

Edward's blindness represents not only his moral blindness but an inability to see or to imagine himself in anyone else's skin, namely, the Matchseller's. Physical blindness in Pinter's plays, formerly associated almost exclusively with the subservient character—Rose and Stanley—here manifests itself in the person who has the uppermost position initially. Flora, however, who gains dominance in the end, like Ruth in *The Homecoming*, is the first of Pinter's major characters to finally achieve power who is also sympathetic and, like Ruth, sees what is going on beneath what is said. Flora's triumph, however dubious her prize, does represent a triumph of the values of life.

While mystery takes a form familiar in Pinter's work with the strange appearance of an outside force, here the Matchseller, Edward's and Flora's different perceptions and responses to him are both more inventively conceived and richly evoked than in earlier plays. In the original radio version, the Matchseller's silence makes his very existence questionable and reduces his potential threat to what might only exist as the projected fears of the observer. But attitude here determines action. Where Edward sees the Matchseller as threatening and is destroyed by him, Flora who views him as harmless gathers strength from his presence.

The attitudes become a major determinant in delivering the final action not by sympathetic magic but as self-fulfilling prophecy, which takes on the force of fate. Where Edward's pessimism breeds failure, Flora's greater optimism results in triumph. If as Kant says we have only three choices—of attitude, intention, and action—then certainly attitude, which is integral here to ethical choice as Pinter dramatizes it, becomes the basis for intention and, ultimately, action.

Time, space, and identity, more elusive qualities than in any previous work, all heighten the mystery and make Edward's attempts to get at the truth a frustrating struggle against a worthy adversary. Time is slippery—but only within limits. In the beginning Flora announces, "It's the height of summer," (11) yet at the end she tells the Matchseller, whom Edward believes has grown younger,

"Summer is coming." (40) But the characters are not growing younger. Life is sliding past, and space and the objects that occupy it are movable; the breakfast furniture simply disappears, focusing the action on the scullery. Finally, the protean quality of identity, dramatized not only in Edward and Flora's exchange of dominant roles but also in Flora's exchange of Edward for the Matchseller whom she calls Barnabas, suggests the fluidity of identity that cannot be posited in time or space upon a person as Edward attempts to fix an identity like a template upon the Matchseller.

Yet the constant is honesty: the importance of confronting and knowing the self, at least not mistaking the persona(ae) for the self. When given that opportunity, Edward, like Goldberg and Ben, prefers not to know, but this time the consequences for a dominant character are dire.

An interesting mix of dominance and subservience, Edward at first dictates orders to Flora when a wasp intrudes upon their breakfast. He commands: "Cover the pot," (11) then resolves "Well, let's kill it for goodness' sake." (12) He himself has no intention of acting but directs Flora to do so.

Edward's blindness or the slight ache in his eye becomes an appropriate ill for one who, like Stanley, perhaps Rose, Disson in *Tea Party*, and Gloucester in *Lear*, is blind to himself. While Edward inhabits his hours and days absorbed in writing about time and space, the Belgian Congo (Zaire), and other topics remote from his life, he has no knowledge of the passing of seasons, of plants in his garden, or any growing things, and, by extension, of himself. "You know perfectly well what grows in your garden," Flora tells Edward who proudly claims ignorance, "Quite the contrary. It is clear that I don't." (10) This time pride in ignorance results in a fall.

Not only is Edward partially blind but, like other subservient characters of Pinter's, fearful, even alarmed by the out of doors. "It's very treacherous weather you know," re-echoes Rose's fear of the world beyond her walls. (10) By contrast Flora glories in its being "the longest day of the year" and "the height of summer." (10) She seems in full bloom while Edward soon appears to wither.

Edward's sense of his own power in the larger community and his attempts to maintain it privately, much like Goldberg's, rely upon his public position, which constitutes his entire identity. Edward has no inner life. But unlike Goldberg, who steps away from the abyss, Edward does attempt to confront it, not, however, with an open-minded quest for truth so much as to prove his own worth by denying any kinship with the dark, destitute side of life witnessed in the Matchseller. As soon as he invites the Matchseller in, he marshals his privilege and possessions as a club to establish his dominant position to impress and distance himself from the impassive Matchseller in the simple gesture of offering him a drink:

> A glass of ale? Curaçao Fockink Orange? Ginger beer? Tia Maria? A Wachenheimer Fuchsmantel Reisling Beeren Auslese? Gin and it? Chateauneuf-du-Pape? A little Asti Spumante? Or what do you say to a straightforward Piesporter Goldtropfschen Feine Auslese (Reichsgraf von Kesselstaff)? (25)

His ostensive largess as host is a barely disguised bludgeon to overwhelm and outclass the man.

The vague indications that Edward, perhaps like Disson in *Tea Party*, may have acquired rather than been born to his social position and married above his station provide one motive for asserting dominance: in Pinter's work such aggression almost always signals a deep fear of exposing some paucity within. Though Edward tries to amaze the Matchseller with his large variety of chairs, (23) he reveals that his furniture was all purchased secondhand at the same sale. (27) After advancing this information, Edward ambiguously suggests, "You too, perhaps, you too." (27) The notion that the vagrant Matchseller also bought or is in possession of an array of chairs is comically ludicrous but introduces the first pass Edward makes into the Matchseller's territory, his skin. Although Edward displays a fleeting sympathy for the mute man who sells matches, when Edward tells him that he, too, was once struggling in commerce, he again like Goldberg, is bent more on affirming his own importance than in extending to the Matchseller any real camaraderie or compassion. (24) First Edward patronizingly addresses the older man as a young, inexperienced subordinate, then he makes him sit. But unlike Goldberg, Edward experiences no victory, only momentary respite when he finally manages to force the man backward until the Matchseller stumbles into a chair:

> Aaah! You're sat. At last. What a relief. (27)

More central to Edward's identity than his position is his masculinity—what it means to be a man. In former times, hinted at in the village setting that until recently boasted of a squire, a man could prove himself in battle. But though Edward claims he struggled "against all kinds of usurpers," his battles are now absurdly reduced to physical combat with a wasp, killed in a cowardly fashion, and to one-sided verbal skirmishes with a matchseller whose silence, like the silence of the crowd against the Woman in *Request Stop*, makes Edward's assertion of dominance appear ridiculously pathetic. (63) Edward projects not only his weaknesses but also whatever strength he has onto the Matchseller, praising his stoic endurance during the summer storm resonant of Lear on the heath:

> There was a storm last week. A summer storm. He stood without moving, while it raged about him. (21)

For Pinter, Lear's heath scene embodies in wonderful combination the heroic, the tragic dread transfigured by gaiety, a point he expresses in *Mac* in his praise for his mentor Anew McMaster's interpretation of *Lear*:

> He understood and expressed totally the final tender clarity which is under the storm, the blindness, the anguish. (15)

The Matchseller succeeds where Edward fails and gains his portion of audience sympathy from his evident stoicism in light of his circumstances. He not only confronts the elements, but perhaps by extension, himself, in ways Edward does not.

In Edward's battle with the wasp that lands on the jam jar, Edward vacillates between trying to coerce Flora to kill it, "Put it in the sink and drown it," and hoping that by doing nothing the problem will solve itself, "It's stuck. It'll drown where it is, in the marmalade"; twice he commands Flora, who refuses: "Bring it out on the spoon and squash it on the plate," then reveals his real fear, "It'll fly out and bite me." (13)

When Edward finally resolves to kill the wasp himself, his method, in contrast to the one proposed to Flora, involves no risk to himself—he pours hot water down the spoon hole and claims he is "blinding him." (14) Clearly relieved by his action, which seems a victory, Edward momentarily transfers his own blindness to the wasp.

Edward's similar attempts to project his blindness onto the Matchseller are unsuccessful, indicating that the essential blindness remains with him; Edward first wonders whether the Matchseller has a glass eye, then, in echo of Goldberg about Stanley, says to Flora:

> He can't see straight (63)

But despite all efforts to posit the blindness with the Matchseller, the problem sticks to Edward who confesses that he looked at the Matchseller from all angles and with all kinds of glasses, as well as "bare eyed" but, despite all efforts "to get to the bottom of it," is still left with the unanswered question and his last gasped utterance:

> Who are you? (39)

His unasked question remains: "Who am I?" In Pinter's plays that question is fundamental to all action. Edward's killing of the wasp, his projected blindness, and the seeming minutia which attract his attention form Edward's attitude that determines each choice and action. Again, through the economy of fractal geometry, a character's least action, imprinted with his larger strength and virtue or lack of it, telegraphs the final action as predictable if not inevitable. Yet in Pinter's work the ending also remains astonishing.

The wasp scene and Edward's interrogation of the Matchseller on his blindness all lead to that overarching question of self-knowledge, in the Pinter canon the *sine qua non*, the formal cause for all choices and subsequent ethical action. Choice becomes the efficient cause, and action the final cause. Edward's inability or refusal to know himself thus limits his ability to know another and to act.

Though Edward has momentary sympathy for the Matchseller, which it may be supposed might lead to subsequent understanding of himself, all compassion ends when he is forced to submit his action to the scrutiny of a third party. When Flora enters and asks how Edward is getting on with him, Edward's undoing begins in his evasions and deliberate lies about himself and the other. Initially Edward seems to have softened when, with wry understatement, he answers Flora: "He's a little . . . reticent. Somewhat withdrawn. It's understandable. I should be the same, perhaps, in his place." (28) But Edward instantly eradicates empathy when he asserts, then defends, till the end:

> Though, of course, I could not possibly find myself in his place. (28)

The horrible truth Edward wishes to avoid provides the great irony: that Edward is precisely in the Matchseller's place in the end. Blind to himself, Edward remains sealed into the skin of his own persona, unconsciously at one with his mask which he fails to perceive is not his best, deepest, or entire self.

Edward's view of the wasp and Matchseller contrasts with Flora's, further emphasizing Edward's inability to "see straight." Where Edward projects volition onto the wasp he fears as "vicious," Flora remains only prudently cautious that the wasp will "bite." Where Edward projects his own failing sexuality onto the Matchseller calling him a bullock (19, 26) with a "great bullock of jelly," (29) conveying negative connotations of "bullock" as castrated bull or a steer, Flora sees the Matchseller a "bullock let loose" (17) and "not at all like jelly," (32) attaching to the Matchseller the more positive connations of a bullock as a young bull.

But the Matchseller is not a mere catalyst for the projections of the others' fears and desires.[1] The Matchseller himself projects a model of strength when contrasted with Edward. He has survived at the margins, and he triumphs at the end through sheer endurance. Edward, much like Goldberg, verges on but finally and desperately avoids any recognition that his being shares any commonality with the Matchseller's. First he attributes any sympathy he might feel for the Matchseller to what the Matchseller feels for him!

> You're shaking with grief. For me. I can't believe it. For my plight. (37)

But instead of confronting the nature of his own "plight," Edward, like Goldberg, retreats into the refuge of asserting his power over another. His very British, masculine stiff-upper-lip response to his perception that the Matchseller is weeping can allow no display of compassion: "Come, come stop it. Be a man." (37) Ironically it is Edward who is having difficulty being a man, being fully human. But like Goldberg, Edward asserts that he himself is in superior health, with "excellent" eyesight as he blames something "in the airs," in the "change of air, the currents obtaining" between him and his object as preventing him from clearly seeing the Matchseller. (38) Edward seems to collapse in exhaustion from the effort of maintaining his veneer of superiority and from his misguided inquiry to the Matchseller, which might have been more profitably directed to himself.

Edward has missed his chance both to know himself and to form a human connection with another through ordinary empathy, and his fall results from choices he makes in defending his difference and his mask.

But Flora succeeds in moving the Matchseller with gentleness where Edward failed by force. Detailing her garden's delights, she entices the Matchseller with promises of seeing her flowers with names laden with sexual connotation: "You must see my japonica, my convolvulus ... my honeysuckle, my clematis." (39) Unlike any previous Pinter character she proposes a mutuality of pleasure: "I want to show you my garden, your garden." (38) She then exchanges the Matchseller for Edward, handing Edward the Matchseller's tray of matches, but is not unsympathetic in her command of the situation as were Goldberg, Bert, or Ben, for she seeks to offer something to a man who might otherwise have been regarded as society's outcast. Moreover she does so only after Edward refuses her favors. Nor is she merely "solicitous" of Edward as Ruby Cohn maintains. (327) Instead, she is throughout more genuinely attuned to Edward's plight and willing to help him than any of Pinter's previous characters were toward another's problem. More important, until the end when Edward proves intractable she remains his ally.

From the first, though Edward obstinately refuses to admit his fear of the Matchseller, ("Of course he's harmless," (16)) Flora understands that her husband is intimidated by the Matchseller's presence at the back gate when Edward admits:

> For two months he's been standing on that spot, do you realize that? Two months. I haven't been able to step outside the back gate. (15)

More important, Flora responds sympathetically to his fear by offering Edward more realistic alternatives to his plight than any previous Pinter character proposed. Several times she counters Edward's request to bring the Matchseller in by suggesting instead they "call the police" to have him removed. (19, 20) And even after she admits the Matchseller into the house, she prudently cautions, "Edward, are you sure it's wise to bother about all this?" (21) But again, Edward refusing her counsel insists on facing him. Even after Edward sees him, then momentarily escapes outside seeking refuge, Flora is still willing to remove the Matchseller herself:

> Is this necessary? I could show him out now. It wouldn't matter. (28)

Only after Edward opposes her counsel, which he takes as a challenge to his manhood ("Me frightened of *him*" (29)), does Flora finally begin to change: to decide, like Edward, to "get to the bottom of it." (30)

Up to this point Edward has rejected not only all Flora's advice, but in his talk with the Matchseller he rejects Flora as well, her sexuality. He tells the Matchseller, "You're no more repulsive than Fanny, the squire's daughter," (27) whom he had earlier described in precisely the same terms he had described Flora when he advised the Matchseller, "Get a good woman to stick by you." (24) Moreover, Flora seems to have been that good woman even up until the time when she tells Edward, "You should trust your wife more." (30)

Edward's seemingly antithetical attitudes to Flora as both desirable and repugnant (like the conflicting attitudes more fully developed in Max's contradictory descriptions of his dead wife Jessie in *The Homecoming*) offer yet another instance of the complexity of Pinter's characters. But Edward tips the balance. It is only after Edward's unremitting rejection of Flora that she dubs the Matchseller Barnabas and prepares to test him as a suitable substitute for Edward.

Barnabas of the Bible means "son of consolation" as Ruby Cohn points out and like Kafka's Barnabas, the only villager admitted to the Castle, this Barnabas "replaces the master of the house and becomes the consolation of its mistress." (372) The name that Flora attributes to the Matchseller further suggests he has more in common with her than Edward does. As Katherine Burkman points out, St.

Barnabas's day in the old style calender was the day of the summer solstice, "while Barnaby-bright is the name for the shortest night of the year." ("Harold Pinter's *A Slight Ache* as Ritual," 333) But if this is a parody of fertility ritual, as Burkman suggests, then the parodic mockery is at base tragic; spring will return each year to the earth but is gone forever from all their lives.

Both Edward's fall and Flora's attempt to recapture the lost love of her youth, perhaps youth itself through the derelict Matchseller, dramatize the inevitably tragic game time plays with living creatures while sounding its *carpe diem* trumpet call to which Flora responds.

What precipitates Edward's fall? Is it simply his time to die, or has the struggle proved too great for him? He raises those same kinds of epistemological questions about what we can know that Gus, Stanley, Rose, Len in *The Dwarfs*, Aston in *The Caretaker* and Disson in *Tea Party* raise but cannot answer, yet Edward has a double edge over all of them as both the character in the dominant position at the outset and possessing more explicitly stated and obvious choices than almost all Pinter's previous and most of his subsequent characters.

Yet it is still possible that had Edward acted differently on Flora's advice the outcome would have been no different if his actions simply unmask already existing qualities. All the possibilities that might account for Edward's collapse remain ambiguously open. But remarkably Pinter evokes through Edward, an initially arrogant, fairly unlikable character, an audience sympathy for the man when he allows us a long intimate look behind the mask to reveal his stance as a subterfuge for fear. Edward's dogged quest to discover the truth about the Matchseller conflicts with his aversion to the truth about himself. That conflict between seeming courage and inner fear invokes audience sympathy even as Edward dramatizes how in shunning truth he disregards responsibility. Isn't his inner struggle between courage and cowardice our own?

But as would-be or surrogate squire his position has moral implications with regard to the Matchseller who may be destitute and whom Edward, by virtue of his position, may therefore have a responsibility to protect rather than destroy. Yet by selecting an adversarial role, Edward ironically is himself destroyed by the man whom it is clear he would rather eliminate than aid. Edward is one of the few, if not the only, initially unsympathetic dominant character in Pinter's plays who is destroyed in the end; yet it is remarkable that by the time he falls the audience has come so close to him that his fall which might have seemed a moral triumph in the first few minutes of the play now gains sympathy.

Is the ending hopeful, an affirmation? Is Flora better off? Her choosing an impoverished, decaying matchseller over her husband, who has revealed himself to be the unworthy opponent of even so frail a chosen adversary, would hardly seem happy. Yet the ambiguity played out through the dense handling of the freshly complex material suggests that the ending is both a negation and an affirmation.

What triumphs is vitality as a primary value in Pinter's ethic and truth, which results from the unmasking of illusion. The silent Matchseller remains the only one of Pinter's characters to triumph with the non-violent tack of total silence. His endurance gains Flora's admiration as an equal. If the morality of friendship, love, and marriage requires that partners remain equals, marriage here is stripped of meaning. Edward, no longer Flora's equal, is exchanged for a decrepit man who may nevertheless be Edward's superior, certainly in endurance. The forces of vitality with their attendant sexuality and strength, clear sight, and action are celebrated here. But there is seldom triumph in Pinter's work without attendant loss. Though Flora and the Matchseller regain the vitality of youth, youth will not come again to them. Edward's life may be draining from him. Yet Pinter for the first time connects a blatant eroticism with vitality which triumphs as a form of poetic justice and of truth over self-delusion.

Notes

1. As Esslin maintains in *The Theatre of the Absurd* (208), Edward, alarmed with the Matchseller whom Flora finds harmless, does not confront himself nor achieve recognition of his inner emptiness (as both Esslin and Burkman [329] maintain). Nor is there evidence that "[i]ndeed, the play moves toward Edward's recognition of his identity with the Matchseller who has come to replace him." (329)

A Night Out: Vitality Vitiated

In sharp contrast to *A Slight Ache's* daylight forces of life, *A Night Out* travels a gloomy exploration of a nether world where entrapment of the self and others results from a stultifying lack of perceived choice. In *A Night Out,* Albert prepares to go out but is restrained by his mother who wants him to put a bulb in the long dead grandmother's room. Albert finally joins his colleagues Seeley and Kedge in a discussion of the office team's Saturday game as it becomes clear that Albert's ranking superior Gidney, the team's coach, is out to get him for his poor playing he blames for the team's Saturday defeat. Later, at the company retirement party for Ryan which Albert resists attending, Albert, unable to match Gidney's favorable impression with the secretaries ends by taking the blame for Ryan's surreptitiously touching Eileen. Ryan's move on Eileen, which may consequently cost Albert his job, sends Albert home where he first transfers his humiliation to his mother by striking her with an alarm clock, then leaves again, meets and humiliates a young woman by exposing her pretense of being a lady with a daughter off at school. When Albert returns home his mother strokes his hand, assuring him he is a good boy.

A Night Out, written and produced in 1960 two years after the revue sketches, remains the only one of Pinter's plays where mystery is wholly absent, all dreams and secrets are revealed, and where battles for dominance are reduced to a son's desperate attempts to gain power over a possessive mother and to assert himself over Gidney, his arrogant superior at work.

Without mystery those who achieve power (the mother, Gidney, and, in a sense, Ryan) like those who do not (the girl and, ultimately, Albert) appear equally pitiful since their motivations, blatantly exposed as stemming from feelings of inadequacy, are further circumscribed within the narrow limits of the lower middle class and white-collar, bureaucratic business world.

But comedy fractally combines with Albert's perceived lack of choice, which is throughout revealed as an attempt to appease or impress those he does not respect. Albert allows his mother, whom he wishes to escape, to treat him like a young boy. Desperately refusing to acknowledge his departure, she communicates only her desire to keep him home:

MOTHER: Cleaning your shoes? I'll have to put the flag out, won't I? What are you looking for?
ALBERT: My tie. The striped one, the blue one.
MOTHER: The bulb's gone in Grandma's room. (8)

The mother's non sequitur here and her "shocked surprise" when she finally exclaims at the end of the beat, "You're going out?" (5) offers one comic touch that lifts the pathos even as she tries to impose her narrow sexual mores on her son. She, like Ryan, is at an age to retire—she from motherhood, Ryan, from the firm—but both attempt to extend their influence by a devious, destructive sexuality: "Are you leading a clean life?" she asks. Albert's denial placates his mother. "Don't be ridiculous," he says, revealing that he is more her son than he may wish to acknowledge. He adds "I don't know any girls," which may be true in several senses. (7) The mother's questions and the son's denial would not be uttered by Flora who asks the Matchseller in *A Slight Ache*, "Does it ever occur to you sex is a very vital experience to other people?" (32)

The only bright light of this play is Seeley, a normative Horatio figure. In conversation alone with Kedge while waiting for Albert to join them to go to Ryan's retirement party, Seeley shields Albert from being made the scapegoat for the team's loss, then later at the party he defends Albert against Gidney's unjust attack. Seeley, the one true friend in Pinter's work, is however powerless but shows an empathy for another character, rare in Pinter's work outside the loyal women in *Mountain Language* and the compassionate doctor in *A Kind of Alaska*.

But before Albert can escape from home his mother must pronounce him a "gentleman" and hangs onto his tie, revealing a blatant sexual attachment. She like Gidney and later the girl he meets all attach narrowly middle-class mores, which they equate with being a good person, believing that those mores define how the "respectable" (30) "gentleman" (13) and "lady" (30) with "breeding" dress and perform. (30, 39)

Kedge opens with a taunt at Albert's not wanting to go to the party: "You frightened Gidney'll be after you, then, because of the game?" (15) Albert, like Stanley, is unable to assert his will to avoid the party; meanwhile his mother, alone at home, plays patience beside a clock.

The party tests the office gamesmanship as Gidney establishes his position as top man over even the senior member of the department, King. When King asserts the merits of bicycling to work, Gidney instantly challenges, "Not so good in the rain." (18) When King then fails to impress Gidney and the women in the office with the fact that he also owns a car, he moves on to the junior colleagues Horne and Barrow with an empty offer intended only to impress them with his boat: "You're quite welcome to come down to my boat at Poole, any weekend—."[1] (23) The level of office politics reduces all to pettiness. Gidney puts Joyce, a secretary, up to embarrassing Albert by asking him to dance, finally revealing that Gidney is little better off than Albert:

> Anyway, I'm thinking of moving on. You stay too long in a place you go daft. After all, with my qualifications I could go anywhere. (22)

"Then why don't you?" Albert asks. (22) Though Gidney answers by repeating his claim and asserting he could be a "professional cricketeer," he concludes "I don't want to." (22) Whatever Gidney's possibilities are compared to Albert's, they are not many. He and the others, save Seeley, position Albert as the even more pathetic scapegoat for their own inadequacies. Ryan's touching Eileen, then allowing the blame to fall on Albert is only the last sad effort of another company man to make his slight presence felt once before he retires.

When Gidney in the guise of gallantry is unable to goad Albert into battle to defend the "lady's" honor, he calls Albert a "mother's boy," which results in Albert's striking him. (30) Albert's violence, like Stanley's, results from utter frustration, but, given Gidney's influence and vehemence, it only further jeopardizes Albert's job.

When Albert returns home only to be accused by his mother of "mucking about with girls," he finally "lunges to the table" and "violently raises" a clock. This action, followed by "a stifled scream from the mother," evokes audience expectation, as Stanley's violence does against Lulu at the birthday party's blackout, that he may have killed her. (33)

Albert seeks refuge with a young woman who, like Lulu, shares many of his mother's affectations. When Albert coughs she says, "Oh please don't do that! Use your handkerchief!" (38) But when she "belches," she excuses it as a hiccough from not eating. She may be starving, and her plight becomes more pitiful as she tries to impress Albert with her notions of "breeding" even as she wonders how "solicitor's wives go out and pick up men when their husbands are out on business!" and is "fascinated" with the question, "How far do men's girlfriends go? I've often wondered." (39) Yet as a prostitute she lacks even the business acumen to conclude the transaction. Twice she says without finishing her sentence or acting: "Yes, I suppose we might as well. . . ." (39)

Albert, also too preoccupied with his problems to follow through, responds only with a freewheeling catalog of his own free associated complaints touched off by her clock which reminds him of his mother. The woman's scolding, "Mind your ash!" her command, "Sit down, sit down," and her final cutting remark, "There's something childish about your face, almost retarded," (42) finally provoke Albert to "hand screw his cigarette out" before he "lets it fall on the carpet," releasing his flood of frustration. "Just because you're a woman you think you can get away with it," (42) he says, followed by an inventory of all his recently suffered injustices: "It's the same business about the light in Grandma's room." (43) Then referring to the secretary he supposedly touched, "You haven't got any breeding. She hadn't either." Responding to Gidney's last insult, "I've got as many qualifications as the next man," he returns to the subject of his mother: "I finished her," (44) yet admits, "I loved her." (44)

That rare admission of love, especially a son's for his mother, is followed almost instantly by an attempt to strip the young woman's desperate sham: the photograph she claims is her daughter away at school is really herself. But the worst ignominy he makes her suffer is to make her put his shoes on him.

His momentary power over her vanishes when Albert returns home to find his mother hurt only because her son raised his hand against her.

The richly complex possibilities that account for character motivation in Pinter's plays which contain mystery are lost here as characters act from accurately perceived but familiar predictable motives that reflect their individual inadequacies. They are all held hostage by class and economic constraints, and ultimately Albert's motivation is shared by all except Seeley. While the play creates some hint of compassion, some understanding of each character, what remains fresh is that the petty quotidian domestic and workplace mores and bullying are unmasked for what they are. But the ethic and the mores are not confused. Even if the two blend inextricably in life, acting like a "lady" or "gentleman" is not equated here with being a good person. Nor is Albert praised for his failure to consummate the seduction with the young woman. What is missing is that vitality in Pinter's former work, even a character in this play who can match Gidney's energy. Albert simply caves in. However much sympathy he evokes, when he transmits his being scapegoated to scapegoating others, he reduces to a sad sack. Even Gidney no more escapes the firm than Albert flees his mother's home. Without well-matched opposition to produce the delight and danger customarily coupled in Pinter's early work, the very tension gained collapses the conflict to a spat, and with it insight dissolves into didacticism. Yet even in its shortcomings, the play adds inventive variety and complexity to the ethic in Pinter's work, though the larger questions of love and justice are stifled whenever vitality is vanquished.

Notes

1. Empty invitations to boats and vacation homes are similarly issued in both *Old Times* and *Party Time.*

The Hothouse: Madness and Violence

Pinter, who eschewed didactic work lacking complexity, attempted "out of irritation" he said, "a play with a satirical point." But he dismissed it as "heavily satirical, and quite useless," because "I never began to like any of the characters, they really didn't live at all. So I discarded the play at once." (Bensky, 361) That play was *The Hothouse.* It would be twenty-one years before he brought the play out and produced it himself. But at the time, cognizant of the importance of characters who are fully alive, Pinter found, "The characters were so purely cardboard," he put the play aside, perhaps wisely for the reception and reputation of his work and his career. (361) Yet when the play was produced, it proved an engrossing, delightfully disturbing play.

The Hothouse remains an aberration for Pinter, his most blatant portrayal of the dominant/subservient theme in any of his full-length plays. Written between *The Birthday Party* and *The Caretaker* the play dramatizes the unhinged responses of a mental hospital administrative staff during Christmas toward unseen patients assigned numbers rather than names. Pinter's compassion comes to play in the portrayal of the staff who are almost equally imprisoned during this holiday. The one affirmative act, the birth of a child by one of the patients (presumably raped by a staff member), is however swiftly countered at the end by the administration's wholesale attack upon the unseen, offstage patients.

The madness that runs from Stanley's catatonic immobility in *The Birthday Party,* Aston's reported madhouse stay in *The Caretaker,* Jerry's threatened catatonia in *Betrayal,* Sarah's bout and recovery from melancholia in *The French Lieutenant's Woman,* to Nicolas the torturer whose mother believes his love of death is mad in *One for the Road* and the sadomasochistic couple who commit lust murder in *Comfort of Strangers* all extend the boundaries between sanity and madness, revealing there are no clear lines.

What could be more crazed than the torture we witness in the recent plays, the slaughter of a child in *One for the Road?* In *The Hothouse* what complicates the question is the lack of boundary between the inmates and staff. Pinter's sympathy for the inmates may have sprung from actual experience. When Pinter was asked about the origin of his fascination with the portrayal of madness, he replied that as a young out-of-work actor he had briefly worked in a mental institution.[1]

Pinter's intention in *The Hothouse*, to present the staff as a collective insane force of destruction, contrasts with patients as agents affirming life, witnessed in the birth of the child. Consistently his work equates madness with depression, despair, and destruction, even when coupled, as in *Betrayal*, with passion.

Despite the distant sympathy *The Hothouse* evokes for the off-stage patients, Pinter takes no romantic view of madness as offering the sufferer superior vision but portrays torment suffered as springing forth to torment others. More important, none of his characters touched by madness or wholly overtaken by it can be fully conscious of their motivation and choices and are therefore robbed of the ability to make fully ethical decisions. Those who are mad, even momentarily so, must struggle so hard to stay afloat they can scarcely attempt to assist anyone else. Because their actions must center on survival they can rarely act or extend influence beyond the private sphere except in destructive capacities.

Pinter saw a connection between *The Hothouse* and *The Caretaker* in "certain features, certain outpourings of wild, bravura which remind me vaguely of Mick [in *The Caretaker*]." (Gussow, "I Started with Two People in Pub," 5) Mick, the only character whose sanity remains largely unquestioned, may be the maddest of them all in his flights of fancy and desperately cruel acts to defend them. All three characters in the end are solipsistically sealed into their own skins, and their inability to form and maintain human contact walls them each into a kind of solitary confinement bordering on madness that permits little action and no influence beyond their private selves.

The Hothouse draws to a close in slaughter and destruction that would find fuller expression in later work. But *The Hothouse* reserves for itself a highly qualified happy ending, which may be another reason Pinter withheld it from production. In an internal uprising the most barbaric of the staff are killed off while the kinder forces remain to tell about it and are cited for bravery. The internal insurrection might have been easily quelled by the superior force of the staff, who have revealed themselves as no less fearful than the powerbrokers subduing the external revolt in *Party Time*, but Pinter allows the anti-erotic forces, Miss Cutts and Roote, to be stabbed in their bed (and makes a point of noting that "bed" is singular). If madness is aligned throughout Pinter's work with forces of repression and destruction, sanity remains an expression of the forces of life and liberty and, as such, informs ethical action. Ultimately, Pinter's portrayal of madness here and throughout dramatizes the individual responsibility to retain what sanity we can if we are to preserve life, to continue to survive, and to thrive as human beings.

Notes

1. Louis Marks, BBC drama director, in an address at the 1991 Pinter Festival.

The Caretaker: Dominance and Subservience Equated—The Human Connection

In *The Caretaker,* Aston, who lives in a dilapidated house in a slummy suburb of London, invites in this play's intruder the tramp Davies, who quickly asserts command of the home till Aston's brother Mick offers Davies the job of caretaker. As a work-shy man Davies refuses and is thus in the end expelled from the last shelter that may be offered to him. As Pinter points out, Aston makes an effort to form a human connection, "When he turns his back at the end, you know he'll never try again." He adds, "You sympathize with both," (Herridge, 9), and that sympathy throws into focus the human relationship. That private attempt to form a private human connection has, in turn, public, ethical repercussions as a basis for any community and action beyond the private level.

Few of Pinter's plays have evoked such a Rorschach test of diverse responses as *The Caretaker,* balanced by Pinter's own quite consistent views about audience and critical response to the three people whom he insists the play is about:

> I've gotten a number of letters I've had to respect about the symbols in this bloody play, but I feel very strongly about the particular, not about symbolism. People watching plays tend to make characters into symbols and put them up on the shelf like fossils. It's a damned sight easier to deal with them that way. (Morgenstern, 4)

Instead, Pinter emphasizes the characters' relationship to one another.[1] Yet more diverse than the critical reaction to the play as a whole is the critical response to the characters who have each been termed sympathetic or menacing by those trying to separate the good guys from the bad. But for any audience searching for and seizing easy labels such as villain or victim, then opting for an either/or interpretation, the great virtue of the play may be lost.

The Chekhovian shifting of sympathies in the characters' relentless battle for power in almost every line offers few resting places as the fractal geometry distributes responsibility for failure in the relationship equally. To conclude that one character is momentarily more sympathetic is not to conclude that the other must, therefore, be unsympathetic. Pinter never intended so simple a response and he details how our sympathies are drawn to both:

> Aston isn't crazy. It's difficult for him but he makes an attempt to be friendly and it just doesn't work …
>
> The tramp in turn, is too suspicious, too selfish to respond. When he finally realizes it's his only chance to escape loneliness, it's too late. You sympathize with both. (Herridge, 9; material in ellipses quoted above)

The Caretaker becomes a play about human connection, about friendship, loneliness, isolation, and distantly, about love. Written in the wake of World War II's supposed post-war affluence when the urban homeless were less omnipresently visible than today, the play speaks to that affluence as a veneer disguising the war's destruction and shows how easily, when connection fails, chaos can come again. Because these characters come so close to forming human alliances, when they cannot their loss becomes ours for reasons Pinter details with subtle brilliance.

Pinter's own experience may account for his sympathetic and complex portrayal of the relationship between the tramp and the two brothers. Pinter had worked as a caretaker, had logged time as an out-of-work actor employed in an asylum, and, like Davies, had taken another name, David Baron, not a far remove from Davies's. While writing the play he was living in Chiswick: his neighbors included an Indian photographer, whom he acknowledged to actor Donald Pleasence as the original for "them Blacks" and two brothers, the older of whom invited in an old tramp later thrown out by the younger brother. (Knowles 1990, 81; 1991, 65) When he wrote *The Caretaker*, "Pinter by now married and with a child on the way, was living at that time in near-destitution as the caretaker of a Notting Hill basement." ("Profile: Playwright on His Own Success," 13) The birth announcement for Pinter's son Daniel in *The Stage* (3 February 1958) lists David Baron as the father.[2] (8)

Pinter equally appreciates Aston's desire to help the vagrant as well as the tramp's aversion to work—his fierce pride and admitted difficulties with his name and identity. When asked if anything in *The Caretaker* had been drawn from actual experience, Pinter replied:

> I'd met quite a few tramps—you know, just in the normal course of events, and I think there was one particular one ... I didn't know him very well, he did most of the talking when I saw him. I bumped into him a few times, and about a year or so afterward he sparked this thing off. (Bensky, 353)

During rehearsals Pinter ran into the man again who was washing up at the Black and White milk bar. (Knowles 1991, 65)

The power in the play comes from raising the stakes in the encounter between Davies and Aston to life-and-death levels:

> At the end of *The Caretaker* there are two people alone in a room, and one of them must go in such a way as to produce a sense of complete separation and finality. I thought originally that the play must end with the violent death of one at the hands of the other. But then I realized, when I got to the point, that the characters as they had grown could never act in this way. ("Harold Pinter Replies," 9).

Pinter thought it might be the tramp who dies violently but concluded that his writing had developed beyond those earlier theatrics:

> The original idea was to end the play with the violent death of the tramp. It suddenly struck me that it was not necessary. And I think that in this play I have developed, that I have no need to use cabaret turns and blackouts and screams in the dark to the extent that I enjoyed using them before. I feel that I can deal, without resorting to that kind of thing, with a human situation. (From an interview with Kenneth Tynan, *Theatre of the Absurd*, 212)

But the tramp's exile may be worse than death: he must now remain forever an outcast, a choice Socrates declined for hemlock. As *The Caretaker* matures in an aging world, it continues to illuminate core failures in human relationships—dramatizing not only how they fail but why.

Written and produced in 1960, the same year *A Night Out* was first presented, Harold Pinter's second full-length produced play, *The Caretaker* contains the most subtle and complex portrayal of Pinter's power struggle to that date. Aston, whose only stated aspiration in life is to build a toolshed, invites Davies into his room but is almost forced out before he finally withdraws his offers of a room, friendship, and job as caretaker, an offer Aston's brother Mick also extends, then withdraws. Davies's initial subservience only briefly conceals his true feistiness, nevertheless a form of vitality which allowed him to survive on the streets but destroys him inside a home. Yet the final dominant position gained by the two brothers who expel him is hardly different from the final subservience of the tramp. While the brothers retain their shelter, their position and the tramp's are equally forms of failure to establish human relationship.

In the play human connection forms the focus of Pinter's ethical concern as both the reason for being and a defining element of justice. Without relationship justice has little value.

The play opens with an act of justice. Aston has just rescued Davies from an unjust attack by others in a pub and extends to Davies the mercy of a room which, however, dissolves into the only on-stage "justice" we witness: Davies's expulsion at the end, synonymous and synchronous with the failure of friendship.

In the shifting relationships between the three men, Aston at first appears to have power over Davies, who at first appears obsequiously grateful but soon becomes diffident and tries to pull rank over Aston by virtually taking over his room. Realizing that he is being pushed out, Aston regains his room but to do so must turn his back upon Davies, a gesture that communicates his failure to make human contact with the man he invited in.

Mick on the other hand, an erratic mix of dominance and subservience, is at first wholly dominant over Davies, terrorizing the old man till he screams. Mick introduces himself to Davies via a strong-arm hold, then frightens Davies by flipping on a vacuum cleaner in the dark, but proffers a kind of friendship by extending a sandwich to him and finally humbles himself before Davies by requesting his counsel:

> Uuh . . . listen . . . can I ask your advice. I mean, you're a man of the world. (48)

But Mick's final rejection of Davies, no less than Aston's, is a show of power that reflects inner failings to sustain a human relationship.

The identity of each character is so protean that it prohibits bonding—what self can another bond with when both are shiftingly slippery? Here the answer to the question, Who am I? becomes even more elusive than in earlier plays. On the surface it is unclear what Mick does, though Pinter when asked replied, "All I know is that whatever he did, he had his own van." (Hewes, 97). Davies confesses to Aston that Bernard Jenkins is an assumed name but insists it is his real name to Mick. Throughout he is anxious to get to Sidcup to get his papers because he exclaims, "They prove who I am!" (19) A name, of course, is not a self. But the name shifts are only symptomatic of deeper identity problems reflecting the illusion and pretense Davies must maintain to avoid realizing that he is a tramp who does probably stink. (70)

At a deeper level the name changes not only display the inadequacy of the outward position to provide an outward identity but also explain why each character fights so fiercely to maintain what he desires. Their desires remain one of the few constants to provide continuity defining who they are. Aston may furnish Davies with shelter and goods, but the compromise, negotiation, and concern for another which might promote affiliation are all absent or simply overwhelmed by desires of the self. Yet the very attempt to secure those desires, when protecting the illusory self, destroys even the possibility of attaining them.

Aston, like Davies and Mick, cherishes illusions about himself. He believes he once had but has now lost clear vision and an ability to talk to other people easily ("I used to get the feeling I could see things . . . very clearly") but adds, "It was . . . but maybe I was wrong." (55) Quickly he covers his own possible error with the conjecture that "some kind of lie must have got around," which precipitated his being committed to an asylum. (55) And while he details his asylum experience at length, monologuing rather than engaging Davies, his discourse is not aimed at discovering truth so much as rehearsing blame he assigns to others for the loss of his true self.

Like Davies, who blames his failure to provide himself with a pair of shoes on others, Aston then blames the doctors and the shock therapy to which his mother consented and which he believes robbed him of his faculties. Electroshock therapy, a primitive therapy then and still not well understood, can produce short-term memory lapses, and some patients, like Aston, report long-term memory loss as well. But while Davies and Aston both center attention in the sad, lost, futureless past, Mick's mania, aside from sentimental childhood remembrances, thrusts him into fantasies about a sparkling future without a past. The men seem grounded in the present only when a contest ensues and the self is threatened, but conflict leads to no productive realization of deeper desires.

Mick's grandiose illusion to transform the slum dwelling into a "penthouse," even a "palace," allows dreams to displace action in the dreary present where he blames Davies for failure to realize his dreams. (60) First casting Davies into the inflated role of a decorator, he confesses his renovation dream for his slum:

> I'd have teal-blue, copper and parchment linoleum squares. I'd have those colours re-echoed in the walls. I'd offset the kitchen units with charcoal-gray worktops. (60)

He suggests, "You could put the dining-room across the landing, see," then launches into raptures over his imagined "armchairs in oatmeal tweed, beech frame settee with a woven sea-grass seat, white topped heat-resistant coffee table, white tile surround." (60) He pictures the bedroom overlaid with the slick magazine, postwar consumer values which hold Mick in thrall. But, having confessed his private dream, he dismisses Davies, accusing him of misrepresenting himself, because he is not an interior decorator who can execute his plan.

Identity, when equated with rank as the basis for relationship, destroys relationship as soon as it is challenged. The relationship between Aston and Davies thrives only so long as Davies responds gratefully to Aston's Samaritan kindness, which, in turn, ratifies Aston's station in the house and positions him over Davies who first appreciatively acknowledges, "If you hadn't come out and stopped that Scotch git, I'd be inside the hospital now" (10) and says he is "grateful" for "a bit of a rest, like . . . for a few minutes." (10–11)

The "few minutes" respite threatens to become permanent even as Davies, unable to abide the submissive role, despite Aston's humility and good intentions, allows his praise and gratitude to transform into insult. Assuming an attitude of superiority to "them Blacks," "Greeks," and "Poles," (8) Davies inflates his image of himself, then imports his arrogance into his attitude that he uses to turn upon Aston: "You think you're better than me you got another think coming." (8)

Communication essential for relationship fails as Davies's further need to assert himself leads him to misunderstand Aston. When Aston confesses he was once approached by a woman who said, "How would you like me to have a look at your body?", (24) Davies misreads Aston's shy discomfort at being the target of a strange woman's advances as a boast which he feels compelled to match: "They've said the same to me." (25)

Davies's only fleeting moment of empathy for Aston dissolves into the final taunt that marks the turning point of the relationship. When Davies proposes they exchange beds, his sympathy is quickly overlaid with insult and an attempt to manipulate Aston. In order to assert his own importance he blunders onto the painful madhouse subject:

> I'll be out of the draught see, I mean you don't mind a bit of wind, you need a bit of air, I understand that, you being in that place that time, with all them doctors and all they done, closed up, I know the places, too hot, you see they're always too hot, I had a peep in one once, nearly suffocated me, so I reckon they'd be the best way out of it, we swap beds. . . . (76)

Aston's simple but direct refusal, "I like sleeping in this bed," anticipates his final expulsion of Davies.

Davies aims directly for Aston's most vulnerable point: "They had you inside one of those places before, they can have you inside again! All they have to do is get the word." (67) When he gloats, "I never been inside a nuthouse!" Davies's taunts only destroy his own chances of remaining in the room.

Even before that fatal taunt Davies rejects Aston's favors in ways which also increasingly eat away at the relationship. Aston, who spends most of his time collecting and repairing junk and who claims he hardly speaks to anyone offers a sort of friendship to Davies whom he also tries to repair and set in working order, offering him a cigarette, a bed and room, money so he can get himself "fixed up," shoes so he can get to Sidcup to claim his papers, clothes, and more shoes. But Davies does not smoke cigarettes (though he accepts the tobacco for his pipe that he never lights), finds the bed draughty, forgets almost at once about the money and asks for more the first morning, rejects the first pair of shoes out of hand without trying them, and though he later accepts the red velvet smoking jacket out of the bundle of clothing Aston buys for him, he refuses the shirt because he says, "I need a kind of shirt with stripes, a good solid shirt with stripes going down." (41) Davies can attend only desultorily to his own welfare as Pinter's comic touches which cut much deeper than their vaudeville origins suggest.

Each of Davies's comically arrogant rejections of Aston's kind offices, from his refusal of the shoes to the shirt, restores Davies's pretensions about himself as much as his acceptance of tobacco for his pipe and the smoking jacket. The comedy could not work if the audience did not form some identification with the tramp. In the tradition which Chaplin entered as a lovable circus tramp/ clown (in stories whose fairy tale endings endorse capitalist comfort and consumption) and which Beckett altered with homeless, vaudeville tramps who fart and never see Godot, Pinter offers a real, destitute tramp who stinks and exudes arrogance but remains nevertheless likable enough. Through the comedy and his simple aspiration to seek shelter and join others in fellowship, we are forced to recognize his pretensions in his attempts to maintain them as our own. But his self-centered inflexibility, prefigured when he rejects the draughty bed, finally destroys him:

> It isn't me has to change, it's that window. (53)

Again the fractal geometry in this smallest beat efficiently telegraphs the source and consequence of conflict at all levels through to Davies's larger rejection (and being rejected) at the end.

Just before Aston returns with a second pair of shoes, Davies turns on his benefactor, registering his litany of complaints against him to his brother Mick. Davies charges, "Couple of week ago . . . he sat there, he give me a long chat," recognizing, "he wasn't talking to me, he don't care about me. He was talking to himself!" (59) Although Davies reads Aston correctly, he fails to see that his accusations aptly apply to himself: "He's got no feelings." (62) With a single exception, the only feelings Davies expresses are for himself.

Aston's arrival with shoes on the heels of Davies's complaint that Aston's jabbering in his sleep wakes him so he has no energy ("And on top of that I ain't got no clock") nullifies Davies's criticism, as it neutralizes his further comic grievance that the shoes have no laces. When Aston produces a pair, Davies complains they are the wrong color: he can't wear black shoes with brown laces. (65)

When Davies does begrudgingly accept Aston's last favor, it is too late.

> I'll tell you what though ... , them shoes ... them shoes you give me ... they're working out all right ... they're all right. Maybe I could ... get ... down ... (78)

By the time he recognizes his ingratitude as a mistake, his last plaintive effort to remain goes unheard.

But Aston, too, lacks a certain sensitivity, and the ending reflects not only the tramp's failure but Aston's as well. Aston's offers, however kind and reasonable, are always on his own terms. Davies, even before he is offered the bed, claims he is "very sensitive to draughts." (11) More important Aston does not offer his guest the room on equal terms or in the spirit of hospitality, nor does he allow discussion about the window he permits Davies to close only once briefly when it rains. What is more, Aston's several confessions reveal more about himself to the stranger than Aston can comfortably live with. When Aston's self-disclosure becomes the target of Davies's taunts, which Aston cannot endure, Aston withdraws from the uncomfortable proximity.

After Aston recounts his madhouse story, his withdrawal from Davies may indicate their mutual discomfort at this intimate disclosure, yet had Davies responded to the story differently, he might have been permitted to stay. Pinter points out that "it isn't necessary to conclude that everything Aston says about his experience in the mental hospital is true." (Bensky, 18). He adds:

> They've so much in common with all of us. It's almost impossible for one person to enter into another's life, don't you agree? When someone tries to share his experiences or disasters with us we listen to them, but always with detachment. And he wants so much more. (Herridge, 9)

Aston, too, lacks sympathetic understanding of the tramp's weaknesses, withdrawing at the end when the old man needs him most.

The characters' actions express a conflicting desire for both intimacy and autonomy, both qualities necessary to relationship, but their failure to strike a balance between them parallels their inability to center between dominance and subservience to attempt to locate any equality necessary for relationship.

Mick's failure occurs for similar reasons to Aston's. While his aloofness to his own brother keeps him at a comfortable, though protective, distance from Aston, Mick's erratic, arbitrary behavior to Davies alternates between violence and friendship. Where Aston uses Davies primarily as a sounding board for his own quandaries, Mick relates to the old man only as he imagines him—as an uncle, a confessor, an advisor, an interior decorator, what Kant would call as a means only rather than as an end.[3] Mick never sees the man himself. Like Aston, Mick, who would rather blame someone other than himself for his inability to realize his dreams, turns on Davies:

> You're the only man I've told, about my dreams, about my deepest wishes, you're the only one, and I told you because I understood you're a first class professional interior and exterior decorator. (72)

Mick's inability to see and accept Davies as the tramp he is reflects his inability to see himself and his dreams for what they are. He may enjoy more worldly success than his brother, may own his own van, and probably holds the deed to the house. But when enraged against Davies because the homeless vagrant is not an interior decorator, Mick gratuitously smashes the Buddha, his brother's one cherished possession and only attempt to decorate the room. Mick's violent rejection of Davies also rejects his brother. That violence, a result of frustration released as anger against Davies, finally reduces Mick to a man less feared than pitied. Mick's erratic violence also shifts audience sympathy to Aston the way seeing a child's favorite toy smashed might. Mick, the only character in *The Caretaker* whose sanity remains largely unquestioned, may be the maddest of them all in his desperately cruel acts to defend his imagined self.

When Aston returns for the last time and discovers his prized Buddha smashed, he has no way of knowing his brother destroyed it. Assuming it was the tramp, Aston turns toward Mick, and the brothers exchange a glance and passing smile, suggesting a bond, however fleeting. Their brief bond extends no friendship to others but erects a wall against the tramp. Aston turns away from Mick, and Mick quickly exits, leaving him alone with the old man. Aston, formerly attached to the clay Buddha, had attempted an attachment with a man but now, like the autistic child in Bruno Bettleheim's "Joey the Mechanical Boy," retreats to his corner to repair a broken electrical plug. The old man he invited in required more than mechanical repairs in his need to be out of the draught, not to be reduced wholly to subservience. Is Aston's rejection of Davies less cruel than the pummeling from which he initially rescued Davies in the pub? When Davies's requirements and demands prove intolerable and Aston turns his back on him, it is a mutual failure to make human contact. But Pinter takes no sentimental view of Davies's departure. When Donald Pleasence asked him how he felt about the old man at the end, Pinter replied, "I think, thank God he got rid of the bastard." (Knowles 1990, 81)

The complex handling of identity and friendship where responsibility for the failure of relationship is almost equally distributed among all three characters represents a clinamen, a slight but decided swerve in Pinter's work. The three characters, on a treadmill of action end as they began but with a terrible finality: for each, a personal failure. Mick will not realize his dreams for renovating his house; Davies can no longer remain in it; Aston may never get his toolshed built. But most important, each fails to form a human connection, and that attempted connection acknowledges the importance of community necessary for further choice and action.

In this play Pinter places the microscope on the private level of human relationship to show once again the inevitable destruction that occurs when self-knowledge is absent, consciousness, unawakened, and characters are driven by a need to supplant any inner identity with an exterior label constructed of illusion. The need to inflate an insubstantial inner self which has implications for the ethical action, revealing that if the basis for human connection is lacking the larger structure will not endure.

NOTES

1. Pinter says, "I have never been conscious of allegorical significance in my plays, either while or after writing. I have never intended any specific religious reference or been conscious of using anything else. 'Mankind caught between the Old Testament God and the New Testament God,' makes no sense whatever to me in relation to *The Caretaker*." (Hewes, 97)
2. Daniel Pinter took his mother's family name, Brand, changing his name to Daniel Brand.
3. Kant's moral injunction is that people ought to treat others as an end, not a means only. (Kant, 91)

Night School: Possible Justice Without Love

Where *The Caretaker* presents the most subtle and complex handling of the ethic that Pinter had yet achieved, *Night School* presents the least. Although it offers a novel take on ethics and criminality, the one-act *Night School* contains one of Pinter's more realistic and stereotypical depictions of the dominant/subservient theme. Walter, a petty forger, returns from a short prison term to reclaim his bed and room in the home of his maiden aunts Annie and Milly, only to discover his claim challenged by the present occupant, Sally Gibbs. While she maintains she is a teacher going to night school, she may work as a nightclub hostess. Walter's attempts to regain his room are ironically successful. By showing Sally's picture to the nightclub owner Solto, who then wins her away from Wally, Wally regains his room. But he loses the woman who has fled.

Pinter felt he was repeating himself in this play which he called "the worst thing" he had written, "slipping into formula," claiming, "The words and ideas had become automatic, redundant. That was the red light for me and I don't feel I shall fall into that pit again." ("Harold Pinter Replies," 7) The dialogue is without resonance, the comic sexual puns are obvious, weak, and serve little purpose beyond themselves. When Wally's aunt Annie serves him a tart with the comment, "I bet you never had a tart in prison, Wally," he returns, "No, I couldn't lay my hands on one." (64)

Pinter's general use of mystery to intensify the illusive identity of each character reduces the question of self-knowledge to superficial roles here, thus eliminating deeper questions of self that form the basis for ethical choice and action in his other plays. Similarly, power plays reduce here simply to everyone's dominance over Wally. But in revisions which subtly, yet rather powerfully improve the play, Pinter increased mystery, strengthened Wally's character to heighten suspense so it is not absolutely certain, as in the original, what the room stands for, nor when someone is lying or telling the truth.

In the revision it is less clear that Wally is attracted to Sally and less likely that Sally would ever return Wally's affection. Perhaps all Wally can really hope to win is his room. But what delivers the play from such a dreary, one-dimensional conclusion is that in the revision it is now just possible that Wally repossesses his room not as a result of his accidental and unfortunate loss of Sally but instead through a carefully calculated removal of her by his private plot which required Solto's successfully winning her away. The revisions instructively reveal Pinter's shift from portraying Wally as victim to focusing on Wally's possible agency and partial responsibility for the outcome of the play.

Pinter's remarkably few revisions—several deft omissions—release Walter from being a merely more comic version of the unfortunate Albert in *A Night Out*, a man who is precisely what he appears to be, without available choices except those that lead to failure. The original television version shows Wally up in Sally's room discovering both Sally's photograph as a nightclub hostess and his post office books (he has just returned from prison for forging such books). While the post office books firmly establish Wally's former and possibly future identity as petty forger and the photograph leaves no doubt as to Sally's evening occupation, the revision without those discoveries opens the possibility that Wally may be the more romantic gunman he describes himself to Sally and that Sally may also be the school teacher she claims to be. The kiss in the original after Sally models for Wally, omitted in revision, removes any evidence of mutual affection between Sally and Wally, making the nature of their relationship more elusive. Sally may or may not care for Wally, may or may not hope he is the romantic gunman he poses as, and may or may not be disappointed to learn from Solto that Wally is only a petty forger. Wally may not really care for Sally but only for himself and his room which he desires to regain. But if he wishes merely to regain his room, as the original portrays, his end is hardly noble, nor are the stakes high.

Yet the increase in the revision's mystery, used chiefly as a technique to increase suspense rather than thematically to amplify character complexity, suggests only that one person may have several identities, or more correctly, several roles. In contrast to earlier plays, identity, here unambiguously reduced to role, encourages the unquestioned equation of role and identity. Where Goldberg's position is dramatized as only a faint representation of his whole identity as a human being, and even minor characters in *The Birthday Party* exhibit interesting complexities, *Night School* distills minor characters like Solto to a single quality or two and explores only the more shallow and less provocative aspects of multiple roles in the main characters.

Solto may be rich or poor. To his tax collector and to Wally who wants to borrow money to "go straight," Solto represents himself as poor. To Sally, whom Solto invites away for a weekend, he represents himself as the wealthy owner of a private beach and a little hut which he says is neither little nor a hut. (83–84) In his relations with Sally, Solto is like Goldberg, possibly Ryan, and others of Pinter's older men who seduce young women through power, assurance, experience, or skill where younger men, such as Wally, Stanley, and Albert fail. But where Albert and Stanley may be unwitting losers, Wally may have calculated his loss to win his room.

Sally may be a school teacher or a nightclub hostess, the only role in which she actually appears, or she may be both. She may leave in the end because she is embarrassed that Wally has discovered her work as a nightclub hostess or because she no longer cares for Wally now that Solto told her Wally is only a petty forger.

Wally may be merely the petty forger he appears and claims to Solto, (68) or he may be, as he tells Sally, an armed robber. (73–75) Wally's roles are less open to multiple interpretation than Sally's and Solto's because most of the evidence seems stacked against interpreting Wally as anything more than an unfortunate, unsuccessful petty bungler.

Interestingly, however, the play presents no ethical injunction against his criminal activity. Written by a man who admittedly enjoyed American gangster films in his adolescence, it may reflect the cinema's glamorizing attitude toward a gunman's power. The maiden aunts' one stroke of comic iconoclastic complexity reinforces that attitude. When they remove Wally from his room, Aunt Milly expresses little respect for Wally's abilities as a criminal, not because his activities might be illegal or wrong, but because Wally is unsuccessful at them:

> Listen, I've told you before, if you're not clever in that way you should try something else, you should open up a little business—you could get the capital from Solto, he'll lend you some money. I mean every time you put your foot outside the door they pick you up, they put you inside. What's the use? (56)

Solto claims to be a better forger than Wally though he himself is no forger at all and advises Wally to quit forging. The message the play conveys is that legitimate business is for failed criminals.

Moreover Sally, like Solto, has no difficulty maintaining the upper hand with Wally. She possesses the room so long as she wants possession and so frightens Wally in their first encounter on the stairway, she throws Wally off balance, stammering backwards away from her.

When Wally later brings a bottle up to Sally, it is more because he needs courage than because he desires her company for a drink, either to initiate a relationship or to offer a conciliatory apology or even to test whether she is the schoolteacher she claims. Only after he gains confidence to speak does he begin to ask her to model for him but gains only momentary authority over Sally when he orders her to cross her legs, stand, and sit, hardly producing tension or a life-threatening conflict. But ironically, Sally is the first of Pinter's characters to gain power not by *resisting* but by *obeying* the command of another: to sit! Here sitting (that familiar act) is for the first time freed from its equation with subservience. Sally executes his orders with such aplomb she reduces Wally's commands to ineffectual foolishness. Does Wally wish merely to gaze at her?

Sally asserts herself, like Flora, as another forerunner of Pinter's strong silent, enigmatic women—Stella in *The Collection*, Ruth in *The Homecoming*, Wendy in *Tea Party* and Jane in *The Basement*—who quietly and without seeming effort gain power over those who wish to dominate them.

When Wally reclaims his room in the end, finding the photograph which Sally leaves of herself as a teacher, the discovery simultaneously answers Wally's inquiry about her and communicates her rejection of him. Yet, because there are no final directions to indicate Wally's response to Sally's sudden departure, it is impossible to determine with certainty whether he is saddened by the loss or secretly gleeful. He may in fact simply be happy to have his room back. What he says cuts both ways. When Milly observes, "It looks as though she's gone for good," Wally merely replies, "Yes," then after a pause adds, "That's what it looks like." (88)

Without stage direction, Wally's deadpan response reinforces the indication that he actually tried to get rid of Sally by the devious route of Solto, that he knew Solto would invite Sally away so that he could recover his room, thus making him far more clever than the mere victim of chance he appears. But whether Wally regains his room by accident or by design, he gains a physical victory at the expense of a moral defeat: he loses the woman and any possibility of love or friendship. The question of justice only incidentally enters into the final action and only if we assume Wally recovers his room by a cleverly convoluted subterfuge.

Yet what is also fresh is Pinter's disregard for Wally's crimes or misdemeanors, his disassociation of the law and justice from the ethic. Cicero said, "The law is but a faint representation of perfect justice," and Talmudic law would not regard Wally's thievery as criminal or a sin but as a tort to be addressed through a retributive justice that would require Wally to repay what he stole rather than to serve a sentence. Pinter's larger concern is with success and failure, endorsing success in a chosen field and denigrating failure even in crime. But even this potentially intriguing spin on the topic develops without resonance because without character complexity there can be no depth charge.

If developing consciousness, a knowledge of self, and an awareness and caring for others are inextricably wed in Pinter's work to how one acts, how that action is interpreted and evaluated by other characters and audience, then most of his subservient characters have only a limited access to developed consciousness and the dominant characters, even less. But in this play characters are not even supplied with a nascent consciousness of self or others, aside from Milly's and Solto's observations and assessment of Wally's criminal talents. While in Pinter's other plays the authorial vision supplies what is lacking and the audience is made to feel what is missing via sympathy and concern for the characters, this work remains a two-dimensional play rather than fully developed drama.

As in *A Night Out*, his other play where for a moment a master relents, *Night School* bears close reading. Here the fractal geometry and the ethic converge in a double irony. Each beat of the play seems driven by everyone's desire to direct or to overpower

Wally until, ironically, Wally gets what he wants—his room—becoming the first of Pinter's seeming victims threatened with the loss of shelter to regain it unequivocally. That shelter, as a basic need, provides the base for gaining any other success, even if, as in Wally's case, the success is ironically likely to be illegal. Hereafter in Pinter's work the threatened loss of a physical shelter lessens as emphasis shifts elsewhere to focus on the self. But even here we can see the function of ambiguity upon individual attitude, intention and action. If we can assume that the perception of Wally as a failure (as he is as perceived by others) may be erroneous, that he regains his room by design, then possibly his own attitude, intention, and action may be other than they seem, and the audience is thrown back into the play to look again, to revise first conclusions, and credit him with volition and ethical choice in his action which reclaims what belongs to him.

The Dwarfs: Dominance as Betrayal

The 1963 stage version of *The Dwarfs*, a one-act which derives from a 1960 radio version adapted from Pinter's first and only novel written from 1952 to 1956 but not published till 1990, swings to the other extreme from *Night School* as the least realistic, most stream-of-consciousness of Pinter's plays. It places ethical emphasis on the most private portion of the self: the nature of inner identity as a basis for action. The play, an inward journey to that private self through the character Len, returns to the outward world of action to dramatize the need for some balance between those two worlds. Len, a train station porter, and two boyhood friends Pete, an accountant, and Mark, an actor, meet to discuss subjects ranging from their close friendship to the church. When Len reveals he sees dwarfs, Pete confesses to nightmares. But Len, in his quest for verification and truth, betrays Pete to Mark. In doing so he destroys the friendship, rids himself of his imagined dwarfs, but also possibly exiles himself to a sanitized reality of mundane order.

Pinter viewed the play as about "betrayal," a defining strategy for maintaining dominance here, which, however, loses for the characters what they most hope to annex to the self: friendship or love from another. Betrayal enters when one character does not share and sustain another character's illusions of the self. In *The Dwarfs* both the causes for betrayal and the resultant loss of friendship with its obvious moral dimensions seem almost wholly negative, yet betrayal may inevitably occur in a triangle where characters seek dominance no matter what actions are taken. But betraying another, a friend in this play also betrays the self, not in the commonly held sense where a friend is defined as another self, but the self proper. Each loses what he most seeks in the fractal geometry of the conflict. But one character, Len, breaks free of the conflict at the end.

The play omits much of the novel's biographical material, long conversational essays that pay homage, through imitation, to Joyce's portmanteau words and free associative language. The play also deletes Virginia, Len's girlfriend, who, as he increasingly shuns her, turns to the more sympathetic Mark. Len initiates this play's betrayal, but Len's loss of his friends at the end in both the novel and play is palpable. Yet Len may gain a clarity of vision which permits him greater interaction in the concrete world around him. Len also struggles to know himself. In doing so he now sets the stage among Pinter's characters for the merging of the conflict with the consciousness necessary to develop an ethic in the larger world.

In stark contrast to *Night School*, where identity is dramatized superficially as mere role, *The Dwarfs* seems to be Pinter's last attempt to date to explore identity as essence. "The essence" of identity may be non-existent or, as Len argues, indistinguishable from "the scum." Where Len tries to dismiss the notion that identity is equivalent to one's "reflection" in the eyes of others, in later plays like *The Homecoming,* identity will re-emerge largely as it is perceived by other characters as exterior role, illusion, reflection and in *The Lover*, as deliberate pretense.

The central character Len in *The Dwarfs* permits us private access to his fantasies, fears, and hallucinations far more fully than any other Pinter character can or does. The most sensitive of the three characters, Len seems to have a heightened sense of reality which transforms into a heightened imaginary life inhabited by dwarfs whom Len temporarily joins:

> I've not been able to pay a subscription but they've consented to take me into their gang, on a short term basis. I won't stay long. (94)

Like a small child, or an artist without an art, Len lacks the ability to abstract, to organize, or to gain distance on the empirical data that bombards his senses. As Pete says, Len may also lack the ability to distinguish between the real and imaginary:

> You've got no idea how to preserve a distance between you and what you smell and what you think about. You haven't got the faculty for making simple distinctions between one thing and another. Everytime you walk out of this door you go straight over a cliff. (93)

Pete encourages Len to "nourish the power of assessment," admonishing him, "How can you hope to assess and verify anything if you walk about with your nose stuck between your feet all day?" (93) But Pete and Mark are hardly superior for their powers of assessment, which Len describes as a reductive, pigeonholing mentality: "You've got me pinned to the wall before I can open my mouth." (99) His echo of Prufrock's complaint that others have him "pinned and wriggling on the wall" (Eliot, 5) suggests that others view him (and perhaps we view one another much of the time) through the diminishing, judgmental lens of a label.

Len, interpreted in a wide variety of ways, both claims and denies a hole-in-the-side (drawing critics to label Len a Christ figure, which Pinter says he did not intend, (Hewes, 97)) and his illness, interpreted as everything from kidney infection to appendicitis and psychosis has drawn diverse speculative interpretation, all leading away from the play's focus on reality and the difficulty of maintaining balance between the inner and outer identity.

Appreciating the play centers on at least three questions that cannot be easily answered. Is Len mad or sane but possessing a heightened, perhaps superior, awareness? Does Len change? If so, for the better, entering a world in which there is a flower, or for the worse, shunted off to a bare and sterile reality stripped of dwarfs, but also without value? Or are both worlds imaginary? There are, of course, other difficulties resulting from the incomplete translation of the private world in the novel to the private world of the play, and Pinter knows that much that is missing is not communicated in the play:

> From my point of view, the general delirium and states of mind and reactions and relationships in the play—although terribly sparse—are clear to me. I know all the things that aren't said, and the way the characters actually look at each other, and what they mean by looking at each other. (Bensky, 357)

The play does successfully communicate the central issues, not the difficult unanswered questions, but emphasis on the illusive qualities of reality, each character's identity, and as Pinter notes, the resultant "betrayal and distrust."

Betrayal becomes the form that the assertion of dominance assumes in this play. Mark and Pete betray one another to bolster themselves against their inherent limitations. Lacking Len's imaginative perception of reality, both young men separately vie for Len's friendship. First Pete, then Mark, play Len off against the other. Pete tells Len, "You knock around with Mark too much. He can't do you any good." (93) Mark later echoes, "You spend too much time with Pete." (95) But in the natural tension of a triangle, Pete claims *only* he knows "how to handle" Mark, and Mark, that *only* he can "get on with" Pete. Each wishes to position himself as "the only one" in his relationship with the other, understandable enough but impossible within a triangle.

Len, perhaps realizing that his relationship with Mark and Pete is nearing an end, unconsciously or deliberately betrays Pete to Mark by telling Mark that Pete, whom Mark idolized, thinks him a fool. Their individual limitations—their distrust of one another and their illusions about themselves—do not permit them to nurture and sustain the more difficult triangular relationship of equals let alone repair Len's damage.

The three characters' betrayal of each other results in the isolation of each and the breakdown of their friendship, which is at first quite close. In the end they are severed from one another with the same finality that closed *The Caretaker*. But their separate views of reality and, by extension, the self are in conflict.

Len, the main spokesman for the view that all reality is illusive, seems preoccupied with the subject which on the surface merely denotes a natural desire for verification but on a deeper level signifies first an avoidance then perhaps a recognition of his own morality which he first refuses to confront. Attributing mutability to everything except himself allows Len to perceive himself as a fixed and immutable center:

> Things do change. But I'm the same. (86)

His remark, like Goldberg's assertion that he never lost a tooth, (77) signals his deepest unspoken fear (he is mutable, therefore mortal, and will die). But instead of stepping away from the abyss, Len first grounds himself in the immediate reality around him, moving inward from those things just outside himself ("There is my table. There is my chair") to a close up on something attached to him, his shoes, and finally to himself, his feet. As Len plays with words trying to discover their relation to the reality they signify, his focus moves interiorly finally entering his own mind with an "I'm-me" self-recognition.

But empirical reality remains in a flux, like the hallucinatory movement of a Van Gogh painting where molecules and the systems they compose seem scintillatingly alive, but as frequently experienced on an LSD trip, he crashes to a dead halt, yet he continues to see himself as fixed:

> This is a journey and an ambush. This is the centre of the cold, a halt to the journey and no ambush. (88)

He concludes:

> I have my compartment. I am wedged. Here is my arrangement, and my kingdom. There are no voices. They make no hole in my side. (88–9)

Others may change, yet Len still insists he remains fixed. When he says of Mark, "Of course he may have changed," he again implies that he himself has not. (86) The dwarfs in Len's world remain an interior analog of other people, specifically of Pete and Mark. When Pete and Mark leave, Len says "They've gone on a picnic." (98) Only later does it become clear that Len is referring to the dwarfs; the momentary conflation of Pete and Mark with the dwarfs is enough to establish a connection between them.

Len's physical illness leads him closer to the recognition of his mortality that is essential for self-knowledge. When Mark returns, Len admits that he, too, may change, but with that recognition comes his simultaneous realization that his relationship with Mark and Pete is over:

> Both of you bastards, you've made a hole in my side, I can't plug it! [*Pause*] I've lost a kingdom. (99)

After Mark exits, he has lost his world of friends. Len next imagines Mark alone in his own home watching himself:

> Mark sits by the fireside. Crosses his legs. His fingers wear a ring. (102)

As Len's imaginary camera eye dollies in, he projects his own essential aloneness upon Mark, but the real bond between them remains broken as communion and communication are now limited to imagination, the place formerly reserved for his dwarfs. Watching Mark watch himself, Len concludes Mark "[s]ees himself speaking, the words arranged on his lips, sees himself with pleasure." (102) That disassociation or standing apart from one's own life is implied in many of Pinter's other characters such as Goldberg, in *The Birthday Party*, Edward in *A Slight Ache* and Disson in *Tea Party*, but all remain without the self-reflective knowledge Len gains.

Len's quest for identity leads him to conclude that it is after all impossible to know who you are and that all reality is illusive, echoing again Pinter's assertion, "A moment is sucked away and distorted, often even at the time of its birth." Len dismisses the possibility that identity is equivalent to role, "what you are," or to what you or others imagine or recall you are:

> The point is, who are you? Not why or how, not even what. I can see what, perhaps, clearly enough. But who are you? It's no use saying you know who you are just because you tell me you can fit your particular key into a particular slot, which will only receive your particular key because that's not foolproof and certainly not conclusive. . . . Occasionally I believe I perceive a little of what you are but that's pure accident on both our parts, the perceived and the perceiver. It's nothing like accident, it's deliberate, it's joint pretense. (104-5; ellipses mine)

Len however also must concede that the "joint pretense" of a constructed identity is nevertheless indispensable to existence and human community:

> We depend on these accidents, these contrived accidents to continue. It's not important then that it's conspiracy or hallucination. What you are, or appear to be to me, or appear to be to you, changes so quickly, so horrifyingly, I certainly can't keep up with it and I'm damn sure you can't either. (120)

He concludes with the question: "What scum does the tide leave?" and answers with a question: "What have I seen, the scum or the essence?" (105)

In this play Pinter deploys an outrider to explore the outer boundaries of the solitary life of the mind, the spirit, psyche and imagination in a quest for answers about the nature of identity. Len ends in striking some balance between that interior life and the life of action in the outside world when he discovers one cannot live at the edge too long without experiencing that dizzying vertigo, that magnetic attraction and pull to leap into the abyss of solipsism.

Len chooses to return to reality. Not till *Landscape* and *Silence* will Pinter again so fully probe the interior of the mind. But next time the questions are different. Where *Landscape* and *Silence* explore memory's function in the formation of who one is in the present, *The Dwarfs* questions the very essence and nature of identity.

Once Len draws his conclusion, he acts. He has gone as far as he can go. He observes the leavings of the dwarfs, then returns to the world of reality as it is generally perceived, and he names what he sees: a shrub and a flower. He does not impose an ideal nor does he accept received attitudes about an integrated identity or fixed reality. He simply grounds himself in the present reality of everyday objects. And that is enough.

Len's values, like Pinter's throughout, seem akin to Keats's theory of negative capability, in which, without imposing an ideal by which reality is measured, it is enough that something exists, simply is. The late director Alan Schneider once said that all contemporary drama is about the impossibility of living with illusions. And the impossibility of living without illusions. Pinter does not seek to impose ideals or illusions upon his work. He may wish human beings better, more conscious, kinder, but he does not ignore the mystery, the flux, the unknowable. Nor does he gloss over the dark side in all human beings or fail to confront it. If, as Jung contends, to ignore the dark side is to be ruled or even destroyed by it, then the mirror Pinter holds up to life allows us to see ourselves with a wholeness rarely offered by Western playwrights since the classical Greeks.

These young men, captured in that rapid-growth, liminal state between boyhood and manhood, shed their childhood adolescent identities like snake skins as they enter responsible adulthood. In any change something is lost, something else, gained, and here the youthful, unselfconscious camaraderie is gone forever, a loss that remains felt after the play's close. Yet the choices Len makes do not seem to imprison him in a confining solipsism but allow him to move out into the world beyond himself.

The Servant: Paradigmatic Powerplays

In 1962, between *The Collection* and *The Lover*, Pinter wrote his first screenplay, *The Servant*, his baldest evocation of the dominant/ subservient conflict which, more closely than any other screenplay, resembles the paradigmatic portrayal of that conflict fractally conveyed in *The Dumb Waiter* and *The Birthday Party*. After *The Servant* the Pinter screenplays generally marked a respite from the strict fractal geometry of the dominant/subservient conflict, but here that conflict assumes full force. In *The Servant*, adapted from the novel by Robin Maugham and directed by Joseph Losey, Tony, a young bachelor of independent means, hires Barrett as his butler. Barrett then usurps Tony's position as master by fostering Tony's total dependence and bringing in as a maid his own lover, Vera, who poses as Barrett's sister to win Tony's affection from his fiancee, Susan.

Although Barrett is among the most sinister and diabolical of all Pinter's characters, Pinter marks the film with that exceptional sympathy he extends to almost all his characters to allow appreciation for the thwarted intelligence and passion of the man placed by his underclass birth in a servant's role as well as for the privileged but guileless young man whose position and seeming soul his servant usurps.

In this, as in later screenplays, Pinter takes the focus of a current concern, identity, and pushes it to a new level. Justice remains a purely private matter, while the erotic, as a force of dependence rather than independence, becomes a destructive power. Tony's destruction dramatizes the loss of self to which one can be lead as a result of erotic desires. *The Servant* dramatizes the very real interchangeability of servant and master in that already familiar chiasmic reversal which here tracks the process of exchange and explodes much that is myth about inherent identity. When

Barrett and Tony reverse roles in the end, nothing in Tony's position protects him against Barrett, and nothing in Barrett's inherited station prevents him from becoming master.

The Collection and *The Lover*: Identity Gained by Deliberate Pretense

Like *The Dwarfs*, both *The Collection* and *The Lover*, which were frequently staged as a double bill, continue to attempt to verify the illusive qualities of identity, but unlike *The Dwarfs* both plays involve deliberate pretense which intensifies problems of verification that determine choice and action. Stella in *The Collection* tells her husband James she slept with Bill, then denies that she did, refusing to say more, while Richard in *The Lover* pretends to be Max, his wife Sarah's lover. The characters in these plays have developed a consciousness of self Pinter's earlier characters rarely display, and they cleverly employ that consciousness and wit to gain what they want from another. The deliberately assumed guises here again expose each character's role as but a faint representation of larger identity, but these plays go further in realizing ethical dimensions within the questions of identity.

The simple act of lying about who one is or what one has done raises one moral question which produces its own resonance. But what becomes more important than the truth or falsity perpetuated are the reasons for the lie. Moreover, by clothing the precise nature of truth in mystery (we never learn whether Stella slept with Bill or whether Sarah has a real lover), Pinter throws into the forefront the larger importance of love where the question of what is love becomes implicitly linked to ethical questions involved in telling the truth as well as justifications for lying.

The Collection

The Collection depicts a self-appointed protagonist-intruder, James, as a husband trying to discover the truth behind his wife Stella's confessed affair with Bill at a recent out-of-town clothing convention. But James's task of uncovering the truth is frustrated when he intrudes upon Bill only to discover that Bill is gay and living with his lover Harry. That discovery furnishes neither refutation nor certainty about his wife's confession but leaves the question unanswered.

Pinter saw the play as "about a woman alone in an alien world of men and her keeping to herself her secret—which is that she is terribly lonely." (Zolotow, 3) Her loneliness remains unmitigated by her ineffectual husband's eventual humiliation and his inability to discover the truth. His quest for verification deflects the real question which is never posed to his wife: Do you love me?

Pinter's portrayal of love here embraces passion and the erotic in some measure but largely as an issue discussed and remembered rather than an act realized in the present. Where James initially seeks affirmation of his wife's love or at least her fidelity, the goal soon shifts to a desire to win Bill's respect and admiration.

But when James's frustration at the unanswered questions hits an impasse, like Stanley and Albert, he strikes the first blow. His violence, in turn, provokes Bill's verbal slap, which surpasses James's mere physical attack. Bill says:

> Every woman is bound to have an outburst of . . . wild sensuality at one time or another. That's the way I look at it, anyway. It's part of their nature. Even though it may be the kind of sensuality of which you yourself have never been the fortunate recipient. (74)

The erotic elements and the quest for the truth that will eventually merge to couple love and justice in Pinter's later work fully announces itself in these two early plays. Here questions of identity couple with the erotic at the private level to form the basis for all other choice and action in the larger world of the characters.

In both *The Collection* and *The Lover* characters deploy deliberate identity shifts to gain an advantage over another and to prove self-worth in order to stem a sense of inadequacy, insecurity, or pain. Even before *The Collection* begins Stella may have fabricated her story that she slept with Bill in order to provoke or to re-engage her husband's attention and affection. James, too, as his erratic behavior and challenge to Bill indicate, initially seeks Bill out because he is hurt by his wife's confessed infidelity:

> When you treat my wife like a whore, then I think I'm entitled to know what you've got to say about it. (54)

James's desire for revenge also motivates his aggression against Bill, which begins when he sets Bill up by complimenting him: "You're a wag, aren't you" (56) and "I'll bet you're a wow at parties." (57) He then shoves Bill to a position below mere sitting, startling Bill backwards down onto the floor, threatening:

> Tell me the truth from there. (58)

But Bill transforms his humiliating position to advantage as a weapon. Although Bill has consistently maintained he did not sleep with Stella, he now imports an allusion to his forced recumbent position on the floor as revenge to correct James. When James says he knows Bill was sitting on the bed beside his wife when James telephoned her in Leeds, Bill replies:

> Not sitting. Lying. (59)

Bill's lover Harry, meanwhile, whose jealousy is aroused by James, reveals similar impetus for his aggression when he reports that someone stopped by, probably James, describing him in grotesque terms:

> Oh . . . lemon hair, nigger brown teeth, wooden leg, bottle green eyes and a toupee. Know him? (62)

Though the description could hardly fit the young husband, it dramatizes another aspect of the nature of identity and its relationship to language; here words form no connection to the subject. Yet quite clearly it is James to whom Harry alludes. Harry's denigrating description communicates quite precisely both James as the subject and Harry's attitude toward James as a perceived threat, the proof of which comes not in Bill's acknowledging the truth but in denying it so vehemently. But Harry, as an older, slighter wiser man chooses to discontinue engaging in pretense and states directly:

> I don't like strangers coming into my house without an invitation. (63)

James, returning briefly to Stella, wishes his wife to believe that he is not at all hurt by her alleged infidelity. Language is employed to convey connotations opposite its denotative value. James coolly thanks his wife for giving him the opportunity to meet Bill, with whom he claims he had dinner—another lie:

> No, really, I think I should thank you, rather than anything else. After two years of marriage it looks as though, by accident, you've opened up a whole new world for me. (67)

That closing *double entendre* leads into a virtual exchange of partners in the next two scenes where objects carry sexual connotations—Harry goes to James's home and strokes the white kitten in Stella's lap, while Bill forces a cheese knife on James—only to convey the failure of any real sexual exchange. When Harry says, "Oh, what a beautiful kitten, what a really beautiful kitten," (72) Pinter, directing the play with Michael Hordan as Harry, indicates his intention that these lines convey a meaning quite opposite the literally stated:

> Michael, you see it's not your taste at all. The whole thing's horrid. (Zolotow, 3)

Harry, of course, prefers men.

James is similarly reluctant to touch a cheese knife which Bill then presses on him upon him:

> Try it. Hold the blade. It won't cut you. Not if you handle it properly. Not if you grasp it firmly up to the hilt. (73)

When Bill challenges James, "What are you frightened of?" James free associates from this phallic object to his wife's supposed infidelity: "I'm not frightened. I was just thinking of the thunder last week, when you and my wife were in Leeds." (73) He finally challenges Bill to a mock duel and seizing both available cheese knives, throws one at Bill and cuts him. James's worst violence follows in direct response to Bill's provocative "Every woman is bound to have an outburst of . . . wild sensuality" speech.

If Stella, in stirring her husband's jealousy intends to regain a hold on him, initially her plan fails because James is, or claims to be attracted to Bill, "wowed" by the belief that Bill is the wealthy owner of his home and the impressive collection of vases, both in fact belonging to Harry. Bill's own insecurity allows, even encourages James's error. Moreover James arouses Harry's jealousy, a fear of losing Bill which becomes apparent when Harry attempts to humiliate Bill before James to disengage James's obvious admiration for Bill:

> Bill's a slum boy, you see, he's got a slum sense of humor. That's why I never take him along with me to parties. . . . That's what Bill is. There's something faintly putrid about him, don't you find? (78; ellipses mine)

For James the sudden realization that Harry, not Bill, owns the house and collection and that Bill may be a "slum boy" is enough to override whatever budding feelings he may have for Bill. When James abruptly departs, it is fairly clear he will not return again.

Rejoining or rather retreating to his wife, James returns to his initial unverified position. Stella seems to possess the upper hand, without, however, gaining her husband's affection as she leaves James's question unanswered:

> You just sat there and talked about what you would do, if you went to your room. That's what you did.
> [*Pause*]
> Didn't you?
> [*Pause*]
> That's the truth . . . isn't it? (79–80)

Mystery, Stella's only trump card, remains her only power. The title *The Collection* is a three-way reference leading directly to questions of love and justice. The collection initially refers to the clothing collection at the convention where Stella meets Bill, but equally, later to Harry's collection of vases displayed in his home along with his slum boy who is not fit to display at parties out of the house. Harry's jealousy of James is impelled less by any love for Bill than a desire to continue to possess him as a kept creature among his collection of possessions. Stella seems similarly kept and valued by James whose jealousy is prompted less out of desire, admiration, or love than fear of losing a possession. *The Collection* defines itself by what is missing in all the relationships—any evidence of love. Without love the desire for justice, in this case the simple truth and the retribution James seeks, becomes almost inconsequential. Pinter pursues his exploration of love as a basis for justice at the private level of marriage in *The Lover.*

The Lover

The Lover opens when Richard, leaving for work, asks his wife Sarah if her lover is coming today. Instead of the expected lover, first the milkman appears, making advances she repels, then Richard arrives in the guise of the lover Max dressed in leather jacket. Rather than confront and risk exposing the fiction they are almost unable to regain in the end, Richard, addressing his wife as "You lovely whore," falls back, like Goldberg and others, on ordering her about, insisting that his wife change her clothes. His command to "Change" requires her to be equally responsible for the habits that have deadened the relationship.

In *The Collection* and *The Lover,* the necessity of reintroducing the erotic into a love relationship to connect the lovers as well as to reconnect the individuals through their relationship or marriage to the larger world is germane to understanding Pinter's fusing of love and justice in his recent work culminating in *Moonlight.* In *The Lover,* however, all questions remain sealed into the private world.

In *The Lover* Sarah and Richard deftly play a game of continually shifting pretense which Richard generally dominates by initiating most of the change, but he wants in Sarah a strong, not merely passive partner. He leads Sarah like a dancer, insisting she change the step as soon as the old one becomes pat, and Sarah's ability to follow his lead, to be all women to him, rarely falters. Near the end she surpasses Richard by taking the lead when Richard [illegible] not seem to know what he wants.

Richard initiates the game, then continues it when he returns from work and inquires whether Sarah's lover has come. (7) But Richard seems to find the subject in and of itself less provocative than necessary to hold his erotic interest, and so, on the offensive he introduces an apparently new attitude toward his wife's supposed infidelity:

> Does it ever occur to you that while you're spending the afternoon being unfaithful to me I'm sitting at a desk going through balance sheets and graphs? (9)

Unperturbed and remarkably undefensive, Sarah remarks that she occasionally thinks of him. When Richard then asks whether she thought of him this afternoon, Sarah assumes the offensive replying that the picture "wasn't a terribly convincing one." When Richard asks why not, she answers:

> Because I knew you weren't there. I knew you were with your mistress. (11)

Sarah's introducing Richard's mistress provokes Richard's denial: that she is not a mistress but a whore who lacks the grace, elegance, and wit of his wife. But he admits, tipping the scales, she does "engender lust with all its cunning." (13) When Sarah inquires about dignity, he replies, "The dignity is in my marriage." (11) When Sarah inquires why he even looked elsewhere, he declares, "You did." (14) His retort is ambiguous enough to suggest that the game may have begun in response to Sarah's having taken a real lover but might equally refer to his own incarnation as Max.

Talk about lovers provides the nexus of Sarah and Richard's after hours and bedtime activity, which remains unaccompanied by any display of affection. The bedroom scene ends with Sarah's seeking Richard's assurance that he is not jealous, a subject introduced to provoke precisely that. Sarah's adding, "Good, because I think things are beautifully balanced," also only heightens awareness of the opposite. (17)

Balance is not, however, what Richard seeks. In the dynamic of this relationship (and of drama), Richard's next several attempts to upend the balance are fairly well matched by Sarah's meeting or besting his challenge.

The next afternoon when John the real milkman comes and tries to press Sarah into buying cream, she coldly refuses. The brief scene, included in part so that the cast list contains two men's names, postpones the knowledge and the surprise that Richard is Sarah's lover. More important, the second man also reveals how Sarah behaves with a an actual and potential lover, the proverbial milkman—she wants no part of him or his offer of cream.

As soon as the milkman leaves, Richard appears as Max, and together he and Sarah play a bongo drum in what may be intended to symbolize actual love making or may reveal literally that their relationship as lovers is as devoid of love making as is their marriage witnessed in the bedroom scene.

The actions after the bongo scene suggest both afterplay, in the post-coital cigarette, and again foreplay, when Max pursues Sarah who now shyly withdraws exclaiming: "I'm waiting for my husband!" (21)

Following Sarah's lead, tables turn as Richard-turned-Max, switches into the role of the kindly park-keeper come to rescue her from the clutches of Max.

To keep the relationship in motion Sarah drops her reserve and turns aggressively on him as "her fingers trace his thigh," and he "lifts them off." (22) Richard, as park-keeper and now the shy one, repels her: "Look now, I'm sorry, I'm married," only provoking Sarah's aggression until Max, almost cornered, regains the advantage by switching roles. (22) He calls her Dolores.

But again Sarah returns his serve, not with further aggression but its opposite. She becomes reticent yet also admits the deeper truth, within the bounds of the game: "Trapped! I'm a married woman. You can't treat me like this." (23) Again Max calls a switch as he calls her Mary. She responds, not sensually as in the earlier bongo drum scene but, "She grits her teeth," as Max advances and draws her out of audience sight behind the table.

Perhaps having exhausted his routine of possible combinations, Max now tells Sarah that he is terminating the affair because his wife would object if she knew. He says, however, he would first like to see Sarah's husband because he is a man and, he complains, "You're just a bloody woman." (27) He then claims, "You're too bony." (28)

Perhaps like James, Richard thinks he might prefer a man to a woman, or would like some androgynous combination of both:

> You know what I like. I like enormous women. Like bullocks with udders. Vast great uddered bullocks. (28)

But Sarah, unable or unwilling to attempt this new role, retaliates against his attack upon the givens of her body structure by announcing she has no dinner ready when Richard next returns home from work.

He accuses her of "falling down" in her "wifely duties," action he finds consistent with her "debauchery." (32-33) Assuming the offense with a business-like paternal tone, he forbids her to entertain her lover. Sarah falters in her first attempt to redeem herself by apology, admitting that she does after all have dinner ready: "Boeuf bourguignon." (36) In Pinter's early work the only fatal error is assuming the defense rather than the offense.

Assuming a subservient position only intensifies an attacker's fury. Incensed and disengaged, Richard angrily whispers, "adulteress." (36) He reengages when he finds the bongo drums, evidence of Sarah's infidelity, but Sarah cunningly checks his mounting aggression as she turns on him with one last surprise:

> Do you think he's the only one who comes! (37)

Her sudden move catapults them beyond the bounds of the game. While she may be bluffing, referring only to Richard in his multiple roles as Max, park-keeper and, presumably, others, her obvious, intended meaning is that she has a real lover.

She details her activities with other men she claims come for tea and to whom she offers strawberries and cream, an echo of the milkman's offer. Her conflation of fact and fancy, like Meg's confabulated description of Stanley's career, would seem to indicate she has no lover. Yet Richard follows her lead as if it were truth and together they begin slipping back into their afternoon roles as Sarah asks: "Would you like me to change my clothes? I'll change for you, darling." (40) Her offer signals the beginning of the end. Having checked his advancing offensive, she can afford a mock groveling stance.

By occasionally initiating change in order to preserve the relationship, Sarah can at other times accept a subservient role without losing dignity. Richard's emphasis on the word "change" in the end seems to indicate that so long as he and Sarah continue to change, to keep up the illusions, and so long as she does not cave in or lose ground the attraction between them will continue to thrive: "Yes," he says, "Change," and adds, "Change your clothes." But it's more than the clothes that require changing. Richard's closure, "You lovely whore," simultaneously imparts approval and denigration. (40) Using a received derogatory address to convey his approbation, even as he expresses his pleasure, Richard's saying "lovely whore" cuts two ways: both as an erotically charged term of endearment and as a moral indictment. Her offer to change has been met by his insistence that she *must* change. The ending suggests that they are now able to import the erotic afternoon game into the evening marriage. While it may appear easy to fault Pinter as chauvinistically gazing at Sarah only from the male vantage, it is necessary to note the degree to which Sarah willingly engages, initiates, and takes her own pleasure from the relationship. Rather than viewing *The Lover* as a patriarchal and therefore limited take on male-female relations in the West, as Sakelleraidou does in *Pinter's Female Portraits*, it seems instead more accurate and discerning to note the astute perception Pinter offers of Western relationships which encourage the splitting off of the erotic from the legal, morally correct, and more important, love relationship that Western marriage ideally is.

The two plays *The Lover* and *The Collection*, propelled by pretense in service of a quest for love, investigate with witty and amazing thoroughness not only the surface of relationships at the private level but resonate at depth with implications about public relationships beyond the sealed confines of the private rooms the characters inhabit. In both plays in each fractal beat, where the conflict appears as a quest for love disguised as a quest for a truth which only disguises deeper truths, Pinter begins that larger connection between love and justice. Through a close look at marriage, what truths it yields, what justices and injustices it endures beneath the mere legalities and morality of sexual exclusivity, Pinter in these plays and in the film script for *The Pumpkin Eater* which he drafted next, exposes larger truths: the need for love if there is to be any justice at the private level of marriage. In both plays where love is dramatized as questionable at best, where the self is a tissue of deliberate pretense, and where self-knowledge necessary for truth and ethical action is therefore impossible to arrive at, the truth necessary for the justice which James seeks and the truths Richard and Stella both try to confront and escape from cancel any possibility of a just resolution. Only in *The Pumpkin Eater*, where love becomes a relationship between equals and where an animal vitality of desire remains does a relationship endure infidelity for a just outcome.

The Pumpkin Eater: Married Love and Justice

Increasingly concerned with married love, between *The Lover* and *Tea Party* Pinter adapted *The Pumpkin Eater,* directed by Jack Clayton from the novel by Penelope Mortimer. The play and the novel depict Jo as a woman who has too many children but who refuses victimization after she discovers her husband Jake's infidelities. Instead she sets out on a brief odyssey of entanglements with several men in explorative, defensive retaliation, before returning, more nearly her husband's equal, at the end. But again in Jake's desire for the children's nanny Philpot, Pinter continues probing questions of reality and the imagination. Jake's desire for Philpot is sufficiently intense that it hardly matters whether he consummates it, the intensity of desire so overwhelms the act. The actual consummation of Jake's multiple infidelities and their aftermath become trivial in the larger context of Jo and Jake's marriage which seems able to sustain itself though a buffeting which returns in the end balanced on both sides.

Where *The Collection* and *The Lover* toyed with marital infidelity and only flirted with sanctioning a woman's being unfaithful (we do not know whether or not Stella is, and Sarah probably is not), *The Pumpkin Eater* confronted the endorsement of female infidelity directly at a time when it was regarded a far more egregious, even unforgivable, fault than it is currently regarded in the West. The whole question is nicely subordinated to the larger issue of the preservation of the marriage. Jo's infidelities permit her to return to the marriage more nearly her husband's equal than if she had remained faithful, and in doing so she gains a kind of rough justice. What appears permissible for Jake is also for Jo, albeit on a much more constrained level. Jake's lovers may be unnumbered, Jo's, limited to two. His are an unprompted aside from feeling trapped in a household with so many children he doesn't know what else to do; Jo's are prompted only in reaction to her husband's infidelity as well as by some affection for her lovers. The ending resolves rather than endorses further infidelity.[1] When Jo returns to Jake her wandering days are over, yet given Jake's habits, energy, interests, and track record, his may not be. Interestingly, although *The Pumpkin Eater* appears before *The Homecoming,* where Jo on screen generally escapes censure for her multiple, though rather dreary infidelities, Ruth on stage is roundly condemned for anticipated infidelities. Perhaps because of the different media and *The Pumpkin Eater*'s happy ending, what was acceptable at the time of the writing in film was still shocking on stage. But while the film pursues the issue of infidelity to the hilt, it is the play rather than the film that allows the topic to generate larger ethical implications.

Notes

1. Joanne Klein in her excellent analysis of Pinter's early screenplays, *Making Pictures: The Pinter Screenplays,* details what she calls director Jack Clayton's "mishandling of the script," especially his cutting and reordering of scenes, and the imposition of the happy ending which she calls "[h]opelessly out of synchronization with his material...disfiguring Pinter's finest contribution to the story, and rendering the entire incongruously sentimental." (29) Her point, however well taken, misses Pinter's larger contribution, his sympathetic treatment of Jo's infidelities which seem consonant with a feminist ethic such as would later be defined by Carol Gilligan in her book *In a Different Voice,* which insists upon examining the context of a situation before evaluating its ethical correctness. Pinter's ethic from the start, has insisted upon examining context.

The Homecoming: Dominance, Choice, and the Ethic Revised

The Homecoming is a pivotal work between the early and middle plays, the first of Pinter's plays where a woman, an underdog and initially a subservient character, is attacked on all sides, becomes dominant and wins something positive—her freedom. Her freedom contrasts with the constraints, often self-imposed, the others subscribe to. As choice is a necessary basis for justice, freedom becomes a cornerstone for the ethic in Pinter's work.

Teddy, a university professor, returns home with his wife of five years, Ruth, to introduce her to his family, two brothers, Lenny and Joey, their father Max, and their uncle Sam, but they are verbally attacked before they are welcomed and Ruth is invited to stay but to pay her own way, it is suggested, as a prostitute.

Ruth's strength, given the attack mounted against her, is remarkable, and among the realm of choices Pinter's characters generally seize or allow to slip past, the choices she makes gain what is wanted against great odds.

Ruth, the most misunderstood of all Harold Pinter's characters, is generally condemned as a shocking, licentious woman, even a nymphomaniac, and it is almost unanimously assumed by her critics that in the end she agrees to become a prostitute.[1] Austin E. Quigley's otherwise most careful reading of Pinter's plays goes even further to promote the unsupportable assumption begun by Martin Esslin (70) that Ruth was a prostitute even before she married Teddy: "Ruth is indeed coming home to her former self. . . ." (205)

The text, however, establishes what Pinter himself affirms: "She does not become a harlot." (Hewes, 58) The most perceptive reading proves to be Pinter's own as he concludes:

> At the end of the play she is in possession of a certain kind of freedom. She can do what she wants, and it is not at all certain she will go off to Greek Street." (57)

A corrected interpretation offers a greater appreciation of all the characters in their struggle for identity, love, power, and some justice as these elements find expression through precisely balanced multiple ambiguities. Again, in the fractal geometry, even the smallest moment of conflict mirrors those larger concerns in the ethic as each of the men strives to win, subvert, and subordinate Ruth, who, though she stays with Teddy's family, may in the end escape them all.

Except for Teddy's uncle Sam, all of the others including Teddy himself encourage Ruth to remain with the family in England and to earn her keep, they propose, as a prostitute. But the best textual evidence indicates that Ruth will neither remain nor agree to their proposal. She deliberately skirts commitment by conducting negotiations in the strictly conditional or contrafactual tense throughout:

> I *would want* at least three rooms and a bathroom. (77)
> You *would have to regard* your original outlay simply as a capital investment. (78)
> All aspects of agreement and conditions of employment *would have to be clarified* to our mutual satisfaction before we finalized the contract. (78; emphasis mine)

Ruth only conditionally concludes, "Well it might prove a workable arrangement," (78), and when Lenny asks if she wants "to shake on it now or later," she refuses to finalize the agreement: "Oh, we'll leave it till later." (79)

Although Ruth's erotic engagement with Joey on the sofa and her expressed approval of their plan ("Yes, it sounds a very attractive idea" [77]) suggest she might consent to their proposal, nothing she says or does commits her to agreement.

Sufficiently cogent evidence also raises doubt that she will remain with the family. Max, who at the outset claims that he could "smell" whether a filly in a horse race was a "stayer" or not, in the end "smells" that Ruth will not stay: "Listen, I've got a funny idea she'll do the dirty on us, you want to bet? She'll make use of us, I can tell! I can smell it." (81) Max's suspicion that she will leave, coupled with Ruth's command of herself and the family at the end (she makes Lenny bring her a proper glass for water and demands food from Joey), confirms that Ruth is in charge of her life and may exercise the option to leave.

Ruth's very self-command at the end and her seeming silence prior to her takeover have drawn nearly as much critical opposition as the shocked response to the possibility of her becoming a prostitute.

Because Ruth expresses no "Ah-ha" recognitions, no faked or genuine moral outrage when the family springs their plan, she is often deemed immoral. But Pinter nicely suspends Ruth's felt *re*action, and instead allows Ruth to act. Like Diana in *Tea Party*, Flora in *A Slight Ache*, Sally in *Night School*, Beth in *Landscape*, Ellen in *Silence*, and later Kate in *Old Times*, Emma in *Betrayal*, and all of Pinter's women whom men cannot dominate, Ruth, once she understands what is at stake, silently waits for the best moment to defend herself, then takes over. What she also gains is justice against those who would suborn her.

Although her command at the end is often viewed as evidence that she is "using" the family, just the opposite occurs. The family's actions which culminate in the invitation are all aimed precisely at using her. Not one of the men understands Ruth—or perhaps understands women at all, including the dead mother Jessie—whereas Ruth does understand them, and contrives to assert her superiority which leaves them unfulfilled, defeated, baffled.[2] Her command, as Pinter observes, is simply her defense against their attack:

> She's misinterpreted deliberately and used by this family. But eventually she comes back at them with a whip: she says "If you want to play this game I can play it as well as you." (Hewes, 143)

In the first three scenes in which she appears, Ruth is misinterpreted, unconsciously by her husband, then deliberately by Lenny, and finally brutally by Teddy's father, Max. When Teddy and Ruth first enter in the middle of the night Ruth announces that she is tired, yet twice after that Teddy asks, "Tired?" revealing how out of touch and indifferent to his wife he is. (21, 22) When Ruth answers "No," Teddy replies, "Go to bed, I'll show you to your room." (22) He may seem concerned when he asks "Are you cold?" but when she says she is not, he offers her "something hot to drink." (21)

Teddy's inappropriate responses, the innocent misinterpretations of one too self-preoccupied to listen, contrast with Lenny's deliberate distortions. When Ruth meets Lenny he begins, like Teddy, by ignoring her information. Twice he conjectures, "You must be connected with my bother in some way," (28) then, "What you sort of live with him over there, do you?" (29). But when Ruth corrects him, with "I'm his wife," and "We're married," he ignores her by switching the subject: "Eh, listen, I wonder if you can advise me. I've been having a bit of a tough time with this clock." (29)

Lenny's deliberate misinterpretations attempt to supplant his brother by redefining Ruth as his woman. His competition with Teddy manifests itself in his mention of the clock which becomes a pretext to deliver academic-sounding jargon rather than information: "So all things being equal . . . this question of my saying it was a clock that woke me up, well that could very easily prove something of a false hypothesis." (28) But then Lenny becomes openly aggressive: "Do you mind if I hold your hand?" (30) His move is at least three ways equivocal. He exposes his aim of repulsing Ruth with words which on the surface would seem aimed at gaining her affection. But when Ruth asks why, his description of his violent response to a woman who once made overtures to him belies the fact that he might actually like to hold her hand, but he is also careful to protect himself from her refusal with his attack: "So I just gave her another belt in the nose and a couple of turns of the boot and sort of left it at that." (31) His mixed signals, the thinly disguised threats which simultaneously communicate attraction, repulsion and fear take the form of a bullying that masks Lenny's cowardice, which Ruth uncovers when she turns to defend herself.

Her defense, or whip as Pinter calls it, is her wit—both her intelligence and her comic humor, and it happens that Ruth is the only witty character in the play who scores off the others; they are merely sarcastic or threatening or unintentionally comic, while she is intentionally so.[2] Lenny unwittingly initiates the final round in this scene's struggle for dominance when he proposes, "And now perhaps I'll relieve you of your glass," but he meets his match in Ruth, who understands what is really at stake. (33) To maintain self-respect and to gain Lenny's she must avoid slipping into subservience, which in Pinter's work and because Lenny can brook no equal, requires nothing less that gaining dominance over him. Ruth does so by topping each of Lenny's threat/proposals with a counterproposal/attack which finally calls his bluff: "If you take the glass . . . I'll take you" (35) Ruth's wit which wins her the dominant position baffles Lenny, who shouts after her as she goes upstairs: "What's that supposed to be? Some kind of proposal?" (35)

Finally Ruth appears to be most viciously misinterpreted by Max the next morning. Before Teddy can introduce Ruth as his wife, Max shouts, "Who asked you to bring tarts into this house?" (41) His tirade derives both its shock and humor from verbal abuse pushed to imaginative extremes in a context of mistaken identity: "We've had a smelly scrubber in my house all night. We've had a pox-ridden slut in my house all night." (41)

Max, like all in Pinter's work who fight most fiercely, is trying to maintain rather than gain a position of dominance. Max's abuse of patriarchal authority is an attempt to maintain his patriarchal position, and his overbearing delivery does momentarily stun, rendering all of the others ineffectual. But once underway, the sheer momentum of his tirade, rather than reason or emotion, propels his continued abuse. Ignoring Teddy's second outburst, "She's my wife! We're married!" Max continues with a double-edged cut: "I've never had a whore under this roof before. Ever since your mother died." When Teddy again interjects, "She's my wife," Max steamrolls ahead, "Chuck them out." (42) Such is Ruth's initial introduction to the family.

The Homecoming requires that careful attention necessary to appreciate any highly complex work, but some minor reading into the text has resulted in the proliferation of misconceptions. Critics frequently assume Sam, who collapses in the end, dies, although Joey states that he is not dead and Max says he "has [a] diseased imagination." (79) Paul Rogers, who played Max in the London, Broadway, and film versions, warns:

> There's an appalling fact about Pinter. You may not allow a single word he writes to pass unnoticed. There's no moment when you can have a quiet doze-off or go searching after complications that are irrelevant. (Hewes, 57)

Indeed irrelevant are the misreadings aimed against Ruth that perpetuate error. Ruth's saying to Max, "I think he [Teddy] wondered whether you would be pleased with me" is almost always interpreted literally as guilty self-criticism, whereas the context reveals just the opposite, exposing the dramatic irony that Teddy is afraid Ruth will not like them! (49) Teddy's elaborate assurances to Ruth when they enter immediately disclose that fear: "They're very warm people, really. Very warm. They're my family. They're not ogres." (23) Ironically, we have just seen Max and Lenny in the opening scene behave precisely like ogres.

Ruth's halting speech is also commonly interpreted as evidence that she is hiding a guilty secret. When she says, "I was . . . different . . . when I met Teddy . . . first," both her hesitant delivery and information are literally taken to mean she is hiding her past guilt, namely, that she was a prostitute before she married Teddy. Quigley, like Esslin, blatantly misreads Ruth's information that she was "A photographic model for the body," (57) as "nude photographic model," which, without evidence, Esslin translates as "a widely known euphemism for prostitute." (*The Peopled Wound*, 159; Quigley, 197–204) Nothing Ruth says suggests that her posing was done in the nude; she says only that she "changed" her clothes. Moreover the scattershot condemnation of Ruth ignores the context in which her information is offered and misses the irony and the deeper truth about how she is regarded by herself and others.

Ruth mentions that she was a model only after Teddy has just been praised for his "Doctorship in Philosophy" and after each of the others except Lenny, a pimp, has asserted as his identity his work label outside the house—Max as butcher, Sam as chauffeur, Joey as demolition worker and boxer. She resists the labels cook-mother-wife which they try to attach to her by asserting that she, too, once had a work-related identity out in the world not circumscribed by her home and family and, more important, that she was once attractive, a point which apparently requires asserting after Lenny implies his assessment of her body when he wonders what she modeled, "Hats?" (57) Only in the context of correcting him does Ruth say, "A model for the body," but must add, "Before I had all my children." (57)

As Ruth recalls her former career ("Oh, just . . . wait . . . yes. . . ."), her halting speech, rather than concealing a guilty secret is more accurately described as simple difficulty remembering coupled with regret. (57) As Teddy's academic wife it is unlikely that she has had recent or frequent occasion to discuss her former work as a model, and now she can never return to that work.

Less easily dismissed here is the censure against Ruth's actions, namely, the two we witness: her behavior with Lenny and Joey on the couch and her decision to leave her husband and children. Like almost all of the complex actions in the play, these acts can neither be assessed out of context nor finally condemned.

Ruth's most shocking behavior begins when she accepts Lenny's invitation to dance, his kiss, and then a roll on the couch with Joey that concludes in an upstairs bedroom two hours later. Joey's admission that they "didn't go the whole hog" emphasizes the arbitrary lines of demarcation in received sexual mores of the time, even while Lenny simultaneously ridicules anything less than going "the whole hog." (68) Similarly Teddy's insistence, "We're married," retains only arbitrary, merely legal meaning although in this family's eyes marriage is all that distinguishes Ruth from a slut or a whore.

Among all the brutal acts in Pinter's work to the time of *The Homecoming,* nothing else has drawn such moral reproach as Ruth's erotic behavior, and of course it is only Ruth who is censured, not the brothers who participate equally with her nor Teddy who simply looks on.

Pinter himself defines sexuality as a form of vitality and in a jovial endorsement of Ruth's behavior exposes attitudes to love, sex, and marriage that run counter to almost all finger wagging critical condemnation:

> As for rolling on the couch, there are thousands of women in this very country who at this very moment are rolling off couches with their brothers, or cousins, or their next-door neighbors. The most respectable women do this. It's a splendid activity. It's a little curious, certainly, when your husband is looking on, but it doesn't mean you're a harlot. (Hewes, 57–8)

Pinter, who rightly cautions against issuing Ruth the easy label "harlot," or "whore" on the basis of an isolated action, also explicitly discloses an attitude toward sex as one of the fundamental goods of life which is, however, circumscribed by a morality that cannot always justify restricting its expression. One of the larger dramatic ironies of the play is that this family, which contains and uncritically tolerates Lenny as a pimp, at the outset condemns Ruth without evidence as a "slut" and "whore." It is one of the failures of the criticism of the play not to recognize that irony and how it functions to reduce "wife" to a mere label and to annul the very term "marriage" in this relationship without any visible bonds.

By the time Sam, the outraged representative of received morality, exclaims against the family's proposal to keep Ruth, ("But she's his wife" [68]) the label "wife" has become meaningless and the marriage dramatically devalued by the family's attack on it, Teddy's inability to defend it, and Ruth's growing indifference to a husband who is indifferent and almost wholly unresponsive to her. As Pinter points out, Ruth's actions with Lenny and Joey originate not in lust but in despair.

> In *The Homecoming* the woman is not a nymphomaniac, as some critics claimed. In fact she's not very sexy. She's in a kind of despair which gives her a kind of freedom. Certain facts, like marriage and family, for this woman have clearly ceased to have meaning. (Kathleen Tynan, 8)[3]

Ruth's freedom, more accurately a stoic freedom, derives from having nothing more to lose. Teddy's inability to defend his marriage against the family and to claim his wife's attention, which he does not even attempt, ends in his betraying her. It is not astonishing, as many critics claim, that Teddy does not try to defend Ruth physically against Lenny and Joey. Pinter argues:

> Look! What would happen if he interfered. He would have a messy fight on his hands, wouldn't he? And this particular man would avoid that. (Hewes, 57)

Michael Craig, who played Teddy on Broadway, argues:

> Teddy is probably the most violent of them all, but his violence is controlled. They play this awful game with him to try to make him break, and he turns it around. He shoots it right at his father. He says, "I'll call your bluff. If you want a woman in this house, here she is if she wants to stay." He's an awful man, Teddy. He's rationalized his aggressions, but underneath he's an Eichmann. (Hewes, 57)

Teddy is no Eichmann, but, outnumbered and outsmarted by his less well-educated family, he withdraws rather than attempt to engage in a match he lacks the wit, intelligence or physical prowess to win.

What is surprising and unfortunate is that Teddy as a philosopher will not or cannot adequately defend Ruth or himself verbally against the family's onslaught. Max simply ignores Teddy's best argument, "We're married you know," which only echoes Sam's empty defense of Teddy. (69) Moreover, when Ruth first proposes they return to the children, Teddy dismisses her. But to his family his only other feeble argument is to assert what he earlier denied to Ruth: ". . . we've got to get back to the children." (69) Even here the ineffectual Sam protests more loudly: "She's a mother. She's got three children," which Max humorously dismisses by equivocating: "She can have more. Here. If she's so keen." (69) Teddy's reply, "She doesn't want any more children," misses both the point of Sam's protest and Max's rejoinder, which elicits Max's significant retort: "What do you know about what she wants, eh, Ted?" (70)

Teddy's concern centers almost exclusively on his own wants. He returns from America seeking his father's "blessing," his family's approval and praise but offers them nothing in return except insult. When he describes them as "just objects," Teddy asserts as his own superiority his "intellectual equilibrium," which on examination is really an emotionless solipsism. Failing to defend himself against the family, he capitulates and becomes one of Ruth's attackers.

It is Teddy who tattles on Joey to his father ("He had her up there for two hours and he didn't go the whole hog," [68]), yet when Max wonders if she might therefore be a tease, Teddy reverses attitude and, by *defending* her behavior with Joey, is the first to promote her merits as a potential prostitute: "It was just love play . . . I suppose. . . . That's all I suppose it was." (73)

Certainly Ruth might be condemned for abandoning her children. But that action, too, which seems unforgivable, cannot be separated from leaving Teddy, her best available choice as Pinter assesses it:

> If this had been a happy marriage it wouldn't have happened. But she didn't want to go back to America with her husband, so what the hell's she going to do? (Hewes, 58)

For almost a century theatergoers, drama critics, and scholars have praised Nora in *A Doll's House* for her courage in her similar decision to leave a husband, which also meant leaving her children. While Nora steps out into the world, perhaps less equipped to confront it than Ruth, she, like Ruth, acts for reasons of self-preservation, and both leave only after their husbands, revealing their own cowardice, betray them under trial and prove themselves incapable of change. Unlike Nora, Ruth neither idealizes Teddy as a hero beforehand nor demands miracles from him afterward, yet both Ruth and Nora hold out some hope for their marriages, Ruth perhaps more than Nora. Where Nora flatly says she will not "accept anything from a stranger," Ruth's final admonition to Teddy, both addresses and reverses Nora's: "Eddy. Don't become a stranger." (80)

To assume that Ruth leaves her children easily or willingly and is for that reason a bad mother is equally a mistake. When she first arrives she tells Teddy she wants to return home soon and gives as her only reason: "I think . . . the children . . . might be missing us." (22) Because of her halting delivery, this information is frequently dismissed as a lie. Yet given the tension of the situation—Teddy's anxiety and Ruth's caution when they first enter—it seems more accurate to describe her delivery as Pinter interprets halting speech, as an expression of deeply distressed emotion: "The more acute the experience the less articulate its expression." ("Writing for the Theatre," 82)

Teddy shows far less regard for the children than Ruth, scoffing at her concern by dismissing it: "Don't be silly." (22) But when it becomes convenient to win his father's approval, he reverses his position insisting that the children do miss their mother. (51) Teddy's inability to hold to a position is finally symptomatic of his overwhelming self-concern. He will do what he can do to win the family's approval, even if it requires dishonesty and the betrayal of his wife.

It is *Teddy* who delivers the family's proposal to her: "Ruth . . . the family have invited you to stay, for a little while longer. As a . . . as a kind of guest." (75) His offer, carefully clothed in euphemism, reveals his cowardice which is underscored when Ruth, taking him literally, is momentarily flattered. He actually encourages Ruth to accept! "If you like the idea I don't mind. We can manage very easily at home . . . until you get back." (75) While Teddy's encouragement might be the impotent gesture of a defeated man, his most seductive offer, "You can help me with my lectures when we get back," would hardly entice anyone to stay with him. (55)

Ruth's invitation from the family entails some equally attractive opportunities. Not only can she work as a prostitute, but Max and Lenny offer her a chance to "do a bit of cooking here if you wanted to. . . . Make the beds. . . . Scrub the place out a bit," and Teddy chimes in equivocally with, "keep everyone company." (55)

It is in response to this moment, when Teddy has wholly joined the family against Ruth, that Sam, who has counted Teddy as his favorite and his ally in morality, blurts out his nasty little secret about Max's best friend Mac and Jessie: "He had her in the back seat while I drove along." (78) He then collapses. Sam's retaliation, like McCann's in *The Birthday Party,* is suspended from Max's earlier silently endured insults: "You'd bend over for half a dollar on Blackfriars Bridge" and from Max's assertion that Mac was a better driver. (48)

Only after Ruth has been wholly betrayed by her husband's proposal, does she, without expressing a flicker of shock or recognition, turn against him to gain power over the entire family by attaching to their proposal a series of conditional demands for clothing, rooms, and a personal maid, which, given this family, they are as unlikely to meet as is Joey to "hit the top as a boxer." Yet unless they meet her demands, she says she will not agree.

While there is considerable doubt that Ruth will remain with the family and work as a prostitute and lackey for four grown men, it is also necessary to acknowledge the possibility that she might. The final point, Ruth's dominance, is of course ambiguous, and this central ambiguity,[4] like the multiple meanings throughout this and other Pinter plays, functions both aesthetically and ethically.

Aesthetically the ambiguity enriches character. No Pinter character can be defined by a single quality. Not only do all exist dynamically along a continuum balanced by opposites, it is a portion of Pinter's genius that he allows us to sympathize with some strength in each of them. And what makes his characters seem fully alive is that he allows each of them to express their own dark side, the private, even the unconscious that is often kept hidden from others and even the self. All of Pinter's characters also struggle for power over others, and beneath the surface that struggle is again an attempt to assert identity in order to gain attention, admiration, love. Ethically the ambiguity dramatizes how the attempt to gain love, if it is sought through a battle for dominance, must necessarily be self-defeating. *The Homecoming* not only explores the powerful nature of the struggle for love as it questions some assumptions about received morality, but it extends appreciation for the varieties of love and finally examines connections between desire, love, and human happiness.

Some of the minor ambiguities throughout enrich individual character and dissolve apparent differences between characters. The coincidence that Teddy and Max both have three sons suggests that the father and son have more in common than their outward appearances indicate, and Teddy's retreat at the end cancels his claim to any superiority over his father. Max's insistence upon identification with his dead friend Mac, whose name, ambiguously a near homonym of his own, consigns to Max some of Mac's spirit and a vitality, however crude-sounding and raucous, that informs the play's deepest values.

One among the many remarkable qualities of this, as of all of Pinter's plays, is that this play belongs to each of the characters. It is as commonplace as it is unenlightening to label Ruth a wife-mother-whore as it is to ask whose homecoming this is, Teddy's or Ruth's. Although Ruth is central at the end, each of the characters is a protagonist in a struggle that all at least partially lose. Like Ruth, the others are often dismissed after a cursory glance at a single or obvious characteristic. Max's desire for Ruth wins him the label old lecher. Sam is generally praised for his good manners or else dismissed as a "wet wick."

To isolate a single quality to define character is to diminish and falsify that character, because each exhibits qualities opposite to his most predominant. Max the butcher, who seems most savage, may be the kindest with some concern for the "human considerations." Sam, the play's Polonius, with his veneer of fastidious good manners and prudish aversion to the mention of sex, when he blurts out his secret he also unwittingly confesses his own complicity (if he can be believed) in cuckolding his brother: he "drove them along." Lenny, who deals in sex and is the first to make overtures to Ruth ("Isn't it funny? I've got my pajamas on and you're fully dressed." [29]) shows himself sadly incapable of fulfilling his own expressed desires. He asks Ruth to dance but turns her over to Joey, then voyeuristically prods Joey for details about what went on upstairs and finally boasts not of his own but of Joey's sexual prowess with women. Ruth sees through and dismisses Lenny's sexual overtures/attack from the outset with summary wit; and later when Lenny asks if she wants the drink she demanded "on the rocks or as it comes"—her rebuff equivocates on the slang sexual innuendoes when she answers: "What would you know about rocks?" (61) Teddy's titles—Ph.D., philosopher, and professor—certify nothing about his intelligence, truth-seeking, love of wisdom, or ability to teach others by word or example. Joey, the boxer and man in demolition, seems the gentlest, least destructive of the group.

The ambiguity that creates characters in Pinter's work is organic and intuitive, never contrived or artificial. Though the attitudes and actions of the characters may at first seem arbitrary, ambivalent, erratic, and even confusing, the ambiguity finally describes the art that results in characters who are among the most complex in twentieth-century drama. It is never possible to summarize and dismiss even a lesser character like Teddy in the way Torvald is summed up and dismissed at the end of *A Doll's House*.

Most important, Pinter allows each character some dignity, some quality to admire and like. Max, the aging patriarch, struggles to retain his position, to maintain the household, and the fact that he struggles in a worthy purpose is significant and evidence of an admirable vigor. He does keep the family together, and though he does not foster dependency, his two sons and brother require his shelter, and Teddy, his approval. His vitality and mind are remarkable, and he reveals his strength when he takes over from the others. It is Max who initially proposes keeping Ruth and who steers the final action toward its conclusion—until Ruth takes over from him. Joey, too, exhibits strength. He does defend Ruth against the others who call her a tease and reveals some generosity and even gentleness in his desire to retain her. Sam, however ineffectually, tries to express his love to Teddy when he confesses that Teddy was his favorite and that he cherished Teddy's letters so much he did not share them with the others. He is also the only one to oppose the family's proposal. Teddy, who fails to defend himself against his family, did manage to escape once, and in the end, leaves open the possibility, however unlikely, for Ruth's return to the family in America. Lenny may prostitute his own identity by assuming, chameleon-like, the character of the person he happens to be with in order to assert his superiority over others—to his father he shouts, "Plug it you stupid sod," but to Sam and Teddy he affects mock deference. Yet Lenny shows himself to be in fact superior to Teddy on Teddy's own turf, outmaneuvering and instructing the philosopher in ethics. Lenny is not wrong when he accuses Teddy of failing to provide the family with a model of virtue, "grace," with that "generosity of mind, a bit of liberality of spirit," anciently regarded as the crowning virtue without which a person has no virtue. (65) Ruth asserts her intelligence and returns attack with some kindness by turning neither upon those who attack her nor away from those who seek her.

That Ruth's behavior has provoked so much outrage, however misguided, among critics is a mark of the high seriousness of the play, but the grimly humorless commentary that already encrusts the play fails to recognize *The Homecoming* as one of the greatest contemporary comedies, if not the greatest. Ruth is taken seriously because the comedy in Pinter's work intensifies the seriousness which is informed by terror without pity, and ultimately by a tragic vision that both recognizes the chaos beneath the ordered surface of custom and received morality and glimpses the looming entropy of ultimate static order—silence, which is momentarily dramatized as the final curtain drops on the static snapshot pose of the family. *The Homecoming* reflects a quality of mind that has contemplated what Hannah Arendt calls "ultimate things" (Max's references to death and the origins of the earth) and returns to dramatize human action and betrayal in ways which nevertheless hold to an ethical center.

Reductive attempts to separate "good guys" from the "bad (woman)," villain from victim, are out of place here as throughout and clearly only limit appreciation. However, while Pinter's ambiguities can embrace multiple and contradictory qualities within each character, ambiguity does not endorse moral fence-sitting or ethical relativism. Certain acts are reprehensible. When asked about evil in the play Pinter replied:

> There is no question that the family does behave very calculatedly and pretty horribly to each other and to the returning son. But they do so out of the texture of their lives, and for other reasons which are not evil but slightly desperate. (Hewes, 57)

Pinter pronounces the family's attack "Harsh and cruel to be sure" but, as always, insists upon examining the context and causes to assess it:

> Still, they aren't acting arbitrarily, but for very deep-seated reasons. (57)

Knowing why they act as they do, while not excusing their behavior, does make it understandable.

Every conflict in the play is, or also results from, an assertion of dominance, yet when asked what the play is about Pinter replied:

> It's about love. And about lack of love. (143)

One most remarkable quality of Pinter's work is that it rivets our attention at every moment not with a conflict between idealized good pitted against embodied evil but one which arises from each character's desire for attention, respect, approval, some affection and love from another. Hence the conflict forces focus to the source of action.

The struggle to win dominance over another which provides the moment-to-moment dramatic tension (Who will win, Lenny or Max? Ruth or Lenny?) remains the primary means by which characters gain identity. These characters assert identity only one other way—by claiming the right of title conferred by work outside the house. Max boasts of his being a butcher, Sam, "the best chauffeur in the firm," and Teddy enjoys Lenny's references, however sarcastic, to his being a professor of philosophy. Both forms of identity rely upon the recognition, and ideally the respect, even admiration, of others.

Again, the awful paradox is that the struggle for dominance destroys precisely what it seeks, love. No instances of self-sacrificing, subservient, or obsequious behavior to successfully gain love exist in Pinter's work.[5] Nor are there examples of unconditional love aside from several wives and relatives of torture victims in *Mountain Language,* nor that middle ground of mutual respect, admiration, and attraction which traditionally defines love and friendship. Other than the already noted friendship between Seeley and Albert in *A Night Out,* exceptions may seem to occur between Max and Mac, or Robert and Jerry in *Betrayal*, but the irony remains that those friendships are scarred by betrayal, the seduction of a "best" friend's wife, an act repeated in references in *No Man's Land*.

That struggle for dominance over another is paradoxically dramatized as both life-affirming and destructive. Because there can be no equals in a dominant/subservient relationship, the struggle inevitably destroys the possibility of love or friendship and leads to betrayal which arises, as it must, when the desire is thwarted and unfulfilled.

We see Teddy betrayed by his family, who in turn act out of their feelings of having been betrayed by his leaving them earlier. Teddy returns asserting his superiority to seek admiration from his family who deny it by revealing him to be no better than what he sought to escape. Were they to acknowledge his superiority, in Pinter's work, the family would be admitting their own inferiority. That Teddy should even need to elicit his family's approval, a mark of Teddy's own immaturity, is also a natural and humanly understandable desire for respect.

Each of the men also harbors a personal sense of betrayal which, because it generates distrust that neither fosters self-respect nor claims the respect of others also destroys human relations. Max claims he was betrayed by the butchers who turned out to "be a bunch of criminals like everybody else," (47) Lenny, by women who make demands upon him, and Sam, perhaps by Mac. But in a larger context all of the men might seem betrayed by the circumstances of their birth. The trades—butcher, chauffeur, pimp—which bestow title to each man's identity and which each, save Lenny, boasts of are hardly professions of choice but are among the few choices available to these men. Pinter, however, neither patronizes nor pities any of his characters for their circumstances, and as soon as one realizes that Teddy, the one man in the family to break from his British inherited class, is no better off, even worse, one recognizes that what is finally being dramatized is again not only the questionable value of mere outer identity but even relative economic security as a primary concomitant of happiness. Teddy's insistence that he is successful and happy, expressed in banalities matched only by Sam's description of his own superlative driving skill, raises the issue of his success and happiness only to cast doubt upon it.

Throughout Pinter's work to *No Man's Land, À la Recherche du Temps Perdu: The Proust Screenplay,* and *Betrayal* is the reminder that comfort, even fame and luxury, may make one person only relatively superior to another. The attainments of the acclaimed poet Hirsch are only subtly and ambiguously superior to the continued vitality possessed of the apparently "failed" and bereft poet Spooner. In Hirsch's no man's land of "silk" and "cloth bell pulls," as well as in the opulent drawing rooms of *The Proust Screenplay,* old age is the leveler that mocks equations of wealth with happiness. Robert and Jerry, as bright, successful young men in *Betrayal,* scoffing at the waiter's foreignness and lowly occupation, only evoke sympathy for the waiter and awaken realization of his greater happiness and joy in his life, family, and work. Robert, who has only recently learned of his wife's betrayal with his closest friend Jerry, must at that moment conceal both his knowledge and his pain, while Jerry must hide his uncomfortable guilt. *Old Times* offers one rare attempt to define happiness in Pinter's work, which Deeley describes as the "looking forwardness" to rather than the attainment of desire. Ruth, with her newly acquired freedom, among all of the characters in *The Homecoming,* indeed in the Pinter canon of plays, may be the only one who can hope to look forward to something different and perhaps better. Yet this single quality, freedom, only partially contributes to happiness as it is depicted in Pinter's work.

Happiness, when it is portrayed at all, seems primarily contained within the self as an attitude of optimism and high self-esteem that constitutes an inner identity not contingent upon circumstances or approval of others. Ruth, like Kate in *Old Times* and Emma at the opening of *Betrayal,* embodies that attitude in her strength, a fortitude that radiates out and suggests a kind of self-contained happiness. Although neither Kate nor Ruth proclaims her happiness, it finds expression in attitude and action. But Kate and Ruth achieve power in the end and are surrounded by others who seek their strength as if hoping to acquire it by osmosis. Ruth and Kate do virtually nothing else, have no work or achievements to hold out for public or private admiration, and what happiness they possess does not seem much able to extend itself to contributing to the happiness of others on the private or public levels. Only when pressed to define herself does Kate express contentment in merely existing, which like almost all expressions of self-regard in

Pinter's work is also tinged with irony. Yet her quiet inner strength, like Ruth's, expresses an inner vitality from which others seek comfort.

Through characters such as Ruth and Kate the struggle for dominance also becomes a vital force, a quest for something portrayed as more laudable than its opposite, passivity. In *The Homecoming* Max and Ruth are finally larger and more admirable than the ineffectual Sam or Teddy, and through Pinter's largest characters the struggle for dominance becomes, however partially, a contemporary analog of the quest theme in Western literature. To struggle for something, given a proper end and means, was once the enactment of heroic human fulfillment.

The struggle here, which in lesser characters often has survival as its primary end, may at first seem selfish or petty (even if self-preservation is minimally necessary for getting anything else). But at the core of Pinter's work in his greatest characters, the struggle for dominance as an expression of vitality is finally linked to virtue—both in the root sense of strength and power, and in its common usage, the coupling of right reason with right action. Those such as Sam who proclaim themselves virtuous because they comply with prescribed moral codes may in fact only parody virtue by parroting qualities they do not possess. Although there are no Horatios in Pinter's work, as there perhaps cannot be unequivocal models of virtue in twentieth-century literature, Pinter's *The Homecoming* celebrates strength, courage, great feeling, and vitality combined with intelligent choice executed in effective action.

Characters such as Goldberg in *The Birthday Party* are hardly held up for much praise. But nowhere does Pinter celebrate failure, and he reserves pity for those who fail to achieve power and are subsequently destroyed by continuing to suggest, however subtly, that each one (except for Gus in *The Dumb Waiter* and his torture victims) is partially responsible for his own destruction. Teddy in *The Homecoming*, through misguided or wrong use of reason, is finally unable to act to get or perhaps even to know what he wants and in the end loses his wife. Yet despite the terrible injustice he perpetuates by taking a lead in the family's conspiracy against her, she keeps open the door of relationship and even the possibility of love.

All of the characters struggle for love, but more important all express love to one another. Their many expressions of love establish its central importance in *The Homecoming*, a point Pinter reaffirmed after *Old Times* opened: "Well, as they say, it's a very important element in all our lives, isn't it? And I think it's the most misunderstood, maltreated matter, too. . . ." (Gussow, "A Conversation. . . ." 126; ellipses in original)

Without professing a definition of love, the characters collectively evoke an ideal to admire through their actions, and by dramatizing what love is not and where it fails, they also define love by negation and contrast as a supreme desire which ideally must be balanced by reason and intelligent action. We can understand this by observing the opposite in Teddy. His failure to keep his wife might be a failure of desire. But it is also a failure of reason that has atrophied his emotion and a failure of intelligence that renders him unable to act to get what he wants.

What is central to Pinter's portrayal of love as a virtue may be best understood by importing and applying one of Pinter's fullest public expressions of love in *Mac*, his tribute to Anew McMaster, the actor-manager with whom Pinter toured Ireland at the beginning of his acting career. In Pinter's tribute, as in his plays, the virtues of a man, if they are sufficiently strong, are never destroyed by ugliness in appearance or unaesthetic behavior. Pinter never diminishes a man by idealizing him, and in his tribute to Mac, his stature and greatness of his performance are enlarged by Pinter's honesty, his inclusion of his savagery, repellent qualities, and other failings. In that complexity that encompasses extremes and requires a full disclosure of truth, Pinter captures the prodigious vitality of the man who, like so many of Pinter's characters, is worthy of attention and admiration for the vitality which he embodies.[6]

The Homecoming does less to define love than to extend appreciation for the rich variety of expressions and forms of love ranging from friendship and familial love to the erotic, through the past and into the future from conception, through old age and death. Lenny inquires of his father, however malicious his intention, about the night of his conception, and his father and Sam both cherish the memory of Jessie however much feelings of love mingle with its opposite. All express love for another.

Max richly details his love for Mac, his feelings for animals, the fillies whose manes he stroked, his love for his dead wife, and now, for his returning son. While his love for Mac is wholehearted, his feelings for the fillies is mixed with distrust, and his love for Jessie, with loathing: "Mind you, she wasn't such a bad woman. Even though it made me sick just to look at her rotten stinking face, she wasn't such a bad bitch." (9) Max's language raises the question, "Did Max really love his wife?" If this question is answered in the facile psychologizing that explains his marriage as a love-hate relationship, the complexity of Max's feelings is overlooked. Between the extremes Max also expresses tenderness for his wife, joy in his sons as young boys, and pain in the disappointed hopes he held for his family. Moreover, Max applies the same language to himself when he rebukes Lenny: "Talking to your lousy filthy father like that." (9) Max attacks Teddy at first by attacking Ruth, but later he offers Teddy "the cuddle and the kiss" of reconciliation. Max's exclamation, "He still loves his father," (44) brings down the curtain on Act One just as his "kiss me" to Ruth brings down the final curtain.

Max's desire for Ruth, generally condemned as lecherous, simply because Max is old, challenges the traditional dictum that erotic desire has no place in old age. Lenny views his father as "sexless" but Max dramatizes what one of Pinter's favorite poets, Yeats, at fifty in "The Tower" questioned, celebrated, and lamented about old age's passions and thwarted possibilities:

> What shall I do with this absurdity—
> O heart, O troubled heart—this caricature,
> Decrepit age that has been tied to me
> As to a dog's tail?
> Never had I more
> Excited, passionate, fantastical
> Imagination, nor an ear and eye
> That more expected the impossible— (192)

Mutability, lamented throughout Pinter's work, is increasingly and emphatically portrayed in the more recent *No Man's Land*, the *Proust Screenplay*, and *Family Voices* as a horrifying trick that attacks from without and may wholly mask and therefore negate the passions and possibilities that continue to live within. What finally distinguishes an audience's attitudes toward Max from his sons' is merely his age.

Even Sam claims that he is not beyond having a woman, not too old to get a wife, but his tenderest expressions of love are to his nephew Teddy when he whispers his love as boldly as he can: "You were always your mother's favorite. She told me. It's true. You were always the . . . you were always the main object of her love," says Sam, expressing his own love for Teddy. But when Lenny enters a moment later, Teddy ignores Sam's proffered affection, brushing off his invitation to "stay a few more days." (63)

Lenny may make overt passes at Ruth, but it is also to Teddy that he expresses love as familial feeling:

> But nevertheless we do make up a unit, Teddy, and you're an integral part of it. When we sit around the backyard having a quiet gander at the night sky, there's always an empty chair standing in the circle, which is in fact yours. (65)

Like much of what Lenny says, his declaration, made while Joey and Ruth are upstairs together, is cut by sarcasm. Later Joey's crudely expressed defense of Ruth's behavior offers the nearest declaration of love combined with sexual desire and pleasure in the play. Joey, unfettered by stock responses toward love and sex, suggests that "just a touch . . . just a tickle" may at times be a fuller, even more satisfying expression of love than "going the whole hog": "I've been the whole hog plenty of times. Sometimes . . . you can be happy . . . and not go the whole hog. Now and again . . . you can be happy . . . without going any hog." (68)

Even Teddy evinces some feeling for others, but usually to invite their admiration or love for himself. He opens his arms to his father, "Come on, Dad. I'm ready for the cuddle," (44) but when he excuses Ruth's behavior by blaming Joey, "Perhaps he hasn't got the right touch," he implies that he himself may have it. (66) He makes a semihumorous bid for Ruth's approval like a child for a teacher's good opinion: "You liked Venice, didn't you? It was lovely, wasn't it? You had a good week. I mean . . . I took you there. I can speak Italian." (55) He also attempts to fend off the family's attack by suggesting to Ruth that they cut their trip short.

But when Ruth, asking why, observes that Teddy does not like his family as much as he imagined, Teddy denies that, lying to her and to himself.

The philosopher, by definition a lover of truth, lies throughout. Though we see no evidence of it, he claims that Ruth is unwell. When Lenny asks if Teddy offers the family a model of virtue, Teddy immodestly answers "Yes." But his greatest lie may be in denying his feelings by asserting the superiority of the intellect over emotion, of acting "on things not in things," (61), which in Teddy's case simply excludes emotion altogether and renders him unable to act in his own behalf, dramatizing the importance of human feeling balanced by understanding and action.

Only Ruth, though she responds to the needs of others, does not express love as a need, and she cannot be taken with the others as incapable of love, because there is no possibility of a test. No one in the play can equal or match her in strength, wit, or wisdom. She returns attack with understanding and tempers assertions of power with compassion and some affection. Drawing attention to Ruth's virtue does not negate her already well-mapped darker side but points to strengths which have been ignored and to the final ambiguity which has been overlooked. If Ruth fails to achieve dominance and complies with the family's proposal, as is commonly assumed, then she cannot be admired, and the power and complexity of the play is greatly diminished.

The ambiguity in the struggle for dominance creates a dialectic that yields no unequivocal synthesis and prevents easy definitions of love or virtue. Yet the play explores the difficulties, not the impossibility, of gaining and expressing virtue or love. Although Ruth's position at the end is ambiguous, the text suggests, without didactically affirming it, that her assertion of power wins her a highly qualified freedom.

Ruth comes closest of all of Pinter's characters to a model of virtue, one whose strength is threatened and tested from without but who understands her circumstances, herself, and the people around her and then acts wisely to gain the best available end. In Ruth comedy and high seriousness combine in proportions they rarely do in drama, and through her actions *The Homecoming* becomes, like the act of writing as Pinter regards it, "a kind of celebration" of vitality, where understanding balanced with emotion combine to result in action that gains freedom, placing this play among Pinter's finest work. ("Writing for Myself," 85)

NOTES

1. Almost without question most critics assume Ruth becomes a prostitute: Hinchliffe, 150; Kerr, 35; Gordon, 61; Esslin, 70; Hollis, 101; Sykes, 114; Burkman, 108; Quigley, 225; Gale, 138; only Sakellaridou cites Pinter's denial that Ruth becomes a prostitute but only gives it a hearing. (110)
2. I am indebted to my reader at *Twentieth Century Literature* for this suggestion.
3. Esslin assumes that Ruth is a nymphomaniac, 150; Sakellaridou merely raises the issue without addressing it except to castigate Pinter for defending Ruth against the charge and, like most, fails to define that term which has no male equivalent. Are we to assume the charge that Ruth is a nymphomaniac marks her as a woman of insatiable sexual appetite, unfulfilled desire or, as the term denotes in this context, simply a woman who overtly expresses any sexual desire?
4. Like Empson's seventh, or extreme type of ambiguity, ambiguity is used here to suggest opposites, seemingly self-contradictory but in reality possibly expressing truth. (Empson, 171)
5. One exception may occur in *The Comfort of Strangers*, in Caroline's fawning attitude toward her husband who remains faithful in his fashion but breaks her back during lovemaking.
6. Pinter's naming his half-admired, larger-than-life, off-stage character Mac, Max's doppelgänger, seems an oblique, but further extension of Pinter's tribute to McMaster. (*Mac*, 19)

The Quiller Memorandum: *Torture without Threat*

In *The Quiller Memorandum*, adapted by Pinter from *The Berlin Memorandum* by Adam Hall, this early screenplay already addresses the issue of torture that has become the centerpiece of Pinter's recent plays. Yet this early in his career and for more than a decade afterward Pinter would maintain, "I find nothing more boring than an ideological work." (Marks, 17) He said he looked for ways to find other levels of a work he considered an "unabashed thriller," as Quiller, a Western agent, penetrates a Nazi spy ring and is drugged, tortured, then seduced by a woman who, ambiguously, may be a spy. Interestingly, however, Pinter stripped the novel of many of its Holocaust references in order to forward the story line, a point nicely detailed in "Pinter's Spy Movie" by Bernard Dukore, whose analysis of Pinter's transposition of the story from the novel to film provides insight into Pinter's art of adaptation generally. (Dukore, 10–16)

In the film, Pinter found ample opportunity to explore his own traditional powerplays in the domineering behavior of interrogators and in Quiller's admirable resistance to victimization. What separates Quiller from his recent counterparts in Pinter's plays is Quiller's colossal, indomitable will, which allows him to spring back to life with the ease of a cartoon character no matter how severe his torturers' beating or drugging, then to triumph unequivocally in the end. Here Pinter still pulls punches so that Quiller is never broken, his tongue never cut out. Pinter is able to indulge in some cinematic stereotypes coming as close as he ever would to allowing the good guy/bad guy dichotomies free reign. But Pinter's own experience and involvement with Amnesty International later would instruct him that in real life under brutal torture the human body and spirit can be scarred, squelched, reduced to pulp.

Tea Party and *The Basement:* The Illusive Qualities of Power

It had been five seemingly long years since Pinter had written a full-length play, *The Homecoming,* and it would be another five before the next, *Old Times,* appeared. In the interim he wrote one pair of one-acts, *Tea Party* and *The Basement,* followed by another, *Landscape* and *Silence,* the two plays that would separate his early work from the next phase. While *Tea Party* and *The Basement* retain the early work's primary focus on dominant/subservient relations, *Landscape* and *Silence* almost sever him from that concern entirely, turning in his work to what have been called the memory plays, a term which Pinter during a 1988 public interview, agreed was apt.[1]

Tea Party returns full force to the dominant/subservient relationship with battle lines drawn across class. The self-made Disson, the foremost bidet manufacturer in England, marries his second wife Diana, a socialite, and becomes the interloper/intruder entering into an unequal battle with her, her brother Willy, and his own twin sons as he begins to suffer a growing sense of impotence manifested finally in his blindness. *The Basement,* originally a screenplay, set primarily in Law's room opens as the intruders Stott and his girlfriend knock at the door, enter, take over, and eventually expel Law in a chiasmic reversal which concludes with Law's appearance at the door, about to intrude on his own premises. The play returned to youthful concerns, and Pinter admitted, "Those two men have been with me for about twenty years. But I'm tired of writing about characters who exist in one room!" (Gilliott, n.p.) In *Landscape* and *Silence* he would escape.

Tea Party and *The Basement* are the last plays written in the early mode where the fractal geometry adheres to each molecule of the dominant/subservient conflict and where that conflict, propelled by a desire for love and respect, fueled by physical or moral blindness equated with a lack of self-knowledge, leads characters to make choices which are most often destructive. When that conflict vanishes in *Landscape* and *Silence*, it returns stripped of excess baggage as a more elegant, complex, subtly driven but also more powerful conflict. That new power, when the conflict returns, is also mingled with the characters' proprietary attitude toward love which nevertheless retains a myopia as destructive as blindness.

Tea Party

Tea Party, the richer of the two plays, adapted from Pinter's short story of the same title, returns once again to all of his former concerns: the illusive nature of power and Disson's subtly dramatized choices that lose what power he begins with. Disson's growing blindness parallels his loss of dominance begun at once in his choice of secretary, but both blindness and dominance are connected with mystery—it is never wholly certain whether Disson's eye trouble is real or imagined, whether what he "sees" or suspects about the relationship between his wife and her brother is true or false. Moreover, Disson's blindness and his protean identity (reflecting working-class origins which contrast sharply with the more stable, privileged assurance of his wife and her brother) provide him with an erratic, self-destructive basis for decision making and action. The flux of his private, inner, emotional being conflicts with his more rigid outer, social self with its attendant action till the warring factions dismantle him. Disson, like Teddy and Edward before him, denies his feelings and approaches problems with a prescriptive rationality that renders him inflexible, emotionally blind and empty. He simultaneously thwarts and encourages his growing attraction and eventual preference for his secretary Wendy over his new wife Diana, but as he does so his lovemaking with his wife becomes perfunctory, coldly rational, finally devoid of feeling, as his eyesight begins to fail him. His physical blindness becomes an analog for his moral blindness—his responsibility to himself and others, but in the three-way interior battle he wages and loses with his feelings, thoughts, and actions, he nevertheless garners some sympathy for the unequal, exterior battle he also fights.

The precarious nature of Disson's power is apparent at once in the opening lines of his interview with Wendy whose reserve and complete confidence contrasts with Disson's lack of it. His evasive euphemisms concealing his embarrassment about the products he manufactures sets off his slight stammer: "We manufacture sanitary ware . . . but I suppose you know that?" (43) He evades naming the products he manufactures before her asking instead: "Well, do you think you'd be interested in . . . in this area of work?" (44) Wendy on the other hand stammers only when answering questions about her previous employer who she claims never stopped touching her, information which fairly provokes invitation. Without requiring proof of her qualifications, Disson precipitously hires her with fulsome praise that reveals an imprudent lack of reserve.

The wedding reception raises one of the play's central ambiguities, the relationship between Disson's bride Diana and her brother Willy, which may be quite innocent or, as Disson later suspects, incestuous. Diana twice kisses her brother before she finally kisses Disson only in gratitude for his having offered Willy a position in the firm. Willy's praise for his sister during the speech in honor of the groom (given extemporaneously to fill in for Disson's absent best friend Disley) is couched in suggestively sensuous terms. Willy praises his sister's swimming, "the grace of her crawl," her piano playing, "the delicacy of her touch," and her "long fingers moving in exquisite motion on the keys," then ends in calling her, "the flower, the blossom and the bloom." (48) After a only few stray words about Disson, Willy's speech heaps more praise on Diana "who in all probability has the beating of her husband in the 200 meter breast stroke." (49)

Disson overrides any injured feeling to Willy's slighting remarks with a socially polite mask: "Marvelous." (49) Moreover Disson invites trouble when on seeming impulse, he invites Willy into the firm as "second in command," showing a continued lack of prudence for a man in a position of power. Whether his invitation to Willy is impulsive or one of the unspoken goods of the marriage contract it represents (like Stanley's sitting and Rose's admitting Riley to her room), the mistake which determines all else. As in chaos theory where order depends on sensitive disturbance to initial conditions, the disturbance in this initial condition determines the order, the shape, or what in chaos theory is referred to as the "space phase tempo," of subsequent, repeated action; with repeated elegance Disson meets challenge after challenge, real or imagined attacks against his inner self, by buttressing his outer self till his inner identity collapses toward entropy.

In contrast, Willy's gracious, dignified acceptance of the position Disson offers reveals Willy's superior command of himself, and all by itself establishes Willy's ability to turn a subordinate position quickly to advantage.

Like Othello's prophetic, "To die now were to die most happy," Disson's closing line to his new wife at the end of the wedding reception, "This is the happiest day of my life," provides ironic foreshadowing for the rest of the play, which proceeds for him down hill. (50)

In the passionless bedroom scene immediately following, Disson's deliberately assumed mask, his guise of a gentleman, begins to crack, increasingly revealing Disson's insecurity and growing self-absorption as the rift between his inner and outer self opens to a chasm. When he asks Diana, "Have you ever been happier? With any other man?" he seems less interested in her happiness than in his score with her as a lover. (50) Her perfunctory responses, "Yes" and "Never," indicate that the answers Disson seeks cannot best be given in words. Yet Disson's attempt to develop an intimacy with his wife, who seems happily disposed to formalities and retaining the distance between them, renders him some audience sympathy. The morning after, when he asks why Diana did not marry Jerry, she replies, "Because he was weak." (51) Disson's self-reassurance, "I'm not weak," offers one of those self-declarations that almost always signal the opposite in Pinter's work. (51)

The first bedroom scene contrasts markedly with the second, and both contrast with the scenes at the office between Disson and Wendy who seems to arouse him more than does his wife. In the second bedroom scene one year later Diana complains, with characteristic ironic Pinter understatement, "You seem a little subdued . . . lately," indicating that Disson is no longer able or willing to meet Diana's desires which still seem actively focused upon Disson. (70)

Disson's business and home life continue to erode as his actions and words become more contradictory. In his briefing to Willy, first Disson notes that their two offices are "completely cut off from the rest of the staff," adding: "Equally, I dislike fraternization between the two offices." (52) But he then concludes by countermanding himself to Willy: "Interdependence is the key word, it's your job to understand me, mine to understand you." (53) Through closed doors?

In view of Disson's closed door policy, Willy's request to Disson that Diana come to work as his secretary "to be closer to you" is ironic. When Disson says, "I don't like indulgence. I don't like self-doubt. I don't like fuzziness. I like clarity. Clear intention. Precise execution," and then, referring to tea, asks, "Black or white?" he underscores his limited, binary thinking process which parallels Edward's and Teddy's but opposes Pinter's own attitude that reality is infirm. (53) Disson nevertheless attempts to fix reality's flux through senseless adherence to the arbitrary rules he creates.

Although Disson is only gazing out the window when Willy buzzes for him, Wendy announces, "Mr. Disson does not want to be disturbed until 3:30." (54) He fails to comply with his own strictures to which he makes others adhere. At the office his growing rigidity mirrors his diminishing interaction with his family; he shuts others off from himself at work and cuts off his family at home. At home, though Diana may only be attempting to get on with the boys, he looks from one to the other as if they are in league with each other against him.

When Diana tells the twins that they mean a great deal to their father, John wonders what "a great deal means," while Tom wonders what "*mean* means."[2] The question turns in upon this play where traditional values recur to reconfigure the dramatization of the dangers in the lack of self-knowledge and the necessity to confront rather than to shun conflict.

At the office Disson's incipient blindness, which begins immediately after he openly begins to notice, then, to touch Wendy, seems to proceed in concrete ratio to the growing three-way disparity between Disson's feelings, his rational attitude, and his actions toward Wendy, now all in conflict. He believes touching his secretary is forbidden, the stuff of cheap fiction which he is above:

> One would have thought this . . . tampering . . . this interfering . . . with secretaries was something, of the past, a myth, in fact something that only took place in paperback books. Tch. Tch. (45)

But his inviting Wendy to sit on the leather on his desk ("It will be softer . . . for you") communicates suggestive sexual overtures and brings Wendy within his reach. (56)

Disson's actual eye trouble begins that evening when he sees two Ping-Pong balls, though Willy apparently served only one. Disson's double vision nicely mirrors the double ambiguity: his suspicion that Willy is double dealing with Diana and Disson's own suppressed double dealing with his secretary. Disson's seeing his doctor is as futile as K.'s seeking a doctor in Kafka's "The Metamorphosis." Though his eye doctor Disley pronounces Disson's sight perfect, Disson in the next scene has difficulty tying his necktie in the mirror (reflecting, like that similar image in *A Night Out*, sexual inadequacy).

But Disson's eye trouble is central to all else—how he views himself and others and how he envisions others view him to ratify his identity. Disson as a self-made man is more peripherally aware of himself as a construct than are Diana and Willy, born to a position they neither have to strive for nor construct. Kimball King's insights into the many levels of Disson's self as construct, especially through his material possessions, reveal the degree to which Disson buys the essentially "commercial medium" Pinter satirized in "the mass-marketing of assumed identities." King concludes: "Disson is all *poseur*. He is financially successful, an ideal employer, a fine husband, a loving father—only because *he* says so and because he expects to be believed." (45) King further concludes that the subjective camera angles which reveal Disson's inner vulnerable state (Disson sees two Ping-Pong balls as does the audience) lead the viewer to question "whether anything is what it appears to be." (43) His conclusion goes beyond what is usually meant by that notion and reverberates back and forward through all Pinter's work on the central issue of self-knowledge and identity.

Pinter never underestimates the difficulty of attaining knowledge of the self. As he acknowledged in an interview before the recent revival of *The Caretaker*:

> There have been a lot of assumptions of clear and definite behaviour but I don't find my own behaviour definite and clear. To pretend to find your behaviour clear is to engage in a conspiracy with other people who would like to find their own behaviour clear. Most of the time we're elusive, evasive, destructive. (Lewis, 1–2)

Disson, in his growing blindness, cannot acknowledge that self honestly and in fact refuses to. Nor does he see the destruction done to himself. Instead his problem persists and multiplies.

Diana offers one wholly realistic solution to Disson's stated problem that he sees less of her than he wishes now that she is Willy's secretary. But he rejects it out of hand. When Diana asks, "Would you prefer me to be your secretary?" Disson replies, "No, no, of course not. That wouldn't work at all." (62) Diana's entry into his office would put an end to his pleasurable games with Wendy and force him to confront his confusion. For Disson, who had previously kept business and pleasure neatly separate, the two are inextricably and confusingly bound together. So long as Wendy, a subordinate, does not draw his attention to them, he can continue to ignore his own attitudes and action. The boundaries between brother, sister, husband and wife, employee and employer and lover also blur uncomfortably for Disson, a man who demands clarity. Willy counters Disson's complaint that he seldom sees his wife with, "But we all meet at lunch time. We meet in the evening." His protest draws explicit attention to the fact he sees more of Diana than Disson does. Disson's rigidly compartmentalized life crumbles as his eyesight continues to fail. (62)

With the pattern established, the rest of the play repeats more intensely the conflict already set in motion. Wendy at times now openly invites Disson's attention: "I've put on my new dress." (63) The more he notices Wendy, the more difficulty he has seeing. After Disson sits upon Wendy's chair, he goes home and nearly cuts off his son's finger while woodworking, a phallic castration telegraphing his own guilt. When Disson next requests that Wendy bind his eyes with her scarf to alleviate the pain, he uses his blindfolded eyes as an excuse to touch Wendy seemingly by accident. Becoming ostrich-like—as if once his eyes are wrapped in darkness his body were out of sight—Disson deliberately chooses blindness. Unlike any prior Pinter character who resists going blind, Disson augments his blindness by using his blindfolded eyes to hide from his own feelings.

Disson's and Wendy's lively office game of catch played with Disson's table lighter contrasts with the second "subdued" bedroom scene where there is no longer even any talk of love. When the blindfolded Disson next touches Wendy, she openly accuses him, "You're playing one of your games, Mr. Disson. You're being naughty again." (72) Disson's blindness may be real enough, however psychosomatic in origin, but he certainly takes advantage of his blindfolded state.

During his next trip to Disley's office Disson cries out, "Help me," but Disley, who earlier protested, "I only deal with eyes, old chap. Why do you come to me?" now simply ignores Disson's plea: "Who made the speech?" (73) Disson asks referring to his wedding. Disley changes the subject, and Disson, rather than admit his weakness, insists, "I don't want you to think I'm not a happy man. I am." (73) Disson's outburst only calls into question what he claims, reveals even greater feelings of inadequacy as the disparity between Diana's former life at her childhood home, Sunderly, contrasts with Disson's less advantaged background.

Willy and Diana's discussions about Sunderly exclude him, and a visit from Disson's lower-class parents emphasizes his progressive alienation. This time when Diana asks him, "Come to bed," no bedroom scene follows. Instead Disson exclaims, "You can say that in front of him?", referring to Willy who is now apparently an ever-present specter. (75) And this time when Disson requests assurances of Diana's love, she avoids mentioning "love" as she instead catalogs, in the past tense, her reasons for marrying him:

> I found you admirable for your clarity of mind, your surety of purpose, your will, the strength your achievement had given you— (75)

Willy draws Disson aside for what is probably going to be a little chat about Disson's drinking, which Diana already addressed to no avail. But Disson circumvents rather than confronts Willy's possible attack by offering Willy a partnership. Again, Disson's hasty overture, a high-priced defense, clashes with what he certainly must desire for Willy.

The final scene at the office tea party, the most intriguing of all, depicts Disson blindfolded at his request, while half of the scene portrays his point of view as what he imagines or intuits is happening, and the other half presents a presumably objective view conveying none of the sinister implications of Disson's view. In the television version Disson "sees" or imagines his guests in conspiratory postures at the tea party with Willy caressing his wife and secretary in turn. The objective viewpoint reveals only the most ordinary activities that might occur at the most respectable tea party, but Disson collapses to the floor.

When in the end Diana says to the fallen Disson, "It's me. It's me, darling," then after a pause adds, "It's your wife," Diana's plea may be the legitimate cry of a loving wife, and all of Disson's suspicions may be imaginary projections of his own feelings denied in himself and attributed to Willy and Diana. (80)

What constitutes Disson's power? How does he lose it? Disson's position is exposed once again as façade without foundation. Neither Willy nor Diana can be accused of actively usurping Disson's place, yet because of the class differences Willy and Diana have command of themselves and others that Disson simply lacks. Once again Pinter portrays through ambiguity the impossibility of knowing whether power is lost through external or internal forces or even which forces are real or imagined. The widening gulf created by Disson's perceptions of what he ought to feel and what he does feel for his wife, secretary, brother-in-law, and family is further enlarged by Disson's repeated choice to ignore his own feelings. Throughout, the overriding choice Disson makes is to bolster the façade rather than confront his true feelings or any one else's. When he chooses to promote Willy rather than to allow Willy to bring up the topic of his excessive drinking, a rather elaborate defense, he further disempowers himself. In this play it is still at the private level, the base, that Pinter explores corruption.

But already his characters have entered new social strata, a change that began with Edward and Flora. Diana and Willy are born to inherited privilege, and assumptions that proceed from a power leaving them no knowledge of the vulnerabilities of those who might envy them their assurance. In this play where the nature of power itself is elusive, it is impossible to assign blame but again, given what we see, possible to regard Disson's choices as precipitating his own fall.

The Basement

The Basement also dramatizes the more illusive qualities of power and what justice is gained, like the justice lost in *Tea Party*, remains on the private level. Although most critics view the play as a battle between Law and Stott for possession of Law's room and the girl, there is hardly any real struggle. Stott, an old friend, enters with Jane and simply takes over the room from the unprotesting Law who actually seems happy enough to welcome company even if the guests take over his bed. But as Stott changes the room by removing Law's watercolors and imprinting his own image on the decor, he also changes Law who gradually absorbs Stott's tastes, including his attraction to Jane, and more important, by seeming osmosis, some of Stott's strength.

Except at the very end, there is no real struggle for Jane who simply gravitates to Law for companionship during the day and to Stott for lovemaking at night; after the second love scene, however, Jane smiles at Law. (92) But when Jane makes overt advances to Law, he spurns her, revealing how apt is his name for one who inflexibly adheres to rules. When she asks how he can resist her, Law cries, "We can be seen! Damn you." (100)

Stott's underlying jealousy of Law may be implied when he attempts to deprecate Law in front of Jane. "Your style was deceptive," he says to Law who agrees: "It still is." But Stott turns on him, "Not any longer." (102) Yet in view of the ending, where Law returns to reclaim his flat, Law may be right. Jane, who gradually cools in her affection for Stott, evidenced when she pulls away from his kiss and, later, his touch (104–105), then pleads with Law, "Why don't you tell him to go?" She adds, insinuating that she knew Law even before she knew Stott, "Then we could be happy again, like we used to be." (105)

Law still resists her as he betrays her confidence to Stott: "She has no loyalty," he complains, then speaks of her as if he found her repulsive: "She's savage. A viper. She sullies this room. She dirties this room. All this beautiful Scandinavian furniture. She dirties it. She sullies the room." (106)

Someone must leave. According to Law's rules of propriety and conduct, "the Council would object," and "so would the Church." (194) Law's attitude to Jane might seem to indicate that in this relationship she prefers Stott. Yet in the very next scene when Stott momentarily appears to be breathing his last, Law and Jane suddenly get on mysteriously well, "snuffing each other like animals." (197)

Law develops some of Stott's animal liking for Jane, but when Stott unexpectedly recovers, two battles ensue for the girl and the room. Stott takes a few shots at Law with some marbles and lands one on Law's forehead, an illusion to Cain's mark on Abel, brother pitted against brother. The final battle with broken milk bottles ends when the bottles smash together, hailing the last scene, a repetition of the first—with the reversal: Law appears at the door with Jane. Law and Stott have exchanged positions. But throughout are allusions to the earlier youthful bonding between the two men who played the recorder together and read Proust in the original but who have developed divergently—Law, primarily with an intellectual prowess witnessed in his reading, and Stott, primarily in an animal strength we see (in contrast to his First in Sanskrit that we only hear about).

The reversal of position is complete as indicated in the forms of address. In the opening scene Stott evinces power when he addresses Law by his first name, Tim, while Law addresses him as Stott (92); in the end Stott welcomes Law as Law who now calls Stott Charles, the first we learn of Stott's given name. (112)

For the first time in Pinter's work, the character who is expelled from the room, Law, refuses to remain the subservient loser and returns to regain dominance. The recursive structure of the play, which suggests that the exchange of roles may occur again, implies that easy interchangeability of dominant and subservient characters already dramatized in *The Servant.* But it is no accident that Law, as a force of reason, first and finally wins out over the sheer brute strength of a Stott. Law develops beyond Stott, combining Stott's strength with his own intellect.

Tea Party and *The Basement*, grounded in the illusive and precarious nature of power which can so easily be exchanged for its opposite, reflect different times in life. Law, young enough and flexible, makes choices and changes Disson fails to make. Though Jane, as a catalyst in the youthful triangle, both reunites the young men and keeps them apart, it is *her* choice which determines who will be the dominant man. Pinter again dramatizes position as a result of a complex combination of choice and chance where choice still determines power. Stott remains the carrier of animal strength who turns his back on his own strength, refusing even to race when his strength might win the woman he seeks. (103) Law's development from someone who merely follows rules to someone who allows his attitude to embrace feeling and his thought to form intention allows him to seize power, making Law one of Pinter's first largely rational characters who develops, seeks justice, then gains what he wants.

Notes

1. Mel Gussow during the 1988 YMHA reading and interview asked whether the term "memory plays," which had been applied by others, might be used to describe plays such as *Old Times*, and Pinter agreed it might.
2. Several years prior to this play, Pinter was asked by New York critic Andrew Sarris the meaning of *The Homecoming*. Pinter replied, "I'd understand questions about meaning if I knew what the word 'meaning' meant." (Wetzsteon, 25) Sarris was later incensed to hear that line issue from the little boy's mouth in *Tea Party*. (Sarris, 53) Pinter's remark does, however, seem apt for those who would inquire into meaning in his work or anyone's.

Accident: Death, Desire and Birth

Accident, adapted from the novel by Nicholas Mosley, directed by Joseph Losey, is set at Oxford among philosophy professors, Stephen and Charley, vying for the favors of Anna, Stephen's student William's girlfriend. Stephen is disenchanted with his pregnant wife, Rosiland, his social circle, and even his former lover, Francesca. All seems dull, constrained, exhausted, as he becomes infatuated, even obsessed with Anna, a student who is seduced by his colleague and friend Charley. In the end (and in the opening sequence) William is killed in an accident from which Anna escapes, only to have to escape Stephen's desperate, clumsy, ineffectual attempt to seduce her.

Pinter explores the seemingly natural dominant/subservient relations between professor and student and the rivalry between professors but with an interesting reversal: Stephen is awed and outclassed by the student he becomes enamored of. The sparring male lovers of a single female object witnessed in *The Basement* would be a familiar triangle from *Monologue* through *Betrayal.* Pinter was attracted to the novel by the very ordinariness of the characters and the "unforgivable, unforgettable things that are never said" but are nevertheless searingly communicated in the film: Rosiland's knowing about her husband's passion for a student, his awareness of her knowing, and their simply continuing on with life. (John Taylor, 184)

The dominant/subservient contest assumes subtle but decidedly ethical dimensions with public ramifications: Stephen's attempt to seduce William's girlfriend colors his relationship with his student William as the contest also takes several interesting turns allowing Pinter to comment upon the sexual mores of the time.

Stephen's desire for Anna, which at that time may have seemed shocking, is soon mitigated by the slightly more shocking news that his colleague Charley has been sleeping with Anna all along—a disclosure rendered yet more shocking by Charley's off-hand, insouciant delivery of the inconsequence of that information. Where Stephen is consumed by guilt from mere desire, Charley remains nearly indifferent to the act. But most shocking of all is perhaps Stephen's attempt to seduce the hysterical Anna following her escape from the automobile accident which killed William. Even that shock, however, diffuses to pity in Stephen's inept failure to get near the young woman. That failure transforms to a sympathy for both Anna and Stephen as *Accident* raises questions surrounding some of the same received sexual mores tackled in *The Pumpkin Eater*, *The Homecoming*, *A Slight Ache*, indeed, in many of Pinter's plays and films that challenge the ethics of a code of sexual conduct.

When the received code colors and threatens to overshadow all other ethical considerations, Pinter returns it to perspective within a larger picture without, however, diminishing the erotic force which informs the characters' action. The birth of Stephen and Rosiland's baby at the end, registered only as a happy fact, signals the continuance of life and opens the film out to other important aspects of life. By placing questions of sexual ethics which threaten to become paramount here and in *The Homecoming* in proportion, Pinter raises more important ethical issues than sexual codes while celebrating love as fundamental to all other issues.

Questions of loyalty, fidelity to another person cannot, in Pinter's work, be so easily teased apart from loyalty and fidelity to one's self. Stephen is not better and is even perhaps less admirable than Charley in his inability to fulfill his own greatest desires. Yet the authentic depth of Stephen's feeling for Anna enlarges his character as Charley's lack of real emotion reduces his. These early works which confront the topic of sexual ethics open the way for larger ethical issues in the third phase of Pinter's work. But before that would happen Pinter entered what might seem a fallow period, developing, however, perhaps at subterranean levels and preparing for his powerfully shocking recent work.

PART TWO

The Liminal Plays of the Middle Period

Landscape, Silence, and *Night:* Where Powerplays Vanish

The second phase of Pinter's work begins with two plays so radically different from anything Pinter had previously written there might seem to be no connection. The dominant/subservient conflict nearly vanishes but with startling consequences—when the conflict resurfaces in *Old Times*, it does so with a vengeance and without skipping a beat as the driving force of all else. The fractal geometry, that quality in Pinter's plays in which the overall arc of the play's conflict is mirrored in each act, each scene, and each beat, also returns with a difference: this time with public consequences. Never, throughout the whole of Pinter's work, does the conflict expressed through the fractal geometry become repetitive or assume a merely mechanical form. For each play its function and form are specific to the nature of the dominant/subservient conflict. The full-length plays of the middle period *Old Times*, *No Man's Land*, and *Betrayal* all contain the experimentation with both form and memory begun in *Landscape* and *Silence* but now give voice to some public consequences of the private conflict at the heart of all Pinter's plays.

Landscape and *Silence* both broke Pinter out of one room and away from his reliable power-play source of tension. In *Landscape* a middle-aged couple Beth and Duff speak at rather than to each other in a counterpoint that consigns speech to an extension of private memory. The characters communicate their thoughts, memories, and daydreams of past loves aloud to the audience but not to each other. Pinter described the genesis:

> I've started a couple pages of something quite different. A new form, and I'm diving. It's simply, as it stands, about a woman around fifty. She's talking. That's all I bloody well know. I don't know where she is. Certainly not in a room. So the characters can't open a door and come in, but I think they're there. (Kathleen Tynan, 8)

In *Silence* Ellen, a young woman in her twenties, recalls relationships with Rumsey, a man in his forties, and Bates, a man in his thirties. Her dialogue crosscuts theirs as she conflates the men, moves forward and back in time. They make parallel focus shifts, evoking a lyrical, erotically charged remembrance of times past. Pinter was excited with this break from past constraints, claiming that the one-act *Silence* took longer to write than any of his full-length plays.

Only in the most subtle sense do these plays dramatize the characters' play for power; more obviously they portray Pinter's concern with time, space, and the mystery of identity as choice continues to connect with self-knowledge. But the absence of power-plays here develops with unexpected ramifications: not as a good but its opposite. The implication which is dramatized—that the absence of the conflict may be as destructive as its presence—may account for the fresh vigor the conflict takes on when it reappears in *Old Times.*

Landscape

In *Landscape* Beth and Duff are engulfed by silence. Stage directions indicate that they do not "appear to hear" each other's voices. Duff's patter about trivia in the present, his recollections of the past, and Beth's internal monologue solely about the past hardly hint at their relationship as husband and wife, nor are their present identities contained in their separate illusions about one another.

The subjects of their separate monologues converge at times, most noticeably at the end when Beth and Duff describe sexual encounters. But even in their separate recollections of a shared intimate experience there is no communion. Where Duff recalls "banging the gong," claiming, "I would have had you in front of the dog like a man," hoping, "You'll plead with me like a woman," Beth recalls a time past on the beach when, "He lay above me." (29) She then brings down the final curtain with "Oh my true love I said." (30) In neither case does the love recalled absolutely reference one another nor is it clearly fulfilled. Duff switches from the conditional past to the future tense, describing what he wishes would have happened or will occur, while Beth recalls a long-past, almost girlhood, memory detached from the living, aging woman of the present.

In the fragmenting and telescoping of time, the identities of the characters in both plays, cloaked in mystery, remain in flux. Is Beth really different from the young girl whom she recalls as herself? She knows she will be different in the future:

> Of course when I'm older I won't be the same as I am, I won't be what I am, my skirts, my long legs, I'll be older, I won't be the same. (24)

Nor is it clear that her man, as she refers to him, is Duff. He may be their former employer Sykes, gone—presumably dead. Pinter, in a letter to the director of a German production, maintains that the man in Beth's memory is Duff, infused with recollections of Sykes whom Duff jealously detests:

> [T]he man on the beach is Duff. I think there are elements of Mr Sykes in her memory of this Duff, which she might be attributing to Duff, but the man remains Duff. I think that Duff detests and is jealous of Mr Sykes, although I do not believe that Mr Sykes and Beth were ever lovers. I formed these conclusions after I had written the plays [letter refers also to *Silence*] and after learning about them through rehearsals. (Esslin, *The Peopled Wound,* 187)

Elsewhere in the play the two monologues contrapuntally echo one another. Immediately following Duff's description of stopping off at a pub for a pint, Beth speaks of stopping off at a hotel for a drink. (15) A dog wanders in and out of both their narratives, but even in these tenuous connections, Pinter dramatizes the separateness of these two people who have presumably lived together for many years but whose lives no longer touch. Duff's explicit statement about what really matters only further emphasizes their separateness:

> That's what matters, anyway. We're together. That's what matters. (24)

In what sense are Beth and Duff together, or does it possibly matter aside from their proximity and the fact that they share a breathing space? Pinter here evokes the horror of the shared/

unshared existence between two people without intimacy or even relationship. Except for their advancing ages, which limit other more attractive choices, would they be better apart? Although the landscape of each of their narratives takes us beyond the walls that are traditionally associated with Pinter's rooms, Beth and Duff seem more obviously walled into the isolation of their separate recollections of their shared romance. Yet romance remains paramount to both.

Hints of the dominant/subservient conflict, subtly retained in Duff's relation to Sykes, to Beth, and in Beth's relation to the man of her memory, continue to portray the destructive qualities of hierarchy from the vantage point of those forced to assume the yoke of service in a hierarchal society— the servants. Duff, first speaks quite respectfully of his former employer, Sykes: "That's where we're lucky in my opinion. To live in Mr Sykes' house in peace, no-one to bother us." (17) But he soon discloses hostility: "Mind you, he was a gloomy bugger," he says with unintended irony that equally comments on his own life, adding: "I was never sorry for him at any time, for his lonely life." (20) He admits his relief now that Sykes is gone:

> At least now . . . at least now, I can walk down to the pub in peace and up to the pond in peace, with no-one to nag the shit out of me. (24)

Duff resents his subservient position but salvages some dignity by recalling his one area of mastery, his position as a trained cellerman: "That's why I could speak with authority." (25)

In his relationship with Beth, he is gentle at times, as when he recalls her among the flowers or when he describes his confession of infidelity to her. But though he confesses his desire to take Beth by force, expressed in commanding, raucous terms, he seems oddly unsure of his ability to have her "like a man" and describes only how he "would" have liked to behave with her and have her respond to him. (25) Sadly, he does not seem to achieve "what matters" to him.

Beth's relation to her man is quaintly passive, played to a courtly but sensuous love, imagined as much as remembered, who spends much time asleep on the beach. The man she describes seems so different from the Duff we see that it is easy to suppose

Beth is speaking of another man altogether. It hardly matters. Duff is becoming the sleepy dormouse Sykes may have become in old age, and *this* Duff of her memories and dreams is not the real living, here-and-now man anyway. That seems to be the point as Pinter explores how, in even a single instant of memory, an image can displace reality, the living moment.

It is not necessary to suppose these two people *never* speak to one another. The dramatic device of the internal monologue simply allows Pinter to dramatize what is occasionally common to any conversation—one person's being on his or her own track while the other is privately shut off or engaged elsewhere. Here he also dramatizes what is most important to each character: not each other, not even themselves as they presently exist, but how each conceives the self and imagines the other, generally in the past.

Beth may or may not have been unfaithful to Duff as he confesses he was to her, yet her ongoing infidelity with her imaginary man of her youth is a far more palpable and salient part of her life now than Duff's real infidelity is to him. In a sense then, these characters who are out of touch with each other are beyond any quest for power. Power requires relationship. But though they have escaped the confinement of the walls of a room, they are also beyond exerting any power even in their own isolated private lives, which seem to drift on chance remembrance rather than be driven by any volition. The absence of powerplays reduces these characters to a static landscape blending with the background and generating only a lyrically recalled past. What is best in their lives is already over except for what is savored in memory and imagination.

Silence

Silence, in which time remains a movable function of memory in the minds of Ellen, Rumsey, and Bates, pushes the boundaries of memory and silence even further by means of a wholly non-realistic setting where the three lives intersect only briefly, primarily to underscore failure and parting. The three characters move forward or back in time at will, illuminating the nodes of failure in their relationships which we see but they miss.

Where *Landscape* obliquely hints at death in the allusion to Sykes, and the play's silence dramatizes a dead relationship between two living people, the silence of *Silence* reverberates with a reminder of mortality although the characters in *Silence*, like almost all of Pinter's characters, remain as unconscious of death as they do the source of failure in their relationships. But the failure is at once apparent in Rumsey's insistence that he is content to be alone:

> I've lost nothing.
>
> Pleasant alone and watch the folding light. My animals are quiet. My heart never bangs. I read in the evenings. There is no-one to tell me what is expected or not expected of me. There is nothing required of me. (35)

But being alive requires something. Only the heart of the dead "never bangs." Rumsey's self-proclaimed peace is really a terrible isolation grown out of a choice he made when he spurned Ellen. Moreover, his rejection appears an outgrowth of defensiveness (which damages more than it preserves). When Ellen approached Rumsey, he told her, "Find a young man," suggesting he quit before he was fired. (35) Rumsey, like others in Pinter's plays who do not get what they want, avoids risks. He remains unaware that time in old age will further reveal his safe choices as cowardice and a retreat that turns his existence into a nondescript shell.

When he earlier asked Ellen to cook for him, she coyly responded, "Next time I come. I will," but next time may be never since the last time, as Rumsey reminds her, "You were a little girl." (41) Even the erotically charged suggestions of lovemaking between Ellen and Rumsey, though joyful, seem to occur between disembodied, ethereal beings without grit who do not touch:

> ELLEN: When I run . . . when I run . . . when I run . . . over the grass. . . .
> RUMSEY: She floats . . . under me. Floating . . . under me. (40)

Ellen as an old woman also insists she is content to be alone: "I like to get back to my room." (36) Though she is described in the cast list as "a girl in her twenties," she clearly moves forward in time into her old age when she says:

> It isn't something that anyone could ever tell me, could ever reassure me about, nobody could tell from looking at me, what was happening. (37)

She seems almost unaware that she is aging, that time is passing as she continues to insist:

> But I'm still quite pretty really, quite nice eyes, nice skin. (37)

She needs to be told, to be convinced she says:

> I seem to be old. Am I old now? No-one will tell me. (43)

How does it feel to be seventy? In many ways no different from twenty. Yet as viewed from the perspective of her old age, Ellen's relations with the men in her past no longer matter, for when asked by a friend "for the hundredth time" if she had ever married, she arbitrarily decides:

> This time I told her I had. (46)

Bates, the only one to admit vague discontent, happily recalls life in the country though he now lives in the city where his youthful neighbors make too much noise and too much love. But he, too, finally concludes, "It's of no importance." (45) Unlike Rumsey in his relations with Ellen, Bates actively pursues her. But he allows his indecisiveness and hers to rule, finally permitting Ellen to elude and spurn him. When he asks Ellen what she wants to do and she says she doesn't know, he offers her a drink and a walk:

> ELLEN: No.
> [Pa*use*]
> BATES. All right. I'll take you on a bus to the town. I know a place. My cousin runs it.
> ELLEN No.
> [Silence]

Does she want something more? Does he fail to propose or provide it? Does she? The exchanges between them mark missed opportunity. *Silence* ends their brief encounter. Whatever wounds Bates suffered in youth may or may not have left marks—his fondest recollections as an old man are of his walks in the country with a little girl. Ellen? Perhaps a walk in the country holding a little girl's hand was the extent of his heart's desire, in contrast to Rumsey, the older man who nevertheless does not trust his own greater desire enough to seize the young woman he wants.

The assertion of power in these plays, so subtle it seems almost absent, occurs primarily at junctures to underscore the failures in the relationships, junctures where Rumsey spurns Ellen, (45) where Ellen spurns Bates (39), and when Bates impotently cries out at his noisy young neighbors (35) and is reminded of his own (mis)spent youth.

The two plays together form a *momento mori* portraying those who not only sit out their lives (rarely a posture to be admired in Pinter's work) but who sleep through life. Like those fence-sitters in Dante's *Inferno*, these characters suffer from unlived lives; failure to choose, inability to act, however lyrically recalled, consigns them to a living purgatory they choose to interpret as contentment. The characters remain without influence in the public sphere, and hardly exert impact on the private. They remain as out of touch with one another as with themselves. But their loss momentarily illumines our own.

Perhaps not surprisingly the near absence of the dominant/subservient conflict does not produce a paradise but a life devoid of that vitality that seems a concomitant of the desire for love and power. These characters, who may seem to represent an ethical advancement toward peace in Pinter's work, have simply retreated from the conflict rather than confront their own desires.[1]

Night

Night, written when Pinter was thirty-nine, his first wife, forty, portrays a couple in their forties who recall their first meeting, though in the mild resumption of the powerplay for dominance, they each recall a different shared experience. Again, rather than struggle for power as is typical in Pinter's work, the two argue, acquiesce, but finally agree to disagree.

She remembers they walked to a corner of a field and stopped at a railing, he, that it was a bridge. She claims: "That was someone else." (56)

They reach accord as they dispassionately rehearse the first time they made love, but it is she who speaks his part:

> And you had me and you told me you had fallen in love with me, and you said you would take care of me always, and you told me my voice and my eyes, my thighs, my breasts, were incomparable, and that you would adore me always. (60–1)

He concurs as she continues to supply his lines in the present: "And you adore me always." (61)

The dialogue at the end progresses to their accord to disagree about the past, but they do agree about the present feelings. When he introduces a memory of other men "holding your hands" and men "looking into your eyes," he seems to require, for his own continued interest in the woman, other admiring eyes upon her. (61) Both express their feelings as ventriloquists speaking for one another, and their emotions only ambiguously are aimed at each other as the Woman recalls other men:

> WOMAN: And they said I will adore you always.
> MAN: Saying I will adore you always. (61)

Love, common to all three plays, *Landscape, Silence,* and *Night* is increasingly portrayed as failing to connect the lives of the characters whose separateness is further emphasized in past, often failed attempts to love. Even those who apparently loved and married, Beth and Duff, the Man and Woman, are no closer than those who have lost their chance to love, Ellen, Rumsey and Bates. *Landscape, Silence* and *Night,* all autumn plays, portray characters past youth without the hopeful springtime and summer of love, seasons which are nevertheless suggested in the lush rain wet landscapes of Duff's narrative, in Rumsey's and Bates's talk of the little girl and the birds, and in the dialogue of youthful passion in *Night.*

The noticeable near absence of the powerplays in these one-acts poses an interesting question. Does the absence of the struggle for dominance reflect an absence of a quality essential not only to drama but to life?

The thematic implications of the dominant/subservient conflict in Pinter's early work suggest that the struggle grows out of feelings of inadequacy and results generally in destruction rather than creation or growth of human relationships. Conversely it might be supposed the absence of the struggle for dominance would signal a positive turn in his work. Yet these plays hardly project a hopeful quality, nor does the absence of that conflict enhance the characters' lives. Without the struggle and without the correlative desire to attain a position or role, however artificial or arbitrary, these characters seem only half alive. Without attempts to fulfill desires, they remain isolated into an almost death-in-life existence.

Love in Pinter's plays seems both integrally connected and opposed to blood lust and violence. The only peace in Pinter's work, purchased in these plays at the expense of powerlessness, is portrayed as self-delusion. Pinter's portrayal of love and violence mirrors the most fundamental physical structure in the human brain governing love and violence to convey a force resembling fate. Deep within what some term the primitive brain resides the core of strongest emotions, the amygdala, center of love and rage. Where Pinter's early plays show how the quest for love and respect, when thwarted, can so easily trigger anger and violence, the reverse applies here—without a quest neither love nor anger is fully activated in the present living moment, and action thus dead ends. These characters who claim to be complete within themselves, as is typical in Pinter's work, only to call that completeness into question.

Where in *The Dwarfs*, confronting identity called attention to the balance required between an inner- and outer-directed identity in order to function in the world, these plays, directly confronting the power conflict by suspending it, signal a shift in attitude toward that conflict. Even more disturbing than the battle for power is the dramatization of how quickly one can inhabit one's routine and assume habits not consciously chosen, but simply fallen into. The characters remain blithely innocent of the choices they made in their lives which gained them their current identities. The younger Ellen says she does not know what she wants; Bates wants her; Rumsey rebuffs her. We see that at some level they all desire love, yet each in the end each is left touting a happy isolation which evinces the opposite: an unresolved loss.

These three plays, written by a master of dramatic conflict, take an audience further to the edge of life lived in the absence of conflict than any of his work written after. Implicit in such wholly solipsistic, inner-directed identities is some recognition that the healthy woman and man exist in a larger society, requiring some balance between the inward- with the outward-directed self, some vital engagement with the world, what Bertrand Russell simply calls "zest." Thus the near absence of Pinter's concern with dominant/subservient relationships in these plays calls for a person possessing an honest self-knowledge, a consciousness of choices, and an ability to confront conflicts in the larger community in order to act to gain what is desired for the self and others.

Notes

1. Jean Baker Miller in her work *Toward a New Psychology of Women*, written almost two decades ago, noted that women (as a subservient group and as nurturers and keepers of peace in a society which does not value those virtues) must not only confront conflict but initiate it. Her conclusion aptly addresses the seeming peace these characters gain at the expense of all else. The failure to confront any conflict here results only in perpetuating illusion.

The Go-Between: Freedom Reborn

The Go-Between, adapted from the novel by L.P. Hartley, directed by Joseph Losey, straddles the world of memory and the dominant/subservient class relations traditional to turn-of-the-century and pre-war Britain. Like *Silence*, the screenplay moves back and forth in time in what might seem to be flash forwards. The central love story, Marian's passionate entanglement with the hired man Ted, is framed by Colston, who as a child, acted as her go-between with Ted. Colston, the child, half enamored of Marian, believes he cast a spell on her love, and when, after she becomes pregnant, she is eased into a marriage with Lore Trimmingham, Ted kills himself. The middle-aged Colston, who revisits the aged Marian at her invitation, bears witness to the son she had with Ted and raised as her husband's, dramatizing a triumph of love over class relations. She represents yet another of Pinter's women characters who wrest some justice and victory from circumstances that would oppress her as love again returns as a vital center of all else.

As with almost any victory in Pinter's work, Marian's is tainted with a darker side. The youthful beauty has become a slightly foolish, old woman, empty of all else save her title as Lady Trimmingham, and her past love for Ted—the great event of her life that gave her a grandson. In her cruel prattle she tells Colston (perhaps rightly), "You're all dried up inside, I can tell that." (359) Though his boyhood moment which we witnessed seemed unconsciously possessed by his crush on her, she seems insensitive to his onetime devotion when she asks, "Don't you feel any need of love?" and adds "Everyone should get married." (359) She then commands the aged go-between, who her fiance once dubbed "Mercury, the messenger of the gods," to assure her grandson that there is no curse on him (which the young man believes prevents him from asking the woman he loves to marry him). She implores Colston to tell her grandson the truth about her love for Ted, "Speak to him, tell him there's no spell, or curse, except an unloving heart." (360) The go-between ends by walking to the young man as bearer of the message of love, the story which began the film (along with, perhaps, a confession of his "spell"). His story, to be told after the film ends, both continues and concludes the fracturing and dislocation of time with a spiral return to love and passion, a formal technique that would also mark the end of *The Proust Screenplay* and the beginning and end of *Betrayal*.

Old Times: Triple Dominance

Old Times pushes the boundaries of traditional form further with the fierce re-emergence of the dominant/subservient conflict. This time conflict connects the private level with the public sphere as each momentary skirmish sustains the tension that runs the whole arc of the play. The play also combines Pinter's fascination with memory with his new fluidity of form developed in *Landscape* and *Silence.* Though it is contained in two rooms, Anna's ambiguous presence at the beginning (she is both there and not there) opens the play out beyond the four walls of the house and breaks a time barrier as well, thrusting the audience into both past and future. But the very conflict which re-invigorates and restores vitality to the play also destroys the relationships which it seeks to preserve in the comfortable lives of these characters, initially secure in shelter and position. They are finally revealed as no less vulnerable to the destructive force of the unconscious conflict for power than the characters living at the margins of life in Pinter's early work. What justice is achieved comes from the truth revealed after all illusions are stripped away.

Old Times opens upon a middle-aged married couple, Deeley and Kate, awaiting the visit of Anna, Kate's roommate of twenty years ago. As they recall their refracted past, what happened in the past and what may be happening in the present remain equally ambiguous, conveying Pinter's continued interest in "the mistiness of the past."

The three entertain one another with a combination of serious remembrances, comically sentimental rounds of the popular love songs of their youth and an increasingly competitive vying for position—who saw *Odd Man Out* with Kate, Deeley or Anna? Whose alliance is strongest, Kate and Anna's, Anna and Deeley's, or Deeley and Kate's? The play closes as Anna lies on one divan while Deeley momentarily collapses across his wife's lap on the other. The three then separately remain together in the room even after Anna's exit. What happened?

Written the previous winter, *Old Times* appeared in London and New York in 1971 to win over most critics at the same time it still left them bewildered. What *really* happened? Did Deeley know Anna in the past? Did Anna and Kate have a lesbian relationship?

Harold Pinter finds such questions "a waste of time" (Gussow, "A Conversation . . .," 43) and directs critical attention instead to the play's more central concern—What is happening now? He points out that what really happened in the past does not really matter in the present:

> I think it's terribly difficult to define what happened yesterday. So much is imagined and that imagining is as same as real. (43)

Anna affirms that point:

> There are some things one remembers even though they may never have happened. (31–32)

As in *Landscape, Silence, and Night,* one of Pinter's main concerns here is with time. But *Old Times* is more than a variation of Pinter's former portrayal of time—that memory is faulty, that the line that separates the imaginary from the real is movable, that youth and a lifetime pass swiftly, and that what is lost in youth can never be wholly recovered, even in memory. In *Old Times* the past penetrates the present, the present, the future, as the private self thrusts itself into the public sphere. Pinter himself defines an almost Eastern attitude to time:

> I think I'm more conscious of a kind of ever-present quality of life. (132)

He adds, "I certainly feel more and more that the past is not past, that it never was past. It's present." (132)

The meaning of self takes on added dimension when the layered past of memory unconsciously exerts power in the present. Pinter says: "So much is imagined and that imagining is as true as real" and argues that the characters discussion of something that may or may not have taken place "actually seems to me to recreate the time and the moments vividly in the present, so that it is actually taking place before your very eyes—by the words he is using." (49)

The opening scene evokes the ever-present quality of time Pinter describes as Anna, standing at a distance in half-light in the moments before her anticipated arrival, is already both there and not there. On the purely realistic level she is not, but within the audience sightlines, in Kate's memory, in Deeley's present imagining as the two speak of her, and in their combined, immediate future, Anna is there. The final scene symmetrically suggests that the present intersects the future as Anna remains at the end even after she switches off the lights signaling her departure. Pinter says of the future:

> Well, it ought to be fanciful really. I know the future is simply going to be the same thing. It'll never end. You carry all the states with you until the end. (Gussow, 131–2)

Kate, Deeley, and Anna carry into the future their shared yet separately perceived experiences. Hence when Pinter was asked whether the relationship between Anna and Deeley would be less meaningful if it never occurred in the past, he answered, "No"—but again returns emphasis to the characters' present relationships:

> By the end of this particular section of the play, they are sharing something in the present. (43)

The relationships the characters create and share in the present are difficult to define for three reasons that also make *Old Times* such a richly complex, provocative drama. What the characters say when they appear together often has a triple significance—a different meaning for each of them; the relationships are protean—ever kaleidoscopically changing; and the play has no single central character—sympathies shift throughout as the three each attempt to gain center stage, to maintain or to gain a more powerful position over another.

Peter Hall who directed the London production put it more simply:

> The play dramatizes the fact that everyone is different with different people, that we put on different faces before we meet different people. (Hastings, n.p.)

As Anna's entering remembrance illustrates, the characters often wear three different masks simultaneously. While Anna attempts to renew her old friendship with Kate by recalling their shared past she deliberately excludes Deeley by ignoring him, which, however, only provokes him to take a more lively interest in her. At the same time she asserts (and creates for herself) her past and present identity: formerly a poor and innocent young woman with culturally refined tastes which had led her and Kate on trips to Covent Garden, Albert Hall, and the Tate, but she lives comfortably now with her husband in a villa in Sicily. When Anna concludes her long monologue with questions addressed to Kate (" . . . and does it still exist I wonder? do you know? can you tell me?" 18) it is Deeley, not Kate who replies, punctuating and puncturing Anna's ballooning reverie with: "We rarely get to London." (18) He simultaneously deflates Anna's fond raptures and inserts himself into the growing alliance between Anna and Kate.

Not only does each character relate to the other two in a slightly different way and to him or herself in yet a third, but the relationships are never static—no sooner is one formed, defined, nailed down than it immediately shifts slightly. Thus *Old Times* becomes for each of the characters a different play. Kate at first half welcomes, then rejects Anna's attempts to renew their friendship while she also quietly preserves a bond with her husband through her reserved, then more assertive, strength. Anna, though she later denies that she came to disrupt, half succeeds and half fails to wedge between Kate and Deeley while he consistently maneuvers to break up any alliance between the two women. Finally, weary from the effort and perhaps realizing his folly, Deeley collapses momentarily.

Deeley's recovery restores the opening symmetry where all the characters have roughly equivalent weight and importance. *Old Times*, like others of Pinter's plays, most notably *The Caretaker*, *Landscape*, *Silence*, and *Night*, is without a single protagonist. Although each of the characters asserts self-importance before the other two, shifting audience sympathies are fairly equally divided among the three, each bearing a share of different strengths and human weaknesses. Thus attempts to look for *the* odd man out, generally supposed to be Deeley, are as fruitless as attempts to figure out what *really* happened in the past. Each character does time as odd man out: as audience-observer to the antics of the other two; and each has moments of power upstaging the others to gain momentary entrance in the spotlight.

The original title of the play *Others with Dancers* underscores the dynamics of action and the nature of dominance in this play. The characters move as dancers around a spotlight they each aim for and enter, sometimes in alliance with another, or singly, thrusting the other out into the audience position to observe. A short poem Pinter wrote six months before the play not only describes an author's relationship to his characters entering the spotlight but, salient to understanding this play, also illuminates the relation of each of these characters to the other two. Each character authors the text of the other two characters' separate and joined past, where text is created by memory, projection, fancy, and verbal utterance (the poem/play's dialog):

poem

they kissed I turned they
 stared
with bright eyes turning to
 me blind
I saw that here where we
 were joined
the light that fell upon us
 burned
so bright the darkness that
 we shared
while they with blind eyes
 turning to me turned
and I their blind kiss formed.[1] (Gussow, 132)

Old Times is so rich in multiple meanings, delayed reactions, shifting alliances and sympathies that any analysis can only suggest some of the broad general relationships and changes. But the ethical implications return focus full force to the destructive consequences of the struggle for dominance at the private and now the public levels.

Where Deeley and Anna rival one another throughout, Kate asserts herself at the end. But the natural tension of the triangle forces one or another to the margins.

The opening scene, before Anna enters into the action, establishes some of the qualities of the private relationship and tensions between the husband and wife who chat elliptically, as people who have lived together long will. The tension defines desire: his is a slight nervousness, hers, an impatience. Kate is not anxious to see Anna; Deeley is curious. He asks the questions she answers with perfunctory precision:

> DEELEY: Did you *think* of her as your best friend?
> KATE: She was my only friend.
> DEELEY: Your best and only.
> KATE: My one and only. (9)

What remains unspoken is the desire to preserve the self and the relationship. Throughout the opening scene Kate generally maintains a slight edge over Deeley. When his questions about Anna threaten to go on and on, Kate terminates inquiry with, "Ask her," (9) adding, "Do you want me to ask your questions for you?" (13) Deeley persists. Kate refuses. He then challenges her, "Haven't you any curiosity?" Kate counters with, "You forget, I know her." (14)

Kate releases the growing tension with the amusing tale that Anna used to steal her underwear. But Deeley gains the last word by dismissing Kate's reluctance to answer his questions: "Anyway, none of this matters." (17) The play, however, ironically dramatizes precisely the opposite—all that happens matters very much to Deeley as the subtly ferocious battle escalates to a near life-and-death struggle for survival. What also matters is that what the characters do to one another actually creates and remains a living moment as they are no less stripped of their comfortable illusions at the end than the characters of Pinter's early work.

After Anna enters chatting about her past with Kate, Kate and Deeley as good host and hostess momentarily vie for Anna's attention; Kate brings coffee, and Deeley offers brandy.

Deeley soon upstages Kate for Anna's attention during the first act as Kate gradually, but never wholly, withdraws as audience to Deeley and Anna. At first when Kate's silence registers as a loss of interest, Deeley insults Kate before Anna. "She lacks curiosity," he says, a delayed reaction echoing his earlier unanswered, "Haven't you any curiosity?" (23) Anna's, "Perhaps she's happy," momentarily rouses Kate out of her silence to inquire, "Are you talking about me?" "Yes," Deeley answers but he and Anna continue to speak of Kate in the third person invisible. As though Kate were not there, Anna remarks, "She was always a dreamer." (23)

The alliance between Anna and Deeley strengthens as Deeley offers an indulgently lyrical description of Kate's face:

> Yes, I look at it, holding it in my hands. Then I kind of let it go, take my hands away, leave it floating. (24)

When Kate objects quite literally, "My head is quite fixed. I have it on," Deeley this time ignores her and says to Anna, "It just floats away." (24)

But next, instead of simply ignoring Kate, Deeley turns on her. When Anna tells Deeley that Kate once thought she slept through Friday, Deeley asks (in a borrowing from a song foreshadowing his round of singing with Anna), "You mean she literally *didn't know what day it was?*" but Kate interjects, defending herself, "Yes I did. It was Saturday." (25; italics indicate lyrics) He marginalizes her as if she were a child with, "What month are we in?" When Kate answers, "September," he reverts to his alliance to with Anna: "We're forcing her to think. We must see you more often. You're a healthy influence." (25)

Kate withdraws as Deeley now directs his barbs against Anna, who free associates on Deeley's remark to strengthen her alliance with him: "Sometimes I'd look at her face, but she was quite unaware of my gaze." (26) But Deeley checks her advance. "Gaze? Don't hear it very often," he says indicating that her vocabulary is dated. Anna and Deeley nevertheless entertain one another with a medley of sentimental love songs that amusingly threaten to go on and on until Deeley again checks Anna, this time by withdrawing his participation: "They don't make them like that anymore." (29)

But he thrusts Anna out of the spotlight which he refuses to share when he tells her how he met Kate. His compliment realigns him with his wife by indicating his preference for Kate over Anna:

> And there she was, very dim, very still, placed more or less I would say at the dead centre of the auditorium. I was off centre and have remained so. (30)

Parodying the marriage ceremony he says that they reached accord on the subject of Robert Newton's talent in the film *Odd Man Out*:

> So it was Robert Newton who brought us together and it is only Robert Newton who can tear us apart. (30)

When Anna intrudes, "F. J. McCormick was good too," Deeley dismisses her: "I know F. J. McCormick was good too. But he didn't bring us together." (30)

Throughout, disagreement elicits immediate, reflexive defense. Deeley reaffirms his alliance with Kate who joins him:

> DEELEY: (*To* Kate.) Remember that film?
> KATE: Oh yes. Very well. (31)

Deeley continues his narrative, "I think I am right in saying the next time we met we held hands," then pays Kate a supreme compliment: "I thought she was even more fantastic than Robert Newton." (31)

As in *The Lover*, no sooner are alliances established, than they must change. Driving his recollections of Kate beyond the merely polite, Deeley plunges into more intimate recollections of their erotic interactions:

> And then at a slightly later stage our naked bodies met, hers cool, warm, highly agreeable, and I wondered what Robert Newton would think of this. What would he think of this I wondered as I touched her profoundly all over. (31)

When Deeley turns to Anna with, "What do you think he'd think?" his comic quip, denoting a desire to be gazed upon by an audience, relieves any embarrassment. (31)

Nonplused by his oddly aggressive maneuver, Anna deflects it by responding openly, literally and with apparent sympathy, "I never met Robert Newton but I do know what you mean." (31) She then moves to regain the spotlight with a competing love story intended to spurn Deeley. Her story, about a man who came to visit Kate and lay across her lap, is intended to make Deeley jealous of some former lover of Kate's and at the same time, by implying that the lover was Deeley, Anna ousts Deeley from her shared past with Kate. Her story which ambiguously posits Deeley as Kate's lover who also made advances to her, allows Anna to reject Deeley: ". . . I would have absolutely nothing to do with him, nothing." (32)

Anna's recollection of their intimacy prefigures the future, the last scene with Deeley folded across Kate's lap. "A man in the dark across my wife's lap?" Deeley asks. Anna reports only that he returned and left again: "It was as if he had never been." (30) Her dismissal of the man in her story (as a surrogate for Deeley) anticipates Deeley's final impact on Kate and Anna at the end: he is reduced to near non-existence despite all his aggression.

But here Deeley returns with an adolescent bit of humor to cancel Anna's dismissal: "Of course he'd been. He went twice and came once." (33) When he sarcastically concludes, "Well, what an exciting story that was," (32) Anna's reaction, delayed until the second act, comes in her response to his story about his failure to reach Anna at the other side of a room at a party he claims they both attended: "I've rarely heard a sadder story," she says. (52) The three run right past the possibility that had he reached Anna at that juncture in their lives, Kate and Anna might have occupied reverse positions.

Kate interrupts, "You talk of me as if I were dead." (32) Anna then deliberately misunderstands: "No, no, you weren't dead, you were so lively, so animated, you used to laugh—." Deeley joins in, "Of course you did. I made you smile myself, didn't I?" (34) But when Anna carries misunderstanding too far, Deeley arrests Anna, then leaps to his wife's defense with: "Stop that." (35)

No sooner does Deeley defend Kate than he mitigates any virtue in having done so by returning to his narrative with even more intimate revelations about his wife, making up to Anna at the same time he abandons Kate to defend herself. He describes Kate in unflattering but perhaps apt terms as a woman "whose only claim to virtue was silence," then in unkindly intended reminder of her age adds:

> A classic female figure, I said to myself, or is it a classic female posture, one way or the other long outworn. (36)

Picking up on Deeley's slight aimed at Kate, Anna attempts to regain attention by returning to the subject of Kate's youth:

> When I heard that Katey was married my heart leapt with joy. (36)

Anna's sentiments, whether sincere or not, more unfortunately are mocked by her very tone that gives them expression. When she continues with a confused metaphor about testing the water before jumping, Deeley derides her. Yet Anna perseveres, "But in this case she did jump and I knew therefore she had fallen in love truly and was glad. And I deduced it must have happened to you." (36) Deeley again deflates her inflated rapture, "You mean the ripples?" (37)

Kate, too, mocks Anna's tone. When Anna says, "And later when I found out the kind of man you were I was doubly delighted because I knew Katey had always been interested in the arts," Kate ridicules her words, tone, and clichéd expression: "I was interested in the arts, but I can't remember now which ones." (37)

In response to the double attack from the other two, Anna maneuvers against Deeley by claiming she and Kate saw *Odd Man Out* at Kate's insistence. Deeley's deliberate attempt to side-step the implications of Anna's information indicates that he recognizes her counterattack: "Yes I do quite a bit of traveling in my job," (38) he says to Anna who follows his lead as she solicitously condescends to Kate, "Is he away for long periods?" (39) Kate, however, subtly cuts both Anna and Deeley with a vague, "I think, sometimes. Are you?" she asks Deeley. (39)

Deeley deflects Kate's slowly mounting attack with an inquiry about Anna's husband for whom, he says, they prepared a vegetarian dish. His remark dramatizes the distortion of even recent events by memory; in the opening, Deeley merely inquires whether Anna's husband was a vegetarian. But Anna continues to defend against attack by boasting about her present life: her husband a gourmet, their villa in Sicily.

Anna and Deeley realign with competing assertions recounting their successes in life. If there is a secondratedness in all Anna describes there may also be in Deeley's description of his work and self-proclaiming insistence, "As a matter of fact I am at the top of my profession, as a matter of fact. . . ." (42) Eager to top everything Anna says, he first establishes that he knows Sicily slightly, then ends in belittling it: "There's nothing more to see, there's nothing more to investigate, nothing." (42)

Deeley and Kate conspire to insult Anna who begins to show signs of slipping when she insists on remaining indoors for the evening. Unlike Kate who enjoys her night walks alone, Anna, like Rose in *The Room*, fears going out and fairly begs to remain in. Kate asks, "What shall we do then?" (44) But she softens her challenge by joining Anna in one last bit of shared reminiscence that again excludes Deeley:

> ANNA: Would you like me to ask someone over?
> KATE: Who?
> ANNA: Charley . . . or Jake.
> KATE: I don't like Jake.
> ANNA: Well, Charley . . . or . . .
> KATE: Who?
> ANNA: McCabe. (45–6)

Kate regains control by deferring her decision: "I'll think about it in the bath," she says to Anna who suddenly assumes full subservience, "Shall I run your bath for you?" (46) Kate declines, leaving Anna and Deeley looking at each other to close Act One.

The loaded closure between Anna and Deeley hooks into the second act set in the bedroom. A more intense, quicker paced, denser repetition of the shifting relationships in the first act, the second act, like the first, builds slowly after the initial overture to a nearly frenzied exchange of partners whose relationships several times break down before the final seeming collapse and separation of all at the end.

Without Kate as audience, Deeley and Anna establish an alliance which is at once closer and more hostile. Deeley insists he knew Anna too in the past, then draws her attention to the beds he describes as, "susceptible to any amount of permutation." (48) The erotic overtones disguise a barely veiled hostility, such as Lenny's asking Ruth if he minds if he holds her hand, and the focus on the beds may also communicate the present state of his marriage: "They can be separated as they are now," he says. (48) From here Deeley abruptly leaps into the middle of his remembrance of Anna in the past: "Yes I remember you quite clearly from the Wayfarers." (48) What he remembers, he says, is looking up her skirt.

Although Anna at first denies any past connection, she later reverses position when there seems some profit in it—an opportunity to make Kate jealous or a last ditch effort to retain the bond with

Deeley in the present. She even defends their past connection after Deeley doubts it and mutters, "If it was her skirt. If it was her." (71) Yet Anna's initial denial of a past connection is as much an attempt to put Deeley off, or to seem to, as it is an attempt to deny her more humble origins. But when Deeley flatters her, "You were the darling of the saloon bar," she softens her protest: "I wasn't rich, you know. I didn't have money for alcohol." (49)

Deeley quickly smudges his flattery and the image she tries to sustain as he says she didn't pay for drinks herself, that she had "escorts," and that he even bought her a few drinks. Whatever pleasure he took from an evening spent looking up her skirt at a party in the past, he offers no flattery in the present:

> That's something that's all over now, of course, isn't it, nothing like the same palpable profit in it now, it's all over. (51)

He then lightens his attack as he adopts the word "gaze" he earlier dismissed as archaic:

> But it was worthwhile then. It was worthwhile that night. I simply sat sipping my light ale and gazed . . . gazed up your skirt. You didn't object, you found my gaze perfectly acceptable. (51)

Anna begins to come round, "I was aware of your gaze was I?" (51) When Deeley finally says he never saw her after and asks what became of her, she asserts her more genteel identity, without now, however, wholly denying her past affiliation with him—she says she probably saw him at concerts or the ballet.

Anna then initiates a discussion of Kate's bath taking which Deeley plays for all its sexual innuendoes. He first complains that Kate doesn't dry herself properly; "I've got a brilliant idea. Why don't we do it with powder?" he proposes to Anna. She derails his enthusiasm with, "Is that a brilliant idea?" then adds, "It's quite common to powder yourself after a bath." (56) Deeley redeems his suggestion, besting Anna:

> It's quite common to powder yourself after a bath, but it's quite uncommon to be powdered. Or is it? It's not common where I come from, I can tell you. My mother would have a fit. (56)

And he pushes his suggestions to the limit positioning himself to relate simultaneously to both women:

> Listen. I'll tell you what. I'll do it. I'll do the whole lot, the towel and powder. After all, I am her husband. But you can supervise the whole thing. And give me some hot tips while you're at it. That'll kill two birds with one stone. (56)

He might like to kill both birds, but a moment later he redresses Anna's resistance to him. By withdrawing his verbally sexual flattery and positioning himself with comic effect in the past, he counters with another reminder of her age:

> You must be about forty, I should think, by now.
> (*Pause*).
> If I walked into the Wayfarers Tavern now, and saw you in the corner, I wouldn't recognize you. (57)

Fresh from her bath, Kate emerges apparently pleased that Anna and Deeley appear to be getting on. But instead of joining them she asserts her strength as independence. Kate walks to the window while Deeley and Anna, anxious to regain Kate as audience, join in another round of singing, re-establishing their alliance that pointedly excludes Kate. But it is not possible to exclude someone who has excluded herself.

Still smiling, Kate turns to them as their singing continues "faster on cue, and more perfunctorily." (58) From now until the end of the play Kate gains a steadily stronger influence over the other two than they generally do over her; Anna admits being affected by Kate, "Doesn't she look beautiful." (59) Although she still addresses Kate indirectly, Kate continues to assert her strength by voicing her preference for the country in opposition to Anna's preference for London:

> There aren't such edges here. And living close to the sea too. You can't say where it begins or ends. That appeals to me. I don't care for harsh lines. I deplore that kind of urgency. (59)

Kate prefers tranquil, inner contentment to what she perceives as aggressive ambition, which both Anna and Deeley exhibit in their mutual attempts to impress one another:

> I would like to go to the East, or somewhere like that somewhere very hot, where you can lie under a mosquito net and breathe quite slowly. You know . . . somewhere where you can look through the flap of a tent and see sand, that kind of thing. (59)

Then echoing Deeley's cadence when he repudiated Sicily, Kate squelches Anna's enthusiasm for the city:

> The only nice thing about a big city is that when it rains it blurs everything, and it blurs the lights from the cars, doesn't it, it blurs your eyes, and you have rain on your lashes. That's the only nice thing about a big city. (59)

Anna's attempt to defend city life, reveals a deeper preference for the cozy shelter of a room:

> That's not the only nice thing. You can have a nice room and a nice gas fire and a warm dressing gown and a nice hot drink, all waiting for you when you come in. (59)

Both Kate and Anna make a virtue out of neither engaging with nor making an impact upon the outside world. But where Kate's preference for solitude is redeemed as an extension of an inner, even courageous strength to remain true to herself, at least to her own desires, Anna reveals her choice as a fearful retreat from the world. Moreover, Kate's strength which others seek seems to strengthen others. Kate defers to Anna's preference for interiors but maintains control of the situation when she decides that they will stay in tonight. Anna, apparently grateful, continues her obsequiousness to Kate where she left off before Kate's bath: "I could hem your dress." (60)

Deeley, meanwhile, never consulted, is not long able to tolerate the growing alliance between the women. When he interjects his double intended, "Have you dried yourself properly, Kate?" which can only have real significance to Anna, he communicates an attempt to subordinate Kate as if she were a child. (60) But Kate avoids engaging with him by smiling at Deeley who again positions himself simultaneously to relate to both Kate and Anna by offering the last word on the *Odd Man Out* topic:

> That's the same smile she smiled when I was walking down the street with her, after *Odd Man Out*, well, quite some time after. (61)

He commands, "Do it again," but when Kate, unable to remain disengaged, replies, "I'm still smiling," he criticizes, "You're not. Not like you were a moment ago." (61) Kate deflects his criticism to Anna who made the coffee. "This coffee's cold," she complains to Anna who dutifully apologizes, "Oh I'm sorry. I'll make some fresh." (61)

Kate, positioning herself as guest in her own home, withdraws her attack against Anna by returning to the subject of Charley, McCabe, Duncan, and Christy whom she likes best and describes as gentle and sensitive with a sense of humor she then praises. All this excludes Deeley so when Kate proposes, "Why don't you ask him round?" Deeley quickly pronounces, "He can't make it. He's out of town." (63) Moreover, Deeley fairly invites Anna to leave when he asks whom else she intends to visit; but before her dismissal he engages Anna in another round. "Do you find her changed?" he asks Anna, who then describes Kate as still shy:

> I put it down to her upbringing, a parson's daughter, and indeed there was a good deal of Brontë in her. (64)

Anna adds an indirect overture to Deeley, also revealing her desire to break through Kate's reserve:

> But if I thought Brontë I did not think Brontë in passion but only in secrecy, in being so stubbornly private.[2] (64)

Anna continues her overture with her version of the stolen underwear story—she borrowed it she says. She uses the story of Kate's first blush (a vicarious blush for Anna's misdeeds) as a vehicle for half affirming her past connection with Deeley with a slightly barbed twist aimed against both Kate and Deeley:

> But I told her that in fact I had been punished for my sin, for a man at the party had spent the whole evening looking up my skirt. (65)

Deeley understands the double connection and apparently the allusion to his recent chat with Anna when he parries: "Looking up *your* skirt at *her* underwear. Mmnn." (65) When he then encourages Anna to tell more, "What was she in passion?" Anna backs off returning an insult, "I feel that is your province." (66) Although he initiated the topic Deeley now angrily voices his distaste for it:

> You feel it's my province? Well, you're damn right. It is my province. I'm glad someone's showing a bit of taste at last. Of course it's my bloody province. I'm her husband.
>
> [*Pause*]
>
> I mean I'd like to ask a question. Am I alone in beginning to find all this distasteful? (67)

When Anna demurs, claiming innocence, Deeley momentarily glimpses the ridiculousness of being sucked into the immediate situation:

> I mean let's put it on the table, I have my eye on a number of pulses, pulses all around the globe, deprivations and insults, why should I waste valuable space listening to two—(67)

While his reference opens the play up to a larger sphere, Kate swiftly closes it down by interjecting an alliance with her guest, "If you don't like it go." (67) But Deeley responds, in distant echo of Stanley, "Go? Where can I go?" (67) Kate humorously offers, "Oh China. Or Sicily." But responding reflexively, Deeley rejects both Sicily, "I haven't got a speed boat. I haven't got a white dinner jacket," then China, "You know what they'd do to me in China if they found me in a white dinner jacket. They'd bloodywell kill me." (68) Deeley's references to the larger world, reveal at the same time the ornamental position Deeley plays in that world.

Anna attempts to continue her faltering relationship with Deeley and Kate by extending an empty invitation they almost certainly would reject: "You are welcome to come to Sicily at any time, both of you, and be my guests." (68) At this point Kate and Deeley who have been operating roughly parallel courses, reform their unspoken alliance as they stare at Anna, a distant echo of Aston and Mick's exchanged stare before they expel *The Caretaker*'s Davies.

Anna reads the implications of their silent stare and defends herself in a reverse echo of Antony's funeral oration:

> I would like you to understand that I came here not to disrupt but to celebrate. (68)

All her immediate actions belie her assertion; she continues to disrupt by appealing to Kate in a way which both excludes and angers Deeley: "To celebrate a very old and treasured friendship, something that was forged between us long before you knew of our existence." (68) She blunders on, "I found her," repeating the story about her shared past with Kate, the coffeehouses they frequented where artists and "others with dancers" gathered.

Deeley not only re-inserts himself into the alliance Anna is trying to maintain, but he remains a step ahead of her. "We've met before," he tells Kate and offers his distorted recollections fabricated from Anna's story, like Meg's garbled version of Stanley's musical success recounted to Goldberg and McCann and like Sarah's description of her lover. More important, Deeley attempts to assert his own youthfulness by deploying contemporary 1960s hippy slang which only emphasizes his age:

> We had a scene together. She freaked out. She didn't have any bread, so I bought her a drink. (69)

Together Kate and Deeley move to exclude Anna. Deeley defends Kate as he dismisses Anna's flirtation in the past saying she was "pretending to be you at the time." (69) Kate cues right in on his tactics by verbally making love to her husband via Anna: "What do you think attracted her to you?" Kate asks Deeley then offers, "She found your face sensitive, vulnerable," and finally, "She wanted to comfort it, in the way only a woman can," (70)—which is perhaps what Kate does in the end offer Deeley: comfort.

Kate's stronger dismissal of Anna comes in the form of another delayed reaction (like Sam's in *The Homecoming*). To Anna's speaking of her as if she were dead, "I remember you dead," Kate cues in on Deeley's tactics to attack with an imaginatively unflattering sketch of Anna:

> You tried to do my little trick, one of my tricks you had borrowed my little slow smile, my little slow shy smile, my bend of the head, my half closing of the eyes, that we knew so well, but it didn't work, the grin only split the dirt at the sides of your mouth and stuck. (71)

More than a reminder of mortality, Kate's vicarious killing expresses her understanding of Anna's attempted alliance with Deeley in the present as an effort to expel Anna from her remembered past: "After all, you were dead in my room." (72) Kate now co-opts their shared room as hers alone. She asserts that her own past alliance with Deeley was stronger than hers with Anna when she notes that he, unlike Anna, resisted her ritual burial: "He suggested a wedding instead, and a change of environment." (73) Finally, when Deeley had asked her who had slept in the bed before him, Kate's answer—"I told him no one. No one at all,"—deletes Anna, just as Anna expunged Deeley from her memory of their room. (73)

Anna, however, never quite exits from their lives. Their different reactions to the same experiences and their distorted remembrances of possibly shared experiences all remain. To describe the dominant/subservient tactics, the alliances that are formed and nearly destroyed, the multiple meanings, and delayed reactions all reduce the play to a game—and it is so much more. Peter Hall notes, "It's a very funny play, and also very erotic." (Hastings, n.p.) When Pinter was asked if *Old Times* was about love, romantic love, he asserts that so were others of his plays. (Gussow, 126)

Old Times is a complex dramatization of friendship and love, neither of which wholly fails or succeeds. The only moment two characters touch, when Deeley seeks silent comfort in his wife's lap, suggests a bond reaffirmed—they together, like Kate alone, will "continue." But their relationship is hardly one of equality, and in the end Deeley's collapse signals an irreversible loss of his private but central position in the household. Moreover the final separation of all the characters within the same room suggests the incompleteness with which the alliances were formed or will continue. Attempts to assert power for Anna and Deeley are more than attempts to assert their worth; but for Kate, it is also an attempt to maintain the relationship that is most important to her: her marriage. Deeley's effort to sabotage the relationship between the women, to claim his own greater importance to Kate, only sabotages his relationship with Kate, and at the end he is reduced rather than enlarged in his attempts to destroy or at least to damage an old friendship.

Old Times is not, however, a dramatization of the pathetic time in these characters' midlives when the "looking forwardness of it all," as Anna defines happiness, has slipped past. The play that might easily border on the sentimental is redeemed by the vitality of the present actions of the three—actions which are no less engaging to view than are their remembrances of youthful passion they attempt to recapture.

The play extends the dramatization of destructive consequences of the lack of self-knowledge by portraying that lack of consciousness it springs from—the conflict can only work with willing participants and what keeps these characters willingly engaged is their lack of conscious choice to act otherwise. They respond instead with a knee-jerk reflex to every taunt and innuendo which threatens what they regard as the self and its relations with others. Even the reserved and reticent Kate proves herself a worthy and willing opponent not long able to remain aloof from contest. The contest only obliquely references the world beyond the walls that contain these people but does so to register their outward comfort and success as no indicator of inner strength or happiness. But, obversely, the private dismantling will have repercussions on their public selves.

The conflict holds in abeyance any question of justice except the injustices inflicted unconsciously upon one another and ultimately themselves. But something is affirmed in the end when illusion is stripped away to reveal some truth characters must now face, or fail to confront in themselves. Truth becomes the justice sought in the fractal geometry of this unrelenting conflict whose colors here begin to include the full spectrum in which love and what limited justice can occur are intimately interwoven.

Pinter, with his infallible sense of theatre, ear for the comic in the quotidian, and poet's economy, precision, and layered meanings, exposes and conveys the depths and limitations of love and friendship when contest enters, takes over, and destroys. He concludes: "I'll tell you one thing about *Old Times.* It happens. It all happens." (Gussow, "A Conversation . . . " 49)

Notes

1. The poem appears in *I Know the Place* with more prose like line breaks:

   they kissed I turned they stared
   with bright eyes turning to me blind
   I saw that here where we were joined
   the light that fell upon us burned
   so bright the darkness that we shared
   while they with blind eyes turning to me turned
   and I their blind kiss formed. (n.p.)

2. Pinter played Rochester to Vivien Merchant's Jane Eyre before they were married.

Langrishe, Go Down, *À La Recherche Du Temps Perdu: The Proust Screenplay*, and *Monologue*: Remembrances of Things Past

Langrishe, Go Down

In the interim between *Old Times* and his next full-length play, *No Man's Land*, Pinter wrote two screenplays and the brief *Monologue*. Again concerned with memory and time, *Langrishe, Go Down*, adapted, from the novel by Aidan Higgins, produced as a television film flashes back to Imogen's youthful affair with Otto, a Bavarian graduate student living on the Langrishe land. The film's focus on love through Imogen's past set against her old age, alone with her sister Helen, offers the flip side of *The Go-Between* but connects with it: both dramatizing the power of youthful love to persist throughout a lifetime and remain possibly a consolation of old age.

À La Recherche Du Temps Perdu: The Proust Screenplay

Pinter's fascination with the relation between time past and present culminates in *À la Recherche du Temps Perdu: The Proust Screenplay*, adapted from the novel by Marcel Proust, and written in 1972 with the collaboration of Joseph Losey and Barbara Bray. The screenplay dramatizes a distillation of the entire seven-volume Proust novel. Like Beckett's slender monograph *Proust*, it relives for a reader the major experience of the novel, a sensitive young man's entrance into love and a society he outgrows and transcends but sets out through writing to recapture as the memorable center of his life. From the love affairs to the societal sparring matches, each beat remains infused with the Pinter tension of the grand gesture toward power.

Undercutting Marcel's desires which drive the screenplay—his love for Albertine and for Gilberte, his obsessive (unsuccessful) attempts to verify the truth, his suspicions of Albertine's lesbian infidelities which horrify him, but which he can neither rival nor counter—is time. Pinter, with Proust's magnificent indirection, turns the narrator's stated homophobic revulsion for lesbianism (and by analogy homosexuality) into a felt (rather than merely rational) apology for what he condemns by protesting too much and by his (and our own) fascination with explicit, sexually provocative actions we witness. As Marcel observes Albertine and Andree dancing, Marcel listens to an older man remark, "It's not sufficiently known that women derive most excitement from their breasts. Theirs are completely touching." (99) Time's inexorable advance transforms the entire society he once admired into a gathering of aging, painted, vacuous masks, horrifying not only at the surface but also for its lack of substance beneath. The pleasure-seeking, frivolous, decaying aristocracy, who prefigure the privileged party seekers in *Party Time,* is, however, dotted with composers, musicians, scholars and lovers whose work and vitality, though often misunderstood, or unacknowledged in its time, give their living dimension the others lack and supply the screenplay with multiple lenses with which to view the artist. In the end Marcel withdraws from life and society to recapture, in a massive labor of love, the mystery and intrigue, the love and passion he, and we as audience, have already witnessed. He concludes, "It was time to begin." (171)

In the introduction Pinter notes that those working on the film script decided "that the architecture of the film should be based on two main contrasting principles: one, a movement, chiefly narrative, toward disillusion, and the other, more intermittent, toward revelation, rising to where time that was lost is found, and fixed forever in art." (ix) Pinter tried to find cinematic expression for memory that could offer a more acute experience than life. The vast scope of the novel and, simultaneously, both the distance and proximity gained allow Pinter a fresh perspective on the grand sweep and futility of the all-consuming gestures to power in the social sphere.

Monologue

Monologue, in which Pinter played the Man in the radio broadcast, continues to intertwine memory with the dominant/subservient contest as the comfortably situated middle-aged Man, addressing an imaginary interlocutor recalls his motorbike, their youth, a particularly erotic moment with a black woman the Man will obviously never forget. Even in the friendly, nostalgic banter resides the ubiquitous kernel of tension derived from a sparring competition over a past romance. The Man's concluding line, "I love your children," cuts two ways: suggesting an embracing, unconditional generosity and, at the same time, a proprietary appropriation of the other man's children.

No Man's Land: Past Dominance Regained

In *No Man's Land,* Hirst and Spooner continue Pinter's interest in competitive gamesmanship combined with memory in a play which explicitly takes virtue as its stated theme. When the famous, now dead-ended poet Hirst invites the seedy, failed poet Spooner into his home where they are joined by a pair of spiny, houseboy-bodyguards and lovers Foster and Briggs, Hirst hints he may have killed the woman he loved (at least in spirit), while Spooner proudly admits he has never been loved. But when Spooner attempts to insert himself into their domestic scene, Foster and Briggs counterattack with all the force of thugs. Yet with the greatest economy and subtly, it is Hirst who delivers the cruelest blow. When Spooner in the end offers his life in service to Hirst, Hirst dismisses him with "Let's change the subject." (91) Here in a gray world without women, where an acclaimed position cannot protect the private self, love again asserts itself in the forefront, displacing name and fame and fortune as the remembered greatest good.

As Hirst enters ushering Spooner into his home and offers drinks, *No Man's Land* announces itself as a play about virtue, where virtue is defined etymologically as strength. From the opening moments the fractal geometry of this play explicitly begins to link love and justice remembered in the past and enacted in the present through the failure of both. Spooner's opening line resumes a discourse on the topic of strength. He promotes a belief that there are "some people who appear to be strong, whose idea of what strength consists of is persuasive, but who inhabit the idea not the fact." (16) He dismisses such apparent strength as "expertise," and "calculated posture," which, he nevertheless concedes, "half the time works." (16) Yet he also claims to know the real thing: "It takes a man of intelligence and perception to stick a needle through that posture and discern the essential flabbiness of the stance. I am such a man." (16) The play moves forward as a test to Spooner's hypothesis, his own virtue and his ability to lance Hirst's posture.

Spooner garrulously monopolizes all talk as he pronounces his host "kindness itself," compliments his home as "[s]afe from all danger," and defines the source of his own "security," "solace," and "comfort" as resting "in the confirmation that I elicit from people of all kinds a common and constant level of indifference." (17)

In fact, however, Spooner reveals only that he has schooled himself in a stoic's course of diminished expectation training: to expect nothing is to fail at nothing. His position which he perceives as "fixed, concrete" places him among the most subservient of Pinter's great many subservient characters. But Spooner attempts to make of subservience a virtue.

He further describes himself as futureless, beyond "the looking forwardness" that defines happiness in *Old Times*, indeed "beyond expectation." (18) But he is not without a quest, at least a question. As a man who has devoted his life to language addressing another who has done the same, he tells Hirst, "All we have left is the English language." (18) Then he asks, "Can it be salvaged? That is my question." (18) Hirst pronounces that responsibility Spooner's: "Its salvation must rest in you." (19)

But Spooner, as the play on his name indicates, demonstrates how language can remain stalled in mere words, expressing mere attitude and intention where language falls short of action. In contrast, as Hirst deploys language, mere words can transform into action: a weapon, a bludgeon and power. Yet as Hirst enters battle to reclaim lost glory through victory over Spooner, past loves remain unforgotten, and betrayal becomes the one unforgivable offense.

Pinter's set-up for *No Man's Land* resembles the ironic closure of Proust's *À la Recherche du Temps Perdu.* The Proustian narrator after nearly seven volumes of what appears to be one of the wisest, deeply insightful explorations of the life of his time and society, now poised to begin to recapture his observations in writing, happens across the Goncourt journal where he discovers to his despair that what he hopes to write has already been written—and better. He reports Goncourt's attention to detail and minutia he missed: down to patterns on the china at a dinner party. But Proust's fear is a scholar's fear, not an artist's whose vision remains individual. The Goncourt journal, for all its trivia mirrored, only serves as a foil to the greater depth and insight in the dramatic observations of Proust's narrator. But that wonderfully heart-sinking moment, like Wordsworth's epiphany "*That we had crossed the Alps*" in *The Prelude,* throws the protagonist into a void whose only exit requires not merely scaling the wall out but surmounting a mountain peak beyond. (684; italics in original) Wordsworth transcends his deep despair which assails him when he realizes he has passed the peak without even knowing it, by taking an infinite perspective, a view through nature outside that lifts him above mere temporal and earthly existence. He finds consolation as a teacher: "What we have loved others will love and we will teach them how." In Proust's case the discovery remains earthly, more concrete and immediate, and belongs equally to the reader and narrator. The attentive reader already knows what Proust's narrator has yet to learn: that he has already transcended mere surface detail by offering up the heart, the mind, the soul of each of his multitude of characters, moreover he has allowed them to reveal themselves through their own speech and actions filtered through the eye of a narrator whose generosity of spirit has allowed us as reader to care deeply for him, for his welfare, and to some degree for all those he casts his eye upon. Finally Proust knows the impossibility of transcending mutability. But in allowing the reader full confrontation with its human horrors he achieves the only human catharsis possible: a felt realization of the value of the present moment and of life itself.

Pinter's Spooner and Hirst can admit no such mediation of a narrator. Only the authorial vision allows us to see what is missing in both poets, the failed and the famous wordmonger: some deeper connection and commitment to love. What can be the value of their published words, given the lives their words must express and reflect? Ironically it may be the apparently more cruel Hirst who comes closer to recognizing and acknowledging that such a failure of spirit more than any failure of language is what condemns him to no man's land, where there can be neither love nor justice.

Spooner's verbosity is initially matched only by the taciturn Hirst's silence. Spooner insists the aim, in virtue and in writing as it conveys virtue, is to "keep the proper distance between yourself and others . . . an objective relation to matter" or "the game's not worth the candle," and that "what is obligatory to keep in your vision is space." (19) His self-advertised aims and intentions prove the opposite in action.

Spooner dismisses the commonly held assumption that virtue is tested in action. He also rejects the value of his own past actions. When Hirst observes, "You speak with the weight of experience behind you," Spooner's humor diminishes and dismisses its value: "And beneath me." (20) He instead discourses on "experience as a paltry thing," and wittily offers to "leave experience to psychological interpreters, the wet dream world." (20)

The snares, dangers, and traps are set not in past action but, as they must be in drama, in the present moment, and as Spooner observes: "The present is truly unscrupulous." (20) Yet in the same breath he introduces himself as a poet, living in an almost Zen relationship to reality: "I am interested in where I am eternally present and active." (20) The ending proves otherwise as his actions belie his aim. Too late Spooner discovers he is indeed interested in his future, which his present has almost no power to direct. Yet his "point" he says, "in case you've missed it":

> I am a free man. (21)

What is the nature of his freedom? Spooner believes he has nothing to lose. He momentarily enjoys a chiasmic exchange of position with Hirst by acting the host to his host, offering him a whiskey. When Hirst, who takes it "as it comes," asks Spooner if he finds the Jack Straw as "beguiling a public house" or "much changed," Spooner claims "it changed my life." (24) His seemingly aimless chatter wanders to recollecting a Hungarian emigre whose "serenity the like of which I had never encountered," but which so impressed Spooner he says, "I am quite sure, made me what I am." (24) Significantly, Spooner notes, "It was not what he said, but possibly the way he sat which has remained with me all my life." (25)

By now the very mention of sitting, which in Pinter's work precludes action, carries with it ethical connotations. It is in what Spooner chooses to admire and to emulate, a posture rather than an act, that his downfall begins. Sitting in Pinter's work is rarely equated with virtue as strength which Spooner espouses or with action which virtue entails.

When Spooner returns to his opening gambit, the topic of virtue, he asks if Hirst knows where "I derive my strength," then answers himself: "I have never been loved." (26) The failure to love or to inspire love in another connects here with strength, or rather the lack of it, at physical and intellectual levels to become one defining feature of no man's land.

Mid-discourse Spooner interjects: "Perhaps it's about time I introduced myself." (27) He then describes himself as "a staunch friend of the art of poetry, and a guide to the young." (27) Detailing the open house he keeps for writers, Spooner next links art to virtue when he asks, "What quarrel can be found with what is, *au fond*, a gesture towards the sustenance and preservation of art, and through art to virtue?" (28)

Finally entering the conversation, Hirst more narrowly, almost puritanically limits definition of virtue to sexual prohibition. Free associating from the country cottage where Spooner and his wife entertained young poets and gave them tea, Hirst describes his village church's custom of hanging garlands to honor young women who die virgin, and young men "all who die unmarried, wearing the white flower of a blameless life." (29) He equates "blameless," solely with innocence of sexual experience, prompting one of Spooner's several humorously goading remarks: "Tell me more about the quaint little perversions of your life and times." (30) Then with barely a beat, Spooner asks Hirst to tell him about his wife.

But before Hirst responds, Spooner describes his own. Indulging in adolescent humor he says his wife had everything: "Eyes, a mouth, hair, teeth, buttocks, breasts, absolutely everything. And legs," to which Hirst significantly retorts: "Which carried her away." (31) Spooner wonders where his wife now is, "Cowering in a locked room, perhaps?" an echo of the mad woman imprisoned in the attic in *Jane Eyre*.[1] Spooner (ambiguously conflating their two wives) asks whether Hirst "truly did love her" and "did truly husband her, falsely dreamed or did truly adore her." (31) When he interjects, "I take it her eyes were hazel," Spooner has finally struck an open wound: a reminder of Hirst's wife. (32)

Roused, Hirst says, "Tonight ... my friend ... you find me in the last lap of a race ... I had long forgotten to run." (32) But Hirst's seeming confession is met by Spooner's sarcasm, the lowest form of wit but one which Spooner seldom transcends: "A metaphor. Things are looking up." (32) Spooner then offers to "salute what I take to be your impotence," having just confessed to his own, he claims sex as a thing of his past. (33)

Nevertheless Spooner offers, "I am a relevant witness. And could be a friend." (33) But could he be a friend if he refuses or is unable to be Hirst's equal? This rare reference to friendship in Pinter's work only briefly conceals Spooner's real desire: to be Hirst's Charon, his "boatman" to ferry him across the river Lethe into the land of the dead. We soon learn why. Spooner's wife had been carried away by Hirst.

Yet Hirst confesses that he is in "No man's land," which he says, "does not move ... or change ... or grow old ... " but "remains forever ... icy ... silent." (34) He staggers to a chair and ends in crawling out of the room. Spooner, in humorous echo of T.S. Eliot's "Prufrock," remarks, "I have known this before. The exit through the door, by way of belly and floor." (34)

The play continues to question a simplistic view of Christian virtue which equates chastity with the whole of morality. Hirst's and Spooner's repeated references to betrayal with a best man, a theme which will carry over again into *Betrayal*, link and color definitions of virtue as friendship and love. In this seemingly static play in which nothing very much seems to happen, everything happens and mocks pretensions of virtue that fail when tested by chance and action.

Foster enters, infusing a chill of fear: "I don't carry a gun in London." (35) His denial is a threat and a weapon. He is joined by Briggs who says that he knows Spooner as a cafe busboy, who collects the beer mugs. But he only momentarily squelches Spooner's pretension to prove himself their better. While Foster and Briggs can claim acquaintance with Siam and Bali, probably as seamen, Spooner pipes up, "I've been to Amsterdam." (39) Flinging out a barrage of language, Spooner describes a landscape he would have liked to paint in a speech which serves as a transparent smoke screen to keep at bay the unspoken threat of violence from these men. As long as Spooner can keep talking, he believes he can forestall harm.

But beneath Spooner's desperate monologue lurks his attempt to regain his own superior position, lost when he was outdistanced by the underclass men on the topic of travel. He mobilizes a lofty vocabulary, slings its weight into the description of a picture he planned but never painted, titled "The Whistler." This echo of one of the most familiar names in Western art suggests the derivative nature of Spooner's work and the impossibility of his matching that painter's fame. Seeming to engage the men as equals, he asks if the title might have baffled them. Foster maintains ground, agreeing he might have been baffled, but adds he might have "appreciated the picture" and "even been grateful for it." (39) For all Spooner's eloquent but dusty, academic-sounding verbiage on art as virtue, only the thug hits upon that quality essential to all art if it is to survive. Foster is the only one who offers a measure of what must be a *sine qua non* of art: "A good work of art tends to move me." (39)

Foster confronts Spooner's unspoken attempts to keep him at bay and in his place with a characteristic verbal violence. Aimed at the game beneath the exchange, he returns fire: "I'm not a cunt you know." (39) Aesthetics and sex mingle for Foster as aesthetics and virtue do for Spooner, but Foster's use of the word "cunt," a denigrating synecdoche, denies and denigrates the feminine in himself as well as some portion of his own sexuality.

Hirst, recovered after a brief nap, reenters to reveal himself more direct, honest, and less compelled to use language as subterfuge and camouflage than Spooner. He prefers, he admits, human company: "I've tried laughing alone. Pathetic." (44) But his thugs, as an extension of himself, prevent any great outflow of audience sympathy for him, his lonely life, or bereft position.

Hirst extends a small degree of intimacy to Spooner, offering him the privilege of seeing his photograph album. But the momentary warm impulse dissolves into a request for a drink, "Who is the kindest among you?" (45)

Hirst wonders if without his bodyguards he would have to wait for a stranger to fill his cup. Briggs answers with a glass:

> You'd crawl to the bottle and stuff it between your teeth. (45)

Hirst deflects insult by turning upon Spooner: "Who is this man?" (44) When Foster responds, "He says he's a friend of yours," Hirst retreats to the past, the photograph album where the past is still alive in the present as "true friends" and where "youth, which can never leave me." (45) But after a swig from the bottle, he twice reverses attitude: "It's gone. Did it exist? It's gone. It never existed. It remains." (45) When he remembers his wife, it is primarily as loss, "When I stood my shadow fell upon her," and in echo of Len with the hole in his side, her absence now leaves "a gap in me.

I can't fill it." (46) But he later tries to fill it by taking action: by doing battle with Spooner.

Did he kill his own wife? He does not seem to distinguish between her death and a dream which conflates her death with his own: "Who was drowning in my dream?" he asks, saying he feels a "flood running through me. I can't plug it," then exclaims simultaneously as both attacked and attacker: "They're blotting me out. Who is doing it? I'm suffocating." As a ventriloquist he speaks for the victim: "Someone is doing me to death," but he quickly transforms the topic of death into the lovedeath ecstasy of poetry: "She looked up. I was staggered. I had never seen anything so beautiful." (46)

The freshly singular use of "staggered" is echoed in one of Pinter's most striking love poems, the 1975 "Paris" where "the light/ Staggers in her eyes," as the lover's gaze fuses the lover with the beloved through the look in her eyes:

> The curtain white in folds,
> She walks two steps and turns,
> The curtain still, the light
> Staggers in her eyes.
>
> The lamps are golden.
> Afternoon leans, silently.
> She dances in my life.
> The white day burns. (*I Know the Place*, n.p.)

When Spooner interposes himself to rescue Hirst from his own scenario, "It was I drowning in your dream," Foster slams back, "Bugger off." (47) Spooner still seems to be the man of enlarged sympathies when he says, "There's no pity in these people," (47) but he soon assumes an increasingly servile posture, while claiming, "I am your true friend. That's why your dream . . . was so distressing." (49)

His gesture of seeming compassion in fact only invites attention and sympathy to himself as he interprets the drowning man (not woman) in the dream to be himself. He then assures Hirst he is not drowned. But Spooner merely takes a small step toward *feeling* compassion; when he finally offers to *act*, it is only to make coffee. Spooner's assuming a traditionally woman's task only underscores his inability to take a woman's place or any place as Briggs offers a swift comeback: "He thinks he's a waiter in Amsterdam." (48)

Foster and Briggs cannot allow their position to be threatened by a character who gives new definition to Pinter's subservient characters—becoming one of the most subservient of all. But Spooner is also fighting to maintain his life and thus gathers audience sympathy as Foster ups the ante and the threat. Foster claims that he and Briggs offer Hirst more than friendship—they offer love:

> Listen chummybum. We protect this gentleman against corruption, against men of craft, against men of evil, we could destroy you without a glance, we take care of this gentleman, we do it out of love. (49)

Foster reminds Spooner he is outclassed: "It's a world of silk," he says, "Flower arrangements. It's a world of eighteenth century cookery books. It's nothing to do with toffeeapples and a packet of crisps. It's milk in the bath. It's the cloth bellpull. It's organisation." (49) Briggs and Foster jealously guard Hirst's world because their only entrance and continued commerce in this world may be as servants in this man's household. The relish with which Foster catalogs the goods of Hirst's world indicates his own identification with those goods and with his position. Like all servants Foster derives rank via his master's.

Foster pushes the privilege of position to the limit as a weapon against Spooner: "We deal in originals. Nothing duff, nothing ersatz, we don't open any old bottle of brandy." (49) But his mention of "organisation," suggesting both order and the notion of an organization, arcs from *The Dumb Waiter* and *Birthday Party* through to *Party Time*, *The New World Order* and *Moonlight*. Here the organization is comprised of three against the intruders of the world. Their organization is supported by the larger economic and class privilege that Pinter's characters for the first time make explicit: distinguishing those it supports from those it expels. Spooner as a poor man will remain as excluded from the castle as Davies the tramp is from the dump.

Foster proposes to Briggs, "Why don't I kick his head off and have done with it?" (49) The verbal violence and physical threat barely mask Foster's own insecurity. Foster then lords Hirst's credentials as "a creative man" over Spooner, a comically ironic reference to the old man slumped drunkenly in a chair. Foster's assertion, "He's an artist," (49) only reduces the too-familiar term "artist" in this context, nullifying its ability to convey a reflexive reverence or automatic kinship to virtue as Spooner earlier argued. But Foster further threatens Spooner by calling their arrangement a family, not intended to open out to or enter the larger communal world but to exclude it: "Don't try to drive a wedge into a happy household. . . . Don't try to make a nonsense out of family life." (50; ellipses, mine) This symbiotic arrangement of three men could only be regarded as family as an underworld mob might regard itself, yet it would seem to be all the family any of the three men has.

Where Spooner earlier said he was beyond expectation, Foster, in marked contrast, claims he "could do something else," believes he "could make another life," and he is young enough to do so. (52)

Foster's threat culminates physically.[2] "You know what it's like when you're in a room with the light on and then suddenly the light goes out? I'll show you." (53) Snapping out the lights, his simple gesture closes the act with a scabbard of impending violence hanging over Spooner's head, revealing how small a gesture is required to frighten a death-threatened man.

The second act, however, opens on a slightly lighter note as Spooner alone, again echoing Eliot, resumes, "I have known this before. Morning. A locked door. A house of silence and strangers." (59) Briggs enters, in a suit, one of the official uniforms of power, to offer Spooner the breakfast left from the financial advisor who has canceled his housecall. Though Spooner first refuses, saying he never takes food, at the mention of waste, he acquiesces and consumes the breakfast: "I abhor waste." (60) Ironically, one of the larger wastes may be his life expressed in wasted verbiage. Briggs downs the champagne eliciting Spooner's claim that he knows his wines. Reminded of winetastings in Dijon and of Hugo, Spooner uses the occasion for another chance to introduce himself:

> You will wonder of course what he translated. The answer is my verse. I am a poet. (63)

Briggs' ingenuous retort could hardly be more devastating: "I thought poets were young." (63)

Spooner, eager to escape, asks why the room was locked, claiming he is urgently needed at a board meeting of a "newly inaugurated poetry magazine."[3] (65)

Indifferent to Spooner's urgency, Briggs puts his partner Jack forward as a poet. Spooner's fussy, archaically phrased reply offers a business-like: "Well, if he'd like to send me some examples of his work, double spaced on quarto, with copies in a separate folder . . . I'll read them." (67) Briggs admits, "The boss could be his patron, but he's not interested. Perhaps because he's a poet himself. It's possible there's an element of jealousy in it, I don't know. Not that the boss isn't a very kind man. He is. He's a very civilized man. But he's still human." (67) The topic of jealousy opens a suggestion of rivalry between Spooner and Hirst. Though Spooner seems surprised to learn Hirst is a poet, he repeats for the third time in this act, "I have known this before." (68) And indeed, we learn he has.

Spooner and Hirst together transmit the unconscious poles of an artist's two worst fears: Spooner, the failed poet, that his work will be forever unrecognized, and Hirst, the famous poet, that he has outlived his fame.

In the next instant Hirst reenters, refers to Spooner as Charles, and in a freshly energized, jovial tone welcomes Spooner, "How nice of you to drop in." (68) Hirst, in uninterrupted monologue, details their acquaintance at Oxford and inquires, "Did you have a good war?" After dismissing Briggs, whom he refers to as Denson, he inserts a left-field remark, "How's Emily?" (68)

Hirst then describes how he seduced Emily, Spooner's wife, plying her "with buttered scones, Wilshire cream, crumpets and strawberries." (68–9) Hirst's boasting resonates with *The Collection* and *The Lover* and anticipates *Betrayal*:

> Proposed that she betray you. Admitted you were a damn fine chap, but pointed out I would be taking nothing that belonged to you, simply that portion of herself all women keep in reserve, for a rainy day. (69)

Hirst's affability at his entrance transforms to a threatening boast, however jovially expressed:

> She would come to me at tea-time, or at coffee-time, the innocent hours. That summer she was mine, while you imagined her to be solely yours. (70)

What triggers Hirst's gratuitously vicious attack upon Spooner that begins when he glibly confesses his affair with Emily? Since nothing Spooner does elicits Hirst's defensive reaction (save Spooner's endless chatter and claims for his virtue), Hirst's offensive strike against him can only have been motivated by some deeply felt need to assert his superiority through battle, any battle, even against a hapless poet.

That Hirst regards his artistic achievement as a competition becomes apparent when he notes that, "When you were doing your exercises she came to me." (70) And though he is explicitly referring to Spooner's running and being a "Natural athlete," when he says, "Once a man has breasted the tape alone, he is breasting the tape forever," he refers equally to himself and to his reputation which admittedly helped him win Emily whose "ardor was, in my experience, unparalleled." (70) He explicitly connects his seduction and betrayal with the privilege of power as an acclaimed artist, adding offhandedly:

> Of course I was successful awfully early. (70)

When Hirst next catalogs at length other women he and Spooner knew and enjoyed, he reduces Emily to one among many in his collection. Spooner's own confessions, an attempt to best Hirst's, culminate in Hirst's astounded, "Are you trying to tell me that you had an affair with Arabella?" (76) Spooner's circumlocution clothes oral sex in a quaint, Victorian garb:

> A form of an affair. She had no wish for full consummation. She was content with her particular predilection. Consuming the male member. (76)

When Hirst attacks Spooner as a "scoundrel" for attacking Arabella's honor, Spooner lists other women and one man whose reputations Hirst reputedly ruined.

But the two real issues have been skirted: Emily and their writing rivalry, which Spooner reserves for his final attack. First Spooner addresses Hirst's dishonoring him:

> It is you who have behaved unnaturally and scandalously, to the woman who was joined to me in God. (77)

Yet whatever pain still exists Spooner glosses over with humor in the exchange that begins when Spooner says, "She told me all," to which Hirst returns, "You listen to the drivellings of a farmer's wife?" Spooner replies: "Since I was the farmer, yes." (77)

Hirst returns a double insult aimed both at Spooner's virility and his aesthetic prowess: "You were no farmer, sir. A weekend wanker." (77) Spooner defends only his poetry by dropping mention of his nineteenth-century-sounding title as uninviting as it sounds uninspired: "I wrote my Homage to Wessex in the summerhouse at West Upfield." (77) Hirst's surface politeness barely veils the depth charge of his more cruel attack: "I have never had the good fortune to read it," which triggers Spooner's first frontal assault against Hirst's poetry: "It is written in terza rima, a form which, if you will forgive my saying so, you have never been able to master." (77)

But Spooner has gone too far, overstepped his bounds as guest and groveler, and Hirst signals the change with, "This is outrageous! Who are you? What are you doing in my house?" (78) Hirst calls for a drink, followed by a two page monologue during which he repositions himself as the famous poet condescending to one of the failed: "I might even show you my pen, and my blotting pad. I might even show you my footstool," he offers, then drinks. (78)

Hirst's second offer to show Spooner his photograph album, now with a faintly pathetic, hollow ring, dissolves into a recollection of youthful friends' faces reminiscent of the Dylan Thomas "Fern Hill" closure: " … who knows they may quicken … in their chains, in their glass jars." (79) Hirst concludes with a complex metaphor revealing the competitive edge of his superior intelligence; he nicely interstices the golden rule admonition with attitudes toward the lost past as dead, while at the same time he summarily insults Spooner:

> And so I say to you, tender the dead, as you would yourself be tendered, now, in what you would describe as your life. (79)

Spooner, who at the top of the act wished to escape but is now expelled as a guest, applies for the position of secretary. Foster checks his advance with, "I am his secretary." (83)

Spooner desperately attempts to flatter Foster into leaving Hirst's employ by referring to his supposed poetic aspirations: "A secretarial post does less than justice to your talents." (83) He then patronizes him with clichéd advice: "A young poet should travel. Travel and suffer. Join the navy, perhaps, and see the sea. Voyage and explore." (83) Spooner's advice only illuminates his own lack of experience in a wider world. Foster replies, "I've sailored. I've been there and back. I'm here where I'm needed." (83)

Hirst's secrets, unlike Spooner's, will remain his own: "There are places in my heart ... where no living soul has ... or can ever ... trespass." (84) But it is now Hirst who echoes but reverses Eliot's Prufrock, announcing, "Today I shall come to a conclusion." (86)

When Spooner offers, "I'll help you," Foster preempts him by claiming that he was "called" to this job from "that beautiful isle" of Bali:

> I was only a boy. But I was nondescript and anonymous. A famous writer wanted me. He wanted me to be his secretary, his chauffeur, his housekeeper, his amanuensis. How did he know of me? Who told him? (86)

Spooner's fanciful reply acknowledges the power of chance and talent in Hirst's position: "He made an imaginative leap. Few can do it. Few do it. He did it. That's why God loves him." (86) Briggs's down-to-earth description of Foster's coming, "You came on my recommendation," deflates Spooner's rhetoric, revealing how out of touch Spooner is with the simple practicalities of any job, including husbanding his own work, possibly his wife or, finally, simply surviving. (86)

Foster extends Spooner's opening claims for art, asserting that his work puts him "in touch with a very special intelligence," he finds "nourishing" and is "enlarged" by, and comically adds, more practically, he finds the demands "natural":

> And they're legal. I'm not doing anything crooked. It's a relief. (87)

He ends with rhapsodies about his "dignity," and "sense of honor," concluding: "It never leaves me. Service to a cause." (87) He believes his work provides meaning for his life.

Briggs, defending their sanctuary, threatens Spooner with an onslaught of sexual and excremental epithets. But Hirst intercedes with a defense, kindness rare, almost nonexistent, among Pinter's other characters:

> Yes, yes, but he's a good man at heart. (88)

Spooner quick to stay his slight advantage bluntly asks:

> Let me live with you and be your secretary. (88)

The echo of Marlowe's "Come live with me and be my love" in "The Passionate Shepherd to His Love," renders Spooner's request as absurdly humorous as it is slightly pathetic given his qualifications, which should but do not give him advantage over the thugs.

Hirst's devastating reply reduces Spooner to an insect, "Is there a big fly in here? I hear buzzing." (88)

In a last, long, desperate, lonely plea Spooner places his life in service to Hirst as a knight and parades before Hirst his list of virtues:

> I offer myself not abjectly but with ancient pride. I come to you as a warrior. I shall be happy to serve you as my master. I bend my knee to your excellence. I am furnished with the qualities of piety, prudence, liberality and goodness. Decline them at your peril. It is my task as a gentleman to remain amiable in my behaviour, courageous in my undertakings, discreet and gallant in my execution. (89)

But Spooner is not a knight, and nothing he intends has proven itself in action. His antique, bombastic rhetoric escalates into empty mimicry of the old knightly virtues: "I am your Chevalier." He reveals how dated, empty, and useless are both the highminded rhetoric and values of other centuries, for clearly Hirst would prefer his bodyguard/thugs whose service and protection (if they do not enable Hirst to swill himself to death) seem guaranteed.

Stripped of all pride, Spooner, the man for whom language is his only shield and now his only sword, continues his hopeless plea for yet another two pages reducing himself to a sycophant. What can he offer besides himself? An offer as enticing as Teddy's to let Ruth help him with his scholarly papers in *The Homecoming*.

Spooner offers Hirst a place at his poetry readings "reasonably well attended, mainly by the young." (90) Hirst brushes him aside as he might a gnat:

> Let us change the subject. (91)

Spooner's reference to the young and their future, which assails Hirst's own age and fading or faded reputation, hardly seduces Hirst to hire him. Spooner's blind fawning, no less than Davies's assault in *The Caretaker*, fails to win him a place in another's man's home.

Yet the play ends with that final revelation that Hirst, for all his aggressive malevolence, and Spooner, for all his obsequiousness, are not so different after all. Again audience sympathies are with both as the two great levelers, time and drink, condemn Hirst no less than the outcast Spooner to no man's land. Hirst's decision, unlike Prufrock's, to force "a conclusion" ends as Briggs says, "For the last time," and Foster concurs "so that nothing else will happen forever. You'll be sitting here forever." (94) Spooner further defines that space in the penultimate speech:

> You are in no man's land. Which never moves, which never changes, which never grows older, but which remains forever icy and silent. (95)

And Hirst concludes:

> I'll drink to that. (95)

Spooner's intention to connect the aesthetic with the ethical remains unfulfilled, only to raise further questions: is the good writer assumed to be expressing what is good? Is the good writer a good person? Spooner's intention, which fails to resolve into action, belies that connection despite his "high sentence." While Hirst, through some combination of intelligence, talent, action, and chance, achieved some power, the audience discovers, that aside from the creature comforts of his domestic situation, his power gains him little more than what Spooner has. Both are in the end cast upon the scrap heap of a world without the gentling presence and influence of women, who now remain only fond remembrances of a passionate, painful, but vital and sometimes happier youth. A half-world descends on both poles of a writer's worst fear, one that strikes equally failure or fame. For all Spooner's good intentions to help the young, Hirst's practical refuge which he offers Foster and Briggs may be more substantial. Hirst's influence, which at least acknowledges the darker side from which Spooner averts his gaze, may be more productive of a whole human being, a more complete vision than Spooner's banner of heralded but untried virtue.

Though they both began on equal footing in their careers at Oxford, they soon diverge. Where Spooner claims he was never loved, Hirst may have in some sense murdered his love, but in the end Hirst absolves himself of all responsibility for the body drowning in his dream: "But I am mistaken. There is nothing there." (95) His virtue, in his own mind, remains intact, but he began without the illusions Spooner has now lost.

Spooner, whose name derives from the slang "spoon," denoting a foolish person given to exuberant demonstrations of affection, half redeems himself through the heroic effort of his quest to test his virtue, but like Pinter's description of Shakespeare's tragic heroes overtaken by their strengths, Spooner is conquered by the very thing he has sought to master—language. Overtaken by language, though he could not take over command of his own life with it, he devolves into a critic-poet, full of theory he cannot conjoin with his art. He has not lived. Hirst espouses no theories but has lived, acted, loved, and largely succeeded in the eyes of the world at what he has attempted. Spooner, like others of Pinter's loveless characters, will attempt to destroy in others what he could not create or inspire for himself.

Did Spooner deliberately seek this invitation and entrance into Hirst's home to destroy Hirst? Is Spooner, like Wally in *Night School* who may have regained his room by design, redeemed by an intention so subtle it could easily be ignored? In the end it hardly matters.

The game might seem to be between two old knights jousting in a tournament of antiquated and nearly forgotten ceremony with little influence in the larger world beyond the walls which contain their battle. No evidence indicates that either still writes. Hirst seems better positioned to wield his tongue as a sword in verbal battle than his pen. The oblique references to Marlowe and Dylan Thomas and the more explicit multiple references to Eliot and other poets remind the audience that neither Hirst nor Spooner are numbered among Western poets whose work casts a shadow over the whole twentieth century: a single line or parody of one phrase of Eliot's work might be instantly recognized as his by anyone in the West who reads. After all, Hirst and Spooner are only poets in a world which at the moment, for all Foster's fulsome praise of Hirst, little values or reads poetry. Yet even in the sealed room the play concludes with a question of a writer's relation and responsibility to the larger world.

Notes

1. Again, the play *Jane Eyre,* a distant reference to the play in which Pinter played opposite his first wife.
2. Although after he wrote *The Caretaker* Pinter claimed he was beyond "blackout turns in the dark," he employs precisely that to end the scene.
3. Pinter was instrumental in work on the literary magazine *Aquarius.*

The French Lieutenant's Woman and *The Last Tycoon:* Love Gained and Lost

The French Lieutenant's Woman

Pinter continued to concern himself with memory, the past, "the mist" in which things take place—the inability, however vigorously one tries, to make "any connection with a thing or person," concluding: "To arrive at a lucid appreciation of what is taking place is impossible. Perhaps it can only be achieved through art. In life I don't think it can be achieved." (Kroll, 78) His work which best dramatizes that point, his screenplay for *The French Lieutenant's Woman,* allows the only happy ending to occur between the lovers in the film within the film, in contrast to the two "real life" actors playing those characters who part in the end.

Love and passion are again central to this film adapted from the novel by John Fowles and directed by Karel Reisz. The film opens on the nineteenth-century Sarah Woodruff, a destitute, outcast English woman of a recently deceased employer, played by the twentieth-century American actress Anna. Sarah, forced for her survival to rely upon her intelligence and education, secures a post with Mrs. Poultney as a lady's companion, but escapes her harsh Victorian household and the reputation she has encouraged as the French Lieutenant's woman—the abandoned mistress of a married man. Her gifts, along with her very reputation which might have destroyed her, win Charles Smithson, whose love rescues her even as it saves him from a loveless marriage with Earnestina. In their one night of love, more nearly a consensual rape—such is Charles' rush and ineptitude—he discovers that Sarah is a virgin after all. But reputation weighs more heavily than fact in the community.

Intersticed with Sarah and Charles' love story is the ongoing love affair between Anna and Mike, the twentieth-century British actor who plays Charles, and also Mike's wife Sonia who, like Stephen's in *Accident*, knows but does not know about her husband's passion. As Pinter sought to find a way to transfer the novel's two endings to the film, he ingeniously hit upon the film within the film cutting back and forth between the film set in Victorian England with those making the film in the present, dramatizing the contrast between the two centuries' values and actions.

The film not only offers a breakthrough in structure, allowing the audience to appreciate differences between nineteenth- and twentieth-century sexual ethics, but it also offers a portrayal of madness that elucidates madness throughout Pinter's work. The nineteenth-century mores which nearly drive Sarah to madness, once they are lifted, allow the twentieth-century Anna a freedom without commitment. But it is Sarah's desire to escape madness and the constrictions of her time and to find love and freedom which drives the film.

The film opens with the camera crew focusing on Sarah ascending the cobb, the jetty in Lyme, to gaze out to sea, cuts to Smithson going to propose to Earnestina, then cuts to the twentieth century lovers, Mike in Anna's bed, taking her make-up call. Where the twentieth-century actress can laugh off her concern that everyone will know she is sleeping with Mike, (that she will be fired for immorality, and that people will think her a whore) is precisely what earns Sarah her nineteenth-century society's censure and drives her to the verge of madness. Anna discovers that Sarah, (for actions not unlike her own) as an unprotected, "fallen" woman in England in the previous century was in danger of being forced for survival into prostitution, thus making Sarah's escape into independence all the more heroic. In contrast, the two actors Anna and Mike who play Sarah and Smithson hardly reveal themselves or their love as remarkable, however passionately Mike imagines he loves Anna.

In the end when Anna leaves the cast party after the shooting finishes, she also leaves her lover Mike who shouts out the window after her: "Sarah," revealing that his real-life love for Anna is inextricably bound up with his character's love for the character Anna plays. Perhaps Anna knows this, and that is one reason why she leaves Mike.

In contrast, the happy ending between Charles and Sarah in the film also depicts Sarah's recovery from a situational madness (imposed by the extraordinary Victorian constraints on her life) as she becomes one of the few women in all of Pinter's work to truly equal, even surpass, her male counterpart. By contrast Smithson, a gentleman, extends small understanding for his servant's hardships, displays understandably a gentleman's disdain for work when offered a job by his fiancee Ernestina's father, and offers an ungentlemanly but polite lie to extricate himself from his engagement. A paleontologist with an interest in Darwin, Smithson is in danger of becoming a fossil himself until he is energized by his love for Sarah. But what ennobles this otherwise ordinary British gentleman of his time, even elevates him as a character worthy of Sarah at the end, is his unalloyed passion for her. Yet it is Sarah who eloquently defines the power of love: "Now I know there was truly a day upon which you loved me, I can bear anything. You have given me the strength to live." (73) She indeed gathers strength and does.

For Sarah, however intelligent, educated, talented a lady's companion, to be worthy of a gentleman's love requires much more: an inner strength and confidence to act. Sarah, even in the depths of an outcast's despair, had replied to Smithson's compliment that she is a remarkable person with, "Yes, I am a remarkable person," then proves it. (56) With a triumphant transformation that requires only Smithson's coach fare out of Lyme, the memory of his love, and her own determination, she gains a position as a children's tutor in a home allowing, even encouraging, her development and her drawing.

How does Sarah effect her recovery from her melancholia?

The French Lieutenant's Woman challenges one of the masternarratives of the Western world with another masternarrative that has become a cliché of Western fiction and film. All conspire to support the first masternarrative: the necessity to speak to relieve the self from mental anguish. Charles, while pursuing Sarah along the undercliff (ironically, as his servant is delivering his flowers to Ernestina) is the first to propose that Sarah unburden her mind: "Permit me to insist. These matters are like wounds. If no-one dares speak of them they fester." (32) Perhaps taking her cue from him, Sarah arranges a meeting at night in a churchyard to ask Charles for help. When he refuses, demanding to know what she wants,

Sarah replies: "I want to tell you of what happened to me eighteen months ago." (38) Sarah, with no one to talk to, is reported to Charles by Dr. Grogan to have divulged the contents of her mind to no one. If she would? Charles asks. The physician answers in authorial baritone, "She would be cured." (41) The film immediately cuts to Sarah and Smithson in the woods, their backs to one another as if in confession where Sarah describes her admiration for the wounded, handsome, but married French Lieutenant whom she nursed to health, a man who found her beautiful but called her cruel for withholding her affection. It is Charles who supplies, "Till one day you were no longer cruel." (43) Sarah neither affirms nor denies the seduction but concludes her confession supplying the reason for her action: she says she chose to be an outcast to retain her freedom—because she could never marry an equal, she chose to marry shame.

Pinter seems to subscribe to the masternarrative that Sarah's confession results in her recovery. But Pinter knows better. He does not confuse confession with catharsis. For it is only later after Smithson gives her fifty pounds to escape Lyme and pursues her to Exeter, where they seduce one another, that we learn that Sarah is a virgin and her confession, a fabrication. Pinter's experience must have taught him that madness is neither so easily confronted nor cured.

Ultimately Pinter's portrayal of madness dramatizes individual responsibility to know ourselves and to retain sanity if we are to continue to survive and to thrive as human beings.

While Pinter may question language alone as supplying a cause or a cure for madness, he nevertheless dramatizes the necessity to confront the self, even owning madness, with the same honesty required for any human change to occur. Sarah confronts herself far more powerfully than with mere words—she draws charcoal portraits of herself, as unflattering as Edvard Munch's "The Scream," which nakedly reveal the horror of her interior weakness and madness.

The film challenges confession as catharsis by subscribing to yet another Western masternarrative which works a far more effective cure: the transformative power of love. But here again Pinter's portrayal of love reverses the traditional formula, that the man pursues the woman, by allowing Sarah the primary agency of her escape from madness to freedom and love. The film reveals that it is Sarah who seduces Smithson: first through sight then through touch.

Love enters through the eye. After the traditional fateful meeting between Charles and Sarah on the cobb, (she looks at him/he looks at her, as love is traditionally first conveyed in film), Charles becomes fascinated and embroiled with her despondency, desperation, and derangement. They meet again near the undercliff in the woods, but she tries to escape his overtures. Of course we, as audience, with our superior perspective, can see that the surest way Sarah can hope to win Charles is to shun him, and she does at first, insisting he allow her to walk alone. Then, in the scene Anna and Mike rehearse, Smithson comes upon Sarah for the first touch, (which Ovid, in *The Art of Love,* deemed a necessary first step toward seduction). Mike reads the filmscript directions aloud to Anna, noting that Sarah sees Smithson, frees her dress caught in the brambles, approaches him, slips, and he picks her up: the first touch. Twice Anna and Mike rehearse the scene. The second time slips Anna into the nineteenth century and, as Sarah, she adds one important action—when Anna as Sarah falls, she grabs hold of Smithson, bringing him down with her. *Her* touch is prior to what is directed: in the script, *his* to help her up. Not only does Sarah initiate the love, first by exhibiting herself on the cobb at the outset, but she also makes the first physical contact. That single act that brings him down with her serves as an analog for the rest of the film to explain her flight. Were Smithson and Sarah to have proceeded in their love unimpeded, Sarah would have dragged them both down.

Instead, Sarah runs away from Mrs. Poultney, telling only Smithson, who finds her, where she is. They kiss. He gives her the money to escape Lyme, where there is talk of committing Sarah to an asylum—such are Sarah's transgressions against society. But despite Smithson's promise never to see her again, he pursues her to Exeter where they make love. Though Smithson declares he will break his engagement, when he returns to Exeter, nearly mad himself with love for Sarah, she is gone, and it is another three years before he finds her again. When he does she is a person transformed.

Pinter's portrayal of her necessary confrontation with madness links recovery with love, not as a Freudian confession told to a masterinterpreter, the analyst, but aligns with Rogerian and

Ericksonian congruence and compassion, where a compassionate listener with unconditional positive regard bears nonjudgmental witness to facilitate the client's *action* to achieve what the client seeks. Smithson becomes such a witness.

The transformative power of love radiates at the end when Smithson finally discovers Sarah, an artist living on a sunlit, glittering bay into which the happy couple row out from a dark grotto betokening a remarkable fairy tale rebirth of love. Their happiness momentarily transcends the contemporary reality in which the two actors Anna and Mike have parted.

The double ending has been interpreted to mean that love and happiness can flourish only in art but not in life. But the brilliant editing, a function of the script, allows the spaces between the nineteenth-and twentieth-century scenes to resonate on the topic of freedom. Throughout we see society's constraints on Sarah in sharp contrast to Anna's twentieth-century freedom. Sarah can find no work, is condemned as sinful for staring out to sea, can neither walk alone nor speak to nor be seen with or touch the man she loves. Anna has gained a comfortably situated film career, sleeps with her married leading man with impunity, and is discovered by the audience in her room or bed with him nearly as often as elsewhere. But all this only points to a larger freedom, fiercely maintained by Anna, but gained by Sarah in her extraordinary battle to overcome madness. Love and justice combine here as love is equated with the goods of life—health, happiness, comfort, ease, and freedom. What is achieved in the film within the film is a poetic justice where those who most deserve one another in the end get together.

Yet even in the happy ending Pinter has added one signature touch: if it is the case that he shows compassion for all his characters "even a bastard like Goldberg," he also allows his most attractive romantic hero to show himself momentarily a bastard in his treatment of his servant Sam and his fiancée Ernestina.

The two endings do not merely provide the film within the film a fairy-tale escape from reality, but rather together they celebrate the rare but remarkable power of love and the necessity of two people to be equal for love to exist and to thrive. The two endings allow both realities equal validity within their specific contexts. Anna has no wish to remove Mike from his happy home and family, and besides she has a lover, David, whose name she sometimes calls out in her sleep. Given the nature of Sarah's obstacles, her extraordinary victory over madness and her transformation become the one heroic battle of the film, and her independence becomes a touchstone for all Pinter's subsequent women characters.

The Last Tycoon

The French Lieutenant's Woman, however tempered with reality, hit a peak of romantic optimism in Pinter's work. More and more Pinter shows that the edge a powerfully dominant man might hold in public life could not insure private happiness. *The Last Tycoon,* adapted from the novel by F. Scott Fitzgerald, directed by Elia Kazan, traces Monroe Stahr's quest for the elusive Kathleen as a possible surrogate for his lost wife. Kathleen eludes the movie tycoon, in the end insisting she wants to live a private life. Again the most powerful is thwarted from getting what he most wants—love.

In the anatomy of lost love and missed chances, Pinter dramatizes Stahr's choices—the failure to commit to love—that begin his own destruction on both private and public levels. Kathleen is not merely inaccesible, else there would be no story. She several times signals openings that Stahr fails to seize, and, despite his overt passion, reveals himself not a far remove from the "dried up" Colston of *The Go-Between* who chooses to side with Lord Trimmingham (the forces of gentility) rather than Ted the force of passion and man of his own heart. Kathleen, describing the man she plans to marry, claims, "He saved my life," but Stahr never inquires about her life, or what needed saving, because his interest is not in her life but in his illusion of her. Her subtle invitation to intercede to obstruct the marriage is missed. Where love, as the erotic, can open a life, teach and even lead those to wisdom who are open to embracing and acting upon it, to those who fail to act upon love (and prefer to retain the illusion), that failure can spell ruin. The distinction between embracing Eros and a mere erotic embrace is nicely delineated in this screenplay where Stahr makes love to Kathleen who permits his overture, but the transaction remains virginal, without reciprocity—his failure to commit to her meets her lack of engagement. Even when he finally embraces her, she eludes him.

In his search for a "perfect gift" for a screenplay (and life) Stahr commandingly telegraphs to a staff scriptwriter Boxley his formula for "making pictures" which, echoed in the end, boomerangs to reveal how totally Stahr has conflated life with art. Stahr tells Boxley: you are in a room, a girl enters, dumps her purse onto a table—two dimes, a nickel, a matchbox, a pair of gloves, then goes to a stove and throws in the gloves, lights a match, tosses it in as the telephone rings and she answers. She says she never owned a pair of black gloves. She lights another match, tosses it in the stove. Suddenly you notice another man standing in the room. When Boxley asks what happens, Stahr answers, "I don't know. I was just making pictures." (117; Klein, 243) After Stahr loses Kathleen and is about to lose the studio, he repeats the story for the camera (for us). This time, answering Boxley's voiceover question, What happens? with his confession/response "I don't know. I was just making pictures," Stahr nakedly reveals to us how little his power and the pictures (a masternarrative of our time) have taught him about life or love.[1]

Notes

1. Stahr prefigures Mike in *The French Lieutenant's Woman* who in the final words of the film calls out to the woman he loves, but calls out not her name but the name of the character she plays in the film. Moreover, Klein rightly notes, both the story's analogy to Pinter's own writing method, and the film's revelation of the self-destructive elements inherent authoritarian power: "Stahr legislates all the variables in his professional dominion. Inevitably, however, the world beyond Stahr's jurisdiction tempts him with its promises of risks and stakes capable of rendering deeper satisfaction; but his effort to maneuver in these autonomous provinces is doomed because he cannot escape the habits and appetites of a movie tycoon." (144)

Betrayal: The Past Regained

Betrayal, a play in nine scenes, represents yet another major breakthrough in structure. Here Pinter takes his concern with the past and changes the form of drama: to allow the happy beginning of the affair to color the ending and illuminate how the past persists into the present. *Betrayal* begins after the end of an affair between Emma and her husband's best friend Jerry and ends with the seduction that brought them together at Emma and Robert's anniversary party nine years earlier.

The choice was not altogether a conscious one. Pinter said:

> When I realized the implications of the past of the play, I knew there was only one way to go and that was backwards. The actual structure of the play seemed to dictate itself. When I realized what was going on, this movement in time, I was very excited by it. (Gussow, "A Conversation . . . ," 5)

The "implications of the past" are too complex to be easily summarized. No play of Pinter's seems so fiercely driven by passion. Only his screenplay of *The French Lieutenant's Woman* can match its portrayal of desire, and *The Last Tycoon,* its erotic obsession. Yet for the last time in a serious, full-length play to date, Pinter allows himself to focus upon love divorced from global, political considerations. The play is infused throughout with ethical implications which extend influence beyond the private level of desire and the consequences of betrayal and, like *No Man's Land,* maintain locus on the virtues of love and friendship. As in all his plays, Pinter deploys ambiguity to examine the tangle of questions raised in the classic triangle of love, passion and its inevitable betrayal. Audience sympathy can be counted upon to attach almost reflexively to lovers, as it does here, but with two differences: the lovers are not irreproachable, nor the husband without some portion of audience sympathy for his strengths and a certain stoicism. All betray. All are betrayed.

Robert's allusion to Ford Maddox Ford, recalling *The Good Soldier* with its brilliant ambiguities, its seering yet restrained passion, and its heartbreakingly revealed betrayal, suggests one source in the play's inspiration, just as Emma's name suggests another. (82) Whereas many of Pinter's earlier central women characters carry Biblical names—Ruth, Jesse, Sarah—the central woman in this play invites a Western audience's comparison with Emma Bovary, who like her nineteenth-century counterparts, Anna Karenina and Tess of the d'Ubervilles, must pay with her life for her infidelity. Pinter does not kill off his twentieth-century heroine. Although Emma may privately suffer diminished circumstances in the end, she does so almost equally with the two men in her life, and all remain publicly successful.

Every beat in the play, almost every line fractally delivers an ambiguity, often multiple ambiguities which serve to create simultaneously a triple level of complexity and focus in the play as a whole. The double entendres raised to triple entendres establish and retain a triple balance of audience sympathy for each character individually and for the impossible triangular relationship they form together.

Betrayal opens with an awkward meeting over drinks long after the close of the affair between Jerry and Emma. Jerry admits he has a hangover, Emma that she is fine, and as she looks around the bar says, "Just like old times," an allusion both to their shared past and to Pinter's play by that name. (12) Jerry steers the topic deliberately clear of references to himself and their affair when Emma asks, "Do you know how long it is since we met?" He skirts the issue with, "Well I came to that private view, when was it—?" (13) But she directs focus back with: "No, I don't mean that." (13) Instead of providing us with narratives of their past, we see them enter the past till the past not only comes alive as the present but, within the play's structure, becomes their future.

When Jerry, during this meeting which Emma called, attempts to forward the conversation with small talk, "How's it going? the Gallery?" Emma interjects a note of discord to direct conversation to another level: "How do you think it's going?" (13) When he remarks, "Funny lot, painters, aren't they?" she counters, "They're not at all funny." (13) Jerry maintains ballast with a saving humor, "Aren't they? What a pity." (13)

Emma is obviously distraught but without knowing anything more about her, it is already clear that her momentary graininess stands apart from her customary contained spirit. If any doubt remains that these two were lovers, they nicely clarify it. When Emma asks how long it's been since Jerry's seen her husband Robert and inquires about Jerry's son Sam, Jerry corrects her, "You mean Judith," then adds, "You remember the form. I ask about your husband, you ask about my wife." (15) When Jerry volunteers, "Ned's five, isn't he?" (16) and Emma remarks, "You remember," he replies, "Well I would remember that." (16)

In this remarkably spare exchange, constituting almost the whole of their opening dialogue, Pinter establishes the length, duration, and intensity of the affair—as well as signaling its demise. Emma's gambit, "Ever think of me?" prompts Jerry to protect himself against exposing any vulnerability. He places himself in the superior position with, "I don't need to think of you," and with faint praise, Jerry compliments Emma's appearance as "very pretty." (17) "Pretty" is not "beautiful."

Emma pursues the offensive, "You think of me sometimes?" Jerry concedes, "I think of you sometimes." (18) But he free associates to Emma's daughter Charlotte whom he remembers recently seeing, and that image carries with it the play's sense of the inexorable flow of time, of Emma's being displaced in the passing of time by her own daughter. With the mention of Charlotte, now thirteen, Emma recalls a long-past moment that will be echoed twice in the play: "Do you remember that time . . . oh god it was . . . when you picked her up and threw her up and caught her?" (18) When Jerry recalls, "It was in your kitchen," Emma corrects him, "It was in your kitchen." (20)

Emma warms him up but, when Jerry, finally opening up calls her "Darling," Emma slams the door in his face: "Don't say that." (20) It is enough for the audience to see that they are both wary of being hurt, and that while the affair is over, they both still care for one another. Moreover, the passionate affair is unlikely to be repeated in either of their lives. The great love of both their lives is over.

Emma recalls driving past their rented flat, where significantly the name they took, Green, was no longer there; Jerry quips: "That's because we're not there any more. We haven't been there for years," but his humor shifts to caution with, "I hear you're seeing a bit of Casey." (22)

Rather than admit any expected jealousy, he claims he feels only "irritation that nobody gossiped about us like that, in the old days. I nearly said, now look, she may be having the occasional drink with Casey, who cares, but she and I had an affair for seven years and none of you bastards had the faintest idea it was happening." (23) Jerry's desire to have his secret conquest publicized is wounded. Emma, however, wonders if everyone knew. Jerry says, "Don't be silly. We were brilliant." (23)

When Jerry reminds her that she did not like Casey's writing, Emma claims that either she or Casey's work has changed. But when Emma wonders if Jerry is jealous, Jerry positions himself hierarchically above Casey, "I couldn't be jealous of Casey. I'm his agent." (25) Then, reducing Casey to public cash flow, marks him as his own private property: "He's my . . . he's my boy." (23) But he also makes a larger observation that capitulates to Emma's notion that Casey may have developed: "I discovered him when he was a poet, and that's a bloody long time ago now." (24) His saying so becomes the first of the play's observations about the development and decline of a writer's life span in the Western literary marketplace. Early in the play (later in Casey's career), Jerry and Robert find him over the hill, but later, Robert pronounces Jerry's "boy" (earlier in Casey's career) "first rate," though Jerry's surprise at this renders Robert's pronouncement a matter of opinion rather than a professional judgment.

Jerry intercepts his own irritation at Casey, pulling back with, "Anyway it's not as if we're having an affair now, is it?" But his slight insistence that he is not jealous "doth protest too much," and his self proclaiming, as almost always in Pinter's work, disclaims what it attempts to disclose: "Really, I'm very happy if you're happy." (24)

When Jerry inquires about Robert, Emma announces that she and Robert are separating, claiming that she found out only last night that he has betrayed her "for years." (25) Jerry is shocked. Then reconsiders, "But we betrayed him for years." Emma protests, "and he betrayed me for years." (25) The comic exchange dissolves into Emma's inadvertent confession of feeling for Jerry when Jerry asks if Casey knows: "I phoned *you*. I don't know why." (26) Mystery is for the first time acknowledged in a Pinter play—there are emotions, Emma admits, she does not understand. Yet she clearly exposes her continued feelings for Jerry, who either unthinkingly misses the point or deliberately cuts her when he says with a zeugma that yokes together her intention and his 180° turn away from her: "What a funny thing. We were such close friends, weren't we," he says, "Robert and me, even though I haven't seen him for months. . . ." (26) Here Pinter nicely sets up the expectation that Jerry is talking about his intimate relationship with Emma but reverses expectation by referring to his close friendship with Robert. Jerry ends in feeling betrayed (by Robert!), complaining that through all their time together in pubs he never honed in on Robert's secret.

Emma's insistence that her seeing Jerry was not "for nostalgia," elicits only Jerry's obvious self-concern, "You didn't tell Robert about me last night, did you?" (29)

Emma's wholly unexplained and inexplicable, "I had to," only further alarms Jerry. Her only explanation, "He told me everything. I told him everything," suggests that her confession, which came when both her marriage and affair were over, could only have been intended to hurt Robert. In fact, however, we later learn that the confession came much earlier—although Jerry is the last to find out. Her saying, "I told him everything" has a triple significance; on first reading or viewing it registers not only her intention to hurt Robert but a way both of keeping Jerry's attention and of covering her own bases in the likely event he discovers Robert knew for years. But at another level, it is a lie.

If it is Emma's intention, conscious or otherwise, to re-ignite her relationship with Jerry, she encounters some flicker of old passion ("Darling") but also a cautious man ensconced in his family and unwilling to take any risks for her despite his strong feeling for her equally divided by concern for himself and his friendship with Robert. Emma, also preoccupied with herself, discounts Jerry's protest, "But he's my oldest friend," when she says, "It doesn't matter. It's all gone." (29)

But it matters deeply to Jerry. He calls Robert in the next scene, which moves forward in time. The tensely emotional, comic confrontation between Jerry and Robert reveals both the depth of Jerry's feeling for Robert and for Emma as well as his double sense of betrayal by Emma and Robert. The ironies begin almost at once when Robert consoles his wife's ex-lover with, "You look quite rough," then soothes Jerry with assurance, "It's not about you and Emma, is it?" he asks before dismissing it as "not very important," then adding, "I know all about that." (35)

When Jerry asks why Emma told Robert "so suddenly" and "[w]ithout consulting me. Without even warning me," Robert corrects Jerry. (37) He says Emma did not tell him last night but four years ago, in Venice. It is Jerry who now feels betrayed that Robert had not told him! "We've had lunch," Jerry protests, but Robert returns, "Never played squash though." (39) Squash becomes a measure of the bond Robert extends to close friends or withdraws from his wife's lovers. He later admits he no longer plays squash with Casey. Robert again consoles his wife's former lover, chastising him: "Oh, don't get upset." (39) Jerry, who doubtless hoped to salvage the friendship by trying to explain, feels doubly betrayed. "Why didn't she tell me?" he asks Robert, who says, "I thought you might know." (39) Then turning on Robert, the man he betrayed, Jerry demands, "Then why didn't you tell me?" adding, "That you knew. You bastard." (40)

Robert, appearing better able to allow reason to control his expression of emotion, returns, "Oh, don't call me a bastard, Jerry." (41)

"What are we going to do?" Jerry asks. Robert replies, "You and I are not going to do anything." (41) Robert recites his arrangements to end his marriage as if reading a balance sheet and dismisses Jerry's alarm that Robert might tell his wife Judith, by brushing Jerry aside: "It's true I've hit Emma once or twice. But it wasn't to defend a principle. I wasn't inspired to do it from any kind of moral standpoint. I just felt like giving her a good bashing." (41) However controlled Robert appears, his admitted gratuitous, physical violence in his marriage alone would provide grounds for Emma's leaving. By discounting Jerry's affair as an insignificant factor in his divorce, Robert also reduces both Jerry and Emma's love to inconsequence.

Jerry leaps to Emma's defense, "But you betrayed her for years, didn't you?" (42) As if he were defending her honor, Jerry claims she did not know, but when Robert asks, "Didn't she?" Jerry replies, "I didn't," opening himself up to Robert's quip, "No, you didn't know very much about anything, really, did you?" (42)

Whatever amends Jerry hoped to proffer reverse as he leaps to the insult with a boast, "I lived with her." (42) Robert's "Yes," is qualified by, "In the afternoons." But Jerry holds the offensive boasting: "Sometimes very long ones. For seven years." (43)

It is Robert the betrayed husband who holds together the friendship with his betrayer. Not without irony he says, "I hope she looked after you all right." (43) When Jerry says, "We used to like each other," Robert replies, "We still do." (43) Why should a little betrayal ruin a friendship? But Robert adds another dig when he mentions Casey, "I believe he's having an affair with my wife," and he adds, "We haven't played squash for years." (43) Robert's reference to Emma as "my wife" may be a reflexive habitual response, a reclaiming of territory, even signaling remaining feeling. Yet, some balance has been restored between Jerry and Robert as both agree Casey is over the hill as a writer. Acknowledging that there is no necessary correlation between what is good and what sells implies there is little connection between Casey's ability to write and his worthiness to elicit Emma's admiration. Casey is selling well.

Jerry steers the subject of good books to Yeats, one of Pinter's favorite poets, reminding Robert that he once read Yeats on Torcello. The point can only have significance on a second viewing or reading. It was alone on Torcello that Robert sought refuge with Yeats after his wife first confessed her affair with Jerry. On a second viewing the scene reads as Jerry's innocently reopening that wound.

Moving back in time, the third scene between Emma and Jerry marks the end of their affair. Dramatizing the disparity between their rational and emotional aims, nothing they do can halt its demise. Once the direction to terminate is set in motion, like Pinter's clashes generally, the conflict develops a life of its own. The crux of the argument, that they never see each other, results in mutual blame: he complains she is at her gallery, never free afternoons, and she, that he is out of the country. But Emma comes closer to disclosing the true nature of her dissatisfaction when she says, "We haven't spent many nights … in this flat." (53) She complains that she cannot bear the waste, the "crockery and the curtains and the bedspread … And the tablecloth I brought from Venice." (54)

Jerry penetrates to the truth of her irritation—a desire to live together. When she protests, "It's just … an empty home," Jerry counters with, "It's not a home." (54) Jerry who seduced Emma, also keeps her carefully at arm's length:

> I know … I know what you wanted … but it could never … actually be a home. You have a home. I have a home. With curtains, etcetera. And children. (55)

Emma pursues the point, "It was never intended to be the same kind of home. Was it?" finally revealing that her real reason for the break is not her stated displeasure that they are never together but the opposite: that they are not permanently committed exclusively to one another. (55) When Jerry replies, "No, I saw it as a flat ... you know," Emma says, "For fucking." She is the first woman to use the term "fucking" in Pinter's work, and the fact that it comes from a woman wins audience sympathy for Jerry, whose response bespeaks a tenderness and generosity when he corrects her: "No, for loving."

His convoluted response to their separation further telegraphs the depth of his love:

> I don't think we don't love each other. (55)

The scene, electrically charged with emotional tension, discloses that what is said on the surface runs counter to what is really intended. As a master of indirection, Pinter allows Emma's impatience, which precipitously terminates the affair, to reveal her deeper desire not to end it at all. When she tosses her keys to the flat to Jerry she says: "Do you realise this is an afternoon? It's the Gallery's afternoon off. That's why I'm here. We close every Thursday afternoon." (58) But it is too late. The direction of the action, once set in motion, has reached its own irreversible conclusion.

Irony strikes the closure as Jerry catches the keys, and Emma snaps the scene shut with what can only be the opposite of what she really means:

> Thanks. Listen I think we've made absolutely the right decision. (58)

Scene four sustains the tension as Robert and Emma entertain Jerry for drinks sometime during the year following Emma's Venice disclosure. The topic of betrayal is subverted as Jerry and Robert banter about whether boys or girls are more anxious and discuss Casey. With a slam at those who depend upon autobiography to fuel their fiction, Robert indulges in a bit of metawriting in describing Casey who has just left his wife as:

> Writing a novel about a man who leaves his wife and children and goes to live alone on the other side of London to write an novel about a man who leaves his wife and their children— (66)

Casey's last novel, *Drying Out,* (67) may ironically point to Emma as a subject of Casey's next novel.

But at this point Robert is still playing squash with Casey whom he describes as a "brutally honest squash player," a hidden slam at Jerry. (68) When the conversation shifts to Robert's suggestion that he and Jerry play, a suggestion he twice prompts with obviously no intention of following through, Emma interjects herself into the conversation: "Why can't I watch and take you both to lunch?" Robert's swiftly decisive response viciously excludes her at the same time it extends his bonds to Jerry:

> You really don't want a woman buying you lunch. You don't actually want a woman within a mile of the place, any of the places. You don't want her in the squash court, shower, pub, or the restaurant. You see, at lunch you want to talk about squash, or cricket, or books, or even women, with your friend, and be able to warm to your theme without fear of improper interruption. (70)

The scene ends carrying the tension of an unexploded bomb. After Jerry leaves, Robert kisses Emma who puts her head on his shoulder, crying as he holds her. Once again audience sympathy extends to all three.

In Venice, the scene five turning point, Emma's discloses her affair to Robert. After that nothing is the same again.

As Emma sits in bed in their hotel reading a book by Spinks, whom Jerry recommended to her, Robert, returning from the post office, mentions he turned Casey's book down because there is not much more to be said on the subject. When Emma asks what he takes to be the subject, he replies, "Betrayal." (78) The exchange reflects its own commentary upon the play which dramatizes the subject with a fresh sympathy for all.

Robert attacks the postal system, outraged because he was offered a letter for Emma which he refused: "I could very easily be a total stranger," he says, adding, "What they of course did not know, and had no way of knowing, was that I am your husband."

(80) In the only fountain of verbiage to occur in the entire text, he deflects his pain and anger with Emma to the post office. Stalling the inevitable confrontation, his diatribe concealing his real fear raises questions, redefining what it means to be a husband, a wife, betrayed, or betrayer. Quizzing Emma on the contents of the letter which she herself retrieved, he postpones her disclosure through his barrage of words, signaling the hope that he desperately wants: a denial of his fear, which the letter from Jerry to her has already affirmed. Circling the subject he recounts his history with Jerry as student poetry magazine editors, "Him at Cambridge, me at Oxford," then he asks, "I've been trying to remember when I introduced him to you." (83) As in *Tea Party* and *No Man's Land*, where a best man betrays the groom and best friend, Robert says he thinks that it was at his wedding that he introduced Emma to Jerry who served as his best man.

Finally, wondering whether the letter contained a message for him, he asks: "No message. Not even his love?" Emma drops the ax: "We're lovers," (84)

But that wasn't his question. Why does she tell him? Because Robert clearly already knows? Because the letter from his best friend to her makes her guilt self-evident? Or does she feel compelled to be honest, to hurt Robert? Or is she simply inexperienced in extramarital deception? It may be for all those reasons, but it should also be clear from the indirection of Robert's discourse and carefully worded questions skirting the issue that there is *no absolute necessity* for Emma to disclose anything.

Until she speaks, the question remains unasked.

That moment contains the beginning and the end of their relationships and the play. It registers as a mistake, an example of *hamartia* that sends a shock wave through the play to mark the unraveling of all of the relationships.

Robert answers: "Ah. Yes. I thought it might be something like that, something along those lines." (84) But he admits he only thought so the day before when he saw the handwriting on the letter.

The aftershock hits when Emma says, "I'm sorry."

"*Sorry*," he replies, then asks, "Where does it . . . take place? Must be a bit awkward. I mean we've got two kids, he's got two kids, not to mention a wife. . . ." (84)

When she says, "We have a flat," the full weight of her disclosure hits Robert. When she admits to its five year duration, Robert protests with a traditional concern about paternity, "Ned is one year old," but Emma assures him, "Yes. He's your son. Jerry was in America. For two months." (86)

The degree of Robert's pain can be measured in part by the cruelty of his attack upon Emma:

> I've always liked Jerry. To be honest, I've always liked him rather more than I've liked you. (87)

He softens with biting wit, "Maybe I should have had an affair with him myself." (87)

The scene closes with apparent accord: "Tell me, are you looking forward to our trip to Torcello?" (87) But that trip, like his squash games that exclude his wife's lovers, will not include her.

With the terrible tension momentarily released, the overlay of irony in Emma's next scene with Jerry which *follows* her return from Venice contains a fresh source of comic tension underscoring the impact of the previous disclosure.

Jerry recounts his alarm at their narrow escape when he briefly misplaced one of Emma's letters. In the tensely humorous scene only Jerry does not know he has already been found out (nor does the reason they have been discovered, his letter to Emma in Venice, ever surface in the play). Instead, the eroticism, laced with wine, his anxiety and Emma's fear of inevitable confrontation between Jerry and Robert when they meet for lunch, carries over to the bed. Emma finally accepts the men's lunch meetings as unavoidable, and for the first time we see her lie. When Jerry asks about Torcello, Emma says she didn't go because "[t]he speedboats were on strike, or something." (93) Her lie to Jerry poses an interesting contrast to her full but unprompted disclosure to her husband. Her lie may be an attempt to protect Jerry from the truth, a desire to avoid the consequences of confrontation, or simply not to ruin the day, but that lie which keeps the truth secret from Jerry only makes Jerry appear both innocent and foolish here and in earlier and subsequent scenes where Robert knows the truth but he does not.

Emma shifts discussion to Spinks's book which Jerry gave her but Robert refused to publish, and when she asks what Spinks is like, Jerry describes him in starkly ascetic, almost Beckettian terms as a thin man, "About fifty. Wears dark glasses day and night. He lives alone, in a furnished room." (97) Here is a ghostly reminder of the writer, not unlike Spooner, whose life is consumed wholly by his work, but who narrowly escapes anonymity—astonishingly his book arrived, Jerry says, in the unsolicited manuscripts.

The scene ends with the bonding device of memory, which nevertheless divides them—Jerry remembers tossing Charlotte up in Emma's kitchen, but Emma reminds him, "It was your kitchen, actually." (101) While Jerry confesses that the specter of that moment with her husband and his wife all looking on haunts him even as they embrace on the bed, Emma chooses to secret the burden of her husband's knowledge from her lover in silence.

Jerry's lunch with Robert in scene seven again breaks with strict regression: like the previous scene, it also follows Robert's return from Venice. Robert extends another squash invitation to Jerry which it must be clear by now Robert has no intention of meeting. When Robert announces he went to Torcello, Jerry nearly slips, "Ah. I thought—" (112) but catches himself from saying that the speedboats were on strike in time, as Robert describes his trip to Torcello alone, reading Yeats on the grass as the "[h]ighpoint, actually, of the whole trip." (113)

Only once when Robert mentions his decision not to publish Spinks does Robert hint at the depth of his feeling of betrayal and his own loss:

> Tell me, do you think that makes me a publisher of unique critical judgment or a foolish publisher? (115)

Robert tenders publishing only as an oblique metaphor for his private agenda: assessing himself as a husband. When Jerry pronounces him only a foolish publisher, Robert concurs: "I agree. I am a very foolish publisher." (115) Though Jerry protests that Robert is being too hard on himself, Robert reveals the extent to which Emma's disclosure has soured his vision. He confesses a cynical, exhausted view of writers and writing at all levels, from aesthetics to commerce—from a writer's reputation and fame, to the private influence of writing on the public spheres of the marketplace:

> I'm a bad publisher because I hate books. Or to be more precise, prose. Or to be even more precise, modern prose, I mean modern novels, first novels and second novels, all that promise and

> sensibility it falls upon me to judge, to put the firm's money on, and then to push for the third novel, see it done, see the dust jacket done, see the dinner for the national literary editors done, see the signing in Hatchards done, see the lucky author cook himself to death, all in the name of literature. (116)

He almost allows his real agenda to reveal itself in his next outburst:

> You know what you and Emma have in common? You love literature. I mean you love modern prose literature, I mean you love the new novel by the new Casey or Spinks. It gives you both a thrill. (116)

Subtextually his topic remains Jerry and Emma's affair, but Jerry, confounded by the outburst says, "You must be pissed." (116) Robert skitters dangerously close to confrontation: "Really? You mean you don't think it gives Emma a thrill?" But when Jerry answers, "How do I know? She's your wife," Robert, a touch relieved, agrees and backs off: "Yes. Yes. You're quite right. I shouldn't have to consult you. I shouldn't have to consult anyone." (116) In Jerry's single line "She's your wife" Robert has received assurance that his marriage remains intact, not likely to be attacked by Jerry as an outside raider.

Robert relaxes expansively into a confessed admiration for Casey and, delivering encomiums on Casey, Jerry, and Emma, pronounces Casey, "First rate. I'm proud to publish him and you discovered him and that was very clever of you." (116) Robert responds to Jerry's efforts to salve his ego by returning Jerry's compliment with his own, restoring balance both to his marriage and his alliance with Jerry, even offering approbation for Jerry as his wife's lover: "You've got a good nose and you care and I respect that in you. So does Emma. We often talk about it." (118) Jerry responds with a lie. Although he has just seen her he asks, "How is Emma?" Robert responds with an invitation laden with wryly comic irony and multiple meaning in a closure that snaps the scene shut as tight as a Shakespearean rhymed couplet: "Very well. You must come and have a drink sometime. She'd love to see you." That evening has already taken place in scene four.

The penultimate scene presents the younger, more erotically charged, but slightly unsure lovers. Emma opens with a request for a vodka, signaling an impending confrontation she postpones till completing a series of inquiries: whether Jerry's wife Judith, a busy physician, has a lover (Jerry insists, just an admirer), whether Jerry has ever been unfaithful, to her, Emma, and what Jerry would do if he discovered Judith were unfaithful. Jerry makes his position clear, as in the opening scene, and later echoed again in their break-up: "She loves me," he says, adding, "All that means something." (129)

Once his position is clear, Emma takes his hand and supplies the context for the discussion of fidelity and betrayal confessing: "I'm pregnant. It was when you were in America." She hastens to add, "It wasn't anyone else. It was my husband." (130) Jerry, who must be at least slightly stunned by the news covers any trace of feeling with: "I'm very happy for you." (130)

The final scene, Jerry's initial seduction during Emma and Robert's anniversary party, proceeds along a fairly traditional assignment of roles. He pursues her. She resists. Jerry follows Emma into the bedroom and reeling from drink and desire opens his suit with a memory of Emma in white at her wedding, expressing his wish to have "blackened" her in her "white wedding dress, . . . as your best man." (135; ellipses mine) Emma stays his advance with a correction, "My husband's best man. Your best friend's best man." (135) But she cannot shield herself with her position which Jerry reconstructs: "No. Your best man." (135) His expression of passion might seem the ravings of a madman, except within the larger context of Pinter's work it is characteristic that extreme emotion overwhelms expression. Jerry calls her his "jewel" says, "You dazzle me," and claims her refusal will condemn him to "a state of catatonia," where "the reigning prince is the prince of emptiness, the prince of absence, the prince of desolation," and in rare utterance in Pinter's work he says, "I love you." (136)

Emma holds to her traditional defenses: "My husband is on the other side of that door." (136) Jerry at the edge of coherence continues, "I adore you. I'm madly in love with you. I can't believe that what anyone is at this moment saying has ever happened has ever happened," adding, "This is the only thing that has ever happened. Your eyes kill me. I'm lost. You're wonderful." (137) From the outset Jerry seeks to encapsulate her and their love in a solipsistic world, like a dream shut off by sleep from the waking world of reality. Her complicity will register only after their decision becomes a *fait accompli.*

Twice Jerry kisses her. Twice Emma breaks away. When Robert enters, Emma declares, "Your best friend is drunk." (137) Jerry denies nothing, but instead lavishes praise on Emma's beauty: "As you are my best and oldest friend, and in the present instance, my host, I decided to take this opportunity to tell your wife how beautiful she was." (137) Robert twice assents, "Quite right." (138–9) And when Jerry repeats, "I speak as your oldest friend. Your best man," Robert has the last word in the play, "You are, actually." (138)

Robert then clasps Jerry's shoulder and exits. As Emma turns to follow her husband, Jerry grasps her arm. "She stops still. They stand still, looking at each other" in a final tableau that places them standing together as a matched pair.

Whether Pinter would want to argue here, as he did of *The Homecoming*, that had this been a happy marriage, this wouldn't have happened seems beside the point. Robert confesses multiple betrayals, to having hit Emma more than once, when once might have sufficed to terminate any marriage. But even a year after the confession we see a brief expression of married love between Emma and Robert after Jerry leaves in scene four as they hold one another in their arms.

But what Pinter has constructed here is a play in which it is possible to feel sympathy, even deep compassion, for *all* the characters. If Jerry and Emma had not betrayed Robert, they might have betrayed their own deeper feelings. Robert's and Jerry's mutual admiration forms the basis for friendship, and Robert's acting with a certain magnanimity to preserve it on both the public and private level requires silently swallowing his own pain. Moreover, Robert's otherwise guileless and true affection for Jerry in what appears to be his oldest and perhaps his only close friendship, survives both the affair and the marriage. In the end love and friendship are equally strong, neither privileged over the other.

Jerry and Emma when they break up, are still obviously in love, and Jerry's "Darling" after the break up is not a mere *pro forma* utterance but one which Emma finds almost too powerful to bear. It is also a reminder that the relationship terminated when she forced it to a conclusion because she could not make it permanent. The love and erotic feeling which survives the breakup by years will remain for both Jerry and Emma the greatest love of their lives.

In the wake of the breakup of the affair and their marriage, available choices are not superb for any of them. Casey is no great prize. We know he drinks too much, and that Jerry, too, judging only from his hangover in the opening scene, is not immune to serious drinking bouts or its effects. Emma's relationship with Robert has the finality of complete closure bridged only by their children. There is no hint in the opening scene that Jerry has had other lovers after Emma, but his marriage is never presented as being more than reliable, even perhaps dreary. For Robert the loss is double if not triple: he loses a wife and the unconditional bond with his best friend, his two closest ties, lost already, in some sense, years earlier.

It is difficult to imagine how a man whose play entitled *Betrayal* which opened in the wake of a scandal that rocked British society could wholly condemn betrayal, yet with a customary compassion, neither denouncing nor licensing infidelity, Pinter dispenses an evenhanded evocation of sympathy for each as betrayed and betrayer. There can be no easy assignment of blame and no pure innocence. While Jerry remains closer to a traditional seducer (not unlike Emma Bovary's), steadfastly without intention to make any commitment to the woman he so passionately entices, he is redeemed by the honesty of his love.

These three characters are the most grown up, comfortable, and secure in Pinter's work, and Emma remains the most independent of his women. She is neither needy nor a seductress. But is Emma, like the Emma of Flaubert or her literary sisters Anna Karenina or Tess, placed in a work in which there are no men who can equal her? Jerry's profession of passion might be interpreted as his own wished-for strengths projected on to her. In the end, which is the beginning, when Emma turns to Jerry he responds to meet her—but only halfway on an erotic level, at least verbally. Emma wants something more—friendship perhaps, a permanent alliance. But Jerry reverts to self-concern.

Yet Emma's telling Robert the truth could be counted the largest betrayal, because it is from that point that the relationships unravel. Where before that moment she might have had both a marriage and lover, she now forces her marriage and Jerry's resistance to "rescuing" her from it to be less tolerable. In the end none of the three retains much more than his or her work on the public level, a career. A gallery or publishing house do not displace or fulfill private desires. After that moment it is Robert who preserves the marriage and friendship, while he endures his wife's continued infidelity for another two years (made palatable by his own infidelities). Never does he request, nor does she volunteer, to terminate her affair.

There can be no truth, no honesty in betrayal that does not also damage and destroy. Seven years is no small stint for a love affair, and these days, even a for marriage. But perhaps the affair's undoing also resulted distantly from the strain produced by Emma's confession.

What remains remarkable is the depth of passion and pity such a spare work evokes while it plumbs the old topic freshly, and with wit and grace finally summons from the audience beyond forgiveness, beyond understanding, an appreciation of all the characters and the power and importance of friendship and love.

PART THREE

"This Is the End My Friend": The Lovedeath Apocalyptic Vision Revised: Love, Justice and Power Reclaimed

Precisely and *Family Voices*: Lovedeath

For the next decade after *Betrayal*, Pinter's work for the stage took a darker turn, more and more toward political and global concerns in eight one-acts and sketches. More than a decade after his last full-length play, Pinter wrote *Moonlight*, a work which weds love and death to dramatize how each choice made by the most ordinary human being may become a choice between life and death. Private choice becomes public responsibility for life-promoting or destructive acts as the play links private love to the ethics of global justice and injustice. The sketch *Precisely* signaled an abrupt shift in that direction, followed by four plays, *Family Voices* and three others featured in a triple bill entitled *Other Places: A Kind of Alaska, Victoria Station,* and *One for the Road.*

Where *A Kind of Alaska* and *Victoria Station* returned to private concerns, *One for the Road* ushered in the onslaught of work inveighing against global injustice in three other deeply disturbing plays which bring together Pinter's focus on justice, love, and power: *Mountain Language, Party Time,* and *The New World Order.*

The most recent phase, beginning with *One for the Road,* Pinter's most violent portrayal of the abuse of authority in a hierarchical relationship, continues with *Mountain Language,* which relentlessly develops his concern with the horrors of torture. The fractal geometry played out along the spine of the dominant/subservient relationships loosens, fractures in *A Kind of Alaska, Family Voices,* and *Victoria Station* only to return cemented to these torture plays but with odd imbalance—there is little possibility for contest in a conflict where the powerful can so easily squelch the powerless. But even in this losing battle, justice and even its connection to love rise to the forefront.

Moonlight restores the balance lost in the torture plays by demonstrating how responsibility is our own. In this play love and justice are wedded to a new end, inviting the audience into the familiar, private world of Andy, a very ordinary middle-class civil servant who happens to be dying. His deathbed questions lead us to examine ultimate things in the comic, raucous, and often touching moments. Though Andy comes to little conscious awareness himself, the play awakens in the audience awareness of his responsibility for the violent consequences of his choices, which becomes a legacy to his children. *Moonlight,* thus, awakens our own accountability. The play raises questions of human nature to examine our perceptions of the limits of human change. His wife, who calls him a "loud mouth," excuses his behavior as his "nature," only to call into question the lack of individual responsibility such an attitude encourages.

Rather than reflecting the human animal as powerless to make choices but at the mercy of nature, *Moonlight* shows how all choices may be life-or-death choices and reveals that characters have many choices they never guess but are seen and felt by the audience. Almost all choice thus becomes ethical. It either feeds or impedes the machinery of power, maintaining a destructive status quo. Thus, through its larger vision *Moonlight* dramatizes not a lack of choices but a lack of *consciousness* of choices when informed by an outmoded vision that promotes destructive rather than constructive private or global policy and action. *Moonlight* awakens in the audience the need for a new vision and reveals how simple consciousness of choices may inspire and empower just action.

Precisely, a brief sketch, frontally addresses the issue of global annihilation by nuclear warfare as two men argue over the kill power of atomic weaponry. Roger and Stephen, over drinks, discuss global annihilation and become the first characters in Pinter's work who agree rather than dispute: in a nuclear war precisely twenty million would die. Their agreement and its horrifying absurdity throws responsibility out to the audience. *Precisely* remains divorced from any larger questions of justice or love, topics which Pinter will almost redefine in close examination in the plays of this period dealing with private life, beginning with *Family Voices.*

In *Family Voices,* a young man speaking in an epistolary style, addresses his distant mother whose voice intersects his as she recalls picnics at seaside cliffs, then reports the death of the young man's father. But their voices pass one another without colliding. Prompted by her belief that he has abandoned her, evidenced by his failure to answer her letters, she moves from a warm concern for her son to anger and detestation. Pinter continues to explore the chthonic forces of both the dead and the past as dead time which threatens to inundate and overtake the present, living moment. The play, speaking with all the force of nightmare, traverses an underworld without gods where the dead who speak are finally dead, speechless and where what is unsaid "will never be said." (296)

This play appropriately without action, dramatizes the failure of action, or more precisely, the failure of intention to translate into action. With deadly irony each missed communication effects a shift in each speaker that communicates the failure to act to the audience. The play casts that failure of transaction in the context of the private moral level of family: a child's duty and responsibility to parents in the face of a desire and quest for a larger "family" out in the world.

The son takes rooms with a new family who contrast with the family he leaves in the past. The missed connection between the young man and his birth family poses questions about the nature of familial love and duty, the present's overpowering ability to obliterate past ties as well as the past's capacity to remain ever present. But the surprising turn at the end, when the son chooses to do the seemingly right thing—to return home—ironically registers like a death knell.

Family Voices, a radio play with three voices, opens with the voice of the young man in an internal monologue that might be the written voice of a postcard: "I am having a very nice time." (281) But postcard cliché dissolves into something more familiar, darker, yet comic: "I hope you're feeling well, and not as peaky as you did, the last time I saw you." (281) Discord lingers in the suggestion that the other party was unwell, perhaps angry, and the parting, less than amiable. But the next line qualifies the point with unintended humor, allowing the audience to laugh at, rather than with the young man and his imaginary interlocutor: "No, you didn't feel peaky, you felt perfectly well, you simply looked peaky." Then he asks, "Do you miss me?" (281)

The young man contradicts himself three times, first claiming he is "dead drunk," cataloging his intake at "five pints" and "three double scotches" at The Fishmongers Arms but quickly denies it (281):

> When I said I was drunk I was of course making a joke.
> I bet you laughed.
> Mother?
> Did you get the joke? You know I never touch alcohol. (282)

This is the first self-referential admission to joking in Pinter's work, and the comic point is heightened by his third contradiction: as the "solace" of his landlady he reports, "I have a drink with her at lunchtime and another one at tea time and then I take her for a couple in the evening at The Fishmongers Arms." (283) His triple reversal describing his drinking might make nothing he says appear to be trusted as truth. But what he describes is less important than what happens. And what happens is that he, like Albert in *A Night Out* may succumb to the forces of death and the past rather than to life and love if he returns home to his mother.

His dialogue moves swiftly from suggestion of the ribald to the erotic. He assures his mother his new "room is extremely pleasant" as is the bath as well as the other inhabitants who "all lie quite naked in the bath." (281) Erotic suggestion heightens when he says he expects to make friends, "to make a girl friend," and promises to bring her home to meet his mother. He closes at dawn, "And so I shall end this letter to you, my dear mother, with my love." (283)

The mother interjects, "Why do you never write?" Wondering whether he changed his address, she worries then admonishes him about selecting his friends now that he is away in the big city, and interjects a bizarre desire to interject herself into his fairy-tale romance which she imagines: "I often think I would love to live happily ever after with you and your young wife." (183)

Her Victorian mores contrast with his erotic disclosures. She reports a remembered scrap of ritual chat from family picnics where the father would recall, "We had a damn good walk," and she would correct and soften his language with: "You mean you had a good munch munch," her prim joke providing the family laughter. (284) The mother's function as a judging superego has become so internalized by the son that he might hardly need to keep contact to hear her scolding.

She closes however with an emotional stab that gains power from its understatement. "I wrote you three months ago, telling you of your father's death. Did you receive my letter?" (284)

Oblivious to his mother's grief and concern, the son's voice returns: "I'm not at all sure that I like the people in this house, apart from Mrs. Withers and her daughter Jane." (284) Lady Withers wears red dresses, but the son is unable to discover whether one of the two men in the house, Benjamin Withers, is related. He then corrects his observation that Jane must be Mrs. Withers's granddaughter, because Mrs. Withers is seventy, and Jane, fifteen, a school girl continually engrossed in her homework, though she does not attend school.

Pinter skillfully orchestrates a growing audience sympathy for the mother, who evokes a palpable desire for the son's return. In the momentary silence—the interstices between the son's reports and the mother's greetings—the maddening cross talk creates in the audience both a continued curiosity and sympathy for the son's explorations as well as a desire for the son to respond to his mother. The terrible irony in the end is that he does so, all too well.

Attempting to assuage her son's grief, the mother reports that in the end his father spoke of him "with tenderness and bewilderment," as she "consoled him with the idea that you had left home to make him proud of you." (285) Among his father's last words were, "Give him a slap on the back from me." (285)

The son, in contrast, reports that Mrs. Withers now functions as a surrogate mother, "Sometimes she gives me a cuddle . . . ," yet he hastens to add, "But I haven't forgotten that I have a mother and that you are my mother." (286) Like other definitive statements from a Pinter character, this one functions to suggest its opposite. The displacement in space from his birth family creates a disjunction in time. As the present takes over, occupying more and more of the young man's time, his aging mother reverts to taking up residence in the past.

The power of the present is augmented by the force of the son's erotic encounter. What happens at tea with Lady Withers on her sofa where he reports Jane was "sitting doing her homework" is equally comic and erotic when he happens to notice "[h]er stockinged toes came to rest on my thigh," and later in his lap, that she chewed "almost dreamily," licked her lips "without haste . . . her toes were quite restless, even agitated," till he bit into his "rock solid" bun, which bounced into his lap, but "Jane's feet caught it," and he reports, "It calmed her down." (286–7; ellipses mine) The scene takes its titillating force from its attendant adolescent innocence coupled with an almost Victorian denial of what is actually happening sexually. He seems unaware of any erotic innuendoes. The oddly unlit, nightmare interior suggests that rather than a life-enhancing encounter this is an erotic dead end.

The mother's response, "Darling. Where are you? Why do you never write?," first suggests her unanswered letters are never received, but that suggestion proliferates into multiple interpretations that either his letters were never sent, or, what becomes more likely, that they were never written. The son's "letters" may remain entirely in his head. The point speaks to several issues, not the least of which become the son's growing concern with his present circumstances and the mother's equally diminishing focus on the present, a return to the past as she looks toward death. In her anger she revises her earlier version of the father's last moments saying, "On his deathbed your father cursed you. He cursed me too, to tell the truth." (287) She concludes, "He died in lamentation and oath." (287)

The duration of her son's absence, measured by the mother's report that her only consolation is his sister Millie, now married with a "very lovely little boy," transforms the mother's concern for her son into guilt-eliciting threats. "When he is older he will want to know where his uncle is. What shall we say?" (287) But her concern remains tempered with hope or fantasy that perhaps her son will arrive "in the not too distant future" in a new car and suit. (287)

The son reports that while he was taking his bath, Riley, one of the tenants, announced that two women claiming to be his sister and mother asked for him, but Riley denied knowing him and unceremoniously sent the women away. Riley's information, quickly subordinated to the son's observation that Riley is enamored of the his "wellknit and slender body" in the bath, registers no response from the son except for the zinger, "It interests me that my father wasn't bothered to make the trip." (289)

The mother's voice returns with a classic widow's lament that she hears his "father's step on the stair . . . , his cough," but she says, "He does not open the door." (289) Memory slowly envelops her present to encase her in tender recollections of bathing her child, careful to cause him no "discomfort or unease," of their exchanged trusting gaze, and of his exclusive desire for her, "knowing that you wanted no-one else, no-one at all, that you were entirely happy in my arms." She remains aware, "that I was at the same time sitting by an indifferent fire, alone in winter, in eternal night without you." (290)

This mother, a distant descendent of the over-protective mother in *A Night Out*, allows her possessive love to displace all other love, including that for her husband. The disassociation she describes, watching herself and her son in the past even as she recognizes herself alive in the present, places the competing moments on equal footing, but always the past, for the aging mother threatens to consume the present, while for the young son the present overtakes the past, becoming his whole concern. He confesses himself happy and, in rapture, admits, "Oh mother, I have found my home, my family. Little did I ever dream I could know such happiness." (290)

Yet almost nothing he says is not laden with several levels of irony. The son, after describing a momentary high point in his encounter with this new household now reports Lady Withers and Jane as the growing locus of his attention. Where the mother remains in "eternal night," the son gleefully exclaims, "I am in it. I will never leave it." (290) His expressed zenith of happiness contrasts with his mother's nadir of despondency which now finds expression in language far removed from her former "munch munch" lady-like euphemisms. Appropriating the coarser language of her dead husband, the mother, with all the passion of a spurned lover, now curses her son: "Oh I pray, I pray your life is a torment to you. I wait for your letter begging me to come to you. I'll spit on it." (290)

The son's drifting blithely past her curse introduces the first dark note into his otherwise happy scene linking love with death as he solicits his mother's advice about the man who calls himself Mr. Withers. What he learns about love in this sexually ambiguous household only confuses him and points him toward death. Mrs. Withers deflects his questions about Mr. Withers by recounting her days in the armed forces, a topic which carries with it the suggestion of warfare and killing. Meanwhile Riley describes keeping his "inclinations" toward his own sex in "tight rein," subverting his carnal desire "towards religion" with the result, he says: "I walk about in a constant state of spiritual, emotional, psychological and physical tension," and he refers to his own sexually repressive discipline as "breathtaking." (292) Riley is among the first of Pinter's characters to link love with death in his desire to "crush a slip of a lad such as you to death." But Riley also claims his love for the son is expressed in classic poetic terms: "I mean that death that is love, the death I understand love to be." (292) Riley is gay but can only express his crushingly violent desires by placing them in "leg irons" and himself in church and, as a respected man on the force, in a policeman's uniform. Infusing a bit of Lawrencian adolescent humor, the son wonders whether Lady Withers is Jane's mother, making her "Lady Jane Withers?" He raises the suggestion of sexual vitality only to quash it. (293)

Despite the disturbing mysteries growing in his life, the son claims, "My life possesses shape," yet another assertion, like his professed happiness, that calls itself into question. (293) The darker side of his expressed earthly paradise emerges as he reports Lady Withers receives guests whose steps he hears on the steps all night. Nested within this household, the son's developing sexuality reinforces the deadend love/death equation.

Voice 3, the father enters at the end to deny the mother's assertion that he is dead. The wonderfully comic interlude both conceals and speaks to the deepest terror of the play: "I know your mother has written to you to tell you that I am dead. I am not dead." (294) The father's entrance offers an imaginative projection of coming to terms with death. He accuses the son of having prayed for his death, claims to have heard the prayers, as he smiles at his "loving son" from his "glassy grave," then signs off with a postcard closure, "Lots of love, son. Keep up the good work." (294) But he returns with the information that he is disturbed by only one thing: the sound of a barking dog, which frightens him.

Beneath the surface appearance of happiness in the son's new home, the borders between life and death collapse as his new family appropriates his identity by assigning him a new name, Bobo. The only exception is the old man, perhaps conflated at some level with the father, but "[h]e is old and will die soon." (295) The others address him in backslapping terms: "How's tricks in the sticks, Bobo," (295)

The mother's alarm at her son's absence expands to paranoia. "The police are looking for you," she says: "I have stated my belief that you are in the hands of underworld figures who are using you as a male prostitute." (295) Reminding her son he is not yet twenty-one, she says, "Women were your downfall, even as a nipper." She cites the French Maid Françoise (an obliquely echoing reference to the maid central in Proust's work) and a governess, Miss Carmichael.

The growing unresolved tension of the quarrel between the mother and son, her disapproval, and his escape from her is addressed only by the son's humorous accusation that his father's disappearance is *her* responsibility: "What have you done with him, mother?" (296)

Her last words significantly resonate with what is central to the play: "Do you think the word love means anything?" (296)

The son's astonishing response, gratuitously announcing that he is returning to her, collides with her question as a challenge when he asks: "What will you say to me?" (296)

His question remains unanswered as the piece ends with the father's final reminder of the finality of death to bring down the curtain on the past, present and future: "I have so much to say to you. But I am quite dead. What I have to say to you will never be said." (296)

The cross talk, miscommunication, incomplete action during a play encompassing the arc of life from infancy through budding adulthood to death situate the ethical concerns within the context of love-and-death issues. If the son, about to enter the larger world, does his duty and returns home, he allows himself to be sucked back into the vortices of his birth family's, specifically his mother's, retreat from the world. The stunning reversal, turning on death and love—both erotic and filial love—unmasks what is worse than the son's unexplained long absence from his family: the possibility that he may return—forever.

A Kind of Alaska: Identity Unresolved

A Kind of Alaska was inspired by the neurologist Oliver Sacks's compassionately written book *Awakenings*, detailing the extraordinary promise but only partial recovery offered to patients suffering from the sleeping sickness *encephalitis lethargica*. Pinter's Deborah, a patient who has been awakened from a twenty-nine-year sleep, fractally dramatizes throughout the near impossibility not only of knowing the self but, in instances of neurological damage, of having a self at all. Deborah's hopefully begun awakening, witnessed by her doctor Hornby (played by Pinter for a BBC radio broadcast) who has stood by her throughout, together with her sister Pauline, is followed by the disappointingly limited fulfillment of L-DOPA's promise as a new drug. That limited, sometimes broken, promise of a psychiatric cure, reflected already in *The Hothouse* and *The Caretaker*, serves as a contemporary analog for the similar unfulfilled promise of almost all the major breakthrough psychiatric cures of the twentieth century (save lithium and perhaps Prozac): from electroshock therapy, lobotomy, and thorazine to the designer neuroleptic and psychotropic drugs which helped empty Western mental institutions in the nineteen sixties and seventies. Each new therapy, like L-DOPA, brought with it the promise of a miracle—briefly. But none are without side effects, sometimes as disturbing as the deficits they seek to address. What was astonishingly hopeful about L-DOPA's promise was that after its initial administration patients awakened from a coma-like sleep often achieving a startling level of normality that momentarily made the drug appear to be indeed a miracle cure. But the miracle was short-lived: no patient ever again attained that level of normalcy, and a few were beset with Parkinsonian-like tics which were far less tolerable than the catatonia-like coma from which they had emerged. As the world's population ages, with many now living decades beyond the life expectancy of only a century ago, and as we witness the loss of "self" that currently can accompany old age's diseases—Alzheimer's, stroke, and senility—the questions raised in this play will take on a significance now primarily reserved for the beginnings of life: what does it mean to be human? On the surface Pinter's play imaginatively telescopes the promise and disappointment of weeks and months into minutes to ask what it means to be a self when the self has slept through half a life. But more significantly, dramatizing the protean nature of identity, the play addresses the audience asking what constitutes a self and what it means to be awake to life.

Deborah, awake for the first time in decades but confused, wonders why her sister has aged, when she grew breasts. At the end when Deborah concludes, "I think I have the matter in proportion," she addresses any normal person's inability to recall the past accurately and raises further questions about what would be meant by accuracy.

Rarely, if ever elsewhere, has Pinter in his writing acknowledged being directly "inspired" by another, here Oliver Sacks, nor has he provided an introduction to explain a play's theme or content, here the sleeping sickness epidemic which early in the twentieth century struck five million people, confining them to a trance, coma, and Parkinsonism through stages which left a third dead and those who lived, conscious of their surroundings but unable move or to speak. Not until the introduction of L-DOPA fifty years later, Pinter reports, did they come back to life but without full recovery of their faculties. The sleeping sickness, according to Sacks, is not a new disease but has recurred for centuries, passing through dormant periods so lengthy that mention of it dropped out of medical record only to reappear again as if it were an undiscovered disease.

What is remarkable about Sacks's original account is his own extraordinary compassion, his ability to penetrate the rigid or sometimes drooling, scabby masks of people encased in tics or catatonic trances and trapped in "sleep" twenty-five years. Yet he remains able to discern the humanity beneath. Pinter captures the spirit of Sacks's compassion in Doctor Hornby's response and extends his own authorial compassion evenly among the three characters, especially to the newly awakened Deborah.

Without romanticizing the forty-year-old woman, whose life stopped when she was fifteen and now confronts the horror of having missed her prime years, Pinter dramatizes the inner world of a woman to let us glimpse what it might feel like to be catatonic, in a coma, or living a death-in-life existence for twenty-nine years. She describes herself as dancing in narrow spaces:

> The most crushing spaces. The most punishing spaces. . . . Like dancing with someone dancing on your foot all the time, I mean *all* the time on the same spot, just slam, slam, a big foot on your foot, not the most ideal kind of dancing, not by a long chalk. (26; ellipses mine)

That almost solipsistic confinement harks back to Pinter's portrayal of Stanley in *The Birthday Party*, but where Stanley's exile is largely inflicted by choice or habit, her affliction is imposed by circumstances wholly beyond her control. Yet both raise similar questions about identity, his an identity lost, then stripped away, and hers, an identity undeveloped. At one level she remains a precocious fifteen-year-old practicing a newly acquired vocabulary as she describes her younger sister Pauline, who she believes is only thirteen:

> I keep telling her I'm not prepared to tolerate her risible, her tendentious, her eclectic, her ornate, her rococo insinuations and garbled inventions. (21)

Nor does Pinter romanticize her even at fifteen as wholly pure in mind or spirit. When she first awakens, wondering who Hornby might be, she proposes, "You are my Prince Charming. Aren't you?," but when he doesn't answer, she turns on him with the full force of a 1980's, not a 1950's adolescent woman: "Silly shit. All men are alike." (19) But after a pause she turns again, "I think I love you." (20) When the doctor says, "No, you don't," humor releases the tension even in the face of the terror she faces when she replies, "Well, I'm not spoilt for choice here, am I?" (20)

When she asks how long she's been asleep and he tells her twenty-nine years, she says, "You mean I'm dead?" (15) Death and love again merge. Her erotic impulses are unchecked by received social convention or even age. Still imagining herself fifteen, she hurls a ferocious torrent of accusations undercut only by desire for the doctor before he can identify himself:

> You've had your way with me. You made me touch you. You stripped me. I cried ... but ... it was my lust made me cry. You are a devil. My lust was my own. I kept it by me. You took it from me. Once open never closed. Never closed again. Never closed always open. For eternity. Terrible. You have ruined me. (12)

Spewing forth a garbled tirade mingling desire and Victorian sexual mores, she nevertheless owns responsibility for what she imagines she remembers has happened. Yet trying to make sense of her circumstances, she also persists in imagining herself a young girl in a hotel and with comic effect wonders if she's been taken into the White Slave Traffic or if she is in prison and what offense she has committed.

Time for her is fluid. When she first awakens she claims she is twelve, then sixteen, then seven, and later that she is eighteen. But Deborah is no longer a girl. Yet as Sacks observed, patients even in a coma often continued to learn from surroundings they seemed oblivious to, and Deborah as a grown woman tries to discover who she might be by navigating through the only markers she has: family.

Her recollections of her sisters Estelle and Pauline express her rich mix of admiration, love, jealousy, envy, and annoyance, but her sisters, along with Jack her boyfriend remain the centerpiece of her earth-bound existence, while her parents, another anchor to reality, operate on the periphery.

When the full realization of her age comes to her she vows, "I certainly have no intention of looking into a mirror." (39)

The promise of a happily-ever-after ending after her awakening is transient, fleeting. Her sister Pauline's entrance confounds and confuses as much as it clarifies.

When the middle-aged Pauline asks the doctor whether she should tell Deborah the truth or lies, Hornby replies, "Both," an attempt to shield Deborah from truths he believes she may not yet be prepared to accept. (27) Rather than launch into the facts that their mother is dead, their father, blind, and that their sister Estelle, who never married, looks after him, Pauline invents a world cruise to account for the family's absence, tells Deborah they are in Bangkok, that she spoke with them, "And they all send so much love to you. Especially mummy." (28)

But Deborah remains incredulous: "So you say you're my sister?" When she asks, "Did a sudden shock age you overnight?" (29) She observes, "Well if you're Pauline you've put on a remarkable amount of weight in a very short space of time. I can see you're not keeping up with your ballet classes." (31)

The comic turns build to Deborah's blurting out, "My God! You've grown breasts!" (31) With great difficulty Deborah struggles to understand that she and her sister are grown women. But when Pauline says, "I am a widow," Deborah replies, "This woman is mad." (33)

Only when the doctor corroborates Pauline's claim, then tells Deborah the truth about her family's circumstances, explaining that she has been living in suspension, "in a kind of Alaska," does Deborah begin to understand. Describing his devotion to Deborah he says, "I have never let you go," and adds, "I have lived with you." (35) In that same spirit he describes himself as having married Pauline, a marriage of a shared vigil:

> Your sister Pauline was twelve when you were left for dead. When she was twenty I married her. She is a widow. (35)

Deborah's experiencing the fracturing and disjunction of time dramatizes its fluidity—a woman at seventy may feel thirteen, just as Yeats at fifty saw himself wearing his aging body as a mask, a scarecrow, tied to him "as to a dog's tail"—having little or nothing to do with the younger reality and identity of the person within.

Not only does the initial soaring effect of L-DOPA never return, but worse than the former sleep are side effects. Deborah exhibits tics, flicking her fingers at her face uncontrollably during one long speech. She is attacked from within and without; her internal development is checked in the quick fade of the medication's efficacy.

At the end Deborah is faced with difficult choices, untangling lies from truths to understand who she is in order to situate herself within the context of her family and the world.

Where earlier she describes herself with "all the world before me" (20) and might as easily be the small child she remembers, the tomboy playing with Peter, with his trains, "Cowboys and

Indians." (20) She remains an adult as she asks, "Any chance of a dry sherry?" and requests a party with "[l]ots of cakes and lots of booze." (24)

She is not without strengths. She claims, "I have a laughing nature" (24) and is in possession of a larger, even profound wisdom of events in the larger world when she says, "I suppose the war's still over," then asks, "They haven't started another one?" (25)

A whole view of human nature presents itself in this brief play, one that sees this girl/woman child frozen into an adolescence yet already in possession of a full spectrum of adult human feelings, desires, and purpose, but within such narrow confines her quest will be limited to sorting out who she is, hampered by the aftermath of her disease and encroaching side effects of the drug. The choices she makes show that she selects what is least repellent and most attractive from among the lies and truths she had been told, constructing yet a third reality for herself, that is no longer a dream but an awakening:

> You say I have always been alive and am alive now. You say I am a woman.
> *She looks at PAULINE then back to HORNBY*
> She is a widow. She doesn't go to her ballet classes any more. Mummy and Daddy and Estelle are on a world cruise. They've stopped off in Bangkok. It'll be my birthday soon. I think I have the matter in proportion. (40)

What we see is precisely the opposite. Like other proclamations of self-knowledge in Pinter's work, her having "the matter in proportion" is a fabrication selected from the fabric of lies she is told and from the truths she has chosen to weave into her own story—a commentary, however oblique, about declaring truth to a patient, however unpleasant. Her choices resonate with the nature of our own realities constructed from what others tell us and what we have selected to know about ourselves, others, and the world. Deborah's awakening speaks to the larger issue Pinter more recently addressed, suggesting that most of us, like himself, may sleepwalk though a portion or the whole of our lives.

Victoria Station: Love and Power Revisited

In *Victoria Station* Driver 274 resists his Controller's order to pick up a passenger at Victoria Station, claiming he never heard of it and that he is parked near the Crystal Palace with a passenger on board. The Controller with increasing verbal abuse orders the Driver to deposit the passenger and take up the assignment. But the Driver reveals that his passenger on board is asleep and that he has fallen in love with her. The Controller orders the Driver to promise to wait there for his arrival. *Victoria Station* returns to the classic dominant/subservient relationship to dramatize the triumph of love over a position of power.

The Controller voices deep dissatisfaction with his own position long before the end. By his own account he has less power than the lowly Driver, who at least has control of the wheel in front of him:

> I'm just talking into this machine, trying to make some sense out of our lives. That's my function. God gave me this job. He asked me to do this job, personally. I'm your local monk, 247. . . . I lead a restricted life. I haven't got a choke and a gear lever in front of me. I haven't got a cooling system and four wheels. I'm not sitting here with wing mirrors and a jack in the boot. And if I did have a jack in the boot I'd stick it right up your arse. (50)

The semi-erotic, semi-violent references to car parts harks back to *Trouble in the Works* and *The Room*, but the Controller's references to a god-appointed position, as a recent introduction of religion in Pinter's plays, links back to his novel, to the re-emergent mention of it in *No Man's Land* and *Family Voices*, and links forward both to *One for the Road*, where the torturer Nicolas claims a direct line to god, and to *The New World Order*, where the torturers proclaim their purity with all the fervor of religious fanaticism.

When the Controller threatens: "I'm going to tie you up bollock naked to a butcher's table and I'm going to flog you to death all the way to the Crystal Palace," the Driver suddenly identifies his location as the Crystal Palace, gratuitously adding that his wife is probably in bed and that he has a little daughter. (54–5)

When the Controller points out that the Crystal Palace burned down, he also threatens increasing malice unless the Driver follows orders:

> Otherwise I'll destroy you bone by bone. I'll suck you in and blow you out in little bubbles, I'll chew your stomach out with my own teeth. I'll eat all the hair off your body. You'll end up looking like a pipe cleaner. Get me? (58)

But the Controller also confesses: "You're beginning to obsess me," and his self-pitying lament no doubt garners some audience sympathy despite his verbal abuse:

> I think I'm going to die. I'm alone in this miserable freezing fucking office and nobody loves me. Listen, pukeface— (58)

Driver 247 continues to refuse the assignment but opposes anyone else being selected for it: "They're all bloodsuckers. I'm the only one you can trust." (58)

Love enters when the controller indulges in a fanciful plan to take an imagined holiday to Barbados, offering to take the Driver: "Just the two of us. I'll take you snorkelling (sic). We can swim together in the blue Caribbean." (59) But when the Driver confesses: "I think I've fallen in love. For the first time in my life," (60) the Controller's tone changes, first to sarcasm ("I'll have to make a note in my diary not to forget your Golden Wedding, won't I?"), then an offer to shake his hand. When the Driver inquires about the man coming in at Victoria Station, the Controller, in an about face replies, "He can go and fuck himself," then orders the Driver to promise to stay put and says he will be right there. (61) Although the Driver promises, "No, I won't move," and closes with "I'll be right here," it is not at all clear he will do so, but it is clear that what he has, love, surpasses what his superior possesses: power.

This slight sketch which polarizes love and power dramatizes those polarities as a rare instance, and the last in Pinter's recent plays, where romantic love triumphs over an abusive power. Equally interesting, the Controller's violent verbal abuse matches the torturers' in Pinter's next several plays, but given the Controller's inability to inflict real damage, and the Driver's near indifference, awash as he is in the euphoria of love, the verbal violence as violence remains impotent and comically ignorable.

One for the Road: The End of the Road

One for the Road, is Pinter's first extended dramatic confrontation with violence as a global, political issue. But Pinter also saw the play's connection to earlier work such as *The Dumb Waiter* and *The Hothouse*, which also dramatize the abuse of authority. The change, which began eleven years earlier with Pinter's shocked response to the West's hypocrisy to the overthrow of the Marxist Allende regime in Chile, took shape in his recent work. Steadily, in the ensuing years Pinter found himself increasingly engaged—joining CND, the Campaign for Nuclear Disarmament, and crusading on behalf of prisoners of conscience, participating in rallies—but this was his first play explicitly attacking those issues.

Gila and her husband Victor, coolly and separately interrogated by Nicolas, have been tortured, their lives irreparably broken. In the end they learn they are free but also that their child Nick is dead.

Writing in outrage against Turkish academics unfairly detained and tortured for political views, Pinter dramatizes for the first time people without choice or any way to defend themselves against the abuse of authority. In the unequal contest between the torturer and people he can so easily squelch, the fractal geometry operates here to reveal even more nakedly the insubstantial identity of the brutalizer who must borrow meaning and confidence from a cause which he is unable to see is as dead-ended for him as the road he closes for those he tortures. The forty-five minute play could be set in any one of the ninety countries, documented by the United Nations and Amnesty International, in which torture is routinely practiced during imprisonment. Pinter's stated aim was to make the audience see the human truth behind such statistics. (Appleyard, 13)

Commenting upon the source of play's violence, Pinter says: "It's to do with my fascination with our separation between reality and our interpretation of it. Our human experience can be totally dislocated by these facts and it happens every day of the week," He adds, "It's exactly the same as when people talk about nuclear war. The words have simply become abstractions—people can't face them":

> Before you recognize what the words mean there's nothing you can do about them. You're always going to be separated from that reality. The words and statistics that are used are not understood. People prefer not to think we are facing the end of the world, that torture involves the gravest humiliation that can happen to an individual. (13)

Pinter's concern over the abrogation of human freedom translates into his recent work as a plea to act: "I think all the plays I've written are attempts to understand people behaving in certain contexts," adding: "You see now I do feel that there will be no writing, no entertainment, no drama whatsoever in a very short time unless we recognize the realities of the world in which we live." (13)

Yet Pinter refuses to fashion his torturer from cardboard; Nicolas is a man who believes "that it is right, for him, to possess this power," because he believes "he's acting for his country legitimately and properly." (Hern, 17) Nicolas also cheerfully identifies himself as liking the ordinary living things of life, "Nature. Trees, things like that. A nice blue sky. Blossom." (12)

Danger enters when identity, the self, is so inextricably equated with country and cause that country and cause supply the whole identity and meaning of life. The torturer, lacking the consciousness of the falsity of that equation—basic to any other self-knowledge—remains unable to act otherwise than as he does. Danger is compounded by habit. Inertia of motion applies throughout Pinter's work either to stifle or to propel human action. Once set in motion to destroy, the very momentum hurls characters forward with the force of irreversible necessity.

Pinter acknowledges that *One for the Road*, witnessed in the child's murder, is "pretty remorseless." (15) Pinter consistently insists upon viewing it with all its specificity, not through the comfortable remove of symbol or abstraction: "I don't really see *One for the*

Road as a metaphor. For anything. . . . You have a torturer, you have the victims. And you can *see* that two of the victims have been physically tortured." He tried to "make the names non-specific," but almost certainly is not unaware that both the torturer Nicolas and the child Nick share a common name, suggesting perhaps that different circumstances might interchangeably find them in reversed positions. (15) ("Nick" was traditionally a common name for the devil.)

Pinter's recent work have all attempted to waken audiences "to recognize the realities" of our world, especially the grimmest and most destructive realities. That recognition, however, can only be a starting point for action.

His recent work provokes more than intellectual or even emotional response. It engages the audience as an equal participant in the play's action by calling for action. His work does so by forcing identification with both tortured and torturer—a familiar technique in his work, which here serves a new end.

Pinter recognizes that, in addition to the discomfort we feel watching the tortured, "It is also, however, true that a good deal of the natural sadistic qualities, which we all possess, are given free reign in the play." (17) When Pinter's work pushes beyond identification with victim to identification with torturer it brings into our consciousness the dark, destructive, chthonic forces in us all. That consciousness which self-knowledge also requires is demanded not merely from the characters but from the audience as well in the double fear the audience feels. Pinter believes the audience fear is not only for the victim, but "fear also born of recognition of themselves as interrogator. Because think of the joy of having absolute power." (Hern, 17)

One for the Road, like Tennessee Williams's *Streetcar Named Desire*, is a difficult play for actors to perform for reasons which also give the play its power. Just as several leading American actresses suffered near or actual psychological breakdowns playing Blanche, as all her escape routes close, the actors in this play, Pinter says,

> found themselves in danger of being taken over by the characters. Because there's no escape once you're in there. Jenny Quayle, for example, who played Gila, broke down at one point in rehearsal and said, "You can't understand what it's like." She was

> telling me how humiliating it was to be treated this way, to be quite helpless. Certainly all three actors, having done it, couldn't face the idea of doing the play again for anything but a very short run. They found the experience too oppressive. . . . (Hern, 17)

The play steamrolls remorselessly forward, sustaining the tension of threatened destruction, beginning with the opening moment when Nicolas aims his fingers at the eyes of Victor seated before him then says: "This is my big finger and this is my little finger," adding "I can do absolutely anything I like." (7) When Nicolas asks, "Do you think I'm mad?" he himself answers, "My mother did." (7)

But Nicolas instantly attempts to purify his action by equating what he does with a spiritual quest. Remarking that the eyes are the windows of the soul, he poses the question, "Which side do you think God is on?" (7) He answers, after taking a drink, by identifying himself as the man who runs the place: "God speaks through me," qualifying that as "The Old Testament God," then adds, "although I am a long way from being Jewish." (8) Why does Pinter have Nicolas disavow his links with Judaism when surely, given the larger context of such statements in Pinter's work, his saying so may only reinforce that link?

The religious references in *One For the Road* reverberate back to the beginning of Pinter's career. The earliest references on the topic occur in the novel *The Dwarfs*, where characters raise questions about the existence of a Judeo-Christian God and Christ to examine one another's beliefs. The subject is vestigially retained in his play of the same title but vanishes in the other early and middle plays only to re-emerge thematically in the recent work as a vengefully destructive force of simplistic dichotomous, fundamentalist belief, which allows and promotes eradication of all who do not subscribe to the belief in absolute dualities and participate on the correct side.

Pinter's recent portrayal of religion consistently aligns religion with that fanaticism which provides those in power with moral justification to oppose those who do not subscribe to their religious beliefs. Nicolas establishes one cause for Victor's detention with the accusation, "You're not a religious man, I take it?" (9)

For Nicolas, religion and national patriotism are fused. He says he confesses to God, that he was never more moved than when the man running the country announced to the country: "We are all patriots, we are as one, we all share a common heritage," but he adds, addressing Victor, "Except you, apparently." (13)

The subtle undercurrent revealing Nicolas's disturbance and perhaps disgust at his own destructive behavior registers only in his excessive drinking signaled by the play's title which Nicolas announces with his third drink: "I think I deserve one for the road." (10) But this, already his second "for the road," also underscores that there is no road ahead for Victor or Gila. At another level, given the claustrophobically sealed interrogation room, only a one-way road opens for Nicolas. But he has no way of knowing that. The very sources which supply his total power set him upon a fixed course which admits no change in direction or self.

Nicholas, however, opens the play out to the larger community of the organization's operation in the building. His remark that Victor's wife is upstairs, like Nicholas's every comment or question, calculated to inflict pain, advances the torture. He asks Victor if his son is all right, then says, "Silly of him to behave as he did." (10) Victor can have no way of answering the question and can only dread the consequences for his child. "Prepared to be frank, as a true friend should," Nicolas proclaims, "I love death." (11)

Where his admission might seem to reflect a self-knowledge, it instead registers as an index of his ethical and spiritual blindness. Death for Nicolas surpasses the erotic in beauty as, "The purest, most harmonious thing there is," as he concludes, "Sexual intercourse is nothing compared to it." (11)

To appreciate the long tradition out of which this seemingly outrageous statement grows, it is helpful to recognize the present context of our own Western tradition which sanctions and has legalized only three forms of killing: war, capital punishment, and self-defense. Pinter's recent work focusing on death by torture and, what may be worse than death, the irreparable and irrevocable brutalization of those who survive torture—that gray area, an extension of undeclared war, self-sanctioned by those appareled in the vestments of power seized in political and religious conflicts around the globe.

But Pinter's work goes even further. In Nicolas's equation of death and Eros, sanctioned and unsanctioned killing are erotically thrilling, and for him the torture deaths, sanctified. American playwright Emily Mann, whose documentary drama *Still Life* dramatizes an actual returning Viet Nam veteran's love of killing as the greatest sex he has ever had, illustrates that point. In an interview she cites a poem which nicely elucidates Nicolas's love of death that has grown into habit that becomes addiction:

> The sad thing is
> When we send our young men to war
> The young men die
> The sad thing is
> When we send the young men to war
> The young men kill
> And the sad thing is that
> When we send our young men to war
> They learn to love to kill.

Emily Mann adds that the poem is Greek, two thousand years old. (Betsko and Koenig, 287)[1]

In Pinter's recent work, love and death, the forces of Eros and Thanatos, square off against each other as Thanatos invariably seizes all power to destroy whatever Eros can build, then claims Eros's desire and ecstasy for its own. The seemingly irreconcilable warring opposites require that the forces of Eros recognize the extraordinary and tantalizing power of Thanatos. Pinter's work shows that if Eros is to seek and secure power, it must not only *resist* forces of the death-lovers' unjustifiable destruction but also use that power to *promote* life.

Nicolas is not without ordinary erotic inclinations and desires, but they do not extend to serving vitality beyond his own lust. He tortures Victor with references to his wife: "I couldn't help noticing she didn't look her best. She's probably menstruating. Women do that." (12) This first mention of menstruation in Pinter's work, coupled with references to her rape, funnels all attention to Gila's sexuality. In the London and New York productions the full horror of her torture visually assailed the audience when Gila turns her back to the audience, revealing a large brown stain on the back of her tattered skirt.

But Nicolas also communicates his own desire for love when he says, "I think your wife is. Beginning. She is beginning to fall in love with me." (12) The truth can only be the opposite. If there is any victory for Gila and Victor in this play, it may remain in Gila's unspoken love and respect for her husband, which Nicolas cannot wrest from Victor.

"Kill me," is Victor's first unprompted utterance, and from that we glimpse the extremity of his agony and despair.

Nicky, the child, appears next, a fresh, spirited young boy, as yet unharmed, who when prompted admits he likes aeroplanes. Unafraid he asks, "Where's mummy?" Nicolas replies by asking if he'd like to be a soldier when he grows up, both an allusion to his mother's being upstairs with the soldiers and a test. When Nick answers, "I don't mind," he reveals himself in no way inculcated by his parents' political views. When Nicolas reprimands, "But you spat at my soldiers," (16) Nicky's animated reply, "I didn't like those soldiers," is met with Nicolas's, "They don't like you either, my darling," and we see Nicky for the last time. (17) Nicolas's "darling," a term of endearment, here ominously conveys the child's death sentence.

Despite the obvious dismantling effects of her torture upon her, Gila's subtly spirited responses to Nicolas, like Nick's, contrast with Victor's despair, and her spirit very slightly relieves tension which might otherwise become unbearable. At first evoking the topic of love as romance, Nicolas asks her seemingly innocuous questions about how she met Victor. When she answers at her father's, Nicolas falls viciously upon her with: "Your *father*? How dare you? Fuckpig." (19) Nicolas sings her father's praises as a man who "would die, for his country, for his God," then closes, "How dare you speak of your father to me? I loved him, as if he were my own father." (19) This exchange clarifies the point that her guilt results not by association, that is by the fact that she was born to an educated and privileged class, but rather for values she embraces. When Nicolas asks what's upstairs, Gila replies, "No nuns." (21) Given the physical brutality she obviously has endured, the fact that Gila stands her ground without cowering before his verbal onslaught dramatizes her extreme courage. Nicolas discloses the precise nature of what is upstairs and of her torture when he asks, "How many times have you been raped." (21)

His compliment, "You're a lovely woman," he quickly corrects: "Well, you were." (21) His viciousness then lights upon her son: "He's a little prick. You made him so," and though the audience has already seen otherwise, he accuses: "You encouraged him to spit, to strike at soldiers of honour, soldiers of God." (22)

When Victor returns, Nicolas offers a drink to "put lead in your pencil," emphasizing all the more that Victor may be forever beyond the pleasures of this world, so complete is the violation inflicted upon him and his wife. Nicolas explains they have "a first class brothel upstairs. . . . They'll suck you in and blow you out in little bubbles. All volunteers. Their daddies are in our business. Which is, I remind you, *to keep the world clean for God*." (23; ellipses and emphasis mine) His conclusion accentuates the need an abuser of power has to believe that his abuse serves a higher cause and gives transcendent meaning to his life.

In almost any other context what might be a happy ending, Nicolas's announcement that Victor and his wife are free, only intensifies the horror of the broken future awaiting them. Nicolas dismisses Victor: "I trust we will always remain friends, Go out. Enjoy life. Be good. Love your wife," adding "She'll be joining you in about a week, by the way. If she feels up to it." (24) The hidden violations inflicted upon Gila only magnify the horror of their present and future. When Victor asks about his son, Nicolas's closing line unveils the worst: "Your son? Oh, don't worry about him. He was a little prick." (24) The simple past tense makes unnecessary explicit statement of the child's death, which is made all the more horrifying by omission.

Nicolas takes some joy in subverting the powers of an intellectual and in gaining power over Victor when he reports that his soldiers "pissed on" his books. But is it by chance that Victor's name is Victor? Is he in any sense victorious? If any victory remains to him it can only be in winning the audience to some awareness that engenders action. In the end, because these are the first among Pinter's characters who bear no responsibility that we can see for their plight, the responsibility is turned to the audience.

What, if anything, separates Pinter's work from the agitational propaganda drama he earlier deplored? It is not simply the depth of insight into the causes of brute violence at all levels, the artistry and resonance, but more significantly the fact that his work does not merely point the finger of responsibility outward—at the other—but equally at the self. In a deeper sense he does not, as in agitprop drama, point fingers at all. Instead his work eloquently allows, rather than forces, us to see how the images we construct to form identity can destroy.

Toni Packer in her 1991 book Th*e Work of this Moment* elucidates the point. A trained psychologist, a survivor of Nazi Germany, and the first American woman Zen Master, Toni Packer left Buddhism to found the Springwater Center for Peace in New York, and in her writing she confronts the dangers of equating self with image. In the chapter "Freedom from Images,"[1] she asks, Who is the self, the source of both peace and destructive conflict? Her process of questioning arrives at an answer which begins by acknowledging:

> It is a fact that one is a woman or a man. Also that one has an image of oneself as a "woman" or a "man." Not just one image, but a whole host of images. . . . [T]o think of oneself as an American, a Buddhist, and a woman is to be tied up with images, emotions and feelings of separateness. (47; ellipses mine)

She says:

> The work of questioning deeply into the human mind is . . . not doing what we normally do and have been doing for hundreds of years: rushing to solve problems in a more or less violent way. This work is to *understand* a problem, not just superficially, or even deeply, but totally. It is to understand so completely that the problem may be resolved through this understanding and not through any "solution" at all. (48)

To demonstrate what she means by that understanding, she cites what happens during the Olympic games, for example, when a member of one's country receives a gold medal. She asks, "Does one's patriotic heart feel a boost? A boost to what? A boost to an image!" (48) Her questions that confront what one feels when one's religion or organization it attacked speak directly to Nicolas's identification with his country and his god, where he and his cause are one: "Does one feel defensive . . . , personally attacked and hurt?" Does praise of one's group flatter one's vanity, "one's identity—'this is me'." (49)

Finally positioning the question within the context of the feminist debate, Packer raises the central question:

> Many people say to me that women have such a negative image of themselves, that one has to work on this bad image, improve it, empower it, which means substituting a good image for a bad image. But why does one need *any* image? (49)

She acknowledges the desire to hold on to good feelings that an image can provide. But noting the inseparability of mind and body: "Anything that goes on in this mind, a single thought, is totally connected with the whole organism—electrically, neurochemically" she concludes: "The self image is easy to confuse with the self." (49)

From there it is easy, she says, to see how in the Middle East it is "possible in the place where three of the greatest religions were born, all of them preaching peace, that people kill each other." (51)

When she asks, "What are you going to do about it?" she answers, "It is a simple fact that this work can only start with oneself. When images dominate the mind, motivating our actions and creating goals of what we want to be or become, confusion reigns. How can we resolve confusion in the world if we are confused ourselves?" (51)

Acknowledging that peace requires questioning of the self, Packer appreciates both the "fundamental anxiety of being nobody" and the "danger of being somebody" as problems in this process of self-deception. (51) When she asks, "Is it possible to see and be free of images from moment to moment, really being no one and therefore completely open and related to everyone and everything, with a lovingness?" no doubt many will suggest that to be free of images and open to everyone simply goes against "human nature." (51) But Packer goes further. On the assumption that change is possible, she rephrased the question to ask instead: "How do we wake people up?"[2]

The process of change has already begun in the work of all those who address the issue. Pinter's work has done so from the start. It is unlikely Nicolas will awaken to his blindness. But by evoking audience sympathy for all the characters, and like all who engage in the process of awakening the self and others in their work and lives, Pinter communicates an optimism in the fundamental necessary paradigm shift requiring a new worldview.

But Pinter's anger and impatience also come through in a recent poem "American Football," which dramatizes Packer's point. Here he couples image-identification in sports with religion to link that identification to violence. In his poem the desire for transcendence is supplied and met by identifying the self with the winning team. The brutally crude language of the poem, "We blew the fucking shit out of them," combines sexual and excremental epithets, crosscut with a religious "Hallelullah," and "Praise the Lord for all good things," only to end in a demand—a shocking slant-reference for love: "Now I want you to come over here and kiss me on the mouth." (41)

His plays raise questions rather than provide answers (commonly associated with agitprop and any lesser work), and also waken an audience to greater awareness of both self and other, and, in a larger sense, call for and celebrate action.

Notes

1. See also Tich Nhat Hanh, the Vietnamese Buddhist monk at the Paris Peace Talks, instrumental in shaping Martin Luther King's philosophy. In his 1991 book *Peace Is Every Step: The Path of Mindfulness in Everyday Life*, he says peace in the world begins with peace in the self and, "the absence of clear understanding is the basis for every knot," every obstacle. (64–65)
2. In conversation during a private meeting November 1991.

Mountain Language: Torture Revisited

After *One for the Road* there might seem little more to say about the brutalities of torture. But *Mountain Language*, which continues to explore the conflict between Eros and Thanatos, offers further insights into the causes for such brutality and strengthens insights into further links between love and violence. Love or its opposite, fractally referenced and infused in each moment, drives the play's conflict. Love, devalued and deployed in brutal language and acts of the torturers as one weapon in the arsenal to destroy, is also a bond which can sustain the tortured and their families. Inspired by the plight of the Kurds who were forbidden to speak their language, *Mountain Language* is the bleakest, most pitiless, and remorseless of Pinter's plays.

The action in the play alternates between women in line waiting outside to see their men being held prisoner inside and the brief visits they are permitted: between a mother and son, a husband and wife, a woman and her lover.

The initial focus on the waiting women throws a spotlight upon their men being held prisoner and tortured. The play levels distinctions between age, education, and class: the young intellectual wife who has come to see her husband and the old peasant mother, to see her son. Both are equally humiliated, both, equally courageous. The near hopelessness of the women's plight, their stoical defiance of authority to support their men dramatizes a courage informed by love.

That love, which sustains the men and women through some of the worst outrages remains, however, impotent to save the men. Love without power is not enough.

As the play opens the Young Woman at the head of the line exhibits defiance as soon the Sergeant demands "Name?" She repeats her reply, "We've given our names," each time he asks. (11) Her refusal to comply with his senseless demands prompts the Officer who enters to engage in the familiar "good cop/bad cop" ploy by turning upon the Sergeant with, "Stop this shit." He then asks the Young Woman, "Any complaints?" Momentarily releasing tension and raising hope, he notices the Elderly Woman's wounded hand and asks, "Has someone bitten your hand?" The term "someone," one of the few grimly humorous turns in the play, both relieves and heightens tension. When the old peasant woman fails to answer his repeated question, the Young Woman finally says, "A Doberman pinscher." (15)

Full dread begins to dawn when the Officer observes, "I think the thumb is going to come off," as he again asks the Elderly Woman (whom we will only later learn does not understand his language), "Who did this?" (16) Her failure to answer his question again prompts the Young Woman to reply, "A big dog." (17) He instantly demands, "What was his name?" and with another desolate trace of humor lights into the Young Woman with a lengthy diatribe:

> Every dog has a *name!* They answer to their name. They are given a name by their parents and that is their name, that is their *name!* Before they bite, they *state* their name. It's a formal procedure. They state their name and then they bite. (17)

In contrast to the dogs who have names, the men being tortured and women waiting in line to see them remain nameless. The point of the Sergeant's repeatedly requesting the women's names serves only to remind them that they have none.

The Sergeant, with permission to speak, pronounces the men they have been waiting to see "shithouses" and "enemies of the State." (21) The Officer reminds the line of waiting women that by "military decree" and by "law" they are forbidden to speak their language: "Your language is dead." (21)

The Young Woman tries to identify herself as apart from the others: "I do not speak the mountain language." (23) The Officer levels any distancing she attempts even in his "good cop" role; when he reminds his subordinate, "These women, Sergeant, have as yet committed no crime," he allows himself to be corrected by his Sergeant who says, "Sir! But you're not saying they're without sin?" (23)

Their denying the equation of "crime" and "sin" only melds the values of church and state for the persecutors. The Officer agrees and the Sergeant further concurs, "This one's full of it. She bounces with it." (23) When the Young Woman declares, "My name is Sara Johnson. I have come to see my husband. It is my right," the word "right" is stripped of all meaning as she is asked for her papers, then informed, "He's in the wrong batch." The Sergeant remarks, "So is she. She looks like a fucking intellectual to me," adding, "Intellectual arses wobble the best." (25) His remark, which cuts at her softer life, also reduces her to a slab of meat, reminding her that she is without distinction from the other women in line and that neither her mind, education, nor knowledge of the law can privilege her above the other women. This enforced leveling of hierarchy by those in command does not destroy hierarchy but distills it to the simple dichotomy of an us vs them duality.

The introduction of her Anglo name, which must garner greater sympathy from an Anglo- or Eurocentric audience, also functions to ambush the audience, reroute and subvert any distancing belief, "This could never happen to me." Her name all by itself also gives weight to her individuality to enhance audience sympathy. (But would a name such as Gingra Razzu serve the same function as Sara Johnson?) This second central Sara in Pinter's plays (though a variant spelling on Sarah of *The Lover*) serves to emphasize the biblical connotations not only of Sarah's lost children, but here, Sara's lost husband, and through his death, of their lost children.

The Elderly Woman with the wounded hand, now in the visitor's room with her son, is twice jabbed by a guard and forbidden to speak her language when once she says, "I have bread—" (27) and another time, "I have apples—" (29) Only then does the Guard realize she does not understand him. Nevertheless his message has been effectively conveyed—she does not speak again.

Pinter departs from his customary realism, transmitting to the audience the thoughts of the prisoners and visitors which they have been forbidden to speak. We hear in the Elderly Woman's thought/voice attempts to encourage her son as she sits mutely across from him to "tell" him in her mind that the baby is waiting, that everyone looks forward to his homecoming. The Prisoner's thought/voice also conveys love and concern as he notices that his mother's hand has been bitten. This invention conveys the depth of feeling the characters bear one another and the significance of their meeting—of her having made the visit and his having survived despite all odds. Their acts of love that sustain them endure to stand in stark contrast to the lack of any human kindness from those in authority.

But beneath their different exteriors and opposing circumstances, Pinter links the prisoners and the guards by a common thread of humanity: family. When the Guard remarks, "I've got a wife and three kids," the Prisoner volunteers the information that he does, too. (32) Even though the prisoner's attempt to form a human connection only prompts the Guard to telephone in the complaint, "I think I've got a joker in here," and though The Guard refuses to recognize any commonality between himself and the man he holds prisoner (as, to continue his work, he must), the link has been forged for the audience. (33)

In the penultimate scene, "Voice in the Darkness," when a Young Woman enters, the Sergeant barks "Who's that fucking woman?" conveying anti-erotic sexual overtones which nevertheless parallel the thought/voice erotic communion between the Young Woman and her lover, who stands before her supported by two guards and with a bag over his head. The Young Man's and Young Woman's intertwining "voices" recall making love. Even here at the edge of the abyss their love sustains them as his thoughts import their past lovemaking into the present, sustaining him to withstand this intolerable situation and transforming it: "I watch you sleep. And then your eyes open. You look up at me about you and smile." The Young Woman's voice in perfect consort responds: "You smile. When my eyes open I see you above me and smile." (39) Even though the hooded Young Man collapses without seeing his young lover, this scene of awakening to love transmits the larger point of the play.

The Sergeant terminates her visit: "Yes, you've come in the wrong door. It must be the computer. The computer's got a double hernia." (41) The horror of that mistake, the irreversible human damage perpetuated upon a man wrongly imprisoned, resonates on the larger scale with the horror of the irrevocable human error in the whole situation: the imprisonment and torture of people who have committed no crime.

The Sergeant tells the Young Woman to come back in a week to see a man who comes in to answer questions. "His name is Dokes. Joseph Dokes." (41) The authority, masked by a protected John Doe identity, reminds us that the only names the guards and officers bear in this play are their anonymous titles: Guard, Officer. Torturers and tortured alike are equally stripped of identity.

The brief moment of love between the young woman and man is quickly supplanted by the Sergeant's returning to his opening level of discourse: addressing love only as fucking. Sex further reduces merely to an animal act to be bartered. When the Young Woman asks of Dokes, "Can I fuck him? If I fuck him, will everything be all right?" Though the Sergeant replies, "Sure," the audience knows that no human currency these women tender can release their men from their suffering. (41)

The final scene, image, action, and language all conspire to reinforce the split between the destructive animality of the term "fuck" as the authorities deploy it and the love between those linked by mutual affection, family bonds, and marriage. The mother and son are brought back together and this time told that the law has been changed, that they are now free to speak their language: "New Rules. Until further notice." (47)

But when the son, now with blood on his face, tries to translate this news to his elderly, wounded, silent mother, she no longer speaks. The earlier action of the guard to prohibit speech speaks more forcefully than any words.

The son finally collapses to the floor in his effort to make his mother understand as the play closes with the Sergeant's, "Look at this. You go out of your way to give them a helping hand and they fuck it up." (47) The double cliché "helping hand" and "fuck it up" seal into a single image the love/violence connection—referring focus both to the mother's wounded hand and to all the violence perpetuated in the name of love for a cause. The word "fuck" here, stripped of all sexual and erotic connotation, any connection to love, reduces it to its function as an intensifying epithet in the weaponry of language and finally means almost nothing at all.

The violence in Pinter's plays, as entertainment, raises ethical questions. Pinter's admission that he opens himself to that charge and that at some level the audience takes some pleasure in the absolute power of the authorities does not divert the charge. Drama as a voyeuristic medium even encourages that, and some argue it provides an escape valve for real aggression. But Pinter's aim is obviously other. The responsibility, since it cannot be claimed or borne by the innocent victims, again transfers to the audience. But how? By raising consciousness.

At the very least these plays serve to raise conscious awareness of the plight of a great many innocent people worldwide. But the insight they offer into the impulse to violence and torture raises even larger questions about human nature which is portrayed as so easily brutalized to become brute. Pinter does that here by fairly conventional means. Nowhere else in Pinter's work are dominant characters drawn with so few or without any redeeming qualities, nor are the characters forced into submission, so wholly pure.

The question of responsibility thrown at the audience requires examination. It is not enough merely to *know* that such things happen. Pinter's recent plays are a call to action. But what action? What direction do I offer students when I teach, audiences, when I direct Pinter's plays? What ought I call upon myself to do in my writing and life? No doubt some classicists will ask of his work, but is this art? Is any call to action art? I would have to wait until *Moonlight* to fully answer these questions. *One for the Road* and *Mountain Language* cannot be lumped with and dismissed as mere diatribe.

In the subtext and the thematic connections between love and justice, the issues Pinter is raising are much larger: his plays provoke in audiences not merely specific emotional and intellectual responses to the injustice in the specific acts of torture but an attitude of sympathy, an empathy, a regard for the other as the self—even the torturer in the self. Without that perspective, humans who hold radically different views can be encouraged to continue to regard themselves as superior to all others who hold different religious or political views and can treat those others as vermin, lice to be smudged out and erased. Interestingly, such an attitude must also extend to the torturers. By extension, a happy ending to the torture plays would hardly be to see the torturers merely dead or themselves tortured but to see them awakened; the extermination of a torturer, even all those in such positions of power, resolves little beyond the moment.

Consistently Pinter's work reveals that how one regards the other remains a measure of how one regards the self. But again in this play we see that love is not enough. Love must assert itself in taking power necessary to defend itself or else the death-loving forces "triumph." Because power is not something asked for, given, or granted, it must be seized. But before it can be exercised to promote the life-enhancing forces of growth and development rather than death and destruction, it must develop at that private level where awakening begins in self-knowledge.

What enhances the power of Pinter's work is that he acknowledges the dark, destructive but passionate Dionysian powers and weds them to the Apollonian, coolly rational quest for order and authority. He gives them equal play, blurring the traditional boundaries of each so that in the end, except for the torture plays, the two forces end in a stand-off. But brute physical power will always claim victory over mere love until love can develop its own sources of power and reclaim that power of attraction that death has appropriated as its own.

Pinter's portrayal of his authority figures' claims of doing good raises the ultimate issue, What does it mean to be good? What are the qualities necessary?

Pinter offers no easy answers. The virtues portrayed as admirable, when inner awareness and lesser strengths remain undeveloped and informed only by insecurity and fear, turn, in excess, to destructive forces loosed upon others that also turn inwardly against the self and outwardly on, the society it seeks to preserve and promote.

Death does not promote life, but the destructors in these plays remain blind to that and to what is mutilated, destroyed, and dead in themselves. Yet love remains powerless to contain, restrain or counter the forces of destruction. Like Good Deeds in *Everyman*, love's power seems nearly extinguished. What is necessary to reawaken love as a life-enhancing power which is justice? Perhaps the simple awareness that Pinter's work evokes and with that awareness action may follow.

Turtle Diary, Victory, The Handmaid's Tale, Reunion, The Heat of the Day, The Comfort of Strangers, Remains of the Day and *The Trial:* The Screenplays of the 1980s and Early 1990s

Following *One for the Road* and *Mountain Language*, Harold Pinter turned more and more to adapting novels for the screen in his most prolific cinematic output in any half decade, with six screenplays in five years. Pinter's screenplays, rather than providing an aside from writing for stage, supplement and often heighten a current concern, pushing it in a provocative and innovative direction. In his first screenplay, *The Servant*, for example, he was able to push the dominant/subservient conflict to some melodramatic extremes but with a fresh insight and twist on class relationships extending beyond what he had confronted in his plays. *The French Lieutenant's Woman* embraces and heightens a variety of themes: from madness to recovery, from individual memory to memory as collective history, from the erotic components of private relationships to ethical considerations of community. While his screenplays suspend the strict fractal geometry of his plays, they continue to delve into public consequences of private acts where love, friendship, and freedom remain the highest goods.

His screenplay for *Turtle Diary*, the most playful of his recent writing for cinema, heightens two issues from his plays in fresh ways: freedom and, for the first time, a close, non-erotic friendship between a man and woman. Adapted from the novel by Russell Hoban, directed by John Irvin, the film depicts Neaera, a children's books writer, and William, a bookstore clerk, independently attracted to the sea turtles in the London Zoo. They meet by chance. Then with full cooperation of the keeper, conspire to set them free, and in doing so themselves re-awaken to life and the possibility of a loving friendship between two very independent and solitary people. The comedy throughout vies with the constant threat the eerie tension produces. The film centers on freedom not merely in the obvious quest to free the turtles to return them to their natural mating grounds in the sea but also on freedoms between classes dramatized in William's physical clash with a foreign tenant over the cleanliness of the common bathroom and the larger freedom of any of the characters do to what they desire. Failure to exercise freedom, to gain what one wants, can result in death—Miss Neap, a tenant in William's building, unable to overcome her lonely isolation and depression, suicides in the end. Here freedom is counterpoised against death, dramatizing that those not choosing to live are somehow dying. The freeing of the turtles becomes for William and Neaera a life-affirming act, a form of saving their own lives.

The unproduced *Victory*, adapted in 1984 from the Joseph Conrad novel, pits death against the erotic when Heyst rescues Lena and becomes the object of pursuit by thug killers unable to inspire or participate in love aside from the thrill of destruction. Pinter's screenplay recasts the Lena-Heyst erotic bond with heightened ambiguity till Lena declares a love that transcends what the intruder killers, "gentleman" Jones and Ricardo, destroy—she proves her love to Heyst in the end by saving his life with her own in a triumph of love over death.

The Handmaid's Tale, adapted from the Margaret Atwood novel, directed by Volker Schlöndorff, portrays the abuse of authority at its extreme delineating one woman's quiet, possibly triumphant, escape to freedom and love from a reactionary, fundamentalist government. Here Pinter allows a more optimistic, less ambiguous ending than the novel or than he might have in any play dramatizing such a repressive regime.

Reunion, directed by Jerry Schatzberg, was adapted from the Fred Uhlman novel which Pinter's mother recommended to him when she was eighty-five. By chance, three years later French producer Ann François asked Pinter's agent if he would like to adapt it. *Reunion* is Pinter's first direct lengthy confrontation with the Holocaust and healing in his writing, and he says, "I did more research on this script than I have ever done in my life." (Ciment, 21) Two childhood, pre-war friends, Hans and Konradin, straddle opposite sides. Hans, a Jew, discovers that the friendship, destroyed by external events, was not betrayed by his friend, who gave his life for what Hans believed. Here friendship becomes the love which attempts to address destruction. Hans learns that Konradin was executed following an attempt to assassinate Hitler. At another level the returning Hans also discovers, in reliving his past, the collective insecurity which produced and promoted anti-Semitism. Scenes portraying the swaggering Hitler youth contrast markedly with the easy friendship between Hans and Konradin. Although Konradin's love for his friend, exhibited in embracing his values and in acting to seek justice, failed to destroy the opposition or save his own life, Konradin's commitment becomes the landmark in Pinter's work of such sacrifice to a cause.

But love, as the heart's intuition, cannot always be trusted to read another accurately. *The Heat of the Day*, adapted from the World War II novel by Elizabeth Bowen and directed by Christopher Morahan, depicts the terrible ambiguity and its results when Stella is informed by an unappealing but lovelorn government agent, Harrison, that her war-time lover Robert is a spy whose fascist values ultimately appall her. When she is finally convinced of the truth about her lover, she allows the forces which conspire to converge upon him. Both the novel and the film explore links between love and justice, but in the film that link is interestingly strengthened in Pinter's surprising addition to the novel: Harrison's attraction to Stella, a point nicely detailed by Ronald Knowles, who concludes that "in the midst of bomb sites, love's embers smoulder. . . ." ("Harold Pinter 1990," 83)

Like *Reunion*, *The Heat of the Day* challenges conventional notions of retributive justice as does *The Comfort of Strangers*. In *Reunion*, Konradin's attempt to stop Hitler becomes one of the greatest attempts to seek justice in Pinter's work, though it results in his execution, which however affirms the bond of friendship and shared values. Robert's death at the end of *The Heat of the Day*, while it puts an end to his activities, is not there to satisfy the audience balance sheet, for we have gained some insight into the economic constraints and forces which led Robert to his fascist position. In *The Comfort Of Strangers* Pinter takes real liberties with the novel by bringing the murderers to justice, but in doing so only raises further questions about the nature of retributive justice which can neither stop these people from continuing to kill others if they are released nor redress the death of a human life by serving time with their lives or even through their own deaths. *The Comfort of Strangers*, discussed at greater length in the next chapter, is adapted from the novel by Ian McEwan, directed by Paul Schrader. The film portrays Mary and Colin, an unmarried English couple on a holiday in Venice, capturing the novel's hermetically sealed claustrophobia of being a tourist trapped within a hotel room isolated in a relationship with only one other person. The two drift into a relationship with Robert, an Italian, and his Canadian wife Caroline one night when they are lost looking for an open restaurant. Their desire to see the "real Venice" and lack of any other positive desire drives them into a relationship which prudence would dictate they extricate themselves from, till in the end they are led seemingly unwittingly into a liaison with Caroline and Robert which ends with Colin's brutal death. Unexamined friendship and love makes mistakes, and what justice is attained only raises further questions about the nature of retributive justice.

The Trial, adapted from Kafka's novel and directed by David Jones, drew Pinter's attention because of K's valiant struggle to retain his freedom against his interrogators. In all its ambiguities the screenplay again raises further questions about justice. In *The Remains of the Day*, adapted from Kazuo Ishiguro's novel, the English butler, the victim of class difference, heartbreakingly imagines himself victorious because he so unswervingly keeps to his servant's place and the rigid rules of decorum imposed by British nineteenth-century manners. But in a larger sense, through an English butler's restricted vision, we are able to see the limitations for the ordinary, responsible citizen to be informed let alone to transcend national values when the justice between nations is at stake.

The Comfort of Strangers: Love and Justice

Detailed analysis of any of Pinter's screenplays yields an illustration of how his screenplays heighten focus of his recent plays, his re-examination of love and destruction expressed through received values, but none does so perhaps so simply or subtly as his dramatization of the erotic as an ethical concern in *The Comfort of Strangers.* The film, which may seem a slight work, dramatizing the kinky cruelty of aberrant beings who little illuminate ordinary human life, in fact opens toward a better appreciation of links between love and justice. Love and death converge here where, again, the seemingly innocent, the couple Colin and Mary who are destroyed, are subtly portrayed as partially responsible for that destruction: Colin's death at the hands of his murderers Robert and Caroline.

The Comfort of Strangers explores the boundary between erotic pleasure and pain, a sado-masochism that in the end unleashes Robert's horrifying lust murder of Colin whom both Robert and Caroline find very beautiful and a stimulant to their sexual pleasures and intimacy. The film opens as Mary and Colin wake at night in Venice and, driven into the night streets by hunger, look for an open restaurant. As Mary chances upon wall posters calling for the castration of rapists, Robert, in white, appears out of the shadows and damns the feminist expression, misogynistly asserting, with all the authority of a tour guide, "All these—are women who cannot find a man. They want to destroy everything that is good between men and women," then he offers to show Colin and Mary some "beautiful Venetian food." (13) Although Mary admires the Italian feminists, when Robert denigrates their political activity, she remains silent, and instead of exercising her freedom to redress his remark is delighted that they have found "the real Venice" (a phrase in the film, not in screenplay's text). But Colin and Mary soon discover there is no food in the restaurant, only wine and breadsticks, and eerily, they also learn that Robert seems to possess intimate knowledge of their lives: that they are not married and that she has children. Rather than *act*—to extricate themselves from Robert to find food—Mary asks Robert how he met his wife Caroline. Robert recounts a childhood incident, which stands beside Sarah's confession in *The French Lieutenant's Woman* as one of the longest narratives in Pinter's filmscripts. Robert reports how he once informed on his sisters after they secretly applied their mother's cosmetics, then how they revenged themselves on him. They fed Robert forbidden sweets and an emetic, let Robert gorge himself, then tied him up in his father's study to vomit and excrete over their father's carpets and walls. Robert incurred his father's wrath, which he recasts by naming himself the favorite of his "fearful" and "revered" father who "nearly killed" him. Robert concludes his narrative:

> I have never forgiven my sisters. (18)

Robert's rage at his father, displaced to his sisters, is later routed through his mother and wife. The mother's role in the father's brutal rage, a conspicuous omission, speaks to her complicity and participation through her perceived powerlessness and addresses her responsibility (any woman's) beyond offering her child comfort after the fact. After his father's violence Robert slept in his mother's bed, and later when his sisters taunt him about doing so in front of Caroline, Caroline replies, "I think that's really awfully sweet." (18) They are eleven years old. The childhood sweethearts marry and, we learn much later, go on to a career of private sexual pleasures that culminate in Robert's breaking Caroline's back while they are making love. Rather than ending their intimacy, it only drives them to seek other sources of stimulation.

Mary and Colin end the first evening after wine and breadsticks asleep in an alley, drunk and possibly drugged. When they go to breakfast in St. Mark's Square the next morning they "chance" upon Robert who, "horrified" that they slept outside, invites them to his house where they finish their sleep and again wake to dinner. While Mary and Caroline are out of the room, Robert displays his father's personal possessions to Colin explaining that his father and grandfather "understood themselves, clearly," adding, "They were men and they were proud of their sex. Women understood them too. Now women treat men like children, because they can't take them seriously." (29) But when Colin quips, "So this is a museum dedicated to the good old days," Robert gratuitously punches Colin hard in the stomach. Again, rather than leaving the premises or addressing Robert's violence, Colin ignores it.

At dinner when Robert exclaims that the society must be "protected from perverts," to "purify society," he explains his "simple" solution: "Put them all up against a wall and shoot them." (30) Mary and Colin again ignore rather than address his verbal assaults. As they leave Mary discovers among Robert's collection a photograph of Colin whose significance registers in her consciousness only in nightmare the next day. At some level, though she never articulates it, Mary may realize Robert has deliberately singled them out and has been following them. But again, both Mary and Colin choose to ignore any clues that signal impending disaster.

Instead, during their own innocently inane love banter, Mary proposes to have Colin's arms and legs cut off and keep him "just for sex," (35) while Colin imagines a machine that "will fuck you—not just for hours and weeks, but for years and years and years. For ever." (36) In fact Robert will cut Colin's throat to heighten his sexual excitation with his wife.

While the contrast between the two couples seems obvious, Pinter again challenges traditional dichotomies between seeming good and evil, innocence and perversion. Robert and Caroline seem to align with the demonic forces of destruction, but Colin and Mary are not wholly blameless victims in Colin's death. The love the two couples express bears strangely similar limitations.

Pinter dramatizes in both couples a love that does not extend beyond the immediate relationship. Colin, at first, cannot even extend his love to Mary's children, although he later buys them both souvenirs. And though Mary in a moment of irritation and boredom says she should have brought the children on the trip, "It would have made all the difference. To me anyway," children would have only ironically made a great difference to their honeymoon holiday schedule of sleeping, drinking and love-making. (21) But where Robert and Caroline know what they want, Mary and Colin do not or do not acknowledge it or act on it. Nor do they know precisely why they selected Venice till it is too late.

After the initial encounter with Robert, Mary wants to go home because she finds Venice "a prison." (21) While it is in part a prison of circumstance—of being a tourist couple in a foreign country—it is also a prison of their own making.

Pinter three times repeats as an echoing device Robert's perverse story of gorging himself on forbidden sweets and his father's brutal vengeance. His narrative resonates with Mary's confession of the worst thing that ever happened to her in childhood—she was ostracized from a gang because, without bothering to discover that she was the subject of the gang's vote, she unwittingly endorsed her own expulsion by voting herself out. Her brief story fractally reflects the choices she and Colin make in Venice, illuminating not only how these characters carry their long-past childhood states and choices with them into the present but the ways in which they detoxify old wounds by glorifying victimization. That kind of self-absorption becomes a drug almost as powerful as the actual drugs Caroline gives Mary which prevent her from aiding Colin when Robert and Caroline set upon him. The real drugs in turn emphasize Colin and Mary's encapsulated, soporific state. Mary and Colin fail to follow their own best intuitions on the best available evidence to promote their own survival. Their vague desire for some excitement outside themselves overpowers their desire for self-preservation.

But the screenplay holds out some hope for an awakening consciousness and change that the novel does not. In the three generations of women Pinter depicts in the screenplay, that change is already occurring, marked in different choices Caroline, Mary, and Mary's off-screen daughter make. Caroline, a generation older than Mary and least likely to awaken to change, cannot comprehend the idea of doing anything in life without men. Mary's mention of her participation in an all-female production of *Hamlet* seems incomprehensible to Caroline (nor is she familiar with the play, a further comment on her education and insular life). Caroline cannot imagine anything can happen until a man enters and, as such, contrasts with Mary who, in a liminal state between Caroline and her own young daughter, is only vaguely clear about what she wants. Mary may admire Italian feminists but neither acts nor even speaks to endorse her own views on the issue. Mary thus contrasts with her own daughter, who, she tells Colin, has just made the school football team, entering a formerly all-male domain. (29–30)

But ultimately real change can occur only through development of consciousness, effecting a paradigm shift where desire can translate into action. Caroline acts on her desires, however perverse; Mary does not fully know or acknowledge hers, however well intended; but her daughter acts, although we have no access to her level of consciousness. But we watch Mary and Colin's lack of conscious knowledge of their own desires precipitate their destruction.

The final horror in the film and the novel turns on a coincidence otherwise rare or nonexistent in Pinter's work. The last morning on return from the Lido, the beach, Colin and Mary decide to disembark on the opposite side of Venice to walk straight across to their hotel to avoid the long boat ride around the island but immediately chance to see Caroline waving from her second-story window. Where past experience, prudence, and actively acknowledged purpose might lead them past this point of no return with polite apologies, Mary says, "We can't be rude," and they are thus taken in by Caroline and Robert for the last time.

Robert parades Colin through the streets near his restaurant while Caroline drugs Mary at home, but not before showing Mary their bedroom where Robert's photographs of Colin line one wall. It is suddenly, but too late, apparent to Mary that Robert had followed and photographed Colin, deliberately bringing him home. "It was as if God was in our dream," Caroline says. (24) Any suggestion of Colin as god is pure projection compared with the rather ordinary Colin we see but serves as a comment on the imaginary fuel that sustains Robert's and Caroline's lust.

In the end when Colin asks what they want, Robert says "I'll show you what we want," then he slits Colin's throat, steps over the twitching legs after Colin has sunk to the floor, and walks off to the bedroom with his wife as the stupefied Mary sits across the room looking on at her dying lover seated on the floor. (48) Their final sitting positions facing each other—Mary's drug-induced catatonia in a chair, Colin's dying on the floor—may not be without significance. In a later interview Pinter will suggest that most of us, including himself, often sleep through life.

This time the police interrogation, in contrast to that in *The Birthday Party* and the torture interrogations, has a valid point. The officer begins by asking Mary, "What did you want from these people?" In the end Mary is not lying when she answers his questions, "Why did you come to Venice," and "What were you looking for," with: "We were going to get married." (49–50) Too late does she voice her intention.

Drama is driven by desire, but these two people do not even know that they want—or let themselves articulate it. While Mary is initially eager to establish a closer tie with Colin, when he finally proposes that they live together, she retreats—she has just had a nice swim she says, adding, "We'll see." While her retreat may reflect genuine indecision, it may equally be a ploy, resulting from her disappointment that he does not propose a more permanent relationship, a commitment she herself seems momentarily unwilling to make.

The obvious bond of attraction that holds Colin and Mary together is that of two people who continue to find one another irresistibly beautiful, which may seem more forgivable in two who are young and on holiday when compared with Robert and Caroline, who are older but no further developed in their love except in perversion. If love is, as Aristotle defines it, a relationship between equals in beauty, strength, and wisdom, none of the people here has a love that progresses beyond physical attraction. That point will be voiced more obviously in *Party Time*.

Although Caroline recounts how Robert broke her back while making love, all in the end are broken by love or lust that does not even coalesce into a clearly articulated desire except in those who desire destruction. Yet Pinter evokes some sympathy for all of them.

The film, which dramatizes the failure of desire to develop or to translate into positive action, concludes as a commentary on retributive justice. Unlike the novel which ends with Caroline and Robert's escape, Pinter allows the murderers to be caught, interrogated, and probably sentenced. While the happier ending may have increased the film's commercial value, it also makes a larger point—nothing justice can mete out can compensate for Colin's lost life. The traditional happy ending of seeming evil people getting a just reward is challenged as resolving nothing at all. By contrast, the Italian feminists' call for the castration of rapists could at least prevent further crime. But no justice can prevent such a murder happening again if Robert and Caroline are ever released. The crime here is not entirely of two perverted, evil people plotting against two innocents, nor is the point to promote distrust of strangers (the film's title, an ironic echo of Blanche's *Streetcar Named Desire* assertion that she has always relied on the kindness of strangers). But rather, the screenplay dramatizes survival predicated on a need to trust one's own best insights coupled with some knowledge of what one wants and what one ought to want. Here only the destructors express clear desires. As often in Pinter's work, only the destructors act to gain what they want, but in neither relationship does love productively extend beyond the two people involved.

The final scene belongs to Robert who sees himself as innocent and not responsible for his own actions. As in *The French Lieutenant's Woman*, Pinter again challenges the cherished Western masternarrative that confession provides both catharsis and change or that it can supply an explanation for current action. Where Sarah confronts herself more honestly and deeply than through a talking cure—by drawing brutally honest portraits of herself revealing her internal weakness and understandable despair given the constraints of her circumstances—Robert's "confession" effects no change but is used only to provide an excuse. When the police ask why Robert has murdered Colin, Robert answers by telling for the third and last time the same story of his father's brutal retribution which by now has become an artifact that no longer needs to be believed. Robert's final words, a commentary on the limits of language and psychoanalysis to provide a past cause for a present effect, again dramatize Pinter's assertion that an explanation is "necessarily false." Here the story becomes meaningless, except as an construct of Robert's mind.

None of Pinter's recent screenplays wholly departs from his concerns that turn toward confrontations with the worst that human beings can do to one another in their relationships, almost always in the name of doing good, but here in the name of love that is lust, that focus on love transforms into that larger question of love which is justice.

Party Time and *The New World Order:* Love and Justice Revisited

In *Party Time* and *The New World Order,* two plays written in 1991, Pinter moves out into the global arena, pursuing the twin subjects of love and justice as he relentlessly continues to explore the abuses of power. Both plays, which protest the underlying values behind the Persian Gulf War, present an ethical reaction to what Pinter views as the false morality reflected in current political power struggles. But the erotic also surfaces to call for a redefinition of love and to reunite love and justice.

The ethic at the center of these plays calls for a redefinition of love that can include Eros, the passionate and the romantic, yet it points toward a more enduring, comprehensive, and mature love that encompasses friendship extended to include justice in action.

The larger implication is that whether human beings treat one another as equals on the private level may be equally important for survival on all levels. To attempt to dominate another person is not perhaps, finally, so different from trying to dominate another nation, and the results, are not surprisingly, similarly destructive. *Party Time* explicitly draws attention to such destruction from the private to the public and global levels and, for the first time, simultaneously offers focus and insight on all three levels—into the blindness, the lack of consciousness, which abets injustice and advances destruction.

In all of Pinter's most recent plays, the torturers, bureaucrats, and powerbrokers remain as innocent and blind as Ben and Goldberg in *The Birthday Party,* both to their injustice and to the injury it does by reducing their own lives. Even if in *One for the Road,* the torturer Nicolas and the innocent murdered child Nick share the same name, implying that, in other circumstances, they might find themselves in reversed positions, Nicolas never realizes that.

While many of Pinter's recent plays concern themselves with the worst injustice, torture, his work continues to awaken audiences to the importance of understanding the source of the desire for dominance in the self if it is to be confronted anywhere else and on any other level.

Once conflict is ignited, all Pinter's characters fight blindly to assert dominance to preserve identity, yet at heart, even the coldest seem driven by some desire for love and respect. From Lenny in *The Homecoming* asking his brother's wife Ruth, "Do you mind if I hold your hand?" (both a desire and a threat), to the torturer in *One for the Road* asserting, "I think your wife is. Beginning. She is beginning to fall in love with me," characters convey a desire for love that impels action but expressed through a desire to dominate the other. That action carried to an extreme, destroys the very thing desired.

In *Party Time* and *The New World Order,* whose title is ironically lifted from a line in one of former President Bush's speeches, Pinter places the magnifying glass on those in power to mark responsibility on the global level, dramatizing yet again fear masquerading as force to perpetuate violence against the "other"—those outside the party or the club. Here the magnitude of the force is out of all proportion to the actual threat which is, however, perceived as pervasive, and the cause, therefore, as transcendently noble. The result is a gathering of force greater than any other in Pinter's work—a sledgehammer to swat a gnat—without a radical shift in worldview such a force might seem invincible. Here at the communal and global levels Pinter again dramatizes what he so masterfully executed decades earlier at the private level: dramatizing that the greatest force is exerted not by those trying to *gain* power but, again, by those attempting to *maintain* power.

In *Party Time* eight people at an exclusive party celebrate their exclusivity, while outside an insurrection is in progress, and the dissidents are being rounded up. Terry issues his host Gavin an invitation to join his club. In the end Gavin accepts. Against the bleak background of violent injustice, Pinter again pushes definitions of love beyond the old romantic bounds of individuals, to encompass something larger which does more than titillate the fancy of the one or two involved, and for the first time he explicitly links love and power, or more correctly here, the abuses of power with the lack of love. Charlotte and Liz, two marginalized women in their thirties at the periphery of the party, define love by showing what it is not.

Charlotte, a widow whose husband died significantly not from an illness but quite likely at the hands of some of those attending the party, and Douglas's wife Liz, discuss a man Liz happens to find "So beautiful. The mouth, really. And of course the eyes," although he was carried off by "that bitch" who "had her legs all over him."[1] (10) But, Liz adds, "He looked back, I swear, at me, like a wounded deer. . . ." (11) Charlotte responds, "How beautiful," concluding, "Think of the wonderful side of it. Because for you it was love, it was falling in love. That's what it was, wasn't it? You fell in love." (12)

Liz agrees, "I did," and offers as evidence of her love, "I haven't slept all night." Here that comically adolescent litmus test of love dramatizes a love that does not extend beyond the self and private level to action or even to any engagement with the other. Liz never connects with the nameless man she "loves," nor does connection seem her primary end; rather, she seems narcissistically content to wallow in her own imagined erotic passion, to think and to talk about it without necessarily acting.

The play opens with two men who may have power over local, and possibly state, affairs. Terry, a man of forty, extends to Gavin, a man of fifty, the party's lavish host, an invitation to join his exclusive club. The only dissonant note at the party comes from Terry's own wife, Dusty, a woman in her thirties, who, each time she asks her husband where her brother Jimmy is, is dismissed with what becomes a series of increasingly brutal rebuffs which culminate in her wondering if her husband Terry will kill her. At the end of the play we find out where Jimmy is; alone and isolated, he delivers an internal monologue which reveals that he is in a quiet place, that he once had a name, sometimes hears things, his own heart, except when the terrible noises come, and that he sits "sucking the dark." (44) We know, without being told, that he is one of the people who has been rounded up outside, imprisoned, and that he is being tortured possibly for crimes he did not commit in seeking justice against those at the party.

Despite the fulsome disquisitions delivered by various members of the party on the worthy purpose of the club (and by association its members), the comfortably pointless private lives of the party seekers are heightened by their stark contrast with Jimmy's horrifying plight. The rare hint of love as concern for another comes only from Jimmy's sister Dusty in her occasional inquiries about him.

For the first time Pinter uses two words he does not couple elsewhere in his plays— "love" and "morality" —and he does so here only to call them into question. If didacticism ranks with self-defense as the most invidious form of discourse, one which almost always turns the audience opposite the intended direction, Pinter here uses didacticism to do precisely that, to turn the audience against the speakers who defend reprehensible positions which they embrace as "moral."

The spokesperson at the party for what Pinter most vehemently opposes, Dame Melissa, a woman of seventy, is the only woman in the play applauded by the male guests for what she says or publicly accorded their respect. In contrast, Dusty's questions about her brother's circumstances bring down not only her husband's wrath but Gavin's cool remark, "So odd, the number of men who can't control their wives." (21) At the end Melissa extols the virtues of Terry's club, making it superior to all the mere tennis and swimming clubs of her past which had "no moral foundation." (40) She champions his club as "activated" and "inspired by a moral sense, a moral awareness, a set of moral values, which is—I have to say—unshakeable, rigorous, fundamental, constant." (40) What morality? the audience might ask. Absolute power. Clearly this is a man's world, and the men at this party mean to maintain and perpetuate their power as Douglas, one of the powerbrokers of war machinery declaims: "We want peace and we're going to get it. But we want that peace to be cast iron. No leaks. No draughts. Cast iron. Tight as a drum. That's the kind of peace we want and that's the kind of peace we're going to get. A cast iron peace." (15)

The party and the club represent yet another aspect of the dichotomous relationships that promote a destructive, dominator society. But we can also see the almost desperate need these people have to infuse meaning into their lives through identification with an abstraction, specifically the noble idea of peace, which they believe gives noble purpose to their lives despite the means they employ.

Dame Melissa capitulates to the demands and values of the dominating men around her rather than confronting, even initiating, conflict that might challenge such dichotomous morality as destructive or that might promote concord and the welfare of others. Dame Melissa subscribes to their values, as she must, to maintain her own position. For the first time in Pinter's plays we see a group dynamic, a herd instinct, a contagion of shared value systems that becomes the prerequisite for belonging to that group or club.

Douglas's and Dame Melissa's speeches acclaiming the club's morality finally succeed in persuading Gavin to join. Subtly, yet powerfully, we as audience who participate in their values are already members of the club.

The conflict fractally evokes a double audience response where love, justice, and power fuse. By placing the opposition to the conflict off stage, the conflict conspires both to engage the audience in sympathy with the off-stage insurrection and to enlist audience identification with the perpetrators of the violence where we as audience must recognize the self as unjust conspirator in the name of self-preservation, love, and morality, promoting the status quo without real understanding, compassion, or love for the other.

Pinter finally links love and power with justice by dramatizing how that love which does not extend beyond the private level and private concerns, that does not act for the justice of others, is not love. Where love is a relationship between equals, as Pete proposes in Pinter's novel *The Dwarfs*, and, as Aristotle states, develops from beauty, strength (physical and moral) to wisdom, here again it does not proceed beyond physical attraction. The wounded deer whom Liz claims to love, while he is not Jimmy, seems linked through animal imagery to Jimmy who is a kind of sacrificial lamb slaughtered to insure the greed necessary to support the comforts and dominant position of the few who have life-and-death power over others.

Until Victor and Gila, tortured in *One for the Road*, the son and husband, tortured in *Mountain Language*, and Jimmy, held captive and tortured in this play, Pinter's work portrayed the seeming victim, from Gus, in *The Dumb Waiter*, Stanley in *The Birthday Party*, to Davies in *The Caretaker*, as at least partially responsible for his own destruction. But where his previous plays focus on those brutalized and destroyed by the real, though sometimes off-stage forces of power, *Party Time* focuses on-stage on the men who are in power and responsible, who denigrate women, who, in turn, like almost all Pinter's other submissive characters in part allow themselves to be diminished. Charlotte's wry irony may communicate her deep rift with the group probably responsible for her husband's demise, but she does not leave the group or subvert from within. She may be able to hold her own in a verbal skirmish with Fred, possibly a former lover, who gave her "a leg up in life," but she is without power or authority that extends beyond such private matters. (23) She does not even possess Dame Melissa's male *manqué* stance which might gain her a male audience nor that power which might transcend Melissa's mere capitulation to the dominator power structure. Charlotte's power is almost solely sexual. But during a fleetingly resuscitated flirtation with Fred, when Charlotte says, "I think there's something going on in the street," Fred terminates the topic, "Leave the street to us." (23) Whatever love these one-time lovers possessed is powerless to sustain a connection between them, let alone extend beyond them in service of others.

Instead, identity cathects to an image: here, of belonging to the club. That image is expressed by Liz: "I think this is such a gorgeous party." (24) While people are being slaughtered in the streets, she rhapsodizes, "I think it's such fun. I love the fact that people are so well-dressed. Casual but good. Do you know what I mean?" (24) Her fulsome praise of that image no doubt mirrors the unexpressed feelings of the others:

> Is it silly to say I feel proud? I mean to be part of the society of beautifully dressed people? Oh, God I don't know, elegance, style, grace, taste, don't these words, these concepts, mean anything anymore? I'm not alone, am I, in thinking them incredibly important? (24)

Pinter never underestimates the extraordinary power of images or of those at the party, the force of their club used to bludgeon others into submission, but he aims to do more than demonstrate the seeming futility of attempting to reclaim power from such a force.

Instead, Pinter dramatizes both how power, which does not encompass that larger love and justice, lacks any ethical basis and, equally, how it is imperative for the just to seize power. Since Jimmy, possibly the only just person in *Party Time*, is imprisoned and powerless, responsibility is again, as in *One for the Road* and

Mountain Language, diverted, to the audience. Pinter raises questions about love, power, and justice that suggest that to live responsibly means to possess and to act upon virtue at all levels.

The New World Order

An even starker portrayal of torture as the ultimate form of dominance and one practiced by the most impotent comes through in the nine-page typescript sketch *The New World Order,* where Lionel and Des threaten, in the third-person invisible, a nameless seated, blindfolded man:

> DES: Do you want to know something about this man?
> LIONEL: What?
> DES: He hasn't got any idea at all of what we're going to do to him. (1)

Since the man can supply no counter threat to their threats, which become blatantly sexual, the verbal violence must sustain the tension. The sexual references strike to the core of survival but, without any erotic charge, exclusively threaten violence and impending destruction:

> DES: Let's put it this way. He has *little* idea of what we might do to him, of what in fact we are about to do to him.
> LIONEL: Or his wife. Don't forget his wife. He has little idea of what we're about to do to his wife.
> DES: Well, he probably has *some* idea, he's probably got *some* idea. After all, he's read the papers.
> LIONEL: What papers?
> *Pause.*
> DES: You're right there.
> LIONEL: Who is this cunt anyway? What is he, some kind of peasant—or a lecturer in theology?
> DES: He's a lecturer in fucking peasant theology.
> LIONEL: Is he? What about his wife?
> DES: Women don't have theological inclinations.
> LIONEL: Oh, I don't know. I used to discuss that question with my mother—quite often.
> DES: What question?

LIONEL: Oh you know, the theological aspirations of the female. (3–4)

As in *Mountain Language*, deploying the term "cunt" does several things at once: it derogates the threatened man, deprecates women, but also subtly denigrates the speaker, revealing the limits of his vocabulary no less than Goldberg's clichés. Within this context the term also links sex, religion, and power. Further along, the torturers' abuse of sexually charged language becomes reminiscently evocative of comedian Lenny Bruce's skit satirizing his trial resulting in his incarceration for saying "blah blah blah." Bruce's comic skit derided the relish his judge and prosecuting attorney enjoyed from the license his case gave them to say "blah blah blah" publicly and in court, and in doing so dramatized as Lionel and Des do, the power of repetition to diminish the power of language. Lionel turns to address the blindfolded, nameless victim for the first time with: "Motherfucker," varied by Des's, "Fuckpig." (5) The terms and contempt escalate, creating a tension released in a comic skirmish over a punctilious semantic point of consistency in usage reminiscent of a similar point argued in *The Dumb Waiter*:

LIONEL: You know what I find really disappointing?
DES: What?
LIONEL: The level of ignorance that surrounds us. I mean, this prick here—
DES: You called him a cunt last time.
LIONEL: What?
DES: You called him a cunt last time. Now you call him a prick. How many times do I have to tell you? You've got to learn to define your terms and stick to them. You can't call him a cunt in one breath and a prick in the next. The terms are mutually contradictory. You'd lose face in any linguistic discussion group, take my tip.
LIONEL: Christ. Would I?
DES: Definitely. And you know what it means to you. You know what language means to you.
LIONEL: Yes, I do know.

In the comically fastidious distinctions these two men make over how much "language means," language is reduced to destructive weaponry which further reduces truth to meaninglessness when it is without any possibility of reciprocal communication. The blindfolded man cannot speak, and Lionel's ecstasy at the end is little different from the "love" Charlotte feels for her "wounded deer"—a solipsistically contained dead end. When Lionel suddenly covers his face and sobs, and Des asks why he is crying, Lionel says:

> I love it. I love it. I love it. (8)

Lionel's tears of ecstasy couple love with death in this first instance in Pinter's work of the repetition of the word "love," though as a subversion of what is meant by that term within the ordinary discourse of love. Yet for Lionel, as for Nicolas who admits in *One for the Road* that he loves death, torturing people is more ecstatically and transcendently charged than love between human beings. He explains:

> I feel so pure.

And Des responds:

> Well, you're right. You're right to feel pure. You know why?

Des answers his own question as the sketch draws to a close:

> Because you're keeping the world clean for democracy. (9)

His closure, a variant of Nicolas's belief that he is keeping the world clean for god, shows that for these two men, identity has become cathected, attached to the point of identification, to something they perceive as larger than themselves. Lionel and Des operate in the belief that they are serving the abstract notion of democracy, which they in turn perceive as enlarging their own beings. While it may be difficult to imagine these men using the term "love" in the ordinary sense of erotic or family romance, no doubt they do. Pinter addressed the perversion in such use of language at all levels and the connection between language and action when he drew comparisons between his own language use and that of novelist the late Graham Greene:

> What he was really referring to it seems to me was in fact language, the language used in relation to the action that is also used; in other words the vileness and rottenness of Central American policy I know in his view, and certainly in mine is that it still insists on using terms of rhetoric such as freedom and democracy which in a way apparently justifies the deaths of countless hundreds of thousands of people. ("Graham Green 1904–1991: A Tribute to the Late Writer," n.p.)

The play propels itself toward a dramatization of the empty rhetoric of democracy, which links love and justice by dramatizing the obvious lack of both. Pinter allows the audience to witness the essential lovelessness in some hollow center of their lives, to see the connection to the larger issue of global justice such lovelessness engenders.

Notes

1. Page references to text of *Party Time* and *The New World Order* are to the typescript.

Moonlight: Lovedeath Wedded

More than a decade after his last major play Harold Pinter wrote *Moonlight,* and, as with each new recent play of his, it takes us some place new—this time on a dark moonlit journey to the abyss, a ride to the borders of death's kingdom. But it is a journey made and taken in the service of love.

The play is both more comically delightful than almost any other recent Pinter play to date and more universally disturbing. In *Moonlight,* Andy, a bedridden, dying man in his fifties, and his wife, Bel, who sits beside his bed embroidering, occupy one portion of the stage in Andy's well-furnished bedroom discussing love, death, and the absence of their three children. Their sons, Jake and Fred, in their late twenties, appear in Fred's shabby bedroom making plans for unspecified, secret activities. Their daughter, Bridget, two years younger than her younger brother Fred, appears arrested in the past at age sixteen when she is alone on stage, in yet a third space, an unspecified no man's land, addressing the audience from her conscious and unconscious mind. Bel's best friend Maria, enters to address Jake and Fred, as does Ralph, who Andy claims is his closest friend. Near the end, Maria, who was both Andy's lover and Bel's, enters Andy's room with her husband Ralph, also Bel's former love, prattling about the details of their married life.

In the face of death, the multiple betrayals become almost inconsequential—Bel tells Andy, "Death is your new horizon." (54; all references are to the typescript) Pinter, once again, explicitly joins love and death. Jake says he will pay "the full price of love," and Fred concurs, "Which is the price of death." (67) Although they mouth received words they scarcely understand, their aphorisms of ceremony, literature, and cliché lead us to see what they do not—what is missing, and what we, as audience, must supply.

Paradoxically, through these fairly ordinary characters and the questions that their actions raise, *Moonlight* is also both more accessible and more deeply enigmatic than any of Pinter's other previous plays. Mystery keeps audience curiosity alive in the scramble to untangle the many questions (Who are Fred and Jake? Why do they not come to their father's deathbed? Why does Bridget appear before us alone, only in the past, and at age sixteen?). Mystery ultimately leads to the realization that some questions remain unanswered. But, through the recognizably familiar characters, not at far remove from our lives, the play trusts the audience to appreciate how the unanswered questions provoke life's most profound mysteries—love and death questions. At the end, *Moonlight* leaves us with questions only we, as audience, can address and answer, but the play offers a guide and some direction: transmitted through Bridget, and through the received values and vision informing all the characters' actions. Through the tension between the limited vision of the characters, and the play's larger vision directed through Bridget to the audience, *Moonlight* offers and requires a new way of seeing, a new vision which it trusts us to see. Through the coupling of death's destructive force with love's vitality and delight, *Moonlight,* like all of Pinter's plays, celebrates freedom, choice and responsibility which enhances life.

Just as the title *Moonlight* carries the suggestion of love, the play's vital center remains the spirit of love and love-lust, not only in the sense that "lust, too, is an art," but, more important, akin to Blake's notion of the lover as a *seer* of truth. For Blake, the seer, one who sees truly, is a visionary, and anyone, if unhampered by limited human sight, might perceive the truth as it is, infinite. (*Marriage of Heaven and Hell,* plate 14) Ecstatic experience provides one way to gain transcendent knowledge. Blake saw erotic love as one route that is open to almost anyone to cleanse "the doors of perception." For most of these characters, as for Emma and Jerry in *Betrayal,* their erotically ecstatic moments remain the high points of their lives. At the end of the play, when we stand with Bridget before a different door, our perception shifts. The questions raised become a key the play offers to open the door to claim fuller perception—our own vision.

Vision, defined at the outset of this inquiry, addresses the question, What actuates human beings? *Moonlight's* response remains the same as we have seen throughout Pinter's work—characters are driven to act by a desire for love, respect, a desire to survive. Here, in a world reflecting individual powerlessness and an ever-lessening possibility for heroic or extraordinary action or even the power to guide the course of one's own life, the love that these rather ordinary characters demand becomes transcendent love. The love expressed by these characters, however unconscious and limited, is not divorced from the love which inspires the heroic quest which cleanses destructive elements from a community's life and renews a vision of hope. *Moonlight* at no time minimizes or denigrates the power or the goods of transcendence which humans access from the daily, momentary "ah ha's" to larger awakenings. Yet for these characters, however intense the erotic ecstasy, ecstatic love remains the only available and momentary escape from the self and merely lifts these characters out of the mundane without affecting change in their lives or in others'. Seeking transcendent love as an escape from the awful ordinariness of life turns the self in *Moonlight* not into "passion's slave" but into a blind, impotent and destructive creature serving "the eternal footman," Death.

Moonlight explores the negative space between Eros and Thanatos, the tension in that space that connects love and death. In the end, the play comes out on the side of love, the underdog in this unequal match. That is not to say that in the end love triumphs, but through the emphasis on love's vital power, the play asks us the question at the center of all the world's great literature: "How are you living your life?"

The play, tighter than almost all Pinter's other full-length plays, covers more ground and goes further than any of his other work to dramatize how each human attitude, intention and action becomes a choice between life or death's destruction. *Moonlight* combines the outcry against global savagery and violence in Pinter's recent torture plays with his focus on love central to most of his work but allows the forces of love and death to coalesce to a new end. The *Moonlight* journey becomes a reminder of love's wedded kinship to death—of destructive forces which must be acknowledged in the self if love is to embrace the other and to maintain its power to sustain life. To deny death is to deny love and life.

Moonlight opens and closes with Bridget who frames the play referencing moonlight. It begins on a moonless night as Bridget is about to slip downstairs hoping not to wake her parents. She views insuring their rest as her "task" because they have given "[a]ll their energies and all their love" to her and her brothers. (1) What her parents need, however, is precisely awakening. The awful irony and the play's central motif, as we shall see, is that neither she nor anyone else is able to wake them. She says she is "all they have left of their life," simultaneously connoting generation, parental sacrifice, and the estrangement of Jake and Fred. (1) Her suggestion of generation, implying an earthly immortality (the possibility that one's children can continue one's own life), becomes a notion which Bridget, by making it explicit, negates. The play ends with Bridget's moonlit recollection of herself as a child invited to attend a party down the block but directed to wait to come until the moon set. When she could wait no longer, she says she left for the party but remained standing outside the dark house bathed in moonlight, waiting for the moon to set.

Life, embraced in the context of this moonless/moonlit frame, becomes an antechamber for death or the space between two deaths—the one before birth and the one after life: the one which Bel describes as the death before life begins and the other which Andy tries to imagine as he leaves life.

Moonlight is a stunning *memento mori* where the only sunlight in the moonlit landscape comes from love, love remembered in stark contrast to the love refused from the children who do not visit their father's deathbed. The only ostensive glimmer of love as a vital force in the present slips in near the end with Maria and Ralph, now married with three children. Their love is cast in shadow by their denial that Andy is dying, and denying death denies them depth. Ralph insists, "He looks in the pink," and Maria parrots, "A bit peaky perhaps but in the pink." (85) *Moonlight* subtly reveals many other deaths in the lives of those who, like Andy, have not fully lived, like Bridget, have withdrawn into a death-like past, like Bel, have retained only vital memories of life and loves past, like Maria and Ralph, have denied some portion of love in giddily denying death, and like Jake and Fred, who have so loved destruction and death they chose it for their life's work.

Throughout Pinter's early and middle work, his characters' vision is myopically constricted by a lack of self-knowledge—almost all of them live as if they are never going to die. Without acknowledging death, they are subsequently prevented from even the beginnings of self-knowledge, are also robbed of choice, and, thus, of fully living. Even in the later torture plays, where the imminent death of a torture victim cannot be denied, those who deal out the torture view death as happening to other people, not to the self. With Andy comes the first head-on recognition of death's inexorable approach to the self, and love is viewed from a fresh perspective where past infractions against the laws of love are subsumed under the larger pervading spirit of life.

Love, for these characters, neither bonds them nor increases in time, nor does it enlarge them in wisdom that extends love to others and embraces them. Instead, love, like life, may have a life span. Bel recalls, "the early and lovely days of our marriage," a phrase Andy later echoes, denoting a love now dead but once so vital it spilled over to include Maria, also, then, Andy's lover, and Ralph, Bel's. (23, 79) Although Bel and Andy repeat the same words, she does not mean the same thing, nor does she reciprocate the intensity of his love. Current confessions of betrayal remain less important than the light and vital heat that the memory of past love still engenders. But where erotic love between Bel and Andy exists primarily in the past, filial love in the present from Jake and Fred is largely absent, displaced to a superior and colleague, Lieutenant-Colonel d'Orangerie. In words devoid of meaning, Jake promises to love his father. But it will not happen in Andy's lifetime.

Moonlight dramatizes varieties of love from the erotic—heterosexual, homosexual and incestuous—and familial to love of friend, as well as love of a cause, exemplified in Jake and Fred's dedication to their work, communicated through Jake's professed love for d'Orangerie. But his love, a destructive image-identification with a power group, which is perceived as larger than the self, only inflates the ego. A love which serves only the self and not another is not, in Pinter's work, love, but desire in service of destruction. The sons' love contrasts with the erotic love Andy and Bel celebrate. The tension between the two forms of love, one a love of death, the other incomplete, along with the momentary surface conflicts in each scene, creates the outer aesthetic that is wedded to the deeper ethic it conveys in Pinter's larger vision.

The play ultimately dramatizes love not only as an attitude composed of emotion, desire, and intention but also as the knowledge and values that inform the vision which impels action that serves life rather than destruction. Jake's intention to love his father stops short of action. By the time he can act it will be too late, and his love for his work, though we do not learn precisely what he does, is productive only of perpetuating injustice through violent destruction. Jake, like all of the other characters, at some level acknowledges the great "they" controlling their lives: the "oughts" and "shoulds" informing the received vision. Even Bridget has so internalized society's injunctions and prohibitions against questioning that she at first obeys culture's (issued probably through her parents) command, given without reason, not to attend the party till the moon sets.

In the second scene, Andy's wryly comic opener to Bel from his bed, "Where are the boys? Have you found them yet?" elicits her equally comic, "I'm trying." (2) His angry edge allows the pathos to enter: "You've been trying for weeks. And failing. It's enough to make the cat laugh. Do we have a cat?" (2) Giving the audience permission to laugh at the outset opens the play up to the core's greater darkness and depth, allowing a closer proximity to death than might be comfortably tolerated later. A character who can make an audience laugh makes them care for him, and in that caring, audience identification begins. Andy, grounded on the bed of illness, birth, sleep, love and his own death, does not use comedy to distance himself from his pain of dying. Instead, he deploys the laughter flash point, which signals recognition of insight, opening audience awareness to small and larger truths: from his deathbed confessions of infidelity (and his innocence), to unknowable truths about death. Like Andy's feisty combativeness that signals his reserves of vitality, his cracking jokes in the face of his death becomes an act of courage.

Bel accepts responsibility for her "ineptitude" in locating and bringing the boys "to their father's deathbed," and she and Andy alternate between pugnacious skirmishes, resolution, and acceptance which peaks in mutual praise, and even in expressions of love. Andy, dying young, at an age when the political philosopher only begins to come into prime, initially takes the lead in the inquiry into the nature of love and death. *Moonlight* reverses the position of the caregiver husband and dying wife in Tillie Olsen's, "Tell Me a Riddle," where a husband finally recognizes the destructiveness in his corrosive complaints to his wife. Now that she is dying he wishes to desist but realizes he must continue the old quarrelsome habits to sustain the seeming normality of their relationship that allows them to acknowledge their pain only in the small doses they are able to tolerate. Andy, however, as the dying partner, conveys both the contentious and the comic in ways which ease the pain for Bel (and the audience) and peel away successive layers of hypocrisy and dishonesty to reveal a core of more important truth.

Andy claims that Bel is "the proper target for the cat's derision," but he recalls, "How I loved you." (3) Employing the past tense invisible, Andy continues to commend her "great heart," which, he adds, "You still have, of course. I can hear it from here. Banging away." (3)

Bel's disjunctive response, her long, disinterested inquiry asking whether Andy feels hot or cold, is met by his scorn:

> Is this a joke? My God, she's taking the piss out of me. My own wife. On my deathbed. She's as bad as the fucking cat. (4)

Bel shields herself against attack with prudery, her "convent school education," which, she claims, left "we girls" ignorant of the meaning of the phrase "taking the piss out" and now leaves her "nonplussed." Andy's sarcastic rejoinder is a demand for a greater truth—the acknowledgement that he is dying. His "We girls! Christ" disallows her hypocrisy of prudery in the guise of female gentility. (5) His insult, which implies that Bel is the opposite of the prudish self she describes, also registers the depth of Andy's pain at her betrayals:

> You've never been nonplussed in the whole of your voracious, lascivious, libidinous life. (4)

Bel refuses to permit his dying to give him license to be "*totally* ridiculous." (5) In the first in a series of metaphysical speculations about death, Andy wonders why he, who has "never harmed a soul," is dying: "You don't die if you're good. You die if you're bad." (5) Andy, a civil servant who has led the unlived life of a bureaucratic functionary, a man who, following orders, imagined himself a leader ("I was an envied and feared force in the temples of the just." (20)), is a near relation of Auden's "Unknown Citizen" and dramatizes an observation Albee made of his own work, "[S]o many of my plays are about people that are avoiding living their own lives, so the first real experience they have is their dying." (55) Albee's further injunction speaks to the way *Moonlight*'s reminder of death awakens an audience:

> I think we should think about our dying and be aware of it very young, very early on, but live so fully that the dying is not the only full experience we have. (55)

After Andy explains to Bel that "taking the piss" is a slang idiom meaning to mock and Bel wonders if there is "a rational explanation" for the phrase, Andy inveighs against the limits of rationality and its efficacy in seeking truth. (6) He says rationality was deep sixed "years ago" and proclaims, "All that famous rationality of yours is swimming about in waste disposal turdology." (6) He concludes, "That was always the destiny of your famous rational intelligence. . . ." (6) The truth which Bel has been avoiding is Andy's death.

Andy fails to see that the choice is not between rationality and something else or that denigrating or disposing of rationality misses the larger point. Ironically, Ralph disparages Andy as being a thinker, who, in turn, dismisses Ralph as the same, although we see little of the thinker in either man. All the attacks on the rational only prompt awareness of the dichotomizing illogic that excludes the rational from fully taking its place with emotion and the psyche in directing human action. *Moonlight* dramatizes a need not for less thinking, but more, fresh and better thought wedded to human action. The play also flags rationality to signal rationality's limitations in perceiving any new vision.

Responding to *Moonlight* with the intellect alone is to discover only a bleak reminder of death that leaves us stranded at death's door outside a bleak house. Regarded only as a doomsday warning, the play offers no news we have not already internalized but reduces the journey to a pointless, "enervating charade" (Andy's description of life without an after light [54]). More importantly, through its delight and raucous vitality, *Moonlight* is a provocative reminder of life. To awaken to the pleasures and possibilities of life that it celebrates, however, requires another way of seeing than from our comfortable, customary distance in the audience as passive but judging spectator.

To seek answers to *Moonlight*'s many mysteries through reason unaided by emotion and imagination is to sit back and complain that there are no Horatios here as a guide—a character long gone from this century's literature—or to complain that Pinter has removed all the Hamlets as well—but that misses the point that Eliot already did that earlier in the twentieth century: "I am not Prince Hamlet, nor was meant to be;/Am an attendant lord. . . ." (7)

The *Hamlet* reference in *Moonlight* reminds us that the play is about attendant lords/all of us—who believe they/we do no harm. Gone from this play are the large, terrifyingly malicious displays of torture in *One for the Road*, *Mountain Language*, and *The New World Order* as well as the malignant violent street warfare provoked by the powerbrokers of *Party Time*. Yet *both* the torturer and powerbrokers are retained in *Moonlight* through Jake and Fred's unspoken and unspeakable violence, a contagion passed down from the self-proclaimed harmless father and a mother who does not, because she believes she cannot, intercede to confront conflict to promote concord either at the private level of family or at the public. The only larger-than-life character, the sons' respected, feared and beloved d'Orangerie, described as unbelievably violent, has been removed off stage.

In that shift from Pinter's recent torture plays, *Moonlight* has taken a fresh turn, evoking a fresh vision. That shift, begun in *One for the Road*, was rooted in the global shift in Pinter's own consciousness outraged by state and individual injustices in South and Central America. Propelled by his subsequent engagement in public affairs, *One for the Road* began to engage the audience in a new way as equal partner in the collaboration by giving the play greater agency and by requiring greater agency from the audience. Informed by Pinter's awakened consciousness, Pinter's vision, for the first time, invited our participation, at the play's core, through identification not only with the torture victim but, inescapably, with the torturer—the "joy" of having all that power—in order to recognize the torturer in us all.

The vision, played out and communicated through the surface dominant/subservient conflict, consistently dramatizes the destruction not only of the other but also the self in any transaction where one person delimits another human being's life. While his early and middle work demonstrated the partial responsibility of both dominant and subservient character for destruction (Stanley and Goldberg in *The Birthday Party*, Hirst and Spooner in *No Man's Land*), beginning with the later torture plays, where victims are stripped of almost all agency and responsibility, Pinter drew the audience into collusion to recognize our complicity, through our own actions which contribute to any system which supports hierarchy, brutalities and destruction. But where, as noted, in his earlier plays, he could refer to Goldberg as a "bastard" and thus still regard him as other and apart from the self, Pinter now acknowledges himself as "a bastard human being."

Moonlight offers no sadistic displays of torture, only the barest mention of violence at all. Anyone who fails to attend to the clues might not guess that Fred is probably a hit man, but once seen, that information serves to remind us that hit men are often good family men and that torturers are best made from the ranks of those unquestioningly obedient in following orders (see Amnesty International's *Torture in the Eighties*). Fred is the son of such a man. Through these characters, who are more recognizably familiar and mundane than Pinter's torturers, *Moonlight* summons us to acknowledge the bastard in us all. But the purpose is not to assign blame nor to elicit guilt but to awaken an audience to assume responsibility. By acknowledging responsibility for contributing to state sanctioned violent destruction, even in our smallest attitudes and actions, comes the attendant recognition of agency that can empower us, as audience, to act.[1]

As "a mirror and chronicle of our time," reflected in the marked contrast between Andy's plush bedroom and his son Fred's seedy room, *Moonlight* registers the current realities of the diminishing monetary possibilities, power, and expectations of the younger generation in the West. Against the present ensuing world clamor for leadership (defined by the traditional vision as one human being, a big Daddy, who can insure a nation's safety against attack and economic destruction), *Moonlight* becomes a counter voice which extends a subtly expressed hope, at depth, to each of us. If there are no Hamlets here it is because we must each assume the hero's responsibility. The end desired and the required effort in that quest for human survival and development are no less heroic, in fact more so. Such a quest extends freedom not merely to one's own group of people but to others. A free society demands informed, questioning, empowered citizenry and neighbors—which Pinter's work has always called for.

This play's core offers an acknowledgement that the individuals making up the masses in a crowded world have unclaimed power and privilege and that assuming individual responsibility to that privilege can empower action that directs larger policy and decisions. That privilege and power come not merely from democracy's consensus, individuals joining in a single voice, but, at depth, from a shift in vision which informs all action and determines outcomes.

Yet, presently, the freedom necessary to effect such core change may be little valued, even rejected, so long as any human being or population feels stunned by an apocalyptic vision of hopelessness. If that were *Moonlight*'s vision, the play would offer only a dangerous endorsement of paralysis. Pinter's work has never endorsed sitting down, let alone embraced despair. The powerlessness that ensues from such hopelessness can impel people and nations to seek safety in a reversion to a familiar and traditional vision.[2] Pinter's work consistently exposes such apparent safety as destructive to everyone entering into that relationship with fear. His plays portray the resultant deathlife of his many characters who sit out their lives, blindly unconscious of the choice to do otherwise, like Jake in *Moonlight*, now forced to sit in bed. Pinter's plays show that resigning responsibility for one's own life only postpones inevitable destruction whenever the driving force of life is fueled by dominant/subservient relationships.

The tension in *Moonlight* might seem to be scrappy rather than scathing and its source often *kvetching* rather than true conflict. But the fractal geometry in *Moonlight* plays out beyond the lines of Pinter's typical dominant/subservient conflict to go for other, larger, truths. For the first time, as we shall later see, *Moonlight* targets for destruction the dominant/subservient relationship itself at all levels: both at the most private (parental authority and inherited, right-of-birth order) and at the most public (globally drawn gender lines that divide half the world from the other half). The core truths, which these surface conflicts convey, come in the form of questions pointing to a revised vision.

At the surface of the conflict, each utterance of each character fractally signals, like a genetic stamp, the history and, in most cases, the future of each speaker's deeper character; almost all except Bridget, are given to those now famous platitudes in Pinter's plays that reflect the stale, deadening thought informing a character's discourse, actions, and vision. Once, however, as Bel, in their next scene, takes occasion to comment, Andy rises above cliché. When Andy asks Bel if he is dying, she responds, "If you were dying you'd be dead." (21) Her remark distances the topic of death, but Andy refuses: "I sometimes think I'm married to a raving lunatic!

But I'm always prepared to look on the sunny side of things." (22) Voicing his will to live, Andy tosses Bel a comically lyrical question: "You mean I'll see spring again? I'll see another spring? All the paraphernalia of flowers?" (22) Bel responds with a rare compliment from a Pinter character: "What a lovely use of language. You know, you've never used language in such a way before." (22) When he denies her assertion by defending himself ("I've said other things . . . ."), Bel, as a worthy opponent able to return insult in kind, derides Andy with a backhanded compliment by claiming that her praise is just:

> Yes, it's quite true that all your life in all your personal and social attachments the language you employed was mainly coarse, crude, vacuous, puerile, obscene and brutal to a degree. Most people were ready to vomit after no more than ten minutes in your company. (22, ellipses mine)

Later, his sons, describing him as a man "spiritually furtive, [and] . . . intellectually abject," refer to his language as "poetically downtrodden." (73) Both their concord and their conflict, conveyed in clichés, disclose their dead vision informing their action. Yet, increasingly, throughout Andy's crude, clichéd, but sometimes freshly inventive phrases, he probes for truths from which those who deny death, shrink.

In Fred's bedroom, Fred and his older brother Jake seem blissfully unaware of their father's dying except as a distant, now long-past event at the far edges of their lives. Jake advertises himself as without a father who, he says, left him his fortune on the day of his birth. Yet the two young men, in their first words, address one another as "Brother." Fred wonders what kind of holiday Jake is giving him "this year. Arts or the beach?" which metaphorically encompasses the two poles of most holidays and is also a distant reference Goldberg's reminder, in *The Birthday Party,* to McCann (speaking possibly as a crime boss to an underling, saying that he has brought McCann to the seaside, and he orders him to relax). (7) Jake maintains, "a man of your calibre," needs both "to keep your pecker up." (8) Fred deflects the topic (of sex rarely attached to him) by returning all adulation aimed at him to his brother: "You were writing poems when you were a mere child, isn't that right?" (8) Jake pushes the question of prodigy back earlier, "before I could read," which Fred tops, "before you could speak." (9) Jake concludes, "I was writing poems before I was born." (9) The absurd sarcasm relates, perhaps distantly, to Bel's notion of death before birth and suggests, however comically, a stamp of fate: "So you were the real thing. . . ?" says Fred. Jake accedes calling himself, "The authentic article." (9) But saying so, in this comic context, only calls fate into question. Jake, the poet-thug, like Foster in *No Man's Land*, claims an innate creative talent we never see in this man of destruction.

When Fred says he has been thinking about "the whole caboodle," an unnamed enterprise for which they will require "capital," Jake claims that he has got it. (10) When Fred asks where he found it, Jake answers, "Divine right." Fred replies "Christ," and Jake says, "Exactly," linking the economics of destruction to divinity. (10) First, Jake details his inheritance, the way his father "weighed it all up carefully the day I was born" and left "without codicil or reservation—his personal fortune to his newborn son the very day of the baby's birth." (14) Pinter links birth and death allowing birth to register the way the death of a parent places the child next in line; the birth of a child here also registers as the beginning of death as the parent is pushed along the line.

Earlier Jake described his father as a modest man who "adhered strictly to the rule of law," (12) did not seek "pleasure or glory," and for whom [a]pplause . . . [g]ratitude. . . .[and m]asturbation came not his way . . ."; he corrects himself, "I meant approbation. . . ." (11) This rare reference to masturbation in Pinter's work allies the sons to their mother's prudery toward language: the hypocrisy that prompts Jake's apology for speaking a word which does no harm while dedicating his life to violence that may harm many. (11–12) Jake next extols his father's legacy as an act which for "sheer undaunted farsightedness, unflinching moral resolve, stern intellectual vision, classical philosophical detachment, passionate religious fervour, profound emotional intensity, bloodtingling spiritual ardour, spell binding metaphysical chutzpah—stood alone." (14) Punctuating the closure with a rare use of Yiddish, Pinter allows his characters to indulge in lyricism and repetition but rescues language from going over the top. Fred, with another comic turn, caps Jake's praise for his father's act with comic brevity, "Tantamount to a backflip in the lotus position." (14) For all the references to Jake's poetic prowess, Fred's language is frequently more imaginative, tighter, and his thought processes more brutally honest. Fred notes that everyone was impressed with their father except Uncle Rufus who knew "that your father was just a little bit short of a few krugerrands." (15) Praise for the father instantly diminishes to pity for the man without fortune: "His casino life had long been a lost horizon." (16) Economic status becomes a barometer for respect and love. Yet Jake concludes with a more complex praise for his father as either "a mountebank—a child—a shyster—a fool—or a villain" to which Fred adds: "Or a saint." (17) For Jake and Fred the truth hangs in a mirror spinning between two polar opposites. Without admitting a middle ground, their truth reduces to an either/or fallacy. But the audience has a wider perspective. While the characters see themselves and others from continually shifting perspectives and often draw contradictory conclusions about one another, they nicely dramatize the impossibility that any single description can sum up even a single act let alone a human life, a point which bears repeating here with these characters from whom we might so easily be tempted to disconnect. To disconnect from them, to disown their unappealing qualities, is to remain disconnected from most others in life who do not precisely mirror or improve upon our image of ourselves. Only connection creates community.

Moonlight also reveals how denying negative aspects of the self only makes them more pronounced by unconsciously informing action. Although Jake denies his inheritance—claiming he has no father, that his father died at his birth—he claims a divine inheritance economically sanctioned by "Divine right," which he believes supports his secret state activities. Yet the spiritual inheritance he cannot deny is the spiritual void which compels his action.

Maria enters, addressing the boys, "Do you remember me? I was your mother's best friend." (17) She monologues, displaying her chief agenda is herself, even as she applauds her three children. She expresses greater admiration for her husband Ralph who refereed "with such aplomb, such command. Your mother and I were so . . . impressed. He was always ahead of the game. He knew where the ball was going before it was kicked." (18) She calls his gift "osmosis," a quality which, she notes, their father lacked, though, she concedes, he was "[o]ne of the great waltzers. An elegance and grace long gone." (18) Her admiration for Andy's "firmness and authority," effervesces into adoration for their mother, "marvellously young and quickening every moment." Ecstatically, she describes Bel in the language of the generative qualities of love, as "breaking out all over the place" in "buds," and says, "I thought I'd go mad." (19)

Almost all the characters express love for another in terms of transcendent ecstasy that unconsciously acknowledges love's kinship with death. Where Maria nearly goes "mad," Fred "dropped dead at her feet" (31), and Andy says he "can't die" without Maria. (45) Jake and Fred love death through its deputy, d'Orangerie. While ecstatic euphoria can open windows on the world, at least momentarily admitting a bond with the wider world, these characters' expressions of adoration do not bond the self to the beloved, and only Bridget views herself as *being* loved—by her parents who gave her their life. The other characters, expressing ecstatic feeling, miss any other transcendent knowledge that love's knowledge, through connection to the other, can offer. That "death which is love" (which Riley expresses in *Family Voices*), the dying to oneself to admit another into one's life, never surfaces here to serve anyone. The characters remain solipsistically walled in, wallowing, in *Moonlight*, in their own briefly heightened emotions, often, only remembered.

Andy's view of himself as a "first class civil servant" is hardly such a fond remembrance as Maria's: "I sweated over a hot desk all my working life and nobody ever found a flaw in my working procedures." (19) He maintains fierce pride for inspiring clichéd postures in those under his command:

> to put their shoulders to the wheel and their noses to the grindstone and to keep faith at all costs with the structure which after all ensured the ordered government of all our lives which took perfect care of us, which held us to its bosom, as it were. (20)

His greatest pride is not in inspiring extraordinary, let alone transcendent action, but in his role for maintaining the status quo that sustained him and subordinated others. Is it wholly surprising that his sons fight so fiercely to maintain what they have, though it appears to be less than their father has?

Andy admits to Bel that he was respected at work but not loved, which he eschewed. He contrasts to d'Orangerie who at least inspired the love of Andy's sons. From left field, Bel interjects,

"But you never swore in the office?" (20) With comic honesty, Andy answers, "Certainly not. I kept my obscene language for the home where it belongs." (20) Freely associating from obscenity to Maria, Andy confesses that he went to Maria's flat just before he was stricken, and Bel replies, "Yes you always entertained a healthy lust for her." (21) Andy says that Bel did, too, but that he is not jealous. "Why should you be jealous?" Bel responds, "She was your mistress. Throughout the early and lovely days of our marriage." (23) Though Andy compliments Bel ("She must have reminded me of you"), he concludes, "The past is a mist." (24) He recalls "a woman walked towards me across a darkening room," but when Bel says, "That was me," he merely asks, "You?" (24) His question links to Bridget.

Their daughter, in the second of three Bridget interludes, immediately enters and describes herself as in a jungle, "hidden but free" where "[n]o-one in the world can find me." (26) As the sixteen-year-old Bridget, she becomes the mediator between the play's vision and the audience, delivering it to our unconscious psyche. Like *Everyman's* Good Deeds' voice, hers is small from disuse. We can understand her, but just barely, for she speaks nearly in tongues, as she must, to convey the mystery of her larger truths which only we can bring fully into consciousness through action. In evoking a territory reminiscent of *No Man's Land*, she returns the play to the death zone, grounding it in the grim reminder both of Andy's dying and of living a death-in-life.

Her withdrawal to this dark place in the past may be variously interpreted as escape, enervation, madness, death, or a survival of a wild untamed or untamable spirit that exists preserved beneath her ordinary, off-stage, outer self as a grown woman and mother of three children. Bridget's jungle could be Eden or a paradise where generation, as an overpopulated, "unweeded garden," has gone rampant nearly smothering her in "[h]ibiscus, oleander, bougainvillea" but which, nevertheless, provides a shelter she reached by crossing "so many fierce landscapes . . . [t]horns, stones, stinging nettles, barbed wire, skeletons of men and women in ditches." (25) Her journey through a war zone brings her to a place where she describes the "velvet odour" that she can still smell "of burning." (26) The image, redolent of cremation (as still done in the open on the Ganges, here, suggests wartime or the concentration camp ovens), evokes the proximity of brutal deaths. Her appearance here in the first third of the play continues our initiation into that nether world of the Eleusinian mysteries. She remains our guide, imprisoned in unconsciousness—that zone which, by definition, cannot be known—until it comes to light, awakened in consciousness. Whatever change can occur at the end, as we shall see, can only come from the audience.

In what at first appears another puzzling exchange, Jake, at a table, asks his brother Fred his name. Fred replies, "Macpherson," to which Jake answers, "I thought it was Gonzalez." (27) Fred says he came at Jake's "urgent request," but when Jake says, "You mean Kellaway," Fred says he doesn't know Kellaway. (27) Jake suggests Fred might know him by the name of Jim Sims. The multiple names that characters assume, which, in Pinter's earlier work, point up questions of identity, are here also used to underscore the subterfuge these men must maintain to protect themselves in their endeavors.

Pinter pushes the horror behind that point further with an added twist. Jake insists, "Yours was the name they gave me." (28) When Jake asks what name, Fred says "Saunders," but Jake veers the subject to, "Manning's popping in to see you," information that carries a barely veiled threat. (30) When Fred says he does not know Manning, Jake proposes he might know him under the name Rawlings. Fred concedes that he knows Rawlings but returns discussion to Kellaway, asking Kellaway's other name. Jake replies, "Saunders." After a pause Fred says, "But that's your name." (31) Closure comes full circle to bring two points home. The deliberately assumed multiple aliases of each brother telegraph that their clandestine activities conceal nefarious deeds. Their not knowing one another's names or aliases emphasizes how these men, immersed in death yet who do not come to their father's deathbed and do not seem to acknowledge one another as kin, will so easily become brother pitted against brother.

Ralph's entrance interrupts anything that might clarify the concealed mystery of their activities: "Were you keen on the game of soccer when you were lads, you boys? Probably not." (32) Ralph, like Maria, monologues, claiming an ability to recognize a "natural athlete" which, he says, their father was not, classifying Andy instead as "a thinker." But he does so only to disparage the efficacy of thinking: "The trouble with so much thinking, though, or with that which calls itself thinking, is that it's like farting Annie Laurie down a keyhole. A waste of your time and mine." (32) This is the second warning light flashed on the limits of rationality, again provoking audience attention to the need for action. It also dramatizes how each man points to the other, rather than the self, to posit blame for failing to act. When Ralph asks the boys what they think, he himself answers by detailing his own active life at sea before he "decided to give the arts a chance generally," citing his "amateur refereeing," which "didn't work out," but he claims a "natural talent for acting," for the piano, and painting, though he wishes he had been "an architect. That's where the money is." The self-proclaimed artist reveals himself as an artist *manqué*, unconsciously aligned with those devoted to material goods. (33) He credits their parents who "woke me up to poetry and art" and "changed my life." (33) He admits he married a "demanding" woman who was after "fibre and guts" with eyes "black and appalling" and then expresses his ecstatic love, "I dropped dead at her feet." (33) Ralph defines himself now through his early life with Maria, "It was all go at that time. Love, football, the arts, the occasional pint." (33) Ralph admits to succumbing to a bureaucrat's way of allowing other people to define his pleasures: he preferred "fruity white wine but," he says, signaling his own underclass origins, "you couldn't actually say that in those days." (33) Andy, in contrast, never acknowledges that anyone defines him.

The forces which define human preferences, values, and action raise the question of nature versus nurture which comes into sharper focus in the next scene: a close-up on Bridget, Fred, and Jake as teenagers. Time and space are fractured during that one brief moment when it is possible to sympathize with each of them as they display familiar youthful desires and remarkably typical sibling contention, nothing that portends the sons' adult attitudes or actions.

The eighteen-year-old Jake refuses to take his tag-along younger brother Fred to a "gig," and his fourteen-year-old sister Bridget begs Jake not to leave him alone with her. Fred, who views not being able to go as "tragic," chides Bridget for her desire to be alone to read a book: "Greta Garbo!" He asks, "Are you going to be a film star when you grow up?" She says he knows that she is going to be "a physiotherapist." Bridget, one of the few main Pinter characters whose chosen work springs from caring for others, reminds Fred that she recently released his neck spasm. His question and her acknowledgement of her gift resonate with much deeper questions of hereditary talent, pointing to a fate motif that runs through the play. (36)

The following scene advances that motif further when Bel accepts Andy's "nature" but, subtly, only affirms her belief that he cannot change. When Andy says, "I'd be lost without you," she nearly returns his compliment:

> You're not a bad man. You're just what we used to call a loud mouth. You can't help it. It's your nature. (39)

Her unconditional acceptance of his "nature," which subscribes to a fixed, immutable notion of human nature, is not the compliment she intends nor that Andy believes he receives but merely ratifies his disempowerment.

Kissing her hand in response to her perceived compliment, Andy next wonders where their sons are. In answer, Bel proceeds in the same accepting tone: "They were good boys. I've been thinking of how they used to help me with the washing up." (41) Andy counters, "They were bastards. Both of them. Always." (41) He cites Jake's defiance—a childhood incident when Jake refused to clean a broom cupboard—and then he labels them both, "Lazy idle layabouts." Andy concludes, "And look at them now. . . ! A sponging parasitical pair of ponces. Sucking the tit of the state." (41–42) His assessment confirms that his sons' nefarious deeds are conducted under government sanction. Although Andy accuses Bel of collusion (feeding "them a few weekly rupees from your little money-box. . . ."), nowhere does he acknowledge his own connection or contribution to their endeavors nor that he was "sucking" at the same "tit." (42)

Instead, he terminates the distasteful topic of his sons by leaving to watch a football game, which, by association, reminds him of his "old chum" the referee. Andy next displaces his outcast status, (to which his sons have relegated him), to the referee, by assigning the referee even lower status, expressed through pity.

> Charming bloke. They treated him like shit. A subject of scorn. No decision he ever made was adhered to or respected. They shouted at him, they screamed at him, they called him every kind of prick. . . . I'll always remember his impotent whistle. It blows down to me through the ages, damp and forlorn. (43; ellipses mine)

But saying that his "whistle" was "impotent" does not make it so. When Andy surmises that the referee must be dead by now, Bel says he is not. He wants to know, "Why not?" and when Andy does not remember his name, Bel instantly supplies it: "Ralph." (43) Her doing so suggests a relationship easily guessed. Andy, however, immediately appropriates Ralph for himself, waxing rhapsodic about Ralph, "My oldest friend." Instead of expressing friendship as a relationship between equals, he regards Ralph as a means to inflate his own self-regard. He calls him "pathologically idiosyncratic" noting that the speed of Ralph's thoughts was reflected in Ralph's gait that ranged from "wading through apricot jam" to "greased lightning," impossible to keep pace with. (44) At some level, Andy is intuiting Bel's forthcoming explicit profession of love for Ralph when he expresses sympathy for Ralph's "sexual partner whoever she may have been." Andy, then, imaginatively employs a turn of a cliché to a fresh end that makes the erotic explicit: "Poor girl. There must be easier ways of making ends meet." (44) Though he reduces Ralph's sexual encounters to "ends" that "meet," Bel will later insist it was love. Andy free associates to Maria, insisting, "I can't die without her." (45)

The pathos quickly gives way to the comic with Bel's reply, "Of course you can. And you will." (45) Andy counters with swift retaliation:

> But think of our past. We were all so close. Think of the months I betrayed you with her. How can she forget? (45)

Andy's comically erotic praise heaped on Maria places betrayal in a diminished context, distancing him from any pain of jealousy:

> Think of the wonder of it. I betrayed you with your own girlfriend, she betrayed you with your husband and she betrayed her own husband—and me—with you! She broke every record in sight! She was genius and a great fuck. (45)

Andy never acknowledges Bel's similar "genius," nor does she. Instead, Bel quickly checks his exuberance with her lady-like, "She was a very charming and attractive woman," a more pristine phrasing demanded by civilized society, which, however, again registers the hypocrisy of prudery. (45) Andy admits, "I was a man at that time," revealing that sexual performance defines, for Andy, what it means to be a man. (46) He demands to know why Maria isn't there "to console you in your grief." (46) Maria will later prove little consolation. Bel answers, "She's probably forgotten you're dying. If she ever remembered." (46) In typical Pinter *lex talionis* retort, Andy's reminder that he had Maria in their bed is an offensive move that de-escalates with his recognition: "You probably had her in the same place, of course." (46) Bel claims she doesn't "'have' people," but when Andy corrects her, "You've had me,"[3] Bel retains the offensive, "Oh you. Oh yes. I can still have you." (47)

Andy wonders how Bel plans to mount her "[a]ssualt" and asks, "How much sexual juice does a corpse retain?" but deflates his attack entirely by confessing that he is "basically innocent," knows "little of women," but has "heard dread tales," from his "old mate, the referee." (47) When he dismisses those tales, however, as "probably all fantasy and fabrication, bearing no relation whatsoever to reality," Bel retains the offense with a closure that leaves in little doubt her relationship with Ralph: "Oh do you think so? Do you really think so?" (47)

Although further discourse is interrupted by Fred and Jake, the dominant/subservient conflict continues, through them, to a crescendo of implied violence. As the two brothers discuss an upcoming undefined meeting with a long list of men including Lieutenant-Colonel Silvio d'Orangerie who "will speak off the record," they leave the audience in no doubt of their connection to state matters but, at the same time, emphasize their growing distance from one another. (49) Fred turns from his earlier genially obsequious praise of his older brother's poetic genius to threatening him: "Listen son. I've come a long way down here to attend a series of highly confidential meetings in which my participation is seen to be a central factor." (51) He demands that Jake produce three men he says he must see: "Frustrate any of this and you'll regret it." (51) Jake's defense, a reminder that he has a steady job, "which is more than can be said for you" (implying his free-lance status) transforms to a counterthreat: "I can only hope Lieutenant-Colonel Silvio d'Orangerie won't find you as offensive as I do. He's an incredibly violent person." (51) His threat cannot deflect Fred's: "I know Silvio." (51) Dismissing Jake by emphasizing his own intimacy with the man underscores Fred's threat as the reverse side of his earlier fawning and reveals how easily a blood link that once bonded the brothers can be severed. Now, like Cain and Abel, one is prepared to kill the other. Death and love, increasingly polarized in the split-scene dialogue, in the end also converge.

Where Fred and Jake continue the focus on implied destruction and death, Bel and Andy focus on love, the topic which allows Andy to confront death openly and Bel to accept and to admit to her friends and family that Andy is dying. By the end, love and death merge in a wedding, a uroboric ring imaging the contiguous relationship of love and death.

Andy, in the next scene, returns focus to love. In the first of two scenes conveying a touch of incestuous desire, he conflates his own daughter Bridget with Maria.

When Andy asks, "Where is she?", he seems to be resuming the thread of his last conversation with Bel about Maria: "Of all the people in the world I know she'd want to be with me now. Because she I know remembers everything." (52) He adds, "How I cuddled her and sang to her, how I kept her nightmares from her, how she fell asleep in my arms." (52) Only when he asks, "Is she bringing my grandchildren to see me?" is Bridget clearly the subject (primarily referred to as a vessel to produce his grandchildren). The conflation serves to question what is meant by family, which, by extension, includes Maria and extends, through the play's vision, to include the larger family of man and woman within the larger community.[4] Similarly, the suggestion of incest, which acknowledges other sexual possibilities, examines the taboo. Is Andy's subtextually expressed desire unconscious and innocent of any action? What, if anything, occasions Bridget's withdrawal into an inner world where "no-one in the world" can find her? Why is Bridget absent from his deathbed, and why isn't Andy surprised or outraged that Bridget doesn't come to comfort her mother? What does her mother know and possibly fail to address? The hints are so subtle the answers can only remain elusive, but it is Bridget who, like Charon, ferries us to the underworld, and it is her name that is on Andy's lips at the end. Yet Andy withholds his sentimental reserves for the "[p]oor little buggers," taking their "last look" at their grandfather and receiving his "blessing." (53) He says they are losing him just "when he was about to stumble upon new reserves of spiritual zest, when the door was about to open on new ever-widening and ever-lengthening horizons." (53) This is the first explicit, self-referential suggestion of spiritual development in Pinter's work, but only awakens awareness of its absence.[5] Bel checks Andy's excess, "But darling, death will be your new horizon." (53) Andy acquiesces, and, what is more, bravely pursues speculation on the nature of death:

> But the big question is, will I cross it as I die or after I'm dead. Or perhaps I won't cross it at all. Perhaps I'll just stay stuck in the middle of the horizon. In which case, can I see over it? Can I see the other side? Or is the horizon endless? (54)

While he engages the rhetoric of religious myth (remaining hopeful of participation in some after light), his speculations on death are without awareness of what light might enter or emanate from his present, living, human spirit. He wonders if the weather will be "sunny" or "unceasing moonlight ... ? Or pitch black forever," then Andy concludes that it will not be pitch black. (54; ellipses mine) His belief that light exists in death, a reminder of the play's title, *Moonlight*, is deduced from his question about the purpose of life: "[W]hat would have been the point of going through all these enervating charades in the first place?" His life described as "an enervating charade" reveals how much of his life was lived unconsciously in death's thrall. Yet his assertion that death will not be pitch black, leads him to suppose, "There must be a loophole." (54) "The only trouble is," he admits, "I can't find it." (54)

If he could find the loophole, he speculates, the result might be a circular return to life (a recurrence akin to what Bel proposes as death-before-birth). "If only I could find it I would crawl through it and meet myself coming back," Andy says, but his picture hardly offers consolation or comfort: "Like screaming with fright at the sight of a stranger to find you're looking into a mirror." (54) This self-reflective horror, more terrifying than Hamlet's vaguely imagined sleep or hell, allows Andy to confront his worst fears and signals an important shift. Confronting the worst finally opens Andy to express concern for others: the grandchildren: "They'll cry or they won't, a sorrow too deep for tears, but they're only babies, what can they know about death?" (55)

His "sorrow too deep for tears" question, a semicomical echo of Wordsworth's closure to his "Ode: Intimations of Immortality from Recollections of Early Childhood," (205) prompts Bel's assertion, "[T]hey know more about death than we do." (55) She says that while we have forgotten death, they remember it:

> Because some of them, those who are really very young, remember the moment before their life began—its [*sic*] not such a long time ago for them, you see—and the moment before their life began they were of course dead. (55)

Bel's notion of the quickening of life, also distantly echoes Wordsworth's "Ode," describing life entering "trailing clouds of glory," (65) where "birth is but a sleep and a forgetting." (58) The provocative moment is punctuated nicely by the phone ringing, unanswered, in Fred's empty room. While the call could be from any of the many men Fred and Jake discuss, given Bel's later call to them, most likely the call confirms both their absence from home to participate in their work cloaked in intrigue and their total alienation from their family.

Stumbling through the dark, in the next scene, Andy pours himself a drink. He rails against loosing life's pleasures, now reduced to three, but already robbed of two, smoking and sex: "No fags, no fucks" as "[g]rowing moonlight" reveals Bridget standing in the background. Andy's "no fucks" conjoins sex with Bridget as she appears. This second conflation scene between Bridget, Maria, and Bel merges Andy's trinity of women but includes Bel only to exclude her. After Andy says, "Ah darling. Ah my darling," a suggestion that Bridget is death in the guise of a young girl and a beloved, Bel appears and "walks into moonlight," but Andy and Bel "turn away from each other." (57) Bridget, as an emissary of his own unconscious, is death as the dark shadow of all that deadened Andy's life. As she steps forward into light, a coming into consciousness, love and death converge. Bridget remains alone "in the moonlight," a momentary suggestion that the younger generation remains as the older disappears in death. (58)

The ending of the next scene mirrors that same point: (moon)light inserted into a death-black night. But the images are reversed. Where Bridget, remaining alone in moonlight, exposes human mutability, Jake and Fred perceive light as a force of the eternal. Jake extrapolates from the eternal properties of light to affirm human immortality. When Jake asks the bedridden Fred, "How's your water consumption these days?", Fred claims to have given it all up "to eschew the path of purity and abstention and take up a proper theology." (59) Through the mention of theology, water (a need basic to life and healing) is quickly coupled to the gods. When Jack admits he, too, once lived "the life of Riley" a man "known under his other hat as the Sheik of Araby," whose people, Jake claims, were made the men they were by the water they drank, made not just men but "Gods," Fred claims that he has "always wanted to be a God." (60–61) In the coupling of light with the desire to be a God, the suggestion of Lucifer reveals how Fred's misguided quest for transcendence, through death and killing, has flung him into a purgatory of a sick bed. When Jake offers him water in bed, Fred worries, "Do you think my nerve is going? Do you think my nerve is on the blink?" (61) Hardly an eternal god, Fred, in his sick bed, paralleling his father's deathbed, opts to stay in bed claiming, "Bridget would understand." (62) Jake proposes that science can diagnose Fred's ills with "things like lightmeters . . . ." (63) When Fred, playing the clichéd line, asks, "They can find whatever light is left in the dark . . . ? And will it serve me as a light at the end of the tunnel?", Jake assures him, "It will serve you as your own personal light eternal." (64)

Where Andy, who says, "You don't die if you're good," sees death as punishment, Jake views death as a compensation for a good life. In a parody of the Christian notion of heaven, he glibly asserts that the light "they find" is "a reward for all your labour and faith and all the concern and care for others you have demonstrated so eloquently for so long." (64) We have seen only the opposite of such eloquent "care and concern for others." The union of "eternal" and "light," which resonates with the moonlit landscape of death's dream kingdom, is a territory Andy has already imaginatively begun to explore more deeply. Talk of eternal light only leads Jake back to deriding their father, disparaging him with pity as "subjected to hatred and vituperation . . . [and] persecuted by a malignant force . . . resisting definition or classification." (67; ellipses mine) Anger bonds them to their father more obsessively than love could.

Jake suddenly withdraws his attack, "I pray for your understanding" and calls his father "an innocent bystander to his own nausea." (67) He inches toward acknowledging connection between himself and his father. The prodigy he claims for himself (a boy who wrote poetry before he could read) he now extends to his father: "At the age of three that man was already at the end of his tether. No wonder he yearned to leave to his loving son the legacy of all that was best and most valuable of his life and death." (67) The legacy they claim is not love but death and destruction.

Jake finally espouses to reciprocate his father's love—in the future: "He loved me. And one day I shall love him. I shall love him and be happy to pay the full price of that love." (67) Fred notes, "Which is the price of death" ("than which there is no greater price").[6] (67) Here, in their inversion, "Death ... [w]hich is the price of love," love and death, circle into a wedded band. (68) The brothers concur, in empty rhetoric reminiscent of Polonius, that that price is "strictly in accordance with the will of God," with "the laws of nature," with "common or garden astrological logic," and is "the first axiom ... And the last." (68) Jake closes with a caveat: "It may well be both tautologous and contradictory." (69) The tone of their reductive, rhetorical banter signals their distance from the real death in which they deal.

Like the complexity betokened in their multiple names, their alternating scorn and adulation expressed for the father, admits the polarity and fragmentation of character, which becomes, from the audience's superior perspective able to connect and integrate the factions, a kind of wholeness that disallows any assignment of hero or villain. Their praise for the man they called "Dad" peaks with Fred's borrowing from Hamlet's reverence for his dead father, "I shall not look upon his like again." (70) This reminder of Andy's distance from the noble king also underscores our own distance from the worldview in *Hamlet* which permits no stain upon the portrayal of the royal king and no saving grace for his villainous brother who murders him. (70) The larger end which the *Hamlet* quotation serves reinforces audience recognition of the hero and villain in us all.

The sons swerve back to heap more violent invectives on their father as "politically bankrupt, morally scabrous," and "spasmodically rampant," yet they resume an unprompted laudatory crescendo of acclaim for the man who "remained proud and fiery" and "a leader of men." (73) The comical closure, that he was referred to by the nickname "The Incumbent," emphasizes the opposite—Andy as a supporter of the status quo. The sons, unable to admit that their father exhibited an ordinary mortal's combination of commendable and destructive qualities, disclose their vision as subordinate to an ideal beset by an either/or fallacy. They must regard Andy as all good or all bad. Following a post-mortem spasm of selective amnesia that filters out all but the praiseworthy memories, they end in tribute that admits their one clear bond with their father: violence. Jake proffers praise for his father's "classic formula for dealing with troublemakers":

> A butcher's hook. (73)

As recipient of his father's abuse (meted out to him on one occasion as a child for his defiant refusal to clean out a broom cupboard), Jake shows how violence can be so easily passed down and perpetuated. When Fred then says, "Tell me about your mother," Jake terminates their talk with, "Don't talk dirty to me." (73) He turns upon her as an abused child frequently turns more unforgivingly, not upon the abusive parent, but upon the one who did not intercede to stop abuse or violence. Here, also, the mother's betrayals remain unforgiven while the father's, described as "spasmodically rampant," are whimsically dismissed. (73)

Bel, in the next section, returns to a loving remembrance of Maria who took her to lunch, squeezed her hand, and "asked about [her] girlhood." (74) Bel describes Maria's listening as so seductive that Bel confesses she could speak to her "in a way I had never spoken to anyone before," discovering that in Maria's presence she was "another person." (75) The passivity Bel exhibits, in allowing Maria to order her food at lunch, gives over to one reminiscence of her childhood where Bel briefly joined in the world of boys, running on the cliffs with her brothers. Being with Maria, one of the few expressions, here, of the transformational power of love, accessed that reminder of a more active self denoting a now long-forgotten agency. (73) But the transformation is momentary. That memory does not inform present action.

Andy, reminiscent of Deeley in *Old Times*, interjects himself as a spy on this girlhood scene, claiming that he was there behind a volume of *The Brothers Karamazov* and could read Bel's thoughts. Bel excludes his intrusion by reporting that Maria once confided, "women had something men didn't have," confessing that she had also thought to herself, "Men can be beautiful too." (77) Andy, who says he heard every word Bel thought, concludes, "She's the one we both should have married." Bel counters, "I think I should have married your friend Ralph." (77)

Only briefly annoyed at his wife's explicit profession of love for Ralph at his deathbed, Andy returns to happier memories—his love for Bel, a love long past, "And how I loved you. I'll never forget the earliest and loveliest days of our marriage. You offered me your body." (79) Andy does not resist an adolescent comic take. When Bel offered, "Do what you will," he says he replied, "I tell you what, hold on to it for a couple of minutes, will you? Hold on to it while I call a copper." (79) The superego as policeman intervened to inhibit his pleasure while Bel, now rhapsodically recalls hers: "Ralph had such beautiful manners and such a lovely singing voice." (79) Andy dismisses Ralph by asserting that she "got the wrong bloke," that his Ralph was "pedantic and scholastic . . . . Big ears but little feet." (80) Then, to vindicate and elevate himself, Andy echoes Bel, "Do you know what he said? He said men had something women simply didn't have." (80) He clinches his argument by aligning with Ralph to ratify male superiority, "Referees are the law. They are the law in action . . . . And that whistle is the articulation of God's justice." (80; ellipses mine)

Ralph next enters Andy's room with Maria who effusively asserts, "How wonderful you both look." (80) Together she and Ralph gleefully recount their life as lived largely through their children. The description of their country cottage on a lake or pond where they "made friends with so many cows" betokens a bucolic withdrawal from public affairs. (81) Ralph recalls he gave up refereeing without a regret, admitting he wasn't "born for it." (82) Andy seconds Ralph's self-assessment, "Well, you were no bloody good at it." (82) Theirs is, yet again, one of the many exchanges sprinkled throughout the play that promotes one's nature as a kind of fate. References range from Bridget's acknowledgement of her gifts as a physiotherapist, Jake's assertion that he wrote poetry before he was born, Ralph's claiming a natural talent for acting, painting, and the piano, and Bel's acknowledging that Andy is a loud mouth by nature. The play, however, convincingly counters with contradictory suggestions that characters have qualities and choices to allow change but that they lack the self-awareness to imagine them. Though Ralph concedes and Andy affirms, that he had no talent for refereeing, Maria asserts that she and Bel were dazzled by Ralph's gift of knowing where the ball would go before it was kicked. What is the truth?

The complexity finally gained in the many conflicting references throughout the play dramatizes not only how a single label diminishes and falsifies but, more important, exhibits the multiplicity of the self. The layered opposing references cumulatively build to a motif imparting a view of human life that recognizes a ying-yang wholeness. Both polar opposites may be true (as well as the implied, unacknowledged middle ground along the continuum between them); as Pinter has noted of the conflicting references in *Old Times*, "It all happened." *Moonlight*, in raising profound questions about innate talent, seeming fate, self-knowledge, and choice, comes out, as always in Pinter's plays, on the side of choice, freedom, and responsibility.

Self-knowledge in the West traditionally commences in knowledge of the self in the past. But where does the past self reside? When Ralph declares he often thinks of the past, Andy claims he remembers nothing, "I was a civil servant. I had no past." (83) Maria and Ralph as a chorus contend, "Lots of things happened," but Andy remains steadfast.

Andy even raises questions about a present self. When Maria inquires about their children, speculating that Bridget "must be a mother by now," Andy affirms, "I've got three beautiful grandchildren," yet he asks Bel for confirmation, "Haven't I?" (83) Bel sustains the focus on the present and directs it to Andy, "By the way, he's not well," and when Maria and Ralph refuse to acknowledge his dying, she states bluntly, "He's on the way out." (84) They contradict her with a shower of clichés insisting that Andy is "fit as a fiddle," with a "[c]onstitution like an ox." (85) Maria goes so far as to deny death entirely:

> People like Andy never die. That's the wonderful thing about them. (85)

Maria's denial of his death is as breathtakingly heartwrenching as Proust's similar depiction of the mortally ill Swann when he comes to the Guermantes seeking recognition that he is dying and they spin out to a party, focused only on their attire.

What the characters in *Moonlight* fail to realize is that self-knowledge is grounded in a vision and that their knowledge of self is limited by their present vision, which, furthermore, they fail to see and understand. Seeing and revising the present vision transforms the past, analogous to the way, in modern physics, the angle of the viewer changes what is viewed. The lens through which these characters view themselves is clouded by a received vision which demands of Andy, as he sums up his past life, a view of himself as good—all good—just as Jake and Fred wish to view him (and see themselves as better—even transcendently so). A revised vision, which relinquishes that dichotomizing and polarizing need and can own the whole self, allows relinquishing a view of the future-self as identified with a specific, finite—often limited and limiting—goal, to admit other possibilities undreamt. These characters do not see that their vision, fastened to a destructive view of the self in the past, cannot enlarge to a constructive view of the self in the present or the future.

The play drives inexorably and remorselessly to the ending as Bel telephones Jake and Fred to inform them, "Your father is very ill," but she is met only with Jake's and Fred's impudent "Chinese laundry?" (86) The comic is no longer funny. A deadly seriousness underlies the grim joke till Bel gives up, "It doesn't matter." (86) In this scene she evinces growing honesty and, regaining dignity, confirms her knowledge of their secret activities before she hangs up: "Do you do dry cleaning?" (87) Her "dry cleaning" question carries the slang suggestion of covert killing. But Bel is off the line when Jake addresses his phone, "Of course we do dry cleaning! What kind of fucking laundry are you if you don't do dry cleaning?" (88)

Andy, in his closing scene, asks where his grandchildren are, "the babies? My daughter?" (88) With only the lightest brushstroke of pathos, he asks, "Are they waiting outside?" (89) We know they will not come. He asks "What's happening?" Bel cannot accompany Andy on his journey, even empathetically, but she remains beside him and continues to develop a growing honesty. She answers him with a question, "Are you dying?" He answers with another question, "Am I?" (90) "Don't you know?" she asks. He says he does not. Andy's final concern, however, is not for himself but his daughter. "Tell Bridget not to be frightened." (90) In that moment we glimpse one of the rare instances of dramatic growth that we witness in the play: a character's expressed concern for another's welfare.

Maria and Ralph exude only a surface vibrancy which remains limited without a recognition of death. Bel's remembered love for Ralph, which may go further than the lust Maria inspired in Andy, may be one crowning expression of love in the play, but her love retains no connection to the Ralph we see when he enters Andy's death chamber with Maria. Bel and Ralph never speak to one another (nor do Andy and Maria) except when Bel addresses Maria and Ralph, asking them to acknowledge the truth, that her husband is dying. In that act she becomes Andy's ally, his comrade in arms in what may be the greatest act of love in the play. Her final words to Andy, also a painful truth, are that his children "haven't come." (90) Even in her simple expression she conveys her sorrow for him as well as her acknowledgement that she will not "still have" him.

The penultimate scene finds Fred out of bed, in shorts, and both brothers energized by Jake's return from the memorial: not for his father but for d'Orangerie. Jake exults, "Everyone was there." (91) His remote echo of Willy Loman's plans for his own death-of-a-salesman funeral emphasizes the contrast to Andy's by reminding us that, unlike Willy, Andy is not even mourned by his children—let alone "Everyone." Jake's brush with power has renewed both brothers' vitality as Jake proudly lists those in attendance, names largely Anglo and European but different from his earlier lists, suggesting that those at the service hold ranking power. The brothers express no grief, only the gain they experience in their proximity to the powerful attending the dead man whose only stated virtue was his violence. Jake and Fred concur, "He was much loved." (93) When Jake suggests, "Well, you loved him yourself, didn't you?", Fred severs himself from filial love of family with horrifying, heartbreaking finality, "I loved him like a father." (93) That the audience can be brought to care in that moment for the lost love between undesirable sons and a rather ordinary father and see Andy's connection to the Lieutenant-Colonel, not merely in death but in their violence (for all Andy's claim that he harmed no one) becomes a measure of the play's fresh vision.

The play closes with a return to moonlight as Bridget recounts a girlhood memory of being invited to a neighborhood party, probably by her parents, but she was not allowed to come with them: "They told me the party wouldn't begin until the moon had gone down." (94) She recalls that strange, aberrant moment, "The house, the glade, the lane, were all bathed in moonlight." (94) The shock comes, however, when she describes her arrival at the party and sees "the inside of the house was dark and all the windows were dark. There was no sound." (94) Her closing image describes what could be a waiting for death, "I stood there in the moonlight and waited for the moon to go down." (94) We, as witness to that image, are with her.

The play, which brightens from a moonless night at the beginning to a description of a flood of moonlight in the end, speaks out for love, once again endorsing the erotic qualities, those forces that enhance rather than destroy life. Andy may be dying and may have lived a largely dead life but in the vitality of his remembrances of love and lust and in his concern for others, however slight, remains the generative force, life. Andy's sons, in contrast, may destroy life in others and seem to be destroying it in themselves. Aside from the gig to which Jake at eighteen alludes and from Fred's needed rest-and-recuperation holiday, their lives seem circumscribed, defined, and strangulated by whatever risky work they do, which remains without the pleasures or goods of life. However thrilling their work seems (in contrast to their father's time-serving civil service) their pursuits unnerve Fred who is unraveling through much of the play to the edge of a burned-out breakdown. He is reinvigorated only by death: the account of d'Orangerie's memorial he was unable to attend "confined to [his] bed with a mortal disease." (91) His facetious tone disclaims his own mortality. Not once do the brother's claim their destruction by naming death as their game.

Contained in their discourse, disclaiming their father, are the blind gropings toward resolving their estrangement from their father. Their fixation on their father, their repeatedly circling back to the topic, almost spiraling to insight is similar to the way in which an audience may experience the play in which layers of ignorance are revealed and lifted. In the recognition that the initial impression of the play's gloom leaves out its real, more liberating, effect, the audience returns to the play to seek the cause of the liberation. In the flashes of disgruntled humor is contained the recognition that these characters are not vicious people. The characters we witness on stage are motivated and driven by ignorance and duplicity but not by malice and fraud. In this work, however, ignorance is malice, the form that human evil takes. Ignorance—of self, others, the world and our vision of it—when it actuates our choice and actions in the world, can be and often is destructive. Ignorance is the form that human evil takes in Pinter's work, yet, ironically, characters all believe their actions spring from love, a desire to do good and to survive. Pinter's plays never even flirt with those characters whose destruction springs from endogenous deficits—those whose innate hardwiring may impel them to destruction. His plays keep focused attention on the greater burden of violence that is born by those who have choices and may intend no harm, but only good which they may also believe requires eradicating those whom they perceive as evil. These characters, as we see, are trying to do what they believe is good, but they are acting out of an ignorance that leaves them blind to themselves and leaves us, finally, more with an impression of their self-estrangement rather than their destructiveness. They, like us, are people trying to glimpse and make sense of their future.

Andy's daughter Bridget, who provides one link with the future through grandchildren, appears before the audience retreated into a frozen past. Are destroyed or destructive children the legacy left by unawakened, enervated parents? Bridget, and the other women, Bel, and even Maria (despite her advanced or adventurous sexuality), all seem reduced, moreover, to radical and prescribed traditional gender roles as daughter, wife, and mother, cut off from participation in state affairs and the world of men. In this play, which is a call to action, we see none of the women choose to enter that world or even praise or encourage their daughters to do so. *Moonlight*, beginning and ending with Bridget, only a generation removed from the highly protected post-second world war women with limited access to the public world, addresses that need through the women here infantalized and devalued by their almost exclusively redomesticated roles. The women themselves, however, bear some responsibility for perpetuating their own imprisonment or exclusion from power. Maria mentions Bridget only as a mother and primarily promotes her son, not her daughters. She specifies her son's work—Lucien is "at the Consulate"—while she twice reports, only vaguely—Sarah is "doing marvelously well," and Susannah, "there's no stopping her." (18, 81) Ironically, she herself may be stopping her in her failure to recognize constraints on both her daughters. As a mirror of our time, *Moonlight*, through Jake and Fred's references to international monetary systems, addresses imperial oppression of women and men in the Third World. If the women here are cut off from agency and its attendant power, the men are cut off from the forces of generation.

Jake and Fred's world, except for one reference to Bridget, to their mother, and to one nameless woman Jake cites primarily to convey his own sexual prowess, seems devoid of women as comrades, lovers, or colleagues and, as such, is exclusive of the erotic—the generative qualities of life. Although Jake claims he was "a very very close friend of the woman Riley ran away with," he is not speaking of friendship at all. (59) When Fred says, "I think she taught you a thing or two," Jake replies, "She taught me nothing she hadn't learnt herself at the feet of the master" (a nice double take that could refer equally to himself or to Riley). (59) Jake's brutal tone reduces sex without love to something less than lust and strips sex of the erotic. The greatest ecstasy Jake expresses comes in the exultation he exudes returning from among the powerful attending the memorial for d'Orangerie, whose violence joins their love to death's destruction. D'Orangerie's power, however, did inspire their love. While their love could be dismissed as identification with his power that fills a desperate void in the brothers, the transcendent rush they feel may be no less ardent than erotic love's, perhaps more so, considering its desperate source. Yet few of us can deny acquaintance with the seductive force of love's euphoria or claim no understanding of its joy. Their ecstatic love may be a false love and destructive. But its power cannot be underestimated.

In *Moonlight*, the erotic, life-enhancing forces again seem unable to equal, let alone to defend against or counter, the destructive forces at any level—the private, the public, or the global. The characters do not even acknowledge such destruction. How can the bureaucratic father, who imagines he has harmed no one all his life, acknowledge that his sons may be thugs or butchers serving the same state he served? His sons at least admit connection to their father through his weapon of choice: the meat hook.

The father's more subtly unacknowledged weapons are of the psyche. Andy never imagines that his withholding parental love in response to his son's refusal, as a child, to clean out a broom cupboard might have done any damage nor that his failure to supply at least an older person's wisdom or perspective, instead of his judging both his sons bastards, might have contributed to making them the men they are. Or are we to imagine they are "bastards" by nature? Given our glimpse of them in their teens it does not seem so. Andy never acknowledges the bastard in himself. To see

Moonlight without recognition of our own destructive bastard that can spring from a desire for transcendent love turns the recognition and naming of those qualities in Andy, Jake, and Fred into character-bashing in the name of rational analysis but leaves us sanctimoniously blind to ourselves. What is worse, without vigilance and insight into the seductive power of the destructive predator in the unconscious, we disempower ourselves. Whenever we are stunned or stopped in our actions, we can easily remain trapped, like Stanley in *The Birthday Party*, cornered, by the mistaken belief that "there's nowhere to go."

Yet those who profess they possess love through their actions, Maria and Ralph, even those who once had love in the past, Bel and Andy, remain like those in *Party Time* who profess to love but remain solipsistically locked into a love which does not extend much beyond the self, unable, here, to extend love to the present or to the borders of family. Moreover, the love expressed by the older generation, rather than growing over time, seems tied to a biological clock that runs down when hormones diminish.

Love and death in *Moonlight* converge in the end, wedded in a partnership where death threatens to engulf love to destroy life. In portraying our three choices which promote survival and destruction—choices of attitude, intention, and action identified by Kant—the play shows both that love requires embracing all three and that attitude, intention and action which promote survival must extend from the private to the public levels if any global justice is to be achieved. Love at the private level, exemplified through Bel and Andy, transmitted to their sons, Jake and Fred, transforms into public injustice. In this way the play finally dramatizes how almost all choice and subsequent action are a choice between life or death. Since Andy at the close of the play may be beyond all choice, the play poses that final choice to the audience.

Moonlight thus becomes far more than a reminder of death that can momentarily reawaken an audience to a joyful awareness of life. *Moonlight* goes beyond awakening the audience to awareness of how everyday choices become life-and-death choices that lead either to survival or destruction. In portraying the link between self-knowledge and consciousness, as Andy gropes toward greater truths by unmasking the hypocrisy in civilization's myths, the play also reveals consciousness as achievable by seeing and understanding the masternarrative we live by and revising (re-seeing) it. The history of human progress can be measured in the development of consciousness. That vision of responsibility, expressed in *Moonlight* by its obvious absence in the characters, can empower an audience by inspiring action.

How *Moonlight* conveys that vision can be appreciated by likening the play to a person, schematically perceived as a series of four concentric circles—the outside circle represents that person's outer being acting and responding to the outside world, the second circle inside, the emotion which sometimes rules those outer actions and reactions, and the third circle in the conscious intellect, which, in Western thought, is perceived as capable of bringing emotions under control and actions to a rational end. At the core of the circle is Psyche's realm, the unconscious self, the dream world, the spirit, what might be called the soul. Through *Moonlight's* fractal geometry, disclosing the core of the play through the surface action of each scene, the play's vision is communicated at depth as one soul speaking directly to another: the play's core communing directly with the audience's unconscious and, through the surface-level drama, bringing what is unconscious into consciousness.

Not all plays, poems, or fiction exhibit a developed inner core any more than all human beings do so. We have traditionally given such names as seer, shaman, Bodhisattva, wise or holy person to people who do so in recognition of the depth of their inner wisdom and ability to transmit their gifts and vision to others. It is not that the surface of such a person is unimportant but, rather, that the whole human being can speak in consort. Each word and act can become a medium for communicating far deeper truths than when a quest is limited by the guidance of reason alone. In the same way, the surface conflict in *Moonlight* conveys the core's truths. That is not to say that *Moonlight* devalues reason, despite Andy's and Ralph's disparaging remarks. Just the opposite. Despite the red flag thrown upon rationality, forcing our reexamination of its limitations, the importance of reason in Pinter's work remains undiminished, emphasizing here how the intellect must act in consort with emotion and action, informed by a fresh vision if action is to serve ethical, life-promoting ends.

The vision at the core in *Moonlight* allows Pinter to trust his audience further than in any of his other work. It is not necessary nor may it be possible to apprehend each innuendo of each scene on a first viewing in order to comprehend the deeper felt/truths

Moonlight expresses. The level-one surface of *Moonlight* remains as important as ever. Through stealth and even seeming scatology, through puzzling, unanswerable mysteries, and through a conflict that threatens to explode shattering characters' lives, each scene's action glues the audience to the journey's end to lead us through death's realm in order to confront the deepest mysteries of love, life, and survival.

Moonlight goes further still. The play's core unfolds a vision that re-awakens the audience to the knowledge that not to confront death is to be controlled by it—to be destructive in one's choices and actions; not to confront the destructive bastard in the self is to act the bastard in life. The play, which presents no answers to survive, poses questions for the audience trusting us to pursue what is needed for individual and global survival. By raising the question of survival to its highest pitch and by leaving us with it at the end to make that final question our own, the play sends us on a living quest, entrusting us to the service of the love and life it celebrates.

Yet, except for poets and the mad, it is easy to lose that moment whose effect might be like hearing an inspiring sermon, then resolving to change, only to break that resolve, or forget, the next day. How is a destructive vision with all its attendant and profoundly ingrained, habitual attitudes and action swept away? A vision is more than a beginning—once seen, it cannot easily become unseen. Pinter's dominant/subservient conflict writes disturbing questions in the blood that can only be dispelled by taking action.

Moonlight engages the dominant/subservient conflict with new subtlety and to a fresh end which weds private love to global justice through questions which celebrate the freedom to question. It addresses, for the first time in Pinter's plays, the destructive, even deadly, qualities inherent in subscribing to what is still perceived by many in the world as seeming natural hierarchy: in birth order, and in the authority granted the father within the family, and in male-female relationships within the private and public world. The play challenges the seemingly natural, hereditary order that automatically grants Jake, as first born, the dominant position over his younger brother. Fred, at first, ingratiatingly compliant to Jake, later defies Jake's primogeniture with his own cunning. His early flattery expressed for Jake's poetic talent later reveals itself as the reverse side of his threats, and his attitude-swings afford us a glimpse of how the malignancy of any relationship which diminishes or destroys another turns against the self—Fred is bedridden through most of the play. Killing others is tough work and is also killing him. He remains blind, however, to the ways exerting destructive power only momentarily inflates the ego but leaves the core of the self deflated, a void that keeps him trapped in one of Psyche's "mortal" illnesses.

Likewise, *Moonlight* questions the seemingly "natural" right of paternity which places Andy in automatic authority over his sons. When Andy blindly lashes out against an infraction of his command by redressing the person not the act (by withdrawing his love and viewing his sons as bastards), he abdicates responsibility as parental leader and guide.

Similarly, through the women in the play, *Moonlight* addresses the blindness to seemingly natural hierarchy in patriarchy. Bel and Maria remain as blithely unaware of their subservience to male tyranny which rules their public world but does not admit their agency in it as they are to their own responsibility for their daughters' exclusion from that world. In their refusal to confront conflict, they sit it out, only to remain, at some level, like the sixteen-year-old Bridget, disengaged and disenfranchised, unable to contribute their strengths fully or effectively at any level, outside, or even within, the family.

In Bel and Andy's contentious banter, and in their references to the unnamed something each sex has that the other does not, *Moonlight* also addresses the surface dominant/subservient conflict as a Punch-and-Judy split between the sexes. At depth, like all the characters, they reinforce that split by unquestioning acceptance of the perceived traditional roles; assigning nurturing qualities to women and destructive qualities to the men. The destructive nature of the split between the sexes to both men and women is reflected in even the smallest unconsciously-made, received choice which allows Bel to condemn Andy's "obscene language" (often the erotic language betokening generative elements of pleasure, birth, and growth) as destructive, and to view herself as superior for eschewing such words. The larger issue Bel fails to see is what Andy's honesty demands but fails to gain by bullying: acknowledgement of the lie and hypocrisy in that split. To endorse the split consciously is to retain it unconsciously and to be imprisoned in a traditional vision which Moonlight reveals denies both men and women ability to claim power to assume responsibility for survival.

Only Bridget comes forward to heal that split. Instead of supplying a Horatio or a young hero to define a normative path that can correct the overwhelming ills of an "unweeded" kingdom, Pinter, through a girl, a maiden, takes us to that nether world not "dreamt of in [Horatio's] philosophy" to revise the vision of anyone who can see and hear her. (*Hamlet,* I, v, 167) Seeing and acknowledging Bridget's vision can summon our own fresh vision. She has entered the dark night of the soul and, like Harold as a child during the Second World War, witnessed death's battlefield. She traversed it, survived, and now becomes our knight and bringer of light, albeit moonlight (classically a feminine source of light) not the primary light of the sun. She is imprisoned, without agency in the public world. Pinter said he believes she is dead. However, though the wonderful irony of *Moonlight,* Bridget, as Psyche's voice, assumes the largest agency in the play: communicating the play's vision to the entire audience. Although in the present time of the play in Andy's mind her outer self has escaped grown up, and had children, she remains, in her own psyche, trapped in the past. Only we can release her dead voices. How? By attending to what she sees.

Literally, she offers us only what she sees. But to perceive and receive the deeper core of that space lit by moonlight we must be wholly present to her, to see that her vision is our own, the underworld's death hold on life, which we share with her, standing with her at the end before the darkened house.

By claiming our own darkness from the unconscious, we bring her into light. When we heal that surface split (the separation between Bridget's dark vision, perceived as other, as our own), we release her vision into our consciousness to begin the return journey to life. Bridget's healing powers are variously acknowledged in the play. Although as a girl she says she wants to become a physiotherapist, a healer of the body who can release physical pain, we never learn whether she entered any other world outside her home; but, significantly, she is acknowledged as a healer of the psyche. When Fred says "She always understood my feelings," Jake and Fred each emphasize that point by repeating, "She understood me too." (62–63) In that understanding, which the play offers the audience, begins the deeper healing to inform a new vision and can change the course of action.

Bridget, as midwife to the plays vision, delivering it to us through the words she speaks, becomes a friend, as the twenty-year old Pinter described a friend in *The Dwarfs,* "an ambassador from yourself to yourself. A go-between. A man of your soul." (177) To deny her vision is to deny friendship in the larger sense of fellowship in the larger community and to reinforce the split. That becomes tragic, as Pinter in *The Dwarfs* defined Shakespeare's tragedy: characters destroyed not by their weaknesses but because they are overcome by their strengths.

Tragedy awaits *Moonlight's* characters and their children who remain blind—unconscious—to how strengths, when developed to excess, exclude and atrophy their opposite qualities. Keeping the shadow side in thrall, the greatest strengths can destroy the other, the self, and both. Andy's "loud mouth . . . nature" may have gained him his power as a man feared at work, but, developed without balance from its opposite, reflective powers, that strength becomes a destructive power, transmitted to his sons who go on to destroy others. Obversely, Bridget has cultivated her own safety in Pysche's realm, but without claiming some of her father's "loud mouth" quality in the public world—at least the power to speak publicly—she may go unheard, or worse, like Cassandra, she may remain unable to effect any needed change in life around her to insure the safety of an other.

The strengths of the men and women in *Moonlight*, as in almost all Pinter's characters, are rooted in survival instincts but, allowed unchecked rein, insure only the ego's survival at the expense of the psyche which, if ignored, unconscious, or unempowered, threatens to destroy civilization. The drive for power to survive, embodied in Jake and Fred as split off from nurturing embodied in a mother, sister, lover, or a brother or father, becomes, when unchecked, a predatory power for destruction. Jake attempts to succor his ailing brother with his promised reward of eternal light, but Jake's narrative only leaves Fred prostrate, choosing to remain, instead, in bed.

Moonlight returns to this book's opening thesis that Pinter's vision, instead of promoting the human as a powerless, already doomed creature on this planet, offers, even inspires, hope, not reflected to us in the characters' actions but as refracted light passing through and illuminating their darkened unconscious, bent through them to us in the way that white light, passing through a prism, bends into a rainbow of color. We are connected to those characters by the same white light of *Moonlight*, though they are denied the full spectrum. Through the limited and destructive, even deadly, dark unconscious vision of the characters, *Moonlight's* light, evoked by Bridget, floods the audience.

Grave danger awaits anyone who refuses the light. To deny our connection to these characters because they are unconscious and see white light where we see color, or worse, to assume our superiority to them becomes an act of overweening pride, *hubris* that can only inspire destruction. Disclaiming our own innate predator, our connection with Jake and Fred remains on par with the reverse, Bel's excusing Andy's behavior as his nature. The former denies the interior destructive qualities of a survival drive which we all share and, the latter excuses the excessive imbalance in the development of those destructive qualities as beyond our power to change. By acknowledging our core kinship with all the characters in *Moonlight*, we become the hero/heroine life demands and Bridget as messenger is sent to summon.

Moonlight's characters may seem a lost, far cry from Hamlet, who, with his superior intelligence and wit, embraces heroic action by weeding the state's rank, unweeded garden, or from Oedipus who embodies heroic action, cleansing his state by acknowledging responsibility, blinding and exiling himself. In blinding himself he accepts and owns responsibility for his actions, even for choices made before his birth. That act, which gives necessity or fate its due, more importantly, dignifies human action by suggesting we are responsible. We cannot reverse his blindness nor revoke his exile, but *Moonlight* can lift our blindness and reconnect us to community by allowing us to see the play's vision, which, by positing choice with us, similarly dignifies our smallest action and affirms our responsibility.

To appreciate what distance Pinter's vision has come it is helpful to recall how, when Richard in the early play *The Lover* commanded his wife Sarah to "change," it is unlikely at that time, that either Richard or Pinter, and least of all the audience, saw those two characters in any relationship except locked into a losing battle flailing blindly against received notions of married lovers—a primary bond, hermetically sealed, that becomes lethal. Moreover, Richard's closing demand, however provocative, remains aimed at Sarah, not the audience.

Saying "change" makes no change happen for the characters and *The Lover* deadends at the close with the growth posited in the husband-wife/lovers of this play. However many identification points occur, they remain other and without engaging the audience at the level that Bridget does in *Moonlight.*

Drama is a reciprocal transaction between the dramatist, who must capture and retain audience attention, and the audience, who must pay attention to the action at the surface if the deeper vision is to be received. If either fails, the transaction is broken. *Moonlight* never loses tension. Paying attention here requires more than attending to the action with eyes, ears, and intellect. It requires being fully present, open to precisely what is happening without the interference of intellect going off, as actor Paul Rodgers cautions, after some irrelevancy.

Close attention leads back to the play's one unanswerable question: Why is Bridget frozen into her sixteen-year-old past? Set apart through lyrical language evoking Psyche's dream world, Bridget never appears to us grown into womanhood. We hear of her only as a mother, which bespeaks her erotic and generative qualities, as the only one of the younger generation mentioned as offering children to the future. Her sixteen-year-old innocence might suggest why she is selected to be the messenger who brings us the light, but in *Moonlight* such innocence is, like Blake's innocence, ignorance. In accepting that light we must ask why she is trapped. Keeping Bridget a *puella/puer* is to deny the erotic, which requires accepting both love and death. For us, as for Bridget, not to grow up becomes a danger we pass on, as Andy does, as our legacy. To choose to remain in an enervated Never Never Land of eternal youth keeps us and our children from recognizing the overwhelmingly attraction of child-like innocence as a destructive predator that can stop us and others dead in our tracks. Who has trapped Bridget and what prevents her from fully growing up? It might be tempting to blame the father, Andy, and by extension, patriarchy. Again we, as woman and man must claim responsibility for trapping her, preventing her from fully growing up. How? Like the characters, by not growing up ourselves, by remaining blind, unconscious to what traps her, and, by extension, us. *Moonlight* illuminates a vision which demands action.

That action begins in questioning which is the form in which the play's vision is delivered. And because the message comes not from the surface, as information or didactic directive, but from the core, it allows us to see, feel, and know how, among the most ordinary of human beings one can be severed from love, from living one's own life, and can engender destructive progeny. Pinter's writing process seems able to access and dredge his own unconscious so that his work avoids what novelist and poet Edna O'Brien cautions against, "that element of strain when the conscious and not the unconscious is seen to be pulling the strings." (1) The play, in recruiting us as witness/participant in its life, continues after the end and breathes hope. Recognition of the light, however, is not enough, and Pinter's vision offers more.

Moonlight's vision reminds us of the limits of language, that mere words are not things in themselves. As a much quoted Sufi proverb reminds us, the word "moon" is not the moon, only a finger pointing at the moon. Bridget stands before a closed door to a darkened house, suggesting, as in the Eleusinian mysteries, the key is under the tongue. It is not enough to be *told* her vision, to hear or even "see" her words as images describing what she sees. We have to take the key and unlock the door. To open the door is to look at death as a mirror and to see the self coming the other way—as Andy describes it before his own vision shifts and enlarges—a "fright" and a fearful experience but it is also freeing. In that terrifying confrontation and acknowledgement of death begins Andy's acknowledgement of caring for others, beyond the self-referential ecstatic ephemeral love for Maria and Bel. That care for another becomes a going out of the self, another kind of ecstasy, that embraces the other, fosters the other's welfare, and promotes it, freeing both the self and other: "Tell Bridget not to be afraid." Stopping short of any action, his last words in this play are not even spoken directly to Bridget. Of course, that journey, out of fear into courage, ("not to be afraid") is one she/we will have to make herself/ourself as [E]very man and woman must.

We can remain standing before the closed door or open the door. Who knows what is behind the door? In questions begin self-knowledge and the wisdom that courage requires. The questions *Moonlight* raises are four questions basic to self preservation, and the preservation of anyone else beyond the self:

> What stands behind the door? What is not as it appears? What do I know deep in my [unconscious] I do not wish to know? What of me has been killed, lays dying [or is killing others]? (Estés, 56)

The play gives us most of the clues we need to answer the riddle central to life and survival. Death stands behind the door, and those who appear and think themselves good, harmful to no one, may be destructive, but I do not wish to acknowledge that destructive force in myself, yet if I fail to, I may remain like Bridget deadened into the past that does not grow up or like Stanley in *The Birthday Party*, with "nowhere to go" and nowhere to take anyone else. Death may stand behind the door as nothing, the dark unconscious, the void, yet, more significantly, it is the place where we remain in life if we deny the light of consciousness.

Although Bridget's journey into her psyche admits us as fellow traveler, we see again how Pinter's work challenges the masternarrative central to psychotherapy that promotes the remembering things past as journey toward healing. Several of Pinter's filmscripts dramatize how rehearsing the past may be either helpful or harmful to the self and others, depending upon whether the journey is taken to serve love or death. *The French Lieutenant's Woman* reveals the healing power of confession when it is coupled with a desire to live and to seek the truth as Sarah is transformed and delivered by love and unburdening herself from melancholic despair (though Sarah's actual narrative of the confession is a fabrication!) into a productive woman who nurtures her lover and inspires young children. Robert's confession in *Comfort of Strangers*, however, becomes a deadly force when driven by an unacknowledged, unresolved desire for revenge. Robert kills the thing he loves. Robert's telling the factual truth, informed only by a darkened unconscious, turns truth as rational fact into a dead, even deadly, artifact.

Moonlight challenges the ultimate masternarrative, the unconscious vision by which we live. Negative qualities of the other are unconsciously presented, in that vision, as different, split off, to be denied and kept separate from the self. Bringing that vision's destructiveness into consciousness suggests what fresh vision is required. Pinter's vision goes beyond words but restores the faith necessary to retain freedom: trust, in this life, that there is somewhere to go. *Moonlight*, as all Pinter's plays, trusts us to find the way. Taking us on a journey through words to that realm like that "from whose borne no traveler returns" offers us the moon—her light—to awaken us in time, and in doing so, Pinter's work no less than Proust's can give the reader/audience another lifetime.

We are finally returned to Pinter's early germane cautionary reminder that no insight, statement, or conclusion can be regarded as "definitive." The characters' statements and our insights, like almost all self-referential statements in Pinter's work, frequently denote a truth that lies in the opposite of what is professed. Ralph's claiming he has no talent for refereeing may be false. The many suggestions of fate as a quality in human nature which one cannot change may also be false, but that does not deny innate gifts or deficiencies in these characters who again dramatize the complex balance between chance and choice in human life. Despite Maria's expressed cheerleader enthusiasm for her daughters' achievements, our recognition that Maria may be stopping herself and her daughters from entering public life is partially correct, but in another sense the reverse is also true: given the entry of women into the public workforce and public life everywhere (amply in evidence in Pinter's own family among his wife and her daughters), there is almost "no stopping" her as a woman from greater participation—except as we stop her/us.

Acknowledging complexity is the responsibility that rests with any interpretation of Pinter's work. Again, the contradictions and unresolved mystery in Pinter's work do not license the conclusion that there is no truth in his work, or none we can finally articulate. The fact that an insight may require qualification does not negate its larger truth. We are cautioned by Pinter's injunction that his statements are not definitive to recognize, instead, how, almost any statement we as audience and interpreter make, may, like the self-referential statements characters make throughout Pinter's work, call up the truth contained in its opposite. These characters are not, finally, ordinary. Andy's extraordinary vitality on the threshhold of death is only one instance. The fact that we do not know what is killing him, however, speaks to what we do not wish to acknowledge, is, at a deeper level, killing us. To say that Pinter has given us a fresh vision is, also, not entirely true. The vision which comes to light in *Moonlight* illuminates a retrospective view of all Pinter's work allowing us to see it was lodged there from the beginning. Nor is Pinter alone in giving this vision voice. Toni Cade Bambara, addressing the First International Women Playwright's Conference, noted that we are all writing the same play—to save the world from the psychopaths. To recognize that we are the psychopath is not as comfortable as recognizing that the psychopath is the other. We, like Andy, shudder at the image in the mirror. Embracing that uncomfortable image and knowledge merely as blame or guilt can arrest rather than inspire action. But accepting it as responsibility becomes empowering, and despite the myriad obstacles, even joyful, as Yeats expressed when he said that impossible tasks make life worth living.

While *Moonlight* delightfully celebrates life, it equally disturbs with pressing reminders of the timeliness and urgency required to expedite change.

A paradigm shift, a core revision of a masternarrative by which we live our lives, can inspire and produce swifter change than attempts at surface changes unconsciously driven by an obsolete destructive vision of the self and other.

Classically, a work of literature has been evaluated in terms of the stature of the hero, the worthiness of his quest, and his actions which cleanse a society of some pollution or destructive force. To confront a worthy opponent in the face of an opposing fate and against impossible odds, in order to secure the safety and peace of a community is the classical enactment of the heroic quest. *Moonlight* does precisely that but with the significant shift that places responsibility not in some extraordinary leader we watch but in the audience. Through this play, we see that to confront the forces of human destruction (a worthy opponent) in the face of our human "nature" and our internalized received laws/vision (an opposing fate) in an overcrowded world threatening itself with a doubled population, with conventional, chemical, and nuclear devastation, and with environmental desolation (impossible odds) in order to secure safety and the peace of the global community all become our task (a revised heroic quest). To accept that quest is not Andy's task but again becomes [E]very man and woman's. To recognize and reclaim the hero's responsibility as our own is to see that we are not choiceless as Pinter's disempowered characters believe but, also, to see that there are limits to the alternatives. His work shows that choices are not infinite and that it is not easy to know which are correct.

The philosopher in quest of a general moral principle, must ask, How *ought* we act? This dramatist addresses that knottiest of all ethical problems—the quest for a fundamental moral principle—by pointing in the direction of life: to make choices that serve life rather than destruction in the larger global, not merely the parochial, community. Self-defense remains one justification for destroying another human being (one cannot serve others when one is dead), but the self-defense that can insure the safety of the future and our children comes from proactive actions that spring from a revised vision which we must communicate through our interactions with others.

Doing good, as ever in the Pinter canon, requires not following orders but asking questions and taking command of the self, a course never absolutely clear and seldom easy. Pinter, as he says of Shakespeare, never throws us a "lifeline." There are no answers here, as offered in modern morality plays which unconsciously present an occluded vision that promotes human beings as separated from parts of the self and as separate from others. The compassion in Pinter's vision, as he has consciously applied it to his characters, embraces the ultimate compassion—regarding the other as another self—and trusts us to find a way to do so. Pinter does allow the approach of Bridget's presence—the play's genius, as the lover who expresses such love for her parents she fears to wake their sleep—to cast the play in an enchantment that can wake us at the end: by returning us to the beginning of the play and like a Genii half escaped from the magic lamp, she awaits our wishes in order to act. In wishes and desires begin all action. Though her parents, asleep in the beginning and perhaps absent from the darkened house at the end, we are reminded that throughout the play the characters are without wishes or desires. More correctly, they wish for sausages and dross where they might wish for gold—the gold of friendship, fellowship, and love. They do not connect love to justice; even though the sons recite a catechism that rejoices in "God's justice," they utter words without meaning to them. The characters here do not think to wish for concord even at the private level. How could such a wish extend, therefore, any further into the larger community? We in the audience, however, harbor such wishes and desires, though they sometimes seem so large and impossible that fearing such wishes cannot come true, we dare not articulate them. Bridget stands incomplete and waiting at the end.

As her brothers say, she would understand. Having evoked her own soulscape, revealing her father's life and the lives of his sons, she has cast a light on our own dark ignorance. By showing us "the steep and thorny" way rather than "the primrose path" and by illuminating that path with *Moonlight's* vision, she has, at the very least, shown us that there is a path, and we are better prepared for the difficult task.[7]

Moonlight's vision, which ultimately defines the paradigm shift required to move from a destructive to a constructive view of the world and of our ways of acting in it, is news in the sense William Carlos Williams spoke of "the news": "It is difficult/to get the news from poems/yet men die miserably everyday/for lack of what is found there." (150–151) Pinter's vision communicates Rilke's injunction, "Du musst dein Leben ändern," that is, "You must change your life." (60) First, however, it is necessary to know the current self.

Pinter's work, which increasingly correlates ignorance with evil, also affirms all knowledge—from knowledge of the self to knowledge of the world—as necessary to the ethic. *Moonlight* further dramatizes a need for knowledge of death. Without death the loveliest flora—hibiscus, oleander and bougainvillea—growing unchecked, can almost suffocate and the denial or fear of death can lead, as it does in the sons and the father, to a worship of death (in the sons) and to destructive acts (in the sons and the father). None who deny death are immune to its destructive effects.[8]

In claiming all generative knowledge necessary for survival as one knowledge, the erotic and the ethic combine in *Moonlight* into an erotic ethic. The erotic ethic, which affirms psyche's knowledge as consort to carnal knowledge and reason's wisdom (all knowledge as one in human flesh), reveals itself as one through love's knowledge. Love's knowledge, all knowledge required to survive and thrive, also addresses the apparent split between the aesthetic and the ethic, the dominant and subservient, the masculine and feminine, and love and death. The erotic ethic, becoming one through love's knowledge, dramatizes love on a continuum with justice: the knowledge, wisdom and action necessary to sustain just life.

Moonlight, finally far less a *momento mori* than a reminder that you must live, remains a reminder of both life and death. To live requires acknowledging kinship with the other. The same extraordinary compassion Pinter expresses for all his characters now extends, through his characters, to us, allowing us to extend it to others. The play, thus, addresses Pinter's earlier question, whether any writing can enlarge our view of the world or change the way we act in it. *Moonlight* answers that, finally, not as a call to change but as a work that can change us. In doing so it becomes an act. As one light among many illuminating our way into a new century, the play assumes its own agency and becomes an act of love.

Notes

1. On the surface *Moonlight* reflects the Thatcher/Reagan-Bush era's endorsement of dominant/subservient conflicts perpetuated between people and nations in the name of creating partnerships. It portrays the recent past, the West's entering an economic landscape on the decline while it fought fiercely to bolster the globally exported imperial American Dream of unlimited economic growth for the world's privileged. And since, in Pinter's work, the fiercest battles are those fought to *maintain* rather than to gain something, Jake and Fred's violence, representing the forces in power, will most likely escalate.

   The play, which looks back at the decade of the eighties, and at the present moment, is poised toward a world threatening to double its population in the next twenty years.
2. Life is replete with instances of abdicating one's own power, giving it over to others. At the moment of this writing, in the wake of the dissolution of the Soviet Union, some opinion poles among Russian citizenry report that fifty percent want a return to dictatorship, expressing a desire to place power in the hands of another rather than claim responsibility at any level in the self. But choosing to return to hierarchy, which dictatorship demands, only postpones inevitably ensuing conflicts and destruction which, Pinter's plays reveal, occur whenever a dominant/subservient relationship defines human transactions. Yet, are our own choices we make entirely different?
3. Andy, in placing himself as subordinate to the audience as a hero-as-schlemiel, dissipates any envy which a character displaying evidence of sexual prowess might evoke and, instead, wins audience sympathy.

4. The suggestion that family includes one's neighbors may sound like the impossible ideals of the French Revolution, the liberty, equality and fraternity implemented in bloody action that sent Wordsworth scurrying back from France to England into the bucolic countryside singing his equally ideal hope of the poet as redeemer: "What we have loved others will love and we will teach them how." But to mock such notions is to forget that free societies are founded on such principles, and if we have not been able to realize them fully in our action, we may question the causes that prevent us from doing so and seek remedy and change.

5. Andy's claim is distantly akin to Nicolas's, the torturer's self-proclaimed direct connection to God in *One for the Road*.

6. Their claim that "that there is no greater price" for love than death distantly echoes what is often interpreted as divine justification and glorification of warfare killing in the Gospels—the defense of friends—and hints at the divine sanction which the brothers believe inspires their work: "Greater love hath no man than this, that a man lay down his life for his friends." (John, 15: 13) See also, footnote 8 below.

7. I am indebted to Carl Dennis for the Genie analogy, for informing the argument that Pinter has stripped away all the Hamlets, and for the distinction drawn between the ignorance and duplicity of these characters rather than malice and fraud.

8. *Moonlight* also dramatizes ways in which death is love's gift to life. Within the larger life/death/life cycle, death is one way of cleansing the old vision to make way for the new. In a death-denying culture it is in this sense that only the lover who has known death can become a true lover. *Moonlight* becomes an initiation into a deeper love. The lover (a lover of this world's greatest gift—life) realizes more than the awful brevity of life and how death deepens love, but through knowledge of death also internalizes an acceptance of one's own death as necessary for sweeping away the destructive vision of the past and allowing the evolving vision its life. In that sense, too, one becomes a friend of the world laying down one's life for a friend. Death becomes midwife to life.

   In many indigenous mythologies such as the Inuit, Lady Death or Skeleton Woman not only enfolds the already dying but as Sedna, she governs birth, midwifery, opening the passages from death to life, the pathways of the mother's milk (Estés, 136–150)

   The new vision *Moonlight* offers, not as a finger pointing to the moon but the real moon, remains for us a reminder that the fat face of the man in the moon was also seen anciently as a stick man carrying a bundle of sticks (bones).

Ashes to Ashes, The Dreaming Child, and *Celebration:* Desire, Destruction, Responsibility and the Complicity of Women

How bored or desperate do you have to be to "remember" being brutalized during a Holocaust atrocity by a man you claim was a lover and then use that "memory" to rouse your partner's jealousy, as Rebecca does in *Ashes to Ashes?* How empty does your life have to be to converse in a restaurant with the host, listen to the waiter's litany of the waiter's grandfather's feats, and purchase their respect, while threatening those who've come to celebrate your wedding anniversary, as Lambert does in *Celebration?* What is it that really prompts Rebecca's remembrances? What ignites the celebrants'animosity?

Why do the characters seek to destroy one another as they do? Questions in Harold Pinter's two most recent plays extend that essential question raised in his last play that appeared before his sixtieth birthday celebration, *Party Time,* which exposes Western power brokers' play for power as paramount. Above all else, even as the party timers party, they jockey for power, elbow aside their marginalized women, easily quash the targets of their guns—the uprising protesters outside their walls—while they themselves, arrogantly settled within cozy assumptions of their own safety and superiority, fiercely focus on retaining power in the name of a greater cause.

Now, ten years later, what fresh perspective does Pinter at seventy advance about the people with guns, drugs, and money who run the world?

Questions in *Ashes to Ashes* and *Celebration* edge closer to "the mystery of life," a phrase used for the first time at the end of *Celebration* exposing a shift from the dialectic of warring opposites that propelled Pinter's conflicts in the past to a tangle of those opposites inextricably wedded in these characters driven by no cause—other than sustaining and promoting self-interested power.

What new insights does Pinter offer his vast audiences of more ordinary citizens, excluded from the party rooms of power, on constructive ways to confront ongoing global conflicts in a world where all of us remain complicit if we do not? These two brief plays more tightly wed domestic conflict to global violence, and sex to power, disclosing how fear, greed, and lovelessness subvert power from socially productive ends to abet global conflict's ongoing destruction. Where Pinter's earlier plays portray destructors as driven by a desire to promote a large, external, overriding cause that links duty to God and country to magnify the importance of the self and to give "meaning" to life, these characters play by rote the power plays, driven neither an overriding desire nor by social conscience; they seek simply power for power's sake.

Without a clear, overriding desire beyond the self to define and propel the conflict, can these plays move us? Characters in these plays express desire so deeply hidden that driving dramatic desire seems almost absent. Yet, drama, like life, is driven by desire. What characters want and do to get it defines both character and conflict and renders drama its power—by wedding audience to characters. When a character's desire becomes our own, it takes on the power to move us. But what if characters desire nothing—beyond winning the immediate, kneejerk, "Who's on top?" powerplay? Can they move us? To do what? That primal desire for love—expressed as a deeply hidden longing for a return to youthful, innocent, romantic love, dramatized as the high point of life—is conveyed as so elemental that without love only destruction and desolation follow. Yet, when Rebecca in *Ashes to Ashes* invents a "remembered" lover out of a man who appears to be from Hitler's Nazi regime, she exposes an erotic rift between her and Devlin in her present relationship that destroys any possibility of real love between them. And when Lambert on his wedding anniversary in *Celebration* recalls a girl he once loved, he excludes, deliberately and cruelly, his wife, Julie, from his affection. Love in these plays exists only in the past, revealing the current soullessness of the loveless, who, unable to create, destroy. But the truths that Rebecca discovers in her invented love-thy enemy story that exposes the falsity in her relationship may allow her to destroy that falsity. However, where *Ashes to Ashes* portrays how those without love remain ineffectual, even impotent, to act for productive end, *Celebration* dramatizes how the loveless destruct.

Responsibility and the Complicity of Women in *Ashes to Ashes*

Rebecca, seated (significantly) in her comfortable living room opening to a sunlit garden, "recalls" for her partner, Devlin, witnessing and being commanded to commit atrocities carried out by a violent man she somehow found attractive. The man she first describes as a tour guide, then later as someone who tears babies from their screaming mothers on train platforms seem images redolent of the Nazi Holocaust. Finally, Rebecca morphs into one of the mothers whose baby was torn from her arms and, interestingly, claims responsibility for the atrocity committed upon her. Yet, in the end she denies the child: "What baby [. . .] ?

Earlier, when Devlin, as puzzled by her "remembrance" as is the audience, wonders where her story originates, she readily admits "nothing has ever happened to me." But through her telling of the story her "remembrance" becomes real in the present, more than a remembrance to *Never forget:* a reminder to remember present responsibility.

The power in the play comes from the conflict between the mystery and menace in Rebecca's story and the seeming kind attention of Devlin's focused determination to understand her story that could never have happened to this women, too young to have experienced the Nazi Holocaust as a grown woman. But it did happen to millions in the past and, in the many forms atrocity takes, continues to happen to countless millions of women and men in the present. Unlike Rebecca, Devlin is focused less on the horror than on his jealousy of her barbaric lover. The play's complex mystery, coupled with the comic tension release, raises questions that give further insight into responsibility and the interconnected interplay of the erotic and the destructive.

"Kiss my fist" is the violently seductive zinger that opens Rebecca's "recollection" of a man's command that rivets the audience to *Ashes to Ashes,* and sets an erotic tone with a promise of sex and violence to come. When the man's "fist grazed my mouth," she says, "I kissed his open palm and said, 'Put your hand round my throat,'" (3) Paradoxically, Rebecca's invitation to violate her becomes her defense, a countercommand that matches her assailant's conjunction of *kiss* and *fist*—together signaling erotic attraction imbedded in physical threat. The play goes beyond acknowledging both the dark and light forces in the self to question the very equation of those forces with good and evil. To counter destructive forces in the self or an other, opposing forces in the human psyche, love and violence, must be further acknowledged as entwined, tangled in every desire, and desire's expression in action. As each line forwards us through a maze of unexpected turns into greater depths of mystery, we reach the illumination of "darkness visible," a kind of hell that might be of our own making, where we are forced to confront what responsibility for violence we have for what may be our future where there may be no children or we may be forced to deny them: "I don't know of any baby," ends the play.

But in the beginning, when Devlin, as much in the dark as the audience, asks if the man put his hands around her throat, she says, "He did.[. . .] very gently.[. . . .]He adored me, you see." (5; bracketed ellipses throughout are mine) When Devlin twice asks, "So your legs were opening?" twice she answers, "Yes." (7) Incredulous, when he finally wonders why she tells her terrible story, asking, "Do you feel you're being hypnotised?" she replies, "I think you're a fuckpig." (9) Each question answered reveals another opening to a larger mystery. Her startlingly unprovoked attack on the man who exhibits great patience in listening to her story signals some seismic disturbance beneath their surface. He says she must be joking, and that if she put herself in his position she'd understand his right to ask such questions.

When Devlin asks her to describe the man, "Does he have eyes?" and she asks, "What colour," he says, "That's precisely the question I'm asking you . . . , my darling," (13) But she attaches further erotic overtones to the man in question when she evades with, "No one has ever called me darling. Apart from my lover," heightening the possibility that this man was her lover. (13) But she terminates the beat she instigated with her insistence, "I'm nobody's darling. It's the last thing I want to be." Devlin lightens the mood with, "That's a song," linking her story to a pop 1940s tune that registers the cliché quality of their conversation as her menacing memories alternate with a comic release of tension that allows tension to build. This alternation between opposites in tone and topic—the familiar and the unexpectedly bizarre, rejection and intimacy, normalcy and nightmare—establishes the dynamic that propels the play's action beyond the force of Hegelian dialectic. What synthesis is achieved? What truths revealed? Each alternation results in greater insight which only raises another question that drives deeper into new mystery.

When Rebecca recalls that the man had a responsible job, as some kind of courier with an agency, a travel agency, as "a guide," and says he took her somewhere, to a factory, her "memory" of the man as a tourist guide mutates into an impression that he was an authority, a prison official. Later, when she calls him her intimate, she absolutely links the violent with the erotic. As she pieces together information she haltingly "remembers," the developing picture more and more resembles a Nazi forced-labor concentration camp, where "the workers were wearing caps, soft caps," doffing them in her presence because of her status in conjunction with this man. (21–23) When Devlin interjects, "I thought you said he worked for a travel agency," she follows immediately with a nightmare, stream of consciousness non sequitur that deflects and changes the tone of the piece utterly—toward the brutal, dark, ugly and very serious as daylight dissolves into night. Her recollection that begins with a familiar desire, to go to the bathroom, "But I never found out where it was," ends abruptly in horror:

> He did work for a travel agency. He was a guide. He used to go to the local railway station and walk down the platform and tear all the babies from the arms of their screaming mothers. (27)

The nightmare quality in "tear" and "screaming mothers" sets the unmistakable stamp of holocaust, stunningly described as routine, repetitive assembly line work.

Rebecca provides the linchpin clue to what led to her assuming the persona of a witness and victim. It originated, she says, when she heard a siren. The sound triggered a free association to the Gestapo sirens signaling people forcibly taken during the Nazi Holocaust. She insists she is "terribly upset, [. . .] incredibly upset," and then asks, "Don't you want to know why?" She adds her single line signaling intimacy with Devlin: "If I can't tell you who can I tell?" Instead of pursuing that line of development, she retreats solipsistically to her own concerns, as she registers her shock of recognition, "It just hit me so hard," and expresses a quite ordinary, familiar observation, "[. . .] as the siren faded away in my ears I knew it was becoming louder for somebody else." (29) Her "ah-ha!" of sudden sympathy for an other that anyone hearing an ambulance siren might feel can be likened in this play's context to Blake's assertion that he cannot be happy so long as he knows that a single person in the world suffers. And when Devlin asks if the siren makes her feel secure or insecure, she makes a rare admission for a Pinter character and says "insecure," registering sympathy with the victim. But we quickly slip from familiar ground.

After Rebecca and Devlin agree the siren will always be heard by someone, her talk veers into the unexpected: "I hate it leaving me. I hate losing it. I hate somebody else possessing it. I want it to be mine, all the time." (29) She suddenly seems to tip into a Jonathan Edward hubris, a self-reflexive superlative expressing self-aggrandizing specialness in his insistence that he is the worst of the worst of sinners in the hands of an angry God. Her desire for specialness inverts that of Pinter's torturers in *One for the Road* and *Mountain Language,* victimizers who claim specialness through a direct pipeline to God. Her desire to be the only one, the only victim, at first indicates she appropriates the story to mark out her specialness as victim, reflecting, perhaps, our own age of victimization where, rather than adopting a stoical or bootstrap approach to minor seismic shocks in otherwise trauma-free lives such as hers, we locate minor wounds and inflate them to trauma status to avoid taking lesser, effective, responsible action where, because we may be unable to resolve a problem in its entirety, we believe ourselves to be powerless.

Her unexpected swerve veers further off, this time to a comic, freshly startling take: "It's such a beautiful sound. Don't you think?" (31) Her odd conjunction of beauty with pain, not unlike Poe's gothic notion that no subject is more beautiful than the death of a beautiful woman, warrants only Devlin's dismissal: "Don't worry, there'll always be another." Here, he underscores his view of police as protectors rather than perpetrators of violence, as in the Nazi Gestapo, implying also a belief in the impossibility of ever doing away with human violence, pain and suffering. (31) If you can't do anything about it, why not ignore it?

That format of exchange that begins with a literal, familiar, recognizable establishing position (that the siren upset her), followed by a swerve to a puzzlingly unforeseen position that leads us into greater mystery (she found the siren beautiful), sets a pattern in both these plays for the comedy and dark laughter. What can she mean that she found the siren beautiful? Does it signal sickness (as an ambulance) and the possibility of healing or violence and death (as the police or Gestapo)? Laughter remains a flash point of insight, so even when we don't quite "get it" all, Pinter, in evoking uneasy laughter uses comedy to a fresh end: to take us as far as we can go in a conflict toward exposing our own pain and truth (the common definition of comedy), and then again, as a master, trusts us to piece together the puzzle to find our own way to go the distance—where others haven't gone before. The comedy that begins with the comic familiar desire to find a bathroom then stops—when Rebecca zaps with babies torn from mothers' arms. Such mystery, delivered through comedy, can reconcile, heal—as it moves us forward, approaching the unknown, toward terror.

Rebecca's name in Biblical terms denotes "a healer." While Rebecca, along with Leah, Rachel and Sarah, is regarded as one of the four mothers of Israel, her name is also taken to mean "captivating," as the chosen woman married to Isaac, Abraham's son who is spared.[1] Here, Rebecca is partnered with Devlin, signifying "fierce," a man who, at her obvious provocation, delves into her past, allowing us to remind ourselves that we are the spared sons and daughters who are now charged with the responsibility to know our own history, to take what responsible action we can in the present, not to perpetuate past destruction now and in the future. Devlin, however, like most of us most of the time, neither acknowledges nor much concerns himself with atrocities he can ignore if they do not occur in his time or place. He would rather "start again," seek diversion, "take in a movie." (31)

This couple, among the world's safely sheltered suburbanites to whom nothing bad has ever happened, seem, significantly, childless, their stake in the future less pointed than their focus on past causes for jealousy and on present pleasures provided by their relative comfort and security. Her story, engaging him primarily at the level of a puzzle, arouses increasing jealousy as their interaction swings between familiar, grounded quotidian details (she couldn't find a bathroom) and her shockingly startling horrors detailing holocaust (tearing babies from their mothers), to reveal the depths of horror and truth she embodies.

Devlin accepts the received view of the police as "very busy" protectors, rather than perpetrators of the worst abuses, to assure

Rebecca she can "take comfort" from the fact that, as he reiterates, "You'll never never be without a police siren." With an unexpected comic inversion, he quips, "You'll never be lonely again." (33)

His more pressing agenda, about "this chap you and I have been talking about . . . in a manner of speaking," is to establish whether her relationship happened "before you knew me or after you knew me?" Exposing arbitrary ways we impugn another, assign blame or feel jealousy, Devlin, at this point, chooses to believe her story, which, until mention of babies torn from their mothers, might seem a desperate attempt, like Sarah's in *The Lover* or Stella's in *The Collection,* to arouse jealousy in a husband whose interests have begun to seriously flag. If she met the man before Devlin knew her, he implies, it is all right—if not, inexcusable. Interestingly, as Susan Hollis Merritt points out, Pinter changed the word "monster" in the holograph for *Ashes to Ashes* to "lover." (*The Pinter Review* 1997–1998, 156) This would certainly be in keeping with Pinter's injunction and intention to kick "language up the arse" (Knowles, *The Pinter Review* 1997–1998, 180) to expose both codified meanings, and here, in the easy transposition from monster to lover, signals the link between opposing qualities contained in a single character. Wisely, Pinter revised "monster" to "lover" in his handwritten draft. We see he is a monster, need not be told, but that Rebecca regards him as a lover remains startlingly puzzling.

But rather than address that question or answer Devlin's, Rebecca again segues into evasion, "Oh by the way there's something I've been dying to tell you," (33) shifting to a seemingly unrelated topic, her inexplicable observation that when she set her pen down on the table, it rolled off: "This pen, this perfectly innocent pen." (35) Devlin, instead of returning to his unanswered question, engages with her new topic—he objects to her assertion: "You can't know it was innocent." However comic his misplaced focus on the innocence of an inanimate object, he tangentially raises the question of guilt and responsibility in Rebecca's main story. When she challenges him, "Why not?" he holds his ground: "Because you don't know where it had been. You don't know how many other hands have held it . . . what other people have been doing with it." While obviously referring equally both to her, sexually, and to the pen, only when he goes over the top, anthropomorphizing the pen with, "You know nothing of its parents' history," (35) does she check him, demanding the literal,

"A pen has no parents." (37) But once confronted, Devlin won't back down, "You can't sit there and say things like that." (37) Rebecca too counters by deliberately misplacing emphasis from his intention, "I can sit here." The argument shifts into a test of wills, returning to the "Who's on top?" game Pinter's characters revert to whenever cornered or threatened. Preserving the self always overrides all other considerations while conflicting positions frequently masquerade as a quest for the "truth," as they did long ago in *The Dumb Waiter,* in Ben and Gus's violent "Light the kettle"/"Light the gas," confrontation. But Devlin and Rebecca's squabbling is slipperier because focus is not on content but merely on what *emphasis* in any given statement each chooses to pursue.

When Devlin counters with, "You can't sit there and say things like that," this time Rebecca holds ground with, "You don't believe I'm entitled to sit here . . . in the place where I live?" Sitting, as always in Pinter's plays and screenplays, denotes stasis, passivity, a position of powerlessness as opposed to agency and action—a *choice* to place oneself in an inferior position, never in his work an admirable choice. When Devlin calls her assertion, "I'm saying you're not entitled to sit in that chair or in or on any other chair and say things like that and it doesn't matter whether you live here or not," and she replies, "I'm not entitled to say things like what?" he simply insists on his literal version as truth: "That pen was innocent." (37) His comically attributing volition to a pen allows him to escape acknowledging his own volition and responsibility and, more importantly, hers, as his real concern.

When she pointedly asks, "You think it was guilty?" he relents, "I'm letting you off the hook," and admits, "I'm letting you slip." But in another rare admission for a Pinter character, he considers, "Or perhaps it's me who's slipping," then confesses, "I'm in quicksand." (39) Instead of acknowledging his distress with compassion, Rebecca says, "Like God." (39)

Provoked, Devlin excoriates her with "God? God? You think God is sinking into a quicksand? That's what I would call a truly disgusting perception." (39) He responds self-reflexively, saying that without a God, the universe, as a "vacuum," is an intolerable game, "like England playing Brazil at Wembley and not a soul in the stadium." His concern is that a godless universe offers no one to bear witness to his life or engage his attention; "apart from the referee's whistle and a fair bit of fucking and blinding," he sees an image of the universe as only "a permanent oblivion." For Devlin, "If you turn away from God it means that the great and noble game of soccer will fall into permanent oblivion. No score for extra time . . . no score for time everlasting, for time without end. Absence. Stalemate. Paralysis. A world without a winner." (40–41) For the first time Pinter links the notion of God directly to the no-win, zero-sum, dominant/subservient game his characters engage in as their primary mode of being: conflict, with the motive for all action, winning. But without a God, what reason is there to win?

To his credit Devlin reconvenes her topic, "your bloke . . . your lover? . . . and babies and mothers, etc. And platforms," but leads to a question aimed less at discovering truth than at assuming ascendency over her, yet deployed in the name of truth: "I inferred from this that you were talking about some kind of atrocity. Now let me ask you this. What authority do you think you yourself possess which would give you the right to discuss such an atrocity?"

She checks his assault, one-upping him with rare but simple truth: "I have no such authority. Nothing has ever happened to me." (41) Is this, like almost all Pinter characters' self-referential statements, registered to question and convey precisely the opposite? Is her life so vacuous that her invention provides vicarious adventure, or, as in James' "Beast in the Jungle," does it prevent her from facing the horror of being someone to whom nothing happens? Albee's admonition to audiences is to live so that death is not the first important event. Is this her event? This does not seem to be Pinter's intent. He sees her as embodying atrocity to communicate it to another.

But her admission that nothing has ever happened to her signals her story as allegory, not the first type, in which surface level can be taken literally, but the second type, not having a literal surface. As allegory her story serves as a warning of the heart. At core, like all allegory, the play embodies mystery. Even though the play turns on that moment when we need not take her literally, more importantly, her assertion that she has never suffered resonates through the rest of the play like a Joycean epiphany. Although she again insists, "I have not suffered. Nor have my friends," is it even possible to live without suffering? Is not her imagined enactment a kind of suffering? Her greatest, but unstated suffering, perhaps embodied in the absence of a child, is telegraphed in her detailed "memory" of the baby torn from her in the final image of the play, yet which she repeatedly denies: "what baby. . . . I don't know of any baby." (83–84)

"Shall we talk more intimately?" Devlin purposes to bring the topic back to reality and to ground discussion in "something more personal, about something within your own immediate experience." (44–45) But when he inquires whether when the hairdresser washes her hair and "he has your entire trust. . . . It's not just your head which is in his hands, is it, it's your life, it's your spiritual . . . welfare," he signals his understanding of her allegorical drift. Linking love with death, he also asks, "when your lover had his hand on your throat, did he remind you of your hairdresser?" He punctuates his point comically while connecting love—and death when he explicitly acknowledges this man as her lover—a murderer: "I'm talking about your lover. The man who tried to murder you." (43) "Murder me?" she asks. He answers doubling his *entendre* with a play on sex, "Do you to death." (43)

When she denies that he tried to murder her, Devlin insists, "He suffocated you and strangled you." (44) But Rebecca only tightens her bond to the man: "He felt compassion for me. He adored me." (45) And of course there may be some truth to this imagined singling her out as a favorite, rather than consigning her immediately to forced labor or the ovens. Her need to clarify also reminds that the whole truth may require acknowledging the attraction in the revulsion, reveals how a story summarized by another can so quickly be torqued into a meaning transformed.

What Devlin views as brutal, she recalls as erotic, provoking Devlin's ire, which inspires a tirade not unlike Robert's in *Betrayal* in that moment when suspicion of his wife's infidelity is confirmed. Devlin demands to know, "Were you unfaithful to me?" He softens, "Why didn't you confide in me," insists that he could have been "[l]ike a priest," then qualifies his plea by wondering when it happened, determining her guilt or innocence within the slightly ridiculously, self-referential comic context of time—their time together: "Unless all this happened before I met you. In which case you have no obligations to tell me anything. Your past is not my business. I wouldn't dream of telling you about my past. Not that I had one." (45)

He plants himself squarely in her camp, as a person to whom nothing has happened, an academic, as if being an academic negates even a whiff of his own infidelity (recall Pinter's screenplay for *Accident*). "When you lead a life of scholarship you can't be bothered with the humourous realities, you know, tits, that kind of thing." (45) Denying his own infidelity on grounds of being an academic only raises the question. "But of course," he comically concludes, being married utterly removes him from any charge of dalliance: "none of this applies when you have a wife. When you have a wife you let thought, ideas and reflection take their course. Which means you never let the best man win. Fuck the best man, that's always been my motto." He expresses his alpha male "guts and application" philosophy of life: "It's the man who ducks his head and moves on through no matter what wind or weather who gets there in the end. A man with guts and application." (47) His view, akin to Pinter's expressed admiration for the perseverance of Kafka's Joseph K, also has to be the method of operation of almost any writer who reaches the widest possible audience. But however much he himself may wish to be "kinder and gentler," when Devlin qualifies his description of a winner with "A man who doesn't give a shit. A man with a rigid sense of duty," he describes better the recent tortures in Pinter's plays. "There's no contradiction between those last two statements. Believe me." (47) Equating a man of duty with a man who "doesn't give a shit," doesn't care, reveals a definition of love by negation: to care, to love, is to act not from duty and will, but from that care, that love, of self and other that contains a consequent desire for justice.

When he does a reality check, asking, "Do you follow the drift of my argument?" Rebecca responds, "Yes," but, after only a comma, she submits a seemingly new agenda with yet another apparent subject shift: "Oh yes, there's something I've forgotten to tell you." She recalls watching a whole crowd of people in Dorset walking across the cliff and down to the sea, led by "guides" who walk them into the water, covered by the tide as "their bags bobbed about in the waves." (49) Like lemmings, the Pied Piper's children, or those led to the gas chambers, she signals a topic swing back to atrocity. Again, Devlin's objection fastens not on her topic, but on a fact that negates the veracity of her story—they've never lived in Dorset. Rather than responding, Rebecca makes another hairpin turn, seemingly off a cliff, "Somebody told me the other day there's a condition known as mental elephantiasis." (49) Again, Devlin focuses on factual irrelevancies—who was the somebody and which "other day?"

But she stays her topic with an ostensive definition to explain what she means and its relevance to the central question of the play—responsibility: "When you spill an ounce of gravy, for example, it immediately expands and becomes a vast sea of gravy [. . .] , which surrounds you on all sides and you suffocate in a voluminous sea of gravy. But," she says, "it's your own fault. You brought it upon yourself. You are not the *victim* of it, you are the *cause* of it. Because it was you who spilt the gravy in the first place, it was you who handed over the bundle." (51) Obliquely in the end, taking responsibility herself for handing over the bundle (the baby), she takes responsibility, perhaps like Oedipus, for an event over which she may have little or no control; a baby demanded and torn from a mother's arms may be no more in her control than her loss of a child through a spontaneous abortion. Yet, however obliquely, Rebecca significantly claims not guilt, but responsibility.[2]

Devlin reads her allegorical meaning well enough, the global ramifications beneath her surface story, but would just as soon not pursue it. "So what's the question? Are you prepared to drown in your own gravy? Or are you prepared to die for your country? Look. What do you say, sweetheart? Why don't we go out and drive into town and take in a movie?" (51) She disregards his dismissal with an apparent dismissal of her own, "That's funny, somewhere in a dream . . . a long time ago . . . I heard someone calling me sweetheart." (51) Yet her mention of "sweetheart," like "darling" earlier, again foregrounds the topic of love. Was she ever loved? She gave her heart, but to a malicious fiend—however imagined (or wished for).

Her dream circles her back to her agenda as she resumes recounting her horrifying story of a walk "into a frozen city," to the railway station, the train with people, among them, "My best friend, the man I had given my heart to, the man I knew was the man for me the moment we met, my dear, my most precious companion, I watched him walk down the platform and tear all the babies from the arms of their screaming mothers," she repeats, describing his act as if it were any assembly line work. (52) Clearly this best friend and most precious companion is not Devlin. A question which her juxtaposition of her lover with such a monstrous act must raise is how could such a woman, any sane person, love a person so maliciously brutal? Is it possible we all love such a person—that is, anyone not actively engaged in confronting such ongoing atrocity, but would rather take in a movie, is such a person. Are we not ourselves, generally, such persons? Of course, as citizens of the world we are responsible for knowing what is happening in it, and Pinter's reading of Gitta Sereny's *Albert Speer: His Battle with Truth* just prior to writing *Ashes to Ashes,* and his extensive research, indicates most German people were aware of the extermination. But if we hold ordinary German citizens responsible and wonder why they did nothing, we must also look to ourselves. By virtue of the fact that most of us today must spend most of our waking hours devoted to work to support ourselves and families, simply being well informed can seem a luxury, and how easily we might argue that caring, concern and confrontation demand more time and discretionary energy than we as otherwise responsible citizens can summon. Quite possibly Rebecca has freedom from material responsibilities, as her next encounter indicates, and with leisure to command can consider, even imaginatively "recall," atrocity that in the end allows her at least to understand responsibility.

Rebecca's admission of a passionate, intimate friendship with another man suddenly does not seem to concern Devlin, who derails her nightmare talk to a seeming irrelevant but parallel track: "Did you see Kim and the kids?" Typical of Pinter's realistic dialog, Pinter can introduce even a mundane topic with the added tension of a question: Who is Kim? Rebecca's sister and her children (who were not torn from their mother's arms), and Kim's estranged husband become a second topic that tightly twins Rebecca's mothers, children and lover. All Rebecca's topics lead to atrocity. While Devlin may not wish to continue to entertain Rebecca's "remembered" passion for another man, Kim's husband's infidelity and Kim's refusal to take him back, "though he says he misses the kids," provides these two a Rorschach upon which they may project their own unspoken discord. When Devlin asks more cogently, "Does he miss his wife?" Rebecca answers, "He says he's given the other one up. He says it was never serious, you know, it was only sex." (59) Devlin assents with an understanding "Ah." But when Rebecca continues, "She says she'll never share a bed with him again. Never. Ever," and Devlin asks why not, Rebecca veers back to his original question, with what amounts to a refusal to answer, creating a typical Pinter gap that exposes unspoken questions about their own relationship: what monster/lover lives here? "Of course I saw Kim and the kids," she says, "I had tea with them." (61)

But even this momentary juxtaposition of normalcy on nightmare (Kim and the kids overlaid on the atrocity of mother's whose babies are torn from them) does not allow Rebecca to escape atrocity and death. Afterward at the cinema, Rebecca, significantly, alone, says she saw a comedy at which others laughed but she did not, signaling perhaps her own inability to "take in a movie," escape into mere entertainment as her consciousness is awakening to the disturbing suffering of the women on the platform. But when she noticed that the man sitting in front of her also never laughed, mirroring her own response, but remained "rigid, like a body with rigor mortis, he never laughed once, he just sat like a corpse," she fled: "I moved as far away from him as I possibly could." (65)

Devlin, unwilling perhaps to entertain another of her flights of fancy, tries to ground her in the here and now, "Now look, let's start again. We live here. You don't live . . . in Dorset . . . or *anywhere else*. You live here with me. This is our house. You have a very nice sister. She lives close to you. She has two lovely kids. You're their aunt. You like that." (65) He compliments her on her "wonderful garden" and, comically, her "green fingers." But no sooner does he repeat, "Let's start again," than Rebecca counters with, "We can't start *again*. We can end again," and they clash in a combat as deadly as the "Light the Kettle"/"Light the gas" argument in occurring at the same point *The Dumb Waiter*—where accord, compromise and reconciliation are no longer possible, but signal the beginning of the inexorable end: a resolution that can only result in a permanent rift. The argument is almost as inane sounding as Ben and Gus's "Light the kettle"/"Light the gas" conflict, except that Rebecca and Devlin, privileged recipients of a more advanced education, give a philosophical-sounding spin to the tone. "End means end," Devlin says. "You can't end 'again.' You can only end once." (67) Where he argues you can start again, she relentlessly insists "you can end again," and giving fresh meaning to the play's title, she begins to sing, "Ashes to ashes." As he joins her, the two reach that momentary penultimate accord, singing alternately, completing the final incantation for the dead with the childish rhyme transformed to music hall ditty:

> Ashes to ashes—
> And dust to dust—
> If the women don't get you—
> The liquor must. (69)

Of course they are dancing together at the edge of the grave, and Devlin's next line joins the topic of death to love: "I always knew you loved me." (69) When she asks why, he reveals the slender basis for their bond, "Because we like the same tunes." (69) However inconsequential sounding his response, not intended entirely literally, what else primarily constitutes the basis for most relationships aside from common interests? Of course one answer is shared values and strengths, and another is attraction, which all here remain at best questionable.

The "conversation," now far beyond questions of whether she is being hypnotized, or whether the lover is real, dramatizes what British psychologist Frederick Bartlett's research on memory concludes, that memories are formed as incomplete fragments, completed afterward as constructs of imagination coupled with prior experience. Rebecca's "memory" of her lover has become real for Devlin. When he asks why she never mentioned her lover before, he threatens, "I have a right to be very angry indeed. . . . Do you understand that?" (71) And the hypnotic quality of her trancelike recollection introduces her story as real into the minds of the audience.

But again, Rebecca disconnects: "Oh by the way there's something I meant to tell you." She launches into one final memory of looking out a window in a building in the middle of town, seeing a man and little boy dragging suitcases, followed by a woman "carrying a baby in her arms." (71) This time the image of the boy and the baby seems to underline the childlessness of this relationship, which also seems to lack commitment—to marriage. As Rebecca makes her transition from the woman as "she" to "I," herself transforming into the woman holding the baby, listening to her breathing, her heart beating, Devlin attempts to appropriate the persona of the lover/monster and supplant him in her psyche. What failure or failures of commitment on his part or hers has torn a baby from Rebecca's arms? Not as a malicious Speer, as so many scholars wish to label Devlin, as Devil[3], but why, at the more obvious, personal level of commitment, does Rebecca have cause to call him a "fuckpig" (73), as she does, unprovoked, at the beginning? (73) Is Devlin a monster without being a lover? He commands Rebecca, "Kiss my fist," but fails to engage her. (75) Rebecca's rejection of Devlin, like Goneril's in *Lear* of her "mild husband," Albany, suggests an echo of Goneril's "Oh, the difference from man and man!" (IV, ii, 27) immediately after a kiss from Edmund, freshly aroused from the news of the putting out of Gloucester's eyes that has elevated the bastard son Edmund to claim the title Gloucester. Devlin's command, "Ask me to put my hand round your throat," can't even engage Rebecca's attention. (75) He has nothing left to say, perhaps never did. Perhaps neither did, till now. But Devlin's failure to engage her as a lover, has rendered him impotent as monster, a persona he reveals himself so willing to appropriate as Rebecca's narrative moves beyond him through the familiar territory of the Holocaust, rendering Devlin irrelevant, invisible.

During her final memory of "the trains [. . . .] They were taking the babies away," each line, followed by an echo, like Webster's dead Duchess of Malfi's an ethereal voice that resonates from the past, reveals a terrible truth. Rebecca continues to create in the present her struggle of trying to protect her baby, to hide her baby in her shawl, but when the baby cried out, a man asked, "what do you have there," and stretched out his hand. "I gave him the bundle," she says, "That's the last time I held the bundle." (81) But at another train station when she met a women she knew who asked, "What happened to your baby?" Rebecca twice denies having had any baby: "I don't know of any baby." With that echo the play ends.

Paradoxically, she is literally telling the truth. But she has so effectively constructed her memory that her statement appears to be a lie. Yet, at another level of meaning, the story is a familiar one, one we should never forget that continues to happen around the world and provokes the unanswered but not unanswerable question that remains. What can we do?

Does the play in production, apart from the printed page, compel us to ask, move us to act?

This brief play *Ashes to Ashes* has the power to engender a nameless fear and a primal terror of a past holocaust, and Rebecca's story becomes a reality in the present, joining that past to a multitude of more recent and current holocaust victims, to dramatize how such acts denied, unconfronted and unresolved, become a future we all inherit.

A close reading of the play reveals some of the many implications of the question, What responsibility do we living now have for the sins of our fathers in whatever fatherland we happen to occupy, a question Hawthorne raised in his fiction to reveal the ongoingness of past crimes infesting the present. Rebecca's internalizing and retelling a story apparently from the Nazi Holocaust keeps the question alive.

But *Ashes to Ashes* exposes another question about drama's efficacy to move us to fresh thought and action. There is a certain necessarily static quality, not only in the near immobility of the characters—Rebecca seated in a near trance state, the Cassandra quality of her speech—but more important in locating the source of power in the drama: what do these characters want—for themselves and from one another? Does this play dramatize the urgency and horror beneath what Rebecca says? Or does it move us primarily through its puzzles, (Who is the man? Is the story real?) questions that may seem intended to conceal as much as to reveal meaning in an attempt, perhaps, to avoid charges of didacticism? What does Rebecca want? That question remains alive and paramount at the end.

The mystery, What do these characters want? is the main mystery, a puzzle that remains unsolved and unsolvable except perhaps by us. Clearly we want to know what Rebecca's story is about. What significance does it have for her? For us? And once "Did it really happen?" (to her) becomes irrelevant, our realization that what is happening before us onstage continues to happen in the world around us is what rescues this play from a talking-heads lecture delivered in code. Her story, told so hypnotically, continues to resonate afterward.

Although we are not told, we know this union was not fruitful. Rebecca's denial of the baby in the end, the bundle foreshadowed earlier, one of the babies torn not merely from the mother's arms as she witnesses, but from her own arms, becomes a denial of the future beyond themselves, beyond ourselves, on both a personal and a public level, if we do not heed her story.

What makes these two new plays so delightful in all their dark disturbance is that the characters say the unsayable, publically, and we as participants join them both, assuming their roles as innocent victim/perpetrator in thinking and feeling the unthinkable. Again it is the fractal geometry, the paralleling and resonance between private and public, performance and audience reception, that conveys to us the possibility of power. Rebecca has come to some degree of honesty through her fabrication, and that truth exposes the lies in the reality of her life. It is in Rebecca's claiming responsibility that her action and ours begins—at end of play. Pinter's work throughout these past decades introduces us to our own dark desires to reveal our power—and our powerlessness, if we remain ignorant both of ourselves and the world in claiming responsibility in designing our own future—or grave.

The Dreaming Child: In Dreams Begin Transformation and Responsibility

Late in 1997, between the 1995 *Ashes to Ashes* and the 1999 *Celebration,* Harold Pinter wrote the screenplay *The Dreaming Child,* adapted from the Karen Blixen/Isak Dinesen story, "The Dreaming Child," in *Winter's Tales.* In *The Dreaming Child,* a wealthy, childless, nineteenth-century couple adopts a slum child, Jack, whom the wife, Emily, later claims as her own natural child, thus claiming her womanhood, love and her whoredom. She courageously insists that her husband accept the child as the fruit of a union with her lover, Charley, a young man not her social equal who died in war, but with whom she'd never, regrettably, consummated her love. She instigates this fabrication not to cast herself into an abyss as a fallen women, but to escape from her remorse at not having made love with Charley, and like Sarah in *The French Lieutenant's Woman,* she seems to triumph as her own self-created, self-affrighted, self-delighting self—but with a difference. Sarah uses her deliberately fabricated story of the French Lieutenant's seduction for productive ends. She transforms herself into an artist and guide to the young claiming her power in order to win Smithson's love. But as Emily slowly, repeatedly, almost obsessively revisits, replays and revises that moment at the garden gate when she refused Charley on his last night home, she transforms her refusal till it becomes an invitation to come inside in what becomes a passionate embrace. Emily's invented passion provides an ongoing pleasurable but only imaginary escape from the truth of her lovelessness which kills and destroys. It might seem that in denying Charley's love, in unexamined accord with the received conventions of her time, Emily has cursed herself to lovelessness.

Dreams as wishes for transformation of the self in *The Dreaming Child* seem a continuation of Sarah's half-fabricated French Lieutenant who becomes a catalyst for change, and also of Rebecca's wholly fictional, but recognizable monster/lover in *Ashes to Ashes*.

In wishes begin transformation and responsibility. All three women dramatize the transformational power of love. But where Sarah claims agency and responsibility till Sarah's dream of love becomes a reality, a triumph that benefits her and Smithson in reality in the present and future in the film (although not in the second story, the "real life" Anna and her lover in reality), Emily's love, without action or agency, remains largely sterile, embedded in the dream state, imaginary, and she remains stunted. She does not fully love the child or her husband, and that tainted dream love can never carry forward into the reality of the present.

Emily's mere dream love, that remains stillborn as a catalyst for full transformation in the future, contrasts with Rebecca's "remembered" past "love" as her touchstone for the passion she wants but cannot have in the present, but Rebecca acts, takes the first step to extricate herself from an unproductive, loveless relationship. She accepts a responsibility of sorts for atrocity in the pregnant possibilities she carries as a result of her self-awakened consciousness of atrocity in the past, and in turning away from Devlin, severs connection (perhaps freeing herself from him). Although her future remains unclear, she can no longer fully share it with a man who neither acknowledges nor accepts responsibility for atrocity, not merely past but as that past implies present atrocity. Such a man neither shares nor arouses passion as does her monster/lover. *Ashes to Ashes* provocatively suggests or questions whether a destructor is a more powerful, potent and even attractive lover than the seemingly more kindly Devlin, who, perhaps like most of us, might rather "take in a movie" than confront the violence and serious destruction of our time. But Rebecca has undergone a brutal and brutalizing imaginary journey back in time before her time to imagine the unimaginable: the erotic love one might feel for a butcher. The awful honesty of her self-knowledge throws her relationship with Devlin (not a bad man, only a man who seeks his own comfort and safety first) into bold relief, and provokes what could be a productive change as it reveals truths about Devlin. He changes, not to accept responsibility as she does, but only to attempt to become, like her "lover," a butcher (one could say he simply acknowledges the butcher in us all). His change allows Rebecca to turn away from an empty and what can only be a loveless relationship, one in no way conducted between equals. Her destruction of a hopelessly unproductive relationship becomes the beginning of a productive act for herself, though not for him. Although he recognizes the monster in himself, he gains no consciousness of its significance. Emily, too, changes, in acknowledging her own lovelessness, but acknowledging alone without action produces no productive change.

What this juxtaposition of the three women reveals is the bidirectional nature of dreams and revisionist possibilities. Where Rebecca revises her present by assuming a persona of the past, Emily revises her own past failure to follow her heart's passion and fully love, briefly, and in doing so reverses her present and Jack's future. After the adoption of Jack, Emily's memory at the garden gate of her failure to love Charley revises into daydreams as "remembrances" of the passion they exchanged. Her dream momentarily transforms her. Her private act of reclaiming her past, failed love as a revised love consummated seems briefly a metaphor for claiming full human status when she claims Jack as the fruit of that "passionate" union with Charley.[4]

Jack, too, has dreams. As a child, born to an impoverished, abandoned woman who dies giving birth to him, he dreams himself out of the slum into the imagined, comfortably wealthy home of long lost parents. He even seems to possess uncanny second sight, able on the first day to "remember" and find things in his room, to inquire about his "father's" medal and ask him to wear it. Yet, although his dreams come true by fortune and chance when he is adopted, after a momentary happiness, he dreams in reverse. His recollections of his slum in his nightmare slumber transform into dreams of returning to that home—to a more tangible, more real life than his present sterile, gilded circumstances offer. Love is not constructed merely of things: a fine house for Jack, a husband of her own station for Emily. Jack comes to believe his dream as truth, that these are his real parents. When he is told the truth, that his real mother is dead, and he can no longer sustain the fantasy to shield himself from the reality of Emily's coldness, he begins to die. But what is revealed is that neither Jack nor Emily have ever been loved, except in dreams. Dreams are not reality—and yet they are. Dreams that become reality in Pinter's work require the truth of some honest action in the present.

Dreams of love operate to construct and destruct a future as Jack and Emily both change their present circumstances. Jack's dreams of a fine life escaped from the drear of poverty end abruptly and after only a brief respite in the fine house as not merely the adopted child but the real child in this gilded cage. He then dreams his way back to his first house, no longer a possible home, and without dreams, reveals an aborted future. But this child's presence awakens a dreaming child in Emily who, instead of regretting her past failure to love, dreams that love into "existence" and "confesses," as does Sarah before her and Rebecca afterward, to an imagined erotic consummation of a love that becomes more real and powerful than anything in Emily's current life. Sarah's "remembered love," and one brief moment of making love with Smithson (clumsily not much more than a rape but which Sarah chooses to regard as love), rescues Sarah from madness and propels her into action that allows her to claim agency and a productive life. Yet, Sarah herself is the stuff of dreams, a character in a fiction, a film, played by Anna, the real-life actress who can walk away from her love affair with the actor playing Smithson, send him back to his less passionate wife, when she returns to her own lover David (interestingly, Pinter's own stage name, the name his first wife called him). Despite the unhappy "real-life" ending, the actors Sarah and Smithson and the audience seem to have given and gained more than a pleasurable moment in film's fiction, the happy ending of the film within the film. The wordless image of Sarah and Smithson that closes the film remains yet another indelible realization of the importance of love in Pinter's work.

While Emily's revisionist dreams claim a past love that Emily insists her husband understand and accept, which he does, it kills Jack. Her fantasy absorbs all her erotic energy. At Emily's core, her lovelessness that she confesses to her best friend continues to manifest itself both in her inability to love or even touch the child, and in her passionless relationship to her husband, who supplies himself with favors from his servant girls. Moreover, Pinter has hinted at a greater complexity beneath Charley's request for Emily's sexual acquiescence, dramatized as synonymous with love. Charley himself, however insistent in his ardor, is also hinted at as a known seducer of women. Yet Emily's denial of real love and of making love remain destructive. Emily's lovelessness beneath her dreamed passion becomes a kind of madness, and in Jack's death, tinged with evil—that which destroys.

Mere dreams of love are not the stuff of a sterner reality and without action cannot supply present happiness that feeds the future. Yet dreams do construct avenues that set a direction, momentarily provide a course for Emily and Jack, a way for us, that the true heart must follow to find love. Rebecca's passion for her fantasy lover becomes more real than her relationship with Devlin and reveals her desire for an equality of shared values. Her story only provokes the stern reality that Devlin meets none of her criteria and could be a monster but not a lover and exposes their lack of love. Aside from the fairy tale contained in *The French Lieutenant's Woman,* Pinter's work, like most fiction and drama, rarely supplies images of true love (a difficult, some might say impossible, task) or even of friendship. But his plays and screenplays illuminate not only past and present causes for failure but the public implications for both the family and community of the failure of private love, and in doing so his work lights many ways toward just love in the future.

Much of Pinter's work celebrates an unforgettable great first love, and his attitude might be compared with Byron's insistence in *Don Juan* that "first love is best." But for Byron beginner's love remains primarily a romantic sensation, the early, passionate rush that can never be recaptured, whereas Pinter sees ethical, productive possibilities in love with implications reaching far beyond two people in love. Without love, as in *The Dreaming Child,* destruction follows. As a woman, Emily's failure to love allows her to abrogate all responsibility to her husband and son. She subordinates that responsibility entirely to indulge in her fantasy of a passionate first love. Her imagined love midway through promises to fully awaken her but later destroys the child. Yet, her fantasy love does in the end bring her a private, solipsistic happiness.

In all three works of the past decade, there is such nostalgia, such longing, for a real love of youth now unattainable, as if that love were sealed off by death. Along life's continuum of first love's passion and death at the end of life remains the pervasive desire for love within the present landscape of reality. And the screenplay of *The Dreaming Child,* anchored at one end in love and its fairy-tale fantasy, at the other in near nightmare poverty, madness and death, provides a stepping stone back and forward through Pinter's work: back to voices speaking from the dead in *Family Voices* and *Moonlight,* back also to the light that opens *Ashes to Ashes* in the imagined but palpable erotic ecstasy Rebecca "experiences" and expresses, and also forward toward the hilarity of light evoked in *Celebration* by celebrants who seem to be almost without dreams. But at bottom all dreams are dreams of love, a wish for love, the passionately erotic and all love's possibilities, and without love, characters cannot function compassionately, ethically, productively. That each character's dominant quality contains its opposite—that love might include a monster, that dreams can kill—reminds us again of the honesty and truths contained in the complexity of Pinter's work that edges toward the greatest mystery of life: love. The larger questions are left for us to answer. But not in easy either/or answers. As Stephen Dunn nicely phrases it in a recent poem: "Some mysteries can be solved by ampersands. *Ands* not *ors*."[5] Here, Emily achieves a half-imaginary, momentary private, erotic victory—more, perhaps, than the women in *Celebration* even dream or seek agency to claim.

Desire, Destruction and the Complicity of Women in *Celebration*

Celebration's very title resonates with the dramatic irony of other paradoxically celebratory titles throughout the Pinter canon from *The Birthday Party* and *Homecoming* to *New World Order,* all dramatizing characters' qualities opposite the titles to illuminate those opposites as overriding truth. *The Birthday Party* ends in the birthday boy Stanley's psychological destruction; *Homecoming* in the expulsion of the returning son, Teddy; and *New World Order* in a relapse into a world viciously primitive.

In *Celebration* three couples at two tables dine in a restaurant described as the most expensive in town. Lambert and Julie, in their forties, celebrate their wedding anniversary with Matt and Prue, while Russell, in his thirties, and Suki, in her late twenties, dine together at another table. In this play the main participants, like Rebecca in *Ashes to Ashes,* significantly remain seated almost throughout, visited by the owner/host, Richard and his hostess, Sonia, who engage in generic owner host questions, and by the Waiter, who interjects recollections of a remarkable grandfather who he claims knew the early- and mid-twentieth-century luminaries in literature, the arts and politics. Suki and Russell briefly join the other table. Lambert picks up everyone's tab, and all exit except the Waiter, who offers one aborted final interjection. In this play nothing seems to happen—except almost every line is edged with a rapier wit designed to destroy a previous speaker and slash into multiple others with a sustained, almost unreleased tension that brilliantly dramatizes how the loveless destruct—in destroying what they cannot create, they destroy others, community and almost imperceptibly the self.

Yet these people hardly seem evil incarnate. Nobody dies in the end. And we as audience grin and laugh all the way up to the final Slow Fade—"not . . . a bang but a whimper." Yet what happens before our eyes is not funny but horrifying, at depth—only if we allow ourselves to look beneath the surface. These, the powerbrokers of the world, grocery clerk bureaucrats who deliver the guns and design strategies of destruction in exchange for millions, scarcely hint at their work. And for good reason. Like Goldberg and McCann, their "job" is conducted clandestinely except for those in the club who know the code words and have the cash and savvy to enter and play.

Celebration, ostensibly celebrating a wedding anniversary as commitment to marriage, reveals human relationships to be a sham, commitment to community, country, even to self, as nonexistent except as practiced at the primal edges of power among the recently moneyed privileged: those who run the guns, drugs and money of the world. Power, as the raw assertion of the self when money as power replaces desire for all else, dramatizes the pervasive destruction that results when such power asserts itself for its own sake with no ethical basis, no real power over the self.

These characters exceed the destructive limits of fanatics driven by personal vision. As David Mamet said, "Political corruption in pursuit of a personal vision of the public good is limited by nothing at all and ends in murder and chaos."[6] These are people, however, who have no vision aside from a reflexive response to sustaining power. Without consciousness of that lack of vision they are without conscience. As such, they are extremely dangerous, perhaps the most dangerous of all Pinter's characters.

The sexually brutal language of Pinter's recent torturers has assimilated itself into the largely upper-bureaucratic classes in both recent plays: men and women calling one another *fuckpigs,* men calling each other *cunts*—this from the writer who once insisted we use such words sparingly because we have so few vivid intensifiers. This decline mirrors the wedding of the erotic with destruction among these characters and parallels, but in a reverse-out, the divine descent in the epic over centuries—the fall from the earliest heroes as gods to the most recent ordinary men: from Gilgamesh, two-thirds a god, through Achilles, immortal save for his heel, to Odysseus, offered immortality, down to Joyce's Leopold Bloom, mere ordinary mortal.

Pinter's characters, begun among outcasts in *The Room,* have steadily risen with his own fortunes, out of the lowest classes to the comfortable middle class in *Betrayal* and, beginning with *Party Time,* to powerbrokers. But as their fortunes continued to rise, here soaring to unimagined heights, the characters have declined in virtue. They increase only in sheer malicious intent. But they have great fun along the way, can make us join them in their laughter. And it might be easy to miss the insidious consequences of such actions that extend far beyond the play. Yet their motive remains the same as that of Pinter's earliest characters: to maintain the status quo—what they possess. These characters cling as fiercely to position and possession as Rose does to her slum room. Pinter's ability to Cinderella himself into the palaces of princes, presidents and their bureaucratic attendants has yielded not happily-ever-after endings. Like Chaucer's work, that employs the saving grace of satire to reveal corruption in the guise of courtliness among the holy orders centuries ago, Pinter's work also wields a comic tone, but he unmasks more than hypocrisy, foibles and corruption. He shows us the faces of outright destructors, laughing at their deals in the name of "peacekeeping." He shows us how comedy in our time can be more deadly serious than tragedy. His characters are caught not in the act of overwhelming destruction but of playing. Pinter's comedy remains in the service of making the terror bearable: to expose evil as annihilation committed by quite ordinary people, despite their extraordinary and delightfully inventive but malicious ribaldry, not so different from us. How better than through comedy to confront ignorance and inaction, face it boldly before it is too late? We are more likely, the recent plays imply, to cling tenaciously like Rose and these celebrants to our familiar room, restaurant or estate, getting news of the outside world at second hand, or remaining ignorant.

Yet, even with his many insights into why characters act as they do, at a larger level puzzling questions and many mysteries of this play for the first time butt up against the very mystery of life, a phrase that first appears here at the end of the play.

What do these characters want?

That question remains central to all else and in the course of the play becomes our own: What do we want? Like Rebecca and Devlin among these characters, a clear, overriding desire remains slender. Perverted from productive ends, power is diverted to destruction. But without consciousness of that desire, every act becomes a brutal exercise of power to put down others. Power for power's sake becomes each character's main objective.

Only Richard, the restaurant owner in his fifties, the hostess, in her thirties, and the Waiter acquiesce to assuming subservient positions. They consistently return lackey courtesy to outrageous overtures, taking on the chin barbs aimed at them, or running from confrontation altogether. And among those three, only the Waiter, to keep from being invisible, interjects into conversations his own brand of self: "recollections" of his grandfather's acquaintance/ friendship with early-twentieth-century household-name greats in literature, Hollywood, the arts and politics. Interestingly, Pinter several years ago mentioned having once been fired as a waiter after engaging clients in an enjoyable discussion about T. S. Eliot. (Knowles, *The Pinter Review*, 1995–1996, 161) Although the Waiter here is brushed aside as an annoying insect by this restaurant's clientele, who all hint at or disturbingly recount violently abusive families, only the Waiter and Richard register fond recollections of family: a grandfather and father.

Among the diners, however, even the most mundane exchange deepens character and delightfully drives us to darker corners of illuminated insight—"darkness visible"—and always forwards conflict. But because nothing beyond the self is at stake, the characters seem to be spinning wheels, going nowhere—furiously. And that seems to be the point. That without an overarching desire, a purpose aimed at a productive end, they careen toward destruction. And they take everything in their wake. But no one seems to notice, perhaps, at first glance, not even the audience. But for an audience the cumulative effect indelibly writes messages in the soul as powerful as Pinter's earlier messages written in the blood.

The Waiter opens with a simple, familiar, "Who's having duck?" Lambert's, "The duck's for me," immediately countered by his wife, Julie, who says it's hers, reveals that the men running the show may not remember what they ordered for dinner less than hour ago. Nor does the Waiter remember what his customers ordered, although that's his job. When Matt announces, "Chicken for my wife, steak for me," the Waiter no sooner serves the chicken than he asks, "And who's having steak?" (1; all references are to the typescript) It's funny and scary—faulty memory, inattention, not listening, only the first of many failings, as dialog quickly hones itself to weaponry to target several at once.

Out of Lambert's, "What did I order?" and his wife, Julie's, "Who cares?" emerges *Celebration*'s theme and technique. *Who cares?* for anyone—self or other—is played out at an accelerating pitch by each character attempting to one-up the other. Aside from temporary alliances formed by the men against the women, the two women in self-defense and retaliation, it's everyone for the self. When Prue, Julie's sister, says Lambert ordered "Osso Bucco" [*sic*], Lambert asks, "Osso what?" Matt, the straight man, Lambert's brother, explains, "It's an old Italian dish." Lambert sets the tone for the rest of the play by introducing the literal translation of "osso buco" as "bone with a hole," to freely associate to "arsehole": "Well I knew Osso was Italian but I know bugger all about bucco." (2) When Matt translates, "I didn't know arsehole was Italian," Lambert asks, "Yes but on the other hand what's the Italian for arsehole?" Prue's "Julie, Lambert" zeugmas as both an answer to Lambert's *What's the Italian for arsehole?* and a break up of the impending conflict with a "peacekeeper" toast: "Happy anniversary." (2) The opening conflict promises fireworks and violence.

The prime motive for the promised destruction to come announces itself at the other table in Russell's opening gambit to Suki: "They believe in me." (3) Russell's declaration of confidence, like Pinter's earlier character's self-referential assertions, refutes what's asserted by dramatizing the opposite: his desperate need to be believed in by others because he does not believe in himself. That pervasive lack of belief in the self in all the characters reveals itself in the bullying of the others. Lack of self-trust, self-respect and self-love discloses yet again how dangerous is a little insecurity. (3) Russell's requiring respect from Suki, a woman he can't respect, like Stanley in *The Birthday Party* dancing for the respect of Meg and Lulu, women he despises, bespeaks Russell's basic insecurity that Suki twists to her advantage. She plays up to Russell, setting him up only to tear him down. "I'm sure they believe in you," she says, then takes deadly aim at his weakness that she uses as her hold on him. Candidly expressing the love/money equation that bonds all these couples, she uses her knowledge that he needs (not wants) her, and wants what she wants—an assured, secure, comfortable financial future—to get what else she wants: "I mean, listen, I want you to be rich, believe me, I want you to be rich so that you can buy me houses and panties and I'll know that you really love me." (3) Her zinger, "panties," tossed into this first mention of love, translates "love" to "lust" that announces the lack-of-love theme that runs rampant throughout Pinter's plays, first most fully realized in *The Homecoming*. But lovelessness quickly links with lust, and with revenge, joining the destructive quest for power. "Panties" sounds vulnerably innocent enough to play Suki as straight, innocent of deliberate, calculated, malicious intent but conciously savvy.

Russell returns fire, registering his knowledge of her jealousy, anger and pain, the real reason for her snide gibe: "Listen, she was just a secretary. That's all." (3) She has him on the defensive. His "just a secretary" intended to proclaim his own power and innocence, in the wake of the Clinton-Lewinsky White House sex scandal, merely reveals, in the destructive links between sex and power, his powerlessness. He blames the secretary for her power over him! When Suki attempts to disarm him with, "Like me," admitting she was once a secretary, Russell denies her equation, "She was a scrubber. . . . They're all the same, these secretaries, these scrubbers. They're like politicians. They love power," he says, pleading innocence in terms of his powerlessness. (4) But when he says, "You don't know what these girls are like," Suki counters his insult by prizing in herself the lust he depreciates, flaunting her knowledge of her way around beds: "I've been behind a few filing cabinets." (4) *Celebration* entertains with the witty repartee of Noel Coward riffs gone scatologically wild to play out in a loveless lustfulness confined more to chat than action.

In a world where money is power, and women remain without power except as adjuncts to men, Suki's task is bolstering Russell's confidence: "Listen. I would invest in you myself if I had any money [. . . .] Because I believe in you." (5) But with sex as her primary currency, Russell wants but cannot demand assurances of her fidelity: "What's all this about filing cabinets?" Suki's sexual prowess, her ability to incite jealousy, is also largely in her past, driven by former hormonal excitability: "Their excitement," she says, "made me so excited, sometimes I could hardly walk from one filing cabinet to another, I was so excited, I was so plump and wobbly it was terrible, men simply couldn't keep their hands off me, their demands were outrageous but," she says, returning Russell to center stage, "coming back to more important things, they're right to believe in you." Her candor and vulnerability, tacit acknowledgment that she too needs him, allow us some sympathy for her. Her repeating, "why shouldn't they believe in you," echoes at the next table. (5)

"I tell him all the time. But he doesn't listen" could be a continuation of Suki's ego-bolstering speech but is Julie's complaint to Prue in a crosscut that reiterates and underscores the marginalized position of all the women: their required buttressing of a male partner's sense of self goes unheeded. (6) How is it possible to fill a bottomless well? Yet, Pinter's characters can always be counted on to rise to rather than neutralize, mediate or ignore provocative comments. Billington notes in the biography that nobody ever registers a blow. (169) True, but they almost always retaliate. When Prue castigates Lambert for not listening to Julie, "You've got a loyal wife there and never forget it," Lambert subverts Prue's compliment to diminish Julie and keep her in her place as a sex toy, "She's really loyal under the table." Julie slams back, "Why don't you go and buy a new car and drive it into a brick wall." Unflappable, Lambert exclaims, "She loves me." (6) With this second mention of "love," Matt's reading of Julie nicely parallel's Suki's assessment of her relationship with Russell, that a man's sexual prowess is in his assets—for what they purchase her: "No, she loves new cars," says Matt, to which Lambert assents, "with soft leather seats." (6) The sexually infused language rarely strays far from bawdy intent. Matt's ditty, "Ain't she neat?/As she's walking up the street./She's got a lovely bubbly pair of tits/And soft leather seat," signals his and Lambert's desires as elsewhere engaged. And they are out of wine.

Russell, at the other table, invites more ego-inflating with, "Do you think I have a nice character?" (8) Suki reliably assures him, "I think you do," but quickly qualifies with an insult that cuts to the quick: "but the trouble is that when you come down to it you haven't actually got any character to begin with—I mean as such, that's the thing." (8) Little she could have said could be more devastating or provoke his full frontal assault. Although she softens her candid appraisal by admitting she's the same, "But I wouldn't worry . . . , look at me. I don't have any character either." (8) Taking no comfort in the downgrade to her class or sex, Rusell retaliates. "You're a whore," he lashes out, "with the wind blowing up your skirt." (8) All the women here have in common the ability to stay their ground. Not one shies away, backs off, freezes or breaks down in tears. Undaunted, Suki replies, "How did you know the sensation . . . ? Men don't wear skirts," reducing Russell to name calling: "You're a prick." (9)

The assault on women continues at the first table on a more generalized level with Matt's singing, "Wash me in the water/Where you washed your dirty daughter." (9) Asked if she knows the song, Julie recognizes the insult to women: "It's not in my repertoire, darling." (10) "Darling," throughout is hardly a term of endearment. Lambert, having scored his hit, terminates the topic announcing, "This is the best restaurant in town." *Best,* equated with *most expensive,* registers in his next, "Do you know how much money I made last year?" (10)

Where Lambert expresses pride in his identity that rests in his money-making prowess, Prue conversely airs her self-loathing by airing grievances against her mother-in-law's disapproval of her: "She never gave me one present in the whole of her life. Nothing. She wouldn't give me the drippings off her nose." (10) Prue, as short on prudence as Miss Prue in Congreve's *Love for Love,* recalls perhaps D'Urfey's more blatantly titled play *Love for Money. Celebration* shares Restoration comedy's guiding trinity of power, sex and money conjoined on the marriage market, a comedy that exposes lies, disguises and deception by dissolving them in laughter. But as in all Pinter plays, the laughter ends—at the abyss—where we stand facing ourselves nakedly. For the men to maintain such bloated power the women are diminished to inconsequence.

Julie sides with Prue, joining her self-deprecating complaint, which she transforms into weaponry targeting both the mother and her sons: their own husbands. Julie sympathizes and then with a dollop of sex on a barb mounts a counterattack equally at both their men. "All mothers-in-law are like that. They love their sons . . . , their boys. They don't want their sons to be fucked by other girls." When Prue pushes it, "All mothers want their sons to be fucked by themselves," the men join together topping the women with assertions that exhaust the ridiculous. "All mothers want to be fucked by their mother," says Lambert. "Or by themselves," says Matt. Yet some embedded truth abides, akin to Jocasta's assurance to Oedipus that all boys have desired to marry their mother's—in dreams. The men steamroll over the women and with sheer tenacity win the point by appropriating the opposition's gambit then raising it. "How old do you have to be . . . ?" Lambert asks, "To be fucked by your mother." Matt concludes, "Any age, mate." (10) "Mate," the slang of another class, reminds us that their lifemates have lost this round.

The women come back with a slight shift from Prue's complaint that her husband's mother gives her no gifts to Julie's insulting refusal of her husband's anniversary gift. "How did you enjoy your dinner, darling," Lambert asks. Julie rebuffs him, "I wasn't impressed." Lambert, equating food with sex, money and power, protests, "This is the most expensive fucking restaurant in town and she's not impressed." (12) Richard, the host, arrives at the table to shmooze with his clients, "Been to a play?" (13) Matt says, "No. The ballet," but Lambert can't remember which one, and Matt makes it clear they're putting him on with, "None of them could reach the high notes." (13)

Their polite replies to Richard's obligatory, rhetorical inquiries, "Good dinner?" halt when Lambert, flexing his power, gets in a double dig at his wife and at Richard with, "My wife wasn't impressed." Julie counters with a thrust to both her husband and Richard: "I liked the waiter." When Richard asks, "Which one?" she says, "The one with the fur-lined jockstrap." Lambert holds his ground, "He takes it off for breakfast." But Julie turns it to her advantage, attacking his sexuality, "Which is more than you do." (14) Richard clings to his professional charm, "Well how nice to see you all." (14) But not to deflect the point, Prue enters to defend her sister and defeat the men. Although she opens with fact, "She wasn't impressed with her food," she quickly slips into the outrageous, "She said [. . .] she's my sister [. . .] she said she could cook better than that with one hand stuffed between her legs [. . .]. She said she could make a better sauce than the one on the plate if she pissed into it." She vouches for her sister's veracity by saying, "I've known her all my life [. . .] since we were little innocent girls [. . . .]" (a reminder that no innocence remains), "when we used to lie in the nursery and hear mummy beating the shit out of daddy." She verifies with, "We saw the blood on the sheets," an intimation that these women have been trained in abuse from childhood, having also learned how to "dis" at their mother's knee. The slot-slipping comic tirade ("one hand stuffed between her legs" for "hand tied behind her back"), aimed at an underling, only registers her own impotence and ends unregistered by Matt: "Well, it's lovely to be here, I'll say that." (15)

Prue, undeterred and not to be dismissed by her husband, walks to Richard to thank him personally, then cuts all the men by announcing, "I'd like to kiss you on the mouth." Her forward move, like Lenny's, "Do you mind if I hold your hand?" to Ruth in *The Homecoming,* is intended to send him reeling back. (15) Julie, too, would like to kiss him, "Because I never said I didn't like your sauce. I love your sauce." (16) But when Prue complains, "We can't both kiss him on the mouth at the same time," Lambert meets her thrust with his parry to end the match, "You could tickle his arse with a feather." Richard, ever professionally charming, takes the subservient, coward's way, and ducks out, "Well I'm so glad [. . . .] See you later I hope." (16)

Lambert and Matt solidify their male bond by heaping praise on Richard as a "Charming man who [. . . .] *insists* [. . .] [t]hat standards are maintained up to the highest standards, up to the very highest fucking standards—," reintroducing the question of values where the highest standards equate merely with the most expensive. (16) Their own perverse values continue to propel the conflict as Prue scores the final point of this round with, "I knew him in the old days." Suggestive of a liaison that parallel's Suki's behind-the-filing-cabinet past, she scores again with, "When he was a chef." (17)

Suki picks up her recitative on her usual male bolstering note, "I'm so proud of you," and Russell's encouraging, "Yes?" registers his need to be proud of. (17) She wonders if the unspecified *they* are "good people. [. . .] And when I meet them, when you introduce me to them, they'll treat me with respect, won't they? They won't want to fuck me behind a filing cabinet?" We soon learn that *they* already have fucked her behind the filing cabinet, yet, it is *she* who introduces Russell to more of *them.*

Sonia, as a good hostess, comes to chat them up and recognize their existence as she pushes dessert, "Are you going to try our bread and butter pudding?" (19) Russell seizes center stage with, "Did I ever tell you about my mother's bread and butter pudding?" echoing the sons-and-mothers' lover talk at the other table. In their most intimate moment Suki says: "Darling. Give me your hand [. . .]. Please tell me about your mother's bread and butter pudding. What was it like?" (20) His faintly sexual response,

"It was like drowning in an ocean of richness," elicits Suki's praise, "How beautiful. You're a poet." But Russell chooses to counter her compliment with complaint; he blames parental rejection as the source that justifies his ongoing, wound-licking insecurity. "I wanted to be a poet once. But I got no encouragement from my dad. He thought I was an arsehole." (20) The seeming compliments and compassion flow in only one direction, from female to male, as Suki, seemingly entrained with the other table's conversation echoes, "He was jealous of you, that's all. He saw you as a threat. He thought you wanted to steal his wife."

The Waiter enters to ask "if I may make an interjection," and commenting that he overheard them mention T. S. Eliot, claims his grandfather "knew T S Eliot quite well." (20) The Waiter lists others, a roster of acclaimed British and American writers his grandfather knew in the early three decades of the twentieth century, many of Pinter's acknowledged favorites: Ezra Pound, W. H. Auden, C. Day Lewis, Louis MacNeice, Stephen Spender, George Barker, Dylan Thomas, D. H. Lawrence, Joseph Conrad, Ford Maddox Ford, W. B. Yeats, Aldous Huxley, Virginia Woolf and Thomas Hardy. He claims his grandfather might have been slated for "Chancellor of the exchequer or [. . . .] first Lord of the Admiralty [. . .], but as things turned out he spent most of his spare time in the United States where he was a very close pal of Ernest Hemingway." (21) As his list grows to outrageous proportion to include, "William Faulkner, Scott Fitzgerald, Upton Sinclair, John Dos Passos—you know—that whole vivid Chicago gang—not to mention John Steinbeck, Erskine Caldwell, Carson McCullers and other members of the old Deep south conglomerate," he ends with a wonderful impossibility: "he was James Joyce's godmother." His secondhand and invented self-importance by association, the power of the powerless, reveals, in this context, fame as another species of power.

Russell brushes aside his interjection with, "Have you been working here long?" and asks, "You going to stay until it changes hands?" The Waiter takes it as a threat, "Are you suggesting that I'm about to get the boot?" (22) Unlike Russell, who requires assurances of his identity, the Waiter admits inadequacies, "To be brutally honest, I don't think I'd recover if they did a thing like that." This second, rare disclosure of vulnerability from a Pinter character (which generally can come only from one who accepts subservience), evokes some sympathy in its honesty. But when he says,"This place is like a womb to me [. . .]. I strongly prefer that to being born," the Waiter, links himself to the long and oldest line of Pinter's characters, Rose and Stanley, self-elected underdogs who prefer to remain entombed in their rooms rather than venture out into life. (22)

Russell, who may recognize unwelcome reminders of his own insecurities in the Waiter's admission, easily dismisses him, "Listen, next time we're talking about T S Eliot I'll drop you a card." (23) The Waiter, taking him literally, further accepts his subservient position, "You would make me a very happy man [. . .]. You are incredibly gracious people." (23) Could anything be further from the truth? And those who dismiss him may be as wedded to this restaurant as he is.

Lambert picks up a variant of Russell's self-congratulatory refrain and need for flattering assurances, bouncing off the others with fulsome self-praise, "I know I'm well liked. [. . .] I trust my family and my friends [. . .]. Deep down they trust me [. . .] they respect me—otherwise I wouldn't say this. I wouldn't take you all into my confidence if I thought you all hated my guts [. . .] if I thought you thought I was a pile of dog shit [. . .] I could never be frank and honest with you if that was the truth. . . ." (24) After this windy prelude, he entrusts them with a confession: "you won't believe this, I fell in love once and this girl I fell in love with loved me back. I know she did." (24)

Love, a fleeting possibility even for Lambert, in an earlier and other incarnation, remains the otherwise unspoken desire that all share, but he uses this trusted confession to erase his wife. When Julie asks, "Wasn't that me, darling?" Lambert, dazed, asks, "Who?" Matt brings him back to the present: "Her." Lambert, responding, "Her? No, not her. A girl. I used to take her for walks along the river," obliterates his wife and love for her.[7] (24) Happy anniversary.

But Julie ignores his recollection by offering her own: "Lambert fell in love with me on top of a bus. It was a short journey, Fulham Broadway to Shepherd's Bush, but it was enough. He was trembling all over." (24) She verifies with Prue: "When I got home I came and sat on your bed didn't I?" (24) The buses and neighborhood suggest that they may have all taken a quick ride up the social ladder, from buses to the best restaurant in town. Lambert, oblivious of his wife's digression, continues to cancel her out, "I used to take this girl for walks along the river."[8] Matt protests that he never knew about that. But Lambert suggests Matt never knew his real self, implying the real self is the self who loves, "You knew nothing about me. You know nothing about me. Who the fuck are you anyway?" (24) Matt's, "I'm your big brother," sounds inadequate as Lambert insists, "I'm talking about love, mate [. . .] , real fucking love." (25)

Throughout, *fucking* appears as an intensifying adjective signaling veracity: what is real, and links almost all topics with sex. Everything is sex. But with this third mention of love, all ties begin to unravel as each speaks from his own memory but remains deaf to the others. While Matt insists he knows his brother Lambert, saw him the day he was born, Prue's attempt to reinforce her bond to Julie, "I mean we were sisters, weren't we?" becomes a comically terrifying assertion—that she should ask for, insist upon, verification, yet set the sibling relationship in the past. Ignoring her question, Julie only recalls, "He was trembling like a leaf on top of that bus," bespeaking, perhaps, Lambert's earlier insecurity and forgotten level of passion. (25) In a contrapuntal recitative, Lambert, on his own track, insists, "This girl was in love with me—I'm trying to tell you," as Prue, on her separate track, asks Julie, "Do you remember what you said?" (25) We never learn what Julie said about Lambert in the past, but she now uses that memory to deride him. The only love in any of the characters' lives is long dead.

At this low point of discord and total alienation, Richard visits the other table as Suki observes the opposite: "Everyone is so happy in your restaurant. I mean women *and* men. You make people so happy." (26) This reminder that food has become a pastime, dining out, an entertainment, and restaurants, a retreat, a sanctuary providing a rare moment of community where people face one another and talk, reveals here only false, ferociously combative fronts. Yet, these people face us so that we can face ourselves. Even as Richard assents, "Well we do like to feel that it's a happy restaurant." (26) Russell accedes and then undercuts them both. He describes himself as "basically a totally disordered personality, some people would describe me as a psychopath" at which he turns to Suki for verification. (27) "But when I'm sitting in this restaurant," he says, "I suddenly find I have no psychopathic tendencies at all. I don't feel like killing everyone in sight, I don't feel like putting a bomb under everyone's arse." (27) Although we later learn he is a banker, the introduction of a *bomb* ties his work metaphorically, and later literally, to violence. But, enraptured, he speaks of the restaurant as a spiritual place of communion: "I feel something quite different, I have a sense of equilibrium, of harmony, I love my fellow diners." This won't last long. On the heels of Lambert's confession of love, Russell admits, "Now this is very unusual for me. Normally I feel—as I've just said—absolutely malice and hatred towards everyone within spitting distance—but here I feel love. How do you explain it?" Suki replies with abandoned but comic banality, "It's the ambience," to register the level of Russell's love. (27)

Russell's honest, if horrifying, admission of his violent desires speaks to us all at odd moments if we are honest with ourselves. With the mention of love, he recollects his "old school master [who] used to say that ambience surrounds you." But he set limits on human connection and love: "but none of us boys were ever invited to tea." (27) Offering a connection, Richard free associates to his own childhood visits with his father to "our village pub," looking in from outside, and his remembrance of the gherkins. "I do hope you noticed that you have complimentary gherkins as soon as you take your seats." (28) That the gherkins in the public house of his youth inspired his own restaurant's welcome Suki finds "very moving." Such is the level of discourse: the maudlin sentimental, the mundane and banal. Yet, it is all very funny because we're not laughing at them, at the shock of it, but at the recognition of ourselves in them.

Lambert, at the other table, toasts, "To my wife. To our anniversary," to which Julie counters, "Oh darling! You remembered[. . .]. I'm so touched by this, honestly." (29) Lambert cuts her off with, "Raise your fucking glass and shut up!" (29) Julie, in one of the rarest calls from a Pinter character, acknowledges another character's point-blank attack, "But darling, that's naked aggression. He doesn't normally go in for naked aggression. He usually disguises it under honeyed words." Lambert returns with honeyed words no less brutal for their obvious opposite intention: "We've been married for more bloody years than I can remember and it don't seem a day too long." (29)

Julie and Prue, bonding to wall themselves off from their men, retreat into sentimental reminiscences of their children, each competitively claiming their love from their children as what love they've known in life: "It's funny our children aren't here. When they were young we spent so much time with them, the little things, looking after them [. . .]. They always loved me much more than they loved him." (30) But again, what love once existed is past, the men claim, evaporated.

Matt quashes their remembered love, disavowing their claim by disparaging the children in the present, their ingratitude: "They have no memory [. . .]. They don't remember who their father was or who their mother was." (30) Only the Waiter and Richard fondly recall family, the Waiter, his grandfather, Richard, his father. Matt's use of past tense "who their father was," like Prue's insistence that Julie "was my sister," suggests that family bonds don't strengthen in time but dissolve.

Again, like the observation of British psychologist Frederick Bartlett whose research on memory concludes that we remember only fragmentary portions of a past occurrence but supply the rest from what we invent or recall from other past experiences, Pinter's characters seem to wander through a past equally invented and remembered, but additionally here used in the present as an arsenal: weaponry to inflict wounds and nearly destroy others. But the target must not be terminated, or the game's over. And so the relationships continue when Sonia enters and learns this is an anniversary celebration when Prue recalls, "I was her leading bridesmaid," and Matt, "I was his best man," continuing the many references to a best man from *Tea Party* and *Betrayal* through Pinter's most recent work. But fact remembered quickly moves to invention when Lambert says, "I was just about to fuck her at the altar when somebody stopped me" and Matt joins in his invention. "I stopped him. His zip went down and I kicked him up the arse. It would have been a scandal. The world's press was on the doorstep." (32) *Celebration's* casual, even comic reference to the world's press brings us a long way from the desire for worldwide fame expressed in *The Homecoming*. Here, in what these men really do in their clandestine work, they seek not notoriety but subterfuge, like the U.S.'s National Security Agency, the NSA, known as No Such Agency.

Sonia, professionally, unflinchingly straight-faced, dismisses Matt's description of Lambert unzipping at the alter quite simply with, "We get so many different kinds of people in here, people from all walks of life." She quotes herself as saying, "'You don't have to speak English to enjoy good food,'" and joins in peripherally likening food to sex, "You don't have to speak English to enjoy sex." (32) Sonia, from Bethnal Green, attempts to reveal her own "worldly" sexual adventures, raising another epistemological question about how we know and how we form generalities, opinions and judgments of the world. She reveals how they come frequently from firsthand, anecdotal, and limited information, limited often to a single, anecdotal remembered window on the world. "Yes, it's funny," says Sonia, veering the conversation from the inane to the maudlin, "I met a man from Morocco once and he was very interested in sex." (33) About to cry, she says he died, "In another woman's arms. He was on the job." A professional sex worker? But she asks only sympathy, "Can you see how tragic my life has been?" (33) No current love touches any of these lives. Sonia registers an *Old-Times* moment when the pleasures of the "lookingforwardness," now lost, rob all pleasure in the present moment. Sonia exits with a variant of that smiley-faced farewell heard round the English speaking world, "Have a happy night." (33)

The Waiter returns to continue his cultural history lesson, moving forward in the twentieth century with a second interjection about his grandfather, who he claims was familiar with 1930s Hollywood: "Clark Gable, Elisha Cook Jr. [. . .] one of the very few native born Englishman to have had it off with Hedy Lamarr." (34) He meets Lambert's "What was she like in the sack?" with an equally startling, "He said she was really tasty." (34) The Waiter's reintroduction of violence and of brutality in his mention of Hollywood's "Irish Mafia" and their friendships among "famous Irish gangsters in Chicago. Al Capone and Victor Mature [. . .]. John Dillinger, the celebrated gangster and Gary Cooper the celebrated film star," reflects Pinter's own youthful fascination with gangster films, and his ongoing exploration of violence and its causes in his plays. "They were Jewish," may also recall attacks upon him as a youthful Jew, along with resonance to the World War II Holocaust. Lambert wrests the spotlight from the nameless waiter by indicating Suki, "You see that girl at that table?" (Not woman, but girl.) "I know her. I fucked her when she was eighteen." (35) His wife, Julie's, nonplussed retort, "What, by the banks of the river?" dismisses Suki as a candidate for Lambert's recalled love.

When Lambert waves, Suki comes to him, and they openly flirt as Russell joins them and accepts Lambert's hospitality, "A drop of that red wine would work wonders." (37) Suki seeks to strengthen their past bond, "Are you still obsessed with gardening." Julie's attempts to split the two apart, "He adores flowers. The other day I saw him emptying a piss pot into a bowl of lilies," dumps water over Suki's advances. Russell's attempt to dip his oar into the current conversation, "My dad was a gardener," only meets with the rebuffed Suki's dismissal, "He was always walking about with a lawn mower," pegging him down a rung in class as a man who mows his own lawn. Julie terminates garden talk with sex talk she draws from her arsenal to shoot Suki down: "Funny that when you knew my husband you thought he was obsessed with gardening. I always thought he was obsessed with girls' bums."(39)

When Prue attempts to detoxify the lethality of these past remembrances, "Oh don't get excited. It's all in the past," Suki repeats another *Old Times*' line, "I sometimes feel that the past is never past." (39)

What would they do if they could live life over? Nothing very different.

Although Julie says, "I wouldn't like to live again, though [. . .]. Once is more than enough," Lambert insists he would: "In fact I'm going to make it my job to live again." In a rare accurate awareness and assessment of a present self for a Pinter character, Lambert proposes, "I'm going to come back as a better person, a more civilised person, a gentler person, a nicer person." But, Julie says, "Impossible." (40)

Jealousy wreaks revenge on all fronts. When Prue wonders where Lambert and Suki met, Russell finally strikes his delayed revenge at Suki, "Behind a filing cabinet." (40) The main table joins forces behind Julie's, "What's a filing cabinet?" (40) However, Julie also reveals she knows very well, when she asks what Suki does and Suki says she's a schoolteacher: "I teach infants," a comic surprise in this context and indicative of the future, the values these people promote to their children. Prue and Julie join together by one-upping her in class, "We run charities"—the women's work in the class that does the cleanup following their husband's "peacekeeping" efforts and economics. (41) We're reminded of Blake's assertion that mercy and pity would be no more if we did not make somebody poor.

When Matt guesses by the way he stands that Russell is a banker, the men begin to dance together even as Lambert mocks, "With a big future before him," and Matt joins in, "Well that's what he reckons." (41) When Suki asks what they do (she's slept with Lambert but never knew what work he did), Matt and Lambert remain illusive: "Well, we're consultants. Matt and me. Strategy consultants [. . .]. It means we don't carry guns." (42) The denial reveals as Matt says, "We don't have to." They broker them. That of course must remain unspoken. "We're peaceful strategy consultants," says Matt, and Lambert concurs with another self-referential descriptor that infers the opposite. "Worldwide. Keeping the peace" dramatizes the main point of Pinter's 25 June 1999 speech to the Confederation of Analytical Psychologists, delivered only months before *Celebration* was written, when he denounced the NATO "peacekeeping" action in Serbia as "yet another blatant and brutal assertion of US power." (1)

Elated, Russell says, "wonderful," and, as a banker with money behind guns brokering, he insists, in double speak cliché, "We need a few more of you about [. . .]. Taking responsibility. Taking charge. Keeping the peace." (43) He wastes no time. Networking to promote his own economic advantage, he attempts to bond with them. "I think I'll have a word with my bank. I'm moving any minute to a more substantial bank. I'll have a word with them." His ego inflated with this brush with power, he confidently proposes, "I'll suggest lunch. In the City. I know the ideal restaurant. All the waitresses have big tits." This final move, marrying "peacekeeping" with guns, money and sex, puts all the men in bed together.

Any seismic disturbances caused by their women now or in earlier liaisons can be dismissed or turned to advantage by an upwardly mobile, insecure young man like Russell now bonding with the more powerful. When Suki registers and replies to his dismissal, "Aren't you pushing the tits bit a bit far?" (43) he flips her aside as an annoyance: "Me? I thought you did that." (43) Again, it was Suki, through her affair with Lambert, who brokered Russell's introduction to these men, and inadvertantly placed them all in bed together. But when Lambert and Matt check Russell, blatantly acting inelegantly out of his pain and jealousy, they signal their own power. "Be careful. You're talking to your wife," Lambert cautions (though he of course has said far worse to his), and Matt joins in, "Have some respect, mate." The reference to *mate,* in the masculine sense, again nicely negates its meaning between these men and their women in marriage.

When Russell attempts to defend himself, deflecting the attack with a diversionary question, "So how is the strategic consultancy business these days?" Matt answers with a nicely ambiguous, "Very good. We're at the receiving end of some of the best tea in China," signaling the third component of their arms and money connections: drugs.

Richard then enters with a legal drug of choice, a magnum of champagne, the Waiter, following with glasses as "Everyone gasps," and Richard toasts, "To celebrate a treasured wedding anniversary," furthering the comic effect with what seems furthest from the truth. (44) Matt exclaims the champagne "the best of the best," as Lambert salutes his ongoing vision of life as a contest, "May the best man win!" (44) Only the worst win here.

Julie and Prue counter his insult by concurring with one another: "The woman always wins." Suki finds that "good news." (44) In what sense can this possibly be true? Is this another self-referential assertion thrown in to call it into absolute doubt and utterly dismiss it? At some level, these women, as kept women, ignorant and perhaps necessarily kept in the dark about their men's financial dealings, seem to live comfortably padded, safe existences, tolerating their marginalization by holding ground, deflecting their husbands' attacks, the primary form of attention and engagement the people in these marriages seem to accord one another. After all, this is the jolly old form of pisstaking, the witty British truth-telling insult of affection honed to a fine art. And the women play nearly as well as the men. But they initiate little action. And they accept themselves as powerless to command their men, to halt or reverse their action or to direct their own in the larger world. Richard pronounces the benediction/toast, carrying an ironic echo of Tiny Tim's blessing at the end of Dickens's *Christmas Carol*. "To the happy couple. God bless. God bless you all." (45)

At another level, however, Pinter seems to be dramatizing the necessary complicity of women, these women, which can allow, even encourage these men to conduct their affairs of the world. The reward is wealth and power. Who would willingly or easily give up such comfort and safety that these women and men enjoy? Does Pinter suggest what might be done? No more than he suggests how we might address the question of how we might stop the ongoing "peacekeeping" conflicts and the slaughter these men perpetuate. While even the precise nature of their work in the world must no doubt elude, puzzle or certainly seem a mystery to many in Pinter's audiences, again, the master trusts his audience. If he has deliberately tapped into mystery (for a great many reasons—to keep their precise work intentionally vague to cover many bases, to reflect the necessity for such secrecy in the clandestine arms brokering in the world), one main reason for the puzzle would seem to ask us to question, and in questioning to begin to seek answers. Almost anyone with the savvy to attend a Pinter play lives in some degree of informed privilege, invested at some level in world markets and with that privilege comes some responsibility: to ask, to seek answers, to act.

Lambert signals the beginning of the end, offering Richard "a cuddle" in boozy affection, a thanks and farewell, a reversal of Julie's and Prue's earlier threat to kiss Richard. He cuddles Sonia, commends them both, "This is so totally rare, you see. None of this normally happens," a comment on the whole play. (45) He discourses on the estrangement of people, "normally [. . .] so distant from each other [. . .] this given bloke doesn't know that another given bloke exists." (45) Nor does Lambert seem to know anyone else exists, except as target practice. His observation and excuse, "It goes down through history, doesn't it?" both exonerates his own license to kill and recognizes self-absorbed, individual isolation as a major contributing factor in global conflict which requires addressing through a knowledge that includes history, politics, economics, psychology, and both chaos and power theory. (45)

Sonia, disregarding Lambert's larger point, illustrates his point precisely by taking this slight pretext for mentioning an estrangement of her own. She tells Julie and Prue, "I'm so touched that you're sisters," adding, "I had a sister. But she married a foreigner and I haven't seen her since." Inclusiveness is not a hallmark of this club. Prue grudges, "Some foreigners are all right." (46) Sonia concedes, "Oh I think foreigners are charming." They're her source of revenue: "Most people in this restaurant tonight are foreigners." She covers her bigotry claiming her reasons for rejecting her sister's husband were personal, not prejudiced, his "enormous moustache. I had to kiss him at the wedding. I can't describe how awful it was." (46)

This time in front of his employer, the Waiter interjects, moving through the century's wars with his references to "the Austro-Hungarian Empire" again, hauling out his grandfather this time as "an incredibly close friend of the Archduke himself [. . . who] once had a cup of tea with Benito Mussolini." (46) Suggesting that the world leaders are all in bed together, he even implicates his own family, and by association, himself as well: "They all played poker together, Winston Churchill included." (46) He admits his grandfather had "a really strange life." He says, "The palms of his hands always seemed to be burning," a reference perhaps to avarice and greed. But as a commentary on the brevity of love and life, he admits, in echo of Lambert's story of lost love and Sonia's of lost lust that prefigures his final story of his own lost grandfather whom he loved: "He was in love, he told me once, with the woman who turned out to be my grandmother, but he lost her somewhere." (46–47) The grandfather is the only one of the bunch we see or hear about here who married for love. Could she have been lost like Rebecca's baby in *Ashes to Ashes?* The Waiter reflects a postmodern complexity in the character of his grandfather, an invented yet collective of all grandfathers, whether or not they visited in the halls of fame and power with men who shaped the century in this peculiarly end-of-the-century, turn-of-the-millennium play. What these many men and few women stood for, valued and acted upon resonates throughout the Waiter's summary catalogs, and his reminiscence of invented remembrance suggests some measure of forgiveness, for they, like all of us, knew not what they did. The waiter insists that his grandfather was an ideal, even Christlike, "everything men aspired to be in those days [. . .], tall, dark and handsome. He was full of good will. He'd even give a cripple with no legs crawling on his belly [. . .] a helping hand [. . . .] He was like Jesus Christ in that respect. And he loved the society of his fellows," the only character in these plays, offstage and long dead who does. (47)

He launches his *De Capo Al Fine,* grandiose summary finale of twentieth-century poets, playwrights, cricket players, pop musicians, singers, writers and comics his grandfather knew: "W B Yeats, T S Eliot, Igor Stravinsky, Picasso, Ezra Pound, Bertholt Brecht, Don Bradman, the Beverley Sisters, the Inkspots, Franz Kafka and the Three Stooges." The Waiter claims his grandfather knew them in their wounds. "He knew these people where they were isolated, where they were alone, where they fought against savage and pitiless odds," and against those same odds one may wonder whether Pinter is speaking out of his own experience, wondering who now is on a par with the household-word famous of the first three decades of the twentieth century, and which ones will continue to endure. At some level the Waiter's declamations remind us that these people in this play, for whatever power they possess, don't even have a shot at such fame. When the Waiter claims his grandfather knew them "where they suffered vast wounds to their bodies, their bellies, their legs, their trunks, their eyes, their throats, their breasts, their balls—," Lambert cuts him off at this sexual juncture, rendering him invisible by turning to his host: "Well, Richard—what a great dinner!" addressing him familiarly and condescendingly by his first name, a liberty Richard dare not take in return—but an action indicative of hierarchy's firm hold. (47)

Lambert's next gesture of even greater condescension solidifies his position as he tosses tips of fifty pound notes, two to Richard (ignoring the custom not to tip the owner), then dangles notes in front of Sonia's cleavage, and even stuffs a note in the Waiter's pocket, punctuating his ostentation with, "Great dinner. Great restaurant. Best in the country." To which Matt adds, "Best in the world." Money ensures position, purchases the assurance that they'll be treated royally upon their return and serves as a weapon to keep those serving at a distance, in their place.[9] When Lambert demands "their bill," taking Suki and Russell's with the announcement "It's for old time's sake," and Suki assents, "Right," Lambert has effectively marked her as his turf. Richard, disregarding all insult, says, "See you again soon?"

Lambert assures him, "Plenty of celebrations to come." For these men who are responsible for the "peacekeeping" lives and deaths of others, he remarks in death imagery: "Rest assured," and "Dead right." Matt and Lambert cap off the evening with a bonding duet that manages to slash out one last time at the women and describe the plays's powerplays in a comic echo of Abbot and Costello's "Who's on first": "Who's in front? Who's in front. Get out of the bloody way. You silly old cunt!" (49)

Suki, put in her place, turns on Russell, putting him in place: "How sweet of him to take the bill, wasn't it?" (49) Russell reads Suki correctly as insulting him as well as Lambert's wife, Julie: "He must have been very fond of you." (50)

Sonia says, "See you soon," only to be met with Matt's comic, "I'll be here for breakfast tomorrow morning." (50) Julie and Suki, with the last words from the group, exit as each says to the other what can only be a honeyed lie: "Lovely to meet you." (51)

The Waiter, alone, has the final word, the first fully human, touchingly warm and genuinely puzzled words of the evening as he recalls perhaps his real grandfather who "used to take me to the edge of the cliffs and we'd look out to sea" with a telescope. He doesn't think they have al but the high-tech telescopes anymore, an odd locution but in a sense he's correct—binoculars have replaced all but the high tech telescopes for distant viewing. He recalls seeing people on a boat, a man, sometimes, and a woman, or sometimes two men. That image of people viewed from a great distance, reinforces a dominant metaphor for the play's dramatization of the bonds between people—as distant, almost, but not quite, nonexistent.

He claims, "My grandfather introduced me to the mystery of life and I'm still in the middle of it," but then he says, "I can't find the door to get out." His reverse echo of Bridget, the dead sister and daughter in *Moonlight* who can't get into the door at the party, becomes an image of death. Here, it is life that the Waiter cannot exit. "My grandfather got out of it. He got right out of it. He left it behind and he didn't look back." (51) But the Waiter can neither find his way out of life nor participate fully in it. Nor can any of the other characters, although their celebration seems a "picnicking at the edge of the precipice," as Lauren Belfer describes in *City of Light* the consequences of early-twentieth-century robber barons' investment in Niagara Falls power plants with the intent of diverting the falls dry for their own gain.

In *Celebration* Pinter has brought us as close as we have come in his work to those picnicking on the global precipice—all of us here—and this time we're laughing all the way through as long as we can avoid looking at our own pain and truth that ignites the flash of comic laughter and the insight we are happier to avoid. Harold Hobson was right those many years ago when he observed, "Mr Pinter has got hold of a primary fact of existence. We live on the verge of disaster." (11) *Celebration* is written with such extraordinary economy that close attention is required not to miss the significance of the destructive wit. This play, another about power and the lack of power, is equally about what almost all Pinter's work is about: love, the desperate desire for it and the resulting destructiveness in the lack of love. But this time he's given us a closer and, in its comedy, a more compassionate look at those more fully responsible for trafficking in the destruction of this planet and its people to awaken us to the primal terror and the delight that illuminates how we are all complicit. And at another level *Celebration* reveals the source of conflict as embedded in the most intimate of human relationships, between friends, lovers and marriage partners, raising great and many questions about the mystery of life. He both dramatizes and asks us *Why—do we act as we do?* He sends us on a quest to seek the most effective means to confront conflict, realizing that our task, like his, is not just that remedial work necessary to effect change, but that the harder task of discovering, implementing change remains ours. The slow fade on the Waiter's unfinished last line, "And I'd like to make one further interjection," tosses the final word to us to ask and answer that conflict with our lives.

Notes

1. Rebecca, along with Leah, Rachel and Sara, is acknowledged as one of the four mothers of Israel; I am indebted to Leslie Fiedler for this insight.
2. Of course, in the absence of a real child in this relationship, she may be talking about a baby or child lost or never born alive.
3. Marc Silberstein, "Talking about some kind of atrocity" *Pinter Review* 1997–1998, 74–85 refers to Devlin as a Devil; Katherine H. Burkman, "Harold Pinter's *Ashes to Ashes*: Rebecca and Devlin as Albert Speer," 86-96. Burkman concludes, "Towards the end of his life Speer had an affair and perhaps learned to love. Perhaps, like Speer, she will now be able to." (94)
4. I am indebted to Francis Gillen for his admirable assessment in "My Dark House."
5. Stephen Dunn, " Some mysteries can be solved by ampersands/*And* not *ors*: that was my latest answer." "Oklahoma City" *American Poetry Review* Sept.–Oct. 1999, 99.
6. Quoted by Garrison Keillor an "The Writers Almanac," WNED-FM, Buffalo, NY November 30, 1999.
7. Lambert's response echoes Andy's in *Moonlight* when, as Bridget stands before him in the dark, his wife approaches and he says, "A woman walked towards me in a darkening room." When his wife says, "That was me," he says, "Who?"
8. Pinter throughout many of his works, recalls a woman in walks along the river especially from his youthful novel *The Dwarfs* and the short fiction "Lola."
9. Jake in Hemingway's *The Sun Also Rises* offers a similar philosophy of a fair exchange, money in exchange for service that approximates fellowship and friendship.

Some Conclusions on Love, Justice and Power in the Pinter Ethic: The Public Consequence of Private Acts

Love, in Pinter's work, without compassion for the other and without understanding of the self and what drives the self cannot engender justice but only furthers continued conflict. As a generative power, love is key to the ethic in Pinter's plays. Not only does the desire for love and respect provide the wellspring for almost all action, but that desire which drives his work points to what is consistently portrayed as a primary end of the ethic: life-enhancing attitude, intention, and action.

Pinter's work most often dramatizes the ethic by negation, through its absence, by showing what it is not: a brutally, destructive force, claiming nevertheless to serve the powers of preservation. Throughout his work, characters fight most fiercely to *maintain* rather than to gain a position of power which is what makes the brothers in *Moonlight* so dangerous. The subsequent conflict ironically most often destroys the larger end it seeks: respect, friendship, love—relationship.

Recent scholars, especially feminists, have spoken of a need to return Eros to our ethic in order to reconnect the self with the whole. Nancy Qualls-Corbett, in her 1988 study *The Sacred Prostitute: Eternal Aspect of the Feminine,* argues for the need to reinstate love and the erotic in the self if justice is to be achieved.[1] Pinter's plays dramatize what Qualls-Corbett argues—the importance of love beyond its current practice:

> The dominant images in the Western world are those of power, wealth and technical knowledge—these are the "gods" we currently honor. . . .Paper hearts and baby cupids hardly suffice; they are symbols of a sentimental romanticism which merely fulfills ego desires. (144; ellipses mine)

Pinter's passionate lovers go beyond "paper hearts" but only to dramatize how much further they must go. What Qualls-Corbett calls for is that wisdom that comes from wholeness that can combine love and justice. In her final chapter, "The Restoration of the Soul," Qualls-Corbett turns to the Wisdom of Solomon: "For wisdom is a loving spirit." (143) But in Pinter's work love is not enough.

Pinter portrays a world which fittingly could only be expressed in drama, where verbal expression and mere intentions may be nothing but where action is all. However much Pinter's work endorses the electrically charged yet highly restrained expression of erotic love and passion, the pleasures and importance of friendship and human relationship, it also acknowledges the power Thanatos gains when it claims the ecstasy of Eros as its own—unless Eros can reclaim its generative power. His is a drama which calls for action. Through the fractal geometry structuring his plays, his work consistently dramatizes how private acts have public consequences. The private battles to maintain power, fought for respect, love and ultimately survival, have repercussions on public justice. Hence, Pinter's work links love and justice, redefining them through action.

If, as Aristotle maintains, love is a relationship between equals in beauty, strength (both physical and moral), and wisdom, then the redefinition of love that Pinter's work calls for is not new but one which realizes development beyond the level of physical attraction to a bond formed through wise action. His plays awaken a necessary consciousness of connection between the other and self in any relationship if love is going to serve justice as a power to promote life.

The fractal geometry in Pinter's work, which reflects and refracts the powerplays from the smallest beat to the work as a whole, links love and justice through the seemingly unlinkable—the world of the microcosmic, the private, to the macrocosmic, the public, and to world powers which sometimes overwhelm. The fractal geometry that reveals how acts on the private level have consequences on the public also conveys optimistic possibility in the simple but important conclusion: that we may have choices at all levels, if we can appreciate our own power on the smallest level which forms the basis for all other action.

Action can, of course, include destructive violence and action seems to be the province of Pinter's dominant characters, whose acts often destroy others and also deaden many levels of their own lives. But the subservient characters, in possession of life-affirming values, often remain unable to act to promote their values.

There is an elegance in the symmetry and simplicity of Pinter's work driven by a dominant/subservient conflict that is the heartbeat of all else. But the beauty may appear to be the violent brute beauty of blood sports, the bull fight, boxing, the cock fight, or surrogate warfare, the life-and-death battles of hockey, soccer, and football that fascinate, like the more subtly combative sports that attract Pinter—cricket, squash, and tennis. Since his plays rely almost exclusively upon the dominant/subservient conflict for tension, Pinter could be accused of exploiting the violence he condemns to ignite his work—unless we recognize the larger end it serves.

Linked to the violence in Pinter's plays are the tender inner workings that drive human existence, a quest for love. The conflict repeatedly dramatizes that the very quest for love, respect, and survival, when driven by the desire to dominate another, inevitably leads to destruction of human relationship by destroying both the other and in many senses the self. Pinter creates characters who must make difficult choices, traveling the razor-thin line between choice and chance, to be judged by what they *do* or *fail to do* either to promote concord or further conflict, violence, and suffering.

In this world of uncertainty the ethic in Pinter's plays extends to the global level, dramatizing how endorsing an authoritarian dominator society, any hierarchical power or superpower, promotes greater uncertainty and inevitable destruction. Pinter has looked back upon his early works as "metaphors" opposing authoritarian political actions at all levels:

> When you look at them, they're much closer to an extremely critical look at authoritarian postures—state power, family power, religious power, power used to undermine, if not destroy the individual, or the questioning voice, or the voice which simply went away from the mainstream and refused to become part of an easily recognizable set of standards and social values. (Hern, 8)

What rescues Pinter's plays from charges of didacticism as modern morality plays? At least the complexity, the comic wit, and that overriding compassion for all his characters which finally directs audience attention to seeking sources of both conflict and concord not merely in the other but first, primarily within the sell. That self in Pinter's plays often seeks meaning in life through transcendent ecstasy as powerful as erotic ecstasy but supplied by identification of the self with a cause or group outside the self—identification with a class, family, nation, religion, or even a football team. Such identification results in both refusing to acknowledge connection between the sell and other and attempting to defeat or destroy anyone who does not endorse one's own group, belief, or values. Such destruction, and its attendant human suffering, is paradoxically done in the name of transcendent good.

But Pinter consistently returns focus to the self as the source of suffering and to the self-knowledge required as a starting point for any productive change. The self-knowledge needed for change requires that we see ourselves nakedly, a point Pinter made in an address praising Graham Greene:

> What he was looking at, his "simplisticness" if that is the proper term, seems to me to consist in being able to look at a tortured naked body. This is a thing that is very rarely done when we are looking at ourselves. ("Graham Green 1904–1991: A Tribute to the Late Writer," n.p.)

Pinter's recent work not only bares the tortured nakedly before us, but forces us to acknowledge the torturer in the self.

Pinter's work evokes a complex but clear constellation of causes for destruction from the reflexive, dominant/subservient conflict and the unconscious impetus that keeps the struggle in motion, the quotidian habits that promote violence or deaden the self to change, the brain chemistry and hardwiring that allow humans to enjoy "all that power" of a torturer, and the quest for respect and love which, when coupled with insecurity and lack of self-knowledge, leads to a struggle for dominance while robbing the self of the knowledge that such a struggle can only self-destruct. Pinter does not dramatize the ravings of the aberrant psychopath, but the actions of fairly ordinary human beings embodying attitudes and actions most humans share. Implied in the dramatized causes for destruction are opposite actions and attitudes which might promote rather than destroy life. Pinter's *Moonlight* takes us beyond his earlier work in revealing a core cause central to all others: the vision. Once made conscious as the source which shapes and drives all else, (attitude, intention and action), a revised vision permits choices and the possibility of change. Pinter's work exposes the traditional heroic vision as requiring a model who stands above the self, out there and other, to inspire and take responsibility. That image identification with a person, a god, or country inherently promotes continued conflict between the self and other. That vision brought into consciousness suggests a revised vision where each self, regarding the other is as another self, recognizes and takes responsibility. Thus, the vision in Pinter's work both dramatizes what destroys and implies what might sustain human life.

The Pinter canon, best appreciated in its totality, combines a unique voice with values tested in action that awaken in the audience self-knowledge and create a fresh vision which is integral to human survival. The ethic in Pinter's work which begins in self-knowledge is informed by traditional Western virtues and values: honor, loyalty, courage, friendship, love, justice, magnanimity, and above all freedom as necessary to all else. Those virtues, however, cannot serve in the old way to promote us-vs.-them attitudes and actions but, as Pinter's work dramatizes, must be enlarged to acknowledge interdependence in all human relationship, to respect and to treat the other like another self—to regard the other's life as one's own. But Pinter's plays, ever acknowledging the bastard in us all, never underestimate the enormity of such a task. Moreover, the values and virtues which his ethic endorses are expressed always through action within very specific contexts.

Pinter is not a theorist but a dramatist, challenging received definitions and dramatizing the supreme difficulty in defining and applying any values. A single virtue such as loyalty is confronted in a multitude of ways in a play such as *Betrayal,* to say nothing of the many dimensions of honor and friendship. In *One for the Road, Mountain Language, Party Time,* and *The New World Order,* love and justice in the discourse of torturers are claimed as their province exclusively. Yet for Pinter, torture and destruction, such as the deaths of one hundred and fifty thousand Iraqis in the Gulf War, are not simply statistics but remain human truths he tries to express in his plays. Salman Rushdie defended "a writer's proper function" in terms that might describe Pinter's own:

> . . . to challenge established descriptions of society, to oppose power with imagination, to set the living language of art against the dead prose of political discourse—and to do so both inside and outside the work. (Rushdie, 43)

Yet finally Pinter's plays continue to remain as apolitical as he claimed for his work at the outset of his career. His most recent plays transcend chauvinistic political concerns in seeking to link justice with Eros and complexity with honesty. *Moonlight,* in revealing the common source of love and destruction and the connection between love, power and justice, dramatizes how those who view themselves as benign, having harmed no one, or doing good, may be the most destructive of all. Most of his characters retain a complexity which produces an honesty rare in drama and literature. Almost all his bastards retain some hint of an admirable quality, and his admirable characters, something of the bastard. His ethic combines with an aesthetic in his plays to produce the depth and integrity that distinguish his work and to extend subtle hope—at the private level his plays force reexamination of individual responsibility. That responsibility allows for the possibility of change.

If the strengths of Pinter's dominant and subservient characters could be combined to create a single being, we might approach an ideal. However much Pinter's work calls for change, Pinter never subscribes to belief in an ideal. Yet significant change—the genius breakthroughs that change the way we view the world or interact with it—as Stewart Brand repeatedly observes in *The Media Lab: Inventing the Future at MIT*—most often come not in seeking either/or solutions but in finding both/and alternatives. As they are, Pinter's characters resemble the two halves of a single sphere that Plato describes in Aristophanes's parable on the origin of love (Symposium, 189–190). Where his subservient characters often possess values which would promote life, it is often only the dominant characters who possess the power to act. However, the rift between those characters, like the split Pinter frequently dramatizes between love and justice, is not an impossible gulf that can only be healed by magic, bridged by some fundamental shift in human nature or by the imposition of an impossible ideal from without but as the recent plays attempt to dramatize, can be healed by attention, awareness, questioning, and by developing consciousness in *both* those who perpetuate destruction and those who stand to be most immediately destroyed by abuses of power. Above all, the split requires a fundamental shift in the vision which informs human life. His plays do not address life as a game of winners and losers but as a seriously disturbing, often delightful, endeavor where finally either both win or both lose.

It is Pinter's insistence upon the whole truth that makes him a reliable witness of the present and trustworthy guide to the future. He gives full play to the darkside of the human life in almost all his characters, not in the sense that a Thomas Pynchon might, often excluding the light, but in that recognition of "the goblins" that E. M. Forster heard in Beethoven and "the panic and emptiness" they engender following "gusts of splendour, the heroism, the youth, the magnificence of life and of death . . . amid vast roarings of superhuman joy." (34) Forster, like Pinter, has no illusions that they can be dispelled:

> But the goblins were there. They could return. He had said so bravely, and that is why one can trust Beethoven when he says other things. (34)

For Pinter the goblins, our darkside, exist concurrently with the light in each of us and are embedded in the unconscious vision which drives attitude, intention and action.

The ethic dramatized throughout Pinter's work requires that attitude and intention follow through to action. A consciousness awakened to our goblins will require necessary action, and Pinter's work is one attempt to awaken consciousness. But his work and his life go further.

Just as the past two decades have witnessed a radical change in Pinter, his work seeks to awaken a dramatic change in his audience. He has admittedly gone from being "an artist in an ivory tower . . . , a rather classic nineteenth-century idea," (Tusa, 13) to a radical exponent of a great many causes for human freedom, campaigning against censorship and the abrogation of freedoms on many fronts: from the brutalities of Nicaraguan Contras and the *intifada* to attempts to prohibit gay expression. His work calls for no less a change. Pinter's most recent play, *Moonlight,* offers a fresh vision, producing a paradigm shift that removes the hero/heroine from the stage/page to the audience, granting the play greater agency and empowering an audience. The values in Pinter's work finally inspire and demand a conscious paradigm shift for right action, not only from his characters but finally from his audience. Ultimately the Pinter ethic dramatizes the need for an awakened, whole human being free to act with awareness and courage upon deeply considered virtues for the welfare of all in order to promote just life.

NOTES

1. She proposes to restore Eros through the eternal feminine which has appeared throughout the ages in many guises from Astarte, Venus, Athena, Sophia the goddess of wisdom to the Black Madonna and Mary Magdalene: "Like the sacred prostitute, she mediated between the world of the divine and the world of humans." (150) Whether or not we subscribe to notions of transcendence or divinity, I believe we acknowledge, as Qualls-Corbett emphasizes and Pinter's plays dramatize, the importance of love beyond its current practice: "We no longer worship the goddess of love; consequently we have no container for sexual ecstasy, the numinous state where the inner core of the individual is awakened and revealed to self and other." (140)

Select Bibliography

Primary Sources: Arranged Chronologically

Essays and Poetry by Harold Pinter: Juvenilia, 1946–1948

"James Joyce." *Hackney Downs School Magazine* 160 (Christmas 1946): 32–33.

"Speech: That a United Europe Would Be the Only Means of Preventing War." *Hackney Downs School Magazine* 161 (Spring 1947): 14.

"Dawn." (poem) *Hackney Downs School Magazine* 161 (Spring 1947): 27.

"Speech: That War Is Inevitable." *Hackney Downs School Magazine* 162 (Summer 1947): 9.

"O Beloved Maiden." (poem) *Hackney Downs School Magazine* 162 (Summer 1947): 14.

"Speech: Realism and Post-Realism in the French Cinema." *Hackney Downs School Magazine* 163 (Autumn 1947): 13.

"Blood Sports." *Hackney Downs School Magazine* 163 (Autumn 1947): 23–24.

"Speech: Supporting the Motion that 'In View of Its Progress in the Last Decade, the Film Is More Promising in Its Future as an Art than the Theatre.'" *Hackney Downs School Magazine* 164 (Spring 1948): 2.

Poetry, Plays, Fiction, and Essays: 1949–2000

Published under the Name Harold Pinta

"New Year in the Midlands" (poem) and "Chandeliers and Shadows" (poem). *Poetry London* 19 (Aug. 1950): 8, 9.

"New Year in the Midlands" (poem reprinted with corrections), "Rural Idyll" (poem) and "European Revels" (poem). *Poetry London* 20 (Nov. 1950): n.p.

"The Second Visit" (poem). *The Window* 2 (1950): 13.

"You in the Night" (poem). *The Glass* 7 (1950): 13.

"So, This Morning of Marvels" (poem). *Poetry Quarterly* 13.1 (Spring 1951): 7.

"One a Story, Two a Death" *Poetry London* 22 (Summer 1951): 22–24.

"Kullus" (dialogue). *Poems*. London: Enitharmon Press, 1968.

Published under the Name Harold Pinter

The Birthday Party. London: Encore, 1959; London: French, 1960; London: Methuen, 1960. Revised 1962; reprinted: New York: Grove, 1969; *Complete Works: One*. New York: Grove Press, 1977.

"The Examination." *Prospect* (Summer 1959): n.p.

The Room. London: French, 1960; New York: Dramatists Play Service, 1961; New York: Grove Press, 1961, revised 1968; *Complete Works: One*. New York: Grove Press, 1977.

The Dumb Waiter. London: Methuen, 1960; London: French, 1964; New York: Dramatists Play Service, 1964; New York: Grove Press, 1964 (with *The Caretaker*); *Complete Works: One*. New York: Grove Press, 1977.

Black and White (revue sketch). *Spectator* 205 (July 1960): 16; (fiction) *Flourish* (Summer 1965) n.p.; *Transatlantic Review* 21 (Summer 1966): 51–52.

The Caretaker. London: Methuen, 1960; London: French, 1960; New York, 1960: Dramatists Play Service; New York, 1960: Grove Press, 1964; *Complete Works: Two*. New York: Grove Press, 1977. *The Caretaker* film written in 1963, opened as *The Guest* in New York, 1964.

Letter. *Times* (London) 9 Dec. 1960: 11.

A Slight Ache. *Tomorrow*. Oxford, 4 (1960): n.p.; London: French, 1962; New York: Dramatists Play Service, 1962; New York: Grove Press, 1962; *The Complete Works: One*. New York: Grove Press, 1977.

"Writing for Myself" (essay) and "Afternoon" (poem). *Twentieth Century* 169 (Feb. 1961): 172–175, 218.

A Night Out. London: Methuen, 1962; New York: Grove Press, 1962; *The Complete Works: One*. New York: Grove Press, 1977.

The Dwarfs (radio play). *Three Plays: A Slight Ache, The Collection, The Dwarfs*. New York; Grove Press, 1962; *Complete Works: Two*. New York: Grove Press, 1977.

Night School. London: Methuen, 1963; London: French, 1963; New York Dramatists Play Service, 1963; New York: Grove Press, 1962; *Complete Works: Two*. New York: Grove Press, 1977.

The Lover and *The Collection*. London: Methuen, 1963, revised 1964; London: French, 1964; New York: Dramatists Play Service, 1964; New York: Grove Press; *Complete Works: Two*. New York: Grove Press, 1977.

Dialogue for Three (revue sketch). *Stand* 6.3 (1963–4): 4–5.

"Writing for Theatre." *Evergreen Review* 8 (Aug.–Sept. 1964): 80–83.

"Tea Party" (fiction). *Playboy* 12.1 (Jan. 1965): 124–125, 218.

The Homecoming. London: Methuen, 1965, revised 1966; New York: Grove Press, 1966, 1967; London: H. Karnac, 1968. Limited edition, 200 copies; *Complete Works: Three*. New York: Grove Press, 1978; the film for The American Film Theatre, 1973.

Tea Party (one-act) and *The Basement* (originally *The Compartment* written 1966 for Grove Press Project 1). New York: Grove Press, 1967; *Complete Works: Three*. New York: Grove Press 1978.

"Beckett." *Beckett at Sixty: A Festschrift*. London: Calder and Boyars, 1967.

That's Your Trouble, That's All, Applicant Dialogue for Three, Last to Go, Request Stop, Interview, Trouble in the Works, The Black and White, (revue sketches from the two revues: *One to Another* and *Pieces of Eight* and from *Pinter People,* the Grove Press cartoon, 1969) London: Methuen, 1967; in *A Night Out, Night School, Review Sketches: Early Plays*. New York: Grove Press, 1967; in *Complete Works: One*. New York: Grove Press, 1977; New York: Dramatists Play Service, 1965, (contains *Trouble in the Works, The Black and White, Request Stop, Last to Go, Applicant, Interview, That's All, That's Your Trouble, Black and White*).

Special Offer. Arnold P. Hinchliffe. *Harold Pinter*. New York: Twayne, 1967; reprinted London: Macmillan, 1976.

A page of typescript from *The Homecoming* in *Writers at Work: Paris Review Interviews*. Third series. Edited by George Plimpton. New York: Viking Press, 1967, 1968.

New Poems 1967: A P.E.N. Anthology. Edited by Harold Pinter, John Fuller and Peter Redgrove. London: Hutchinson, 1968.

"The Knight Has Been Unruly: Memories of Sir Donald Wolfit." *Listener* 79 (18 Apr. 1968): 501.

Landscape. *Evergreen Review* 13 (Jul. 1969): 55–63; *Silence*. and *Landscape*. London: Methuen, 1968: New York: Grove Press, 1968.

Mac. Harper's Bazaar 110 (Nov 1968): 234, 178, 180; Emanuel Wax for Pendragon Press, 1968. (Limited edition 1,000 copies); New York: Grove Press, 1968. (Limited edition, 1,000 copies). *Collected Poems and Prose.* London: Methuen, 1986.

Poems (Selected by Alan Clodd). London: Enitharmon Press, 1968. (Limited edition, 200 copies)

Old Times. London: Methuen, 1968; New York: Grove Press, 1968; *Complete Works: Four.* New York: Grove Press, 1981.

Night. Nova Aug. 1969: 66.

"Memories of Cricket." *Daily Telegraph Magazine* 16 May 1969: 25–26.

"Distressing." *New York Times* 26 Apr. 1970: 180.

Letter. *Times* (London) 9 Dec. 1970: 11.

"Speech: Hamburg." *Theatre Quarterly* 3 (1971): 3.

The Servant. Five Screenplays. London: Methuen, 1971.

The Pumpkin Eater. Five Screenplays. London: Methuen, 1971.

The Quiller Memorandum. Five Screen Plays. London: Methuen, 1971.

Accident. Five Screen Plays. London: Methuen, 1971.

The Go-Between. Five Screenplays. London: Methuen, 1971.

Monologue. London: Covent Garden Press Limited, 1973; London: Methuen, 1973; New York: Grove Press, 1973.

"Pinter on Pinter." *Cinebill* Oct. 1973: 7.

"An Unpublished Speech." *Theatre Quarterly* 3 (Aug.–Oct. 1974).

"The Error of Alarm," "The Table," and "Afternoon Poems." *Poetry Northwest* 8.1 (Spring 1976): 3–5.

Langrishe, Go Down. The French Lieutenant's Woman and Other Screenplays. London: Methuen, 1978.

The Last Tycoon. The French Lieutenant's Woman and Other Screenplays. London: Methuen, 1978.

Harold Pinter: Poems and Prose, 1949–1977. London: Methuen, 1978.

Betrayal. London: Methuen, 1978; New York: Grove Press 1978; *Complete Works: Four.* New York: Grove Press, 1981.

The Proust Screenplay: À la Recherche du Temps Perdu, London: Methuen, 1979; New York: Grove Press, 1979.

The Hothouse. London: Methuen, 1980; New York: Grove Press, 1980.

Family Voices. London: Next Editions Limited, 1981.

Letter to Peter Wood. *Kenyon Review* 3 (1981): 1–5.

Arthur Wellard. London: Villiers Publications, 1981.

No Man's Land. London: Methuen, 1981; New York: Grove Press, 1981; *Complete Works: Four*. New York: Grove Press, 1981.

The French Lieutenant's Woman. *The French Lieutenant's Woman and Other Screenplays*. London: Methuen, 1982.

A Kind of Alaska, Victoria Station and *Family Voices*. London: Methuen, 1983; New York: Grove Press, 1983; *Complete Works: Four*. New York: Grove Press, 1981.

Precisely. *The Big One*. Edited by Susannah York and Bill Bachle. London: Methuen, 1984.

One for the Road. London: Methuen, 1984, 1985; New York: Grove Press, 1985.

P.E.N. Anthology of New Poems. Co-edited by Harold Pinter. London: Methuen, 1986.

100 Poems by 100 Poets. Edited by Harold Pinter, Geoffrey Godbert and Anthony Astbury. London: Methuen, Greville Press, 1986.

Collected Poems and Prose. London: Methuen, 1986.

The Handmaid's Tale. Adapted for screen from the Margaret Atwood novel, 1987.

Letter. *Independent* 30 Nov. 1988.

Mountain Language. New York: Grove Press, 1988.

The Heat of the Day. Adapted for television from the novel by Elizabeth Bowen. London: Faber and Faber, 1989.

The Dwarfs (novel written 1952–1956). London: Faber and Faber, 1990.

Victory. *The Comfort of Strangers and Other Screenplays*. London: Faber and Faber, 1990.

Turtle Diary. *The Comfort of Strangers and Other Screenplays*. London: Faber and Faber, 1990.

Reunion. Adapted for screen from the Fred Uhlman novel. *The Comfort of Strangers and Other Screenplays*. London: Faber and Faber, 1990.

The Comfort of Strangers. Adapted for screen from the Ian McIwan novel. *The Comfort of Strangers and Other Screenplays*. London: Faber and Faber, 1990.

"Oh, Superman" (speech). "Opinion." Channel 4 Television (31 May 1990). *Poems and Prose*. London: Faber and Faber, 1991.

Complete Works. 4 Vols. New York: Grove Weidenfeld, 1990.

"Yanquis Go Home!" *Independent on Sunday* 27 May 1990: "Sunday Review" 10–11, 15.

"The New World Order." The American Theatre 8.8 (Nov. 1991) and *Pinter Review* (1991): 1–3.

"American Football" (poem). *Pinter Review* (1991): 41.

"Graham Green 1904–1991: A Tribute to the Late Writer." Channel 4 Television, 7 Apr. 1991.

Letter. *Independent* 24 May 1991:22.

Address Before the House of Commons [representing the position of "500 Years of Resistance Campaign"]. 10 July 1991.

Letter. *Independent* 1 Aug. 1991:18.

Letter. *Independent on Sunday* 29 Sept. 1991: 21.

Party Time. London: Faber and Faber, 1991.

"The New World Order." *Granta* 37 (fall 1991): 249–254.

Other Places: Pinter: Plays. London: Faber and Faber, 1991.

The Remains of The Day: A Screenplay by Harold Pinter (adaptation of the novel by Kazuo Ishiguro; typescript, 1991).

"The Shameful Truth." *World. BBC Magazine of Mankind* 58 (March 1992): 10–17.

McNamara, Brooks. *Plays from the Contemporary British Theatre* (Includes *Betrayal*). New York: Penguin, 1992.

Ten Early Poems. Warwick, England: Greville Press, 1992.

Moonlight. London: Faber and Faber, 1993.

The Trial: Adapted from the Novel by Franz Kafka. London: Faber and Faber, 1993.

"U.S. Should Admit Role in El Salvador." *Ottawa Citizen* 30 March 1993: A11.

"This House Regrets America's Roles as Policeman to the World." Oxford Union Debate. 21 May 1992. [Typescript courtesy of Harold Pinter, as cited by Knowles, "From London," 1994. *The Pinter Review, 1992:* 94.]

"God" (poem). *Times Literary Supplement)* 24 Dec. 1993: 21.

Party Time and *the New World Order: Two Plays by Harold Pinter.* New York: Grove, 1993.

99 Poems in Translation. Edited by Harold Pinter, Anthony Astbury and Geoffrey Godbart. London: Faber and Faber, 1994. New York: Grove Press Atlantic, 1994.

Schmid, Estella, *et al.* (Ed). *Anthology of Contemporary Kurdish Poetry*. Foreword by Harold Pinter. Translated by Andre Penny, *et al.* London: Kurdistan Solidarity Committee: Y. Ismail, 1994.

The Diaries of Etty Hillesun (unpublished screenplay, unproduced), 1994.

Lolita (unpublished screenplay, unproduced), 1994.

"Early Draft, *The Homecoming*." *Pinter Review (1994): 1–7.*

Letter. *New York Review of Books* 9 June 1996: 60.

and Antonia Fraser. Letter. *Guardian* 13 June 1995: 25.

Letter. Guardian 27 Sept. 1994: Features, 21.

"A War of Words." *Red Pepper* (May 1995): 24–25.

Ashes to Ashes. London: Faber and Faber, 1996; New York: Grove, 1997.

"Order" (poem). *Guardian* 12 Sept. 1997:7

The Dreaming Child: a Screenplay by Harold Pinter: Adapted from the short story by Karen Blixen (typescript, December 1997).

"A note on Shakespeare." *France the Outsider*. New York: Granta: 1997.

"The Old Days" (poem). Observer 29 Sept. 1–7: Review, 18.

"Picking a Fight with Uncle Sam" *Guardian* 4 Dec. 1997: Section 2, 4.

Various Voices: Prose: Poetry, Politics 1948–1998. London: Faber and Faber, 1998.

"Attack on Labour." *Independent* 15 April 1998: 19.

Letter. *Independent* 10 July 1998: 21.

"No Fixed Points" and "The Envy of the World" [History of the Third Programme]. BBC Radio 3, 5 August 1998.

Letter. *Independent on Sunday* 5 October. 1998: 1.

"Global Spin." *Guardian* 5 Dec. 1998: Books, 3.

"NATO Action in Serbia." *Ethical Imperialism: The War after the War*. Ken Coats (Ed.) Nottingham: Spokeman For the Bertrand Russell Peace Foundation, 1999.

Celebration (typescript, 1999).

Getting Acquainted (possibly lost revue sketch from *Pieces of Eight*).

I Know the Place (chapbook of poems). Warwick, England: Greville Press, n.d. (Limited edition: 500 copies)

Celebration London: Faber and Faber, 2000.

Secondary Sources

Bibliographies and Checklists: Arranged Chronologically

Adelman, Irving, and Rita Dworkin. *Modern Drama; A Checklist of Critical Literature in Twentieth Century Plays*. Metuchen: Scarecrow Press, 1967.

Gordon, Lois G. "Pigeonholing Pinter; A Bibliography." *Theatre Documentation* 1 (Fall 1968): 3–20.

Palmer, Helen H., and Anne Jane Dyson. *European Drama Criticism*. Baton Rouge: Shoe String Press, 1968.

Salem, James M. *A Guide to Critical Reviews; Part III; British Drama from Ibsen to Pinter*. Metuchen: Scarecrow Press, 1968.

Palmer, Helen H., and Anne Jane Dyson. *European Drama Criticism, Supp. I*. Baton Rouge: Shoe String Press, 1968.

Palmer, David S. "Harold Pinter Checklist." *Twentieth Century Literature* 16 (Oct. 1970): 287–296.

Prentice, Penelope. *A Checklist of Work by and About Harold Pinter Through 1971: 1300 Titles Including Unindexed Reviews*. Buffalo: D'Youville College.

Imhof, Rudiger. *Pinter: A Bibliography:* XXXXXI Theatre Quarterly Publications, 1975.

Gale, Steven H. *Harold Pinter. An Annotated Bibliography*. Boston: G. K. Hall; London: Prior, 1978.

Merritt, Susan Hollis. "Recent Developments in Pinter Criticism: Harold Pinter Bibliography 1986–87." *Pinter Review* 1987, 77–82; 1988, 83–92; 1989, 112–121; 1990, 133–123; 1991, 79–94; 1992, 92–93, 100–111; 1994, 138–161; 1995–1996, 208–228; 1997–1998, 186–218.

Other Works

Albee, Edward. "Edward Albee." *Bomb* (Winter 1992): 52–55.

Allen, Paul. "Harold Pinter at 60—A Birthday Party." BBC Radio 3, 10 Oct. 1990.

Almansi, Guido, and Simon Henderson. *Contemporary Writers: Harold Pinter*. London: Methuen, 1983.

Appleyard, Bryan. "The New Light That Burns Within Harold Pinter." *Times* (London) 16 March 1984, 13.

Aristotle. *The Basic Works of Aristotle*. Edited by Richard McKeon. New York: Random House, 1941.

———. "From London: Harold Pinter 1994–1995." *Pinter Review* (1995–1996): 1952–167.

Armstrong, Raymond. *Kafka and Pinter Shadow-Boxing: The Struggle between Father and Son*. New York: St. Martin's Press, 1999.

Baker, William, and Steven Tabachnik. *Harold Pinter*. Edinburgh: Oliver & Boyd, 1973.

Bakewell, Joan. "In an Empty Bandstand—Harold Pinter in Conversation with Joan Bakewell." *Listener* 6 Nov. 1969: 630–31.

Batty, Mark. *Harold Pinter*. Plymouth: Northcote House, 2000.

Behera, Charan, Guru. *Reality and Illusion in the Plays of Harold Pinter*. New Delhi: Atlantic Publishers and Distributors, 1998.

Bensky, Lawrence M. "Harold Pinter." *Writers at Work: The Paris Review*. Third Series. New York: Viking Press, 1967.

Betsko, Kathleen, and Rachel Koenig. (eds.) *Interviews with Contemporary Women Playwrights*. New York: Beech Tree Books, 1987.

Billington, Michael. *The Life and Work of Harold Pinter*. London: Faber & Faber, 1996.

———. *One Night Stands: A Critic's View of British Theatre from 1971 to 1991*. London Nick Hern Books, 1993.

Blake, William. "The Question Answered." *The Pomlete Poems of John Donne and William Blake*. New York: Modern Library, 1946.

Bloom, Harold. *Harold Pinter*. New York: Chelsea House Publishers, 1987.

Dold, Alan. *Harold Pinter: You Never Heard Such Silence*. New York: Vision Press and Barnes and Noble, 1984.

Bosworth, Patricia. "Why He Doesn't Write More." *New York Times,* 27 Oct. 1968:IV, 3.

Bragg, Melvyn. "Interview with Harold Pinter." Independent Television, 22 Apr. 1978.

Brand, Stewart. *The Media Lab: Inventing the Future at MIT*. New York: Viking, 1987.

Bryden, Ronald. "Harold Pinter." *Observer* 19 Feb. 1967:9.

Burkman, Katherine H. *The Dramatic World of Harold Pinter.* Columbus: Ohio State University Press, 1971.

———. "Harold Pinter's *A Slight Ache as Ritual." Modern Drama* 10 (1968): 326–335.

———. "Harold Pinter's *Ashes to Ashes:* Rebecca and Devlin as Albert Speer." *Pinter Review* (1997–1998): 86–96.

———. and John Kundert-Gibbs (eds.) *Pinter at Sixty.* Bloomington: Indiana University Press, 1993.

Cahn, Victor L. *Gender and Power in the Plays of Harold Pinter.* New York: St. Martin Press, 1994.

Cardullo, Bert. "Anonymity in *The Birthday Party." Notes on Contemporary Literature* (16 Sept. 1986): 9–10.

———. "Harold Pinter/Poltics." *Around the Absurd: Essays on Modern and Postmodern Drama.* Ed. Enoch Brater and Ruby Cophn. Ann Arbor: University of Michigan Press, 1990.

Cassill, Kay. "Providence (R.I.) Is Divine While the Harold Pinters Briefly Share the Spotlight." *People* 17 (1 Mar. 1982): 64.

"*Caretaker's* Caretaker." *Time,* 10 Nov. 1961, 76.

Cavander, Kenneth. "Filming *The Caretaker.*" *Transatlantic Review* 13 (1963): 17–26.

Chevallier, Genevieve. Introduction. "Harold Pinter" *Cynos* (Special Issue) 14.1 (1997): 1–169.

Ciment, Michael. *"Visually Speaking." Film Comment* 25 (1989): 20–22.

Cleaves, Henderson. "Playwright Pinter Finds Interpretations Odious." *New York World-Telegram and Sun* 6 Sept. 1961: 28.

———. "Voices in the Dark: The Disembodied Vice in Harold Pinter's *Mountain Language." Pinter Review (1991): 17–22.*

Crist, Judith. "A Mystery: Pinter on Pinter." *Look* 24 Dec. 1968: 77–83.

Davis, Barry. "The Jewish Quarterly Interview. The 22 from Hackney to Chelsea: A Conversation with Harold Pinter." *Jewish Quarterly* 38.4 (Winter 1991/1992): 9–17.

De Rham, Edith. *Joseph Losey.* London: André Deutch, 1991.

Dean, Michael. "Harold Pinter Talks to Michael Dean." *Listener* Mar. 1969: 312.

Diamond, Elin. *Pinter's Comic Play.* Cranbury, New Jersey: Associated University Presses, 1985.

Drake, Sylvie. "Acting Is Just Like *Old Times* for Pinter." *Los Angeles Times* 29 Oct. 1985: VI 1, 6.

Dukore, Bernard. *Where Laughter Stops: Pinter's Tragicomedy.* Columbia, Missouri: University of Missouri Press, 1976.

———. *Harold Pinter.* London: Macmillan, 1982; New York: Grove Press, 1982.

———. "Pinter's Spy Movie." *Pinter Review* (1991): 10–16.

Dunn, Stephen. "Oklahoma City." *American Poetry Review* (Sept./Oct. 1999): 99.

Ehrenzweig, Anton. *The Hidden Order of Art: A Study in the Psychology of Artistic Imagination.* Berkeley: University of California Press, 1976.

Eliot,T.S. *The Complete Poems and Plays: 1909–1950.* New York: Harcourt, Brace and World, Inc., 1956.

Empson, William. *Seven Types of Ambiguity.* London: Chatto and Windus, 1963.

Esslin, Martin. *The Theatre of the Absurd.* New York: Doubleday, 1961.

———. *The Peopled Wound: The Work of Harold Pinter.* New York: Doubleday, 1970.

Estés, Clarissa Pinkola. *Women Who Run with the Wolves.* New York: Random House, 1992.

Fay, Stephen. *Power Play: the Life and Times of Peter Hall.* London: Hodder and Stoughton, 1995.

Ford, Anna. "Pinter Politics and Plays." BBC1, 21 Oct. 1988; edited and retitled "Radical Departures." *Listener* (27 Oct. 1988): 406.

Forster, E. M. *Howard's End.* New York: Vintage Books, 1921.

Foucault, Michael. *Discipline and Punish: The Birth of The Prison.* New York: Vintage, 1977.

Freed, Donald "An Interview with Michael Billington, Author of *The Life and Work of Harold Pinter.*" *Pinter Review* (1997–1998): 123126

Gabbard, Lucinda P. *The Dream Structure of Pinter's Plays: A Psychoanalytic Approach.* Rutherford, N.J.: Fairleigh Dickinson University Press, 1977.

Gale, John. "Taking Pains with Pinter." *Observer Weekend Review* 10 June 1962: 9.

Gale, Steven H. *Butter's Going Up*. Durham: Duke University Press, 1977.

———, and Francis Gillen. (eds.) *Critical Essays on Harold Pinter*. Boston: Hall, 1990.

Galens, David. *Drama for Students, Volume three (The Homecoming)*. Detroit: Gale Group, 1998.

———. *Drama for Students, volume 5 (The Bithday Party)*. Detroit: Gale Group, 1999.

———. *Drama for Students, volume 7 (the Caretaker)*. Detroit: Gale Group, 2000.

Ganz, Arthur (ed.). *Pinter: A Collection of Critical Essays*. Englewood Cliffs: Prentice Hall, 1972.

Gillen, Francis. "Harold Pinter's *The Birthday Party:* Menace Reconsidered." Steven Gale (ed.). *Harold Pinter. Critical Approaches*. London and Toronto: Fairleigh Dickinson, 1986.

———. "My Dark House: Harold Pinter's Political Vision in His Screen Adaptation of Karen Blixen's 'The Dreaming Child.'" *Pinter Review* (1997–1998): 110–122.

Gilligan, Carol. *In a Different Voice. Psychological Theory and Women's Development*. Cambridge: Harvard University Press, 1982.

Gillot, Jackie. *Options*. BBC, 15 Nov. 1970.

Gleick, James. *Chaos*. New York: Viking, 1986.

Gomez, Christine. *The Aleinated Firgure in Drama: From Shakespeare to Pinter*. New Delhi: Reliance, 1991.

Gordimer, Nadine. "The Nobel Lecture." *Poets and Writers* May/June 1992: 18–24.

———. *Harold Pinter: A Casebook*. New York: Garland Publishing, Inc. 1991.

Gordon, Lois G. *Stratagems to Uncover Nakedness*. Columbia: University of Missouri Press, 1969.

Grahamyool, A. "Blowing Up the Media." *Index on Censorship* 21.5 (May 1992): 2–3.

Grant, Steve. "Pinter: My Plays, My Polemics, My Pad." *Independent* 20 Sept. 1993: Living, 13.

Grove, Valerie. "Rebel without a Pause." *Guardian* 17 Feb. 1998: 184.

Guralnick, Elissa S. *Sight Unseen: Beckett, Pinter, Stoppard, and Other Contemporary Dramatist on Radio*. Athens, OH: Ohio University press, 1996.

Gursel, Mustafa. "Turkey Censors Blast on Rights by 2 Authors; Miller,. Pinter Say Torture a Fact in Turkey." *Washington Post* 24 Mar. 1985: 27.

———. "A Conversation [Pause] with Harold Pinter." *New York Times* 5 Dec. 1971: VI, 43, 126–146.

———. *Conversations with Pinter.* London: Nick Hern Books, 1995.

———. "Harold Pinter: I Started with Two People in a Pub." *New York Times* 30 Dec. 1979: IV, 5, 7.

Gussow, Mel "*The Hothouse.*" *New York Times* 17 Aug. 1980: 10.

———"Off Broadway's Sparkling Brevity." *New York Times* 31 May 1984: 19.

———. "A Stormy Courtship." *Horizon* Oct. 1981: 37–9.

Hall, Ann C. "A Kind of Alaska": Women in the Plays of O'Neill, Pinter, and Shepard. Carbonale: Southern Illinois University Press, 1993.

Hanh, Tich Nhat. *Peace Is Every Step: The Path of Mindfulness in Everyday Life.* New York: Bantam Books, 1991.

Hayman, Ronald. *Harold Pinter.* London: Heinemann, 1968.

Hern, Nick. "A Play and Its Politics: A Conversation between Harold Pinter and Nick Hern." *One for the Road.* London: Methuen, 1985.

Herridge, Francis. "Across the Footlights; Pinter Talks About *The Caretaker.*" *New York Post* 26 Oct. 1961: 9.

Hewes, Henry. "Probing Pinter's Play." *Saturday Review* 50 (Apr. 1967): 56–58, 96–97.

Hinchliffe, Arnold P. *Harold Pinter.* Twayne English Authors Series No. 51. New York: Twayne, 1967.

Hobson, Harold. "The Screw Turns Again." *Sunday Times* (London) 25 May 1958: 11.

Hollis, James R. *Harold Pinter; The Poetics of Silence.* Carbondale, IL: Southern Illinois University Press, 1970.

Hornby, Richard. "The Careers of Edward Albee and Harold Pinter." *Hudson Review* 47.1 (1994): 109–116.

Housten, Beverle, and Marsha Kinder. "The Losey-Pinter Collaboration." *Film Quarterly* 32 (Fall 1978): 17–30.

Jones, Edward T. "Harold Pinter: A Conversation." *Literature/Film Quarterly* 21.1 (1993): 2–9.

Kamm, Henry. "Two Playwrights Deplore Turkish Rights Record." *New York Times* 28 Mar. 1985: 17.

Kant, Immanuel. *The Moral Law*. Translated by H. J. Paton. New York: Barnes & Noble, Inc., 1948.

———. *Kant's Groundwork of the Metaphysics of Morals*. Translated and analysed by H. J. Paton. New York: Barnes & Noble, Inc., 1948.

Kauffman, Michael. "Actions That a Man Might Play: Pinter's *The Birthday Party*." *Modern Drama* 16 (1973): 167–78.

Kerr, Walter. *Harold Pinter; Columbia Essays on Modern Writers Series No. 27*. New York: Columbia University Press, 1967.

———. *"Betrayal." New York Times* Jan. 1980: C, 13.

———. "The Riveting Counterpoint of Pinter's *Betrayal*." *New York Times* Jan. 1980: IV, 3.

King, Kimball. "Satire on Television: *The Basement* and *The Tea Party*." *Pinter Review* (1991): 42–45.

Kirby, E. T. "The Paranoid Pseudo Community in Pinter's *The Birthday Party*." *Educational Theatre Journal* 30 (1978): 157–164.

Kitchen, Laurence, and Paul Mayersberg. "New Comment." BBC, 10 Oct. 1963.

Klein, Joanne. *Making Pictures The Pinter Screenplays*. Columbus: Ohio State University Press, 1985.

Knowles, Ronald. "Harold Pinter, Citizen." *Pinter Review* (1989): 24–33.

———. "From London: Harold Pinter 1991. *Pinter Review* (1991): 64–73.

———. "From London: Harold Pinter 1993–1994." *Pinter Review* (1993–1994): 115–131.

———. "From London: Harold Pinter 1993–1995." *Pinter Review* (1993–1994): 115–131.

———. "From London: Harold Pinter 1994–1995." *Pinter Review* (1995–1996): 152–1167.

———. "Harold Pinter 1996–1997 and 1997–1998." *Pinter Review* (1997–1998): 165–185.

———. "Harold Pinter—1992." *Pinter Review* (1992): 85. Merritt, Susan Hollis. "Ashes to Ashes in New York." *Pinter Review* (1997–1998): 156.

———. "From London: Harold Pinter 1994–1997 and 1997–1998." *Pinter Review*. (1997–1998): 165–185.

———. "Harold Pinter 1990: BBC Birthday Celebration; Reviews of *Heat of the Day, Family Voices, A Kind of Alaska, Betrayal*." *Pinter Review* (1990): 79–87.

———. "Harold Pinter—1992." *Pinter Review* (1992): 85.

Kroll, Jack. "The Puzzle of Harold Pinter." *Newsweek* 29 Nov. 1976: 74–81.

———. "A Kind of Alaska: Pinter and Pygmalion." *Classical and Modern Literature: A Quarterly* 16.3 (1996): 231–240.

Lahr, John (ed.). *A Casebook on Harold Pinter's The Homecoming*. New York: Grove Press, 1971.

———. *Understanding Harold Pinter*. Columbia: University of South Carolina Press, 1995.

Lewis, Peter. "Tramp's Progress." *Sunday Times* (London) 16 Jun. 1991:, V, 1–2.

Maetre Nontahud, Francisco. *La Habitatación Pinteriana: Formas, Limites y Procesos*. Alicante: Univesidad de Alcante, 1998.

Marks, Sally K. "Pinter's Philosophy of Theatre." *Los Angeles Times* 20 Nov. 1966: 17.

McFerran, Ann. "How Influential Has He Been?" *Independent on Sunday* 20 Oct.1991: 19.

Merritt, Susan Hollis. "*Ashes to Ashes* in New York" *Pinter Review* (1997–1998).

Merritt, Susan Hollis. *Pinter in Play*. Durham: Duke University Press, 1990.

Miller, Jean Baker. *Toward a New Psychology of Women*. Boston: Beacon Press, 1986.

Morgenstern, Joseph. "A Playwright Who Stays Off Stage." *New York Herald Tribune* 10 Sept. 1961: IV, 4.

Morrison, Kristin. *Cantors and Chronicles: The Use of Narrative in the Plays of Samuel Beckett and Harold Pinter*. Chicago: University of Chicago Press, 1983.

"Mr. Harold Pinter—Avant-Garde Playwright and Intimate Revue." *Times* (London) 16 Nov. 1959: 4.

Naismith, Bill. *Harold Piner: The Caretaker, The Birthday Party, The Homecoming*. London: Faber and Faber. 2000.

Nichols, Sunday Caroline. *Creating and Performing the Role of Jamie in Paper Wings*. Virginia Beach, VA: Regent Univeristy, 1997.

Nightingale, Benedict. "Going Back to a Playwright's Source." *New York Times* 24 May 1984; 24.

———. *Harold Pinter: Writers Talk of Ideas of Our Time*. The Roland Collection, ICA Video, n.d.

———. "Merchant-Ivory and Friends: On the Job Again." *New York Times* 24 Jan. 1993: H11–12.

O'Brien, Edna. "It's a Bad Time Out There for Emotions." *New York Times Book Review* 14 Feb. 1993: 1, 20.

Olson, Elder. *Tragedy and the Theory of Drama*. Detroit: Wayne State University Press, 1966.

O'Toole, Tintan. "Our Own Jacobean." New York *Review of Books* 7 Oct. 1999: 29/680.

Ovid. *The Art of Love*. Translated by Rolfe Humphries. Bloomington: Indiana University Press, 1966.

Owen, Michael. "Funny, but Pinter and Coony are Very Similar." *Evening Standard* 6 Oct. 1995: 18.

Packer, Toni. *The Work of This Moment*. Boston: Shambhala, 1991.

Page, Malcolm. *File on Pinter*. London: Methun, 1993.

Peacock, D. Keith. *Harold Pinter and the New British Theatre*. Westport, Ct: Greenwood Publishers, 1999.

Pearson, Kenneth. "News in the Arts: Dramatist Pinter to Direct First Film." *Sunday Times* (London) 8 Mar. 1970: 57.

Pinter People. [Grove Press television film of revue sketches and interview]. 1968.

"Pinterview." *Newsweek* 23 July 1962: 69.

Plato. *The Dialogues of Plato*. Translated by B. Jowett. New York: Random House, 1982.

Preminger, Alex. Ed. *Princeton Encyclopedia of Poetry and Poetics*. Princeton: Princeton University Press, 1974.

Prentice, Penelope. "*The Birthday Party:* Ambiguity, Identity and the Violent Struggle for Dominance." *Pinter Review* (1989): 9–23.

———. *Harold Pinter: Life, Work; and Criticism*. Fredericton, NB: York Press, 1991.

———. "The Ironic Con Game in *The Dumb Waiter*." *Drama and Discussion*. Edited by Stanley A. Clayes. Prentice Hall: Englewood Cliffs, NJ, 1978.

———. "Love and Survival: The Quintessence of Harold Pinter's Plays." *Cithara* 27 (May 1988): 30–40.

———. "Madness in Harold Pinter's Work: Public Consequences of Private Madness." *Cithara* 32 (Nov. 1992): 31–38.

———. "Ruth: Pinter's The *Homecoming* Revisited." *Twentieth Century Literature* 26 (Winter 1980): 458–479.

"Profile: Playwright on His Own Success." *Observer* 15 Sept. 1963:13.

Pugh, Marshall. "Trying to Pin Down Pinter." *Daily Mail* 7 Mar. 1964: 8.

Qualls-Corbett, Nancy. *The Sacred Prostitute: Eternal Aspect of the Feminine*. Toronto: Inner City Books, 1988.

Quigley, Austin E. *The Pinter Problem*. Princeton: Princeton University Press, 1975.

Ramanathan, Geetha. *Sexual Politics and the Male Playwright: The Portrayal of Women in Ten Contemporary Plays*. Jefferson NC: McFarland, 1996.

Rilke, Rainer Maria. *The Selected Poems*. New York: Random House-Vintage International, 1989.

Roof, Judith. "'*A Kind of Alaska*: Women in the Plays of O'Neill, Pinter and Shepard: Hall, Ann C.'" *Pinter Review* (1994): 132–133.

Rose, Charlie. "Harold Pinter Reviews His Career." *Charlie Rose Show,* PBS, 10 Dec. 1993.

Rushdie, Salman. "Speak and be Damned." *Observer* 7 July 1988: 43.

Sakellaridou, Elizabeth. *Pinter's Female Portraits: A Study of Female Characters in the Plays of Harold Pinter*. Totowa, NJ: Barnes & Noble Books, 1988.

Sarris, Andrew. "What Does 'Mean' Mean?" *Village Voice* December 19, 1968: 53.

Schiff, Stephen. "Pinter's Passions." *Vanity Fair* Sept. 1990: 218–222, 300–303.

Sereny, Gitta. *Albert Speer: His Battle with Truth*. New York: Knopf, 1995.

Sexton, David. "The Arts: Life in the Old Dog Yet." *Daily Telegraph* 16 March 1995: 12.

Sherwood, John. "The Rising Generation." BBC, 3 Mar. 1960.

Shulman, Milton. "Sorry Mr. Pinter, You're Just Not Funny Enough." *Evening Standard* 20 May 1958: 9.

Silverstein, Marc. *Harold Pinter and the Language of Cultural Power*. Lewisburg, PA: Bucknell University Press; London: Associated University Presses, 1993.

The Stage. 3 Feb. 1958, 8.

———. Talking about Some kind of Atrocity. *Pinter Review* 1997–1998, 74–85.

Sweeny, Louise. "Confrontation Scene." *Christian Science Monitor* 7 Oct. 1968: 8.

Sykes, Arlene. *Harold Pinter*. St. Lucia: University of Queensland Press, 1970.

Tallmer, Jerry. "2 Playwrights Meet and Improvise a Scene." *New York Post* 8 Nov. 1962: 19.

Taylor, Clarke. "Pinter's World—And Wary of It." *Los Angeles Times* 12 Mar. 1983: 1–2.

Taylor, John Russell. "*Accident.*" *Sight and Sound* 35 (1965–66): 179–184.

———. *Harold Pinter; Writers and Their Work, Series No. 212*. London: Longmans, 1969.

Tennyson, Hallam. "Critic At Large." BBC, 7 Aug. 1960.

Thompson, David T. *Pinter: The Player's Playwright*. New York: Macmillan, 1985.

Thompson, Harry. "Harold Pinter Replies." *New Theatre Magazine* 2. 2 (Jan. 1961, 8–10): 16.

"The *Times* Diary: At Last, Pinter's *Landscape;* Shorter Pinter." *Times* (London) 11 Apr. 1969: 10.

Torture in the Eighties: An Amnesty International Report. London: Amnesty International Publications, 1984.

Trussler, Simon. *The Plays of Harold Pinter, An Assessment*. London: Gollancz, 1973.

Tusa, John. "Growth of an Angry Playwright." *Observer* 16 Oct. 1988: 13.

Tynan, Kathleen. "In Search of Harold Pinter: Part Two." *Evening Standard* 29 Apr. 1967:9.

Tynan, Kenneth. "People Today." BBC, 28 Oct. 1968.

"Two People in a Room." *New Yorker* 25 Feb. 1967: 36.

Wardle, Irving. "The Master and the Muse." *Independent on Sunday,* 20 Oct. 1991: 18–19.

Watt, Stephen. *Postmodern/drama: Reading the Contemporary Stage*. Ann Arbor: University of Michigan Press, 1998.

Wesker, Arnold. *As Much As I Dare: An Autobiography*. London: Hodder and Stoughton, 1995.

Wetzsteon, Ross. "Pinter & Losey; Game and Set, or the Deadly Double." *Village Voice* 20 Apr. 1969: 25.

Whitman, Walt. *Leaves of Grass*. Garden City, NY: Doubleday & Co., Inc., 1926.

Wildman, Carl. "Talking of Theatre." BBC, 7 Mar. 1961.

Williams, William Carlos. *Selected Poems*. New York: New Directions, 1949.

Wolf, Matt. "Happy 60th Birthday, Harold Pinter." *Miami Herald* 7 Oct. 1990: 71.

Wordsworth, William. *The Complete Work*. Oxford: Oxford University Press, 1923.

Yeats, W. B. *The Collected Poems of W. B. Yeats*. New York: Macmillan Company, 1969.

Zarthy-Levo, Yael. *The Theatrical Critic as Cultural Agent: Constructing Pinter, Orton and Stoppard as Absurdist Playwrights*. New York: Peter Lang, 2000.

Zolotow, Maurice. "Young Man with a Scorn; Harold Pinter, Author of *The Caretaker* Vents His Opinions." *New York Times* 17 Sept. 1961: II, 3.

Index

Names and Titles

Themes, Techniques and Topics

Themes and Techniques

Topics